076130

Florida

THE ROUGH GUIDE

There are more than eighty Rough Guide titles covering
destinations from Amsterdam to Zimbabwe

Forthcoming titles include
China • Corfu • Jamaica • New Zealand • South Africa
Southwest USA • Vienna • Washington DC

Rough Guide Reference Series
Classical Music • The Internet • Jazz • World Music

Rough Guide Phrasebooks
Czech • French • German • Greek • Italian • Mexican Spanish
Polish • Portuguese • Spanish • Thai • Turkish • Vietnamese

Rough Guide Phrasebooks
http://www.roughguides.com/
http://www.hotwired.com/rough

Rough Guide credits

Text editor:	Vivienne Heller
Series editor:	Mark Ellingham
Editorial:	Martin Dunford, Jonathan Buckley, Samantha Cook, Jo Mead, Amanda Tomlin, Alison Cowan, Annie Shaw, Lemisse Al-Hafidh, Catherine McHale, Paul Gray
Online editors:	Alan Spicer (UK), Andrew Rosenberg (US)
Production:	Susanne Hillen, Andy Hilliard, Judy Pang, Link Hall, Nicola Williamson, Helen Ostick
Cartography:	Melissa Flack, David Callier
Finance:	John Fisher, Celia Crowley, Catherine Gillespie
Marketing & Publicity:	Richard Trillo, Simon Carloss (UK), Jean-Marie Kelly, Jeff Kaye (US)
Administration:	Tania Hummel, Margo Daly

Acknowledgements

The editor would like to thank Susanne Hillen, Nicola Williamson and Andy Hilliard for their supreme patience and humour in putting the book together, Melissa Flack and David Callier for map revisions, Elaine Pollard for proofreading, Jeanne Muchnick and Narrell Leffman for *Basics* research, and Mark Lewis for indexing. The writers would like to thank Damian O'Grady at the Florida Division of Tourism, Alyce McDaniel at the Greater Miami Convention & Visitors' Bureau, and everyone at the various Visitors' Bureaux and Chambers of Commerce throughout the state.

The publishers and authors have done their best to ensure the accuracy and currency of all the information in *The Rough Guide to Florida*; however, they can accept no responsibility for any loss, injury or inconvenience sustained by any traveller as a result of information or advice contained in the guide.

This third edition published September 1996 by Rough Guides Ltd, 1 Mercer Street, London WC2H 9QJ.

Distributed by the Penguin Group:

Penguin Books Ltd, 27 Wrights Lane, London W8 5TZ
Penguin Books USA Inc., 375 Hudson Street, New York 10014, USA
Penguin Books Australia Ltd, 487 Maroondah Highway, PO Box 257, Ringwood, Victoria 3134, Australia
Penguin Books Canada Ltd, 10 Alcorn Avenue, Toronto, Ontario M4V 1E4, Canada
Penguin Books (NZ) Ltd, 182–190 Wairau Road, Auckland 10, New Zealand

Typeset in Linotron Univers and Century Old Style to an original design by Andrew Oliver.
Printed in the UK by Cox & Wyman Ltd, Reading, Berks.

Illustrations in Part One and Part Three by Ed Briant. Basics illustration by Tommy Yamaha. Contexts illustration by Henry Iles.

A catalogue record for this book is available from the British Library.
ISBN 1-85828-184-9

Florida

THE ROUGH GUIDE

Written and researched by
Mick Sinclair

additional contributions by
Laura Harper, Oliver Marshall and Tony Mudd

THE ROUGH GUIDES

LIST OF MAPS

MAP SYMBOLS

 Interstate
 U.S. Highway
 Highway
 Railway
 Ferry route
 Path/Trail
 International border
 State border
 Chapter division boundary
 Airport
 Accommodation
 Museum

Gardens
Picnic area
Lighthouse
 Information office
 Post office
 Building
 Church
 Cemetery
 Indian reservation
Park
National park/forest
Marshland

CONTENTS

INTRODUCTION

T he cut-rate package trips and photos of tanning flesh and Mickey Mouse that fill the pages of glossy holiday brochures ensure that everyone has an image of **Florida** – but seldom one that's either accurate or complete. Pulling 35 million visitors each year to its beaches and theme parks, the aptly nicknamed "sunshine state" is devoted to the tourist trade, yet it's also among the least-understood parts of the US, with a history, character and diversity of landscape unmatched by any other region. Beyond the palm-fringed sands, hiking and canoeing trails wind through little-known forests and rivers, and the famed beaches themselves can vary wildly over a short distance – hordes of copper-toned ravers are often just a frisbee's throw from a deserted, pristine strand coveted by wildlife-watchers. Variations continue inland, where smart, modern cities are rarely more than a few miles away from steamy, primeval swamps.

In many respects, Florida is still evolving. Socially and politically, it hasn't calmed since the earliest days of US settlement: stimulating growth has always been the paramount concern, and with a thousand people a day moving to the booming state, it's currently the fourth most populous place in the nation. The changing demographics have begun eroding the traditional Deep South conservatism and are overturning the common notion that Florida is dominated by retirees. In fact, the new Floridians tend to be a younger breed, working energetically to shape not only the future of Florida but that of the whole US. Immigration from outside the country is also on the increase, with Spanish- and French-Creole-speaking enclaves providing a reminder of geographic and economic ties to Latin America and the Caribbean. These links have proven almost as influential in raising the state's material wealth over the past decade as the arrival of huge domestic businesses, including sections of the film industry that have opted for central Florida in preference to Hollywood.

Florida does, however, have a number of problems to contest with, the most pressing of which is its growing reputation for crimes against (and even murders of) tourists. While the authorities have devised schemes to reduce such attacks, it is an inescapable fact that visitors are an inviting target for both opportunist and organized criminals. Statistically, it's highly unlikely that you'll become a victim, but you should be wary at all times and pay heed to the safety tips given throughout the book. On the home front, the state is struggling to provide enough houses, schools and roads for its growing population; levels of poverty in the rural areas can be severe; and in an increasingly multi-ethnic society, racial tensions frequently surface. Expanding towns without jeopardizing the environment is another hot issue; large amounts of land are under state or federal protection, and there are signs that the conservation lobby is gaining the upper-hand. Nevertheless, uncontrolled development is posing serious ecological problems – not least to the Everglades.

Where to go and when

Heat-induced lethargy is no excuse not to get out and explore the different facets of Florida, as the state is compact enough to be toured easily and quickly. The

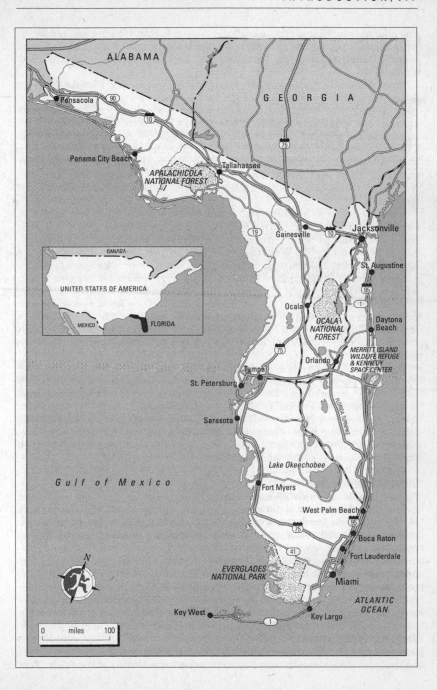

essential stop is **Miami**, whose addictive, cosmopolitan vibe is enriched by its large Hispanic population, and where the much-photographed Art Deco district of **Miami Beach** provides an unmistakeable backdrop for the state's liveliest nightclubs.

From Miami, a simple journey south brings you to the **Florida Keys**, a hundred-mile string of islands of which each has something to call its own, be it sports fishing, coral-reef diving, or a unique species of dwarf deer. The single road spanning the keys comes to a halt at **Key West**, a blob of land that's legendary for its sunsets and anything-goes attitude. North from Miami, much of the **Southeast Coast** is a disappointingly urbanized strip – commuter territory better suited for living in than visiting. Alongside the busy towns, however, beaches flow for many unbroken miles and finally escape the residential stranglehold along the **Northeast Coast**, where communities are often subservient to the sands that flank them.

When you tire of beachlife and ocean views, make a short hop inland to **Central Florida**, whose verdant terrain features cattle farms, grassy hillsides, and isolated villages beside expansive lakes. The sole but rather dramatic disruption to this rural idyll is **Walt Disney World**, which practises tourism on the scale of the infinite. If you're in the mood, you can indulge in its ingenious fix of escapist fun; if not, the upfront commercialism may well encourage you to skip north to the deep forests of the **Panhandle**, Florida's link with the Deep South – or to the art-rich towns and sunset-kissed beaches of the **West Coast**. Explore these at your leisure as you progress steadily south to the **Everglades**, a massive, alligator-filled swathe of sawgrass plain, mangrove islands and cypress swamp, which provides as definitive a statement of Florida's natural beauty as you'll encounter.

Cost-wise, it makes little difference **when** you visit. Intense, year-round competition for your dollar gives rise to tremendous bargains in accommodation and food, though prices are lowest off-season (see below). The best-value plan is to explore northern Florida in March and move south in April – or vice versa during October and November. However, it is also worth considering Florida's climatic variations when planning your trip; winter in northern Florida is unsuitable for beach holidays, while summer in the south is plagued by high humidity, with many of the natural areas infested by mosquitoes.

Climate and seasons

Florida is split into **two climatic zones**: subtropical in the south and warm temperate – like the rest of the southeastern US – in the north. More importantly for the visitor, these two zones determine the state's **tourist seasons**, which are different for Florida's southern and northern halves and have a great effect on costs (see above).

Anywhere **south of Orlando** experiences very mild winters (November to April), with pleasantly warm temperatures and a low level of humidity. This is the peak period for tourist activity, with prices at their highest and crowds at their thickest. It also marks the best time to visit the inland parks and swamps. The southern summer (May to October) seems hotter than it really is (New York is often warmer) because of the extremely high humidity, relieved only by afternoon thunderstorms and sometimes even hurricanes (the southern section of Florida was devastated by **Hurricane Andrew** in August 1992); at this time of year you'll be lucky to see a blue sky. Lower prices and fewer tourists are the rewards for braving the mugginess, though mosquitoes can render the natural areas off-limits. Winter is the off-peak period **north of Orlando**; in all probability, the only chill you'll detect is a slight nip in the evening air, though it's worth bearing in mind that at this time of year, the sea is really too cold for swimming, and snow has been known to fall in the Panhandle. The northern Florida summer is when the crowds arrive, and when the days – and the nights – can be almost as hot and sticky as southern Florida.

The Florida sun: sunbathing and sunburn

Any visitor with sensitive skin should bear in mind that Florida shares a latitude with the Sahara Desert; the power of the Florida **sun** should never be underestimated.

Time spent outdoors should be planned carefully at first, especially between 11am and 2pm, when the sun is at its strongest. A powerful **sunscreen** is essential; anything with an SPF of less than 25 is unlikely to offer the necessary protection. Light-coloured, loose-fitting, lightweight clothes should protect any parts of your body not accustomed to direct sunlight. Wear a hat with a wide brim, carry sunglasses, and keep to the shaded side of the street. Drink plenty of **fluids** (but not alcohol) to prevent dehydration – public drinking-water fountains are provided for this purpose; iced tea is the best drink for cooling off in a restaurant.

AVERAGE DAYTIME TEMPERATURES (°F)											
	Jan	Feb	Mar	Apr	May	Jun	Jul	Aug	Sep	Oct	Nov	Dec
Miami	69	70	71	74	78	81	82	84	81	78	73	70
Key West	69	72	74	77	80	82	85	85	84	80	74	72
Orlando	60	63	66	71	78	82	82	82	81	75	67	61
Tampa	60	61	66	72	77	81	82	82	81	75	67	62
Tallahassee	53	56	63	68	72	78	81	81	77	74	66	59
Jacksonville	52	55	61	67	73	79	82	81	78	70	62	55
Pensacola	52	55	60	67	74	80	81	81	78	70	60	54

THANKS

Thanks are due to all those who wrote in with comments, suggestions and criticisms of the previous edition: Mike Andrushchyshyn, Graham Arthur, Ned Biggs, Jill Binder, King and Mary Bishop, Allison Blankenship, AC Bowker, Ellen Bragg, Elizabeth Campbell, Rory Cashin, M Chadwick, Colin Chapman, Floyd Creamer, Paul and Paula Cretney, Clair Donnelly, Derek Elliot, Sharon and Maria Freedman, Rae Garner, Peter George, Leila Grocharski, Ruth Higgenbotham, Raymond Holland, M Hommes, Phil Hughes, Claire Janes, Michael and Ursula Keating, Pamela Kelly, Martin King, Tim Kisiel, Robin Knowles, JD Lee, Robert Magill, Neil McCabe, Ian McConnell, Michael and Lucy Morris, Pascal Nicolle, Victoria Pittard, B Powell, Dawn Rattray, John Richmond, Gary Spinks, Judith Stutz, Terry Tracey, Sandra Warnock, Alan Westgarth, Fran Williamson, TJ Wood, K Wyatt, Robert Young and Marcia Zerivitz.

HELP US UPDATE

Months of painstaking research have ensured that this third edition of *The Rough Guide to Florida* is as accurate and up to date as possible. Nevertheless, in Florida the changes come thick and fast, so readers' ideas and updates are very welcome. Please mark letters "Rough Guide Florida Update" and send to:

Rough Guides, 1 Mercer Street, London WC2H 9QJ, or

Rough Guides, 375 Hudson Street, 9th Floor, New York, NY 10014, or

florida@roughtravl.co.uk

PART ONE

THE
BASICS

GETTING THERE FROM BRITAIN

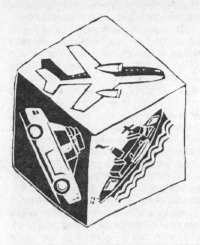

There's never been a better time for British travellers to go to Florida. Price wars between airlines on transatlantic routes are hotter than ever, and many operators are tossing in car rental and accommodation for only a little over the regular airfare. Comparatively few airlines fly non-stop from the UK to Florida, but many have one-stop links, and connections from other US airports are plentiful. Innumerable charter flights from all over the UK to major holiday centres such as Orlando throw up even more low-cost options.

FLIGHTS

Although you can fly to the US from many of Britain's regional airports, the only **non-stop scheduled** flights to Florida are from London, and all of these land either at Miami or, less often, Orlando. The **flight time** is around eight hours, leaving London around midday and arriving during the afternoon (local time). The return journey is slightly shorter, leaving in the early evening and flying through the night to arrive in London around breakfast time.

Specialist agents (see p.4) can offer cut-price seats on direct **charter flights**. These are particularly good value if you're travelling from a British city other than London, though they tend to be limited to the summer season, be restricted to so-called "holiday destinations", and have fixed departure and return dates. Brochures are available in most high street travel agents, or contact the specialists direct.

Many more routings use direct **one-stop** flights to Florida (a flight may be called "direct" even if it stops on the way, provided it keeps the same *flight number* throughout its journey). Obviously, these take a few hours longer than non-stop flights but can be more convenient (and sometimes cheaper) if you're not aiming specifically for Miami or Orlando. All the state's cities and large towns have airports – the other major one is Tampa – with good links from other US cities.

Alternatively, you could take a flight to New York or **another city** on the northern East Coast

FLIGHTS FROM BRITAIN

The following carriers operate **scheduled flights** to Florida from London (all use Gatwick airport unless otherwise stated).

Air Canada (☎ 0990/247226) Daily from Heathrow via Toronto to Miami and other Florida airports.

American Airlines (☎0181/572 5555) Daily non-stop to Miami from Heathrow; one-stop flights to most other Florida airports, usually via Dallas.

British Airways (☎0345/222 111) Daily non-stop to Miami from Heathrow; 1–2 daily via Miami or Orlando to Tampa; 4 weekly non-stop to Miami; daily non-stop to to Orlando; daily to Charlotte from Gatwick then onwards by *USAir* to most major Florida airports.

Continental (☎0800/776464) Daily via Newark to most Florida airports.

Delta (☎0800/414767) Daily to Orlando, connecting with all other Florida airports; also daily via Atlanta to most Florida airports.

Northwest (☎0345/747800) Daily via Detroit to Orlando and (via Orlando) Miami.

United (☎0800/888555) Daily to Miami from Heathrow (via Washington or Chicago).

Virgin Airlines (☎0800/747747) 4–5 weekly non-stop to Miami; daily to Orlando.

and travel on from there – this won't save any money overall but is an idea if you want to see more of the country before reaching Florida. Again, agents have the cheapest offers.

FARES

Whenever and however you go, the most expensive time to fly is **high season**, between June and August and a week either side of Christmas; April, May, September and October are slightly less pricey, and November to March is considered **low season** – cheaper still. It's important to remember, however, that high season in the UK is the low season – the least costly and least busy time – in south Florida, so the extra you might spend on a summer flight may be offset by cheaper deals once you're on the ground. Seasons in north Florida, however, match those of the UK. For more on the seasonal variations across Florida, see the *Introduction*.

Before booking a flight, **shop around** for the best price: scan the travel ads in the Sunday papers, in London's *Time Out* and giveaway magazines, or phone the airlines or one of the agents mentioned below. The details we've given are the latest available, but are sure to have undergone at least subtle changes by the time you read them.

Of the various **ticket types** offered by airlines, the cheapest are, not surprisingly, **economy returns**, which are bookable at any time and work out around £340 for a midweek flight in low season to £440 for a weekend flight in high season. Economy returns have no restrictions regarding length of stay, but a change of your return date after booking entails a penalty of between £35 and £50. Of other tickets, **standby** deals (tickets which you pay for in advance without specifying precise travel dates), and **APEX** returns, which have to be booked 14, 21 or 30 days in advance for a stay of at least a week, are £100–150 dearer than economy fares if bought directly from the airline. However, cut-rate APEX tickets are what you're likely to find offered by **agents** such as *STA Travel* or *Campus* (addresses below) who always have the lowest fares, with special reductions for students and anyone under 26.

FLIGHT AGENTS AND SPECIALIST TOUR OPERATORS IN BRITAIN

LOW-COST FLIGHT AGENTS

Campus Travel, 52 Grosvenor Gardens, London SW1 (☎0171/730 2101). *Also many other branches around the country.*

Council Travel, 28A Poland St, London W1 (☎0171/437 7767).

STA Travel, 86 Old Brompton Rd, London SW7 (☎0171/937 9971). *Offices nationwide.*

Trailfinders, 42–50 Earls Court Rd, London W8 (☎0171/937 5400).

Travel Cuts, 295 Regent St, London W1 (☎0171/637 3161).

SPECIALIST US TOUR OPERATORS

Airtours, Helmshore, Rossendale, Lancs BB4 4NB (☎01706/260000).

AmeriCan Adventures, 45 High St, Tunbridge Wells, Kent TN1 1XL (☎01892/511894).

Bon Voyage, 18 Bellevue Rd, Southampton, Hants SO1 2AY (☎01703/330332).

British Airways Holidays, Astral Towers, Betts Way, London Rd, Crawley, W Sussex RH10 2XA (☎01293/518022).

Contiki Travel, Wells House, 15 Elmfield Rd, Bromley, Kent BR1 1LS (☎0181/290 6422).

Enterprise, Groundstar House, London Rd, Crawley, West Sussex RH10 2HB (☎01293/560777).

Explore Worldwide, 1 Frederick St, Aldershot, Hants GU11 1LQ (☎01252/319448).

Greyhound, Sussex House, London Rd, East Grinstead, West Sussex RH19 1LD (☎01342/317317).

Premier Holidays, Westbrook, Milton Rd, Cambridge CB4 1YQ (☎01223/355977).

Transatlantic Vacations, 3A Gatwick Metro Centre, Balcombe Rd, Horley, Surrey RH6 9GA (☎01293/774441).

TrekAmerica, Trek House, The Bullring, Deddington, Oxford OX15 OTT (☎01869/38777).

Unijet, "Sandrocks", Rocky Lane, Haywards Heath, West Sussex RH16 4RH (☎01444/459191).

Virgin Holidays, The Galleria, Station Rd, Crawley, West Sussex RH10 1WW (☎01293/617181).

Through an agent, provided your plans are flexible and you hunt around, you can often make savings of £100–200 on regular fares, bringing prices down to around £300–350 for a weekend flight in high season. Look out, too, for short-term offers from the major airlines – which can cut fares to any east-coast US city to as low as £250 return.

Many agents and airlines offer **"open jaw"** deals whereby you fly into one US city and out through another: these won't save money if you're sticking to Florida but you could, for example, combine New York with Miami for around £380.

Finally, around £100 can be cut from the cheaper fares if you travel as a **courier**. Most of the major courier firms, such as *CTS Ltd* (☎0171/351 0300), *DHL* (☎0181/890 9393) and *Polo Express* (☎0181/759 5838) – see the *Yellow Pages* for others – offer a cheap return flight as payment for delivering a package or documents; a return to Miami can work out as little as £180. Normally, though, you're required to sacrifice your baggage allowance (only hand baggage is allowed) and fit in with tight restrictions on travel dates.

PACKAGES

Packages – fly-drive, flight-accommodation deals and guided tours (or a combination of all three) – can be a good way of skirting potential problems once you're in Florida and they usually work out cheaper than arranging the same trip yourself. The drawbacks are the loss of flexibility and the fact that flight-accommodation schemes often use hotels in the mid-range to expensive bracket – cheaper accommodation is almost always readily available. There are a great many packages to choose from and your high-street travel agent will have plenty of brochures and information.

FLIGHT AND ACCOMMODATION DEALS

There's really no end of **flight and accommodation packages** to all the major coastal areas and Orlando, and although you can always do things cheaper independently, you won't be able to do the *same* things cheaper – in fact the equivalent room booked by itself will probably be a lot more expensive. *STA Travel* (address on p.4) offers a package deal which includes flight and $15-a-night hostel accommodation (bear in mind not every Florida town has a hostel, see "Accommodation" p.27).

Any number of tour operators offer other, costlier deals. Of these, *Virgin Holidays* has the cheapest and widest selection, averaging £400–500 per person for a week, inclusive of return flight and car hire. See also "Accommodation", p.27, for details of pre-booked accommodation schemes.

FLY-DRIVE DEALS

Fly-drive deals, which combine car rental with a flight booking, can be extremely good value, and should certainly be considered before booking a flight and car rental separately. In fact, many airlines offer seven days' car rental at little, if any, extra cost above booking a flight to Florida with them. *British Airways*, for example, can set you up with a week's car rental and a return flight to Miami or Orlando for £315–£489 depending on season. If you're not aiming for these major centres, several American airlines have even cheaper deals based on smaller Florida cities.

The most obvious drawback of fly-drive deals is that the quoted prices are usually based on **four adults** sharing a car (and, obviously, each booking a flight with the airline involved); two people travelling together will often face a £20 surcharge. Scan a handful of brochures for the deal which suits you best – and be sure to read the small print. Renting a car for longer than seven days can usually be arranged with a minimum of fuss for as little as £23 per week for a subcompact (ideal for two people); around £33 for an intermediate vehicle.

Other important facts to consider when looking for a fly-drive deal are the unavoidable extra expenses such as the Collision Damage Waiver, the Florida surcharge and the cost of fuel, and the fact that under-25s may face problems renting a car in the US (although a pre-arranged booking should prevent this). For complete details on these matters and full car rental and driving facts, see "Getting around".

TOURING AND ADVENTURE PACKAGES

Geographical isolation and scorching summer temperatures mean that Florida tends to miss out on the specialist **touring and adventure trips** that cover much of the rest of the US. Nonetheless, *TrekAmerica* is one UK-based company that does include Florida, offering 8- or 12-day tours (£318 and £425 respectively), which include transport, accommodation and a guide. Other operators worth contacting include *Contiki* and *AmeriCan Adventures*, whose brochures can be found in youth- and student-oriented travel outlets. Once you're in Florida, tours of much shorter length, often just a day or two, can usually be arranged on the spot – details are given throughout the *Guide*.

FLIGHTS FROM IRELAND

It's not possible to fly non-stop from Ireland to Florida, though *Aer Lingus* and *Delta* have services from Dublin and Shannon via New York or Atlanta for IR£500–550. If you're under 26 or a student, the cheapest flights from Eire to Florida are through *USIT* (see below), which offers a return fare of IR£420 with *Northwest* via London.

AIRLINES AND FLIGHT AGENTS IN IRELAND

AIRLINES

Aer Lingus
Belfast ☎01232/314844; Dublin ☎01/844 4777; Cork ☎021/327155; Limerick ☎061/474239.

Delta Airlines
Belfast ☎01232/480526; Dublin ☎01/676 8080 or ☎1800/768080.

FLIGHT AGENTS

American Holidays, Lombard House, Lombard St, Belfast 1 (☎01232/238762); 38 Pearse St, Dublin 2 (☎01/679 8800).

Apex Travel, 59 Dame St, Dublin 2 (☎01/671 5933).

Flight Finders International, 13 Baggot St Lower, Dublin 2 (☎01/676 8326).

Inflight Travel, 92–94 York Rd, Belfast 15 (☎01232/740187 or 743341).

Joe Walsh Tours, 8–11 Baggot St, Dublin (☎01/676 3053).

Thomas Cook, 11 Donegall Place, Belfast (☎01232/240833); 118 Grafton St, Dublin (☎01/677 1721).

USIT, Fountain Centre, Belfast BT1 6ET (☎01232/324073); Aston Quay, Dublin 2 (☎01/679 8833); other branches nationwide.

GETTING THERE FROM NORTH AMERICA

Getting to Florida from anywhere else in North America is never a problem as the region is well serviced by air, rail and road networks. Every major and most minor US airlines fly to Florida, where Miami is the main hub, closely followed by Orlando and Tampa. Flying remains the quickest but most expensive way to travel; taking the train is a close second; and travelling by bus is much less costly but also the slowest and least comfortable mode of transport.

BY AIR

Prices are similar no matter which airline you choose; variations in cost are more dependent on the conditions governing the ticket – whether it's fully refundable, the time and day (midweek is always cheaper than weekends) and most importantly the **time of year** you travel.

Booking directly with an airline tends to be expensive, although it is the best way to take advantage of any car rental and accommodation deals they may offer in conjunction with a flight (see "Packages", p.8). Price-wise, the best outlets for plane tickets are the **specialist operators** such as *STA* and *Council Travel* (see p.8), primarily aimed at students but able to offer competitively priced fares to everybody.

AIRLINES IN NORTH AMERICA

Air Canada ☎1-800/776-3000; in Canada call directory enquiries for local toll-free number

Air South ☎1-800/247-7688

American Airlines ☎1-800/433-7300

America West Airlines ☎1-800/235-9292

Canadian Airlines ☎1-800/426-7000; ☎1-800/665-1177 in Canada

Carnival Air Lines ☎1-800/824-7386

Continental Airlines ☎1-800/525-0280

Delta ☎1-800/221-1212 in the US; in Canada, call directory enquiries for local toll-free number

Kiwi Airlines ☎1-800/538-5494

Midwest Express ☎1-800/452-2022

Northwest Airlines ☎1-800/225-2525

TWA ☎1-800/221-2000

United Airlines ☎1-800/241-6522

US Air ☎1-800/428-4322

Note that the **Canadian directory enquiries number** is ☎1-800/555-1212

Of the **major carriers**, *Delta* and *American Airlines* have the best links with the state's many smaller regional airports. *American Airlines* charges $250 from New York to Miami, and from $187 from JFK. In general, however, travellers can expect to pay about $250 from New York; $240 from Chicago, and anywhere from $330 to $560 from LA.

Of the **smaller airlines**, *Air South* services Newark and JFK to Miami and Jacksonville, often with a few stops but no change of plane. The least expensive return ticket to Jacksonville from New York is around $198, with a high of $398; to Miami from Newark will cost from $264. Look out for their special deals; under the current "Two for One" fare, Newark to Miami costs $399. *Kiwi*, based in Newark and New York, services Orlando, Tampa and West Palm Beach. Fares from New York to Orlando start at $178, rising to $418, and to West Palm Beach from $204. You can also take advantage of *Kiwi*'s deal with *Hertz* which entitles you to a ten percent reduction in the cost of car hire. *Midwest Express* is based in Milwaukee and only services Florida in the winter months, flying mainly to Midwest destinations: Fort Lauderdale, Fort Myers and Tampa. *Carnival* flies to Miami, Fort Lauderdale and Tampa. Their lowest fare from Newark to Miami is $245; from LA $302.

From **Canada**, *Air Canada* flies direct between Toronto and Montréal to Fort Lauderdale, Miami and Tampa; and from Toronto only to Fort Myers and Palm Beach. *Canadian Airlines* fly Toronto and Montréal to Miami; and from Toronto only to Fort Lauderdale, Fort Myers, Tampa and Sarasota. *American Airlines* flies nonstop from Toronto to Miami, Orlando and Fort Lauderdale, and from Vancouver to Miami. In general, the absolute minimum you might expect to pay is about $CND279 from Toronto or Montréal to Miami. From Vancouver, you'll pay at least $CND524.

Again, the place to find the lowest-priced fares is a **specialist flight agent**, such as *Travel Cuts*. If your plans are very flexible, scanning the travel pages of your local newspaper may turn up some bargains; though be sure to read the small print – many seemingly attractive deals are dependent on two people travelling together and using specified hotel accommodation.

BY CAR

How feasible it is to **drive** to Florida naturally depends on where you live and how much time you have. If you're aiming for the tourist hotspots like Orlando, you may enjoy a few days passing through the relaxing scenery of the south east before and after your trip. From the northeast or midwest, reckon on around 26 hours of actual driving to get to Florida; from the West Coast you'll probably need 40 hours behind the wheel.

BY TRAIN

A few years ago, the deregulation of the airline industry helped make domestic air travel as cheap as train travel. In an effort to win back business, **Amtrak** (contactable on a nationwide toll-free number ☎1-800/USA RAIL) has sharpened up its act all round: raising comfort levels, offering better food, introducing "Thruway" buses to link with its trains, and launching new services – most recently the Los Angeles–Miami *Sunset Limited* route. Consequently, travelling to Florida by train can be enjoyable and relaxing, if not particularly inexpensive.

DISCOUNT AGENTS IN NORTH AMERICA

Council Travel, 205 E 42nd St, New York, NY 10017 (☎212/822-2700), and branches in many other US cities.
Student/budget travel agency.

STA Travel, 10 Downing St, New York, NY 10014 (☎1-800/777 0112 or 212/627-3111), and other branches in the Los Angeles, San Francisco and Boston areas.
Worldwide discount travel firm specializing in student/youth fares; also student IDs, travel insurance, car rental, rail passes, etc.

Travel CUTS, 187 College St, Toronto, ON M5T 1P7 (☎416/979-2406), and other branches all over Canada.
Organization specializing in student fares, IDs and other travel services.

From **New York**, the *Silver Meteor* and the *Silver Star* traverse the eastern seaboard daily to Miami or Tampa (each train splits in half in Jacksonville before continuing), and the *Palmetto* charts a similar course from New York to Jacksonville. Fares range from $182 to $408 for a return ticket, and the journey from New York takes around 30 hours. From **Los Angeles** to Miami, the *Sunset Limited* crosses the southerly reaches of the US in a three-day journey. The return fare varies according to season from $278 to $1,156.

If you really can't bear to be parted from your car and you live within driving distance of Lorton, Virginia (just south of Washington DC), the **Florida Auto Train** will carry you and your vehicle to Sanford, near Orlando. The journey time is 17 hours and passenger fares range from $74 to $168; depending on its size, your car will cost a further $131–210.

All the above involve overnight travel. To spare yourself a restless night fidgeting in your seat, upwards of $95 will get you an "economy sleeper", essentially a narrow bed which pulls down from the wall; a family room will cost you $172, and a deluxe bedroom (for two) from $198.

BY BUS

Long-distance travel on **Greyhound** buses (☎1-800/231-2222) can be an endurance test but is at least the cheapest form of public transport to the Sunshine State. Also, if you have the time and inclination to include a few stopovers on the way, you'll find that *Greyhound* operates a more comprehensive service than do planes or trains (they also reach all but the smallest Florida towns). Scan your local newspaper or call your local *Greyhound* station for the special fares which are periodically offered, and remember that midweek travel will usually be cheaper than travelling at weekends.

Presently, the lowest fare from New York to Miami costs $119, allowing no refunds or stopovers. A more flexible ticket costs $139; Chicago–Miami is also $119, with the more flexible ticket (meaning a 15 percent refund clause and stopovers allowed) is $198. From LA to Miami the cheapest fare is $178; $199 with stopovers.

PACKAGES

Pick up the travel section of any newspaper and you'll see dozens of Florida **package deals** on offer. These come in all shapes and sizes, and are designed to appeal to a multitude of budgets and interests (golf enthusiasts, for example, are spoilt for choice). Most, however, simply offer a week or two in the Florida sun for a single price – from around $250–$400 per person per week depending on which part of the country you live in – inclusive of round-trip flights, accommodation and (in many cases) car rental.

Besides independent operators catering to specialist interests, package deals are also offered by most airlines and by *Amtrak*. Contact the nearest office for the latest details.

GETTING THERE FROM AUSTRALASIA

There are no direct flights to Florida from Australia or New Zealand, so travellers should fly to Los Angeles or San Francisco – the main points of entry to the US – and make their way from there.

Other than charter deals, seasonal bargains and all-in-packages that may be on offer from high-street travel agents, the cheapest flights are available from the specialists listed overleaf. Fares vary throughout the year according to **season**: low season for flights to the US is Feb–March and Oct 16–Nov 30; shoulder season is Jan 16–31, April–May and Sept 1–Oct 15; high season is Dec 1–Jan 15 and Jun–Aug. Your local travel agent will give you information on the latest deals; student and under-26 deals, where available, are about ten percent cheaper.

From Australia there are **direct flights** to LA and San Fransisco five times weekly from Sydney, Melbourne and Brisbane on *Air New Zealand* (A$1750 low season/A$2145 high season), daily from Cairns, Brisbane, Sydney, Darwin and Perth on *Quantas* (A$2250/2650), and daily from Sydney on *United Airlines* (A$1750/2145).

Daily flights to LA or San Fransisco via a **stopover** in Asia or the Pacific are operated by *ANZ* (from Sydney & Melbourne via Auckland; A$1750/2150), *Cathay Pacific* (via Hong Kong from Sydney & Brisbane, A$1932/2300; or Cairns, A$1822/2250), *JAL* (from Brisbane & Sydney via Tokyo; A$1650/2010), *MAS* (from Sydney via Kuala Lumpur; A$1868/2800) and *Quantas* (from Sydney &

Melbourne via Hawaii or Auckland & Papeete; A$2250/2650). Other airlines with several indirect flights a week from major Australian airports are *Garuda*, *Korean Airlines*, *Philippine Airlines* and *Singapore Airlines*.

From New Zealand, the best direct deals are from Auckland; add about NZ$100 for departures from Christchurch and Wellington. Daily flights are operated by *ANZ* (NZ$1869/2819 to LA) and *United Airlines* (NZ$1869/2809 to LA or San Fransisco); plus *MAS* and *Quantas* fly to LA several times a week for NZ$1860/2805.

Flights to LA via their homeports are operated several times a week by *JAL* (NZ$2295 flat rate) and *Korean Airlines* (NZ$2250 flat rate); and once a week by *Air Calcdonie-Corsair* (NZ$1980 flat rate) and *Air Pacific* (NZ$2045/2260).

Add-on fares to destinations in Florida cost around A$424 or NZ$450.

Various **coupon deals**, valid in continental US, are available with your main ticket. A minimum purchase of three usually applies, for example *AA*'s Coupon Pass costs US$319 for the first three, and between US$50 and $100 for subsequent tickets (maximum of ten in total); *UA*'s first three are US$49/379 plus US$100 for next two, then US$30 thereafter, with a limit of eight; *Continental*'s prices vary according to the airline, but start from US$319 for the three, with a maximum of nine, and subsequent coupons are US$50 each. *Delta*'s published prices are high with a minimum of three for US$380 and a maximum of ten for US$930; however, discounted fares are available through travel agents. *ANZ–AA* offer a five-coupon deal from US$2199.

Round The World deals from Australasia include *Cathay Pacific-UA*'s "Globetrotter" or *ANZ-KLM-Northwest*'s "World Navigator", two similar packages of six stopovers worldwide, limited backtracking, and additional stopovers (around $100 each in OZ/NZ), for A$2349/2899; NZ$2999/3449. *Quantas-BA*'s "Global Explorer" is more restrictive, allowing six stopovers but no backtracking within the US (A$2499/3099; NZ$2399/2999). More US-oriented, but only available in Australia, is *Singapore-TWA*'s "Easyworld" fare, allowing unlimited backtracking within the US (flat rate A$3023). For unlimited flexibility, *UA*, in conjunction with a variety of airlines, also offers an unrestrictred RTW fare for around A/NZ$4500/4800.

AIRLINES IN AUSTRALASIA

Air New Zealand, Sydney (☎02/9223 4666); Auckland (☎09/357 3000).

American Airlines, Sydney (☎02/9956 7055; toll-free 1800/227 101).

British Airways, Sydney (☎02/9258 3300); Auckland (☎09/356 8690).

Cathay Pacific, Sydney (☎02/9931 5500); Auckland (☎09/379 0861).

Delta Air Lines, Sydney (☎02/9262 1777); Auckland (☎09/379 3370).

Garuda, Sydney (☎02/9334 9900); Auckland (☎09/366 1855).

JAL, Sydney (☎02/9283 1111); Auckland (☎09/379 9906).

MAS Malaysian Airlines, Sydney (local-call rate ☎13 2627); Auckland (☎09/373 2741).

Philippine Airlines, Sydney (☎02/9262 3333). No NZ office.

Qantas, Sydney (☎02/9957 0111); Auckland (☎09/357 8900).

Korean Airlines, Sydney (☎02/9262 6000); Auckland (☎09/307 3687).

Singapore Airlines, Sydney (local-call rate ☎13 1011); Auckland (☎09/379 3209).

United Airlines, Sydney (☎02/237 8888); Auckland (☎09/307 9500).

FLIGHT AGENTS IN AUSTRALASIA

Anywhere Travel, 345 Anzac Parade, Kingsford, Sydney (☎02/9663 0411).

Brisbane Discount Travel, 260 Queen St, Brisbane (☎07/3229 9211).

Budget Travel, 16 Fort St, Auckland; other branches around the city (☎09/366 0061; toll-free 0800/ 808 040).

Destinations Unlimited, 3 Milford Rd, Milford, Auckland (☎09/373 4033).

Flight Centres Australia: Circular Quay, Sydney (☎02/9241 2422); Bourke St, Melbourne (☎03/ 9650 2899); other branches nationwide. New Zealand: National Bank Towers, 205–225 Queen St, Auckland (☎09/209 6171); Shop 1M, National Mutual Arcade, 152 Hereford St, Christchurch (☎03/379 7145); 50–52 Willis St, Wellington (☎04/472 8101); other branches nationwide.

Passport Travel, Kings Cross Plaza, Suite 11a, 4010 St Kilda Rd, Melbourne (☎03/9824 7183).

STA Travel, Australia: 855 George St, Ultimo, Sydney (☎02/9212 1255; toll-free 1800/637 444); 256 Flinders St, Melbourne (☎03/9654 7266); other offices countrywide. New Zealand: Travellers' Centre, 10 High St, Auckland (☎09/309 0458); 233 Cuba St, Wellington (☎04/385 0561); 90 Cashel St, Christchurch (☎03/379 9098); other branches nationwide.

Thomas Cook, Australia: 321 Kent St, Sydney (☎02/9248 6100); 330 Collins St, Melbourne (☎03/ 9602 3811); branches in other state capitals. New Zealand: Shop 250a St Luke's Square, Auckland (☎09/849 2071).

Topdeck Travel, 65 Glenfell St, Adelaide (☎08/ 8232 7222).

Tymtro Travel, 428 George St, Sydney (☎02/9223 2211).

UTAG Travel, 122 Walker St, North Sydney (☎02/9956 8399); other branches nationwide.

SPECIALIST TOUR OPERATORS IN AUSTRALASIA

The Adventure Specialists Floor 1, 69 Liverpool Street, Sydney (☎02/261 292).

Adventure World 73 Walker St, Sydney (☎02/ 956 7766); 8 Victoria Ave, Perth (☎09/221 2300); 101 Great South Rd, Remuera, Auckland (☎09/524 5118). Agents for *TrekAmerica*.

American Travel Centre 2nd Floor, 262 Adelaide St, Brisbane (☎07/3221 4788).

Creative Tours (wholesaler) Level 3, Grafton St, Woollahra, Sydney (☎02/386 2111).

Insight (wholesaler) 39–41 Chandos St, St Leonards (☎02/9437 4660).

Padi Travel Network 4/372 Eastern Valley Way, Chatswood, NSW (☎1-800 678 100). Dive packages to prime sites off the Florida Coast.

Sydney International Travel 75 King St, Sydney (☎02/9299 8000).

Wiltrans Level 10, 189 Kent St, Sydney (☎02/ 9255 0899).

VISAS AND RED TAPE

VISAS

To visit the US for a period of less than ninety days, citizens of Austria, Andorra, Belgium, Britain, Brunei, Denmark, Finland, France, Germany, Iceland, Ireland, Italy, Japan, Liechtenstein, Luxembourg, Monaco, the Netherlands, New Zealand, Norway, San Marino, Spain, Sweden and Switzerland need a **full passport** and a **visa waiver form**. The latter will be provided either by your travel agent or by the airline during check-in or on the plane, and must be presented to immigration on arrival. Prospective visitors from Australia and all other parts of the world not mentioned above must have a valid passport and a **non-immigrant visitor's visa**. To obtain a visa, fill in the application form available at most travel agents and send it with a full passport to your nearest US Embassy

Canadian citizens are in a particularly privileged position when it comes to crossing the border into the US. Although it is possible to enter the States without your passport, you should really have it with you on any trip that brings you as far as Florida. Only if you plan to stay for more than ninety days do you need a visa.

Bear in mind that if you cross into the States in your car, trunks and passenger compartments are subject to spot searches by US Customs personnel, though this sort of surveillance is likely to decrease as remaining tariff barriers fall over the next few years. Remember, too, that Canadians are legally barred from seeking gainful employment in the US.

or Consulate. Visas are not issued to convicted criminals. You'll need to give precise dates of your trip and declare that you're not intending to live or work in the US (if you are intending to do either of these things, see "Staying on", p.46).

IMMIGRATION CONTROLS

During the flight, you'll be handed an **immigration form** (and a customs declaration: see below), which must be filled out and, after landing, given up at immigration control. Part of the form will be attached to your passport, where it must stay until you leave, when an immigration or airline official will detach it.

On the form you must give details of where you are staying on your first night (if you don't know write "touring") and the date you intend to **leave** the US. You should also be able to prove that you have enough **money** to support yourself while in the US ($300–400 per week is considered sufficient) as anyone revealing the slightest intention of working while in the country is likely to be refused admission. You may also experience difficulties if you admit to being HIV positive or having AIDS or TB.

CUSTOMS

Customs officers will relieve you of your customs declaration and ask if you have any fresh foods. You'll also be asked if you've visited a farm in the last month: if you have, your shoes may well be taken away for inspection.

The **duty-free allowance** if you're over 17 is 200 cigarettes and 100 cigars and, if you're over 21, a litre of spirits.

As well as foods and anything agricultural, it's also **prohibited** to carry into the country any articles from North Korea, Cuba, Iran, Iraq, Libya, Serbia or Montenegro, obscene publications, lottery tickets, chocolate liqueurs or pre-Columbian artefacts. Anyone caught carrying drugs into the country will not only face prosecution but be entered in the records as an undesirable and probably denied entry for all time. If you take prescription medicines, it may be a good idea to carry a letter from a doctor stating the exact nature of the pills you are carrying, in order to ease your passage through Customs.

US EMBASSY AND CONSULATES IN CANADA

Embassy: 100 Wellington St, Ottawa, ON K1P 5T1 (☎613/238-5335).

Consulates:

Suite 1050, 615 Macleod Trail, Calgary, AB (☎403/266-8962).

Suite 910, Cogswell Tower, Scotia Square, Halifax, NS (☎902/429-2480).

Complex Desjardins, South Tower, Montréal, PQ (☎514/398-9695).

1 Ave. St Genevieve, Québec City, PQ (☎418/692-2095).

360 University Ave, Toronto, ON (☎416/595-1700).

1095 West Pender St Vancouver, BC (☎604/685-4311).

US EMBASSY AND CONSULATES ELSEWHERE

Australia
Moonhah Place, Canberra (☎62/733 711).

Denmark
Dag Hammerskjöld Allé 24, 2100 Copenhagen (☎31 42 31 44).

Eire
42 Elgin St, Ballsbridge, Dublin (☎01/688 8777).

Netherlands
Museumplein 19, Amsterdam (☎020/790 321).

New Zealand
29 Fitzherbert Terrace, Thorndon, Wellington (☎4/722 068).

Norway
Drammensveien 18, Oslo (☎22 44 85 50).

Sweden
Strandvägen 101, Stockholm (☎08/783 5300).

UK
5 Upper Grosvenor St, London W1 (☎0171/499 7010).

3 Regent Terrace, Edinburgh EH7 5BW (☎0131/556 8315).

Queens House, 14 Queen St, Belfast BT1 6EQ (☎01232/228239).

EXTENSIONS AND LEAVING

The date stamped on the form in your passport is the **latest** you're legally entitled to stay. Leaving a few days after may not matter, especially if you're heading home, but more than a week or so can result in a protracted – and generally unpleasant – interrogation from officials, which may cause you to miss your flight and be denied entry to the US in the future and your American hosts and/or employer/s to face legal proceedings.

Although not a foolproof method, one of the simplest ways to stay on is to make a quick trip to the Bahamas: the least costly way to do this is as a $100 day-trip with *Seascape Ltd* (☎1-800/327-7400), one of many cruise companies operating between Miami and Fort Lauderdale to the Bahamas and the Caribbean – its ads are in all the local newspapers. When you re-enter the US, you may be searched, so make sure you don't have a US library card or anything else that might indicate you have an unofficial, semi-permanent US address; your diary may also be examined. All being well, you'll routinely have a new leaving date stamped in your passport.

Alternatively, you can do things the official way and get an **extension** before your time is up. This can be done by going to the nearest **US Immigration and Naturalization Service (INS)** office (in Miami at 7880 Biscayne Blvd, ☎305/536 5741; other addresses will be under the "Federal Government Offices" listings at the front of the phone book). They will automatically assume that you're working illegally and it's up to you to convince them otherwise. Do this by providing evidence of ample finances and, if possible, an upstanding American citizen to vouch for your worthiness. Obviously you'll also have to explain why you didn't plan for the extra time initially – saying your money lasted longer than you expected, or that a close relative is coming over, are well-worked excuses.

HEALTH AND INSURANCE

HEALTH

If you have a serious **accident** while in Florida, emergency medical services will get to you quickly and charge you later. For **emergencies** or ambulances, dial ☎911 (or whatever variant may be on the information plate of the pay phone). If you have an accident but don't require an ambulance, we've listed casualty departments in the *Guide*; ditto for **dental treatment**.

Should you need to see a **doctor**, lists can be found in the *Yellow Pages* under "Clinics" or "Physicians and Surgeons". A basic consultation fee is $50–75, payable in advance. Medication isn't cheap either – keep receipts for all you spend and claim it back on your insurance policy when you return.

Many **minor ailments** can be remedied using the fabulous array of potions and lotions available in **drugstores**. Foreign visitors should bear in mind that many pills available over the counter at home need a prescription in the US and that local brand names can be confusing; ask for advice at the **pharmacy** in any drugstore.

Travellers from Europe do not require **inoculations** to enter the US.

INSURANCE

Though not compulsory, **travel insurance** is *essential* for **foreign travellers**. The US has no national health system and you can lose an arm and a leg (so to speak) having even minor medical treatment. Bank and credit cards (particularly American Express) often have certain levels of medical or other insurance included, especially if you use them to pay for your trip.

If you plan to participate in water sports or do some hiking or skiing, you'll probably have to pay an extra premium; check crarefully that any insurance policy you are considering will cover you in case of an accident. Note also that very few insurers will arrange on-the-spot payments in the event of a major expense or loss; you will usually be reimbursed only after going home. In all cases of loss or theft of goods, you will have to contact the local police to have a report made out so that your insurer can process the claim.

BRITISH COVER

Most **travel agents** and tour operators will offer you insurance when you book your flight or holiday, and some will insist you take it. These policies are usually reasonable value, though as ever, you should check the small print. The cheapest are generally *Endsleigh*, who charge around £35 for three weeks to cover life, limb and luggage (with a 25 percent reduction if you forego luggage insurance). *Columbus* does an annual multi-trip policy, which offers twelve month's cover for £125.

If you feel the cover is inadequate, or you want to compare prices, any travel agent, **insurance broker** or **bank** should be able to help. If you have a good "all risks" home insurance policy it may well cover your possessions against loss or theft even when overseas, and many private medical schemes also cover you when abroad – make sure you know the procedure and the helpline number.

On all policies, read the small print to ensure the cover includes a sensible amout for medical

---

TRAVEL INSURANCE COMPANIES IN THE UK

Campus Travel or **STA** (see p.4 for addresses)

Endsleigh Insurance, 97–107 Southampton Row, London WC1B 4AG (☎0171/436 4451).

Frizzell Insurance, Frizzell House, County Gates, Bournemouth, Dorset BH1 2NF (☎01202/ 292333).

Columbus Travel Insurance, 17 Devonshire Square, London EC2M 4SQ (☎0171/375 0011).

expenses – this should be at least £1,000,000, which will cover the cost of an air ambulance to fly you home in the event of a serious injury or hospitalization.

AUSTRALASIAN COVER

Travel insurance is put together by the airlines and travel agent groups in conjunction with insurance companies (see box below). They are all comparable in premium and coverage. Adventure sports are covered, with the exception of mountaineering with ropes, bungy jumping (some policies), and unassisted diving without an Open Water licence – check the policy first. A typical insurance policy will cost A$190/NZ$220 for one month, A$270/NZ$320 for two months and A$330/NZ$400 for three months.

TRAVEL INSURANCE COMPANIES IN AUSTRALASIA

UTAG, 347 Kent St, Sydney (☎02/9819 6855; toll-free 1800/809 462).

AFTA, 181 Miller St, North Sydney (☎02/9956 4800).

Cover More, Level 9, 32 Walker St, North Sydney (☎02/9968 1333; toll-free 1800/251 881).

Ready Plan, 141–147 Walker St, Dandenong, Victoria (toll-free ☎1800/337 462); 10th Floor, 63 Albert St, Auckland (☎09/379 3399).

NORTH AMERICAN COVER

Before buying an insurance policy, **North American travellers** should check that they're not already covered for health charges or costs by their current **health insurance**. If, in the event of an accident or illness, you are unable to use a phone or are required to pay the practitioner immediately, save all the **forms** to support a claim for subsequent reimbursement. Remember that time limits may apply when making claims after the fact, so promptness in contacting your insurer is highly advisable. Holders of official **student/teacher/youth cards** are entitled to accident coverage and hospital in-patient benefits – the annual membership is far less than the cost of comparable insurance. **Students** may also find that their student health coverage extends during the vacations and for one term beyond the date of last enrollment. **Bank and credit cards** (particularly *American Express*)

often provide certain levels of medical or other insurance, and travel insurance may also be included if you use a major credit or charge card to pay for your trip. **Homeowners' or renters'** insurance often covers theft or loss of documents, money and valuables while you are on holiday.

After exhausting the possibilities above, you might want to contact a specialist **travel insurance** company; your travel agent can usually recommend one, or see the box below.

Travel insurance **policies** vary: some are comprehensive while others cover only certain risks (accidents, illnesses, delayed or lost luggage, cancelled flights, etc.). In particular, ask whether the policy pays medical costs up front or reimburses you later. For policies that include lost or stolen luggage, check exactly what's covered, and make sure the per-article limit will cover your most valuable possessions.

The best **premiums** are usually to be had through student/youth travel agencies – *ISIS* policies, for example, cost $48–69 for fifteen days (depending on level of coverage), $80–105 for a month, $149–207 for two months, $510–700 for a year. If you're planning to do any "dangerous sports" (skiing, mountaineering, etc.), be sure to ask whether these activities are covered: some companies levy a surcharge.

Most North American travel policies apply only to items lost, stolen or damaged while in the custody of an identifiable, responsible third party – hotel porter, airline, luggage consignment, etc. Even in these cases you will have to contact the local police within a certain time limit to have a complete report made out so that your insurer can process the claim.

TRAVEL INSURANCE COMPANIES IN NORTH AMERICA

Access America ☎1-800/284-8300

Carefree Travel Insurance ☎1-800/323-3149

Desjardins Travel Insurance – Canada only ☎1-800/463-7830

International Student Insurance Service (ISIS) – sold by *STA Travel* ☎1-800/777-0112

Travel Assistance International ☎1-800/821-2828

Travel Guard ☎1-800/826-1300

Travel Insurance Services ☎1-800/937-1387

COSTS, MONEY AND BANKS

To help with planning your Florida vacation, this book contains detailed price information for lodging and eating throughout the region. Unless otherwise stated, the hotel price codes given (explained on p.27) are for the cheapest double room in high season, exclusive of any local taxes which may apply, while meal prices include food only and not drinks or tip. Naturally, as time passes after the publication of the book, you should make allowances for inflation.

Even when the exchange rate is at its least advantageous (see box below), most visitors find virtually everything – accommodation, food, petrol, cameras, clothes and more – to be better value in the US than it is at home. However, if you're used to travelling in the less expensive countries of Europe, let alone in the rest of the world, you shouldn't expect to scrape by on the same minuscule budget once you're in the US.

Your biggest single expense is likely to be **accommodation**. Few hotel or motel rooms in cities cost under $30 – around $50 is more usual – and rates in rural areas are little cheaper. Although hostels offering dorm beds – usually for $12–15 – exist, they are not widespread and in any case represent only a very small saving for two or more people travelling together. Camping, of course, is cheap, ranging from free to perhaps $18 per night, but is rarely practical in or around the big cities.

As for **food**, $10 a day is enough to get you an adequate life-support diet, while for a daily budget of around $20 you can dine pretty well. Beyond this, everything hinges on how much

MONEY: A NOTE FOR FOREIGN TRAVELLERS

Regular upheaval in the world's money markets causes the relative value of the **US dollar** against the currencies of the rest of the world to vary considerably. Generally speaking, one **pound sterling** will buy between $1.45 and $1.80; one **Canadian dollar** is worth between 76¢ and $1; one **Australian dollar** is worth between 67¢ and 88¢; and one **New Zealand dollar** is worth between 55¢ and 72¢.

Notes and coins
US currency comes in **notes** worth $1, $5, $10, $20, $50 and $100, plus various larger (and rarer) denominations. Confusingly, all are the same size and same green colour, making it necessary to check each note carefully. The dollar is made up of 100 cents in **coins** of 1 cent (known as a **penny**), 5 cents (a **nickel**), 10 cents (a **dime**) and 25 cents (a **quarter**). Very occasionally you might come across **JFK half-dollars** (50¢), **Susan B. Anthony dollar coins**, or a **two-dollar note**. Change (quarters are the most useful) is needed for buses, vending machines and telephones, so always carry plenty.

sightseeing, taxi-taking, drinking and socializing you do. Much of any of these – especially in a major city – and you're likely to be getting through upwards of $50 a day.

The rates for **travelling** around using buses, trains and even planes, may look cheap on paper, but costs soon mount up. For a group of two or more, **renting a car** can be a very good investment.

Sales tax of 6 percent is added to virtually everything you buy in shops, but it isn't part of the marked price.

TRAVELLERS' CHEQUES

US dollar travellers' cheques are the best way to carry money, for both American and foreign visitors; they offer the great security of knowing that lost or stolen cheques will be replaced. You should have no problem using the better-known cheques, such as *American Express* and *Visa*, in shops, restaurants and filling stations (don't be put off by "no checks" signs,

For **emergency phone numbers** to call if your cheques (and/or credit cards) should be stolen, see p.36.

which only refer to personal cheques). Be sure to have plenty of the $10 and $20 denominations for everyday transactions.

Major Florida banks – such as *Bank of America, Barnett, First Florida, Southeast* and *Sun* – will (with considerable fuss) change travellers' cheques in **other currencies** and foreign currency. Commission rates tend to be lower at exchange bureaux like *Deak-Perera* and *Thomas Cook*; airport exchange offices can also be reasonable. Hotels rarely, if ever, change money.

Banking hours in Florida are generally 10am until 3pm Monday to Thursday and 10am to 5pm on Fridays.

PLASTIC MONEY AND CASH MACHINES

If you have a **Visa**, **Mastercard** (known elsewhere as **Access**), **Diners Club**, **Discover** or **American Express** card you really *shouldn't* leave home without it. Almost all stores, most restaurants and many services will take some kind of plastic. In addition, hotels and car rental companies will ask for a card either to establish your credit-worthiness, or as security, or both. Even in these dark days for credit buying, some people still get funny about cash.

With *Mastercard* or *Visa* it is also possible to **withdraw cash** at any bank displaying relevant stickers, or from appropriate automatic teller machines (**ATMs**). *Diners Club* cards can be used to cash personal cheques at *Citibank* branches. *American Express* cards can only get cash, or buy travellers' cheques, at *American Express* offices (check the Yellow Pages) or from the travellers' cheque dispensers at most major airports. Most **Canadian** credit cards issued by hometown banks will be honoured in the US.

Thanks to relaxation in interstate banking restrictions, American holders of ATM cards from out of state are likely to discover that their cards work in the machines of select Florida banks

Each of the two main networks operates a toll-free line to let customers know the location of their nearest ATM; *Plus System* is ☎1-800/THE-PLUS, *Cirrus* is ☎1-800/4CI-RRUS.

(check with your bank before you leave home). Not only is this method of financing safer, but at around only a dollar per transaction it's economical as well.

Most major credit cards issued by **foreign banks** are accepted in the US, as well as cash dispensing cards linked to international networks such as *Cirrus* and *Plus* – though it's important to check the latest details with your credit card company before departing, as otherwise the machine may simply gobble up your plastic friend. Overseas visitors should also bear in mind that fluctuating exchange rates may result in spending more (or less) than expected when the item eventually shows up on a statement.

EMERGENCIES

If you're flat broke and at your wits' end as to what to do, there are a few alternatives before making a meal of yourself to the local alligators.

Assuming you know someone who is prepared to send you money in a crisis, the quickest way is to have them take the cash to the nearest **Western Union** office (information on ☎1-800/325-6000 in the US; ☎0800/833833 in the UK; toll-free 1800/649 565 in Australia; and ☎09/302 0143 in New Zealand), and have it instantaneously **wired** to the office nearest you, subject to the deduction of ten percent commission. **American Express MoneyGram** (☎1-800/543-4080) offers a similar service.

It's also possible to have money wired directly from a bank in your home country to a bank in the US, though this is somewhat less reliable because it involves two separate institutions. If you go this route, the person wiring the funds to you will need to know the routing number of the bank the funds are being wired to. Having money wired from home is never convenient or cheap, and should only be considered a last resort.

If you have a few days' leeway, a cheaper method is to have a postal money order sent through the mail; these are exchangeable at any post office. The equivalent for foreign travellers is the **international money order**, for which you need to allow up to seven days in the international air mail before arrival. An ordinary cheque sent from overseas takes two to three weeks to clear.

Foreign travellers in difficulties have the option of throwing themselves on the mercy of their nearest national **consulate**, which will – in the worst cases – repatriate you, but will never, under any circumstances, lend you money.

COMMUNICATIONS: TELEPHONES AND POST

Visitors from overseas tend to be impressed by the speed and efficiency of communications in the US, and for the most part, Florida conforms to this high standard. However, a laid-back attitude is ingrained in certain areas (notoriously so in the Florida Keys), which can frustrate travellers who have yet to adjust to the local pace.

TELEPHONES

Florida's **telephones** are run by several companies, the largest being *Southern Bell*, all of which are linked to the *AT&T* network.

Public telephones invariably work and are easily found – on street corners, in railway and bus stations, hotel lobbies, bars, restaurants – and they take 25¢, 10¢ and 5¢ coins. The cost of a **local call** from a public phone varies according to the actual distance being called. The minimum is 25¢ for the first three minutes and a further 10¢ for each additional three minutes – when

USEFUL NUMBERS

Emergencies ☎911; ask for the appropriate emergency service: fire, police or ambulance
Local directory information ☎411
Long-distance directory information ☎1 (Area Code)/555-1212

Directory enquiries for toll-free numbers ☎1-800/555-1212
Operator ☎0

FLORIDA AREA CODES

305 Miami, the Florida Keys and the southern section of the Southeast Coast.
407 Orlando and surrounds and the central section of the East Coast.

904 Most of the Northeast Coast, North Central Florida, the northern parts of the West Coast and the Panhandle.
941 Most of the West Coast and parts of South Central Florida.

INTERNATIONAL TELEPHONE CALLS

International calls can be dialled direct from private or (more expensively) public phones. You can get assistance from the **international operator** (☎1-800/874-4000), who may also interrupt every three minutes asking for more money, and call you back for any money still owed immediately after you hang up. One alternative is to make a **collect call** (to "reverse the charges"); dialling ☎1-800/445-5667 will connect you with an operator in Britain.

The **cheapest rates** for international calls to Europe are between 6pm and 7am, when a

direct-dialled three-minute call will cost roughly $5.

In **Britain**, it's possible to obtain a free **BT Chargecard** (☎0800/800 838), using which all calls from overseas can be charged to your quarterly domestic account; from Florida, you contact the British operator via AT&T, and your call is charged at standard payphone rates.

The telephone code to dial **TO the US** from the outside world (excluding Canada) is 1.

To make international calls **FROM the US**, dial 011 followed by the country code:

Australia 61	**Denmark** 45	**Germany** 49	**Ireland** 353
Netherlands 31	**New Zealand** 64	**Sweden** 46	**United Kingdom** 44

SPRING CREEK CAMPUS

necessary, a voice will come on the line telling you to pay more.

More expensive are **non-local calls** ("zone calls"), to numbers within the same area code (commonly, vast areas are covered by a single code) but costing much more and sometimes requiring you to dial 1 before the seven-digit number. Pricier still are **long-distance calls** (ie to a different area code), for which you'll need plenty of change. If you still owe money at the end of the call, the phone will ring immediately and you'll be asked for the outstanding amount (if you don't cough up, the person you've been calling will get the bill). Non-local calls and long-distance calls are far cheaper if made between 6pm and 8am, and calls from **private phones** are always much cheaper than those from public phones.

Making telephone calls from **hotel rooms** is usually more expensive than from a payphone (and there are usually payphones in hotel lobbies). On the other hand, some budget hotels offer free local calls from rooms – ask when you check in. An increasing number of phones accept **credit cards** – simply swipe the card through the slot and dial. Another way to avoid the necessity of carrying copious quantities of change everywhere is to obtain an **AT&T charge card** (information on ☎1-800/874-4000 ext 359), for which you have to have an American credit card.

Many government agencies, car rental firms, hotels and other services have **toll-free numbers**, for which you don't have to pay anything: these numbers always have the prefix ☎1-800. Some lines, such as ☎1-800/577-HEAT to get the latest on the Miami Heat basketball team, employ the letters on the push-button phones as part of their "number".

MAIL SERVICES

Post offices are usually open Mon–Fri 9am–5pm and Sat 9am–noon, and there are blue **mail boxes** on many street corners. Ordinary **mail**

within the US costs 32¢ for a letter weighing up to an ounce; addresses must include the **zip code** (postal code), as well as the sender's address on the envelope. **Air mail** between Florida and Europe generally takes about a week to arrive. Postcards, aerograms and letters weighing up to half an ounce (a single sheet) cost 60¢.

Letters can be sent c/o **General Delivery** (what's known elsewhere as **poste restante**) to any post office in the country but *must* include the post office's zip code and will only be held for thirty days before being returned to sender – so make sure there's a return address on the envelope. If you're receiving mail at someone else's address, it should include "c/o" and the regular occupant's name; otherwise it, too, is likely to be returned.

Rules on sending **parcels** are very rigid: packages must be in special containers bought from post offices and sealed according to their instructions, which are given at the start of the Yellow Pages. To send anything out of the country, you'll need a **customs declaration form**, available from a post office. Postal rates for sending a parcel weighing up to 1lb are $9.75 to Europe, $11.20 to Australasia.

TELEGRAMS AND FAXES

To send a **telegram** (sometimes called "a wire") don't go to a post office but to a *Western Union* office (listed in the *Yellow Pages*). Credit card holders can dictate their message over the phone. For domestic telegrams ask for a **mailgram**, which will be delivered to any address in the country the following morning. **International telegrams** are slightly cheaper than the cheapest international phone call: one sent during the day from Florida should arrive at its overseas destination the next morning.

Public **fax** machines, which may require your credit card to be "swiped" through an attached device, are found at photocopy centres and, occasionally, in bookshops.

INFORMATION, MAPS AND THE MEDIA

Advance information for a trip to Florida can be obtained by post from the Florida Division of Tourism at 126 W Van Buren Street, Tallahassee, Florida 32399-2000 (☎904/487-1462); Canadian travellers can call Travel, USA at $2 per minute (☎900/451-4050). Once in Florida, you'll find most large towns have at least a Convention and Visitors Bureau ("CVB"; usual hours Mon–Fri 9am–5pm, Sat 9am–1pm), offering detailed information on the local area and discount coupons for food and accommodation, but unable to book hotel or motel rooms.

In addition there are **Chambers of Commerce** almost everywhere; these are designed to promote local business interests, but are more than happy to provide travellers with local maps and information. Most communities have local **free newspapers** (see p.20) carrying news of events and entertainment – the most useful of which we've detailed in the *Guide*.

Drivers entering Florida will find **Welcome Centers**, fully stocked with information leaflets and discount booklets, at two points: on Hwy-231 at Campbellton, near the Florida–Alabama border and off I-75 near Jennings, just south of the Florida–Georgia line. More convenient for arrivals on I-10 are the **visitor information centers** at Pensacola and Tallahassee, detailed later in the *Guide*.

MAPS

CVBs and Chambers of Commerce give away an excellent **free map** of the whole state (though the *Official Transportation Map* does not, as its name suggests, detail public transport routes). If you're planning to drive or cycle (see "Getting around" through rural areas, use *DeLorme's* highly detailed 120-page *Florida Atlas & Gazetteer* ($12.95). The best commercially available **city plans** are published by *Rand-McNally* (see box on p.20).

Local **hiking** maps are available at ranger stations in state and national parks either free or

MAP AND TRAVEL BOOK SUPPLIERS

AUSTRALIA

The Map Shop, 16a Peel St, Adelaide (☎08/8231 2033).

Bowyangs, 372 Little Burke St, Melbourne (☎03/9670 4383).

Perth Map Centre, 891 Hay St, Perth (☎08/9322 5733).

Travel Bookshop, 20 Bridge St, Sydney (☎02/9241 3554).

CANADA

Open Air Books and Maps, 25 Toronto St, Toronto, ON M5R 2C1 (☎416/363-0719).

Ulysses Travel Bookshop, 4176 St-Denis, Montréal (☎514/289-0993).

World Wide Books and Maps, 1247 Granville St, Vancouver, BC V6Z 1E4 (☎604/687-3320).

IRELAND

Easons Bookshop, 40 O'Connell St, Dublin 1 (☎01/873 3811).

Fred Hanna's Bookshop, 27–29 Nassau St, Dublin 2 (☎01/677 1255).

Hodges Figgis Bookshop, 56–58 Dawson St, Dublin 2 (☎01/677 4754).

Waterstone's, Queens Bldg, 8 Royal Ave, Belfast BT1 1DA (☎01232/247355).

NEW ZEALAND

Specialty Maps, 58 Albert St, Auckland (☎09/307 2217).

UK

Daunt Books, 83 Marylebone High St, London W1 (☎0171/224 2295).

John Smith and Sons, 57–61 St Vincent St, Glasgow G2 5TB (☎0141/221 7472).

National Map Centre, 22–24 Caxton St, London SW1 (☎0171/222 4945).

Stanfords *, 12–14 Long Acre, London WC2 (☎0171/836 1321); 52 Grosvenor Gardens, London SW1W 0AG; 156 Regent St, London W1R 5TA.

The Travel Bookshop, 13–15 Blenheim Crescent, London W11 2EE (☎0171/229 5260).

*Note: Maps by **mail or phone order** are available from *Stanfords*, ☎0171/836 1321.

USA

The Complete Traveler Bookstore, 199 Madison Ave, New York, NY 10016 (☎212/685-9007); 3207 Fillmore St, San Francisco, CA 92123 (☎415/923-1511).

Forsyth Travel Library, 9154 W 57th St, Shawnee Mission, KS 66201 (☎1-800/367-7984).

Map Link Inc, 25 E Mason St, Santa Barbara, CA 93101 (☎805/965-4402).

Phileas Fogg's Books & Maps, #87 Stanford Shopping Center, Palo Alto, CA 94304 (☎1-800/233-FOGG in California; ☎1-800/533-FOGG elsewhere in US).

Rand McNally *, 444 N Michigan Ave, Chicago, IL 60611 (☎312/321-1751); 150 E 52nd St, New York, NY 10022 (☎212/758-7488); 595 Market St, San Francisco, CA 94105 (☎415/777-3131); 1201 Connecticut Ave NW, Washington, DC 20003 (☎202/223-6751).

Sierra Club Bookstore, 730 Polk St, San Francisco, CA 94109 (☎415/923-5500).

Travel Books & Language Center, 4931 Cordell Ave, Bethesda, MD 20814 (☎1-800/220-2665).

Traveler's Bookstore, 22 W 52nd St, New York, NY 10019 (☎212/664-0995).

*Note: For the location of other *Rand McNally* stores, or for maps by **mail order**, call ☎1-800/333-0136 (ext 2111).

---

for $1–2 and some camping shops carry a supply. For travelling around more of the US, the *Rand McNally Road Atlas* is a good investment, covering the whole country plus Canada and Mexico.

Members of the *American Automobile Association (AAA)* and its overseas affiliates (such as both the AA and the RAC in Britain) can also benefit from their maps and general assistance. They're based at 1000 AAA Drive, Heathrow, FL 32746-5063 (☎1-800/336-4357); further offices all across the state are listed in local phone books.

MEDIA

The best-read of **Florida's newspapers** is the *Miami Herald*, providing indepth coverage of state, national and world events; the *Orlando Sentinel* and *Tampa Tribune* are not far behind and, naturally enough, excel at reporting their own areas. **Overseas newspapers** are often a preserve of specialist bookshops, though you will find them widely available in major tourist areas.

Every community of any size has at least a few **free newspapers**, found in street-

> If you're thinking of travelling elsewhere in the US, the **Rough Guide: USA** (Penguin; US $18.95, CAN $25.99, UK £12.99) is essential reading.

distribution bins or just lying around in piles. It's a good idea to pick up a full assortment: some simply cover local goings-on, others provide specialist coverage of interests ranging from long-distance cycling to getting ahead in business – and the classified and personal ads can provide hours of entertainment. Many of them are also excellent sources for bar, restaurant and nightlife information and we've mentioned the most useful titles in the *Guide*.

TELEVISION

Florida's **TV** is pretty much the standard network sitcom and talk-show barrage you get all over the country, with frequent interruptions for hard-sell commercials.

Game shows fill up most of the morning schedule; around lunchtime you can take your pick of any of a dozen daily soaps. Slightly better are the **cable networks**, to which you'll have access in most hotels and include the around-the-clock news of *CNN* and *MTV*'s non-stop circuit of mainstream pop videos.

Especially in the south, Spanish-language stations service the Hispanic communities.

RADIO

Most of Florida's **radio** stations stick to the usual commercial format of retro-rock, classic pop, MOR country, or easy-listening pap.

In general, except for news and chat, the occasional fire-and-brimstone preacher, and Latin and Haitian music, stations on the AM band are best avoided in favour of the FM band, in particular the public and college stations on the air in Tallahassee, Gainesville, Orlando, Tampa and Miami, found on the left of the dial (88–92FM). These invariably provide diverse and listenable programming, whether it be bizarre underground rock or abstruse literary discussions and they're also good sources for local nightlife news.

GETTING AROUND

Travel in the surprisingly compact state of Florida is rarely difficult or time-consuming. Crossing between the east and west coasts, for example, takes only a couple of hours and even the longest possible trip – between the western extremity of the Panhandle and Miami – can just about be accomplished in a day. With a car you'll have no problems at all, but travelling by public transport requires adroit forward planning: cities and larger towns have bus links – and, in some cases, an infrequent train service – but many rural areas and some of the most enjoyable sections of the coast are sadly off-limits to non-drivers.

BUSES

Buses are the cheapest way to travel. The only long-distance service is *Greyhound*, which links all major cities and many smaller towns. In isolated areas buses are fairly scarce, sometimes only appearing once a day, if at all – so plot your route with care. Between the big cities, buses run around the clock to a fairly full timetable, stopping only for meal breaks (almost always fast-food dives) and driver change-overs. *Greyhound*, though not luxurious, is bearable and it's feasible occasionally to save on a night's accommodation by travelling overnight and sleeping on the bus. Any sizeable community will have a *Greyhound* station; in smaller places the local post office or filling station doubles as the stop and ticket office. In the Florida Keys, the bus makes scheduled stops but can also be flagged down anywhere along the Overseas Highway.

Fares – for example $37 one way between Miami and Orlando – are expensive but not staggeringly so and can sometimes be reduced by travelling on weekdays (except Fridays).

Remarkably, in 1993 *Greyhound* stopped publishing **timetables**, with the exception of condensed summaries of nationwide services – which obviously makes detailed route planning for Florida extremely difficult. The only toll-free information service is in Spanish (☎1-800/531-5332); otherwise information can be obtained from local terminals. The phone numbers for the larger *Greyhound* stations are given in the *Guide*.

It's handy to know that a fair-sized chunk of the Southeast Coast can be covered for very little money (if also very slowly) using **local buses**, which connect neighbouring districts. It's possible, for example, to travel from Miami to West Palm Beach for under $3, but doing so takes all day and three changes of bus – the *Tri-Rail* (see below) covers the same route for even less.

BY TRAIN AND THE TRI-RAIL

A much less viable way of getting about is by **train** (run by *Amtrak*). Florida's railroads were built to service the boom towns of the Twenties and, consequently, some rural nooks have rail links as good as the modern cities. The actual trains are clean and comfortable, with most routes in the state offering two services a day. In some areas, *Amtrak* services are extended by buses, usable only in conjunction with the train.

Fares are not particularly cheap – $51 one way between Miami and Orlando is typical.

For **Amtrak** information:	☎1-800/USA RAIL
For **Tri-Rail** information:	☎1-800/TRI RAIL

THE TRI-RAIL

Designed to reduce road traffic along the congested Southeast Coast, the elevated **Tri-Rail** system came into operation in 1989, ferrying commuters between Miami and West Palm Beach with twelve stops on the way. The single-journey flat fare is a very cheap $2.50; the only drawback is the fact that almost all services run during rush hours – meaning a very early start, or an early evening arrival.

BY PLANE

Provided your plans are flexible and you use the special cut-rate fares which are regularly advertised in local newspapers, off-peak **plane** travel within Florida is not much more expensive than taking a bus or train – and will also, obviously, get you there more quickly. Typical cut-rate one-way fares are around $60 for Miami–Orlando and $100 for Miami–Tallahassee; full fares are much higher.

For toll-free airline numbers, see p.7.

DRIVING AND CAR RENTAL

As a major vacation destination, Florida is one of the cheapest places in the US in which to **rent** a car thanks to a very competitive market. Drivers are supposed to have held their licences for at least one year (though this is rarely checked); people under 25 years old may encounter problems and will probably be inflicted with high insurance premiums.

Car rental companies will also expect you to have a credit card; if you don't have one they may let you leave a hefty **deposit** (at least $200) but don't count on it. The likeliest tactic for getting a good deal is to phone the major firms' toll-free 800 numbers for their best rates – most will try to beat the offers of their competitors, so it's worth haggling.

In general, the lowest rates are available at the airport branches. Always be sure to get free unlimited mileage and be aware that leaving the car in a different city to the one in which you rent it may incur a **drop-off charge** of as much as $200 – though many firms do not charge drop-off fees within Florida.

Alternatively, a number of **local** companies rent out new – and not so new – vehicles; in Miami try *Alva* (☎305/4444-3923) or *Inter-America Car Rental* (☎305/871-3030; in Fort Lauderdale, *Florida Auto Rental* (☎305/764-1008). Other companies are listed in the *Yellow Pages*. Rates in Miami range from $25 to $40 a day, and $130 to $165 a week with unlimited mileage. Again, you should always check that free mileage is included in the rental cost.

When you rent a car, read the small print carefully for details on **Collision Damage Waiver (CDW)**, a form of insurance which often isn't included in the initial rental charge but is well worth considering. This specifically covers the car that you are driving yourself – you are in any case

All the main American airlines (and *British Airways* in conjunction with *USAir*) offer **air passes** for visitors who plan to fly a lot within the US: these have to be bought in advance, and in the UK are usually sold with the proviso that you cross the Atlantic with the relevant airline. All the deals are broadly similar, involving the purchase of at least three **coupons** (for around £160; around £55 for each additional coupon), each valid for a flight of any duration in the US.

The **Visit USA** scheme entitles foreign travellers to a 30 percent discount on any full-priced US domestic fare, provided you buy the ticket before you leave home – but this isn't a wise choice for travel within Florida, where full-priced fares are very high.

Greyhound Ameripasses

Foreign visitors intending to travel virtually every day by bus (which is unlikely), or to venture further around the US, can buy a *Greyhound* **Ameripass**, offering unlimited travel within a set time limit, before leaving home: most travel agents can oblige. In the UK, they cost £50 (4-day), £85 (7-day), £125 (15-day) or £170 (30-day). *Greyhound*'s office is at Sussex House, London Road, East Grinstead, West Sussex RH19 1LD (☎01342/317317). Extensions can be bought in the US for the dollar equivalent of £12 a day.

The first time you use your pass, it will be dated by the ticket clerk (this becomes the commencement date of the ticket), and your destination is written on a page which the driver will tear out and keep as you board the bus. Repeat this procedure for every subsequent journey.

Amtrak rail passes

Rail travel can't get you around all Florida, but overseas travellers have a choice of three **rail passes**. The least expensive, the **East Region Pass**, available in 15- and 30-day forms, costs $158 ($178 June–Aug) and $209 ($229) respectively. Alternatively, the **National Pass** entitles you to travel throughout the US, again for 15 or 30 days, for a price of $208 ($308 June–Aug) or $309 ($389) respectively. By combining rail with some other form of travel, you could take advantage of the 30-day **Coastal Pass**, permitting unlimited train travel on the country's east and west coasts; this pass costs $179 ($199 June–Aug).

On production of a passport issued outside the US or Canada, the passes can be bought at *Amtrak* stations in the US. In the UK, you can buy them from *Amtrak*'s UK agent, Destination Marketing Limited, 2 Cinnamon Row, Plantation Wharf, York Place, London SW11 3TW (☎0171/978 5212).

Car rental

UK nationals can **drive** in the US on a full UK driving licence (International Driving Permits are not regarded as sufficient). Fly-drive deals are good value if you want to **rent** a car (see p.5), though you can save up to 60 percent simply by booking in advance with a major firm (*Holiday Autos* guarantee the cheapest rates). You can choose not to pay until you arrive, but make sure you take a written confirmation of the quoted price with you. Remember that it's safer not to rent a car straight off a long transatlantic flight; and that standard rental cars have **automatic transmissions**.

It's also easier and cheaper to book **RVs** (see overleaf) in advance from Britain. Most travel agents who specialize in the US can arrange RV rental, and usually do it cheaper if you book a flight through them as well. A price of £400 for a five-berth van for a fortnight is fairly typical.

insured for damage to other vehicles. At $9 to $12 a day, it can add substantially to the total cost, but without it you're liable for every scratch to the car – even those that aren't your fault. Some credit card companies (*AMEX* for example) offer automatic CDW coverage to anyone using their card to pay in full for the rental; read the fine print beforehand in any case. You'll also be charged a **Florida surcharge** of $2 per day.

If you decide to hire a bottom-of-the-range model, when you go to pick up the vehicle you will invariably be asked if you want to **upgrade** to a better quality car for an apparently small extra charge. Although it may sound like a good deal, bear in mind two things: firstly, if the company has already hired out all of their bottom-of-the-range cars, they are duty-bound to give you a better car at no extra charge (a fact that they will not necessarily inform you of before asking you to upgrade); secondly, the mark-up price for a better-quality car is quoted at a daily rate, which may sound reasonable at first but quickly escalates when totalled for your entire trip, and does not include extras such as tax.

CAR RENTAL COMPANIES

IN THE UK
Alamo ☎0800/272 200
Avis ☎0181/848 8733
Budget ☎0800/181 181
Dollar (Eurodollar) ☎01895/233300
Hertz ☎0345/555888.
Holiday Autos ☎0990/300400

IN NORTH AMERICA
Alamo ☎1-800/354-2322
Avis ☎1-800/331-1212
Budget ☎1-800/527-0700
Dollar ☎1-800/421-6868
Hertz ☎1-800/654-313; in Canada ☎1-800/263-0600
Holiday Autos ☎1-800/422-7737
National ☎1-800/CAR-RENT
Rent-A-Wreck ☎1-800/535-1391
Thrifty ☎1-800/367-2277

IN AUSTRALIA
Avis ☎1800/225 533
Buget ☎13 2848
Hertz ☎13 1918
Renault Eurodrive ☎02/9299 3344

IN NEW ZEALAND
Avis ☎09/525 1982
Budget ☎09/275 2222
Fly and Drive Holidays ☎09/529 3709
Hertz ☎09/309 0989

IN IRELAND
Avis ☎01232/240404
Budget Rent-A-Car ☎01232/230700
Europcar ☎01232/450904 or 01232/423444
Hertz ☎01/660 2255
Holiday Autos ☎01/454 9090

When collecting your car, ensure that it has a **full tank** of petrol, as this is part of the agreement. Likewise, you are expected to return the car with a full tank, and if you don't you'll be charged extra.

Finally, check to see if it is cheaper to arrange car hire and insurance from your own cuntry rather than waiting until you reach the US.

RENTING AN RV

Besides cars, Recreational Vehicles or **RVs** – those huge juggernauts that rumble down the highway complete with multiple bedrooms, bathrooms and kitchens – can be rented from around $300 per week for a basic camper on the back of a pickup truck. These are good for groups or families travelling together, but they can be quite unwieldy on the road.

Rental outlets are not as common as you might expect, as people tend to own their own RVs. On top of the rental fees you have to take into account mileage charges, the cost of gas (some RVs do twelve miles to the gallon or less) and any drop-off charges. In addition, it is rarely legal simply to pull up in an RV and spend the night at the roadside; you're expected to stay in designated RV parks – some of which charge $35 per night.

The *Recreational Vehicle Rental Association*, 3251 Old Lee Highway, Fairfax, VA 22030 (☎703/591-7130 or ☎1-800/336-0355) publishes a newsletter and a directory of rental firms. A couple of the larger companies offering RV rentals are *Cruise America* (☎1-800/327-7799) and *Go! Vacations* (☎1-800/845-9888).

ROADS

The best roads for covering long distances quickly are the wide, straight and fast **Interstate Highways**, usually at least six lanes and always prefixed by "I" (for example I-95) – marked on maps by a red, white and blue shield bearing the number. Even-numbered Interstates usually run east–west and those with odd numbers north–south.

A grade down are the **State** and **US highways** (for example Hwy-1), sometimes divided into scenic off-shoots such as Hwy-A1A, which runs parallel to Hwy-1 along Florida's east coast. There are a number of **toll roads**, by far the longest being the 318-mile **Florida Turnpike**; tolls range from 25¢ to $6 and are often graded according to length of journey – you're given a distance marker when you enter the toll road and pay the appropriate amount when you leave. You'll also come across **toll bridges**, usually charging 10–25¢ to cross, sometimes as much as $3.

Even major roads in cities are technically state or US highways but are better known by their local name. Part of Hwy-1 in Miami, for instance, is more familiarly known as Biscayne Boulevard. Rural areas also have much smaller **County Roads** (given as **Routes** in the Guide, such as Route 78 near Lake Okeechobee); their number is preceded by a letter denoting their county.

RULES OF THE ROAD

Although the law says that drivers must keep up with the flow of traffic, which is often hurtling along at 70mph, the official **speed limit** in Florida is 55mph (65mph on some Interstate stretches), with lower signposted limits – usually around 30–35mph – in built-up areas. A **minimum speed limit** of 40mph also applies on many Interstates and highways. There are no spot fines; if you get a ticket for **speeding**, your case will come to court and the size of the fine will be at the discretion of the judge; $75 is a rough minimum. If **the police** do flag you down, don't get out of the car and don't reach into the glove compartment as they may think you have a gun. Simply sit still with your hands on the wheel; when questioned, be polite and don't attempt to make jokes.

Apart from the obvious fact that Americans **drive on the right**, various rules may be unfamiliar to **foreign drivers**. US law requires that any **alcohol** be carried unopened in the boot of the car; it's illegal to make a **U-turn** on an Interstate or anywhere where a single unbroken line runs along the middle of the road; to **park on a highway**; and for front-seat passengers to ride without fastened **seatbelts**. At junctions, you can turn right on a red light if there is no traffic approaching from the left; and some junctions are **four-way stops**: a crossroads where all traffic must stop before proceeding in order of arrival.

It can't be stressed too strongly that **Driving Under the Influence (DUI)** is a very serious offence. If a police officer smells alcohol on your breath, he/she is entitled to administer a breath, saliva or urine test. If you fail, they'll lock you up with other inebriates in the "drunk tank" of the nearest jail until you sober up – and, controversially, in some parts of the state they're empowered to suspend your driving licence immediately. Your case will later be heard by a judge, who can fine you $200 or in extreme (or repeat) cases, imprison you for thirty days.

AMERICAN DRIVING TERMS

Antennae	Aerial
Divided Highway	Dual carriageway
Fender	Bumper/Car wing
Freeway	Limited access motorway
Gas(oline)	Petrol
Hood	Bonnet
No standing	No parking or stopping
Parking brake	Hand brake
Parking lot	Carpark
Speed zone	Area where speed limit decreases
Stickshift	Gear stick/manual transmission
Trunk	Boot
Turn-out	Lay-by
Windshield	Windscreen

PARKING

Parking meters are common in cities; their charge for an hour ranges from 25¢ to $1. **Carparks** generally charge $2 an hour, $6 per day. If you park in the wrong place (such as within ten feet of a fire hydrant) your car is likely to be towed away or **wheel-clamped**; a sticker on the windscreen will tell you where to pay the $30 fine. Whenever possible, **park in the shade**; if you don't, you might find the car too hot to touch when you return to it – temperatures inside cars parked in the full force of the Florida sun can reach 140°F.

BREAKDOWN

If you **break down** in a rented car, there'll be an emergency number pinned to the dashboard. Otherwise you should sit tight and wait for the Highway Patrol or State Police, who cruise by regularly. Raising your car bonnet is recognized as a call for assistance, though women travelling alone should, obviously, be wary of doing this. Another tip, for women especially, is to rent a **mobile telephone** from the car hire agency – you often only have to pay a nominal amount until you actually use it, but having a phone can be reassuring at least and even a potential life-saver.

HITCHING

Where it's legal, **hitching** may be the cheapest way to get around but it is also the most unpredictable and potentially very dangerous, especially for women travelling alone. Small country roads are your best bet: in rural areas it's not uncommon for the locals to get around by thumb. One place *not* to hitch is Miami; not only is this illegal, but if you do take the risk, the chances are you'll be lucky to live to regret it. Anywhere else, observe the general common-sense rules on hitching: make sure you sit next to a door that's unlocked, keep your luggage within reach, refuse the ride if you feel unsure of the driver and demand to be let out if you become suspicious of his/her intentions.

Hitching is illegal not only in Miami but also on the outskirts of many other cities; indeed it's is always prohibited to wait for a lift by standing on the road (as opposed to beside it on the pavement or grass verge) or by a freeway entrance sign – rules which are enforced. On Interstates, thumb from the entrance ramps only. Another, slightly less risky, technique is to strike up a conversation with likely-looking drivers in roadside diners or filling stations. Safer still is to scrutinize the **"ride boards"** on university campuses, though drivers found this way will usually expect a contribution towards fuel costs.

CYCLING

Cycling is seldom a good way to get around the major cities (with the exception of some sections of Miami), but many smaller towns are quiet enough to be pleasurably explored by bicycle, there are many miles of marked **cycle paths** along the coast, and long-distance **bike trails** crisscross the state's interior. Cycling is gaining popularity among Floridians, too, and a free

monthly magazine, *Florida Bicyclist*, is aimed at the growing band of devoted pedallers; find it in bookshops and bike shops or on street corners.

Bikes can be **rented** for $8–15 a day, $30–55 a week, from many beach shops and college campuses, some state parks and virtually any place where cycling is a good idea; outlets are listed in the *Guide*.

For **long-distance** cycling – anything over thirty miles a day – you'll need a good-quality, all-terrain, multi-gear bike, preferably with wide touring tyres. For safety and visibility, wear a brightly coloured **helmet** and cycling **gloves** (available from most bike shops). Keep your water-bottle filled and drink from it frequently to avoid dehydration – don't forget the power of the Florida sun.

The best **cycling areas** are in North Central Florida, the Panhandle and in parts of the Northeast Coast. By contrast, the southeast coastal strip is heavily congested and many south Florida inland roads are narrow and dangerous. Wherever you cycle, avoid the heaviest traffic – and the midday heat – by doing most of your pedalling before 10am.

For free biking **information** and detailed **maps** ($2–15) of cycling routes, write to the **State Bicycle Program**, Florida Department of Transportation, 605 Suwanee Street, Tallahassee, FL 32399-0450 (☎904/488-3111). You can get the same maps from most youth hostels; the Florida *AYH* also publishes the *AYH Bicycle Hospitality Directory*, a list of local cycling enthusiasts willing to host bike-mad visitors overnight (PO Box 533097, Orlando, FL 32853-3097).

ACCOMMODATION

Accommodation costs inevitably account for a significant proportion of the expenses for any traveller in Florida, though as ever in the US you usually get good value for what you pay. If you're on your own, it's possible to pare costs by sleeping in dormitory-style hostels, where a bed can cost from $12 to $15. However, groups of two or more will find it little more expensive to stay in the far more plentiful motels and hotels, where basic rooms away from the major cities typically cost anything upwards of $30 per night. Many hotels will set up a third single bed for around $5–10 on top of the regular price, reducing costs for three people sharing. By contrast, the lone traveller will have a hard time of it: "singles" are usually double rooms at an only slightly reduced rate. Prices quoted by hotels and motels are almost always for the actual room rather than for each person using it.

Motels are plentiful on the main approach roads to cities, around beaches and by the main road junctions in country areas. High-rise **hotels** predominate along the popular sections of the coast and are sometimes the only accommodation in city centres. In major cities **campgrounds** tend to be on the outskirts, if they exist at all.

Wherever you stay, you'll be expected to **pay in advance**, at least for the first night and perhaps for further nights too, particularly if it's high season and the hotel's expecting to be busy. Payment can be in cash or in dollar travellers' checks, though it's more common to give your credit card number and sign for everything when you leave. **Reservations** are only held until 5pm or 6pm unless you've told the hotel you'll be arriving late. Most of the larger chains have an advance booking form in their brochures and will make reservations at another of their premises for you.

Since cheap accommodation in the cities and on the popular sections of the coast is snapped up fast, always **book ahead** whenever possible, using the suggestions in this book.

HOTELS AND MOTELS

While **motels** and **hotels** essentially offer the same things – double rooms with bathroom, TV and phone – motels are often one-off affairs run by their owners and tend to be cheaper (typically $30–45) than hotels ($45–75), which are likely to be part of a nationwide chain. All but the cheapest motels and hotels have pools for guests' use and many offer cable TV and free local phone calls. Under $60, rooms tend to be similar in quality and features; spend $60–70 in rural areas or $80–100 in the cities and you get more luxury – a larger room and often additional facilities such as a tennis

ACCOMMODATION PRICE CODES

It's a fact of Florida life that the plain-and-simple motel room, which costs $30 on a weekday in low season, is liable to cost two or three times that amount on a weekend in high season. To further complicate matters, high and low season vary depending on whether you're in north or south Florida (see *Introduction*), and some establishments that depend on business travellers for their trade (such as those in downtown areas, distanced from the nearest beach) will actually be cheaper at weekends than on weekdays. Local events – such as a Space Shuttle launch on the Space Coast, or Spring Break in Panama City Beach – can also cause prices to increase dramatically.

Throughout the book, we've graded accommodation prices according to the cost of the least expensive double room throughout most of the year – but do allow for the fluctuations outlined above.

① up to $30	③ $45–60	⑤ $80–100	⑦ $130–180
② $30–45	④ $60–80	⑥ $100–130	⑧ $180+

HOTEL DISCOUNT VOUCHERS

Many of the higher-rung hotel chains offer **pre-paid discount vouchers**, which in theory save you money if you're prepared to pay in advance. To take advantage of such schemes, British travellers must purchase the vouchers in the UK, at a usual cost of between £30 and £60 per night for a minimum of two people sharing. However, it's hard to think of a good reason to buy them; you may save a nominal amount on the fixed rates, but better-value accommodation is not exactly difficult to find in the US, and you may well regret the inflexibility imposed upon your travels. Most UK travel agents will have details of the various voucher schemes; the cheapest is the "Go As You Please" deal offered by *Days Inn* (☎01483/440480 in Britain).

---

court, gym and golf course. Paying over $150 brings all the above, plus a fabulous ocean view, *en-suite* jacuzzi and all imaginable upmarket trappings.

Alternatively, there are number of unexciting but dependable **budget-priced chain** hotels, which, depending on location, cost around $25–45; the cheapest are *Days Inn, Econo Lodge, Hampton Inns, Knights Inns* and *Red Carpet Inns*. Higher up the scale are **mid-range chains** like *Best Western, Howard Johnson's* (now usually abbreviated to *HoJo's*), *TraveLodge* and *La Quinta* – though if you can afford their prices (usually $75–125), there's normally somewhere nicer to stay.

On your travels you'll also come across **resorts**, which are motels or hotels equipped with a restaurant, bar and private beach – on average these cost $70–110; and **efficiencies**, which are motel rooms adapted to offer cooking facilities – ranging from a stove squeezed into a corner to a fully equipped kitchen – usually for $10–15 above the basic room rate.

Since inexpensive diners are everywhere, very few hotels or motels bother to offer **breakfast**, though there's a trend towards providing free coffee (from paper cups) and sticky buns on a self-service basis from the lobby.

OTHER DISCOUNTS AND RESERVATIONS

During **off-peak periods** many motels and hotels struggle to fill their rooms and it's worth **haggling** to get a few dollars off the asking price. Staying in the same place for more than one night will bring further reductions. In addition, pick up the many **discount coupons** that fill tourist

information offices and welcome centres (see p.19), and look out for the free *Traveler Discount Guide*. Read the small print, though: what appears to be an amazingly cheap room rate sometimes turns out to be a per-person charge for two people sharing and limited to midweek.

When it's worth blowing cash on somewhere really atmospheric we've said as much in the *Guide*. Bear in mind the most upmarket establishments have all manner of services that may appear to be free but for which you will be expected to **tip** in a style commensurate with the hotel's status – see "Tipping" in "Directory".

BED AND BREAKFAST

Bed and breakfast in Florida is often a luxury. Typically, the bed and breakfast inns, as they're usually known, are restored buildings in the smaller towns and more rural areas – though the cities also have a few. Even the larger establishments tend to have less than ten rooms, sometimes without TV and phone but always with flowers, stuffed cushions and an almost contrived homely atmosphere; others may just be a couple of furnished rooms in someone's home.

While always including a huge and wholesome breakfast (five courses are not unheard of), prices vary greatly: anything from $45 to $200 depending on location and season; most cost between $60 and $80 per night for a double. Bear in mind, too, that most are booked well in advance, making it sensible to contact either the inn directly (details are given throughout the *Guide*), or one of the agents below, at least a month ahead – longer in high season.

BED AND BREAKFAST AGENCIES

For a list of inns in various areas, contact one or several of the following:

A&A Bed & Breakfast of Florida Inc PO Box 1316, Winter Park, FL 32790 (☎407/628-3222).

B&B Scenic Florida PO Box 3385, Tallahassee, FL 32315-3385 (☎904/386-8196).

Bed'n'Breakfast Central Gulf Coast PO Box 9515, Pensacola, FL 32513-3222 (☎904/438-796).

Bed & Breakfast East Coast PO Box 1373, Marathon, FL 33050 (☎305/743-4118).

Bed & Breakfast of Volusia County PO Box 573, DeLeon Springs, FL 32028 (☎904/985-5068).

Florida Suncoast Bed & Breakfast PO Box 12, Palm Harbor, FL 33563 (☎941/784-5118).

YS AND HOSTELS

At around $12 (a few dollars more for non-members) per night per person, **hostels** are clearly the cheapest accommodation option other than camping. There are two main kinds of cheap hostel-type accommodation in the US: YMCA/YWCA hostels (known as *"Ys"*), offering accommodation for both sexes or, in a few cases, women only; and official *AYH* youth hostels. In Florida you'll find **AYH youth hostels** in Miami Beach, Daytona Beach, St Augustine, Fort Lauderdale, Orlando and St Petersburg. Miami Beach, St Petersburg and Clearwater Beach also have **privately run youth hostels**, of a similar standard and price.

Particularly if you're travelling in high season, it's advisable to **book ahead** through one of the specialist travel agents or international youth hostel offices. Some hostels will allow you to use a **sleeping bag**, though officially they should (and many do) insist on a **sheet sleeping bag**, which can usually be rented at the hostel. The maximum stay at each hostel is technically three days, though this is again a rule that is often ignored if there's space. Few hostels provide meals, but most have **cooking** facilities, and there's sometimes a curfew of around midnight: alcohol, smoking and, of course, drugs are banned.

The informative *American Youth Hostel (AYH) Handbook* ($5) is available from hostels in the US, or direct from the *AYH* national office: 733 15th Street NW, Suite 840, Washington DC 20005 (☎202/783-6161). Specific hostel information for Florida can be had from the *Florida Council*, PO Box 533097, Orlando, FL 32853-3097 (☎407/649-8761).

For **overseas hostellers**, the *International Youth Hostel Handbook* provides a full list of hostels. In Britain, it's available from the *Youth Hostel Association* headquarters/shop, at 14 Southampton Street, London WC2 (☎0171/836 1036), where you can also buy a year's *IYHF* **membership** for £9 (£3 if you're under 18).

CAMPING

Florida **campgrounds** range from the primitive (a flat piece of ground that may or may not have a water tap) to others that are more like open-air hotels with shops, restaurants and washing facilities. Naturally, prices vary accord to amenities, ranging from nothing at all for the most basic plots to up to $35 a night for something comparatively luxurious. There are plenty of campgrounds but often plenty of people intending to use them: take special care over plotting your route if you're camping during public holidays or weekends, when many sites will be either full or very crowded. By contrast, some of the more basic campgrounds in state and national parks will often be completely empty midweek. For camping in the wilderness, there's a nightly charge of $1.50 payable at the area's administrative office.

Privately run campgrounds are everywhere, their prices range from $8 to $35 and the best located are listed throughout the *Guide*; for a fuller list, write for the free *Florida Camping Directory* to the **Florida Campground Association**, 1638 Plaza Drive, Tallahassee, FL 32308-5364 (☎904/656-8878).

State parks – there are over 300 in Florida – are often excellent places to camp; sites cost $8–17 for up to four people sharing. Never more than half the space is reserved, the rest goes on a first-come first-served basis (bear in mind that park offices close at sunset; you won't be able to camp there if you arrive later). **Reservations** can be made within two months of arrival by phone only, and stays are limited to fourteen days. Reservations won't be held after 5pm unless previously arranged. If you're doing a lot of camping in state parks, get the two free leaflets, *Florida State Parks Camping Reservations Procedures* and *Florida State Parks Fees Schedule* from any state park office, or by writing to the **Department of Natural Resources**, Division of Recreation and Parks, 3900 Commonwealth Boulevard, Tallahassee, FL 32399 (☎904/488-9872).

Similarly priced campsites exist in National Parks and National Forests – see the details throughout the *Guide*, or contact the **National Park Service**, PO Box 2416, Tallahassee, FL 32316 (☎904/222-1167) and the **US Forest Service**, Suite 4061, 227 N Bronough Street, Tallahassee, FL 32301 (☎904/681-7265).

However desolate it may look, much of undeveloped Florida is, in fact, private land and **rough camping** is illegal. For permitted rough camping, see "The Backcountry", p.36.

FOOD AND DRINK

Florida has a mass of restaurants, fast-food outlets, cafés and coffee shops on every main street, all trying to outdo one another with their cut-price daily specials. In every town mentioned in this book you'll find reviews of the full range of eating options.

Fresh fish and seafood are abundant all over Florida, as is the high-quality produce of the state's cattle farms – served as ribs, steaks and burgers – and junk-food is as common as anywhere else in the country. But the choice of what to eat is influenced by where you are. In the northern half of the state, the accent is on wholesome cooking – traditional Southern dishes such as grits, cornbread and fried chicken. As you head south through Florida, this gives way to the most diverse and inexpensive gathering of Latin American and Caribbean cuisines to be found anywhere in the US – you can feast on anything from curried goat to mashed plantains and yucca.

BREAKFAST

For the price (on average $3–5) breakfast makes a good-value, very filling start to the day. Go to a **diner**, **café** or **coffee shop**, all of which are very similar and usually serve breakfast until at least 11am (though some continue all day) – though there are special deals at earlier times, say 6–8am, when the price may be even less.

LUNCH AND SNACKS

The Florida workforce takes its lunch-break between 11.30am and 1.30pm, during which hours all sorts of low-cost **set menus** and all-

you-can-eat specials are on offer – generally excellent value. Chinese restaurants, for example, frequently have help-yourself rice and noodles or dim sum feasts for $4–6, and many Japanese restaurants give you a chance to eat sushi much more cheaply ($6–8) than usual. Most Cuban restaurants and fishcamps (see "Dining Out", below) are exceptionally well priced all the time and you can get a good-sized lunch in one for $4–5. **Buffet restaurants** – most of which also serve breakfast and dinner – are found in most cities and towns; $6–8 lets you pig as much as you can from a wide variety of hot dishes. A chain version, *Shoney's*, turns up throughout the state.

As you'd expect, there's also **pizza**; count on paying $5–7 for a basic two-person pizza at national chains and local outlets. If it's a warm day and you can't face hot food, find a deli (see below) with a **salad bar**, where you can help yourself for $3. **Frozen yogurt** or **ice cream** may be all you feel like eating in the midday heat: look for exotic versions made with mango and guava sold by Cuban vendors.

SNACKS

For **quick snacks**, many **supermarket deli counters** do ready-cooked meals for $3–4, as well as a range of **salads** and **sandwiches**. Filled **bagels** are also common, while **street stands** sell hot dogs, burgers or a slice of pizza for around $1: in Miami, **Cuban fast-food stands** serve crispy pork sandwiches and other spicy snacks for $2–3, and most shopping malls have ethnic fast-food stalls, often pricier than street stands but usually with edible and filling fare. Bags of fresh oranges, grapefruit and watermelons are often sold from the roadside in rural areas, as are **boiled peanuts** – a dollar buys a steaming bagful. Southern fast-food chains like *Popeye's Famous Fried Chicken* and *Sonny's Real Pit Bar-B-Q* and Mexican outlets such as *Taco Bell*, will satisfy your hunger for $3–4, but are only marginally better than the inevitable **burger chains**.

FREE FOOD AND BRUNCH

Some **bars** are used as much by diners as drinkers, who fill up on the free **hors d'oeuvres** laid out by a lot of city bars between 5 and 7pm

Monday to Friday – an attempt to nab the commuting classes before they head off to the suburbs – and sometimes by beachside bars to grab beach-goers before they head elsewhere for the evening. For the price of a drink you can stuff yourself on chilli, seafood or pasta.

Brunch is another deal to look out for: indulged in at weekends (usually Sunday) between 11am and 2pm. For a set price ($8 and up) you get a light meal (or even a groaning buffet) and a variety of complimentary cocktails or champagne. We've listed the most interesting venues in the *Guide*.

DINING OUT

Even if it sometimes seems swamped by the more fashionable regional and ethnic cuisines, traditional **American cooking** is found all over Florida. Portions are big and you start with **salad**, eaten before the main course arrives; look out for **heart of palm** salad, based around the delicious vegetable at the heart of the sable palm tree. Main dishes are dominated by enormous **steaks**, **burgers**, piles of **ribs** or half a **chicken**. Vegetables include french fries or a baked potato, the latter commonly topped with sour cream and chives.

Southern cooking makes its presence felt throughout the northern half of the state. Vegetables such as **okra**, **collard greens**, **black-eyed peas** and fried **eggplant** are added to staples such as fried chicken, roast beef and **hogjaw** – meat from the mouth of a pig. Meat dishes are usually accompanied by **cornbread** to soak up the thick gravy poured over everything; with fried fish, you'll get **hush puppies** – fried corn balls with tiny bits of chopped onion. Okra is also used in **gumbo** soups, a feature of **Cajun** cooking, which originated in nearby Louisiana as a way of using up leftovers. A few (usually expensive) Florida restaurants specialize in Cajun food but many others have a few Cajun items (such as red beans and rice and hot and spicy shrimp and steak dishes) on their menu.

Don't be shocked to see **alligator** on menus: most of the meat comes from alligator farms, which cull a certain number each year. The tails are deep-fried and served in a variety of styles – none of which make much of a mark on the bland, chicken-like taste. **Frogs' legs** also crop up occasionally.

Regional **nouvelle cuisine** of the Californian kind is far too pretentious and expensive for the typical Floridian palate, although some restaurants in the larger cities do extraordinary and inspired things with local fish and the produce of the citrus farms, creating small but beautifully presented and highly nutritious affairs for around $40 a head.

Almost wherever you eat you'll be offered **Key Lime Pie** as a dessert, a dish which began life in the Florida Keys, made from the small limes that grow there. The pie is similar to lemon meringue but with a sharper taste. Quality varies greatly; take local advice to find a good outlet and your tastebuds will tell you why many swear by it.

FISH AND SEAFOOD

Florida excels with **fish and seafood** – which is great news for non-meat eaters. Even the shabbiest restaurant is likely to have an excellent selection, though fish comes freshest and cheapest at **fishcamps**, rustic places right beside the river where your meal was swimming just a few hours before; a fishcamp lunch or dinner will cost around $5–9. **Catfish** tends to top the bill, but you'll also find **grouper**, **dolphin** (the fish not the mammal, sometimes known by its Hawaiian name, **mahimahi**), **mullet**, **tuna** and **swordfish**, any of which (except catfish, which is nearly always fried) may be boiled, grilled, fried or "blackened" (charcoal-grilled). Of **shellfish**, the tender claws of **stone crabs**, eaten dipped in butter, raise local passions during their mid-October to mid-May season; **spiny** (or **"Florida"**) **lobster** is smaller and more succulent than its more famous Maine rival; **oysters** can be extremely fresh (the best come from Apalachicola) and are usually eaten raw (though best avoided during summer, when they carry a risk of food poisoning) – many restaurants have special **"raw bars"**, where you can also consume meaty **shrimp**, in regular and jumbo sizes. One crustacean you can't eat raw is the very chewy **conch** (pronounced "konk"); abundant throughout the Florida Keys, it usually comes as fritters but tastes better in a chowder.

ETHNIC CUISINE

Florida's **ethnic cuisines** become increasingly exotic the further south you go. In Miami, **Cuban food** is extremely easy to find and can be very good value. Most Cuban dishes are meat based: frequently pork, less often beef or chicken, always fried (including the skin, which becomes a

AMERICAN FOOD TERMS FOR FOREIGN TRAVELLERS

A la mode	With ice cream	*Hero*	French-bread sandwich
Au jus	Meat served with a gravy made from its own juices	*Hoagie*	Another French-bread sandwich
Biscuit	Scone	*Home fries*	Thick-cut fried potatoes
BLT	Bacon, lettuce and tomato toasted sandwich	*Jello*	Jelly
		Jelly	Jam
Broiled	Grilled	*Muffin*	Small cake made with bran and/or blueberries
Brownie	A fudgy, filling chocolate cake		
Chips	Potato crisps	*Popsicle*	Ice lolly
Cilantro	Coriander	*Potato chips*	Crisps
Clam chowder	A thick soup made with clams and other seafood.	*Pretzels*	Savory circles of glazed pastry
		Seltzer	Fizzy/soda water
Cookie	Biscuit	*Sherbet*	Sorbet
Eggplant	Aubergine	*Shrimp*	Prawns
English muffin	Toasted bread roll, similar to a crumpet	*Sub*	Yet another French-bread sandwich
Frank	Frankfurter (hot dog)	*Soda*	Generic term for any soft drink
(French) fries	Chips	*Surf 'n' Turf*	Restaurant serving fish and meat
Gravy	White lard-like sauce poured over biscuits for breakfast	*Teriyaki*	Chicken or beef, marinated in soy sauce and grilled
Grits	Ground white corn, served hot with butter, often a breakfast side dish.	*Yucca*	Cassava
		Zucchini	Courgettes
Hash browns	Potato chunks or grated potato chips fried in fat		

CUBAN SPECIALTIES

Ajiaco criollo	Meat and root vegetable stew	*Pan*	Bread
Arroz	Rice	*Pan con lechon*	Crispy pork sandwich
Arroz con leche	Rice pudding	*Piccadillo*	Minced meat, usually beef, served with peppers and olives
Bocadillo	Sandwich		
Chicarones de pollo	Fried chicken crackling		
		Pollo	Chicken
Frijoles	Beans	*Puerca*	Pork
Frijoles negros	Black beans	*Sopa de mariscos*	Shellfish soup
Maduros	Fried plantains		
Masitoas de puerca	Fried spiced pork	*Sopa de plantanos*	Meaty, plantain soup
Morros y Christianos	Literally "Moors and Christians", black beans and white rice	*Vaca*	Beef
		Tostones	Fried mashed plantains

crispy crackling) and usually heavily spiced, served with a varying combination of yellow or white rice, black beans, plantains (a sweet-tasting tropical vegetable) and yucca (cassava) – a potato-like vegetable completely devoid of taste. Seafood crops up less often, most deliciously in thick soups, such as *sopa de mariscos* – shellfish soup. Unpretentious Cuban diners serve a filling lunch or dinner for under $6, though a growing number of upmarket restaurants will charge three times as much for identi-

cal food. In busy areas, many Cuban cafés have street windows where you buy a thimble-sized cup of sweet and rich *Café Cubano* – Cuban coffee – for 50–75¢, strong enough to make your hair stand on end; the similarly priced *café con leche*, coffee with warm milk or cream, is strictly for the unadventurous and regarded by Cubans as a children's drink. If you want a cool drink in Miami, look out for roadside stands offering *coco frio* – coconut milk sucked through a straw directly from the coconut, for $1.

Although nowhere near as prevalent as Cuban cooking, foods from other parts of the Caribbean and Latin America are easily located around Miami: **Haitian** food is the latest craze, but **Argentinian**, **Colombian**, **Nicaraguan**, **Peruvian**, **Jamaican** and **Salvadorean** restaurants also serve the city's diverse migrant populations – at very affordable prices.

Other ethnic cuisines turn up all around the state, too. **Chinese** food is everywhere and often very cheap, as is **Mexican**, though many Mexican restaurants are more popular as places to knock back margaritas than for eating in; **Japanese** is more expensive; **Italian** food is popular but can be expensive once you leave the simple pastas and explore the more gourmet-inclined Italian regional cooking that's catching on fast in the major cities. **French** food, too, is widely available, though always pricey, the cuisine of social climbers and power-lunchers and rarely found outside the larger cities. **Thai**, **Korean** and **Indonesian** food is similarly city-based, though usually cheaper; **Indian** restaurants, on the other hand, are thin on the ground just about everywhere and often very expensive. More plentiful are well-priced, family-run **Greek** restaurants, and a smattering of **Minorcan** places are evidence of one of Florida's earliest groups of European settlers.

Whatever and wherever you eat, **service** will always be enthusiastic and excellent. Foreign travellers should note that this is mainly due to the American system of **tipping**, on which the staff depend for the bulk (and sometimes all) of their earnings. You should always top up the bill by 15–20 percent; not to tip at all is severely frowned upon. The only exceptions to this rule are trendy, South Beach-type restaurants, which sometimes add a service charge to the bill. Many (not all) restaurants accept **payment** in the form of credit/charge cards: if you use one, a space will be left to fill in the appropriate tip; travellers' cheques are also widely accepted (see p.15).

DRINKING

While regular **bars** in the classic American image do exist in Florida – long, dimly lit counters with a few punters perched on stools before a bartender-cum-guru, and tables and booths for those who don't want to join in the drunken barside debates – most drinking is done in restaurant or hotel lounges, at fishcamps (see "Dining Out"), or in **"tiki bars"**, open-sided straw-roofed

huts beside a beach or hotel pool. Some beachside bars, especially in Daytona Beach and Panama City Beach, are split-level, multi-purpose affairs with discos and stages for live bands – and take great pride in being the birthplace of the infamous wet T-shirt contest (nowadays sometimes joined by G-string and "best legs" shows), an exercise in unrestrained sexism that shows no signs of declining in popularity among a predominantly late-teen and twenty-something clientele.

To **buy and consume alcohol** you need to be 21 and could well be asked for ID even if you look much older. **Licensing laws and drinking hours** vary from area to area, but generally alcohol can be bought and drunk in a bar, nightclub or restaurant any time between 10am and 2am. More cheaply, you can usually buy beer, wine or spirits in supermarkets and, of course, liquor stores, from 9am to 11pm Monday to Saturday and from 1pm to 11pm on Sundays. Note that it is **illegal** to consume alcohol in a car, on most beaches and in all state parks.

BEER

A small band of Florida **micro breweries** (tiny, one-off operations) create interesting beers, though rarely are these sold beyond their own bar or restaurant – such as the **Sarasota Brewing Company** in Sarasota. It's more common for discerning beer drinkers to stick to imported brews, best of which are the Mexican brands *Bohemia*, *Corona*, *Dos Equis*, *Superior* and *Tecate*. Don't forget that in all but the more pretentious bars, several people can save money by buying a quart or half-gallon **pitcher** of beer. If bar prices are a problem, you can stock up with **six-packs** from a supermarket at $5–7 for domestic, $8–12 for imported brews.

WINE AND SPIRITS

If **wine** is more to your taste, try to visit one of the state's fast-improving **wineries**: several can be toured and their products sampled for free. One of the most successful is also one of the newest: *Chautauqua Vineyards*, in De Funiak Springs (see p.342). In a bar or restaurant, however, beside a usually threadbare stock of European wines, you'll find a selection from Chile, Washington State and Oregon. Probably the most interesting of US wines are those from **California**. *Cabernet Sauvignon* is certainly worth trying – a light, drinkable red; also widespread are the heavier reds – *Burgundy*, *Merlot* and *Pinot Noir*. Among the

COCKTAILS

Bacardi	White rum, lime and grenadine – not the brand name drink	Margarita	The cocktail to drink in a Mexican restaurant, made with tequila, triple sec, lime juice and limes, and blended with ice to make slush. Served with or without salt. Also available in fruit flavours.
Bellini	Champagne with peach juice		
Black Russian	Vodka with coffee liqueur, brown cacao and coke		
Bloody Mary	Vodka, tomato juice, tabasco, Worcester sauce, salt and pepper		
Brandy Alexander	Brandy, brown cacao and cream	Mimosa	Champagne and orange juice
Champagne cocktail	Brandy, sugar and champagne	Mint Julep	Bourbon, mint and sugar
		Negroni	Vodka or gin, campari and triple sec
Daquiri	Dark rum, light rum and lime, often with banana or strawberry	Pina Colada	Dark rum, light rum, coconut, cream and pineapple juice
Harvey Wallbanger	Vodka, galliano, orange juice		
		Screwdriver	Vodka and orange juice
Highball	Any spirit plus a soda, water or ginger ale	Silk Stocking	Gin, tequila, white cacao, cream and sugar
Kir Royale	Champagne, cassis	Tequila Sunrise	Tequila, orange juice and grenadine
Long Island Iced Tea	Gin, vodka, white rum, tequila, lemon juice and coke	Tom Collins	Gin, lemon juice, soda and sugar
Mai-Tai	Dark rum, light rum, cherry brandy, orange and lemon juice	Vodka Collins	Vodka, lemon juice, soda and sugar
		Whisky Sour	Bourbon, lemon juice and sugar
Manhattan	Vermouth, whisky, lemon juice and soda	White Russian	Vodka, white cacao and cream

whites, *Chardonnay* is very dry and full of flavour and generally preferred to *Sauvignon Blanc* or *Fumé Blanc*, though these have their devotees. It's fairly inexpensive: a glass of wine in a bar or restaurant costs from around $2.50, a bottle from $8. Buying a bottle from a supermarket can prove cheaper still.

Spirits generally cost $1.50 a shot. **Cocktails** are extremely popular, especially rich fruity ones consumed while gazing over the ocean or into the sunset. Varieties are innumerable, sometimes specific to a single bar or cocktail lounge, though there are a few standards listed above, any of which will cost $2–5. Cocktails and all other drinks come cheapest during **happy hours** (usually 5–7pm; sometimes much longer) when many are half-price and there might be a buffet thrown in.

PERSONAL SAFETY

No one could pretend that Florida is trouble-free, though outside of the urban centres crime is often remarkably low-key. Even the lawless reputation of murder-a-day Miami is in excess of the truth, though several clearly defined areas are strictly off-limits. At night you should always be cautious – though not unduly frightened – wherever you are. All the major tourist and nightlife areas in cities are invariably brightly lit and well policed. By being careful, planning ahead and taking good care of your possessions, you should, generally speaking, have few real problems.

Foreign visitors tend to report that the police are helpful and obliging when things go wrong, though they'll be less sympathetic if they think you brought the trouble on yourself through carelessness*.

CAR CRIME

Even more than muggings on the street (see below), it's been crimes against tourists driving **rented cars** in Florida that have garnered headlines around the world in recent months and threatened the well-being of the state's number one industry.

Firstly, you'd be advised not to drive immediately on arrival after a transatlantic flight.

---

*One way you might accidently break the law is by **jaywalking**. If you cross the road on a red light or anywhere except at an intersection, and are spotted by a cop, you're likely to get a stiff talking-to – and possibly a ticket, leading to a $20 fine.

Instead, spend the first night at an airport hotel or catch a taxi to a hotel in the city and collect your hire car the following day.

When driving, under no circumstances stop in any unlit or seemingly deserted urban area – and especially not if someone is waving you down and suggesting that there is something wrong with your car. Similarly, if you are "accidentally" rammed by the driver behind, do not stop immediately but drive on to the nearest well-lit, busy and secure area (such as a hotel, toll booth or filling station) and phone the emergency number (☎911) for assistance. Keep your doors locked and windows never more than slightly open (as you'll probably be using air conditioning, you'll want to keep them fully closed anyway). Do not open your door or window if someone approaches your car on the pretext of asking directions. Even if the person doing this looks harmless, they may well have an accomplice ready to **attack you from behind**. Hide any valuables out of sight, preferably locked in the boot or in the glove compartment (any valuables you don't need for your journey should be left in your hotel safe).

Always take care when planning your route, particularly through urban areas, and be sure to use a reliable map such as the ones we've recommended under "Information, Maps and the Media" (see p.19). Particularly in Miami, local authorities are making efforts to add directions to tourist sights and attractions to road signs, thereby reducing the possibility of visitors unwittingly driving into dangerous areas. Needless to say, you should always heed such directions, even if you think you've located a convenient short cut.

STREET CRIME AND HOTEL BURGLARIES

After car crime, the biggest problem for most travellers in Florida is the threat of **mugging**. It's impossible to give hard and fast rules about what to do if you're confronted by a mugger. Whether to run, scream or fight depends on the situation – but most locals would just hand over their money.

Of course, the best thing is simply to avoid being mugged, and there are a few basic rules worth remembering: don't flash money around; don't peer at your map (or this book) at every street corner, thereby announcing you're a lost stranger; even if you're terrified or drunk (or

LOSING YOUR PASSPORT

Few disasters create bigger headaches for foreign travellers than **losing your passport**. You can't get home without it, and it can be an extremely tough process to get a new one. The **British Consulate** in Florida – which can (very grudgingly) issue passports – is in Miami at Suite 2110, S Bayshore Drive, Coconut Grove, FL 33131 (☎305/374-1522). Expect to spend around $40 on fees and waste at least a week.

both), don't appear so; avoid dark streets and never start to walk down one that you can't see the end of; and in the early hours stick to the roadside edge of the pavement so it's easier to run into the road to attract attention.

If the worst happens and your assailant is toting a gun or (more likely) a knife, try to stay calm: remember that he (for this is generally a male pursuit) is probably scared, too. Keep still, don't make any sudden movements – and hand over your money. When he's gone you'll be shocked, but try to find a cab to take you to the nearest police station. Here, report the theft and get a reference number on the report to claim insurance (see "Health and Insurance", p.13) and travellers' cheque refunds. If you're in a big city, ring the local *Travelers Aid* (their numbers are listed in the phone book) for sympathy and practical advice.

Another potential source of trouble is having your **hotel room burgled** while you're out. Some

Orlando area hotels are notorious for this and many such break-ins appear to be inside jobs. Always store valuables in the hotel safe when you go out; when inside keep your door locked and don't open it to anyone you are suspicious of; if they claim to be hotel staff and you don't believe them, call reception on the room phone to check.

LOST TRAVELLERS' CHEQUES

Lost travellers' cheques are a common problem. You should keep a record of the numbers of your cheques separately from the actual cheques and, if you lose them, ring the issuing company on their toll-free number. They'll ask you for the cheque numbers, the place you bought them, when and how you lost them and whether it's been reported to the police. All being well, you should get the missing cheque re-issued within a couple of days – and perhaps an emergency advance to tide you over.

STOLEN TRAVELLERS' CHEQUES/CREDIT CARDS EMERGENCY NUMBERS

American Express (TCs) ☎ 1-800/221-7282; (credit cards) ☎1-800/528-2121
Diners Card ☎1-800/968-8300
Mastercard (*Access*) ☎ 1-800/336-8472
Thomas Cook ☎1-800/223-7373
Visa ☎1-800/627-6811 or ☎1-800/227-6811

THE BACKCOUNTRY

Despite the common notion that Florida is entirely composed of theme parks and beaches, much of the state is undeveloped land containing everything from scrubland and swamps to shady hardwood hammocks and dense forests streaked by gushing rivers. Hiking and canoe trails make the wilderness accessible and rewarding – miss it and you're missing Florida.

The US's protected backcountry areas fall into several potentially confusing categories. **State parks** are the responsibility of individual states and usually focus on sites of natural or historical significance. **National parks** are federally

controlled, preserving areas of great natural beauty or ecological importance. Florida's three **national forests** are also federally administered but enjoy much less protection than national parks.

HIKING

Almost all state parks have undemanding **nature trails** intended for a pleasant hour's ramble; anything called a **hiking** or **backpacking trail** – plentiful in state and national parks, national forests and through some unprotected land as part of the 1300-mile **Florida Trail** (intended eventually to run the full length of the state) – requires more thought and planning.

Many hiking trails can be easily completed in a day, the longer ones have rough camping sites at regular intervals (see "Camping", below), and most periodically pass through fully equipped camping areas – giving the option of sleeping in comparative comfort. The **best time** to hike is from late autumn to early spring: this avoids the exhausting heat of the summer and the worst of the **mosquitoes** (see "Wildlife", below) and reveals a greater variety of animals. While hiking, be extremely wary of the **poisonwood** tree (ask a park ranger how to identify it); any contact between your skin and its bark can leave you needing hospital treatment – and avoid being splashed by rainwater dripping from its branches. Be sure to carry plenty of drinking water, as well as the obvious hiking prerequisites.

In some areas you'll need a **wilderness permit** (free or $1) from the local park ranger's or wilderness area administration office, where you should call anyway for maps, general information on the hike and a weather forecast – sudden rains can flood trails in swampy areas. Many state parks run **organized hiking trips**, details of which are given throughout the *Guide*. For general hiking information, write for the free *Backpacking in Florida State Parks* to the **Florida Department of Natural Resources**, 3900 Commonwealth Boulevard, Tallahassee, FL 32393 (☎904/488-1234) and to the **Florida Trail Association**, PO Box 13708, Gainesville, FL 32604 (☎1-800/343-1882).

CANOEING

One way to enjoy natural Florida without getting blisters on your feet is by **canoeing**. Canoes can be rented for around $12–15 a day wherever conditions are right: the best of Florida's rivers and streams are found in north Central Florida and the Panhandle. Many state and national parks have canoe runs, too; the **Florida Canoe Trails System** comprises 36 marked routes along rivers and creeks, covering a combined distance of nearly a thousand miles.

Before setting off, get a canoeing **map** (you'll need to know the locations of access points and any rough camping sites) and check **weather conditions** and the river's **water level**: a low level can expose logs, rocks and other obstacles; a flooded river is dangerous and shouldn't be canoed; coastal rivers are affected by tides. Don't leave the canoe to **walk on the bank**, as this

will cause damage and is likely to be trespassing. When a **motorboat** approaches, keep to the right and turn your bow into the wake. If you're **camping**, do so on a sandbar unless there are designated rough camping areas beside the river. Besides food, carry plenty of drinking water, a first-aid kit, insect repellent and sunscreen.

Several small companies run canoe trips ranging from half a day to a week; they supply the canoe and take you from the end of the route back to where you started. Details are given throughout the *Guide*; or look out for the free *Canoe Florida* leaflet, available from most state parks and some local tourist information offices. For more on the Florida Canoe Trails System, pick up the free *Florida Recreational Trails System Canoe Trails* (available from the **Department of Natural Resources**, address above).

CAMPING

All hiking trails have areas designated for **rough camping**, with either very limited facilities (a handpump for water, sometimes a primitive toilet) or none at all. Travelling by canoe (see "Canoeing", above), you'll often pass sandbars, which can make excellent overnight stops. It's preferable to cook by stove, but otherwise start **fires** only in permitted areas – indicated by signs – and use deadwood. Where there are no toilets, **bury human waste** at least four inches in the ground and a hundred feet from the nearest water supply and campground. **Burn rubbish** carefully, and what you can't burn, carry away. **Never drink** from rivers and streams, however clear and inviting they may look (you never know what unspeakable acts people – or animals – further upstream have performed in them), or from the state's many natural springs; **water** that isn't from taps should be boiled for at least five minutes or cleansed with a iodine-based purifier before you drink it. Always get advice, maps and a weather forecast from the park ranger's or wilderness area adminstration office – often you'll need to fill in a **wilderness permit**, too and pay a $1.50-a-night **camping fee**.

WILDLIFE

Though you're likely to meet many kinds of **wildlife** on your travels, only mosquitoes and, to a much lesser extent, alligators and snakes, will cause any problems.

From June to November, **mosquitoes** are a tremendous nuisance and virtually unavoidable in any area close to fresh water. During these months, **insect repellent** (available for a few dollars in most camping shops and supermarkets) is essential, as is wearing long-sleeved shirts and long trousers. It's rare for mosquitoes to carry diseases, though during 1991 Florida was hit by an outbreak of **viral encephalitis**, a mosquito-borne disease which can cause paralysis and death. As each generation of mosquitoes dies out during the winter, it's unlikely that this will be repeated – at least not for many years.

The biggest surprise among Florida's wildlife is the apparent docility of **alligators** – almost always they'll back away if approached by a human (though this is not something you should put to the test) – and the fact that they now turn up all over the place, despite being decimated by decades of uncontrolled hunting. These days, not only is it unlawful to kill alligators (without a licence), but feeding one can get you two months in prison and a hefty fine: an alligator fed by a human not only loses its natural fear of people but comes to associate them with food – and lacks the brainpower to distinguish between food and feeder. The only truly dangerous type of alligator is

a mother guarding her nest or tending her young. Even then, she'll give you plenty of warning, by showing her teeth and hissing, before attacking.

Like alligators, Florida's **snakes** don't go looking for trouble, but several species will retaliate if provoked – which you're most likely to do by standing on one. Two species are potentially deadly: the **coral snake**, which has a black nose and bright yellow and red rings covering its body, and usually spends the daylight hours under piles of rotting vegetation; and the **cottonmouth moccasin** (sometimes called the **water moccasin**), dark-coloured with a small head, which lives around rivers and lakes. Less harmful, but still worth avoiding, are two types of **rattlesnake**: the easily identified **diamond-back**, whose thick body is covered in a diamond pattern, which turns up in dry, sandy areas and hammocks; and the grey-coloured **pygmy**, so small it's almost impossible to spot until it's too late. You're unlikely to see a snake in the wild and snake attacks are even rarer, but if **bitten** you should contact a ranger or a doctor immediately. It's a wise precaution to carry a **snakebite kit**, available for a couple of dollars from most camping shops.

For more on Florida's wildlife and its habitats, see "Natural Florida" in *Contexts*.

WOMEN'S FLORIDA

In the state that invented the wet T-shirt contest and which still promotes itself with photos of bikini-clad models draping them-selves around palm trees, first-time visitors may be surprised to find women playing demanding and crucial roles in Florida life – in many respects a mark of the achievements of the women's movement over the last two decades. While the force of feminist politics has dissipated of late, the fact that women's bars, bookstores and support centres – while not on the scale of New York or the West Coast – are well established in the larger cities indicates a continued commitment to female self-determination.

Equally, if not more, effective in this thoroughly capitalist society, are the growing number of women's business organizations seeking ways to further female career advancement and raise (if not destroy) the "glass ceiling" – the invisible sexist barrier halting movement up the corporate ladder. In Florida, some such groups have focused recent efforts on strengthening the female presence in that traditional arena of male-bonding and off-the-record deal-making: the golf course.

Practically speaking, a woman **travelling alone** in Florida is not usually made to feel conspicuous, or liable to attract unwelcome attention. Outside of Miami and the seedier sections of the other major cities, much of the state can feel surprisingly safe. But as with anywhere, particular care has to be taken at night. **Mugging** is nowhere near the problem it is in New York, but you can't relax totally, and should use common sense at all times: walking through unlit, empty streets is never a good idea, and if there's no bus service (and you can afford it), take cabs – if not, an escort. It's true that women who *look* confident tend not to encounter trouble – those who stand around looking lost and scared are prime targets.

In the major urban centres, provided you listen to advice and stick to the better parts of town, going into **bars** and **clubs** alone should pose few problems: there's generally a pretty healthy attitude towards women who do so and your privacy will be respected. Gay and lesbian bars are usually a trouble-free and welcoming alternative.

However, **small towns** tend not to be blessed with the same liberal or indifferent attitudes towards lone women travellers. People seem to jump immediately to the conclusion that your car has broken down, or that you've suffered some terrible tragedy; in fact, you may get fed up with well-meant offers of help. If your **vehicle breaks down** in a country area, walk to the nearest house or town for help; on Interstate highways or heavily travelled roads, wait in the car for a police or highway patrol car to arrive. One increasingly available option is to rent a portable telephone with your car, for a small additional charge – a potential life-saver.

Rape statistics in the US are outrageously high, and it goes without saying that you should *never* **hitch** alone – this is widely interpreted as an invitation for trouble and there's no shortage of weirdos to give it. Similarly, if you have a car, be careful who you pick up: just because you're in the driving seat doesn't mean you're safe. Avoid travelling at night by public transport – deserted bus stations, if not actually threatening, will do little to make you feel secure – and where possible you should team up with a fellow traveller. There really is security in numbers. On *Greyhound* buses, follow the example of other lone women and make a point of sitting as near to the front – and the driver – as possible. Should disaster strike, all major towns have some kind of rape counselling service; if not, the local sheriff's office will make adequate arrangements for you to get help, counselling and, if necessary, get you home.

Specific **women's contacts** are listed in the city sections of the *Guide*, but for good back-up material get hold of *Places of Interest to Women* ($7; Ferrari Publications, PO Box 35575, Phoenix, AZ; ☎602/863-2408), a guide for women travelling in the US, Canada, the Caribbean and Mexico, which is updated annually. And for more detailed country-wide info, read the annual *Index/Directory of Women's Media* (published by the Women's Institute for the Freedom of the Press, 3306 Ross Place NW, Washington DC 20008), which lists women's publishers, bookshops, theatre groups, news services and media organizations and more, throughout the country.

GAY AND LESBIAN FLORIDA

With a thousand people a day moving into the state, it's inevitable that Florida's gay and lesbian communities will grow considerably in the urban areas over the next few years, becoming ever more organized and vocal. At present, the biggest gay and lesbian scene is in Key West, at the tip of the Florida Keys and as far as it is possible to get from the rest of the state. The island town's live-and-let-live tradition has made it a holiday destination favoured by American gays and lesbians for decades and many arrivals simply never went home: instead, they've taken up permanent residence and opened guesthouses, restaurants and other businesses – even running gay and lesbian snorkelling and diving trips.

Elsewhere, Miami's fast-expanding network of gay and lesbian resources, clubs and bars – if not as ubiquitous as in New York or on the West

Coast – is a major indication of what's to come. There are smaller levels of activity in the other cities, and along developed sections of the coast (where the gay tourist dollar is recognized as being as good as anyone else's) a number of motels and hotels are specifically aimed at gay travellers. Predictably, attitudes to gay and lesbian visitors get progressively worse the further you go from the populous areas. Being open about your sexuality in the rural regions is likely to provoke an uneasy response if not open hostility – the hell-and-damnation reaction to AIDS widespread in these parts certainly doesn't improve matters.

For a complete rundown on local **resources**, **bars** and **clubs**, see the relevant headings in individual cities. Of national and statewide **publications** to look out for, by far the best is the free *TWN* (*The Weekly News*), packed with news, features and ads for Florida's gay bars and clubs. Also worth a look are *Bob Damron's Address Book* (PO Box 11270, San Francisco, CA 94101; $12), a pocket-sized yearbook of nation-wide listings of hotels, bars, clubs and resources, available from any gay specialist bookshop, and *Gay Yellow Pages* (Ferrari Publications, PO Box 292, Village Station, New York, NY 100114; $8.95). Specifically lesbian publications are harder to find: the most useful is *Gaia's* Guide (132 W 24th St, New York, NY 10011; $6.95), a yearly international directory with a lot of US information.

DISABLED TRAVELLERS

Travellers with mobility problems or other physical disabilities are likely to find Florida – as with the US generally – to be much more in tune with their needs than any other country in the world. All public buildings must be wheelchair accessible and have suitable toilets, most city street corners have dropped kerbs, and most city buses are able to "kneel" to make access easier and are built with space and hand-grips for wheelchair users.

When organizing your holiday, read your travel **insurance** small print carefully to make sure that people with a pre-exisiting medical condition are not excluded. A **medical certificate** of your fitness to travel, provided by your doctor, is also extremely useful; some airlines or insurance companies may insist on it. Make sure that you have extra supplies of drugs – carried with you if you fly – and a prescription including the generic name in case of emergency. Carry spares of any clothing or equipment that might be hard to find; if there's an association representing people with your disability, contact them early in the planning process.

Use your travel agent to make your journey simpler: airline or bus companies can cope better if they are expecting you. With at least a day's notice, domestic **airlines** within the US, and most transatlantic airlines, can do much to ease a disabled person's journey; wheelchairs can be provided at airports, staff primed to help, and, if necessary, a helper will usually be permitted free travel.

On the ground, the major **car rental** firms can, given sufficient notice, provide vehicles with hand controls (though these are usually only available on the more expensive makes of vehicle); **Amtrak** will provide wheelchair assistance at its train stations, adapted seating on board and a 15 percent discount on the regular fare, provided they have 72 hours notice; **Greyhound** buses, despite the fact that they lack designated wheelchair space, will allow a necessary helper to travel free.

In the **Orlando** area, *B.S. Mini Med* specialize in assisting disabled visitors. They provide wheel-chair or stretcher transportation from Orlando airport to any Orlando accommodation for $75 and trips within the area – to the Disney parks and other attractions, for example – are charged at $20 plus $2 per mile (for the disabled traveller plus up to eight companions). The company are contactable at 551 Little River Loop, Suite 213, Altamonte Springs, FL 32714 (☎407/296-3460).

Many of Florida's hotels and motels have been built recently, and disabled access has been a major consideration in their construction. Rarely will any part of the property be difficult for a disabled person to reach, and often several rooms are specifically designed to meet the requirements of disabled guests.

The state's major **theme parks** are also built with disabled access in mind, and attendants are always on hand to ensure that a disabled person gets all the necessary assistance and derives maximum enjoyment from their visit. Even in the Florida wilds, facilities are good: most state parks arrange programmes for disabled visitors; the **Apalachicola National Forest** has a lakeside nature trail set aside for the exclusive use of disabled visitors and their guests; and, in the **Everglades National Park**, all the walking trails are wheelchair accessible, as is one of the backcountry camping sites.

For further information, get the free *Florida Services Directory for Physically Challenged Travellers* from the Florida Division of Tourism (see "Information, Maps and Media" on p.19 for the address). For general information on travelling in the US, contact **SATH**, the Society for the Advancement of Travel for the Handicapped, 347 Fifth Avenue, Suite 610, New York, NY 10016 (☎212/447-7284).

CONTACTS FOR TRAVELLERS WITH DISABILITIES

AUSTRALIA

Australian Council for Rehabilitation of the Disabled (ACROD, PO Box 60, Curtin ACT 2605 (☎06/682 4333); 55 Charles St, Ryde (☎02/9809 4488).

IRELAND

Disability Action Group, 2 Annadale Ave, Belfast BT7 3JH (☎01232/91011).

Irish Wheelchair Association, Blackheath Drive, Clontarf, Dublin 3 (☎01/833 8241). *A national voluntary organization working with people with disabilities with related services for holidaymakers.*

NEW ZEALAND

Disabled Persons Assembly, PO Box 10, 138 The Terrace, Wellington (☎04/472 2626).

UK

Holiday Care Service, 2nd floor, Imperial Building, Victoria Rd, Horley, Surrey RH6 9HW (☎01293/774535). *Information on all aspects of travel.*

RADAR, 12 City Forum, 250 City Rd, London EC1V 8AS (☎0171/250 3222; Minicom ☎0171/250 4119). *A good source of advice on holidays and travel abroad.*

Tripscope, The Courtyard, Evelyn Rd, London W4 5JL (☎0181/994 9294). *A national telephone information service offering free transport and travel advice.*

US

Directions Unlimited, 720 N Bedford Rd, Bedford Hills, NY 10507 (☎1-800/533-5343). *Tour operator specializing in custom tours for people with disabilities.*

Jewish Rehabilitation Hospital, 3205 Place Alton Goldbloom, Montréal, PQ H7V 1R2 (☎514/688-9550). *Guidebooks and travel information.*

Mobility International USA, PO Box 10767, Eugene, OR 97440 (Voice and TDD: ☎503/343-1284). *Information and referral services, access guides, tours and exchange programmes. Annual membership $20 (includes quarterly newsletter).*

Society for the Advancement of Travel for the Handicapped (SATH), 347 5th Ave, New York, NY 10016 (☎212/447-7284). *Non-profit travel-industry referral service that passes queries on to its members as appropriate; allow plenty of time for a response.*

Travel Information Service, Moss Rehabilitation Hospital, 1200 West Tabor Rd, Philadelphia, PA 19141 (☎215/456-9600). *Telephone information and referral service.*

Twin Peaks Press, Box 129, Vancouver, WA 98666 (☎206/694-2462 or 1-800/637-2256). *Publisher of the Directory of Travel Agencies for the Disabled ($19.95), listing more than 370 agencies worldwide; Travel for the Disabled ($19.95); the Directory of Accessible Van Rentals ($9.95) and Wheelchair Vagabond ($14.95), loaded with personal tips.*

TRAVELLING WITH CHILDREN

Travelling with kids in the United States is relatively problem-free; children are readily accepted – indeed welcomed – in public places across the country and probably nowhere more so than in Florida, where visiting families have long constituted a major part of the state's mighty tourist industry.

Hotels and **motels** almost without exception welcome children: those in major tourist areas such as Orlando often have a games room (usually of the computer kind) and/or a play area, and allow children below a certain age (usually 14, sometimes 18) to stay free in their parents' room.

In all but the most formal **restaurants**, young diners are likely to be presented with a kids' menu – liberally laced with hot dogs, dinosaur burgers and ice-cream – plus crayons, drawing pads and assorted toys.

ACTIVITIES

Most large towns have at least one child-orientated **museum** with plenty of interactive educational exhibits – often sophisticated enough to keep even adults amused for hours. Virtually all museums and other tourist attractions have reduced rates for kids under a certain age.

Florida's **theme parks** may seem the ultimate in kids' entertainment but in fact are much more geared towards entertaining adults than most people expect. Only Walt Disney World's **Magic Kingdom** is tailor-made for young kids (though even here, parents are warned that some rides may frighten the very young); adolescents (and adults) are likely to prefer Disney-MGM Studios or Universal Studios.

Away from the blockbusting tourist stops, **natural Florida** has much to stimulate the young. In the many state parks and in the Everglades National Park, park rangers specialize in tuning formative minds in to the wonders of nature – aided by an abundance of alligators, turtles and all manner of brightly coloured birds. A boat trip in dolphin-inhabited waters – several of these are recommended in the *Guide* – is another likely way to stimulate curiosity in the natural world.

On a more cautious note, adults should take great care not to allow young flesh to be exposed to the Florida **sun** for too long: even a few minutes' unprotected exposure can cause serious sunburn.

No matter how you go, once you get there be sure to take special care in keeping track of one another – it's no less terrifying for a child to be lost at Walt Disney World than it is for him or her to go missing at the shopping mall. Whenever possible agree a meeting place *before* you get lost and it's not a bad idea, especially for younger children, to attach some sort of wearable ID card and for toddlers to be kept on reins.

A good idea in a major theme park is to show your child how to find (or how to recognize and ask uniformed staff to take them to) the "Lost Kids Area". This designated space not only makes lost kids easy to locate but provides supervision plus toys and games to keep them amused until you show up. Elsewhere, tell your kids to stay where they are and not to wander; if *you* **get lost**, you'll have a much easier time finding each other if you're not all running around anxiously.

GETTING AROUND

Children under two years old **fly** for free – though that doesn't mean they get a seat, a pretty major consideration on long-distance flights – and when aged from two to twelve they are usually entitled to half-price tickets.

Once you're in Florida, travelling **by bus** may be the cheapest way to go, but it's also the most difficult with kids. Under-2s travel (on your lap) for free; ages 2 to 4 are charged 10 percent of the adult fare, as are any toddlers who take up a seat. Children under 12 years old are charged half the standard fare.

Even if you discount the romance of the railroad, **taking the train** is by far the best option for long journeys – not only does everyone get to enjoy the scenery, but you can get up and walk around, relieving pent-up energy. Children's discounts are much the same as for bus or plane travel. Recreational Vehicles (**RVs**) are also a good option for family travel, combining the convenience of built-in kitchens and bedrooms with freedom of the road (see pp.23 and 24).

Most families choose to travel **by car**, and while this is the least problematic mode of transport, it's worth planning ahead to assure a pleasant trip. Don't set yourself unrealistic targets if you're hoping to enjoy a driving vacation with your kids. Pack plenty of sensible snacks and drinks; plan stops every couple of hours; arrive at your destination well before sunset; and if you're passing through big cities, avoid travelling during rush hour. Also, it can be a good idea to give an older child some responsibility for route-finding – having someone "play navigator" is good fun, educational and often a real help to the driver. If you're doing a fly-drive vacation, note that when **renting a car** the company is legally obliged to provide free car seats for kids; in reality, however, these are not always available, so you'd be advised to bring your own.

SPORTS

Florida is as fanatical about sports as the rest of the US, but what's more surprising is that collegiate sports are often, especially among lifelong Floridians, more popular than their professional counterparts. This is because Florida's professional teams are comparatively recent additions to the sporting scene and have none of the traditions and bedrock support that the state's college sides enjoy. Seventy thousand people attending an inter-college football match is no rarity. Other sports less in evidence include soccer, volleyball, greyhound racing and Jai Alai – the last two chiefly excuses for betting.

PROFESSIONAL SPORTS

BASEBALL
Until April 1993, when the **Florida Marlins** played their first game, Florida had no professional **baseball** side of its own. Now the Marlins play at the Joe Robbie Stadium, 16 miles northwest of downtown Miami (box office Mon–Fri 10am–6pm; ☎305/620-2578; tickets $10–15).

Many northern baseball teams, however, have long held their pre-season **spring training** (Feb and March) in the state – and thousands of their fans plan vacations so that they can watch their sporting heroes going through practice routines and playing in the friendly matches of the **Grapefruit League**. Much prestige is attached to being a spring training venue and the local community identifies strongly with the team that it hosts – in some cases the link goes back fifty years. Turn up at 10am to join the crowds watching the training (free); of the twenty-odd sides who come to train in Florida, you'll find the country's top teams at the following: the **LA Dodgers**, Holman Stadium, Vero Beach (☎407/569-4900); the **Boston Red Sox**, Chain O'Lakes Park, Winter Haven (☎813/293-3900); **Detroit Tigers**, Marchant Stadium, 2301 Lakeland Hills Blvd, Lakeland (☎813/682-1401); and the **Minnesota Twins**, Tinker Field, 287 S Tampa Ave, Orlando (☎407/849-6346).

FOOTBALL
Of the state's two professional **football** teams, the **Miami Dolphins** are easily the most successful, appearing five times in the Superbowl and, in 1972, enjoying the only all-win season in NFL history. They too play at the Joe Robbie Stadium (see above; most tickets $30). By contrast, the **Tampa Bay Buccaneers** have fared only moderately well; they're based at 4201 Dale Mabry Highway (☎813/879-BUCS; tickets $15–35).

Much greater fervour is whipped up by the University of Florida's **Gators** (in Gainesville) and Florida State University's **Seminoles** (in Tallahassee), both of whom play ten-match seasons in the Southeast Conference – although the Seminoles are planning to join the rival Atlantic Coast Conference. A poor third among the college teams in terms of support but enjoying a record-breaking undefeated home run in 1991, the University of Miami's **Hurricanes** play in the National College League – which they've won on several occasions. Tickets are $18–35 for professional matches; $12–18 for college games. Further details are given in the *Guide*.

BASKETBALL
Both the state's two professional **basketball** teams are infants and have yet to make much of a mark: **Miami Heat** joined the National

Basketball Association (NBA) in 1988, followed two years later by **Orlando Magic**. Top among the college sides are Miami University's **Hurricanes**. Tickets for professional games cost $8–26; college games $6–16. Further details are given in the *Guide*.

ICE HOCKEY

Florida boasts at least one team in the National Hockey League (NHL): **Florida Panthers** (☎305/530-4444), who play at the Miami Arena between October and April. Details are given in the *Guide*.

PARTICIPANT SPORTS

WATER SPORTS

Even non-swimmers can quickly learn to **snorkel**, which is the best way to see one of the state's finest natural assets: the living coral reef that curls around its southeastern corner and on along the Florida Keys. Many **guided snorkelling trips** run to the reef and cost around $25 – details are given throughout the *Guide*. More adventurous than snorkelling is loading up with air-cylinders to go **scuba diving**. You'll need a **Certified Divers Card** to do this; if you don't already have one you'll be required to take a course, which can last anything from one hour to a day and costs $50–100. Get details from **diving shops**, always plentiful near good diving areas, which can also provide equipment, maps and general information.

When you snorkel or dive, observing a few **underwater precautions** will increase enjoyment and safety: wear **lightweight shoes** to avoid treading on jellyfish, crabs, or sharp rocks; *don't* wear any **shiny objects**, as these are likely to attract hungry fish such as the otherwise harmless barracuda; **never dive alone**; always leave your boat by diving **into the current** – by doing this, the current will help glide you back to the boat later; always display the red and white **"diver down" flag**. And, obviously, never dive after drinking alcohol.

The same reefs that make snorkelling and diving so much fun cause **surfing** to be less common than you might expect, limiting it to a few sections of the east coast. Florida's biggest waves strike land between **Sebastian Inlet** and **Cocoa Beach**, and surfing tournaments are held here during April and May. Lesser breakers are found at Miami Beach's **First Street Beach**, Boca Raton's **South Beach Park** and around the **Jacksonville Beaches**. Surfboards can be rented from local beach shops for $8–10 a day.

Cutting a (usually) more gentle passage through water, many of the state's rivers can be effortlessly navigated by **canoe**; these can be rented for around $12–15 a day from most state parks and riverside recreational areas. Additionally, there are a number of long-distance canoe trails and several companies offering inclusive canoe trips; see "The Backcountry" (p.36) for more details.

FISHING

Few things excite higher passions in Florida than **fishing**: the numerous rivers and lakes and the various breeds of catfish, bass, carp and perch that inhabit them bring eager fishermen from all over the US and beyond. Saltwater fishing is no less popular, with barely a coastal jetty in the state not creaking under the strain of weekend anglers. The most sociable way to fish, however, is from a **"party boat"** – a boatload of people putting to sea for a day of rod-casting and boozing; these generally cost $25 and are easily found in good fishing areas. **Sportsfishing** – heading out to deep water to do battle with marlin, tuna and the odd shark – is much more expensive. In the prime sportfishing areas, off the Florida Keys and off the Panhandle around Destin, you'll need around $200 a day for a boat and a guide. To protect fish stocks, a highly complex set of **rules and regulations** governs where you can fish and what you can catch. For the latest facts, get the free *Florida Fishing Handbook* from the **Florida Game and Freshwater Fish Commission**, 620 Meridian Street, Tallahassee, FL 32399-1600 (☎904/488-1960).

FESTIVALS AND HOLIDAYS

Someone, somewhere is always celebrating something in Florida, though apart from national holidays, few festivities are shared throughout the region. Instead, there is a disparate multitude of local annual events: art and craft shows, county fairs, ethnic celebrations, music festivals, rodeos, sand-castle-building competitions and many others of every description. The most interesting of these are listed throughout the Guide and you can phone the visitor center in a particular region ahead of your arrival to ask what's coming up. For the main festivities in Miami and Miami Beach see p.117 and in Key West, p.141.

NATIONAL FESTIVALS

As with everywhere else in the US, the most important of the annual **national festivals and holidays** celebrated in Florida is **Independence Day** (July 4), when the entire state grinds to a standstill as people get drunk, salute the flag and partake of firework displays, marches, beauty pageants and more, all in commemoration of the signing of the Declaration of Independence in 1776. **Halloween** (October 31) has no such patriotic overtones – in fact it's not even a public holiday despite being one of the most popular yearly flings. Traditionally, kids run around the streets banging on doors demanding "trick or treat" and get rewarded with pieces of candy; these days such activity is confined to rural areas, though you will find plenty of evidence of Halloween in cities, with waitresses liable to be disguised as witches or cats and hip city nightspots hosting everyone-dress-in-black specials. More sedate is **Thanksgiving Day** (last Thursday in November), the third big event of the year. This is essentially a domestic affair, when relatives return to the familial nest to stuff themselves with roast turkey in celebration of the first harvest of the Pilgrim Fathers and the start of the European colonization of North America.

The biggest holiday event to hit Florida is the annual **Spring Break**: a six-week invasion (late February through March and early April) of tens of thousands of students seeking fun in the sun before knuckling down to their summer exams. Times are changing, however: one traditional Spring Break venue, Fort Lauderdale, has successfully encouraged the students to go elsewhere; another, Daytona Beach, is planning to do likewise. Panama City Beach, though, welcomes the carousing collegiates with open arms and Key West – despite its lack of beach – is fast becoming a favourite Spring Break location. If you are in Florida during this time, it'll be hard to avoid some signs of Spring Break – a mob of scantily clad drunken students is a tell-tale sign – and at the busier coastal areas you may well find accommodation costing three times the normal price; be sure to plan ahead.

PUBLIC HOLIDAYS

On both Independence Day and Thanksgiving Day, shops, banks and offices will be closed for the day, as they will on most of the **other public holidays**: New Year's Day; Martin Luther King's Birthday (January 15); President's Day (third Monday in February); Memorial Day (last Monday in May); Labor Day (first Monday in September); Columbus Day (second Monday in October); Veteran's Day (November 11); and Christmas Day. Good Friday is a half-day holiday, though Easter Monday is a full-day holiday.

STAYING ON

Far from being the land of the "newly wed and the nearly dead" as many comedians have described the state, Florida's immaculate climate has persuaded people from all over the US and the rest of the world to arrive in search of a subtropical paradise. The following suggestions for finding work are basic and, if you're not a US citizen, represent the limits of what you can do without the all-important Social Security number (without which legally you can't work at all).

FINDING WORK

Since the federal government introduced fines of up to $10,000 for illegal employees, employers have become understandably choosy about whom they hire. Even the usual **casual jobs** – catering, restaurant and bar work – have tightened up for those without a **Social Security number**. If you do find work it's likely to be of the less visible, poorly paid kind – as washer-upper rather than waiter. **Agricultural work** is always available on Central Florida farms during the October to May citrus harvest; check with the nearest university or college, where noticeboards detail what's available. There are usually no problems with papers in this kind of work, though it often entails working miles from major centres and is wearying "stoop" (continually bending over) labour in blistering heat. If you can stick it out, the pay is often good and comes with basic board and accommodation. **House-cleaning** and **baby-sitting** are also feasible, if not very well-paid options.

FINDING A PLACE TO LIVE

Apartment hunting in Florida is not the nightmare it is in, say, New York: accommodation is plentiful and not always expensive, although the absence of housing associations and co-ops means that there is very little really inexpensive accommodation anywhere except in country areas. Accommodation is almost always rented unfurnished so you'll have to buy furniture; in general, expect to pay $500–600 a month for a studio or one-bedroom apartment, $900–1200 per month for 2–3 bedrooms in Miami, Tampa or Orlando, a lot less in rural areas. Most landlords will expect one month's rent as a deposit, plus one month's rent in advance.

There is no statewide organization for accommodation so you'll have to check out the options in each place. By far the best way to find somewhere is to ask around – often short-term lets come up via word of mouth. Otherwise, rooms for rent are often advertised in the windows of houses and local papers have "Apartments For Rent" sections. In **Miami**, the best source is *New Times*, although you should also scan the *Miami Herald* classifieds. In **Tampa** and **Orlando** check out the *Tampa Tribune* and *Orlando Sentinel* respectively.

> ### OPPORTUNITIES FOR FOREIGN STUDENTS
>
> **Foreign students** wishing to study in Florida can either try the long shot of arranging a year abroad through their own university, or apply directly to a Florida university (being prepared to stump up the painfully expensive fees).
>
> *The Student Exchange Visitor Programme*, for which participants are given a J-1 visa enabling them to take a job arranged in advance through the programme, is not much use since almost all the jobs are at American summer camps – of which the state has none. If you're interested anyway, organizations to contact **in the UK** include *BUNAC* (16 Bowling Green Lane, London EC1; ☎0171/251 3472) or *Camp America* (37 Queen's Gate, London SW7; ☎0171/589 3223).

DIRECTORY

ADDRESSES Though foreign visitors can find them confusing at first, American addresses are masterpieces of logic. Generally speaking, roads in built-up areas are laid out to a grid system, creating "blocks": addresses of buildings refer to the block, which will be numbered in sequence from a central point usually somewhere downtown; for example, 620 S Cedar will be six blocks south of this downtown point. In small towns and parts of larger cities, "streets" and "avenues" often run north–south and east–west respectively; streets are usually named (sometimes alphabetically), avenues generally numbered.

CIGARETTES AND SMOKING Smoking is now severely frowned upon in the US, though no government measures have been taken against tobacco advertising. It's possible to spend a month in Florida without ever smelling tobacco; most cinemas are non-smoking, restaurants are usually divided into non-smoking and smoking sections, and smoking is universally forbidden on public transport – including almost all domestic airline flights. Work places, too, tend to be smoke-free zones, so employees are reduced to smoking on the street outside. Cigarettes are, however, still widely sold. A packet of twenty costs around $1.95, though most smokers buy cigarettes by the carton for around $12.

DATES In the American style, the date 6.9.94 means not September 6 but June 9.

DEPARTURE TAX None: airport tax is included in the price of your ticket.

DONATIONS Many museums request donations rather than an admission fee; usually you'll be expected to put $2 or so into the collection as you enter. If you don't, you won't be turned away but will suffer the indignity of being considered a complete cheapskate.

DRUGS Despite the widely accepted fact that much of the marijuana and cocaine consumed in the US arrives through Florida, the state's laws regarding possession of drugs are among the toughest in the country. Recreational drug use is by no means unheard of, but many people, even in the cities, view any kind of drug-taking as an attempt to turn the country over to Satan. Bluntly put, it isn't worth the risk of being caught in possession of any illegal substance in any quantity whatsoever.

ELECTRICITY 110V AC. All plugs are two-pronged and rather insubstantial. Some travel plug adapters don't fit American sockets. British-made equipment won't work unless it has a voltage switching provision.

FLEA MARKETS Beside almost any major road junction, you'll find something touting itself as "Florida's Biggest Fleamarket". The genuinely big ones usually take place on Fridays and weekends, with hundreds of booths selling furniture, household appliances, ornaments, clothes – often hideous and always cheap.

FLOORS The *first* floor in the US is what would be the ground floor in Britain; the *second* floor would be the first floor, and so on.

ID Should be carried at all times. Two pieces should suffice, one of which should have a photo: a passport and credit card(s) are your best bets.

HURRICANES Despite the much publicized onslaught of Hurricane Andrew in August 1992, statistically it's highly improbable that a hurricane will hit during your visit ,and even if it does there will be plenty of warning – accurate tracking of potential hurricanes brewing around the Gulf of Mexico and the Caribbean from June to November (regarded as the hurricane season) being a feature of every TV weather bulletin. Local services are well equipped, most buildings are (supposedly) hurricane-proof, evacuation routes are signposted, and even phone books carry tips on how to survive – and since Andrew,

Floridians have become much less blasé in their attitude to hurricanes. A more likely source of danger are thunderstorms; see below.

LAUNDERETTES All but the most basic hotels will wash laundry for you, but it'll be a lot cheaper (about $1.50) for a wash and tumble dry in a launderette – found all over, including many hotels, motels and campgrounds. Take plenty of quarters.

LOTTERY Every few weeks, the state goes potty over the drawing of the winning six-sequence number in the Florida Lottery. Along with millions of others, you can buy as many tickets as you can afford (at a dollar a time) from any shop displaying the lottery sign. The prize sometimes reaches $17 million.

MEASUREMENTS AND SIZES The US has yet to go metric, so measurements are in inches, feet, yards and miles; weight in ounces, pounds and tons. Liquid measurements differ, too: American pints and gallons are about four-fifths of British ones. US clothing sizes can be calculated by subtracting two from British sizes; thus, a British women's size 12 is a US size 10. Shoe sizes are one and a half more than the equivalent British size.

PUBLIC TOILETS Don't exist as such in the city. Bars, restaurants and fast-food outlets are the places to go, though technically you should be a customer.

TAX Be warned that 6 percent sales tax is added to virtually everything you buy in a shop, and is not included in the marked price.

THUNDERSTORMS Subtropical southern Florida has frequent, very localized thunderstorms throughout the summer. Obviously, if possible you should shelter inside a building to avoid being struck by lightning (which, on average, kills eleven people a year). If you're caught in the open, stay away from metallic objects and don't make a dash for your car – most people who are struck are doing this. On the plus side, the air after a storm is refreshingly free of humidity.

TICKETS For music, theatre and sports, use *Ticketmaster*, whose plentiful offices are listed in the phone book and through whom you can buy tickets over the phone with your credit card.

FLORIDA TERMS

Barrier Island A long, narrow island of the kind protecting much of Florida's mainland from coastal erosion, comprising sandy beach and mangrove forest – often blighted by condos (see below).

Condo Short for "condominium", a tall and usually ugly block of (normally) expensive flats, common along the coast and in fashionable areas of cities. Many are rented out for holidays or owned as timeshares.

Cracker Nickname given to Florida farmers from the 1800s, stemming from the sound made by the whip used in cattle round-ups (or possibly from the cracking of corn to make grits). These days it's also a common term for the state's conservative ruralites: surly, insular types who prefer the company of wild hogs to people they don't already know.

Crackerbox Colloquial architectural term for the simple wooden cottage lived in by early Crackers (see above), ingeniously designed to allow the lightest breeze to cool the whole dwelling.

Florida Ice Potentially hazardous mix of oil and water on a road surface following a thunderstorm.

Hammocks Not open-air sleeping places but patches of trees. In the south, and especially in the Everglades, hammocks often appear as "tree islands" above the flat wetlands. In the north, hammocks are larger and occur on elevations between wetlands and pinewoods. All hammocks make excellent wildlife habitats and those in the south are composed of tropical trees rarely seen elsewhere in the US.

Intracoastal Waterway To strengthen coastal defences during World War II, the natural waterways dividing the mainland from the barrier islands (see above) were deepened and extended. The full length, along the east and southwest coasts, is termed the "Intracoastal Waterway".

Key Derived from the word "cay" – literally an island or bank composed of coral fragments.

No see'ems Tiny, mosquito-like insects; near-impossible to spot until they've already bitten you.

Snowbird Term applied to a visitor from the northern US coming to Florida during the winter to escape sub-zero temperatures – usually recognised by their sunburn.

TIME Most of Florida runs on Eastern Standard Time, five hours behind GMT in winter. The section of the Panhandle west of the Apalachicola River, however, is on Central Standard Time – one hour behind the rest of Florida. British Summer Time runs almost parallel to US Daylight Saving Time – implemented from the last Sunday in April to the last Sunday in October – causing a four-hour time gap for two weeks of the year.

TIPPING You really shouldn't depart a bar or restaurant without leaving a tip of *at least* 15 percent (unless the service is utterly disgusting):

it causes a lot of embarrassment and nasty looks and a short paypacket for the waiter/waitress at the end of the week. About the same amount should be added to taxi fares – and round them up to the nearest 50¢ or dollar. A hotel porter should get roughly $1 per item for carrying your baggage to your room. When paying by credit or charge card, you're expected to add the tip to the total bill before filling in the amount and signing.

VIDEOS The standard format used for video cassettes in the US is different from that used in Britain. You cannot buy videos in the US compatible with a video camera bought in Britain.

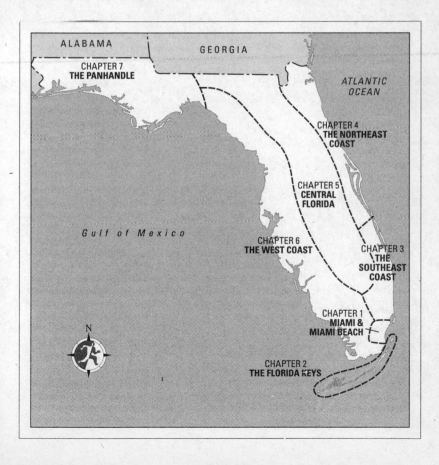

ALABAMA   GEORGIA

CHAPTER 7
THE PANHANDLE

ATLANTIC OCEAN

CHAPTER 4
THE NORTHEAST COAST

CHAPTER 5
CENTRAL FLORIDA

Gulf of Mexico

CHAPTER 6
THE WEST COAST

CHAPTER 3
THE SOUTHEAST COAST

CHAPTER 1
MIAMI & MIAMI BEACH

N

CHAPTER 2
THE FLORIDA KEYS

CHAPTER ONE

MIAMI AND MIAMI BEACH

You tell people you're from Miami and they duck.

Carl Hiaasen.

Far and away the most exciting city in Florida, **Miami** is a stunning and often intoxicatingly beautiful place. Set beside the cool blue waters of Biscayne Bay, with its roads lined by lush tropical foliage, the state's major urban centre is awash with sunlight-intensified natural colours and a delicious scent of jasmine. An emergent city with a sharp, contemporary style (and some horrific social problems), there are moments, such as when the downtown skyline glows in the warm night and the beachside palm trees sway in the evening breeze, when a better-looking city is hard to imagine.

The climate and landscape may be near perfect, but it's the people that make Miami unique. In the antithesis of the traditional Anglo-American-dominated US metropolis, half of Miami's two-million population is Hispanic, of which the majority are Cubans. They form easily the most visible – and powerful – ethnic group in a city that's home to dozens from all over Latin America and the Caribbean. Spanish is the main language in most areas, and news from Havana, Caracas or Bogotá frequently gets more attention than the latest word from Washington. The city is no melting pot, however. Ethnic divisions and tensions are often all too evident. Since the black ghettoes first erupted in the Sixties, violent expressions of rage – most recently among Haitians and Puerto Ricans – have been a regular feature of Miami life.

Some sections are still extremely dangerous, but Miami has cleaned itself up considerably since 1980, when it had the highest murder rate in the country. It has also grown rich as a key gateway for US–Latin American trade, to which a glut of expensively designed banks and financial institutions bears witness. Strangely enough, another factor in Miami's revival was the mid-Eighties cop show *Miami Vice*, which was less about crime than designer clothes and subtropical scenery; its featuring of Miami Beach's **Art Deco** district made this a popular location for fashion shoots.

Miami has very little history to look back on. A century ago it was a swampy outpost where a thousand mosquito-tormented settlers commuted by boat around a trading post and a couple of coconut plantations. The arrival of the railroad in 1896 gave Miami its first fixed land link with the rest of the continent, and literally cleared the way for the Twenties property boom, which saw entire communities appearing almost overnight, forming the basis of the modern city.

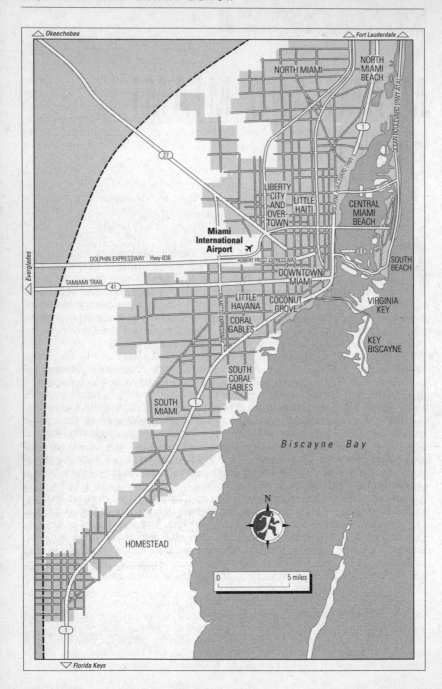

> The area code for Miami and Miami Beach is ☎305.

The Fifties saw **Miami Beach** establishing itself as a celebrity-filled resort area, while at the same time – and with much less fanfare – thousands of Cubans fleeing the successive regimes of Batista and Castro began arriving on mainland Miami. The Sixties and Seventies brought decline, as Miami Beach's celebrity cachet waned and it became a haven for retirees; and the city's tourist industry was damaged still further by the Liberty City riot of 1980, which marked a low point in Miami's black-white relations.

Since then, with the strengthening of Latin American economic links and a younger, more cosmopolitan breed of visitor energizing Miami Beach, the city is enjoying a surge of optimism and affluence – and, as Hispanic immigration into the US drastically alters the demography of the nation, today's Miami could well be a preview of tomorrow's US.

Arrival and information

However and whenever you arrive in Miami, grasping initial bearings will not be difficult. All points of entry are within a few miles of the centre, and public transport links are generally reliable. Numerous offices around the city dispense general tourist information and advice.

By air

All passenger **flights** land at Miami International Airport, a chaotic complex six miles west of downtown Miami. Once through the gate, it's a simple matter to get across the city.

The main **car rental** firms (see "Driving and car rental", p.22) have desks close to the baggage reclaim area and provide free transport to collect a vehicle. If you have pre-booked a car, just leave the terminal and flag down a bus belonging to your rental company. If you're arriving in Miami after dark, especially after a long flight, consider spending your first night at an airport hotel; the rental car-parks are located in a none too safe area, and it can be confusing for first-time visitors to make their way onto the city- or Beach-bound highways. **Local buses** depart from several points beside the airport's concourse; take #7 (every 40mins; Mon–Fri 5.30am–8.30pm, Sat/Sun 7am–7pm) to downtown Miami (half an hour away), or the "J" bus (every 30mins; daily 5.30am–11.30pm) for the slightly longer journey to Miami Beach. The bus stop is indicated by "City Bus and Tri-Rail Shuttle" signs opposite the airport's "E" departure gates. A short cab ride from the airport will deliver you to the Miami West *Greyhound* station, with links to other parts of Miami (see below) and beyond.

Quicker, if more expensive than public transport, the **Airporter**, **SuperShuttle** and **Red Top** minivans (grandly calling themselves "limos") run around the clock and will deliver you to any address in or around Miami for $8–15. Their representatives are easy to spot as you leave the baggage reclaim area. **Taxis** are in plentiful supply outside the airport building; fares are metered and cost around $15 to downtown Miami, $20 to Miami Beach.

By bus

Of several **Greyhound** stations in Miami, the busiest is **Miami West**, near the airport, at 4111 NW 27th Street (☎871-1810). Most *Greyhound* buses, however, including those to and from Key West, also call at the **Downtown** station, 700 Biscayne Boulevard (☎372-7222). Fewer services use the city's other *Greyhound* stations: in **Homestead**, 5 NE Third Avenue (☎247-2040); in **Central Miami Beach**, 7101 Harding Avenue (☎538-0381); and in **North Miami Beach**, 16250 Biscayne Boulevard (☎945-0801). Local bus services are detailed on p.59.

By train and tri-rail

The **train** station, 8303 NW 37th Avenue (☎1-800/872-7245), is seven miles northwest of downtown Miami, with an adjacent **Metrorail** stop that provides access to downtown Miami and beyond; bus #L stops here on its way to Central Miami Beach. The **Tri-Rail** (☎1-800/TRI-RAIL), the cheap commuter service along the southeast coast (see *Basics*), links directly with the Metrorail at 1149 E 21st Street, also seven miles northwest of downtown Miami. For more information on the Metrorail, see p.59.

By car

Most of the major **roads** into Miami take the form of elevated expressways which – accidents and rush hours permitting – make getting into the city simple and quick, if potentially hair-raising. From the north, **I-95** (also called the **North South Expressway**) streaks over the downtown streets before joining **Hwy-1**, an ordinary road that continues through South Miami. Crossing the Everglades from the west coast, **Hwy-41** (also called the **Tamiami Trail**) enters Miami along SW Eighth Street, and you'll save time by turning off north along the **Florida Turnpike** (coming from the north and skirting the city's western periphery) to reach the **Dolphin Expressway** (**Hwy-836**), which meets I-95 just south of downtown Miami. **Hwy-27**, the main artery from central Florida, becomes the **Robert Frost Expressway** close to the airport and intersects with I-95 just north of the downtown area. The slower, scenic coastal route, **Hwy-A1A**, enters the city at the northern tip of Miami Beach.

Information

Although Miami has no single office devoted to providing tourist **information**, several useful outlets for leaflets, free tourist magazines and general practical advice are dotted around the city. In **downtown Miami**, outside Bayside Marketplace, an information stand is open from 11.30am to 8pm (☎1-800/283-2707); at Miami Beach, the Miami Beach Chamber of Commerce, 1920 Meridian Avenue (Mon–Fri 8.30am–6pm, Sat 10am–4pm; ☎672-1270), is a good stop, with a kiosk located at the intersection of Lincoln Road Mall and Washington Avenue (Mon–Fri 9.30am–4pm). Also at **Miami Beach** is the Art Deco Welcome Center, 1001 Ocean Drive, which provides information on South Beach's historic Art Deco district and organizes tours (daily 11am–9pm; ☎672-2014). Useful **Chambers of Commerce** in other districts are detailed throughout the *Guide*. If you're spending time in **Homestead**, or just passing through, be sure to stop at the area's excellent Visitor Information Center, 160 Hwy-1 (daily 8am–6pm; ☎1-800/388-9669).

Most of the free **maps** are useful for only very basic route-finding; it's worth spending $2.50 on the street-indexed *Trakker* map of Miami, available from most newsstands and many shops.

MIAMI MEDIA

TV stations

4 WTVJ NBC
6 WCIX CBS
7 WSVN FOX
10 WPLG ABC

17 WLRN PBS
23 WLTV Spanish-language independent
33 WBFS Independent

Radio stations

RWIOD 610 AM. All-talk: phone-ins, entertainment, sports, news.

WINZ 940 AM. All-news format with magazine shows, sports reports, weather and entertainment.

WDNA 89.5 FM. Innovative music shows.

WVUM 90.3 FM. University radio, dominated by British indie rock.

WLRN 91.3 FM. In-depth news coverage from National Public Radio (NPR), with educational, political and arts programming.

WTMI 93.1 FM. Classical music by day, jazz after midnight.

WLVE 93.9 FM. Pop, jazz and rock.

WZTA 94.9 FM. Classic Sixties rock.

WFLC 97.3 FM. MOR rock.

WEDR 99.1 FM. Soul music, with rap and disco.

WMXJ 102.7 FM. Rock, R&B and soul oldies.

WHQT 105 FM. Black dance music.

The Friday issue of Miami's only daily **newspaper**, the reputable *Miami Herald* (weekdays 35¢; Sunday edition $1) – which includes the Spanish supplement *El Nuevo Herald* – carries comprehensive weekend entertainment listings. Another, better source is the weekly *New Times*, published on Thursdays and available free from street machines and many restaurants and bars. Also free, and easily found around the South Beach, *Ocean Drive* carries handy basic information on local cafés and clubs as well as the celebrities who frequent them. In addition, there's a host of papers geared towards more specialist markets, such as *TWN* (*The Weekly News*) for gays and lesbians.

Getting around

Miami is a city that's easily navigated; while designed for the car, it also boasts a comprehensive public transit system that provides a sound alternative for daytime travel.

Driving and car rental

Driving around Miami is a piece of cake, and certainly the most practical way to get around. Traffic in and out of Miami can be heavy, but the city's **expressways** (see "Arrival", above) will carry you swiftly from one area to another. Before setting off on any journey, plan your route carefully so as not to stray accidentally into an unsavoury area, and if you do get lost, ask for directions at a filling station. Use ordinary streets and avenues for short journeys only, as they're often clogged by local traffic and may have confusing one-way systems. **Rush hour** (7–

MIAMI ADDRESSES AND ORIENTATION

Miami's street **naming and numbering system** takes some getting used to. The city splits into quadrants, divided by Flagler Street and Miami Avenue (which intersect downtown). "**Streets**" run east–west and "**avenues**" north–south, their numbers getting higher the further you go from downtown Miami. "**Roads**" are less common and run northwest–southeast. Streets and avenues change their compass-point prefix when crossing into a new quadrant. For example, SE First Street becomes SW First Street after crossing Miami Avenue, and NW Second Avenue becomes SW Second Avenue after crossing Flagler Street.

In some areas the pattern varies, most obviously in Coral Gables, where streets have names instead of numbers, and avenues are numbered in sequence from Douglas Avenue.

9am and 4–6pm) should also be avoided. Driving between Miami and Miami Beach is straightforward using one of six causeways, each well marked and quickly accessed from the main arteries.

There is plenty of provision for **street parking** in Miami, though actually finding an empty space can prove difficult, particularly at night in Coconut Grove and the South Beach. Parking meters are everywhere and usually require 50c per half-hour; save every quarter you get as you'll need vast quantities. Parking at public **parks and beaches** normally costs $2 per day; **carparks** generally charge $2 an hour, $6 per day. Shopping mall carparks seldom charge but may have a two-hour time limit.

Most of the major **car rental** companies have booking desks at the airport and provide free transportation from the terminals to their offices where your car will be waiting: *Alamo*, 3355 NW 22nd Street (☎1-800/327-9633); *Avis*, 2330 NW 37th Street (☎1-800/331-1212); *Budget*, 3901 NW 38th Street (☎1-800/527-0700); *Hertz*, 3755 NW 21st Street (☎1-800/654-3131); and *Thrifty*, 2701 Le Jeune Road (☎1-800/367-2277). Each charges around $25 a day, $150 a week. To rent a car in another part of the city, call and ask for the nearest branch office or look in the phone book. Depending on the fine print, smaller firms can be cheaper; pick of the bunch is *Value Rent-a-Car*, with an office at 2875 NW Le Jeune Road (☎1-800/327-4847) and a desk at the airport, which charges around $20 a day, $100 per week.

Public transport

An integrated **public transport** network of buses, trains and a monorail run by *Metro-Dade Transit* covers Miami, making the city easy – if time-consuming – to get around by day; night travel is much harder.

Bus routes cover the entire city, most radiating out from downtown Miami. Frequencies vary greatly, but major areas are usually linked by at least two services an hour between 6am and 7pm on weekdays, fewer at weekends. On busy routes, such as Miami–Miami Beach, buses run until 10pm or 11pm; otherwise they finish around 7pm. The flat-rate one-way **bus fare** is $1.25, payable on board by dropping the exact amount in change (no notes) into a machine beside the driver. If you need to transfer to another bus, say so when you get on; the driver will give you a free **transfer** ticket, which you hand over to the driver of the next bus. Transfer tickets are route- and time-stamped to prevent you lingering too long between connections or taking a scenic detour (if you do so, you'll be charged the full fare again).

Considerably quicker is the **Metrorail**, a single, elevated railroad that links the northern suburbs with South Miami; trains run every five to fifteen minutes between 5.30am and midnight. Useful stops are Government Center (for the downtown area), Vizcaya, Coconut Grove and Douglas Road or University (for Coral Gables). Stations do, however, tend to be awkwardly situated, and you'll often need to use Metrorail services in conjunction with a bus. One-way **Metrorail fares** are $1.25; buy a token from the machines (insert five quarters) at the station and use it to get through the turnstile. **Transfers between buses and Metrorail** cost 25¢ from the bus driver or a Metrorail station transfer machine.

Downtown Miami is ringed by the **Metromover** (sometimes called the "People Mover"), a daytime monorail loop that doesn't cover much ground but gives a bird's-eye view of downtown Miami. The flat fare is 25¢, payable into the machines at the stations. Transfers to Metromover from Metrorail are free; to transfer from Metromover to Metrorail, insert $1 in coins into the turnstile between the respective platforms.

Also operated by *Metro-Dade Transit* and running between South Beach and downtown Miami, at fifteen-minute intervals between 7pm and 4am on Friday and Saturday and from noon to 4pm on Sunday, for $1.25, are the **Breeze minibuses**, mainly intended to reduce traffic – and drunken driving – as revellers head to and from South Beach.

Over **long stays** involving regular public transport use, it's economical to buy a **Metropass**, which gives unlimited rides on all services for a calendar month. The Metropass costs $60 from any shop displaying the *Metro-Dade Transit* sign, and is on sale from the 20th of each month.

For **information** and **free route maps and timetables**, go to the *Transit Service Center* (daily 7am–6pm) inside the *Metro-Dade Center* in downtown Miami, or phone ☎638-6700 (Mon–Fri 6am–10pm, Sat & Sun 9am–5pm). Individual route maps and timetables can usually be found on buses.

Besides the official services, **privately run minibuses** (known as "Jitneys") link busy areas for a flat fare of $1. They generally pull up at regular bus stops, but can be waved down practically anywhere: look for the destination board on the front. Note that such buses are unregulated and rarely insured to carry passengers – you travel on them very much at your own risk.

Taxis

Taxis are abundant and often the only way to get around at night without a car. **Fares** average out at $1.80 per mile, hence the trip between the airport and Miami Beach – easily the longest journey you're likely to make – costs around $20–30; from downtown Miami you'll pay around $8 to Coconut Grove and $8–15

MAJOR MIAMI BUS ROUTES	
From downtown Miami to:	**Greyhound within Miami**
Coconut Grove #48.	**From downtown Miami to:**
Coral Gables #24.	Homestead (3 daily; 1hr 15min)
Little Havana #8.	Miami Beach (18 daily; 25–45min)
Key Biscayne #B.	Miami West (18 daily; 15–45min)
Miami Beach #C, #F, #K, #M or #S.	North Miami Beach (18 daily; 20–45min)
Miami International Airport #7.	

to Miami Beach. An empty cab will stop if the driver sees you waving, but it's more common to phone: *Central Taxicab* (☎532-5555), *Metro Taxi* (☎888-8888), *Yellow* (☎444-4444) and *Magic City* (☎757-5523) are all fairly reliable.

Water taxis

If you're in no great hurry, one of the most pleasant ways to get around the city is by **water taxi**. Two routes link to provide an extensive network that stretches from central Miami Beach in the north to Coconut Grove in the south. The **Shuttle Service** (daily 10am–2.30am every 15–20min; $3) runs from the Omni International Mall (north of the Venetian Causeway) to points along the Miami River (ideal for eating out at the numerous riverside fish restaurants). At Bayside Marketplace you can transfer to the **Biscayne Bay Service** (Sun–Thurs 11am– midnight, Fri–Sat 11am–2am; $6) with moorage points on the west shore of Miami Beach, Virginia Key (the Seaquarium), Key Biscayne (Crandon Park), Viscaya and Coconut Grove. An **all day pass** is available for $14 (children under twelve go half price). For precise location of moorage places phone ☎858-6292.

Cycling

Although you won't be able to see all of Miami by **cycling**, Coral Gables and Key Biscayne are perfectly suited to pedal-powered exploration, and there's a fourteen-mile cycle path through Coconut Grove and into South Miami. For details, get hold of the free leaflet *Miami on Two Wheels* from the Greater Miami Convention and Visitors' Bureau, 701 Brickell Ave, Suite 2700 (☎539-3063).

You can **rent a bike** for $12–25 per day from several outlets: in Coconut Grove, *Dade Cycle Shop*, 3216 Grand Avenue (☎443-6075); or in Key Biscayne, *Key Biscayne Bicycle Rentals*, 260 Crandon Boulevard (☎361-5555). For cruising around Miami Beach, you can beat exorbitant hotel bike-rental charges by going to the *Miami Beach Cycle Center*, 923 W 39th Street (☎531-4161), or to *Cycles on the Beach*, 713 Fifth Street (☎673-2055), which also arranges guided **bicycle tours** of the Art Deco district; trips leave at 10.30am on Sundays and cost $6 for the tour plus $6 for the bike – phone ahead to reserve your place.

Walking tours and roller blading

Miamians consider **walking** anywhere a bizarre concept, but some of the city's more enjoyable areas are compact enough to cover on foot – though too far apart to walk between. For an informed and entertaining stroll, take one of **Dr Paul George's Walking Tours** (☎375-1625), which look at a number of areas including downtown Miami, Coconut Grove, Coral Gables, Little Havana, South Beach and the Miami Cemetery; walks last two to three hours and cost $15.

Elsewhere, you shouldn't miss the ninety-minute **Art Deco Walking Tour** of South Miami Beach. A perfect introduction to the area's phenomenal architecture, the tour begins each Saturday at 10.30am from the Art Deco Welcome Center, 1001 Ocean Drive (☎672-2014), and costs $6.

A speedier means of getting around is **roller blading** or in-line skating, particularly popular in South Beach; see "Listings" for rental (or sales) details.

Bus, boat and helicopter tours

Scores of travel companies run **guided bus tours** around Miami's obvious points of tourist interest, but most are overpriced ($25–40 for a day) and only mildly instructive; leaflets are available from any hotel or Chamber of Commerce.

A cheaper and better option is the **Old Town Trolley Tour**: a 90-minute narrated shunt around the main sights of downtown Miami, Coconut Grove, Coral Gables, Little Havana and the Art Deco district. The trolley costs $7 and leaves every thirty minutes between 10am and 4pm daily from the Bayside Marketplace, close to the downtown area.

If you prefer water to dry land – and the downtown skyline is undoubtedly most striking from across the water – several small craft moored along the jetty at the Bayside Marketplace offer **boat tours** around Biscayne Bay; departure times and prices (usually $22 per person for an hour) are chalked up. One of the longest established is *Bayside Cruises* (☎888-3002), whose ninety-minute trips begin daily at 1pm, 3pm, 5pm, 7pm and 9pm.

Accommodation

Finding a place to stay in Miami is only ever a problem over New Year and important holiday weekends such as Memorial Day and Labor Day. It's small enough that you can stay just about anywhere and not feel isolated, though the lion's share of **hotels** and **motels** are on **Miami Beach**: an ideal base for nightlife, beachlife and seeing the city. Prices vary from $20 to $300, but you can anticipate spending $40–75 during the summer, and $60–100 during the winter (or upwards of $100 per night in the ultra-chic South Beach hotels). **Budget accommodation** is restricted to two **youth hostels** in Miami Beach and a **campground** miles out in the city's southwest fringe.

Away from Miami Beach, choice is reduced and costs increase. **Downtown Miami** – interesting by day but dull at night – has few affordable rivals to its expense-account chain hotels; distinctive character and architecture make **Coral Gables** appealing, but its rooms are seldom cheap; the stylish high-rise hotels of **Coconut Grove** are a jet-setters' preserve; and in **Key Biscayne** you'll need $100 a night for the plainest oceanside room. Only in **South Miami**, unremarkable in itself but a feasible base if you're driving, will you find a good assortment of no-frills motels for $40–60 a night. The **airport** area hotels, with just one bargain among them, should only be considered if you're catching a plane at an unearthly hour or arriving late and want to avoid driving into Miami after dark.

During the winter you'd be well advised to **reserve ahead**, either directly or through a travel agent. Between May and November, however, you'll save by going for the best deals on the spot (though you may want to arrange your first night in advance). Don't be afraid to **bargain**, as this can result in a few dollars being lopped off the advertised rate. **Single** rooms are rarely cheaper than **doubles**, and the few exceptions are indicated in "Listings". Prices below are for the winter season; all will be lower during the summer.

ACCOMMODATION PRICE CODES

All **accommodation prices** in this book have been coded using the symbols below. Note that prices are for the least expensive double rooms in each establishment. For a full explanation see p.27 in *Basics*.

① up to $30	③ $45–60	⑤ $80–100	⑦ $130–180
② $30–45	④ $60–80	⑥ $100–130	⑧ $180+

Hotels and motels

Downtown Miami

Hampton Inn-Downtown, 2500 Brickell Ave (☎1-800/HAMPTON). A generic but perfectly adequate chain motel, a mile from the centre of downtown Miami. ④.

Howard Johnson, 200 SE Second Ave (☎1-800/654-2000). Very standard chain hotel but the lowest-priced rooms this close to the heart of downtown Miami. ⑤–⑦.

Inter-Continental Miami, 100 Chopin Plaza (☎1-800/327-0200). Wicker chairs and a Henry Moore sculpture improve the atmosphere of this multinational chain hotel. Very classy and comfortable. ⑧.

Marina Park, 340 Biscayne Blvd (☎1-800/528-1234). A bland exterior shields a personable interior, with views across the Port of Miami and the neighbouring parks. ⑤–⑧.

Miami River Inn, 118 SW South River Drive (☎325-0045). Most of the buildings making up the inn date to 1908 and provide comfortable accommodation in a unique environment a short walk across the Miami River from the centre of town or the Brickell banking district. Rooms have stunning views either of the city or the inn's garden and pool. ⑤.

Occidental Parc, 100 SE Fourth St (☎1-800/521-5000). A good choice, delectably positioned beside the Miami River. All rooms are suites with small kitchens. ⑥–⑦.

Omni International, 1601 Biscayne Blvd (☎1-800/843-6664). Mostly utilized by business people and wealthy Latin Americans on shopping trips to the expansive downstairs mall. ⑥–⑦.

Coconut Grove

Doubletree at Coconut Grove, 2649 S Bayshore Drive (☎1-800/528-0444). Elegant high-rise with cosy rooms and great views, just a quarter of an hour's walk from the area's cafés and bars. ⑦.

Grand Bay, 2669 S Bayshore Drive (☎1-800/327-2788). A glass of champagne on arrival at the hotel sets the tone; expense-account elegance throughout. ⑧.

Mayfair House, 3000 Florida Ave (☎1-800/341-0809). Luxury all-suite hotel, complete with rooftop swimming pool. ⑧.

Coral Gables

Biltmore, 1200 Anastasia Ave (☎1-800/727-1926). A landmark, Mediterranean-style hotel that has endured mixed fortunes since it began pampering the rich and famous in 1926. Show up to pace the echoey corridors and sink into the lobby armchairs, even if you can't afford to stay here. ⑥–⑧.

Colonnade, 180 Aragon Ave (☎1-800/533-1337). Marble floors, oriental rugs and brass lamps fill this showpiece of Mediterranean Revival architecture. ⑤–⑥.

Gables Inn, 730 S Dixie Hwy (☎661-7999). Basic but clean and the least expensive in the area. ③.

Place St Michel, 162 Alcazar Ave (☎444-1666). Small, romantic hotel just off the Miracle Mile, with Laura Ashley decor and copious European antiques. Rate includes continental breakfast. ⑤–⑦.

Riviera Courts, 5100 Riviera Drive (☎1-800/368-8602). Simple, homely motel equipped with a pool, close to the University of Miami and Miracle Mile. ③–⑤.

Key Biscayne

Sheraton Royal, 555 Ocean Drive (☎1-800/334-8484). Upper bracket beachside hotel with all the amenities you can think of, and some good off-season reductions. ⑧.

Silver Sands Oceanfront Motel, 301 Ocean Drive (☎361-5441). Hardly a bargain, but the simple rooms are the cheapest on the island. ⑥.

Sonesta Beach, 350 Ocean Drive (☎1-800/SONESTA). High-rise resort with luxurious rooms, sports facilities, bars and a prime stretch of private beach. ⑨.

South Miami and Homestead

A1 Motel, 815 N Krome Ave (☎248-2741). Basic and clean, with some non-smoking rooms and a do-it-yourself laundry. ③–④.

Coral Roc, 1100 N Krome Ave (☎247-4010). Unexciting but fully functional motel. ③–④.

Everglades Motel, 605 S Krome Ave (☎247-4117). A slightly run-down exterior, but the rooms are okay and there's a coin-operated laundry for guests. ②–③.

Gateway to the Keys, 1 Straus Blvd, Florida City (☎246-5100). One of the most comfortable places to stay hereabouts, and usefully located between the Keys, Miami and the Everglades. ⑤–⑥.

Greenstone Motel, 304 N Krome Ave (☎247-8334). Simple, adequate motel in the heart of old Homestead. ③–④.

Super 8, 1202 N Krome Ave (☎1-800/800-8000). Branch of a plain but cheap motel chain, with clean and reasonably priced rooms. ③.

South Miami Beach

Brigham Gardens Guesthouse, 1411 Collins Ave (☎531-1331). Large rooms with either basic or fully equipped kitchens. A tropical garden patio and friendly atmosphere contribute to make this one of the most pleasant places to stay in South Beach. ④–⑤.

Cavalier, 1320 Ocean Drive (☎534-2135). Recently opened and completely revamped 1930s Art Deco hotel, now featuring neo-Moorish decor. ⑦–⑧.

Century, 140 Ocean Drive (☎674-8855). Stark, deconstructivist chic; a home from home for its predominantly fashion-industry clientele. ⑤–⑦.

Clay, 406 Española Way (☎534-2988). Vintage hotel that functions as the city's only youth hostel (see "Budget Accommodation", below), but has some private rooms. ①–②.

Colony, 736 Ocean Drive (☎673-0088). Beautifully refurbished Art Deco delight. ⑤–⑥.

Essex House, 1001 Collins Ave (☎532-3872). Warm atmosphere and one of the more tastefully restored Art Deco hotels. ④–⑥.

Lafayette, 944 Collins Ave (☎673-2262). Pleasant, airy rooms a short walk from the beach strip. ⑦.

Leslie, 1244 Ocean Drive (☎1-800/338-9076). Excellently located on the beachside Art Deco strip, with striking interior design – bright colours and mirrors at crooked angles. Rooms are equipped with tape-player/radios as well as TVs. ⑥–⑧.

Marlin, 1200 Collins Ave (☎673-8770). Eleven costly but cosy suites stunningly decorated with a Caribbean islands theme, plus a rooftop sun deck. If you can't afford to stay here, at least have a drink at the bar. ⑧.

Mermaid, 909 Collins Ave (☎538-5324). Cost-effective rooms – some with kitchenettes – in a Caribbean-style cottage. ③–⑤.

Park Central, 640 Ocean Drive (☎538-1611). Largest of the Art Deco piles and one of the few with a pool, retaining ceiling fans alongside regular air conditioning. ⑥–⑦.

Park Washington, 1020 Washington Ave (☎532-1930). Quiet and cosy, with a fridge in every spartan room; two blocks from the ocean. ④.

Raleigh, 1775 Collins Ave (☎534-6300). The 1990s refurbishment aped the original 1940s look, but added state-of-the-art electronics in every room. Probably the best run and currently the most glamorous hotel in South Beach. ⑥–⑧.

Villa Paradiso, 1415 Collins Ave (☎532-0616). Fully equipped studios and one bedroom apartments with kitchens, just one block away from the beach. ⑤–⑦.

Waldorf Towers, 860 Ocean Drive (☎531-7684). Another Art Deco landmark, facing the ocean and right in the throng of the fashionable strip. ⑥.

Central Miami Beach and Bay Harbour Islands

Alexander, 5225 Collins Ave (☎1-800/327-6121). Well-equipped suites, free champagne on arrival, mattresses adjusted to your desired firmness. You won't want to leave. ⑧.

Eden Roc Resort & Spa, 4525 Collins Ave (☎1-800-327-8337). A landmark on the Beach since the 1950s, this has been refurbished to the last detail and again ranks amongst Miami's most luxurious hotels. Most of the rooms command spectacular views. Besides the two pools there's a health spa offering everything from shiatsu massage to seaweed and salt scrubs. ⑧.

Bay Harbor Inn, 9660 E Bay Harbor Drive, Bay Harbor Islands (☎868-4141). Low-key elegance in an upmarket residential neighbourhood a few minutes' walk from the beach and 15 minutes' drive from downtown. The most attractive rooms are those with views onto Indian Creek fronting the inn. ⑤–⑥.

Fountainbleau Hilton, 4441 Collins Ave (☎538-2000). Once the last word in glamour, now elaborately refurbished and seeking to regain its lost esteem; a staff of two thousand attends your every whim. ⑦–⑧.

The Golden Sands, 6910 Collins Ave (☎1-800/932-0333). Nothing flash and mostly filled by package-touring Europeans, but likely to turn up the cheapest deals in this pricey area. ③.

North Miami Beach

Beach Motel, 8601 Harding Ave (☎861-2001). Unelaborate motel a short trot from the Surfside beach. ③.

Blue Mist, 19111 Collins Ave (☎932-1000). The cheapest in Sunny Isles; rooms are basic but most face the ocean. ③–④.

Paradise Inn, 8520 Harding Ave (☎865-6216). Neatly tucked into Surfside's main street, this is one of the best bargains around. ③.

Thunderbird Resort, 18401 Collins Ave (☎1-800/327-2044). No frills but handy for both Miami and Fort Lauderdale. Like most hotels around here, you can step straight out of your room into the pool or onto the beach. ③–⑤.

At the airport

Hampton Inn-Miami Airport, 5125 NW 36th St (☎1-800/HAMPTON). Branch of a good-value hotel chain, offering some of the best rates in the airport area. ④.

MIA, Miami International Airport (☎1-800/327-1276). There's no excuse for missing your plane if you stay here; this stylishly designed and fully equipped hotel is located inside the airport. ⑤–⑦.

Miami Airways Motel, 5001 36th St (☎883-4700). Easily the cheapest in the area. ②.

Quality Inn, 2373 NW Le Jeune Rd (☎1-800/228-5151). Well-presented chain hotel with a beckoning pool. ④.

Budget accommodation: youth hostels and camping

Impeccably positioned in the heart of South Beach, the city's AYH **youth hostel**, *Hostel International of Miami Beach*, at the *Clay Hotel*, 406 Española Way (☎534-2988), has beds in small dorms for $10 ($13 for non-IYHA-members), as well as private singles and doubles ($25–35); see "Hotels and motels," above. Also in South Beach, the *Miami Beach International Travelers Hostel*, 236 Ninth Street (☎534-0268), offers beds in four-person dorms for $12 per person.

Staying at either hostel is certainly preferable to **camping** at *Larry & Penny Thompson Memorial Campground*, 12451 SW 184th Street (☎232-1049), twelve miles southwest of downtown Miami and well away from any bus route; $18 per night, $74 per week.

MIAMI

Despite its relatively small population, **Miami** is a diverse place. Many of its districts are officially cities on their own, and each has a distinctive background and character. Some are compact enough to explore on foot, but you'll need a car, or local buses, to travel between them – though the city doesn't stretch far inland because of the natural barrier of the Everglades swamps, distances between northern and southern reaches are considerable. Beware that the mood within a district can switch dramatically from one block to another, making it easy to stray into hostile territory if you don't stay alert.

The obvious starting point is **downtown Miami**, the small, bustling nerve centre of the city. Its streets are lined by garishly decorated shops and filled with a startling cross-section of people, bringing a lively human dimension to an area overlooked by futuristic office buildings. Close to the **downtown area** are regions of marked contrast. Those to the north – with a few exceptions – are run-down and dangerous, infamous for their outbreaks of violent racial unrest. To the south are the international banks signifying Miami's new wealth – and the state-of-the-art residential architecture that comes with it.

Beyond the environs of downtown Miami, the city spreads out in a broad arc to the west and south. The first of Miami's Cubans – who have reshaped the city substantially over the last two decades – settled a few miles west in (what became) **Little Havana**. This is still one of the most enjoyable and intriguing parts of Miami, rich with Latin American looks and sounds but far less solidly Cuban than it used to be. Immediately south, Little Havana's street grid gives way to the spacious boulevards of **Coral Gables**, whose finely wrought Mediterranean architecture – a far cry from cheap pastiches elsewhere – is as impressive now as it was in the Twenties when it set new standards in town planning. South of the downtown area, **Coconut Grove** is mounting a strong bid to become Miami's trendiest quarter; beautifully placed alongside Biscayne Bay, it boasts a plethora of neatly appointed streetside cafés as well as mansions and shops from a bygone era.

Beyond Coconut Grove and Coral Gables, **South Miami** is a lacklustre residential sprawl with little of note, fading into farming territory on Miami's southern edge and into the barren expanse of the Everglades to the west. **Key Biscayne** is a more attractive destination: a classy, secluded island community with some beautiful beaches, five miles off the mainland but easily reached by causeway.

Downtown Miami

DOWNTOWN MIAMI is not a place in which to relax: humanity storms down its short streets, rippling the gaudy awnings of countless cut-price electronics, clothes and jewellery stores, easing up only to buy imported newspapers or to gulp down a spicy snack and a mango juice from a fast-food stand.

Since the early Sixties, when newly released Cuban Bay of Pigs veterans came here to spend their US Government back pay, the predominantly Spanish-speaking businesses of the downtown square mile have reaped the benefits of any boost in South or Central American incomes. The recipients pour

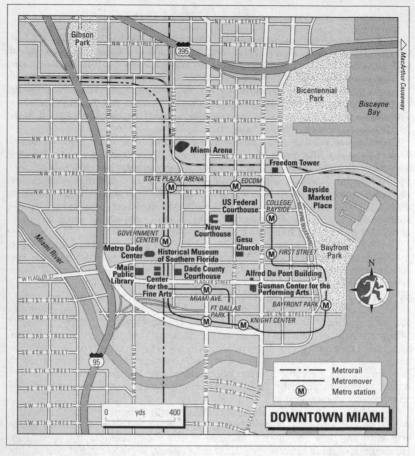

into Miami airport and move downtown in droves, seeking the goods they can't find at home. Minorities in the throng include dazed-looking European tourists, clean-cut Anglo-Americans with local government jobs, and street people of indeterminate origin dragging their worldly possessions with them. Only some solid US public architecture and whistle-blowing traffic cops remind you that you're still in Florida and not on the main drag of a seething Latin American capital.

The nerve-jangling streets (safe by day), and the feeling they induce of being at the crossroads of the Americas, are reason enough to spend half a day in downtown Miami, but added attractions are an excellent historical collection, a well-stocked library and, rather strangely, an old courthouse filled with works of art. When the street melange becomes too much, you can revive your senses with a quick *café Cubano* in one of the many small Cuban cafés (see "Eating", p.100).

Flagler Street and the Metro-Dade Cultural Center

Nowhere gives a better first taste of downtown Miami than **Flagler Street**, by far the loudest, brightest, busiest strip, and long the area's main attraction. Start at the eastern end by glancing inside the 1938 **Alfred Du Pont Building**, no. 169 E, which now houses the Florida National Bank (go up to the first floor); fanciful wrought-iron screens, bulky brass fittings and frescoes of Florida scenes epitomize the decorative style popular with US architects at the end of the Depression.

Nearby, the even less restrained **Gusman Center for the Performing Arts**, no. 174 E, began life in the Twenties as a vaudeville theatre, and displays all the exquisitely kitsch trappings you'd expect inside a million-dollar building designed to resemble a Moorish palace. The turrets, towers and intricately detailed columns remain (having escaped demolitoin in 1972), and a crescent moon still flits across the star-filled ceiling. The only way to get a look at the interior (the exterior is far less interesting) is by buying a ticket for a show: classical and contemporary music and dance are staged here from October to June; details are available from the ticket booth or on ☎372-0925.

Further along the street, at no. 73 W, four forbidding Doric columns mark the entrance to the **Dade County Courthouse**. Built in 1926 on the site of an earlier courthouse – where public hangings used to take place – for fifty years this was Miami's tallest building, its night-time lights showing off a distinctive stepped pyramid peak and beaming out a warning to wrong-doers all over the city.

The Metro-Dade Cultural Center

Little inside the courthouse is worth passing the security check for (the juiciest cases are tried in the new US Courthouse; see "North of Flagler Street"). Instead, you should cross SW First Avenue towards the giant, air-raid shelter-like building of the **Metro-Dade Cultural Center**, entered via a ramp off Flagler Street. This was an ambitious attempt by renowned architect Philip Johnson to create a postmodern Mediterranean-style piazza, a congenial gathering place where Miami could display its cultural side. The theory almost worked: superb art shows, historical collections and a major library frame the courtyard, but Johnson forgot the power of the south Florida sun. Rather than pausing to rest and gossip, most people scamper across the open space towards the nearest shade.

Facing the piazza, the **Historical Museum of Southern Florida** (Mon–Wed, Fri & Sat 10am–5pm, Thurs 10am–9pm, Sun noon–5pm; $4) offers a comprehensive look at the multifaceted past of southern Florida. The section on the indigenous Seminole people has a strong collection of photographs and artefacts that reveal much about the native Americans' lifestyle (the Creek Indians began arriving in what was then Spanish-ruled Florida during the eighteenth century, fleeing persecution further north). Another fine display covers the trials and tribulations of early Miami settlers, enabling you to put faces to names such as Tuttle and Brickell that crop up as street, park or bridge titles all over the city. Also well chronicled are the fluctuating fortunes of Miami Beach: from its early days as a celebrities' vacation spot – with amusing photos of Twenties Hollywood greats – through to the recent renovation of the Art Deco strip. Recent history is also covered, with considerable space devoted to the arrival of Cuban refugees and immigrants.

A few yards from the historical museum, the **Center for the Fine Arts** (Tues, Wed, Fri & Sat 10am–5pm, Thurs 10am–9pm, Sun noon–5pm; $5) showcases outstanding international travelling exhibitions, with a particular strength in Latin

American works. Directly opposite is the **Main Public Library** (Mon–Wed, Fri & Sat 9am–5pm, Thurs 9am–9pm, Sun 1–5pm; closed Sun in summer), which, besides the usual lending sections, has temporary exhibitions on art and literary themes as well as a massive collection of Florida magazines and books.

Adjoining the Cultural Center, the **Metro-Dade Center** (also called Government Center) chiefly comprises county government offices, but useful bus and train timetables can be gathered from the **Transit Service Center** (daily 7am–6pm) by the Metrorail entrance at the eastern side of the building.

North of Flagler Street

The tempo drops and storefronts become less brash as you head north of Flagler Street. A busy Hispanic procession passes in and out of the 1925 Catholic **Gesù Church**, 118 NE Second Street, whose Mediterranean Revival exterior and stylishly decorated innards make a pleasing splash, but otherwise there's nothing else to slow you down until you reach the Neoclassical **US Federal Courthouse**, 300 NE First Avenue (Mon–Fri 8.30am–5pm), a few minutes' walk away.

Finished in 1931, the building first functioned as a post office; Miami's then negligible crime rate required just one room on the second floor for judicial purposes. The room did acquire a monumental **mural**, however: *Law Guides Florida's Progress*, by Denman Fink (the designer behind much of Coral Gables, see p.75), a 25-foot-long depiction of Florida's evolution from swampy backwoods to modern state; if the courtroom's locked, ask a security guard to open it up. In 1985, fresco artist David Novros was commissioned to decorate the building's medieval-style inner **courtyard**, to which his bold, colourful daubs make a lively addition.

By the late Sixties, Miami's crime levels became too much for the old courthouse to handle, and the building of the $22 million **New Courthouse** was started next door (main entrance on North Miami Ave; Mon–Fri 8.30am–5pm). A gruesome creation in concrete and glass, the major advantage of the new courthouse – other than size – is that jurors can pass in and out unobserved: "Getting them out without getting them dead," as one judge commented.

Around Downtown Miami

A few polite parks and shopping precincts lie within easy walking distance, but you'll need a car or a bus to make much progress **around downtown Miami**. To the north lies Little Haiti, one of the most strongly defined ethnic areas in the city, bordering onto a desolate, poverty-stricken district that you'd be well advised to avoid. In total contrast, if you go south, an extraordinary line of swanky modern banks and spectacular apartments show off Miami's freshly found affluence. To the west, the area between downtown Miami and Little Havana (see p.72) is filled with several kilometres of uninspiring houses.

North of Downtown Miami

The Eighties saw the destruction of some decaying but much-loved buildings beside **Biscayne Boulevard** (part of Hwy-1) to make way for the **Bayside Marketplace** (Mon–Sat 10am–10pm, Sun noon–8pm), a large, pink shopping mall providing pleasant waterfront views from its terraces. Enlivened by street musicians and some choice international food stands, the place is less hideous than might be expected, but is clearly aimed at tourists. A number of pleasure trips around the bay begin here (see "Bus, boat and helicopter tours" and "Water taxis" p.60) – and, in case you've ever wondered, it was just to the south, on the yacht-filled marina of Bayfront Park of the Americas, that *Miami Vice*'s Sonny Crockett moored his floating home.

To the north of the Bayside Marketplace, endless lines of container trucks turning into Port Boulevard attest to the importance of the **Port of Miami** – now one of the world's biggest cargo and cruise ship terminals. Just beyond, the perpetual flame of the John Kennedy Memorial Torch of Friendship symbolizes good relations between the US and its southern neighbours, and guards the entrance to **Bicentennial Park**, filled with markers to various US-approved Central American luminaries.

Across Biscayne Boulevard, the **Freedom Tower**, originally home to the now defunct *Miami News*, earned its current name by housing the Cuban Refugee Center from 1962. Most of those who left Cuba on the "freedom flights"* got their first taste of US bureaucracy here. The 1925 building, modelled on a Spanish bell tower, has been closed for some years due to restoration – its Mediterranean features are more impressive from a distance, anyway – and there are no plans at present to re-open it in any form.

Beyond the Freedom Tower, there's little more to see within walking distance, and you're on the fringe of some of the city's most impoverished – and dangerous – neighbourhoods. You might venture a few blocks further to the **City of Miami Cemetery**, on the corner of North Miami Avenue and NE Eighteenth Street, though this should only be undertaken with a **walking tour** (call ☎375-1625 for details). There are historical stories aplenty here, but the graves are littered with used syringes, anything valuable has been stolen, and the family vaults of early Miami bigwigs have had their doors torn off by the homeless seeking shelter.

Continuing North: Little Haiti and the Police Museum

About 170,000 **Haitians** live in Miami, forming one of the city's major ethnic groups – albeit it far smaller than the Cuban population. Roughly a third of them live in what's become known as **LITTLE HAITI**, a two-hundred-block area that centres on NE Second Avenue, north of 42nd Street (buses #9 or #10 from the downtown area). Aside from hearing Haitian Creole on the streets (almost all Miami's Haitians speak English as a third language after Creole and French), you'll notice the colourful shops, offices and restaurants. For a taste of the culture, visit the **Caribbean Marketplace**, 5927 NE Second Avenue (Tues–Sun 9am–8pm), a large, Haitian-style building containing stalls and small stores selling Haitian handicrafts, books, records and food such as goat-stew. Established in 1990 to encourage local entrepreneurs and create a commercial focal-point for the community, the Marketplace has been largely unsuccessful, with much of the space unused. The **Haitian Refugee Center**, 32 NE 56th Avenue, will give you a

---

* Between December 1965 and June 1972, ten empty planes a week left Miami to collect Cubans – over 250,000 in total – allowed to leave the island by Fidel Castro. While US propaganda hailed them as "freedom fighters", most of the arrivals were simply seeking the fruits of capitalism, and, as Castro astutely recognized, any that were seriously committed to overthrowing his regime would be far less troublesome outside Cuba.

greater insight into why Haitians remain one of the more oppressed immigrant groups in Miami, most scraping their living as taxi drivers or hotel maids, hindered by poor education and English-language skills, and by the often racist attitudes of Anglos, Cubans and black Americans alike.

Close to Little Haiti (buses #3, #16 or #95 from downtown Miami), the **American Police Hall of Fame & Museum**, 3801 Biscayne Boulevard (daily 10am–5.30pm; $6), occupies the former local FBI headquarters – a shrine to law and order ironically located near to Liberty City and Overtown, scene of some of Miami's most desperate living. You can easily while away a spare hour here; besides CIA baseball caps and the car from the film *Blade Runner*, the first floor is devoted to a somber memorial to slain police officers. Upstairs you'll find information on gangsters; a dope addict's kit; an arsenal of weapons found on highways; the roadgang leg-irons still used in Tennessee; and moments of humour, including a signed photo of Keith Richards, a member of the museum's celebrity advisory board. Throughout, bad taste abounds; you can even have your photograph taken in the electric chair or gas chamber.

Liberty City and Overtown

In December 1979, after a prolonged sequence of unpunished assaults by white police officers on members of the African American community, a respected black professional, Arthur MacDuffie, was dragged off his motorbike in **LIBERTY CITY** and beaten to death by a group of white officers. Five months later, an all-white jury acquitted the accused, sparking off what became known as the "Liberty City Riot". On May 18, 1980, the night after the trial, the whole of Miami was ablaze, from Carol City in the far north to Homestead in the south. Reports of shooting, stone throwing, and whites being dragged from their cars and attacked or even burned alive, were rife. The violence began on Sunday, roadblocks sealed off African American districts until Wednesday, and a city-wide curfew lasted until Friday. In the final tally, eighteen were dead (mostly African Americans killed by police and National Guardsmen), hundreds injured, and damage to property was estimated at over $200 million.

Incredibly, the "worst racial paroxysm in modern American history" (not the first nor probably the last violent expression of Miami's racial tensions) caused no harm to Miami's broader fortunes, coming just as the city was establishing itself as a hub of Latin American finance and on the brink of becoming fashionable through *Miami Vice*. Even Liberty City soon found a chic international fashion district (see "The Stores", p.114) springing up in the disused warehouses on its periphery – the western edge of Little Haiti. Nonetheless, Miami's African Americans have remained at the bottom of the city's social heap. From the earliest days, "Coloredtown", as **OVERTOWN** was previously known, was divided by train tracks from the white folks of downtown Miami, and by the Thirties – when its jazz clubs thrilled multiracial audiences – conditions were so bad and overcrowding so extreme that Liberty City was built in an adjoining area to ease the strain.

In recent decades, Miami's black–white relations have been complicated by the extraordinary scale of Hispanic immigration, which has caused the city's African-Americans to miss out even on the menial jobs that elsewhere in the US are their traditional preserve. This unique form of political dispossession was borne out by an official snub delivered by the city's Cuban-American mayor, Xavier Suarez, to the visit in June 1990 of the then ANC deputy leader, Nelson Mandela. This incident, which stemmed from Mandela's refusal to denounce Fidel Castro, stimulated a well-organized **African American boycott** of the city's lucrative tourist industry, causing African American professional organizations around the US to cancel conventions planned for Miami. Dubbed the "quiet riot", the boycott cost the city millions of dollars in lost revenue.

Needless to say, these areas (and certain parts of Coconut Grove, North Miami Beach and South Miami) are not only depressing but dangerous, and your very presence may be seen as provocative, particularly if you're white. If you do unwittingly find yourself driving through the area, keep your windows closed, doors locked, be wary when stopping at lights, and do not leave your car.

If you've a serious interest in the African American contribution to Miami and Florida, head for the **Black Archives History and Research Foundation of South Florida**, at 5400 NW 22nd Avenue (Mon–Fri 9am–5pm; free; ☎636-2390), a resource centre that also arranges guided tours for a minimum of ten people through black historical areas.

South of Downtown Miami

Fifteen minutes' walk south from Flagler Street, the **Miami River** marks the southern limit of downtown. If your crossing is delayed by the drawbridge being raised to allow a ship through, glance westwards to the concrete modernity of the *Hotel Inter-Continental*, at the river's mouth, built on the site where Henry Flagler's *Royal Palm Hotel* stood at the turn of the century. At the behest of Miami's biggest landowners, Flagler – a millionaire oil baron whose railroad opened up Florida's east coast and brought wealthy wintering socialites to his string of smart hotels – extended the rail line here from Palm Beach. His luxury hotel and subsequent dredging of Biscayne Bay to accommodate cruise ships did much to put Miami on the map.

One landowner, William Brickell, ran a trading post on the south side of the river, an area now dominated by **Brickell Avenue**. Beginning immediately across the SE Second Avenue bridge and running to Coconut Grove (see p.80), Brickell Avenue was *the* address in 1910s Miami, easily justifying its "millionaires' row" nickname. While the original grand homes have largely disappeared, money is still Brickell Avenue's most obvious asset: over the bridge begins a half-mile parade of **banks**, the largest group of international banks in the US, whose imposing forms are softened by forecourts filled with sculptures, fountains and palm trees. Far from being places to change a travellers' cheque, these institutions are bastions of international high finance. From the late Seventies, Miami emerged as a corporate banking centre, cashing in on political instability in South and Central America by offering a secure home for Latin American money. Among it was a lot of dirty money that needed laundering: there's more than a grain of truth to the tales of dark-suited men depositing cash-filled suitcases.

The sudden rise of the Brickell banks was matched by new condominiums of breathtaking proportions but little architectural merit a few blocks further along. These astronomically priced abodes, featured in the opening sequence of *Miami Vice*, include in their pastel-shaded midst the most stunning modern building in Miami: the **Atlantis**, at no. 2025. First sketched on a napkin in a Cuban restaurant and finished in 1983, the *Atlantis* crowned several years of innovative construction by a small architectural firm called Arquitectonica, whose style – variously termed "beach blanket Bauhaus" and "ecstatic modernism" – fused postmodern thought with a strong sense of Miami's eclectic architectural heritage. The building's focal point is a gaping square hole through its middle where a palm tree, a jacuzzi and a red-painted spiral staircase tease the eye. You won't be allowed inside unless you know someone who lives there, which might be just as well: even its designers admit the interior doesn't live up to the exuberance of the exterior, and claim the building to be "architecture for 55mph" – in other words, seen to best effect from a passing car.

Little Havana

Unquestionably the largest ethnic group in Miami, the impact of **Cubans** on the city over the last four decades has been incalculable. Unlike most Hispanic immigrants to the US, who trade one form of poverty for another, Miami's first Cuban arrivals in the late Fifties had already tasted affluence. They rose quickly through the social strata and nowadays wield considerable clout in the running of the city.

CUBANS IN MIAMI: SOME BACKGROUND

Proximity to the Caribbean island has long made Florida a place of refuge for Cuba's activists. From José Martí in the 1890s to Fidel Castro in the early Fifties, the country's radicals arrived to campaign and raise funds, and numerous deposed Cuban politicians have whiled away their exile in Florida. However, until comparatively recent times, New York, not Miami, was the centre of Cuban emigré life in the United States.

During the mid-Fifties, when opposition to Cuba's Batista dictatorship – and the country's subservient role to the US – began to assert itself, a trickle of Cubans started arriving in the predominantly Jewish section of Miami called Riverside, moving into low-rent properties vacated as the extant community grew wealthier and moved out. The trickle became a flood when Fidel Castro took power, and as Cuban businesses sprang up on SW Eighth Street and Cubans began making their mark on Miami life, the area began to be known as **Little Havana**.

Those who left Cuba were not peasants but the affluent middle classes with most to lose under communism. Regarding themselves as the entrepreneurial sophisticates of the Caribbean, stories are plentiful of high-flying Cuban capitalists who arrived penniless in Little Havana, took menial jobs, and, over the course of two decades – aided by a formidable network of old ex-pats – toiled, wheeled and dealed their way steadily upwards to positions of power and influence (and not just locally – leading Miami Cubans also hold considerable sway over the US government's policy towards Cuba).

The second great Cuban influx into Miami was of a quite different social nature and racial composition: the **Mariel boatlift** brought 125,000 predominantly black islanders from the Cuban port of Mariel to Miami in May 1980. Unlike their worldly-wise predecessors, these arrivals were poor and uneducated, and a fifth were fresh from Cuban jails – incarcerated for criminal rather than political crimes. Bluntly put, Castro had called the bluff of the US administration and dumped his misfits on Miami. Only a few of them wound up in Little Havana: most "Marielitos" settled in Miami Beach's South Beach where they proceeded to terrorize the local community, thereby becoming a source of embarrassment to Miami's longer-established and determinedly respectable Cubans.

The first Miami Cubans settled a few miles west of downtown Miami in what became known as **LITTLE HAVANA**. According to tourist brochures, the streets are filled with old men in *guayaberas* (billowing cotton shirts) playing dominoes, and exotic restaurants whose walls vibrate to the pulsating rhythms of the homeland. The reality is more subdued: Little Havana's parks, memorials, shops and food stands all reflect the Cuban experience – and as such shouldn't be missed – but the streets are quieter than those of downtown Miami (except during the Little Havana festival in early March – see "Festivals", p.117). Like their US peers, as soon as the early settlers acquired sufficient dollars, they gave up the tightly grouped, modest homes of Little Havana for fully fledged suburban living.

Seeing Little Havana

For all the powerful emotions stirred up by its politics, there's not an awful lot to see in Little Havana; the appeal of the place is almost all atmospheric. On the graffitied streets, the prevailing mood is one of a community carrying on its daily business, and while the sights, smells and sounds are distinctly Cuban, many of

Exile Politics

However much Miami Cubans have prospered in the US, for many the "liberation" of their country is rarely far from their minds. Some older Cubans – driven by a fanatical hatred of Fidel Castro and communism – still consider themselves to be in exile, though few would seriously think about giving up their comfortable lifestyles to return, whatever regime governs Cuba.

Within the complexities of Cuban exile politics, there's a major rift: one school of thought holds that the US sold Cuba out to the USSR, beginning when President Kennedy* withheld air support from the invading Brigade 2056 at the Bay of Pigs in 1961, and favours a violent overthrow of the communist regime with a return to the survival-of-the-fittest ethic of the old days. The more pragmatic line runs that the Cuban clock can't be turned back, and that the only way for exiled Cubans to be usefully involved is to face up to the present situation and use their economic muscle to bring about changes.

Fuelled by a mix of *machismo* and hero-worship of early Cuban independence fighters, passions run high and action – usually violent – has been prized more than words. In Miami, Cubans even *suspected* of advocating dialogue with Castro have been killed; one man had his legs blown off for suggesting violence on the streets was counterproductive, and the Cuban Museum of Arts and Culture was bombed for displaying the work of Castro-approved artists.

In 1995, however, there was a break in the violence, as the hostility between exile factions was directed instead towards President Clinton and his policies of returning all future refugees to Cuba; for the first time since Castro came to power, Cubans had lost their special status, and instead were treated as any other economic migrant seeking to enter the US illegally. When the exiled Cuban leadership is eventually able to return to Cuba, one might expect the violent feuding to resume with a vengeance as parties struggle for power in the post-Castro era.

* In 1978, the US government's House Select Committee on Assassinations listed a (still active) Miami-based Cuban "action group", Alpha 66, as having "the motivation, capability, and resources" to have assassinated President Kennedy, and various, if unsubstantiated, links to the alleged assassin, Lee Harvey Oswald.

the people you'll pass – at least those under fifty – are less likely to be Cuban than Nicaraguan or Colombian: the latest immigrant groups in Miami to use Little Havana as a first base.

Only the neighbourhood's main strip, SW Eighth Street, or **Calle Ocho** (a direct Spanish translation), offers more than houses: on its course, tiny cups of sweet Cuban coffee are sold from street-side counters, the odors of cigars being rolled and bread being baked waft across the sidewalk, botanica shops sell *Santeria* (a Voodoo-like religion of African origin) ephemera beside six-foot-high models of Catholic saints, and you'll spot the only branch of *Dunkin' Donuts* to sell guava-filled doughnuts.

Along Calle Ocho

The most pertinent introduction to Little Havana is the **Brigade 2506 Memorial**, between Twelfth and Thirteenth avenues on Calle Ocho. Inscribed with the brigade crest, topped by the Cuban flag and ringed by sculptured bullets, this simple stone remembers those who died at the Bay of Pigs on April 17, 1961, during the attempt by a group of US-trained Cuban exiles to invade the island and wrest control from Castro.

Depending on who tells the story, the outcome was the result either of ill-conceived plans, or due to the US's lack of commitment to Cuba – to this day, sections of the Cuban community hate the then US president John Kennedy only slightly less than they hate Fidel Castro. Every anniversary, veterans clad in combat fatigues and carrying assault rifles gather here to make pledges of patriotism throughout the night.

A less emotionally charged gathering place is **Maximo Lopez Domino Park**, a few yards away on a corner of Fourteenth Avenue; access to its open-air tables is (quite illegally) restricted to men over 55, and this is one place where you really *will* see old men in *guayaberas* playing dominoes.

Besides discussing the fate of Cuba, the domino players might also be passing judgement on the **Latin Quarter** that's replacing a line of old buildings on the north side of Calle Ocho. Described by city planners as an attempt to "create a world renowned showcase of Latin American culture", the development seems destined to be a Hispanicized version of Bayside Marketplace (see "Around Downtown Miami", p.68), with Spanish-style ceramics, plazas and fountains decorating pricey boutiques and eateries aimed at tourists. Most Cuban objections to the scheme are to do with the name, which doesn't, they claim, do justice to the Cuban influence in the area.

Further west, the peaceful greenery of **Woodlawn Cemetery**, between 32nd and 33rd avenues (daily sunset–dusk), belies the scheming and skulduggery that some of its occupants indulged in during their lifetimes. Two former Cuban heads of state are buried here: Gerardo Machado, ousted from office in 1933, is in the mausoleum, while one of the protagonists in his downfall, Carlos Prío Socarras, president from 1948 to 1952, lies just outside. Also interred in the mausoleum (marked only by his initials) is **Anastasio Somoza**, dictator of Nicaragua until overthrown by the Sandinistas in 1979, and later killed in Paraguay.

Around Calle Ocho

With nondescript, low-income housing to the north and modest Spanish Revival Twenties bungalows to the south, there's little to detain you around Calle Ocho. One exception is the **Cuban Museum of Arts and Culture**, 1300 SW Twelfth

Avenue (usually Wed–Fri 10am–3pm, Sat noon–4pm; free; for latest opening times phone ☎858-8006), established by Cuban exiles. Its exhibitions of contemporary work have to be carefully chosen to avoid inflaming local passions; the museum suffered a bomb attack in 1989 for displaying the works of artists living in Cuba, regarded as collaborators by extreme anti-Castro exiles. A permanent collection is in the process of being formed, but there is not yet space to display it.

You might also drop into the *La Esquina de Tejas* restaurant, 101 SW Twelfth Avenue, where you can mull over the signed photos of Ronald Reagan. It was in this otherwise ordinary Cuban eatery that the president, seeking re-election, took a well-publicized lunch in 1983 in an effort to harness the powerful Cuban vote in Miami. Four years later, George Bush called by for a swift *café Cubano* and a drawn-out photo-call. Aside from his right-wing domestic policies, Reagan gained immense popularity among Miami Cubans for his support of the Nicaraguan Contras, viewed as kindred spirits in the guerrilla struggle against communism (it's widely acknowledged that the Contras ran their anti-Sandinista operation from offices in Miami and trained for combat in the Everglades). The community's affection was demonstrated by the renaming of Twelfth Avenue as "Ronald Reagan Boulevard".

There's no point in actually going there (except for a sports event; see "Listings"), but from here you can see the rising hump of the 70,000-seat **Orange Bowl** stadium, about ten blocks north. This is home to the University of Miami's football team, the Hurricanes, but is best remembered by older Cubans as the place where, on a December night in 1962, John Kennedy took the Brigade 2056 flag and vainly promised to return it "in a free Havana".

Coral Gables

All of Miami's constituent cities are fast to assert their individuality, but none has a greater case than **CORAL GABLES**, south of Little Havana: twelve square miles of broad boulevards and leafy streets lined by elaborate Spanish- and Italian-style architecture, which make the much more famous Art Deco district (see p.92) seem decidedly uncouth.

Whereas Miami's other early property developers built cheap and fast in search of a quick buck, the creator of Coral Gables, a local man named **George Merrick**, was more of an aesthete than an entrepreneur. Taking Mediterranean Europe as his inspiration, Merrick raided street names from a Spanish dictionary – by coincidence, many of today's residents are wealthy, Spanish-speaking Cubans – and enlisted his artist uncle, Denman Fink, and architect Phineas Paist, to plan the plazas, fountains and carefully aged stucco-fronted buildings.

Coral Gables land started selling overnight, with the five years following the first sale in 1921 bringing in $150 million, a third of which was channelled into the biggest advertising campaign ever known. The layout and buildings of Coral Gables quickly took shape, but the sudden end of Florida's property boom (see "History" in *Contexts* for the full account) wiped Merrick out. He ran a fishing camp in the Florida Keys until that was destroyed by a hurricane, and wound up as Miami's postmaster until his death in 1942.

Coral Gables, however, was built with longevity as well as beauty in mind. Despite successive economic crises, it never lost its good looks, and these days, boosted by a plethora of multinational companies in the renovated office buildings and by a very image-conscious resident population, it is still a lovely place to explore.

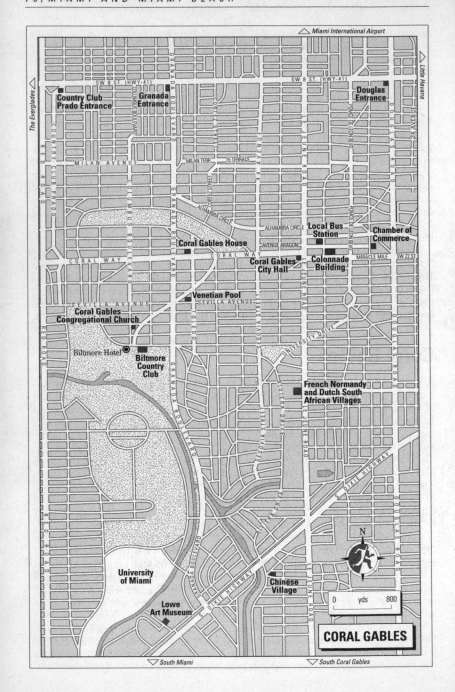

Miami International Airport

The Everglades

Little Havana

SW 8 ST. (HWY-41)

SW 8 ST. (HWY-41)

**Country Club
Prado Entrance**

**Granada
Entrance**

**Douglas
Entrance**

COLUMBUS BOULEVARD

GRANADA BOULEVARD

CORTEZ STREET

LE JEUNE ROAD

DOUGLAS ROAD

PONCE DE LEON BLVD.

COUNTRY CLUB PRADO

RED ROAD

MILAN AVENUE

MILAN TERR.

15 TERRACE

ALHAMBRA CIRCLE

Coral Gables House

ALHAMBRA CIRCLE

AVENUE ARAGON

**Local Bus
Station**

**Chamber of
Commerce**

CORAL WAY

CORAL WAY

**Coral Gables
City Hall**

**Colonnade
Building**

MIRACLE MILE

SW 22 ST

SEVILLA AVENUE

Venetian Pool

SEVILLA AVENUE

**Coral Gables
Congregational Church**

RED ROAD

Biltmore Hotel

**Biltmore
Country
Club**

GRANADA BOULEVARD

TOLEDO

SEGOVIA STREET

UNIVERSITY DRIVE

**French Normandy
and Dutch South
African Villages**

LE JEUNE ROAD

SEGOVIA STREET

ALHAMBRA DRIVE

S DIXIE HIGHWAY

DOUGLAS ROAD

N

**University
of Miami**

GRANADA BOULEVARD

S DIXIE HIGHWAY

**Chinese
Village**

LE JEUNE ROAD

**Lowe
Art Museum**

0   yds   800

CORAL GABLES

South Miami

South Coral Gables

CORAL GABLES: THE ENTRANCES

To make a strong first impression on visitors to Coral Gables, Merrick planned eight grand **entrances** on the main access roads, of which only four were completed before the bust. The three most impressive are to the north, along a two-and-a-half-mile stretch of SW Eighth Street.

The million-dollar **Douglas Entrance** (junction with Douglas Road) was the most ambitious, consisting of a gateway and tower with two expansive wings of shops, offices and artists' studios. During the Sixties it was almost bulldozed to make room for a supermarket, but survived to become a well-scrubbed business area, still upholding Merrick's Mediterranean themes. Further west, the sixty-foot-high vine-covered **Granada Entrance** (junction with Granada Boulevard) is based on the entrance to the city of Granada in Spain. A better appetizer for Coral Gables is the **Country Club Prado Entrance** (junction with Country Club Prado), the expensive recreation of a formal Italian garden bordered by freestanding stucco-and-brick pillars topped by ornamental urns and lamps with wrought-iron brackets.

The "Villages"

Driving (or cycling) around the less busy parts of Coral Gables, you'll catch glimpses of several "**Villages**", small pockets of residential architecture intended to add diversity to the area's Mediterranean looks. These include the brightly coloured roofs and ornately carved balconies of the **Chinese Village**, on the "5100" block of Riviera Drive; the timber-beamed town houses of the **French Normandy Village**, on the "400" block of Viscaya Avenue, at Le Jeune Road; and, perhaps strangest of all, the twisting chimneys and scroll-work arches of the **Dutch South African Village**, also on the "400" block of Viscaya Avenue.

The Miracle Mile and around

Elaborate entrances apart, the best way into Coral Gables is along SW 22nd Street, which on the other side of Douglas Road becomes the **Miracle Mile**, conceived by Merrick as the centrepiece of his business district and still the preferred shopping place of community-conscious locals. It continues to bear the imprint of Merrick's vision, even if the occasional spot of mundane Art Deco makes a bizarre addition to the more fanciful Mediterranean trimmings.

Dominated by department stores, Latin American travel agents and a staggering number of bridal shops, the Miracle Mile (actually only half a mile long) becomes increasingly expensive and exclusive as you head west. Notice the arcades and balconies along its course, and the spirals and peaks of the **Colonnade Building**, no. 133–169: now comprising a smart hotel (see "Accommodation" p.62) and shops, this was completed in 1926 – just a few months before the property crash – to accommodate George Merrick's land sales office.

Cut around the corner to collect info from the **Chamber of Commerce**, 50 Aragon Avenue (Mon–Fri 8.30am–5pm; ☎446-1657), and complete the Miracle Mile inside the grandly pillared **Coral Gables City Hall**, 405 Biltmore Way (Mon–Fri 8am–5pm), whose corridors are adorned with posters from the Twenties advertising the "City Beautiful" and with newspaper clippings bearing witness to the property mania of the time. There's also a caseful of oddments from the Biltmore Hotel (see below), which fall some way short of encapsulating the moneyed elegance that characterized Merrick's spa resort. From the third floor landing you can view Denman Fink's impressive blue and gold mural of the four seasons, which decorates the interior of the bell tower.

About half a mile further west, at no. 907 on Coral Way – a typically peaceful and tree-lined Coral Gables residential street – George Merrick's childhood home, the **Coral Gables House** (Sun & Wed 1–4pm; $2), is now a museum charting his family's history. In 1899, when George was 12, his family arrived here from New England to run a 160-acre fruit and vegetable farm – and, in the case of George's father, to deliver sermons at local Congregational churches. The farm was so successful that the house quickly grew from a wooden shack into a modestly elegant dwelling of coral rock and gabled windows (the inspiration behind the name of the city that later grew up around the family farm). The dual blows of the property crash and a citrus blight led to the gradual deterioration of the house, until restoration began in the Seventies. There's only enough inside to occupy half an hour, but it provides an interesting background on the founder of Coral Gables, who lived here until 1916.

Along De Soto Boulevard

There's no reason to continue along Coral Way, so backtrack instead to the junction with De Soto Boulevard, which curls southwards to three of Merrick's most notable achievements.

While his property-developing contemporaries left ugly scars across the city after digging up the local limestone, Merrick had the foresight – and the help of Denman Fink – to turn his biggest quarry into a sumptuous swimming pool. The **Venetian Pool**, 2701 De Soto Boulevard (June–Aug Mon–Fri 11am–7.30pm, Sat & Sun 10am–4.30pm; rest of the year Tues–Fri 11am–4 or 5.30pm, Sat & Sun 10am–4.30pm; ☎460-5356; $4), an elaborate conglomeration of palm-studded paths, Venetian-style bridges and coral rock caves, was opened in 1924. Despite its ornamentation, the pool was never aimed at the social elite; admission was cheap and open to all, and even today's local residents get a special discount.

A few minutes' walk further south, on land donated by Merrick, stands the **Coral Gables Congregational Church** (Mon–Fri 8am–4pm), a bright Spanish Revival flurry topped by a barrel-tiled roof and enhanced by Baroque features. The building's excellent acoustics make it a popular venue for jazz and classical concerts; ask for details at the church office, just inside the entrance.

Merrick's crowning achievement – aesthetically if not financially – was the **Biltmore Hotel**, 1200 Anastasia Avenue, wrapping its broad wings around the southern end of De Soto Boulevard. The 26-storey tower of the hotel can be seen across much of low-lying Miami: if it seems similar to the Freedom Tower (see "Around Downtown Miami", p.69), it's because they're both modelled on the Giralda bell tower of Seville Cathedral in Spain. The *Biltmore* was hawked as "the last word in the evolution of civilization", and everything about it was outrageous: 25-foot-high frescoed walls, vaulted ceilings, a wealth of imported marble and tile, immense fireplaces and custom-loomed rugs. To mark the opening in January 1926, VIP guests were brought in on chartered, long-distance trains, fed on pheasant and trout, and given the run of the casino. The following day they could fox-hunt, play polo or swim in the US's largest pool – whose first swimming instructor was Johnny Weissmuller, future Olympic champion and the original screen Tarzan.

Although high-profile celebrities such as Bing Crosby, Judy Garland and Ginger Rogers kept the *Biltmore* on their itineraries, the end of the Florida land boom and the start of the Depression meant that the hotel was never the success it might have been. In the Forties, many of the finer furnishings were lost when the hotel became a military hospital, and decades of decline followed. The future looked rosier in 1986, when $55 million was lavished on a restoration programme, but the company involved went bust, and the great building remained closed. Only in 1993 did it finally re-open, after another multi-million dollar refit. Now, once again it is functioning as a hotel; you can step inside to admire the elaborate architecture, take afternoon tea for $10.50, or – best of all – join the free historical tours beginning at 1.30pm, 2.30pm and 3.30pm every Sunday in the lobby.

The neighbouring **Biltmore Country Club**, also open to the public, has fared better. You can poke your head inside for a closer look at its painstakingly reno-vated beaux-arts features, but most people turn up to knock a ball along the lush fairways of the **Biltmore Golf Course**, which, in the glory days of the hotel, hosted the highest-paying golf tournament in the world.

South of the Biltmore: the Lowe Art Museum

One of the few parts of Coral Gables where Mediterranean architecture doesn't prevail is on the campus of the **University of Miami**, about two miles south of the *Biltmore*, whose dismal, box-like buildings have traditionally been filled by students with wealthy parents rather than healthy intellects. In recent years the university has undergone something of a renaissance and now attracts top facul-ties in many fields and a more academic student body.

The sole reason to visit the campus is the **Lowe Art Museum**, 1301 Stanford Drive (Tues–Sat 10am–5pm, Sun noon–5pm; ☎284-3535; $4). Established in 1950, the Lowe underwent major renovation and extension work in 1995, and it now constitutes Miami's foremost art museum. The diverse permanent collection contains Renaissance and European Baroque art, Spanish "Old Masters", nine-teenth-century European paintings, and a considerable number of contemporary American works. Non-Western art is also well represented, including varied pre-Columbian, African and East Asian collections, Guatemalan textiles, and one of the finest Native American art collections in the country. The Lowe also hosts some excellent national and international touring exhibitions; call ahead to find out what's on.

South Coral Gables

Just as the Venetian Pool was a clever disguise for a quarry, so Merrick turned the construction ditches that ringed the infant Coral Gables into a network of canals, calling them the "Miami Riviera" and floating gondolas along them. Although the idea never really took off, the placid waterways remain, running between the university campus and a secluded residential area on Biscayne Bay, just south of Coconut Grove (described below).

Dividing Coconut Grove and South Miami (see p.83), the **Matheson Hammock Park**, 9601 Old Cutler Road (6am–sunset; $3 parking fee), was a coconut plantation before becoming a public park in 1930. At weekends, thou-sands decant here to picnic, use the marina and take a dip in the artificial lagoon, great for small children but with little to offer for adults; the rest of the sizeable park is much less crowded, and you can easily while away a few hours strolling around the wading pond – popular with people catching crabs – or along the winding trails above the mangrove swamps.

Virtually next door, the **Fairchild Tropical Garden** (daily 9.30am–4.30pm; $7) turns the same rugged terrain into lawns, flowerbeds and gardens decorated by artificial lakes. A good way to begin exploring the 83-acre site – the largest tropical botanical gardens in the continental United States – is to hitch a ride on the free tram (departing hourly, on the hour, from inside the garden's entrance) for a forty-minute meander along the trails, with a recorded commentary on the various plants.

The tropical habitats reproduced here – some more successfully than others – range from desert to rainforest, though there's relatively little space devoted to fauna endemic to south Florida. As a research institution, Fairchild works with scientists all over the world to preserve the diversity of the tropical environment; many of the plant species here are extinct in their original environments, and efforts have been made to re-establish them in their places of origin.

Some two-thirds of Fairchild's plants were destroyed or badly damaged on August 24, 1992 by Hurricane Andrew. An area of the garden has been left untouched since then to show the effects of a hurricane and how plants respond to devastation. Following one of several rough trails through here will make the recovery of the rest of the garden seem that much more remarkable.

Food may not be brought into the gardens, but at weekends the **snack bar** is open. At other times you can use the picnic sites in neighbouring Matheson Hammock Park (see p.79) or the café at Parrot Jungle (see p.84) a few minutes' drive away.

Coconut Grove

A stamping ground of down-at-heel artists, writers and lefties through the Sixties and Seventies, today's **COCONUT GROVE** is a glitterati hangout thanks to business-led revitalization. Art galleries, fashionable restaurants and towering bayview apartments mark its central section – clear signs of a neighbourhood whose fortunes are rising. But Coconut Grove, finely placed along the shores of Biscayne Bay, also retains much of value from its formative years. A century ago, a strange mix of Bahamian salvagers and New England intellectuals searching for spiritual fulfillment laid the foundations of a fiercely idiosyncratic community, separated from the fledgling city of Miami by a dense, jungle-like wedge of tropical foliage. The distance between Coconut Grove and the rest of Miami is still very much apparent: cleaner and richer than ever, but continuing to fan the flames of liberalism – and boasting the best batch of **drinking and music locales** outside of Miami Beach.

North Coconut Grove

In 1914, farm-machinery mogul James Deering followed his brother, Charles (of Deering Estate fame, see "South Miami"), to south Florida and blew $15 million on recreating a sixteenth-century Italian villa within the belt of vegetation between Miami and Coconut Grove. A thousand-strong workforce completed his **Villa Vizcaya**, 3251 South Miami Avenue (daily 9.30am–5pm; $8), in just two years. The lasting impression of the grandiose structure is that both Deering and his designer (the crazed Paul Chalfin, hellbent on becoming an architectural legend) had more money than taste: Deering's madly eclectic art collection, and the concept that the villa should appear to have been inhabited for 400 years, resulted in a thunderous clash of Baroque, Renaissance, Rococo and Neoclassical fixtures and furnishings, and even the landscaped **gardens**, with their fountains and sculptures, aren't spared the pretensions. Nonetheless, Villa Vizcaya is one of Miami's more recherche sights, with many diverting details – Chinese figures casting shadows across the tearoom, and a Georgian library, for instance – and one of the most visited. It's also a popular wedding reception venue, hence the brigades of beaming Cuban brides being photographed here. **Guided tours** leave frequently from the entrance loggia – dominated by a second-century marble statue of Bacchus – and provide solid background information, after which you're free to explore at leisure.

Straight across South Miami Drive from Villa Vizcaya, the **Museum of Science and Space Transit Planetarium** (daily 10am–6pm; $6) sets a different mood entirely. Its interactive exhibits provide a good two-hour family diversion, though a more forceful reason to visit is the collection of wildlife at the museum's rear. Vultures and owls are among a number of injured birds seeing out their days here, a variety of snakes can be viewed at disturbingly close quarters, and the resident tarantulas are happy to be handled. The adjoining **planetarium** (☎854-2222; shows around $5) has the usual trips-around-the-cosmos shows, and hosts head-banging rock music laser shows most weekends. Details are available by phone or from the ticket office inside the museum.

Where South Miami Drive becomes Bayshore Drive, close to Mercy Hospital, the road off to the left leads to the **Church of Ermita de la Curidad** (daily 9am–9pm), erected by Miami Cubans. A mural behind the altar traces the island's history, and the conical-shaped church is angled to allow worshippers to look out across the bay in the direction of Cuba.

Back on Bayshore Drive, for the next two miles or so you'll catch glimpses of limestone jutting through the greenery on the inland side. It was on this ridge, known as **Silver Bluff**, that several early settlers established their homes, later joined by the well-heeled notables of 1910s Miami; a few of their houses still stand, though none is open to the public. The area has remained a preserve of the rich, whose opulent abodes are shielded from prying eyes by carefully maintained trees.

Central Coconut Grove

The suggestion of major money around Silver Bluff yields to blatant statements of wealth once you draw closer to central Coconut Grove. Bayshore Drive continues between expensive, high-rise condos and jogger-filled, landscaped parks. Heading up Pan American Drive will take you to the **marina** on **Dinner Key**, a picnic spot for settlers at the turn of the century and now a mooring for lines of hundred-thousand-dollar yachts.

Next door, the **Coconut Grove Exhibition Center** is nowadays a popular venue for top-of-the-range car and interior furnishing shows. Its forerunner was the Dinner Key Auditorium, where in 1969 the rock legend **Jim Morrison**, singer with the Doors, dropped his leather pants to expose himself during the band's first – and last – Florida show; this caused Miami's police to clamp down on local rock clubs, and increased the band's notoriety a hundred-fold.

The gigantic Exhibition Center overshadows the more cheerful **Miami City Hall**, 3400 Pan American Drive (Mon–Fri 8am–5pm), the small and unlikely seat of local government. The blue-and-white-trimmed Art Deco building used to be an airline terminal: from the Thirties, passengers checked in here for the *Pan American Airways* seaplane service to Latin America, and the sight of the lumbering craft taking off used to draw thousands to the waterfront. In front of the City Hall a small plaque records the fact that Dinner Key was the place that veterans of the Bay of Pigs stepped ashore after their release from Cuba in 1962.

Walking from the City Hall across the Exhibition Center's carpark brings you to the *Havana Clipper* restaurant, whose ground floor houses a mildly appealing **historical collection** (11.30am–midnight; free) of photos and old radio parts from the seaplane times (which lasted until improvements to Latin American runways made sea landings unnecessary).

Peacock Park, at the end of Bayshore Drive beside MacFarlane Road, was a notorious hippie haunt at the time of Morrison's misdemeanours in Coconut Grove. More recently it's been cleaned up to fit the area's present smart, sophisticated image, and now features tennis courts and some peculiar abstract rock sculptures. The **Chamber of Commerce** (Mon–Fri 9am–5pm; ☎444-7270), on a corner of the park, has plenty of free leaflets and maps of the area.

Along Main Highway

At the end of MacFarlane Road you hit **Main Highway** and Coconut Grove as most Miamians see it: several blocks of trendy cafés, galleries and boutiques. Though less enjoyable than Miami Beach's South Beach (see "Miami Beach", see p.90), it's a fine place for a stroll, if only to watch the neighbourhood's affluent fashion victims going through their paces. You can eat, drink and pose (for where to do all three, see "Eating" and "Drinking", p.103 and 108) at **CocoWalk** – an enjoyable collection of open-air restaurants and bars, and yet more stylish shops – located between Main Highway and Virginia Street, at 3000 Grand Avenue. Or for a taste of sheer exclusivity, drop into **Mayfair-in-the-Grove** (Mon, Thurs & Fri 10am–9pm, Tues, Wed & Sat 10am–7pm, Sun noon–5.30pm), at the corner of MacFarlane Road and Grand Avenue, a designer shopping mall whose zigzagging walkways – decorated by fountains, copper sculptures, climbing vines and Romanesque doodles in concrete – wind around three floors of expense-account stores.

Heading south down Main Highway you'll come across the beige-and-white **Coconut Grove Playhouse**, at 3500. Opened in 1927 and still going strong on a mixed diet of Broadway blockbusters and alternative offerings, this is the best of the area's several examples of Mediterranean Revival architecture, but warrants only a passing glance as you move on to the most enduring historic site in Coconut Grove, at the end of a path right across Main Highway from the playhouse.

The tree-shaded track leads to a tranquil bayside garden and a century-old house known as the **Barnacle** (Fri–Sun, 9am–4pm; $1), built by "Commodore" Ralph Middelton Munroe: sailor, brilliant yacht-designer and a devotee of the Transcendalist Movement (advocating self-reliance, a love of nature and a simple lifestyle). The Barnacle was ingeniously put together in 1891 with local materials and tricks learned from nautical design. Raising the structure eight feet off the ground in 1908 improved air circulation and prevented flooding, a covered verandah enabled windows to be opened during rainstorms, and a skylight allowed air to be drawn through the house – all major innovations that alleviated some of the discomforts of living all year in the heat and humidity of south Florida. More inventive still, when Munroe needed more space for his family he simply jacked up the single-storey structure and added a new floor underneath. Only with the guided tour (10am, 11.30am, 1pm & 2.30pm) can you see inside the house, where many original furnishings remain alongside some of Munroe's intriguing photos of pioneering Coconut Growers. The grounds, however, you are free to explore on your own. The lawn extends to the shore of Biscayne Bay, while behind the house are the last remnants of the tropical hardwood hammock that extended throughout the Miami area.

Charles Avenue and Black Coconut Grove

The Bahamian settlers of the late 1800s, who later provided the labour that went into building Coconut Grove and nearby areas, mostly lived along what became **Charles Avenue** (off Main Highway, close to the playhouse), in small, simple wooden houses similar to the "conch houses" that fill Key West's Old Town (see *The Florida Keys*). You'll find a trio of these still standing on the "3200" block, though be warned that they are on the edge of **Black Coconut Grove** (not a name you'll find on maps, but one which everyone uses), a run-down area stretching westwards to the borders of Coral Gables. The fact that such a derelict district exists within half a mile of one of the city's most fashionably upmarket areas provides a stark reminder of Miami's racial divisions. Like all of Miami's black areas, white people should only approach with caution; and certainly not without a car.

South Coconut Grove

South of the playhouse, the outlook along Main Highway soon reverts to expansive older homes set back from the street. A couple of easily found minor sites are the only reasons to stop as you pass through towards South Miami. After half a mile, you'll spy the **Ransom Everglades School**, 3575 Main Highway, founded in 1903 for boarding pupils who split the school year between New York's Adirondack mountains and here. Oddly enough, the main school room was a Chinese-style **pagoda** (Mon–Fri 9am–5pm; free), which still stands incongruously in the middle of what's now an upper-crust prep school. Inside the green-painted pine structure are a few amusing relics from the school's past.

A little further on, near the corner of Devon Road, the 1917 **Plymouth Congregational Church** (Mon–Fri 9am–4pm) has a striking, vine-covered, coral rock facade; remarkably, this finely crafted exterior was the work of just one man. Note, too, the 375-year-old main door, hand-carved in walnut, which looks none the worse for its journey from an early seventeenth-century monastery in the Spanish Pyrenees. If the church door beside the carpark is locked, try the church office, on the other side of Devon Road.

South Miami

South of Coral Gables and Coconut Grove, monotonous middle-class suburbs consume almost all of **SOUTH MIAMI**, an expanse of cosy but dull family homes reaching to the edge of the Everglades, interrupted only by golf courses and a few contrived tourist attractions. Mini-malls, filling stations, cut-price waterbed outlets and bumper-to-bumper traffic are the star features of its primary thoroughfare, Hwy-1. You can't avoid this route entirely, but from South Coral Gables a better course is Old Cutler Road, which makes a pleasing meander from Coconut Grove through a thick belt of woodland (see also Matheson Hammock Park, p.79

and Fairchild Tropical Garden, p.80) between Biscayne Bay and the suburban sprawl. Cutting inland from Hwy-1 is unrewarding (and unthinkable without a car), since there are no stops of any major importance.

Along Old Cutler Road: the Deering Estate

Long before modern highways scythed through the city, **Old Cutler Road** was the sole road between Coconut Grove and Cutler, a small town that went into terminal decline in the 1910s after being bypassed by the new Flagler railroad. A wealthy industrialist and amateur botanist, Charles Deering (brother of James, the owner of Villa Vizcaya; see "Coconut Grove", above), was so taken with the natural beauty of the area that he purchased all of Cutler and, with one exception, razed its buildings to make way for the **Charles Deering Estate**, 16701 SW 72nd Avenue (☎235-1668), completed in 1922. Deering maintained the *Richmond Inn*, Cutler's only hotel, as his own living and dining quarters. Its pleasant wooden form now stands in marked contrast to the limestone mansion he erected along-side, whose interior – echoing halls, dusty chandeliers and checker-board-tile floors – is Mediterranean in style but carries a Gothic spookiness. More impressive than the buildings are the three-hundred-acre **grounds**, where signs of human habitation dating back 10,000 years have been found amid the pine woods, mangrove forests and tropical hardwood hammocks.

The buildings were severely damaged or destroyed by Hurricane Andrew, and the estate has been closed for some time while restoration takes place. Phone ahead to see whether it has re-opened to visitors and to enquire about the free **walking tours**; more adventurous are the guided **canoe tours** (Sat & Sun 9.30am & 1pm; $10), some at night, which navigate the mangrove-fringed inlets.

Parrot Jungle, Metrozoo and the Gold Coast Railroad Museum

Parrot Jungle, 11000 SW 57th Street (9.30am–6pm; adults $11.67, children 3–12 $8.47), has parrots, parakeets and macaws of rainbow plumage swapping squawks as visitors wander along delightfully shaded pathways past their cages. The gardens are designed to protect both residents and visitors from the hot Florida sun and include hundreds of varieties of plants, waterfalls and a lake with Caribbean pink flamingos. Apart from birds, the park is home to numerous species of alligators and crocodiles, giant tortoises, chimpanzees and other primates. Even if you don't intend to enter Parrot Jungle, the *Parrot Café* (8am–5pm) offers views into the park and makes a useful stop if you're coming from the nearby Fairchild Tropical Garden (see p.80).

A more extensive display of wildlife – assuming you're not opposed to zoos in principle – is the **Metrozoo**, 12400 SW 152nd Street (daily 9.30am–5.30pm; adults $5, children $2.50), its once lush foliage only slowly recovering from the devastating effects of Hurricane Andrew. Even so, while psychological barriers such as moats and small hills are employed instead of cages, it's hard to imagine that many of the animals enjoy baking heat and humidity any more than their audience; both tend to spend their time here pursuing shade and a cool drink. If you do come, the snow-white Bengal tigers are the prize exhibit, but avoid the usually sweltering midday temperatures of the summer months and rainy days, as most of the zoo is outdoors.

Sharing the zoo's entrance, the **Gold Coast Railroad Museum** (Mon–Fri 10am–3pm, Sat & Sun 10am–5pm; adults $4, children under 12 free) houses a small but intriguing collection of old locomotives that can be clambered around for closer inspection. Among them is the *Ferdinand Megellan*, a luxury Pullman car that was custom-built in 1928 for presidential use and features escape hatches and steel armour-plating. Harry S Truman travelled 21,000 miles in it on his 1948 re-election campaign, giving three hundred speeches from the rear platform.

Homestead and around

Suburbia yields to agriculture as you continue south along Hwy-1, where broad, fertile fields grow fruit and vegetables for the nation's northern states. Aside from offering as good a taste of Florida farmlife – the region produces the bulk of America's winter tomatoes – as you're likely to find so close to its major city, the district can be a money-saving stop (see "Accommodation") en route to the Florida Keys or the Everglades National Park.

Closer in mood to *The Waltons* than *Miami Vice*, **HOMESTEAD** is the agricultural area's main town, and the least galvanizing section of Miami. Krome Avenue, just west of Hwy-1, slices through the centre, but besides a few restored 1910s–1930s buildings (such as the Old City Hall, no. 43 N), there's little to detain you other than the **Florida Pioneer Museum**, no. 826 (☎246-9531), where two yellow-painted train station buildings store photos and objects from Homestead's formative years – this end-of-the-line town was planned by Flagler's railroad engineers in 1904. To the rear, a 1926 caboose keeps moderately entertaining railroad mementoes. The museum was badly damaged by Hurricane Andrew in 1992, so if you're thinking of visiting it, phone ahead to find out if it's open.

Around Homestead

Time is better spent **around Homestead** than actually in it, with plenty of diversions just a few minutes' drive from the town. You can also gather your own dinner in this area; keep an eye out for **"pick-your-own"** signs, where, for a few dollars, you can take to the fields and load up with peas, tomatoes and a variety of other crops.

The Coral Castle

The one essential stop is the **Coral Castle** (daily 9am–5pm; adults $7.75, children $4.50), whose bulky coral rock sculptures can be found about six miles northeast of Homestead, beside Hwy-1, at the junction with 286th Street. Remarkably, these fantastic creations, whose delicate finish belies their imposing size, are the work of just one man – the enigmatic **Edward Leedskalnin**. Jilted in 1913 by his sixteen-year-old fiancee in Latvia, Leedskalnin spent seven years working his way across Europe, Canada and the US before buying an acre of land just south of Homestead. Using a profound – and self-taught – knowledge of weights and balances, he somehow raised enormous hunks of coral rock from the ground, then used a work bench made from car running boards and handmade tools fashioned from scrap to refine the blocks into chairs, tables and beds; odd furniture that suggests the castle was intended as a love nest to woo back his errant sweetheart (last heard of in 1980, still in Latvia). Leedskalnin died here in 1951.

You can wander around the slabs, sit on the hard but surprisingly comfortable chairs, swivel a nine-ton gate with your pinkie, and admire the numerous coral representations of the moon and planets that reflected Leedskalnin's interest in astronomy and astrology; also on display is his twenty-foot-high telescope. But what you won't be able to do is explain how the sculptures were made. No one ever saw the secretive Leedskalnin at work, or knows how, alone, he could have loaded 1100 tons of rock onto the rail-mounted truck that brought the pieces here in 1936.

The Fruit and Spice Park, and Monkey Jungle

The subtle fragrances of the **Fruit and Spice Park**, 24801 SW 187th Avenue (daily 10am–5pm; $1), tickle your nostrils as soon as you enter. Rare exotica such as star fruit and the aptly named panama candle tree are the highlights of a host of tropical peculiarities; at weekends the guided tour (1pm & 3pm; $1) will give you a good introduction to the secret lives of spices.

To the north of Homestead, at 14805 SW 216th Street, **Monkey Jungle** (daily 9.30am–5pm; adults $11.67, children 3–12 $8.47) is one of the few places of protection in the US for endangered primates. Covered walkways keep visitors in closer confinement than the monkeys, and lead through a steamy hammock where several hundred baboons, orang-utans, gorillas and chimps move through the vegetation. Despite a degree of freedom, the animals don't appear a terribly happy lot, possibly because of overcrowding. The monkeys spend most of their time scrounging food from visitors – take care not to get bitten or, just as unpleasant, relieved on by inmates angry if there are no treats on offer.

Biscayne National Park

If you're not going to the Florida Keys, make a point of visiting **Biscayne National Park** (daily 8am–sunset), at the end of Canal Drive (328th Street), east of Hwy-1. The bulk of the park lies beneath the clear ocean waters, where stunning formations of living coral provide a habitat for shoals of brightly coloured fish and numerous other creatures too delicate to survive on their own. For a full description of the wondrous world of the living coral reef, see "John Pennecamp State Park", in *The Florida Keys*.

The lazy way to view it is on the three-hour **glass-bottomed boat** trip (daily at 10am; adults $16.50, children under 12 $8.50; reservations ☎230-1100), but for a fuller encounter you should embark on a three-hour snorkel tour ($28 including all equipment). Gear can also be rented from the **visitor center** (Dec–April Mon–Fri 8am–5pm, Sat & Sun 9am–5.30pm; rest of the year Mon–Fri 10am–4pm, Sat & Sun 10am–6pm; ☎247-7275) near the entrance at **Convoy Point**. For tours and dives, phone at least a day ahead to make reservations.

Another option is to visit the park's **barrier islands**, seven miles out. A tour boat leaves for **Elliot Key** from Convoy Point at 1.30pm on Sundays between December and May. Once ashore, besides calling at the **visitor center** (Sat & Sun 10am–4pm) and contemplating the easy six-mile hiking trail along the island's forested spine, there's nothing to do on Elliot Key except sunbathe in solitude.

Key Biscayne and around

A compact, immaculately manicured community five miles off the Miami Shore, **KEY BISCAYNE** is a great place to live – if you can afford it. Seeking relaxation and creature comforts away from life in the fast lane, the moneyed of Miami fill the island's upmarket homes and condos: even Richard Nixon had his presidential winter house here, and singer Sting chose one of the luxury shorefront hotels for a recuperative pamper between tour dates. For visitors, Key Biscayne offers a couple of inviting beaches, a third within a state park, and a fabulous cycling path running the full length, but bear in mind that much of the shade-producing vegetation was torn out by Hurricane Andrew and that it will take years before the newly planted trees develop. Cheap eats and lodgings are in predictably short supply.

Approaching Key Biscayne: Virginia Key and around

Without a private yacht, the only way onto Key Biscayne is via **Rickenbacker Causeway**, a four-mile-long continuation of SW 26th Road just south of downtown Miami; it soars high above Biscayne Bay, allowing shipping to glide underneath, and provides a breathtaking view of the Brickell Avenue skyline (see "Around Downtown Miami"). Drivers have to pay a $1 toll; otherwise you can cross the causeway by bus (#B), bike or even on foot.

The first land you'll hit is the unexceptional and sparsely populated **VIRGINIA KEY**. The Miami Marine Stadium is the prominent building on the left, but this is now closed due to disrepair and underuse. A few yards beyond it is the beginning of a two-mile lane that winds through a cluster of Australian pines to **Virginia Beach** (daily 8am–sunset; cars $2). During the years of segregation, this was set aside for Miami's black community (chosen, cynics might presume, for its proximity to a large sewage works). Later, flocks of hippies became seriously laid-back around the secluded coves, which provide a private setting for (unofficial) nude sunbathing.

In contrast, on the right of the main road, the **Seaquarium** marine park (daily 9.30am–6pm; adults $20.19, children under 10 $14.86) is a bustling place where you can while away three or four hours watching the usual roster of performing seals and dolphins – and be sure not to miss Lolita, the 8000-pound star of the spectacular killer whale show (daily, noon). The park's most important work – formulating breeding programmes to preserve Florida's endangered sea life and serving as a halfway house for injured manatees and other sea creatures – goes on behind the scenes. Though enjoyable, remember that there are plenty more marine parks in Florida, such as Orlando's Sea World, and much more in Miami on which to spend your time and money.

On to Key Biscayne: Crandon Park Beach

Not content with living in one of the best natural settings in Miami, the people of Key Biscayne also possess one of the finest landscaped beaches in the city – **Crandon Park Beach** (8am–sunset; cars $3), a mile along Crandon Boulevard (the continuation of the main road from the causeway). Three miles of golden beach fringe the park, and you can wade out at knee-depth to a sandbar far from the shore. Filled by the sounds of boisterous kids and sizzling barbecues on weekends, at any other time the park is disturbed only by the occasional jogger or holi-

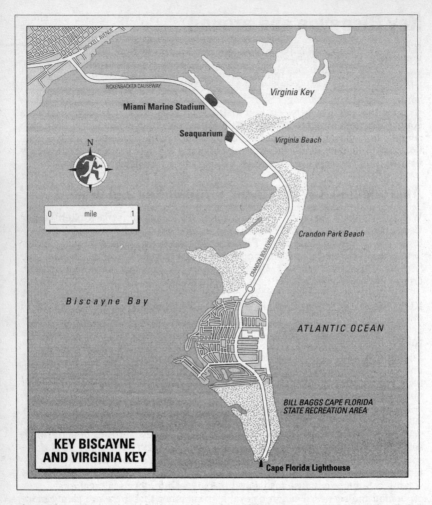

KEY BISCAYNE AND VIRGINIA KEY

day-maker straying from the private beaches of the expensive hotels nearby. Relax beside the lapping ocean waters and keep a look out for manatees and dolphins, both known to swim by, but be sure to bring high factor sun screen and a beach umbrella as Hurricane Andrew tore out almost all of the palms immediately fronting the beach.

Residential Key Biscayne

Besides its very green, manicured looks, **residential Key Biscayne**, beginning with an abrupt wall of apartment buildings at the southern edge of Crandon Park Beach, has little to offer visitors. You'll need to pass through, however, on the way to the much more rewarding Bill Baggs Cape Florida park (see below), and while doing so should make a loop along **Harbor Drive**, turning off along McIntire Drive. At no 485 W stands the former home of ex-president Richard Nixon, who picked up his *Miami Herald* here one morning in 1972 to read of a break-in at the *Watergate Hotel* in Washington; the seemingly insignificant event (only featured by the paper because two Miami Cubans were involved) that led to Nixon's resignation two years later. On the same street, pick up information on the area at the **Chamber of Commerce**, 95 W (Mon–Fri 9am–5pm; ☎361-5207).

Key Biscayne: the southern tip

Crandon Boulevard terminates at the entrance to the 400-acre **Bill Baggs Cape Florida State Recreation Area** (daily 8am–sunset; cars $4, pedestrians and cyclists $1), which covers the southern extremity of Key Biscayne. Once thickly wooded, almost all the trees were destroyed in 1993 by Hurricane Andrew, but a massive planting programme has taken place, including the introduction of native Floridian fauna. Until the trees mature, however, there's no shade from the often scorching sun, so take the usual precautions. An excellent swimming **beach** lines the Atlantic-facing side of the park, and a boardwalk cuts around the wind-bitten sand dunes towards the **Cape Florida lighthouse**, built in the 1820s. Only with the ranger-led **tour** (daily except Tues at 9am, 10.30am, 1pm, 2.30pm & 3.30pm; $1) can you climb through the 95-foot-high structure, which was attacked by Seminole Indians in 1836 and seized by Confederate soldiers to disrupt Union shipping during the Civil War. It remained in use until 1878, and now serves as a navigation beacon.

Stiltsville

Looking out from the park across the bay, you'll spy the grouping of fragile-looking houses known as **Stiltsville**. Held above water by stilts, these wooden dwellings were built and occupied by fishermen in the Forties and Fifties, and enraged the authorities by being outside the jurisdiction of tax collectors. Stiltsville's demise has been signalled by a recent law forbidding repair work on the ramshackle structures, whose state of disrepair was compounded by the destruction wrought by Hurricane Andrew; just one now has a full-time occupant, the others are occasionally used for parties.

MIAMI BEACH

Three miles offshore from Miami, sheltering Biscayne Bay from the Atlantic Ocean, the long, slender arm of **Miami Beach** was an ailing fruit farm in the 1910s when its Quaker owner, John Collins, formed an unlikely partnership with a flashy entrepreneur called Carl Fisher. With Fisher's money, Biscayne Bay was dredged, and the muck raised from its murky bed provided the landfill that helped transform the island into the sculptured landscape of palm trees, hotels and tennis courts that – by and large – it is today.

In varying degrees, all twelve miles of Miami Beach are worth seeing – and its firm, crushed-coral-rock beach offers excellent sunbathing and swimming opportunities – though only **South Beach**, a fairly small area at the southern end, will hold your attention for long. Here, rows of tastefully restyled Thirties Art Deco buildings have become chic gathering places for the city's fashionable faces

APPROACHING MIAMI BEACH: THE CAUSEWAYS & ISLANDS

The setting of countless *Miami Vice* car chases, the six **causeways** crossing Biscayne Bay between Miami and Miami Beach offer striking views of the city, especially so at night when the lights of buildings downtown twinkle over the bay's dark waters. Some of the causeways also provide the only land access to the artificial residential islands that shelter the rich and famous from unwanted attention.

Best pickings are along **MacArthur Causeway**, running from just north of downtown Miami into Miami Beach's South Beach. A mile into it, **Watson Island Park** harbours the **Japanese Garden**, bequeathed to the city by a Japanese industrialist in 1961; pride of place goes to an eight-ton statue of Hotei – the Japanese God of prosperity. On subsequent islands are the former homes of gangster Al Capone (Palm Island), author Damon Runyan (Hibiscus Island), and actor Don Johnson (Star Island).

and the stamping ground of Miami's more creative and unconventional elements: it's no fluke that many of Florida's leading art galleries and nightclubs are found in this compact area. Heading north, **Central Miami Beach** was where Fifties screen stars had fun in the sun and helped cement Miami's international reputation as a glamorous vacation spot. Oddly enough, it's the monolithic hotels remaining from these times that give the area a modicum of appeal. Further on, **North Miami Beach**, despite splitting into several distinctive communities, has even less to kindle the imagination – a long way from the action and mostly overrun by package tourists – but makes a good back route if you're heading north from Miami towards Fort Lauderdale.

South Beach

Miami Beach's most exciting area is **SOUTH BEACH**, which occupies the southernmost three miles. Filled with pastel-coloured Art Deco buildings, up-and-coming art galleries, modish diners and suntanned beach addicts, it attracts multinational swarms of photographers and film crews who zoom in on what has – thanks to the visuals of *Miami Vice* and the fashion photography of Bruce Weber (shooting nudes on the hotel roofs for the 1986 Calvin Klein *Obsession* campaign) – become the hottest high-style backdrop in the world.

Socially, South Beach is unsurpassed. By day, fine-bodied ravers soak up the rays on the beach, and by night the ten blocks of Ocean Drive are the heart and soul of the biggest party in Miami: chic terrace cafés spill across the wide sidewalk amid a procession of fashion models, tropical-shirted existentialists, wide-eyed tourists, tarot card readers and middle-aged trendies. Places worth frequenting are listed under "Nightlife", see p.109. Ocean Drive is also the scene of the Miami Beach cruise; see the box on p.93.

Not all South Beach is so sensuous. Just a few blocks from Ocean Drive, the streets still bear the scars of the area's poverty-stricken Seventies, and the arrival in 1980 of the *Marielitos*, Fidel Castro's gift to the US of Cuban criminals and misfits (see "Little Havana" for more), many of whom ended up here. Provided you stick to the main streets and exercise the usual caution, however, none of South Beach is unduly dangerous.

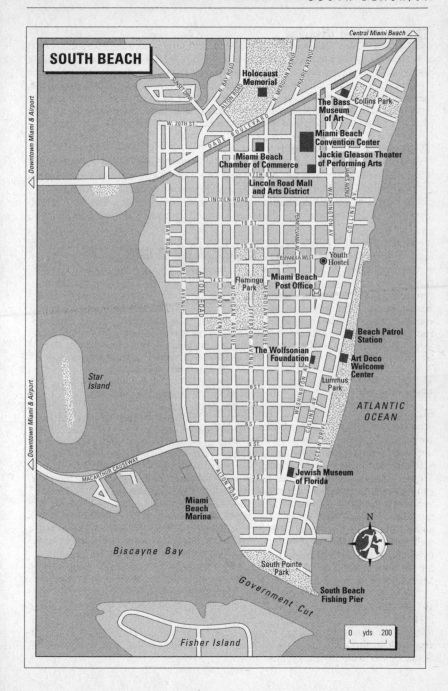

SOUTH BEACH

Central Miami Beach

Downtown Miami & Airport

Downtown Miami & Airport

Holocaust Memorial

The Bass Museum of Art

Collins Park

Miami Beach Convention Center

Jackie Gleason Theater of Performing Arts

Miami Beach Chamber of Commerce

Lincoln Road Mall and Arts District

LINCOLN ROAD

W. 20TH ST

SUNSET DRIVE

BAY ROAD

ALTON ROAD

N MERIDIAN AVENUE

PRAIRIE AVENUE

DADE BOULEVARD

17TH ST.

16 ST

15 ST

PENNSYLVANIA AV

WASHINGTON AV

COLLINS AV

JAMES AVENUE

ESPANULA WEST

Youth Hostel

Flamingo Park

Miami Beach Post Office

14 ST

BAY ROAD

WEST AVENUE

ALTON ROAD

LENOX AVENUE

MICHIGAN AVENUE

MERIDIAN AVENUE

JEFFERSON AVENUE

Beach Patrol Station

The Wolfsonian Foundation

Art Deco Welcome Center

Lummus Park

WASHINGTON AV

COLLINS AV

OCEAN DRIVE

ATLANTIC OCEAN

9 ST

8 ST

7 ST

6 ST

5 ST

4 ST

3 ST

2 ST

Jewish Museum of Florida

Star Island

Miami Beach Marina

MACARTHUR CAUSEWAY

ALTON ROAD

N

Biscayne Bay

South Pointe Park

South Beach Fishing Pier

Government Cut

Fisher Island

0   yds   200

The Art Deco district

As much as the beach and the social life, it's the **Art Deco district**, containing the world's greatest concentration of Art Deco architecture, that brings people to South Beach. Art Deco here is a smorgasbord rather than a gourmet experience; there are no great buildings, just a great number of them – in their hundreds between Fifth and 23rd streets between Ocean Drive and Lennox Avenue – built during the late Thirties in a style that became known as "Miami Beach Art Deco".

Seeing the Art Deco district

Painstaking restoration notwithstanding, little of the Art Deco district looks today quite like it did in the Thirties. Nowhere is this more apparent than in the colours – "a palette of Post Modern cake-icing pastels now associated with *Miami Vice*", according to disgruntled Florida architecture chronicler Hap Hatton – which appeared in 1980 when local designer Leonard Horowitz started adorning the

---

ART DECO IN MIAMI BEACH

Art Deco's roots go back to the Paris of 1901, though in the US it only began to take hold as a building style in the Thirties. With it, the nation shook off the restraints of Classical Revivalism and the gloom of the Depression. Thrilling and new, Art Deco architecture embraced technology, borrowing streamlined contours from the aerodynamic designs of futuristic cars, trains and planes. It also incorporated playful and humorous themes, employing wacky ornamentation and vivid colours, as well as new materials such as aluminium, chrome and plastic. Often derided as vulgar, Art Deco nonetheless became a symbol of a country emerging from economic catastrophe to become the first modern superpower.

In the late Thirties, a small group of architects built prolifically – and fast – in Miami Beach. Employing the trademarks of Art Deco, they used local limestone and stucco to produce buildings that were cheap (and often cramped and uncomfortable) but instantly fashionable – defining the look of the nation's fun and sun mecca with a style soon dubbed **"Miami Beach Art Deco"** (sometimes called "**Tropical Deco**"). Recognizable Florida motifs, such as herons, pelicans, blooming flowers and blazing sunsets, decorated facades and porches. Nautical themes were prevalent, too: windows resembled portholes, balconies stretched out like luxury liner sundecks, and any ungainly bulges on roofs were disguised as ships' funnels. Many of the buildings were painted stark white, reflecting the force of the Florida sun with matching intensity.

It's a sobering thought that Miami Beach almost lost all of these significant structures, which fell into decline from the late Fifties and were sought after by property developers wishing to replace them with anonymous high-rise condos. In the mid-Seventies, the **Miami Beach Art Deco Preservation League** (Art Deco Welcome Center, 1001 Ocean Drive ☎638-6064) – whose first meeting drew just six people – was born with the aim of saving the buildings and raising awareness of their architectural and historical importance. The League's success has been dramatic – a major turning point was convincing the buck-hungry developers of the earning potential of such a unique area. The driving force of the movement, the late Barbara Capitman, failed in her attempt at a similar initiative in Opa-Locka, a socially blighted district in northwest Miami, nowadays better known for its crack dealers than its crazy, Arabesque architecture.

buildings. Furthermore, the details of restoration reflect the tastes of the buildings' owners more than historical accuracy – but Miami Beach Art Deco of the 1990s is a sight to behold in its own right.

Examples of the Art Deco style are too numerous to list (or view) in full; just stroll around and keep your eyes open. For a more structured investigation, try taking the ninety-minute **walking tour** (Sat 10.30am; $6) from the Art Deco Welcome Center, 1001 Ocean Drive, or the **bicycle tour** (Sun 10.30am; $10 including bike rental; reservations ☎672-2014) from *Cycles on the Beach*, 713 Fifth Street .

The district's contemporary look should be assessed from Ocean Drive, where a line of revamped hotels have exploited their design heritage; you can venture into the lobbies for a look, and many are worth visiting for their bars or restaurants (see "Eating" and "Nightlife"). Among them, the *Park Central*, no. 640, is a geometric *tour de force*, with octagonal windows, sharp vertical columns and a wrought-iron decorated stairway leading up to the mezzanine level, which displays monochrome photos of Miami Beach in the Twenties. Nearby, at no. 850, a corner of the *Waldorf Towers* is topped by an ornamental lighthouse. Just across the street in Lummus Park (the grassy patch that separates Ocean Drive from the beach), and more honestly redolent of the old days, stands the boat-shaped **Beach Patrol Station**, unmistakeable for its vintage oversized date and temperature sign, and still the base of the local lifeguards.

Just ahead are two buildings at the centre of the controversy currently raging through South Beach: should its Art Deco buildings be decorated only in officially approved pastel colours, or can they be allowed to evolve a particularly 1990s South Beach style and use much more vivid tones? The purple and orange frontage of the **Cardozo**, no. 1300, and the intense yellow exterior of the **Leslie**, no. 1244, were the recent work of Barbara Hulanicki, who founded London's scene-setting clothes store *Biba* in the 1960s. Hulanicki's exuberant tones have upset many South Beach purists, but seem set to be the look of South Beach to come.

Walk at least once after dark along the beach side of Ocean Drive. This frees you from the crowds and enables a clear view of the Art Deco hotels' **neon illuminations**, casting shimmering circles and lines of vivid blues, pinks and greens around the contours of the buildings.

Away from the image-conscious trappings of Ocean Drive, perhaps the district's most enduring relic, an example of the less ornate Depression Moderne style, is the **Miami Beach Post Office**, 1300 Washington Avenue (lobby Mon–Fri 6am–6pm, Sat 6am–4pm). Inside, streaming sunlight brightens the murals sweeping around a rotunda; there can be few more enjoyable places to buy a stamp.

South of Fifth Street: South Pointe Park and around

South of Fifth Street, a small and shabby area called **South Pointe** is being revamped by a major redevelopment project: more, it seems, to exploit the commercial potential of the location than to benefit the community. A marina and several restaurants have been added, and the luxury 26-storey *South Pointe Towers* leaps skyward from South Pointe Park (see below), dwarfing the stucco-fronted boxes in which most local people live. The best route through South Pointe is the mile-long shorefront boardwalk, beginning near the southern end of Lummus Park, and finishing by the 300-foot-long jetty lined with people fishing off **First Street Beach**, the only surfing beach in Miami and alive with tanned, athletic bodies even when the waves are calm. You can swim and snorkel here, too, but bear in mind that the big cruise ships frequently pass close by and stir up the current.

South Pointe Park
On its inland side, the boardwalk skirts **South Pointe Park** (daily 8am–sunset), whose handsome lawns and tree-shaded picnic tables offer a respite from the packed beaches. The park is a good place to be on Friday evenings when its open-air stage is the venue for enjoyable free **music events** (details are posted up around South Beach).

Seats on the southern edge of the park give you a view of **Government Cut**, a waterway first dredged by Henry Flagler at the turn of the century and now, substantially deepened, the route for large cruise ships beginning their journeys to the Bahamas and Caribbean. You might also witness an impounded drug-running vessel being towed along by the authorities. Don't be surprised, either, to hear the neighing of horses: Miami Beach's police horses are stabled on the eastern side of the park.

North along Washington Avenue

Running through South Beach parallel to Ocean Drive is **Washington Avenue**, much of it lined by small, Cuban-run supermarkets, trendy restaurants and boutiques, and run-down retirement homes. Two of Miami Beach's museums are located here, while a third lies just west of it.

Jewish Museum of Florida
During the 1920s and 1930s, South Beach became an major destination for Jewish tourists escaping the harsh northeastern winters. In response, many of the hotels placed "Gentiles Only" notices at their reception desks, and the slogan "Always a view, never a Jew" appeared in many a hotel brochure. Despite this, by the 1940s South Beach had a largely Jewish population and, though today the centre of the community has moved north along the Beach to around 40th and 50th streets, a considerable number of elderly Jews remain. The **Jewish Museum of Florida**, 301 Washington Avenue (Tues–Sun 10am–5pm; $4, Sat free) bears testimony not only to Jewish life in Miami Beach, but in Florida generally. Housed in an elegant 1936-built Art Deco building, which served as an Orthodox synagogue for Miami Beach's first Jewish congregation, the museum documents Florida's Jewish heritage from the eighteenth century to the present day. Apart from its permanent collection, the museum hosts visiting exhibitions on Jews in Florida, the Caribbean and elsewhere.

Wolfsonian Foundation
Thousands of objects dedicated to design arts have been assembled by Mitchell Wolfson Jnr at the **Wolfsonian Foundation**, 1001 Washington Avenue (Mon–Fri 1–5pm; $1). Anyone with a passing interest in decorative, architectural or politics-inspired arts ought to be able to find something of interest in the galleries, which also provide a wonderfully cool haven from the shadeless avenue outside.

Española Way
Other than the Miami Beach post office (described above under "Seeing the Art Deco District"), nothing along Washington Avenue need delay you until you reach **Española Way**, between 14th and 15th streets. While renowned for its Art Deco, Miami Beach also boasts several examples of the Mediterranean Revival architecture found across much of Miami; most of these are situated on this slender street overhung by narrow balconies and striped awnings.

Completed in 1925, Española Way was grandly envisaged as an "artists' colony", but only the rhumba dance craze of the Thirties – said to have started here, stirred up by Cuban band leader Desi Arnaz* – came close to fitting the bill. Following South Beach's social climb in the Eighties, however, a group of browsable art galleries and art supply stores have revived the original concept; they now fill the first-floor rooms, while above them, small top-floor apartments are optimistically marketed as "artists' lofts".

Lincoln Road Mall and the Lincoln Road Arts District
A short walk further north, between 16th and 17th streets, the pedestrianized **Lincoln Road Mall** was considered the flashiest shopping precinct outside of New York during the Fifties, its jewellery and clothes stores earning it the label "Fifth Avenue of the South". Today, run-of-the-mill consumer durable stockists fill the section closest to Washington Avenue, and the focus of interest has shifted a few blocks west to the **Lincoln Road Arts District**, around Lenox Avenue. Here, among a number of art galleries breathing life into what were, a few years ago, fairly seedy offices and shops, the studios (viewing hours are displayed on their doors) and showrooms of South Florida Art Center, Inc., 810 Lincoln Road, will tune you into the burgeoning South Beach arts scene. The area's increasingly cultured mood is reflected in the many restaurants and cafés along the mall (see "Eating"), and the area is a favourite place for evening strolls.

The Jackie Gleason Theater and the Miami Beach Convention Center
The first of two public buildings immediately north of Lincoln Road Mall, the 3000-seat **Jackie Gleason Theater of Performing Arts**, fronted by Pop artist Roy Lichtenstein's expressive *Mermaid* sculpture, stages Broadway shows and classical concerts. However, it is best known to middle-aged Americans as the home of wholesome entertainer Jackie Gleason's immensely popular TV show, which ran for twenty years from the Fifties.

On the far side of the theatre, sunlight bounces off the white exterior of the massive **Miami Beach Convention Center**, which occupies a curious niche in

---

*Arnaz (later to find wider fame as the husband of Lucille Ball) and his band often performed in the *Village Tavern*, inside the *Clay Hotel*, which is now the city's youth hostel; see "Accommodation".

HOLOCAUST MEMORIAL

At 1933–1945 Meridian Avenue, it's hard not to be moved by Kenneth Treister's **Holocaust Memorial** (9am–9pm), completed in 1990 and dedicated to Elie Wiesel. Depicting an arm tattoed with an Auschwitz number reaching towards the sky, with life-sized figures of emaciated, tormented people attempting to climb it, the deeply emotive sculpture rises from a lily pond in the centre of a plaza, around which are graphic images recalling the Nazi genocide against the Jews.

US political history. At the Republican Convention held here in August 1968, Richard Nixon won the nomination that would take him to the White House. Nixon counted his votes oblivious to the fact that the first of Miami's Liberty City riots had just erupted (see "Around Downtown Miami").

The Bass Museum of Art

A little further north, within a sculpture-studded garden, is the fetching coral-rock building of the **Bass Museum of Art**, 2121 Park Avenue (Tues–Sat 10am–5pm, Sun 1–5pm, 2nd & 4th Weds 1–9pm; $5, Tues donations), whose major expansion, completed in 1995, was overseen by acclaimed Japanese architect Arata Isozaki. The museum's permanent collection – dominated by worthy European works mostly from the fifteenth to seventeenth centuries, with Rubens, Rembrandt and Dürer heading the cast – is a notch above anything you'll find elsewhere in the state. For anyone other than fine-art buffs, the contemporary visiting exhibitions offer greater stimulation.

Central Miami Beach

The energy of South Beach fades dramatically as you travel north of 23rd Street to **CENTRAL MIAMI BEACH**. Collins Avenue charts a five-mile course through the area, between Indian Creek – across which are the golf courses, country clubs and secluded palatial homes of Miami Beach's seriously rich – and the swanky hotels around which the Miami Beach high-life revolved during the glamorous Fifties. These often madly ostentatious establishments are the main attraction of Central Miami Beach; the strand itself is largely the preserve of families and older folk, and is backed by a long and lovely boardwalk that stretches over a mile from 21st Street.

Along Collins Avenue

The southern edge of Central Miami Beach is defined by the garbage-clogged **Collins Canal**, cut in the 1910s to speed the movement of farm produce through the mangrove trees that then lined Biscayne Bay. The canal is a dismal sight, but improves as it flows into the luxury yacht-lined **Indian Creek**, and along Collins Avenue you'll see the first of the sleek condos and hotels that characterize the area.

Unlike their small Art Deco counterparts in South Beach, the later **hotels** of Central Miami Beach are massive monuments to the Fifties. When big was beautiful, these state-of-the-art pleasure palaces drew the international jet set by offering much more than mere accommodation: a price that few could afford also bought access to exclusive bars, restaurants and lounges where film and TV stars cavorted to the envy of the rest of the US. Yet the good times were short-lived. As everyone tried to cash in, cheap imitations of the pace-setting hotels formed an ugly wall of concrete along Collins Avenue; quality sank, service deteriorated and the big names moved on. By the Seventies, many of the hotels looked like what they really were: monsters from another age. The Eighties saw Miami's social star re-emerge once again, and a revival got underway. Many of the polished-up hotels are now occupied by well-heeled Latin American tourists – along with grey-haired swingers from the US for whom Miami Beach never lost its cachet.

The Fontainebleau Hotel

Prior to Central Miami Beach becoming a celebrities' playground, the nation's rich and powerful built rambling shorefront mansions here. One such, the winter home of tyre-baron Harvey Firestone, was demolished in 1953 to make room for the **Fontainebleau Hotel**, 4441 Collins Avenue, a "dreamland of kitsch and consumerism" that defined the Miami Beach of the late Fifties and Sixties. Gossip-column perennials such as Joan Crawford, Joe DiMaggio, Lana Turner and Bing Crosby were *Fontainebleau* regulars, as was rebel crooner Frank Sinatra who, besides starting a scrambled-egg fight in the coffee shop, shot many scenes here as the private-eye hero of the Sixties film *Tony Rome*. Drop in for a look around the curving lobby overhung by weighty chandeliers, and venture through the tree-filled grounds to a swimming pool complete with rock grottoes and waterfalls.

If you can't face the toadying bellhops lurking in the lobby, one feature you shouldn't miss is on an exterior wall: approaching from the south, Collins Avenue veers left just before the hotel, passing beneath Richard Haas' 13,000-square-foot *trompe l'oeil* mural. Unveiled in 1986, it creates the illusion of a great hole in the wall exposing the hotel directly behind – one of the biggest driving hazards in Miami.

More hotels and luxury homes

Truth be told, there's not much more to see in Central Miami Beach. For its place in local folklore, the *Fontainebleau* is easily the most tempting of the hotels, though you might snatch glances inside the *Shawnee*, no. 4343, and the *Castle Beach Club*, no. 5445, both Fifties survivors who've undergone stylized renovation, with marble floors, indoor fountains and etched glasswork. Meanwhile, the ultra-swish *Alexander*, no. 5225, has become a watering hole of Miami's present-day smart set.

Many of the rich people who live in Miami Beach have gracefully appointed homes up pine-tree-lined drives on the other side of Indian Creek. Cross the water on Arthur Godfrey Road and drive (or cycle) around the exclusive La Gorce Drive and Alton Road for an eyeful of what money can buy.

From further down Collins Avenue to North Miami Beach, the scene is dominated by hotels. In 1968, an unrestrained Norman Mailer wrote of the scene: "Moorish castles shaped like waffle irons, shaped like the baffle plates on white plastic electric heaters, and cylinders like Waring blenders, buildings looking like giant op art and pop art paintings, and sweet wedding cakes, cottons of kitsch and piles of dirty cotton stucco. . ."

North Miami Beach and inland

Collins Avenue continues for seven uninspiring miles through **NORTH MIAMI BEACH**, enriched only by a few noteworthy beaches and parks. Confusingly, due to the machinations of early property speculators, the four small communities that make up this northern section of Miami Beach lack a collective appellation, and the area officially titled "North Miami Beach" is actually inland, across Biscayne Bay.

Surfside and Bal Harbour

Untouched for years as big-money developments loomed all around, the low-rise buildings of **Surfside** – the pleasant North Shore Park marks the community's southern limit – retain a rather appealing old-fashioned ambience, though the community is currently in the throes of gradual gentrification, and only the neighbourhood's **beach**, between 91st and and 95th streets, will make you want to stick around; incidentally, it's one of the few in Miami Beach to allow topless sunbathing.

Directly north, **Bal Harbour** – aspirations of "Olde Worlde" elegance reflected in its anglicized name – is similar in size to Surfside but entirely different in character: an upmarket area filled with the carefully guarded homes of some of the nation's wealthiest people. The exclusive Bal Harbour Shops, 9700 Collins Avenue, packed with outrageously expensive designer stores, sets the tone for the area. A better place to spend time is **Haulover Beach Park**, just to the north, whose sprawling vegetation backs onto more than a mile of uncrowded beach – and there's a great view of the Miami Beach skyline from the end of the pier.

Sunny Isles and Golden Beach

Beyond Haulover Park, **Sunny Isles** is as lifeless as they come: a place where European travel agencies dump unsuspecting package tourists and where, due to bargain basement prices, French Canadian tourists choose to return year after year, dominating the fast food restaurants and tacky souvenir shops along Collins Avenue. You'll quickly get a tan on Sunny Isles' sands, but everything around is geared to low-budget, package tourism and, if staying here without a car, you're likely to feel trapped. Of passing interest, however, are some architecturally excessive hotels erected during the Fifties: along Collins Avenue, watch out for the camels and sheikhs guarding the *Sahara*, no. 18335; the crescent-moon-holding maidens of the *Blue Mist*, no. 19111; and the Moorish-Polynesian-Deco-Ultra-Bad-Kitsch style of the *Marco Polo*, no. 19200.

By the time you reach **Golden Beach**, the northernmost community of Miami Beach, much of the traffic pounding Collins Avenue has turned inland on the 192nd Street Causeway, and the anachronistic hotels have given way to quiet shorefront homes. Public beach access here is negligible, and unless you're intending to leave Miami altogether (Collins Avenue, as Hwy-A1A, continues north to Fort Lauderdale), there's a bigger draw to be found directly inland.

Inland: the Ancient Spanish Monastery
The Sunny Isles Causeway (163rd Street) leads across to "North Miami Beach", on the mainland. Despite its name, this area is a continuation of the depressed

suburbs north of downtown Miami, and not a place to linger in unless you're visiting the **Ancient Spanish Monastery** (Mon–Sat 10am–5pm, Sun noon–5pm; $4). Publishing magnate William Randolph Hearst came across the twelfth-century monastery in Spain in 1925, bought it for $500,000, broke it into numbered pieces and shipped it to the US – only for it to be held by customs, who feared that it might carry foot-and-mouth disease. Photos in the monastery's entrance room show the 11,000 boxes that contained the monastery when it came ashore – and a docker standing over them, scratching his head.

The demands of tax officials left Hearst short of ready funds, and the monastery lingered in a New York warehouse until 1952, when the pieces were brought here and re-assembled as a tourist attraction. The job took a year and a half, done largely by trial and error thanks to incorrect repacking of the pieces; pacing the cloisters, as Cistercian monks did for 700 years, you can see the uneven form of the buttressed ceilings and rough, honey-coloured walls. Now used as an Episcopal church, the monastery is a model of tranquility, its peacefulness enhanced by a lush garden setting.

If you're not driving, **getting to the monastery** is relatively easy with buses #E, #H and #V from Sunny Isles, #3 from downtown Miami, or services from the North Miami Beach *Greyhound* station, 16250 Biscayne Boulevard (☎305/945-0801). Each of these routes, though, leaves you with a nail-biting ten-minute walk through some very dodgy streets.

Continuing north: towards Fort Lauderdale

The coastal route, Hwy-A1A (Collins Avenue), and the mainland Hwy-1 (Biscayne Boulevard) both continue into Hollywood, at the southern edge of the Fort Lauderdale area, fully described in *The Southeast Coast*. By **public transport** you can travel north with *Broward County Transit* (☎305/357-8400) buses from the vast Aventura shopping mall on the corner of Lehman Causeway (192nd Street) and Biscayne Boulevard.

PRACTICALITIES

Due perhaps to the cool night-time breeze that blows the humidity out of the subtropical heat, no one in Miami, it seems, can wait to get out and enjoy themselves. Entertainment listings are the most popular section of any newspaper, and the very thought of not devoting evenings and weekends to hedonistic pursuits would bring many locals out in a rash.

Social **drinking** usually serves as a curtain-raiser on the night rather than an end in itself and is seldom allowed to impinge on **eating** time. Miamians think nothing of eating out three times a day seven days a week, and the range of food on offer spans most of the world and suits all budgets – discovering Cuban cuisine is one of the joys of the city. Don't be surprised if the place where you had dinner doubles as a **live music** spot: restaurant back rooms feature significantly on a small local live music network, where reggae shines strongly. The city's effervescent **club** scene is fun to explore, too – set around South Beach's Art Deco strip are some of the hippest nightspots in the whole country. High-brow **arts** fans can choose between several orchestras, three respected dance groups and a diverse programme of drama at several medium-sized theatres. And if these don't appeal, you can burn up excess energy cruising the **shops**, not the country's greatest totems of consumerism, but easily sufficient to slake a thirst for acquisition.

WHAT'S ON TELEPHONE NUMBERS

Call the following numbers for recorded information on what's happening in Miami.

Blues Hotline ☎666-MOJ   PACE Free Concert Hotline ☎681-1470
Folk Hotline ☎595-8042   WTMI Cultural Arts Line ☎550-9393
Jazz Hotline ☎382-3938   WSHE-FM Concert Hotline ☎581-7655
Movie Hotline ☎888-FILM   ZETA Link Concert Hotline ☎372-1442

Miami is virtually impossible to **get around** at night without a car or taxi, though the bulk of the bars, live music spots and clubs are within walking distance of one another in South Beach. If you're staying in South Beach, you won't have to worry about carparks or fret over the city's paucity of late-night buses; if you're not, you might use the *Breeze* minibuses to get there – and back – from downtown Miami (see p.59).

To find out **what's on**, read the listings in *New Times* (published on Thursdays), or in the Friday Weekend section of the *Miami Herald*. Make use, too, of the several **telephone hotlines** – see the box above – giving recorded information.

Eating

With everything from the greasiest hotdog stand to the finest gourmet restaurant vying for business, **eating** in Miami is a buyer's market. All over the city, street stands, cafés and coffee shops offer decent, filling **breakfasts** and all-day **budget food** (a good feed for around $5), and many restaurants dish up huge **lunches** at remarkably low prices; $7–10 is about average. **Dinner** too can be good value, rarely costing more than $10–15, and you don't need to be rich to indulge in the occasional blowout; look out for **early-bird specials**, when some restaurants knock a few dollars off the price of a full evening meal simply to get bums on seats between 5 and 7pm. Be aware, too, of the free food offered at **happy hours** (see "Drinking"), and the ample buffets that constitute Sunday **brunch** (see p.107).

Anywhere that serves breakfast is usually open at 6am or 7am, most restaurants do business between noon and midnight or 1am, some closing between lunch and dinner, and a few operating around the clock (see the box on p.103).

The big fast-food franchises and pizza chains are as plentiful here as elsewhere across the country, and "typical" **American** food, such as thick, juicy burgers and sizeable sandwiches, is easily found. Recent years have seen the development of of a style of cooking termed as **"New Floridian"**, which successfully combines nouvelle cuisine methods and presentation with Caribbean ingredients. Yet Miami is too cosmopolitan for a single food style to be dominant, and only **seafood**, every bit as plentiful and good as you would expect so close to fishladen tropical waters, is a common feature among the city's plethora of cuisines drawn from every corner of the Americas – and beyond.

So common all over the city that it hardly seems an ethnic cuisine at all, **Cuban** food is what Miami does best. A sizeable lunch or dinner in one of the innumerable small, family-run Cuban diners (always pleased to show off their culinary skills to non-Spanish-speaking customers) will cost an absurdly low $4–7, a fraction of the prices charged by fancier Cuban restaurants – mostly in Little Havana and Coral Gables – now lauded by the nation's food critics thanks to the development of a lighter, more attractive "**Nuevo Cubano**" style of cooking. **Haitian** cooking is slowly gaining popularity in Miami, and the restaurants in Little Haiti, just north of downtown Miami, are just some of the places in which to sample it. **Argentinian, Jamaican, Nicaraguan** and **Peruvian** eateries bear witness to the city's strong Caribbean and Latin American elements, though aside from Cuban food, for sheer quality and value for money it's hard to better the many **Japanese** outlets, most north of downtown Miami and a few in South Miami – all much cheaper than their European counterparts – while in South Beach, sushi is the current rage. **Chinese** and **Thai** places are abundant, too, as are **Italian**. By contrast, **Indian** food is having a hard time taking root despite a couple of commendable restaurants in Coral Gables, and **Mexican** food is far less common than in most other parts of the US.

Downtown and around

Aux Palmistes Chez Julie, 6820 NE Second Ave (☎759-8527). Where Little Haiti dances (see "Live Music") and dines on home-cooked fried pork, goat and fish. Closed Mon.

Big Fish, 55 SW Miami Ave Rd (☎372-3725). Lively spot on the Miami River, with folding chairs, benches and picnic tables. Menu includes home-cooked fish sandwiches and fresh seafood chowder. Closed Sun; lunch only June–November.

Bimini Grill, 620 NE 78th St (☎758-9154). Florida country-style food in a wooden shack on a river bank. Barbecued meats and Caribbean conch fritters are among the treats.

Café del Sol, *Crowne Plaza Hotel*, 1601 Biscayne Blvd (☎374-0000). A safe introduction to the varied cuisines of Latin America and the Caribbean for those who don't want to venture into Little Havana. Moderate prices.

Chez Moi, 1 NW 54th St (☎756-7540). Not cheap, but a strong creole menu makes this the top Haitian restaurant in Little Haiti.

Dick Clark's American Bandstand Grill, at the Bayside Marketplace, 401 Biscayne Blvd (☎381-8800). Great collection of rock'n'roll memorabilia, from Fabian to the Beatles, to admire as you munch a chargrilled burger.

East Coast Fisheries, 360 W Flagler St (☎373-5516). The fish goes straight from the boats into the kitchen of this lively Miami River restaurant, but the cooking is plain and rather expensive.

Firehouse Four, 1000 S Miami Ave (☎379-1923). Restored fire station frequented by three-piece suiters walking over from Brickell Avenue for pricey but good American and international fare. See "Drinking."

Fishbone Grille, 650 S Miami Ave (☎530 1915). A busy but friendly restaurant serving the finest budget seafood in Miami. Located next to *Tobacco Road* (see "Drinking" and "Live Music") where many of the diners move on to.

Gourmet Diner, 13900 Biscayne Blvd (☎947-2255). Always a line for a winning Continental daily menu.

Hiro, 17516 Biscayne Blvd (☎948-3687). Miami's only late-night sushi bar, and where the city's sushi chefs hang out after work. Open until 4am.

Joe's Seafood Restaurant, 2771 NW 24th St (☎638-8602). The dockside setting improves the otherwise only adequate seafood. Not to be confused with *Joe's Stone Crab* (see "Miami Beach").

Rita's Italian Restaurant, 7232 Biscayne Blvd (☎757-9470). Family-run Italian diner with check tablecloths, hearty portions, good prices and an owner inclined to burst into song.

S & S Sandwich Shop, 1757 NE Second Ave (☎373-4291). Under the same ownership for nearly fifty years, proffering platefuls of meatloaf, turkey, stuffed cabbage, beef stew, shrimp creole or pork chops for less than $6. Counter service only. Closed Sun.

Shagnasty's Saloon & Eatery, 638 S Miami Ave (☎381-8970). Restaurant section of *Tobacco Road* (see "Drinking" and "Live Music"), its hamburgers, fries and sandwiches consumed by relaxing yuppies.

Shiroi Hana, 12460 NE Seventh Ave (☎891-5160). Excellent Japanese cuisine in roomy, comfortable setting. Extensive menu and polite clientele and staff.

Super Duper Sandwich Restaurant, 206 NE First Ave (☎374-5493). Biggest and busiest Cuban diner in downtown Miami. Closed Sun.

Las Tapas, at the Bayside Marketplace, 401 Biscayne Blvd (☎372-2737). Spanish bar and restaurant in Miami's zestiest shopping mall. Tapas served with sangria and a basket of bread.

Tark's, 13750 Biscayne Blvd (☎944-8275). Fast-and-fresh seafood: shrimp, Alaskan snow crab, stone crab claws, clams and oysters, all at low prices.

Trixie's, 3600 NE Second Ave (☎573-6799). Healthy, natural foods served for breakfast and lunch. Very reasonably priced, and popular with the fashion designers who work nearby.

Little Havana

Ayestaran, 706 SW 27th Ave (☎649-4982). Long a favourite Cuban restaurant among those in the know, especially good value for its $5 daily specials.

La Carreta, 3632 SW Eighth St (☎444-7501). The real sugar cane growing around the wagon wheel outside is a good sign: inside, home-style Cuban cooking is served at unbeatable prices.

Casablanca Cafeteria, 2300 SW Eighth St (☎642-2751). Large family-style Cuban restaurant dispensing ample portions over two horseshoe-shaped counters, with an espresso bar opening onto the busy street.

Casa Juancho, 2436 SW Eighth St (☎642-2452). Pricey, but the tapas are good value at $6–8, and there's a convivial mood as strolling musicians serenade the wealthy Cuban clientele.

El Cid, 117 NW 42nd Ave (☎642-3144). A gargantuan Moorish-style castle where the staff dress as knaves and displays of freshly killed fowl greet you at the door. Lots of drinking, singing and eating, with affordable Spanish and Cuban delicacies.

La Esquina de Tejas, 101 SW Twelfth St (☎545-5341). Where Reagan and Bush both solicited the Hispanic vote, and which turns out dependable Cuban lunches and dinners.

El Inka, 1756 SW Eighth St (☎845-0243). The city's oldest and best Peruvian restaurant, famed for its spicy meats and seafood, and doing extraordinary things with squid.

Hy-Vong, 3458 SW Eighth St (☎446-3674). Tiny, dinner-only Vietnamese restaurant, a favourite of hip yuppies and Vietnam vets. No-frills, slow service, but damn good food. Closed Mon.

Las Islas Canarias, 285 NW 27th Ave (☎649-0440). Tucked away inside a drab shopping mall. Piles of fine, unpretentious Cuban food at unbeatable prices.

Malaga, 740 SW Eighth St (☎858-4224). Inexpensive Spanish and Cuban cuisine, specializing in fresh fish dishes, served inside or in the courtyard.

La Palacio de los Jugos, 5721 W Flagler Ave (☎264-1503). A handful of tables at the back of a Cuban produce market, where the pork sandwiches and shellfish soup from the takeout stand are the tastiest for miles.

Versailles, 3555 SW Eighth St (☎444-0240). Chandeliers, mirrored walls, a great atmosphere and wonderful inexpensive Cuban food.

Coral Gables

Café 94, 94 Miracle Mile (☎444-7933). Serving low-cost lunches and snacks, this makes a fine pit-stop when exploring the area. Closed Sun.

Cheese Villa Café, 264 Miracle Mile (☎446-3133). Does a brisk trade in well-stuffed deli sandwiches and tasty soups.

El Corral, 3545 Coral Way (☎444-8272). An appealingly priced Nicaraguan eatery where anything that isn't beef isn't taken seriously – carnivores' heaven.

24-HOUR EATS

The five below, all in South Beach, are places where you can get reasonably priced **food all night**. See the eating listings for fuller details.

David's Coffee Shop, corner of Eleventh St and Collins Ave (☎534-8763).

Eleventh Street Diner, 1065 Washington Ave (☎534-6373). Fri and Sat only.

News Café, 800 Ocean Drive (☎538-6397).

Ted's Hideaway South, 124 Second St (no phone).

Wolfie's, 2038 Collins Ave (☎538-6626).

Darbar, 276 Alhambra Circle (☎448-9691). Indian restaurant seeking to enlighten local taste-buds with a full selection of basics plus a few specialties. Closed Sun.

Doc Dammers' Bar & Grill, inside the *Colonnade Hotel*, 180 Aragon Ave (☎441-2600). Affordable eating in a spacious, old-style saloon; serving breakfast, lunch and dinner, and offering a happy hour in its piano bar. See the "Happy Hours" box on p.105.

El Farolito, 2885 Coral Way (☎446-4122). Fairly inexpensive seafood restaurant specializing in unusual Peruvian dishes.

Hofbrau Pub & Grill, 172 Giralda Ave (☎442-2730). Three daily specials, but come for the Wednesday night $7-all-you-can-eat fish-fry. Closed Sun. See "Drinking".

House of India, 22 Merrick Way (☎444-2348). Quality catch-all Indian food including some excellently priced lunch buffets.

Mykonos, 1201 Coral Way (☎856-3140). Greek food in an unassuming atmosphere: spinako-pita, lemon chicken soup, gyros, souvlaki and huge Greek salads.

Restaurant St Michel, in *Hotel Place St Miche*l, 162 Alcazar Ave (☎444-1666). Outstanding French and Mediterranean cuisine amid antiques and flowers. Not cheap, but very alluring.

Vatapa, 2415 Ponce de Leon Blvd (☎461-5669). Authentic Brazilian regional cooking at affordable prices.

Victor's Café, 2340 SW 32nd Ave (☎445-1313). Mambo musicians secreted about the palms and fountains make for lively dining, but the Cuban food – while good – tends to be overpriced.

Yoko's, 4041 Ponce de Leon Blvd (☎444-6622). Intimate Japanese restaurant usually packed with students from the neighbouring University of Miami.

Yuca, 148 Giralda Ave (☎444-4448). Currently the rave of food critics up and down the land, serving "Nuevo Cubano" cuisine in a deliberate gourmet-diner setting; great stuff, but don't budget for under $50 each.

Coconut Grove

Café Tu Tu Tango, inside CocoWalk, 3015 Grand Ave (☎529-2222). A quirky and entertaining spot themed as an artist's garret; lengthy menu of good-quality food served in tapas-sized portions and at high speed.

Captain Dick's Tackle Shack, 3381 Pan American Drive (☎854-5871). In the shadow of Miami City Hall and a great find in an otherwise expensive area: filling seafood and salads all at rock-bottom prices.

Cheesecake Factory, inside CocoWalk, 3015 Grand Ave (☎447-9898). A huge variety of cheesecakes to choose from.

Fuddruckers, 3444 Main Hwy (☎442-8164). Where sides of beef hang from hooks before being turned into ultra-fresh burgers.

Grove Café, 3484 Main Hwy (☎445-0022). Succulent burgers to munch as you watch the Coconut Grove groovers swan by.

Hungry Sailor, 3064 Grand Ave (☎444-9359). Pseudo-British pub creates moderately successful fish and chips and shepherd's pie, but does better with its conch chowder. See "Drinking" and "Live Music".

Mandarin Garden, 3268 Grand Ave (☎446-9999 or ☎442-1234). Very tasty, affordable Chinese food. The free parking is a big plus during traffic-jammed weekends.

Scotty's, 338 Pan American Drive (☎854-2626). Tasty seafood and fish'n'chips consumed at marina-side picnic tables in a simple setting.

Señor Frog's, 3008 Grand Ave (☎448-0999). Broad selection of reasonably priced Mexican food, but most people come to gulp down margaritas.

Zanzibar, 3468 Main Hwy (☎444-0244). The burgers and omelettes will erase hunger pangs, but the real attraction is people-watching from the outdoor tables.

Key Biscayne

Bayside Seafood Restaurant, 3501 Rickenbacker Causeway (☎361-0808). Variety of down-to-earth seafood dishes at bargain prices. See "Drinking" and "Live Music".

Beach House, 12 Crandon Blvd (☎361-1038). Gossipy locals' haunt serving three square meals a day.

The Sandbar, at Silver Sands Motel & Villas, 301 Ocean Drive (☎361-5441). Tucked-away seafood restaurant offering easily affordable lunch or dinner a pebble's throw from crashing ocean waves.

Sunday's on the Bay, 5420 Crandon Blvd (☎361-6777). Marina seafood eatery catering to the boats and beer set. Very casual. See "Live Music".

South Miami

Chifa Chinese Restaurant, 12590 N Kendall Drive (☎271-3823). In all probability the only restaurant in Florida specializing in Peruvian–Cantonese cuisine. Tasty deep-fried appetizers, run-of-the-mill main courses, plus a range of Chinese and Peruvian beers are served up at budget prices.

Fountain & Grill, at *Sunset Drugs*, 5640 Sunset Drive (☎667-1807). Large, clean and modern version of the traditional small-town diner. Noted for its grilled cheese sandwiches, burgers and meatloaf.

JJ's American Diner, 5850 Sunset Drive (☎665-5499) and 12000 N Kendall Drive (☎598-0307). Big burgers and sandwiches in a contemporary soda shop setting, complete with blaring rock'n'roll.

Never On Sunday, 9707 S Dixie Hwy (☎662-8739). Friendly joint serving cheap Greek and Italian dishes.

Old Cutler Inn, 7271 SW 168th St (☎238-1514). A neo-rustic country inn that's a neighbourhood fave for its steaks, shrimps and delicious desserts.

Pars, 10827 SW 40th St (☎551-1099). Good Iranian food in a simple setting.

Sakura, 8225 SW 124th St (☎238-8462). Tiny, good-value sushi bar and restaurant that's always packed.

Shorty's Bar-B-Q, 9200 S Dixie Hwy (☎665-5732). Sit at a picnic table, tuck a napkin in your shirt and graze on barbecued ribs and chicken and corn on the cob – pausing only to gaze at the cowboy memorabilia on the walls.

Su Shin, 10501 N Kendall Drive (☎271-3235). Great teriyakis, daily specials and sushi chefs with a sense of humor.

El Toro Taco, 1 S Krome Ave (☎245-5576). Excellent family-run Mexican restaurant, a gem in the centre of Homestead that makes a good place to stop en route to the Keys.

Tropical Delite, 10865B Caribbean Blvd, at the Caribbean Plaza (☎235-5615). Dirt-cheap Jamaican home cooking: jerk chicken and goat curry among the favourites.

Wagons West, 13111 S Dixie Hwy (☎238-9942). Maximum cholesterol breakfasts and other unhealthy fare are consumed in this always-crowded, budget-priced shrine to cowboys and the Wild West; sit at wagon-shaped booths and admire the Western memorabilia on the walls.

HAPPY HOURS

Almost every restaurant in Miami has a **happy hour**, usually on weekdays from 5 to 8pm, when drinks are cheap and come in tandem with a large pile of free food – varying from chicken wings and conch fritters to chips and popcorn. Watch for the signs outside or scan the numerous newspaper ads for the best deals – or try one of our listings, which are consistently among the best in the city.

Crawdaddy's, 1 Washington Ave, Miami Beach (☎673-1708). Cut-price oysters, shrimp and drinks in Miami Beach's most congenial happy hour.

Coco Loco's, in the *Sheraton*, 495 Brickell Ave near downtown Miami (☎373-6000). No better place to finish off a day downtown; the drinks are high, but for a dollar you help yourself to a massive buffet.

Doc Dammers' Bar & Grill, inside the *Colonnade Hotel*, 180 Aragon Ave, Coral Gables (☎441-2600). Where the young(ish) and unattached of Coral Gables mingle after work to the strains of a pianist. See "Eating".

Firehouse Four, 1000 S Miami Ave, downtown Miami (☎379-1923). Happy hour in this 1923 former fire station is a riot of thirty-something yuppies.

Monty's Raw Bar, 2560 S Bayshore Drive, Coconut Grove (☎858-1431). Cheap drinks wash down the seafood, and tropical music complements the bay view at Coconut Grove's best happy hour.

Shagnasty's Saloon & Eatery, 638 S Miami Ave, near downtown Miami (☎381-8970). The hip yuppie's happy hour hangout, with free appetizers and many discounted drinks.

South Beach and around

Las Américas, 450 Lincoln Rd Mall (☎673-0560). Inexpensive, no-frills Cuban food in a cafeteria-style atmosphere.

Blue Star, at the Raleigh Hotel, 1775 Collins Ave (☎534-1775). An intimate restaurant patronized by the famous and fashionable; expensive but divinely chic.

Caffè Cozzolino, 1627 Michigan Ave (☎672-2042). Good, inexpensive Italian food in a loft setting in the Lincoln Road arts district.

Casona de Carlitos, 2232 Collins Ave (☎534-7013). Hearty Argentinian food and live music, lots of Latin-style pasta and grilled red meat.

Chrysanthemum, 1248 Washington Ave (☎531-5656). Superb Peking and Szechuan cooking at moderate prices; a surprise in a city not known for quality Chinese food.

Cielito Lindo, 1626 Pennsylvania Ave (☎673-0480). Low-cost Mexican food is served with a smile in this cosy restaurant, handily placed just off Lincoln Road.

Da Leo Trattoria Toscana, 819 Lincoln Rd (☎674-0354). A reliable Italian restaurant serving authentic fare at budget prices.

David's Coffee Shop, corner of Eleventh St and Collins Ave (☎534-8763). Low-priced Latin food served all day and night to a crowd that's sleazy but discerning. See "24-Hour Eats".

Eleventh Street Diner, 1065 Washington Ave (☎534-6373). All-American fare served around the clock on Fri and Sat; eat inside in cosy booths or outside on the terrace.

Granny Feelgood's, 647 Lincoln Rd (☎673-0408). An interesting selection of vegetarian food and sandwiches plus a few chicken and fish dishes. Inexpensive–moderate.

Joe's Stone Crab, 227 Biscayne St (☎673-0365). Only open from October to May when Florida stone crabs are in season; expect long lines of people waiting to pay $20 for a succulent plateful.

Larios on the Beach, 820 Ocean Drive (☎532-9577). Best known for being owned by singer Gloria Estefan rather than for its sophisticated – and surprisingly affordable – "Nuevo Cubano" food served in a Latin nightclub atmosphere; when the live band strikes up, the diners dance.

Lulu's, 1053 Washington Ave (☎532-6147). Deep-south home cooking: fried chicken, greens, black-eyed peas and more, but you pay for the Elvis Presley memorabilia on the walls.

Maiko Japanese Restaurant, 1255 Washington Ave (☎531-6369). Highly imaginative sushi creations are what make this moderately- priced restaurant so popular.

Mappy's, 1390 Ocean Drive (☎532-2064). Good, cheap Cuban food lures beach bums and tourists, as does the fresh-squeezed-juice bar and the tropical milk shakes.

News Café, 800 Ocean Drive (☎538-6397). Utterly fashionable sidewalk café with extensive breakfast, lunch and dinner menu and front-row seating for the South Beach promenade.

Norma's On the Beach, 646 Lincoln Rd (☎532-2089). Jamaican cooking at its most sophisticated, most tasty – and most expensive.

Pacific Time, 915 Lincoln Rd (☎534-5979). Modern American cooking with strong East Asian influences producing excellent results at moderate prices.

Palace Bar & Grill, 1200 Ocean Ave (☎531-9077). One of the few trendy places for breakfast, opening for a party at 8am. Otherwise general, inexpensive fare including good burgers.

Puerto Sagua, 700 Collins Ave (☎673-9569). Where local Cubans meet gringos over espresso coffee, beans and rice. Cheap, filling breakfasts, lunches and dinners.

Rolo's, 38 Ocean Drive (☎532-2662). Bleach-blonds and tanned Latin surfers breakfast here before surf's up. Also serves Cuban- and American-style lunches and dinners, and stocks a formidable range of beers. See "Drinking".

The Strand, 671 Washington Ave (☎532-2340). A place to see and be seen in; offering nouvelle and regular American food for trendy regulars and slumming celebrities.

Sushi Hana, 1131 Washington Ave (☎532-1100). Large portions of beautifully presented Japanese food at unusually affordable prices.

Tap Tap Haitian Restaurant, 819 Fifth St (☎372-2898). The tastiest and most attractively presented Haitian food in Miami, at very reasonable prices. Wander around the restaurant to admire the Haitian naive murals, and visit the upstairs gallery where exhitibions on worthy Haitian themes are held.

Ted's Hideaway South, 124 Second St (no phone). Downbeat bar that proffers cheap fried chicken, steak and red beans and rice; see "Drinking".

Thai Toni, 890 Washington Ave (☎538-8424). Thai food at moderate prices in a fashionable hangout.

Toni's New Tokyo Cuisine & Sushi Bar, 1208 Washington Ave (☎673-9368). Japanese cuisine for the American palate, such as South Beach roll – eel, salmon skin scallions, cucumber and masago – among many more curiosities.

Wolfie's, 2038 Collins Ave (☎538-6626). Long-established deli drawing an entertaining mix of New York retirees and late-night clubbers – all served generous helpings by beehive-haired waitresses. Open 24 hours, and serving $1.99 "breakfast specials" throughout the day.

World Resources, 719 Lincoln Rd (☎534-9095). Excellent, inexpensive Thai food served in an informal sidewalk café setting. Live Asian, African and other music is played nightly.

Northern Beaches and around

Bangkok Orchid, 2576 Miami Gardens Drive (☎935-1456). Delicious Thai meals along a stretch lacking any other remotely exotic eateries.

Café Prima Pasta, 414 71st St (☎867-0106). One of the best Italian restaurants in Miami – and one of the least expensive. The place is tiny, so arrive early.

Chef Allen's, 19088 NE 29th Ave (☎935-2900). Outstanding "New Floridian" cuisine created by Allen Susser, widely rated as one of America's greatest chefs. Only dine here if money's not a problem.

Nino's Spaghetti House, 6984 Collins Ave (☎866-4102). A great choice for cheap, tasty pasta and polenta dishes.

Pineapples, 530 41st St (☎532-9731). Fresh juices, plus a range of vegetarian dishes and fabulous desserts.

Rascal House, 17190 Collins Ave (☎947-4581). Largest, loudest and most authentic New York deli in town; huge portions and cafeteria ambience.

Salty's, 10880 Collins Ave (☎945-6065). Sophisticated American cuisine at surprisingly affordable rates.

Brunch

Sunday **brunch** in Miami is usually a more upmarket affair than its equivalent in New York or Los Angeles; high-quality buffet food is laid out in a stylish setting, and only occasionally accompanied by cheap drinks. Served from 11am to 2pm, brunch costs $5–30 depending on the quality of the food; again, check the newspapers for up-to-the-minute offers, or simply show up with a big appetite at one of the establishments listed below – all in Miami Beach unless stated.

Brunch spots

Beach Villa Chinese Restaurant, at the *Beach Paradise Hotel*, 600 Ocean Drive (☎532-2679). Excellent dim sum brunch on Sat and Sun.

Biltmore Hotel, 1200 Anastasia Ave, Coral Gables (☎445-1926). Miami's most expensive brunch in the city's most historic hotel; overpriced but a worthwhile one-off indulgence.

Colony Bistro, 736 Ocean Drive (☎673-6776). Gourmet brunch served in a small but stylish sidewalk cafe; great for people-watching.

The Dining Galleries, at the *Fontuinebleau Hotel*, 4441 Collins Ave (☎538-2000). Gargantuan buffet and doting service; also a sneaky way to glimpse the inside of this Fifties landmark hotel.

Grand Café, at the *Grand Bay Hotel*, 2669 S Bayshore Drive, Coconut Grove (☎858-0009). Fine food and lots of it in a very chic dining room – attracts the well-heeled glutton.

Sundays on the Bay, 5420 Biscayne Blvd, Key Biscayne (☎361-6777). The biggest and most enjoyable brunch in Miami; make a reservation to avoid waiting in line.

Drinking

Miami's **drinking** is more commonly done in restaurants, nightclubs and discos than in the seedy bars so beloved of American film-makers. One or two dimly lit dives do capture the essence of the archetypal US bar, however, and a handful of Irish and British pubs stock imported ales. But boozing in restaurant lounges, back rooms of music spots or shorefront hotel bars is more in keeping with the spirit of the city. Most places where you can drink are open from 11am or noon until midnight or 2am, with the liveliest hours between 10pm and 1am. Among the following listings, some are suited to an early evening, pre-dinner tipple, while others – especially those in Coconut Grove and Miami Beach – make prime vantage points for watching the city's poseurs come and go. Prices are broadly similar, though the most pose-worthy places sometimes charge way above the average.

Downtown and around

Churchill's Hideaway, 5501 NE Second Ave (☎757-1807). A British enclave within Little Haiti, with soccer and rugby matches on video and UK beers on tap. See also "Live Music".

Firehouse Four, 1000 S Miami Ave (☎379-1923). By day filled by expense-account eaters (see "Eating"), in the evening Miami's oldest fire station makes a fine spot for a drink.

Tobacco Road, 626 S Miami Ave (☎374-1198). Crusty R&B venue (see "Live Music") that sees plenty of serious boozing in its downstairs bar.

Coral Gables

The Crown and Garter Pub, 270 Catolonia Ave (☎441-0204). Bar food staples plus Guinness, Bass and cider on tap contribute to making this a popular place for resident Brits and Anglophiles of all nationalities.

Duffy's Tavern, 2108 SW 57th Ave (☎264-6580). Pool tournaments and a large TV screen beaming sports events for the athletically minded drinker.

Hofbrau Pub & Grill, 172 Giralda Ave (☎442-2730). A fairly upmarket dining place with a mellow, tavern-like atmosphere.

John Martin's, 253 Miracle Mile (☎445-3777). Irish pub and restaurant with occasional folk singers and harpists accompanying a good batch of imported brews. See "Live Music".

Coconut Grove

Fat Tuesday, inside CocoWalk, 3015 Grand Ave (☎441-2992). Part of a chain of bars famous for fruit-flavoured frozen daiquiris, which you can imbibe while observing the milling crowds.

Hungry Sailor, 3064· Grand Ave (☎444-9359). A would-be British pub with overpriced Bass and Watneys on tap, though the atmosphere is made by the nightly live reggae; see "Live Music".

Monty's Bayshore Restaurant, 2560 S Bayshore Drive (☎858-1431). Drinkers often outnumber the diners (see "Eating"), drawn here by the gregarious mood and the views across the bay.

Taurus, 3540 Main Hwy (☎448-0633). Old Coconut Grove drinking institution, with a burger grill on weekends and a nostalgic Sixties-loving crowd.

Tavern in the Grove, 3416 Main Hwy (☎447-3884). Down-to-earth locals' haunt with bouncy jukebox and easy-going mood.

Key Biscayne

Bayside Seafood Restaurant, 3501 Rickenbacker Causeway (☎361-0808). Friendly beer-drinking crowd beside the bay. See "Eating" and "Live Music".

The Sandbar, at *Silver Sands Motel & Villas*, 301 Ocean Drive (☎361-5441). The poolside bar is a prime site for sipping cocktails as the ocean crashes close by.

South Beach

Clevelander, 1020 Ocean Drive (☎531-3485). The ultimate poolside sports bar, with pool tables, sports-tuned TVs and partially-clothed athletic physiques attacking the brews.

Irish House, 1430 Alton Rd (☎534-5667). Old neighbourhood bar with two well-used pool tables.

Mac's Club Deuce, 222 Fourteenth St (☎531-6200). Raucous neighbourhood bar open until 5am, with a CD jukebox, pool table and a clientele that includes cops, transvestites, artists and models.

Rebar, 1121 Washington Ave (☎672-4788). The South Beach bar for the fashionably grungy.

Shabeen Cookshack, at the *Marlin Hotel*, 1200 Collins Ave. Upmarket Jamaican-style watering hole gently throbbing to recorded reggae.

Ted's Hideaway South, 124 Second St (no phone). Beer for a dollar a can and special reductions on draft when it rains outside; serves basic bar food around the clock. See "Food" and "24-Hour Eats".

Nightlife

Miami's **nightlife** has taken a profound turn for the better since the days when leggy cabaret shows were the high point of the action. Right now, in every sense except the literal one, Miami is a very cool place to dance, drink and simply hang out in **clubs** rated by the cognoscenti as among the hippest in the world. The appeal of the trendiest clubs – few in number and secreted about Miami Beach's South Beach, shifting their name and changing site frequently – may fade once their novelty wears off and too many people come looking for them, but for the time being an air of excitement and vibrancy hangs over the scene and there are plenty of fresh ideas to excite the most jaded clubber. Read *New Times* for the latest raves – or, better still, quiz any likely-looking groover that you encounter around the cafés and bars of South Beach. If you don't give a fig for fashion and just want to dance your socks off, there are plenty of mainstream **discos** – no different from discos the world over – where you can do just that. More adventurously, track down one of the city's **salsa** or **merengue** (a slinky dance music from the Caribbean) clubs, hosted by Spanish-speaking DJs.

Not surprisingly, Fridays and Saturdays are the busiest, but there's a decent choice on any night and some of the mainstream discos boost their midweek crowds by offering cut-price drinks, free admission for women and bizarre asides such as aerobics shows and amateur strip contests. Most places open at 9pm, but don't even think of turning up before 11pm as they only hit a peak between midnight and 2am – although some continue until 7 or 8am and provide a free breakfast buffet for survivors. Usually there's a **cover charge** of $4–10 and a **minimum age** of 21 (it's normal for ID to be checked). Obviously you should dress with some sensitivity to the style of the club, but only by turning up in rags at the smartest door are you ever likely to be turned away on account of your clothes. All the following are in Miami Beach's South Beach unless stated otherwise. (For gay- and lesbian-oriented nightlife, see p.113.)

Clubs and discos

Bash, 655 Washington Ave (☎538-2274). Many revellers get no further than the garden, though there's an intimate bar and a beckoning dance floor in this club co-owned by Madonna's ex Sean Penn and Simply Red's Mick Hucknall; no cover.

Cameo Theatre, 1445 Washington Ave (☎673-8679). Each night this Art Deco one-time film theatre sees different fare, from disco to punk to world beat. Attracts a young crowd; cover varies.

Chili Pepper, 621 Washington Ave (531-9661). Currently one of South Beach's hippest clubs, attracting a mainly young crowd. Features live music most nights, and is one of the few clubs where it's fine to arrive early – from 11.30pm, that is; cover varies.

Club Manhattan, 6600 Red Rd, South Miami (☎666-1335). Reggae, rap and house music most nights; cover varies.

Disco Inferno, Sun at the Cameo Theater, 1445 Washington Ave (☎534-5533). Riproaring Seventies trash disco celebrating the Bee Gees, Village People, Chic and other greats of the genre; $7.

Groove Jet, 323 23rd St (☎532-20020. Very trendy and becoming a place to be seen in. Dress up and arrive late.

Union Bar & Grill, 653 Washington Ave (☎672-9958). Pass through the rooms decorated as an English gentleman's club and you'll find a psychedelic disco room; usually no cover.

Warsaw Ballroom, 1450 Collins Ave (☎531-4555). The dingiest and busiest nightspot in town; Friday is exclusively gay (see "Gay and Lesbian Miami"), but Saturday is "straight night" and Wednesday is a riotous "strip night"; cover $5–10.

Salsa and merengue clubs

Bonfire, 1060 NE 79th St, Little Haiti (☎756-0200). Smooth and very danceable salsa sounds Wed–Sun; $2–5.

Club Tipico Dominicano, 1344 NW 36th St, Little Havana (☎634-7819). Top merengue DJ hosting the sessions Fri–Sun; $5.

El Inferno, 981 SW Eighth St, Little Havana (☎856-5523). Popular local disco with Latin grooves Fri & Sat; $6.

Live music

In a city that still goes crazy over the studio-based Latin-pop of local girl Gloria Estefan, you might not expect to find a **live music** scene at all in Miami. In fact, an impressive number of **locales** – many of them poky clubs or the back rooms of restaurants or hotels – host bands throughout the week. It's often a matter of quantity over quality, however. Be they glam, goth, indie or metal, the city's **rock bands** tend to be pale imitations of the better-known US and European groups who periodically add Miami to their tour schedules. **Jazz** fans fare slightly better, and there's a trustworthy **R&B** site plus a very minor **folk** scene. It's **reggae**, however, that's most worth seeking out; aside from acts flying in from Jamaica, the musicians among Miami's sizeable Jamaican population appear regularly at several small spots. There's a rare chance to hear live **Haitian** music in Miami, but for **country** sounds you'll have to leave the city altogether.

Other than for megastar performers (see below), to see a band you've heard of, expect to pay $6–15; for a local act, admission will be $2–5 or free. Most places open up at 8 or 9pm, with the main band onstage around 11pm or midnight.

The most comprehensive music **listings** are in *New Times*, but if you can't decide where to go on a Friday night, go along to South Pointe Park (see "Miami Beach"), where there's entertainment and usually a **free concert**; look for the posters strewn all over South Beach.

Miami also gets its share of **big performances**, with the venues listed below – none of which has much atmosphere – attracting top names in rock, soul, jazz, reggae and funk; tickets are $18–35 from a branch of *Ticketmaster* (outlets all over the city; phone ☎358-5885 for the nearest) or over the phone by credit card.

Rock, jazz and R&B

Cameo Theater, 1445 Washington Ave (☎532-0922). *The* spot for weird and wonderful lefty arty happenings, poetry readings and interesting bands. Cover varies.

Churchill's Hideaway, 5501 NE Second Ave, Little Haiti (☎757-1807). Good place to hear local hopeful rock and indie bands; $4–6. See "Drinking".

Mango's Tropical Cafe, 900 Ocean Drive (☎673-4422). It's hard to stand still when the Brazilian and Cuban bands who play on this terrace strike up. Usually no cover.

Peacock Café, 2977 McFarlane Rd, Coconut Grove (☎442-8833). Back-room lounge features jazz, blues and occasional rock acts; cover varies.

BIG PERFORMANCE VENUES

James L. Knight Center, 400 SE Second Ave, downtown Miami (☎372-0277).

Joe Robbie Stadium, 2269 NW 199th St, 16 miles northwest of downtown Miami (☎623-6262).

Miami Arena, 721 NW First Ave, downtown Miami (☎530-4400).

Sunshine Music Theater, 5555 NW 95th St, north of downtown Miami (☎741-7400).

Scully's Tavern, 9809 Sunset Drive, South Miami (☎271-7404). Rock and blues bands playing for beer-drinking, pool-playing regulars; free.

Stephen Talkhouse, 616 Collins Ave (☎531-7557). Coffee-house ambience that makes a comfortable setting for semi-established bands of various musical persuasions.

Studio One 83, 2860 NW 183 St, Overtown (☎621-7295). Powerful rap, soul and reggae, but located in a dangerous area north of downtown Miami; $5–15.

Tobacco Road, 626 S Miami Ave, downtown Miami (☎374-1198). Earthy R&B from some of the country's finest exponents. See "Drinking". Free–$6.

Washington Square, 645 Washington Ave (☎534-5019). Showcase for Miami's aspiring rock and glam acts, plus periodic indie-inspired fare; $2–10.

Reggae

Bayside Hut, 3501 Rickenbacker Causeway, Key Biscayne (☎361-0808). Bayside reggae jams on Fri and Sat; free.

Hungry Sailor, 3064· Grand Ave, Coconut Grove (☎444-9359). Reggae bands fill the tiny corner stage of this attempted English pub almost every night; free–$3. See "Eating" and "Drinking").

Rockers Café, 216 Española Way (☎537-7701). Big names from Jamaica, top local talent and, without live bands, a rootsy reggae disco (see "Nightlife"); free–$20.

Sunday's on the Bay, 5420 Crandon Blvd, Key Biscayne (☎361-6777). Unlikely but lively setting for live reggae Thurs–Sun; free. See "Eating".

Folk

JohnMartin's, 253 Miracle Mile, Coral Gables (☎445-3777). Spacious Irish bar (see "Drinking") and restaurant with Irish folk music several evenings a week; free.

Our Place Folk Club, 830 Washington Ave (☎674-1322). Folk musicians and floor singers several nights a week in a wholefood eatery; free–$2. See "Eating".

Haitian music

Aux Palmistes Chez Julie, 6820 NE Second Ave, Little Haiti (☎759-8527). Great live Haitian music from 10pm to 4am on Fri and Sat; free–$5. See "Eating".

Obsession, 69 NE 79th St, Little Haiti (☎756-7575). Best place in Miami for the hottest Haitian sounds; $8–10.

Tap Tap, 819 Fifth St, South Beach (☎372-2898). Best known for its excellent restaurant (see "Eating"), interesting gallery and regular live Haitian music – phone ahead for details.

Classical music, dance and opera

The Miami-based New World Symphony orchestra (☎673-3331) gives concert experience to some of the finest graduate **classical** musicians in the US. Its season runs from October to April with most performances at the Lincoln Theater or the Gusman Center for the Performing Arts; tickets $10–30. For better-known names, look out for top-flight soloists guesting with the Miami Chamber Symphony (☎858-3500), usually at the Gusman Concert Hall; tickets $15–30.

The city's two major professional **dance** companies, the Miami City Ballet (☎532-4800) and the Ballet Theater of Miami (☎442-4840), appear at the Gusman Center for Performing Arts; tickets are $15–45, but the Miami City Ballet also holds cut-price, dress-rehearsal shows at the Colony Theater for under $10. A third group is the Ballet Flamenco La Rosa (☎672-0552), whose frenetic Latin dance productions take place at the Colony Theater; tickets $10–20.

CENTERS FOR CLASSICAL MUSIC AND PERFORMING ARTS

Colony Theater, 1040 Lincoln Rd, Miami Beach (☎673-1026).
Dade County Auditorium, 2901 W Flagler St, downtown Miami (☎547-5414).
Gusman Center for the Performing Arts, 174 E Flagler St, downtown Miami (☎372-0925).

Gusman Concert Hall, 1314 Miller Drive, University of Miami (☎284-2438).
Jackie Gleason Center of the Performing Arts, 1700 Washington Blvd, Miami Beach (☎673-7300).
Lincoln Theater, 55 Lincoln Rd, Miami Beach (☎673-3300).

Opera is the poor relation of classical music and dance despite the efforts of the Greater Miami Opera Association (☎854-1643), which brings impressive names to varied programmes at the Dade County Auditorium; tickets $10–60.

Comedy

Whether it's the difficulty of finding jokes to span Miami's multicultural population, or simply its geographical distance from the stand-up comedy hotbeds of New York and Los Angeles, the city is very short of **comedy clubs**, although those it does have draw enthusiastic crowds and often comparatively big names. Admission will be $5–10; phone for show times.

Comedy clubs

Coconut's Comedy Club, at *Howard Johnsons Hotel*, 16500 NW Second Ave, North Miami (☎461-1161). Showcasing comic talent on the way up – or down. Thurs only.
Improv Comedy Club, inside CocoWalk, 3015 Grand Ave, Coconut Grove (☎441-8200). One of the nationwide chain of Improv comedy clubs and the best place in Miami for comedy, despite the rather formal atmosphere. Reservations required.

Theatre

It may be small, but Miami's **theatre** scene is of an encouragingly good standard. Winter is the busiest period, though something worth seeing crops up almost every week on the alternative circuit. If you're fluent in Spanish, make a point of visiting one of the city's **Spanish-language theatres**, whose programmes are listed in the Friday *El Neuvo Herald*: Bellas Artes (a supplement of the *Miami Herald* newspaper), 2173 SW Eighth St (☎325-0515), *Teatro Martí*, 420 SW Eighth St (☎545-7866), *Teatro Trail*, 3717 SW Eighth St (☎448-0592), are three of the best; tickets are $12–15.

Major and alternative theatres

Coconut Grove Playhouse, 3500 Main Hwy , Coconut Grove (☎442-4000). Comfortable and well-established mainstream theatre that bucks up its schedule with many interesting experimental efforts; $10–35.
Miami Actors Studio, 1150 SW 22nd St, Coral Gables (☎666-6992). Small showcase for the city's best acting talent, going through their paces in a mixed-bag of plays, usually Fri, Sat and Sun only; $5–10.

Minorca Playhouse, 232 Minorca Ave, Coral Gables (☎446-1116). Main base of the Florida Shakespeare Company, with Elizabethan drama throughout the year; $18–25.

New Theater, 4275 Aurora St, Coral Gables (☎595-4260). Sitting neatly between mainstream and alternative, a nice place for a relaxing evening; $8–18.

Ring Theater, at the University of Miami, 1312 Miller Drive (☎284-3355). Assorted offerings year-round from the drama students of the University of Miami; $5–18.

Film

Except for the **Miami Film Festival** (details on ☎444-FILM), ten days and nights of new films from far and wide each February at the Gusman Center for Performing Arts, Miami is barren territory for film buffs. Most **film theatres** are multiscreen affairs inside shopping malls showing first-run American features. Look at the *Weekend* section of the Friday *Miami Herald* for complete listings, call the *Movie Hotline* (☎888-FILM), or try Omni 10, in the Omni mall at 1601 Biscayne Boulevard; Cinema 10, in the Miracle Center mall, 3301 Coral Way; the 8-screen AMC in the CocoWalk, 3015 Grand Avenue; and Movies at the Falls, in the The Falls mall, 8888 Howard Drive; admission is $4–8.

For **arthouse**, **foreign-language** or fading monochrome **classic** films, find out what's playing at the Alliance Film/Video Project, 927 Lincoln Rd (☎531-8504), or at the University of Miami's Beaumont Cinema, 1111 Memorial Drive (☎284-4177), both liable to have interesting films for $2–5. Local **libraries** have screenings, as does the Bass Museum of Art, 2100 Collins Ave (☎673-7530), on Tuesdays – newspaper listings carry details.

Gay and lesbian Miami

Miami's **gay** and **lesbian** communities are enjoying the city's boom times as much as anyone else, with a growing number of gay-owned businesses, bars and clubs opening up around the city. The scene, traditionally focusing on Coconut Grove, has recently gathered great momentum on South Beach. In either of these areas, most public places are friendly and welcoming towards gays and lesbians – though attitudes in other parts of Miami can sometimes be considerably less enlightened. The key source of info is the free *TWN* (*The Weekly News*), available from any of the places listed below and from many of the mixed bars and clubs around Coconut Grove and South Beach.

Resources

Gay Community Bookstore, 7545 Biscayne Blvd (☎754-6900). Copious books, magazines and newspapers of gay and lesbian interest.

Gay and Lesbian Community Hotline, phone ☎759-3661 for a recorded message which gives access – via touch-tone dialling – to more recorded info on gay bars and events, gay-supportive businesses, doctors and lawyers, and much more.

Lambda Passages, 1665 Michigan Ave, South Beach (☎538-5822). A good gay- and lesbian-oriented bookstore with a small general collection as well.

Gay and lesbian bars, clubs and discos

Andrea's, 2890 SW 27th Ave, Coconut Grove (☎444-0200). A women-only disco especially noted for its theme nights – phone ahead for details.

Cheers, 5922 S Dixie Hwy, South Miami (☎667-4753). Cruisy, predominantly gay male bar with video room and pool tables under the stars; Monday is ladies' night, but women also drop in on the Friday disco.

On the Waterfront, 3615 NW S River Drive (☎635-5500). Latino and black gays dancing to salsa; Thurs is the best night.

Paragon, 1235 Washington Ave (☎534-1235). No place for the faint-hearted: the decadent *Paragon* has pulsating music, laser lights, shameless male go-go dancers, drag queens and much, much more; cover $5.

Sugars, 13705 Biscayne Blvd, North Miami (☎940-9887). Predominantly black gay club.

Uncle Charlie's, 3673 Bird Ave, South Miami (☎442-8687). Hardcore gay male bar, with music and much partying; women a rarity.

Warsaw Ballroom, 1450 Collins Ave, Miami Beach (☎1-800/9-WARSAW). While not exclusively gay (see "Nightlife"), this is the busiest and biggest gay disco in town.

Women's Miami

Though it lacks the extended networks of Los Angeles or New York, Miami is steadily becoming a better place for **women** seeking the support and solidarity of other women in business, artistic endeavour, or simply looking for a reliable and inexpensive source of medical care.

Women's organizations

Women's Caucus for Art Miami, 561 NW 32nd St (☎576-0041). Charitable organization striving to raise women's profile in the visual arts; membership open to men.

Women's Chamber of Commerce of South Florida, suite 310, 7700 SW 88th St (☎446-6660). Promoting women-owned and women-run businesses throughout south Florida.

Health care and counselling centres

Eve Medical Center, 3900 NW 79th Ave (☎591-2288). Low-cost medical care and abortions in serene, supportive environment.

Miami Women's Healthcenter, at North Shore Medical Center, suite 301, 1100 NW 95th St (☎835-6165). Education, information, support and discussion groups, physician referrals, mammograms, seminars and workshops.

Planned Parenthood of Greater Miami, 11632 N Kendal Drive, South Miami (☎593-6363). Economical health care for men and women; including birth control supplies, pregnancy testing, treatment of sexually transmitted diseases and counselling.

Women's Care, 68A NE 167th St (☎947-0885). Inexpensive private clinic specializing in abortions and offering complete gynecological services.

Women's Resource & Counselling Center, 1108 Ponce de Leon Blvd (☎448-8325). Friendly clinic providing individual, marriage, group and family counselling, psychotherapy and assertiveness training.

The stores

Shopping for the sake of it isn't the big deal in Miami that it is in some American cities, though there's plenty of opportunity for eager consumers to exercise their credit cards. Bizarre as it may seem, Miami leads the field in **shopping mall** architecture, blowing millions of dollars on environments intended subtly to soften the hard commercialism of the stores which fill them – several malls are worthy of investigation for this reason alone. These days, old-style **department stores**, such as the dependable *Macy's* and *Sears Roebuck & Co*, generally show up inside the malls too, but Miami has one dignified survivor, *Burdines*, that stands alone.

The closer you get to the beach, the wackier Miami's **clothes** shops become – look out for zebra-print bikinis and Art Deco shirts. However, the best places for quality togs at discounted rates are the designer outlets of the **fashion district**, on Fifth Avenue between 25th and 29th streets, just north of downtown Miami; here you'll find classy outfits – most of Latin American origin – at slashed prices. With less finesse, there can be finds amid the discarded garb filling the city's **thrift stores**.

Unless you're existing on a shoestring budget – or are preparing a picnic – you won't need to shop for **food and drink** at all, although supermarkets like *Publix* and *Winn-Dixie*, usually open until 10pm, are plentiful – flip through the phone book to locate the nearest one. You can buy alcohol from supermarkets and, of course, from the many **liquor stores**, but if you're looking for quality grub or booze, only the largest of the supermarkets and a few specialist suppliers will oblige.

Gun shops have long outnumbered **bookshops** in Miami, but large discount chains like *B. Dalton's* and *Waldenbrooks* have arrived, with branches in shopping malls, and there are also a few local outlets stocking quality reading material. Some of the city's **record** shops make good browsing territory, too, their contents spanning everything from doo-wop rarities to the smoothest salsa hits.

The Malls . . . and Burdines department store

Aventura Mall, just north of 192nd St Causeway, North Miami Beach (☎935-4222). One of the largest air-conditioned malls in the state, boasting virtually every major department store: Macy's, Sears, J C Penney. Pick up a map on entry or you'll never find your way out.

Bal Harbour Shops, 9700 Collins Ave, Miami Beach (☎866-0311). Don't come to buy but to watch designer-shopping in a temple of upmarket consumerism.

Bayside Marketplace, 401 Biscayne Blvd, near downtown Miami (☎577-3344). Squarely aimed at tourists, but a good blend of diverse stores – selling everything from Art Deco ashtrays to bubblegum – beside the bay, with some excellent food stands.

Burdines, 22 E Flagler St, downtown Miami (☎577-2191). Run-of-the-mill clothes, furnishings and domestic appliances, but Miami's oldest department store – circa 1936 – is an entertaining place to cruise.

CocoWalk, 3015 Grand Ave, Coconut Grove (☎444-0777). In the heart of Coconut Grove, has a relatively small range of stores, some good places to eat and a decent multiplex cinema.

Dadeland Mall, 7535 N Kendall Drive, South Miami (☎665-6226). More top-class department stores and speciality shops in a totally enclosed, air-conditioned environment conducive to passionate shopping.

The Falls, Hwy-1 and SW 136th St, South Miami (☎255-4570). Sit inside a gazebo and contemplate the waterfalls and the rainforest that prettify suburban Miami's classiest set of shops.

Florida Keys Factory Shops, 250 E Palm Drive, Florida City/Homestead (☎248-4727). Located where the Florida Turnpike meets Hwy-1 and conveniently located for people travelling to the Keys or Everglades. Dedicated shoppers will find huge savings on name brands.

Lincoln Road Mall, South Beach. Not a shopping mall in the usual sense of the word, but, between Washington Ave and Alton Road, a pedestrian-only road lined with stores. Many are given over to art galleries, but there's also a whole range of trendy clothes stores and many excellent sidewalk cafés and restaurants.

Mayfair-in-the-Grove, 3000 Florida Ave, Coconut Grove (☎448-1700). The expensive stores take second place to the landscaped tropical foliage and the discreetly placed classical sculptures.

Clothes and thrift stores

Coral Gables Congregational Church Thrift Shop, 3010 De Soto Blvd, Coral Gables (☎445-1721). After viewing the church (see "Coral Gables"), drop into the interestingly stocked thrift store next door.

Details at the Beach, 1149 Washington Ave (☎672-0175). Interesting clothing and furnishings in a store sure to delight interior designers.

Miami Twice, 6562 SW 40th St (☎666-0127). Department store specializing in vintage clothing, accessories and some furniture.

One Hand Clapping, 432 Española Way, Miami Beach (☎532-0507). Amid a wondrous assortment of antique junk, there are hats, dresses and scarves to delight the time-warped flapper.

Food and drink

Epicure Market, 1656 Alton Rd, Miami Beach (☎672-1861). Tasty morsels for the gourmet palate and a mouthwatering array of hot foods for immediate consumption.

Estate Wines and Gourmet Foods, 92 Miracle Mile, Coral Gables (☎442-9915). Alongside the fine foods, an exquisite stock of wines chosen with the connoisseur in mind.

Books

Books & Books, 296 Aragon Ave, Coral Gables (☎442-4408) and a small branch at 933 Lincoln Rd, Miami Beach (☎532-3222). Excellent stock of general titles but especially strong on Floridian art and design, travel and new fiction; also has author signings and talks: ☎444-POEM for the latest events.

Downtown Book Center, 247 SE First St, downtown Miami (☎377-9939). Large selection ranging from the latest blockbusters to esoteric and academic tomes.

Gables Booksellers, 345 Miracle Mile, Coral Gables (☎446-7215). Used books on all subjects at surprisingly reasonable prices.

Grove Antiquarian, 3318 Virginia St, Coconut Grove (☎444-5362). A relaxing oasis in the heart of lively Coconut Grove stocking quality used books and some valuable first editions covering all subjects.

Records, CDs and tapes

Lily's Records, 1260 SW Eighth St, Little Havana (☎856-0536). Unsurpassed stock of salsa, merengue and other Latin sounds.

KowTow Music, 1249 Washington Ave, Miami Beach (☎538-0938). Comprehensive selection spanning most musical tastes.

Yesterday & Today, 1614 Alton Rd, Miami Beach (☎534-8704). Dusty piles of blues, jazz, R&B and Sixties indie rarities.

Cuban curios

Ba-Balú!, 432 Española Way, South Beach (☎538-0679). Beach towels, coffee mugs and T-shirts sporting anti-Castro slogans or Cuban flags, CDs and tapes of Cuban music, guayaberas and cigars make original south Florida souvenirs.

Coral Way Antiques, 3131 Coral Way, Coral Gables (☎567-3131). Old postcards, books, military items and other Cuban "collectables".

MIAMI AND MIAMI BEACH FESTIVALS

The precise dates of the **festivals** listed below vary from year to year; check the details at any tourist information office or Chamber of Commerce.

January

Mid *Art Deco Weekend*: on Ocean Drive in the South Beach; talks and free events concerning the area's architecture.

Taste of the Grove: Pig out on food and free music in Coconut Grove's Peacock Park.

Late *Homestead Frontier Days*: home cooking and home-made arts and crafts at Harris Field in Homestead.

February

Early *Miami Film Festival*: latest US and overseas films premiered in downtown Miami's Gusman Center for the Performing Arts.

Mid *Coconut Grove Arts Festival*: hundreds of (mostly) talented unknowns display their works in Coconut Grove's Peacock Park and the nearby streets.

Late *Miami Grand Prix*: high-performance motor race which screeches around the streets of downtown Miami.

March

Early *Calle Ocho Festival*: massive festival of Cuban arts, crafts and cooking along the streets of Little Havana.

Carnival Miami: an offshoot of the Calle Ocho festival, with Hispanic-themed events across the city culminating in a parade at the Orange Bowl.

April

Early *Miracle Mile Festival*: parades and floats along Miracle Mile singing the praises of Coral Gables.

Coconut Grove Seafood Festival: an excuse to eat loads of seafood in Coconut Grove's Peacock Park.

June

Early *Goombay Festival*: a spirited bash in honor of Bahamian culture, in and around Coconut Grove's Peacock Park.

Art in the Park: arty stalls and displays in the Charles Deering Estate in South Miami.

August

First Sunday *Miami Reggae Festival*: celebration of Jamaican Independence Day with dozens of top Jamaican bands playing around the city.

September

Mid *Festival Miami*: three weeks of performing and visual arts events organized by the University of Miami, mostly taking place in Coral Gables.

October

Hispanic Heritage Festival: lasts all month and features innumerable events linked to Latin American history and culture.

Early *Caribbean-American Carnival*: a joyous cavalcade of soca and calypso bands in Bicentennial Park.

November

Mid *Miami Book Fair International*: a wealth of tomes from across the world spread across the campus of Miami-Dade Community College in downtown Miami.

December

26–1 Jan *Indian Arts Festival*: Native American artisans from all over the country gather at the Miccosukee Village to display their work.

30 *King Mango Strut*: a very alternative New Year's Eve celebration, with part-time cross-dressers and clowns parading through Coconut Grove.

31 *Orange Bowl Parade*: mainstream climax of the New Year bashes all over the city, with floats, marching bands and the crowning of the Orange Bowl Queen at the Orange Bowl stadium.

Listings

Airlines *Air Canada*, Airport Concourse G (☎1-800-776-3000); *American Airlines*, 150 Alhambra Plaza (☎1-800-433-7300); *British Airways*, 354 SE First St (☎1-800/249-9297); *Continental*, Airport Concourse "C" (☎1-800/525-0280); *Delta*, 201 Alhambra Circle (☎1-800/ 221-1212); *Northwest Airlines*, 150 Alhambra Plaza (☎1-800/225-2525);*TWA*, Airport Concourse "G" (☎1-800/221-2000); *United*, 178 Giralda Ave (☎1-800/241-6522); *USAIR*, 150 Alhambra Plaza (☎1-800/428-4322); *Virgin Atlantic*, 225 Alhambra Circle (☎1-800/862-8621).

Airport Miami International, six miles west of downtown Miami. Take local bus #7 from downtown Miami (an approximately half-hour journey), local bus #J from Miami Beach (around 40min), or a shuttle bus: *Airporter* (☎247-8874); *Red Top* (☎526-5764); *Super Shuttle* (☎871-2000). More details on p.55.

American Express Offices around the city: in downtown Miami, Suite 100, 330 Biscayne Blvd (☎358/7350); in Coral Gables, 32 Miracle Mile (☎446-3381); in Miami Beach, at Bal Harbour Shops, 9700 Collins Ave (☎865-5959).

Amtrak 8303 NW 37th Ave (☎1-800/872-7245).

Area Code ☎305.

Babysitting Central Sitting Agency: ☎856-0550.

Banks See "Money Exchange".

Bike rental See p.60

Boat rental Recreate the opening sequences from *Miami Vice* by skimming over Biscayne Bay in a motor boat. Equipped with 50hp engines, such vessels can be rented at hourly rates – from $45 for one hour – from *Beach Boat Rentals*, 2380 Collins Drive, Miami Beach (☎534-4307).

Coastguard ☎535-4314.

Consulates *Canada*, 1600–2000 S Biscayne Blvd (☎579-1600); *Denmark*, Suite 600, 2655 Le Jeune Rd (☎446-0020); *France*, 200 Biscayne Blvd(☎372-9541); *Germany*, Suite 2210, 100 N Biscayne Blvd (☎358-0290); *Netherlands*, in Houston, Texas (☎713/622-8000); *Norway*, Suite 525, 1001 North American Way (☎441-8780); *UK*, Suite 2110, 1001 S Bayshore Drive (☎374-1522).

Crisis Hotline ☎358-5357.

Dentists To be referred to a dentist: ☎667-3647.

Doctor To call out a physician: ☎945-6325.

Emergencies Dial ☎911 and ask for relevant emergency service.

Everglades daytrips In the absence of public transport, almost every tour operator in Miami runs half- or full-day trips ($20–35) to the Everglades, but these seldom involve more than a quick gape at an alligator and an air-boat ride – or even enter the Everglades National Park. Only *All Florida Adventure Tours* (☎1-800/33T-OUR3) and *Eco Tours Miami* (☎232-5398) operate ecology-centred tours ($80 for a day) to the park and surrounding areas; unfortunately, they rarely have places for individual travellers. The Everglades are comprehensively detailed in Chapter Six.

Gay community hotline ☎759-3661.

Hospitals with emergency rooms In Miami: *Jackson Memorial Medical Center*, 1611 NW Twelfth Ave (☎325-7200); *Mercy Hospital*, 3663 S Miami Ave (☎854-4400). In Miami Beach: *Mt Sinai Medical Center*, 4300 Alton Rd (☎674-2121); *St Francis Hospital*, 250 W 63rd St (☎868-5000).

Launderettes Check the Yellow Pages for the nearest; handiest for South Beach is the 24-hr *Clean Machine*, 230 Twelfth St.

Left Luggage At the airport, some *Greyhound* terminals (phone to be sure) and the *Amtrak* station.

Library The biggest is Metro-Dade County Public Library, 101 W Flagler St (Mon–Sat 9am–6pm, Thurs until 9pm; Oct–May also Sun 1–5pm; ☎375-2665) – see p.67.

Lost and found For something lost on *Metro-Dade Transit*, phone ☎375-3366 (Mon–Fri 8.30am–4.30pm). Otherwise call the police.

Money exchange Bring US dollar travellers cheques or cash, but if you need to change money, facilities are available at the airport and the following: *Barnett Bank*, 701 Brickell Ave (with 42 branches elsewhere; call ☎350-7143 for the nearest); *First Union National Bank*, 200 S Biscayne Blvd (☎789-5000); *Jefferson National Bank*, 301 Arthur Godfrey Rd (☎532-6451) and 18170 Collins Ave (☎935-6911); *Sun Bank*, 777 Brickell Ave (☎591-6000).

Parking fines $18, increasing to $45 if not paid within thirty days.

Pharmacies Usually open from 8am or 9am until 9pm or midnight. 24-hour pharmacies are *Eckard*, at 1825 Miami Gardens Drive (☎932-5740) and 9031 SW 107th Ave (☎274-6776); and *Walgreens*, 5731 Bird Rd (☎666-0757).

Police Non-emergency: ☎595-6263; emergency: ☎911.

Post offices In downtown Miami, 500 NW Second Ave; in Coral Gables, 251 Valencia Ave; in Coconut Grove, 3191 Grand Ave; in Homestead, 739 Washington Ave; in Key Biscayne, 59 Harbor Drive; in Miami Beach, 1300 Washington Ave and 445 W 40th St. All open Mon–Fri 8.30am–5pm, Sat 8.30am–12.30pm, or longer hours.

Rape hotline ☎549-7273.

Road conditions ☎470-5277.

Roller blading Hugely popular in Miami, especially in South Beach. *Rollertech*, at 221 7th St, South Beach (☎538-8408), and *Fritz Skates*, at 117 5th St (532-0054), both sell and rent out roller blades and safety gear, as well as offering lessons. Rental costs around $8 per hour, $24 per day, or $15 overnight (6.30pm–12 noon); to buy, prices range from $55 to $250.

Sports Miami Dolphins (☎620-2578), Florida's oldest pro football team, and the Florida Marlins (☎626-7400), the country's newest professional baseball team, play at the Joe Robbie Stadium, 2269 NW 199th St, sixteen miles northwest of downtown Miami: box office open Mon–Fri 10am–6pm; most seats are $30 for football and around $10–15 for baseball. The football season is August through to December, and the baseball season April through to October. The Miami Heat basketball team plays NBA matches at the Miami Arena, 701 Arena Blvd, three miles north of downtown Miami: info on ☎577-HEAT; tickets $14–21. The basketball season is November through to April. Miami Freedom plays soccer at Milander Park in Hialeah, seven miles northwest of downtown Miami: info on ☎888-0838; tickets $9.50. Professional ice hockey is represented by the Florida Panthers (☎530-4444) who play at the Miami Arena between October and April. Miami University's football, basketball and baseball teams are all called the Miami Hurricanes: game and ticket (usually $5–13) info Mon–Fri 8am–6pm on ☎1-800/GO-CANES.

Thomas Cook In downtown Miami: 155 SE Third Ave (☎381-9525); in Coral Gables: suite 102, 901 Ponce de Leon Blvd (☎448-0269); in Miami Beach: at the *Fountainbleau*, 4441 Collins Ave (☎674-1907).

Ticketmaster Tickets for arts and sports events, payable by credit card: ☎358-5885.

Weather/surf information ☎661-5065.

Western Union Offices all over the city; call ☎1-800/325-6000 to find the nearest.

travel details

Trains
From Miami to Deerfield Beach (2 daily; 52min); Delray Beach (2 daily; 1hr 6min); Fort Lauderdale (2 daily; 34min); Hollywood (2 daily; 20min); New York (2 daily; 29hr); Ocala (1 daily; 5hr 37min); Sebring (2 daily; 3hr 17min); St Petersburg (1 daily; 4hr 51min); Tampa (1 daily; 4hr 16min); Washington (2 daily; 22hr); West Palm Beach (2 daily; 1hr 40min); Winter Haven (2 daily; 3hr 56min).

Tri-Rail
From Miami (5–15 daily) to Boca Raton (1hr); Delray Beach (1hr 7min); Fort Lauderdale (31min); Hollywood (16min); West Palm Beach (1hr 34min).

Buses

From Miami to Daytona Beach (9 daily; 8hr 55min–9hr 50min); Fort Lauderdale (19 daily; 1hr); Fort Myers (4 daily; 5hr 35min); Fort Pierce (9 daily; 4hr); Jacksonville (9 daily; 7hr 30min); Key West (3 daily; 4hr 30min); Orlando (7 daily; 6hr 45min); Sarasota (5 daily; 7hr 35min); St Petersburg (3 daily; 9hr 50min); Tampa (5 daily; 9hr 45min–10hr 35min); West Palm Beach (12 daily; 2hr 30min).

CHAPTER TWO

THE FLORIDA KEYS

Fiction, films and folklore have given the **Florida Keys*** – a hundred-mile string of small islands running from the southeastern corner of the state to within ninety miles of Cuba – an image of sultry romance and glamorous intrigue that they don't really deserve. Throughout their length, and especially for the first sixty-odd miles, fishing, snorkelling and diving dominate – admittedly with great justification – and are ruthlessly hawked at every opportunity. The main attraction here is the **Florida Reef**, a great band of living coral just a few miles off the coast, whose multifarious forms and colours and the dazzling assortment of creatures living on it create an exceptional sight. However, if you're not planning to indulge in watersports you'll be hard pushed to find much else to fill your time. Here and there the islands' idiosyncratic history rears its head in the form of houses built by early Bahamian settlers and seedy waterside bars run by refugees from points north, plus there are some stunning natural areas and worthwhile ecology tours, but these tend to be exceptions.

One of the better places to visit the reef is the **John Pennecamp State Park**, one of the few interesting features of **Key Largo**, the biggest and by far the dullest of the keys. Like **Islamorada**, further south, Key Largo is rapidly being populated by suburban Miamians, moving here for the sailing and fishing but unable to survive without shopping malls. Islamorada is the best base for fishing, but also has some natural and historical points of note, as does the next major settlement, **Marathon** – at the centre of the key chain and thus makes a useful short-term base. Thirty miles on, the **Lower Keys** get fewer visitors and less publicity than their neighbours. Don't dismiss them, though; in many ways these are the most unusual and appealing of the whole lot, home to a tiny species of deer, covered with dense forests – and, at Looe Key, possessing a tremendous embarkation point for trips to the Florida Reef.

However much you enjoy the other keys, they're really only stops on the way to **Key West**, the final dot of the North American continent before a thousand miles of ocean – the end of the road in every sense. Shot through with an intoxicating aura of abandonment, it's a small but immensely vibrant place. The only part of the keys with a real sense of history, Key West was once – unbelievably – the richest town in the US and the largest settlement in Florida. There are old homes and museums to explore and plenty of bars in which to while away the hours.

Key West also has a couple of small **beaches**, something noticeably missing – due to the reef – elsewhere. But the absence of sand and surf is easily made up

---

* A variation on the word "cay", a key is a small island or bank composed of coral fragments. The Florida Keys are the largest grouping, but keys are common all along the state's southerly coastlines.

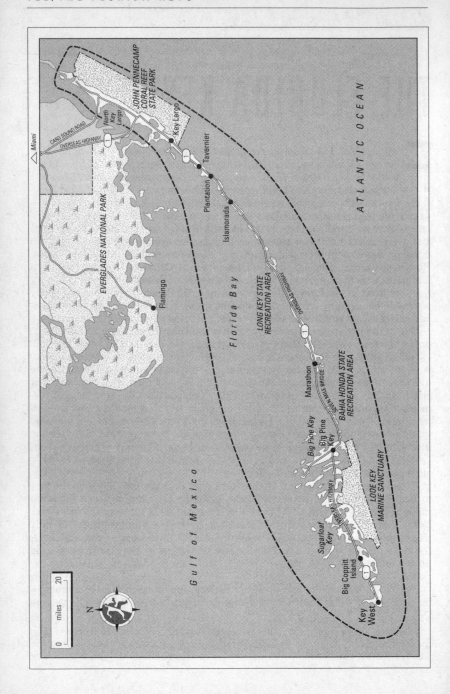

The area code for all numbers in this chapter is ☎305.

for by the keys' spectacular **sunsets**. As one early visitor, the nineteenth-century ornithologist John James Audubon, rhapsodized: "a blaze of refulgent glory streams portal of the West and the masses of vapour assume the semblance of mountains of molten gold".

Practicalities

Travelling through the keys could hardly be easier as there's just one route all the way through to Key West: the **Overseas Highway (Hwy-1)**. This is punctuated by **mile markers (MM)** – posts on which mileage is marked, starting with MM127, just south of Homestead (see *Miami & Miami Beach*), and finishing with MM0, in Key West. Most motels and restaurants are strung along the highway, often using the mile markers as addresses. **Public transport** comprises three daily *Greyhound* buses between Miami and Key West, which can be hailed down anywhere on the route (see "Travel details" at the end of the chapter), and a skeletal local bus service in Key West.

Accommodation is abundant but more expensive than on the mainland. During high season, from November to April, budget for *at least* $50–85 a night, $35–55 the rest of the year, unless you're camping – well catered for along the keys.

Note that throughout this chapter only the most basic **diving information** is given. Always take local advice before venturing into the water, and see p.40 in *Basics*.

ACCOMMODATION PRICE CODES

All **accommodation prices** in this book have been coded using the symbols below. Note that prices are for the least expensive double rooms in each establishment. For a full explanation see p.27 in *Basics*.

① up to $30	③ $45–60	⑤ $80–100	⑦ $130–180
② $30–45	④ $60–80	⑥ $100–130	⑧ $180+

North Key Largo

Assuming you're driving, the clever way to arrive in the keys is with Card Sound Road (Hwy-905A; $1.50 toll), which branches off Hwy-1 a few miles south of Homestead. Doing so avoids the bulk of the tourist traffic and, after passing through the desolate southeastern section of the Everglades, gives soaring views from Card Sound Bridge of the mangrove-dotted waters of Florida Bay (where a long wait and a lot of luck might be rewarded with a glimpse of a rare American crocodile) – and a glimpse of the keys as they all might have looked long ago before commercialism took hold.

The bulk of **North Key Largo**, where Hwy-905 touches ground, is free of development, and human habitation is marked only by the odd shack amid a rich

SWIMMING WITH DOLPHINS

Long before the Sixties TV show *Flipper* brought about a surge in their popularity, **dolphins** – marine mammals smaller than whales and differentiated from porpoises by their beak-like snout – were the subject of centuries of speculation and mythology. According to the wildest notion, dolphins once lived on land but became so disenchanted by the course of civilization at the time of Aristotle and Plato that they took to the sea, vowing to bide their time until humankind was ready to receive their wisdom. Whatever the truth, there's no disputing that dolphins are extremely intelligent, with brains similar in size to those of humans. They communicate in a **language** of clicks and whistles, and use a sonar technique called echolocation to detect food in dark waters and, perhaps, to create "sound pictures" for one another.

The world's dolphin population has been reduced by several factors, including the nets of tuna fishermen, but they are a common sight around the Florida Keys and form the star attraction of the state's many marine parks – though watching them perform somersaults in response to human commands gives just an inkling of their potential. By contrast, at the **Dolphin Research Center** (address below; Wed–Sun 9am–4pm, closed Mon & Tues) they are used in therapy programmes for cancer-sufferers and mentally handicapped children; the exceptional patience and gentleness displayed by the dolphins (all of whom are free to swim out to sea whenever they want) in this work suggest that their sonar system may allow them to make an X-ray-like scan of a body to detect abnormalities and perhaps even to "see" emotions. Take a **tour** (Wed–Sun at 10am, 12.30pm, 2pm & 3.30pm; adults $7.50, under 13s $4.50) of the research centre to become better informed on these remarkable – and still barely understood – mammals. The Dolphin Research Center is also one of three places in the Florida Keys where, by booking well ahead, you can **swim with dolphins** ($80 for around twenty minutes). Averaging seven feet long, dolphins look disconcertingly large at close quarters – and will lose interest in you long before you tire of their company – but if you do get the opportunity to join them, it's an unforgettable experience.

- In Key Largo: Dolphins Plus, MM100 (☎305/451-1993).
- In Islamorada: Theater of the Sea, MM84.5 (☎305/664-2431).
- In Marathon: Dolphin Research Center, MM59 (☎305/289-1121).

endowment of trees. Despite elaborate plans to turn the area into a city called Port Bougainvillea, with high-rise blocks and a monorail (a terrifying prospect ended by sudden bankruptcy), much of the land here is now owned and protected by the state. Scare stories about drug smugglers and practitioners of the Voodoo-like *Santeria* seem designed to ward off visitors, but in reality there's no more drug smuggling here than anywhere else in the keys, and magic merchants come not to sacrifice innocent tourists but to gather weird and wonderful herbs for use in rituals. There's probably more danger from the exclusive *Ocean Reef Club*, whose golf course you'll spot after a few miles if you turn left where Hwy-905 splits; it's regarded by the FBI as the country's most secure retreat for very important people – watch out for nervous, armed men in dark suits. If you want to explore North Key Largo at length, you'll have to eat and sleep in Key Largo or Tavernier; see the listing below.

Further south, Hwy-905 merges with Hwy-1 (from the mainland) near MM109. Known from here on as the **Overseas Highway**, Hwy-1 is the main – and only – road all the way to Key West.

John Pennecamp Coral Reef State Park

The one essential stop as you approach Key Largo is the **John Pennecamp Coral Reef State Park**, at MM102.5 (daily 8am–sunset; cars and drivers $3.75 plus 50¢ per passenger, pedestrians and cyclists $1.50). At its heart is a protected 78-square-mile section of living coral reef, part of the reef chain that runs from here to the Dry Tortugas, off Key West (see p.149). Experts rate this as one of the most beautiful reef systems in the world, despite the substantial damage wrought by decades of ecologically unsound tourism and irresponsible tampering with Florida's ecosystem*. Whether you opt to do it here, which is one of the better spots, or elsewhere in the keys (such as Looe Key, see "The Lower Keys"), make sure you visit the reef – the eulogistic descriptions you'll hear are rarely exaggerations.

Seeing the reef: practicalities

Since most of the park lies underwater, the best way to see it is with a **snorkelling tour** (9am, noon & 3pm; adults $25, under 16s $20) or, if you're qualified, a **guided scuba dive** (9.30am & 1.30pm; $37 excluding equipment; diver's certificate required). If you prefer to stay dry, a remarkable amount of the reef can be enjoyed on the two-and-a-half-hour **glass-bottomed boat tour** (9.15am, 12.15pm & 3pm; adults $14, under 12s $9). You can also rent a boat ranging from a single person kayak to a 22-foot power boat – kayaks cost $8 per hour ($32 all day), 12-foot sailboats -$16 per hour ($48 for half a day) and power boats -$25 or $35 per hour. Note that only during the summer are you likely to get a place on these tours or obtain a boat without booking ahead. To be sure, call ☎451-1621 to make a reservation, or drop into *Sundiver Station*, MM103 (☎451-2220). If there's no room, try one of the numerous local diving shops: *American Diving Headquarters*, MM106 (☎1-800/322-3483), and *Captain Slate's Atlantis Dive Center*, at MM106.5 (☎451-1325), are just two that operate their own trips out to the reef – and cover a larger area than park tours – at around the same rates.

At the reef

Only when you're **at the reef** does its role in providing a sheltered environment for a multitude of crazy-coloured fish and exotic sea life become apparent. Even from the glass-bottomed boat you're virtually guaranteed to spot lobsters, angelfish, eels and wispy jellyfish shimmering through the current, shoals of minnows stalked by angry-faced barracudas – and many more less easily identified aquatic curiosities.

Despite looking like a big lump of rock, the **reef**, too, is a delicate living thing, composed of millions of minute coral polyps that extract calcium from the seawater and grow from one to sixteen feet every 1000 years. Coral takes many shapes and forms, resembling anything from staghorns to a bucket, and comes in a paintbox variety of colours due to the plants, *zooxanthellae*, living within the coral tissues. Sadly, it's far easier to spot signs of death rather than life on the reef: white patches show where a carelessly dropped anchor or a diver's hand have

---

* Only a few decades ago, great sections of the reef were being dynamited or hauled up by crane to be broken up and sold as souvenirs. These days, collecting Florida coral is illegal; any coral seen in tourist shops is likely to be imported from the Philippines.

scraped away the protective mucus layer and left the coral susceptible to lethal disease.

This destruction got so bad at the horseshoe-shaped **Molasses Reef**, about seven miles out, that the authorities sank two obsolete Coast Guard cutters nearby to create an alternative attraction for divers. In as much as the destruction has slowed, this plan worked and today you'll enjoy some great snorkelling around the reef and the cutters. If you prefer diving and **wrecks**, head for **the Elbow**, a section of the reef a few miles northeast of Molasses, where a number of intriguing, barnacle-encrusted nineteenth-century specimens lie; like most of the keys' diveable wrecks, these were deliberately brought here to bolster tourism in the Seventies, which lessens their allure somewhat, and you definitely won't find any treasure.

By far the strangest thing at the reef is the *Christ of the Deep*, a nine-foot bronze statue of Christ intended as a memorial to perished sailors. The algae-coated creation, twenty feet down at Key Largo Dry Rocks, is a replica of Guido Galletti's *Christ of the Abyss*, similarly submerged off the coast of Genoa, Italy – and is surely the final word in Florida's long-time fixation with Mediterranean art and architecture. The glass-bottomed boat trip, by the way, doesn't visit the Elbow or the statue.

Back on Land: the visitor center
Provided you visit the reef early, there'll be plenty of time left to enjoy the terrestrial portion of the park. The ecological displays at the **visitor center** (daily 8am–5pm) provide an inspiring introduction to the flora and fauna of the keys, and the mangrove and tropical hardwood **hammock* trails** within the park will give you a practical insight into the region's transitional zones: the vegetation changes dramatically within an elevation of a few feet. A lazier way to explore the area is to rent a **canoe** ($6 per hour; $30 per day) and glide around the mangrove-fringed inner waterways.

Key Largo and Tavernier

Thanks to the 1948 film in which Humphrey Bogart and Lauren Bacall grappled with Florida's best-known features – crime and hurricanes – almost everybody has heard of **Key Largo**. Yet the film's title was chosen for no other reason than it suggested somewhere warm and exotic, and the film, though set here, was almost entirely shot in Hollywood – hoodwinking countless millions into thinking that paradise was a town in the Florida Keys.

Recognizing a potential tourist bonanza, businesspeople here soon changed the name of their community from Rock Harbor to Key Largo (a title that until then had applied to the whole island, derived from *Cayo Largo* – Long Island – the name given to it by early Spanish explorers), and tenuous links with Hollywood are maintained even today. The steam-powered boat that starred alongside Bogart in *The African Queen* is moored in the marina (when not on promotional

---

*Cropping up all over Florida, **hammocks** are pockets of woodland able to flourish where the ground elevation rises a few feet above the surrounding wetlands. For a fuller explanation, see "Natural History" in *Contexts*.

tours) of the *Holiday Inn*, MM100, and the hotel's lobby displays a selection of stills of Bogart and co-star Katharine Hepburn acting their hearts out – in England and Africa.

One of the area's attractions is the **Maritime Museum of the Florida Keys**, MM102 (10am–5pm; $5, under 13s $3), which draws in visitors by playing up the keys' reputation as a place where pirates buried treasure, but it does have an interesting if small collection of artefacts salvaged from shipwrecks.

Once you see the filling stations, bait-and-tackle shops, shopping plazas and fast-food outlets that dominate the real Key Largo, clutching at tourist-appeal straws becomes understandable; if arriving in the evening, turn right along any road off the Overseas Highway to enjoy the sunset, otherwise keep moving.

You only need travel ten miles before reaching the far more homely **TAVERNIER**, once the first stop on the Flagler railway (the keys' first link to the mainland, see "South of Marathon"). Drop into **Harry Harris Park**, off the Overseas Highway along Burton Drive, on a weekend, and you could well find an impromptu party and free live music – locals sometimes drop by with their instruments for jam sessions – around the picnic tables.

Another reason to stop are the old buildings (a rarity in the keys, outside of Key West) of the **historic district**, between MM91 and MM92. Besides the plank walls and tin roofs of the turn-of-the-century Methodist Church (now functioning as a small visitor center) and post office, you'll see some of the "Red Cross buildings" erected after the 1935 Labor Day hurricane – which laid waste to a good chunk of the keys – with foot-thick walls of concrete and steel intended to withstand nature's fiercest poundings. Unfortunately, the use of seawater in the construction caused the walls to crumble, leaving only these rusting steel frames.

Practicalities

Unless you've already called in at the well-stocked Visitor Information Center near Homestead (see *Miami & Miami Beach*), pull up at the equally informative **Florida Keys Visitor Center**, 105950 Overseas Highway (daily 9am–6pm; ☎1-800/822-1088), for piles of brochures, money-saving vouchers and hotel booking facilities.

Though there's not much else to stick around for, the high-quality snorkelling and diving in the Key Largo area may detain you for a couple of nights. Plenty of **motels** offer diving packages. Look for their signs or try: *Economy Efficiency*, 103365 Overseas Highway (☎451-4712; ②), with a two-night minimum stay; *Largo Lodge*, 101740 Overseas Highway (☎451-0424; ⑤), offering very comfortable apartments in a lovely garden right on the beach; the sea-front cottages of *Sea Farer*, MM97.8 (☎852-5349; ③); or the *Hungry Pelican*, MM99.5 (☎451-3576; ③). Much more expensive, but a one-off, *Jules' Undersea Lodge*, at 51 Shoreland Drive (☎1-800/858-7119; ⑧), is a tiny "hotel", five fathoms deep. Book early – there are only two bedrooms – and bear in mind that you must be a qualified diver. Of the many **campgrounds** in and around Key Largo, the cleanest and cheapest is the *John Pennecamp Coral Reef State Park* (☎451-1202; see above). The *Key Largo Kampground*, MM101 (☎451-1431), is a reasonable alternative but has no grass pitches.

As for **eating**, the area has some excellent choices: *Ganim's Kountry Kitchen*, 99696 Overseas Highway (☎451-2895), has cheap breakfasts and lunches; *Frank Keys Cafe*, 100211 Overseas Highway (☎453-0310), in an attractive cottage hidden away in the trees off the highway, offers slightly more sophisticated seafood and other dishes than are usual hereabouts; *Crack'd Conch*, MM105 (☎451-0732) specialises in conch dishes, but fried alligator is offered as an alternative; *Mrs Mac's*, MM99 (☎451-3722), provides bowls of ferociously hot chilli and other home-cooked goodies; or taste the fresh pasta and seafood at the *Italian Fisherman*, MM104 (☎451-4471). Key Largo has the keys' biggest and cheapest **supermarket**, the *Winn-Dixie* at the Waldorf Plaza Shopping Center, MM100; ideal for loading supplies for the journey ahead.

Assuming the bikers in leather jackets and tropical shorts don't frighten you off, check out the *Caribbean Club*, MM104 (☎451-9970), for a lively **drink**; if they do, *Coconuts*, the bar of the *Marina del Mar Resort*, MM100 (☎451-4107), is mellower.

Heading on: Islamorada and around

Once over Tavernier Creek, you're at the start of a twenty-mile strip of islands encompassing Plantation, Windley and Upper and Lower Matecumbe keys, collectively known as **Islamorada**. More than any other section of the keys, fishing is headline news here: tales of monstrous tarpon and blue marlin captured off the coast are legion, and no end of smaller prey is easily hooked by total novices (and even former president George Bush, who regularly cast a rod in these waters, between crises).

If you've an interest in putting to sea, you'll find plenty to appeal in Islamorada: there's no problem renting fishing boats and guides or, much more cheaply, joining a fishing party boat from any of the local marinas. The biggest docks are at the *Holiday Isle*, 84001 Overseas Highway (☎1-800/327-7070), and *Bud 'n' Mary's*, MM80, which also sports a modest **Museum of Fishing** (Mon–Sat 10am–5pm; free).

There's notable **snorkelling** and **diving** in the area, too. Crocker and Alligator reefs, a few miles offshore, both have near vertical sides, whose cracks and crevices provide homes for a lively variety of crabs, shrimps and other small creatures that in turn attract bigger fish looking for a meal. Nearby, the wrecks of the *Eagle* and the *Cannabis Cruiser* provide a home for families of gargantuan amberjack and grouper. Get full snorkelling and diving details from the above marinas or any dive shop on the Overseas Highway.

On dry land, if the extortionate price doesn't deter you and you're not planning to visit any of the other marine parks in Florida, you might pass a couple of hours at the **Theater of the Sea**, MM84.5 (daily 9.30am–4pm; adults $11.75, under 13s $6.25), whose sea lions, dolphins and half-dozen tankfuls of assorted fish and crustaceans are informally introduced by knowledgeable staff; if you reserve ahead, you can swim with the dolphins ($65; see p.124).

Otherwise, there's little in Islamorada to woo non-fisherfolk. The **Chamber of Commerce** at MM82 (Mon–Fri 9am–5pm, closes for lunch; ☎1-800/FAB-KEYS), in a bright red railway guard's van, is packed with general info and has details on the latest cut-rate accommodation deals (see below). Half a mile further south, an Art Deco **monument** marks the grave of the 1935 Labor Day hurricane's 425 victims, killed when a tidal wave hit their evacuation train. The unkempt state of the stone is perhaps an indication of modern keys dwellers' nonchalant attitude to the threat of a repeat disaster.

Islamorada's state parks

Indian Key, Lignumvitae Key and Long Key, the three **state parks** at the southern end of Islamorada, offer a broader perspective of the area than fishing and diving alone can provide. The **guided tours** to Indian Key and Lignumvitae Key are particularly fruitful, revealing respectively a near-forgotten chapter of the Florida Keys' history and a virgin forest. Both tours begin by boat from Indian Key Fill, at MM78. Departures (daily except Tues & Wed; adults $7, under 12s $3; ☎664-4815) to Indian Key are at 8.30am and to Lignumvitae Key at 1.30pm. In winter, it's strongly advisable to **reserve a place**.

Indian Key

You'd never guess from the highway that **Indian Key**, one of many small, mangrove-skirted islands off Lower Matecumbe Key, was once a busy trading centre, given short-lived prosperity – and notoriety – by a nineteenth-century New Yorker called Jacob Houseman. After stealing one of his father's ships, Houseman sailed to Key West looking for a piece of the lucrative wrecking (or salvaging) business. Mistrusted by the close-knit Key West community, he bought Indian Key in 1831 as a base for his own wrecking operation. In the first year, Houseman made $30,000 and furnished the eleven-acre island with streets, a store, warehouses, a hotel and a permanent population of around fifty. However, the income was not entirely honest: Houseman was known to lead donkeys with lanterns along the shore to lure ships towards dangerous reefs, and eventually he lost his wrecking licence after salvaging from an anchored vessel.

In 1838, Indian Key was sold to physician-botanist Henry Perrine, who had been cultivating tropical plants here with an eye to their commercial potential. A Seminole attack in 1840 burnt every building to the ground and ended the island's habitation, but Perrine's plants survived and today form a swath of flowing foliage that includes sisal, coffee, tea and mango plants. Besides allowing ample opportunity to gawp at the flora, the two-hour **tour** takes you around the one-time streets, up the observation tower and past Houseman's grave – his body was brought here after he died working on a wreck off Key West.

Lignumvitae Key

By the time you finish the three-hour **tour of Lignumvitae Key** you'll know a strangler fig from a gumbo limbo and will instantly be able to recognize many more of the hundred or so species of tropical tree in this two-hundred-acre hammock. A further treat are the sizeable spiders, such as the Golden Orb, whose silvery web regularly spans the pathway. The trail through the forest was laid out by a wealthy early Miamian, W J Matheson, whose 1919 limestone **house** is the island's only sign of habitation and shows the deprivations of early island living – even for the well-off. The house actually blew away in the 1935 hurricane, but was found and brought back.

Long Key State Recreation Area

Many of the tree species found on Lignumvitae can be spotted at **Long Key State Recreation Area**, MM67.5 (daily 8am–sunset; cars $3.25 plus 50c per passenger, pedestrians and cyclists $1.50). There's a nature trail that takes you along the beach and on a boardwalk over a mangrove-lined lagoon or, better still, you can rent a canoe ($2 per hour) and follow the simple **canoe trail** through the tidal lagoons, in the company of mildly curious wading birds. For details of **camping** in the park, phone ☎664-4815.

Practicalities

You're unlikely to find **accommodation** in Islamorada for under $50 a night, although price wars among the bigger hotels can ease the budget strain. The popular *Holiday Isle*, 84001 Overseas Highway (☎1-800/327-7070; ⑤), is just one place with good off-season deals; otherwise, the best bets are *Drop Anchor*, MM85 (☎664/4863; ④–⑥), *Key Lantern*, MM82 (☎664-4572; ③), and *Islamorada Inn Motel*, MM87.8 (☎852-9376; ③). For information on other establishments, check with the Chamber of Commerce (address above). If you have a tent, use either Long Key State Recreation Area (see above) or the campervan-dominated *KOA* campground on Fiesta Key, MM70 (☎664-4922).

Provided you avoid the obvious tourist traps, you can **eat** well and fairly cheaply. *Manny & Isa's*, MM81.5 (☎664-5019), serves high-quality, low-cost Cuban food; *Whale Harbor*, MM84 (☎664-4959), lives up to its name, proffering massive seafood buffets to devil-may-care gluttons; the ramshackle but justifiably pricey *Green Turtle Inn*, MM81 (☎664-9031; closed Mon), has glorious chowders; and the *Hungry Tarpon*, at MM77.5 Lower Matecumbe Key, in a 1940s converted bait shop, serves superb fish according to local recipes.

When it comes to **nightlife**, many people get no further than the huge tiki bar at *Holiday Isle* (address above), which always throbs on weekends to the sound of insipid rock bands. Alternatively, investigate the nightly drinks specials at *Lorelei's*, MM102 (☎664-4656), or sample the raunchy blues and boozing at the much less touristy *Woody's*, MM102 (☎664-4335).

The Middle Keys: Marathon and around

The Long Key Bridge (alongside the old Long Key Viaduct, see "South of Marathon", below) leads south of Long Key to the **Middle Keys**: Duck Key to Bahia Honda Key. The largest of several islands is Key Vaca – once a shantytown of railway workers – which holds the area's major settlement, **MARATHON**. On first sight this is a town as commercialized and uninspiring as Key Largo, but has better features hidden from view a short way off the Overseas Highway.

If you've not had your fill of tropical trees at Lignumvitae Key (see "Islamorada" above), take the right hand turning at 50.5MM (opposite the K-Mart) into 55th Street, which leads to the 63 steamy subtropical acres of **Crane**

SNORKELLING, DIVING, FISHING AND SAILING

Around Marathon, **spearfishing** is permitted a mile offshore (there's a three-mile limit elsewhere), but if you're not planning to skewer the local sealife, you can take advantage of the area's **snorkelling** and **scuba diving** opportunities. The choice locale for these pursuits is around **Sombrero Reef**, marked by a 142-foot-high nine-teenth-century lighthouse, whose nooks and crannies provide a safe haven for thousands of darting, brightly coloured tropical fish. The best time to go out is early evening when the reef is most active, since the majority of its creatures are noctur-nal. The pick of local dive shops is *Hall's Dive Center* (☎1-800/331-4255), in the grounds of Faro Blanco Marina Resort, MM48.5. Five-day Basic Open Water Scuba Certificate courses ($385) are offered to novice divers, and night diving, wreck diving and Instructor's Certificate courses are available to the experienced. Once certified, you can rent equipment ($55) and join a dive trip (9am, 1pm, 5.30pm; $40).

Marathon hosts four major **fishing tournaments** each year: in early May (for tarpon); late May (dolphin, the fish not the mammal); early October (bonefish); and early November (sailfish). Precise dates are available from the **Chamber of Commerce**, 3330 Overseas Highway (Mon–Fri 9am–5pm; ☎1-800/842-9580). You may fancy your chances, but entering costs several hundred dollars and only the very top anglers participate. Just being around during a tournament, however, will give you an insight into the Big Time Fishing mentality, and if you feel inspired to put to sea yourself, wander along one of the marinas and ask about chartering a boat. Boats take out up to six people and charge between $400 and $850 for a full day's fishing (7am–4pm), including bait and equipment. If you can't get a group together, join one of the countless party boats for about $40 per person for a full day's fishing – remember, though, that it's easier to catch fish with fewer people aboard.

Although most of the boats at the local marinas are large power vessels designed for anglers, Marathon is also a major sailboat base, offering vessels for charter – with or without a captain – as well as sailing courses. A reliable source of both is *A–B–Sea Charter* (☎289-0373), at the Faro Blanco Marina Resort, MM48.5.

Point Hammock (Mon–Sat 9am–5pm, Sun noon–5pm; $4). A free text guide gives details of the trees you'll find along its one-mile **nature trail**, which also runs past one of the last examples of Black Bahamian architecture in the US: a house built in 1903 by Bahamian immigrants, currently under restoration.

An authoritative rundown of the area's history – starting with the Caloosa Indians, who had a settlement on this site, and continuing with the story of early Bahamian and American settlers – plus displays on its geology can be found at the hammock's excellent **Museum of Natural History of the Florida Keys**. A large section of the museum features interactive displays designed to introduce kids to the wonders of the keys' subtropical ecosystems, including the hardwood hammocks and reefs. Much the same ground is covered by the adjoining **Florida Keys Children's Museum**, which also houses a tropical aquarium, a terrarium and an artificial saltwater lagoon where you can feed the fish.

For a closer look at the keys' natural life, take the waterborne **ecology tour** (selected days only, 10am & 2pm; $15; ☎743-7000) from the marina of the $200-a-night *Hawks Cay Resort* on Duck Key, reached by way of a causeway at MM61. Led by a radically minded local naturalist, the two-hour trip to an uninhabited island will furnish you with a wealth of information on the make-up of the keys and the creatures who live in them.

If you have a less active time in mind, Marathon has a couple of small **beaches**. Sombrero Beach, along Sombrero Beach Road (off the Overseas Highway near MM50), is a slender strip of sand with good swimming waters and shaded picnic tables. Four miles north, the beach at Key Colony Beach, a man-made island dredged into existence during the Fifties for building pricey homes on, is prettier and quieter.

Practicalities

If relaxation is a priority, spend a night or two at one of Marathon's well-equipped **resorts**, such as *Faro Blanco Marine Resort*, 1996 Overseas Highway (☎1-800-759-3276; ④–⑦), whose small cottages and houseboats offer beautiful views of the mangroves. Similar accommodation is available at *Sombrero*, 19 Sombrero Boulevard (☎1-800/433-8660; ⑤–⑦), or *Banana Bay*, 4590 Overseas Highway (☎1-800/488-6636; ⑤–⑦). The least costly of the plentiful supply of cheaper **motels** are *Sea Dell*, 5000 Overseas Highway (☎1-800/648-3854; ③), and *Seaward*, 8700 Overseas Highway (☎743-5711; ③–④). Good deals can also be found at the *Flamingo Inn*, a motel at MM59 (☎289-1478; ④). The only **camp-ground** permitting tents (others are designed for motor homes and trailers only) is *Knights Key Park*, MM47 (☎743-9954).

Despite the commercial conformity of Marathon's main drag, there are several friendly places to **eat**. Good Cuban fare is found at *Don Pedro Restaurant*, MM53 (☎743-5247); *Herbie's*, 6350 Overseas Highway (☎743-6373), is justly busy on account of its inexpensive seafood; *Porky's Too BBQ*, MM45 (☎743-6637), provides platefuls of beef and chicken; and quality Italian dishes can be enjoyed in the simple setting of the *Village Café*, at the Gulfside Village Plaza, 5800 Overseas Highway (☎743-9090).

Marathon goes to sleep early; the only place with a suspicion of **nightlife** is the tiki bar of *Bacchus by the Sea*, 725 11th Street (☎743-6106), which is also the prime vantage point for sipping a drink as the sun goes down.

South of Marathon: the Seven Mile Bridge

In 1905, Henry Flagler, whose railway opened up Florida's East Coast, undertook to extend its tracks to Key West. The Overseas Railroad, as it became known (though many called it "Flagler's folly"), was a monumental task that took seven years to complete and was marred by the appalling treatment of workers.

Bridging the Middle Keys gave Flagler's engineers some of their biggest head-aches. North of Marathon, the two-mile-long Long Key Viaduct, a still-elegant structure of nearly two hundred individually cast arches, was Flagler's personal favourite and widely pictured in advertising campaigns. Yet a greater technical accomplishment was the **Seven Mile Bridge** to the south, linking Marathon to the Lower Keys. At one point, every US-flagged freighter on the Atlantic was hired to bring in materials – including special cement from Germany – while float-ing cranes, dredges and scores of other craft set about a job that eventually cost the lives of 700 labourers. When the trains eventually started rolling (doddering over the bridges at 15mph), passengers were treated to an incredible panorama: a broad sweep of sea and sky, sometimes streaked by luscious red sunsets or dark-ened by storm clouds.

The Flagler bridges were strong enough to withstand everything that the keys' volatile weather could throw at them, except for the calamitous 1935 Labor Day hurricane, which tore up the railway. The bridges were subsequently adapted to accommodate a road: the original Overseas Highway. Tales of hair-raising bridge crossings (the road was only 22 feet wide), endless tailbacks as the drawbridges jammed – and the roadside parties that ensued – are part of keys folklore. The later bridges, such as the $45-million **new Seven Mile Bridge** between Key Vaca and Bahia Honda Key that opened in the early Eighties, certainly improved traffic flow but also ended the mystique of travelling the old road – and its walls are just high enough to hide the fabulous view.

The old bridges, intact but for the mid-sectional cuts to allow shipping to pass, now make extraordinarily long fishing piers and jogging strips. A section of the former Seven Mile Bridge also provides the only land access to **Pigeon Key**, which served as a railway work camp from 1908 to 1935, utilized until recently by the University of Miami for marine science classes. Its seven original wooden buildings have been restored, and a railway museum is also planned for the site. Cars are not permitted access to Pigeon Key, which contributes to the serene atmosphere of the place. A shuttle bus leaves hourly (9am–4pm; $4) from the Pigeon Key Visitor's Center at MM48.

The Lower Keys

Starkly different to their northerly neighbours, the **Lower Keys** are quiet, heavily wooded and predominantly residential. Aligned north–south and built on a limestone rather than (like the preceding keys) a coral base, these islands have a flora and fauna that's very much their own, a lot of it tucked away miles from the Overseas Highway. Most visitors speed through the area on the way to Key West, just forty miles further, but the area's lack of rampant tourism and easily found seclusion make this a good place to linger for a day or two. The main settlement is **Big Pine Key**, where the **Lower Keys Chamber of Commerce**, at MM31.9 (Mon–Fri 9am–5pm, Sat 9am–3pm, ☎1-800/872-2411), is packed with information on the area.

Bahia Honda State Recreation Area

While not officially part of the Lower Keys, the first place of consequence you'll hit after crossing the Seven Mile Bridge is the 300-acre **Bahia Honda State Recreation Area** (daily 8am–sunset; cars $3.25 plus 50c per person, pedestrians and cyclists $1.50; ☎872-2353), one of the keys' prettiest spots. The northeasterly section of the park rings a lagoon with a natural **beach** and inviting, two-tone ocean waters. While here, you should ramble the **nature trail**, which loops from the shoreline through a hammock of silver palms, geiger and yellow satinwood trees, passing rare plants such as dwarf morning glory and spiny catesbaea; look out for white-crowned pigeons, great white herons, roseate spoonbills and giant ospreys (whose bulky nests are plentiful throughout the Lower Keys, often atop telegraph poles).

The waters at the park's southern end are good for swimming (beware, though, that currents here can be very swift), as well as for snorkelling, diving –

and especially windsurfing; rent equipment from the marina's dive shop. You'll also notice the two-storey **Flagler Bridge**. The unusually deep waters here (Bahia Honda is Spanish for "deep bay") made this the toughest of the old railway bridges to construct, and widening it for the road proved impossible: the solution was to put the highway on a higher tier. It's actually far safer than it looks and there's a fine view from the top of the bridge over the Bahia Honda channel towards the forest-coated Lower Keys.

Facilities in the park include a campground and cabins, a snack bar, and a dive shop offering reef snorkel trips, scuba trips and boat rental.

Big Pine Key and around

The eponymous trees on **Big Pine Key** are less of a draw than its **Key deer**, delightfully tame creatures that enjoy the freedom of the island; don't feed them (it's illegal), and be cautious when driving – signs alongside the road state the number of road-kills to date during the year. The deer, no bigger than large dogs, arrived long ago when the keys were still joined to the mainland; they provided food for sailors and Key West residents for many years, but hunting and the destruction of their natural habitat led to near extinction by the late Forties. The **National Key Deer Refuge** was set up here in 1954 to safeguard the animals – one refuge manager went so far as to burn the cars and sink the boats of poachers – and their population has now stabilized between 250 and 300.

Pick up factual information on the deer from the **refuge headquarters** (Mon–Fri 8am–5pm; ☎872-2239), at the western end of Watson Boulevard, off Key Deer Boulevard. To see them, driving along Key Deer Boulevard or turning east onto No Name Key should turn up at least a few; they often amuse themselves in domestic gardens. Your chances are best in the cooler temperatures of early morning or late afternoon.

Also on Key Deer Boulevard, the **Blue Hole** is a freshwater lake with a healthy population of soft-shelled turtles and at least one alligator, who now and then emerges from the cool depths to sun himself – parts of the lakeside path may be closed if he's staked out a patch for the day. Should the gator get your adrenaline pumping, take a calming stroll along the short **nature trail**, a quarter of a mile further south along Key Deer Boulevard.

Moving on: the rest of the Lower Keys

An even more peaceful atmosphere prevails over the Lower Keys south of Big Pine Key, despite the efforts of property developers. The **Torch Keys**, so-named for their forests of torchwood – used for kindling by early settlers – can be swiftly bypassed on the way to **Ramrod Key**, where Looe Key Marine Sanctuary is a terrific place for viewing the coral reef, and to **Sugarloaf Key**, site of an oddball slice of keys' history.

Perhaps the most expensive thing you'll see anywhere in the keys, if not in all of Florida, is the balloon-like "aerostat" hovering over **Cudjoe Key**. With a budget of $16 million, it was used by the US government to beam TV images of American-style freedom – baseball, sit-coms, soap operas – to Cuba. Called *TV Martí*, the station was named after the late-nineteenth-century Cuban independence fighter, José Martí. In July 1993 the Clinton administration decided to end the broadcasts, and the aerostat's future is uncertain.

Looe Key Marine Sanctuary

Keen underwater explorers should home in on **Looe Key Marine Sanctuary**, clearly signposted from the Overseas Highway on Ramrod Key. Named after *HMS Looe*, a British frigate that sank here in 1744, this five-square-mile area of protected reef is in every part the equal of the John Pennecamp Coral Reef State Park (see "North Key Largo"; above). The crystal-clear waters and reef formations create an unforgettable spectacle; rays, octopus and a multitude of gaily coloured fish flit between tall coral pillars, big brain coral, complex tangles of elk- and staghorn coral, and soft corals like purple seafans and sea whips.

The **sanctuary office** (Mon–Fri 8am–5pm; ☎872-4039) can provide free maps and information. You can only visit the reef itself on a trip organized by one of the many diving shops throughout the keys; the nearest is the neighbouring *Looe Key Dive Center* (☎1-800/942-5397).

Perky's Bat Tower

On Sugarloaf Key, fifteen miles from Ramrod Key, the 35-foot **Perky's Bat Tower** stands as testimony to one man's misguided belief in the benefits of bats. A get-rich-quick book of the Twenties, *Bats, Mosquitoes and Dollars*, led Richter C. Perky, a property speculator who had recently purchased the island, into thinking bats would be the solution to the keys' mosquito problem. With much hulla-balloo he erected this brown cypress lath tower and dutifully sent away for the costly "bat bait", which he was told would lure an army of bats to the tower. It didn't work: no bat ever showed up, the mosquitoes stayed healthy, and Perky went bust soon after. The background story is far more interesting than the actual tower, but if the tale tickles your fancy, you can view it from the bumpy road just beyond the sprawling *Sugarloaf Lodge*, at MM17.

Practicalities

For what they offer, motels in the Lower Keys are expensive. *Looe Key Reef Resort*, MM27.5 (☎872-2215; ③), is ideal for visiting the marine sanctuary, or there's *Parmer's Place*, MM28.5 (☎872-2157; ④). For a real splurge, stay at the idyllic *Little Palm Island*, MM28.5, Little Torch Key (☎872-2524; ⑧), whose thatched cottages are set in lush gardens a few feet from the beach. **Campgrounds** are plentiful, but tents are accepted only at the Bahia Honda State Recreation Area's *Big Pine Key Fishing Lodge*, MM33 (☎872-2351), and *Seahorse*, MM31 (☎872-2443). Three **bed and breakfast inns** along Long Beach Drive on Big Pine Key make cosy alternatives, but book early: *Deer Run*, MM32.5 (☎872-2015; ⑤), *Barnacle*, MM32.5 (☎872-3298; ⑤), and *Casa Grande*, 33MM (☎872-2878; ④).

The best place to **eat** in the Lower Keys is *Mangrove Mama's*, at MM20 on Sugarloaf Key (sometimes closed Tues or Thurs and usually throughout Sept; ☎745-3030), for its rustic atmosphere, great seafood and home-baked bread. Otherwise, on Big Pine Key try *Island Jim's*, MM31.3 (☎872-2017), for good fare from breakfast through to dinner, or grab a sandwich at *Dip N'Deli*, MM31 (☎872-3030).

Nightlife is not a strong card; when locals want to live it up they go to Key West. Take a shot at the *No Name Pub*, at the eastern end of Watson Boulevard on Big Pine Key (☎872-9115), for varied beers and occasional live bands; the *Looe Key Reef Resort* (see above) for weekend drinking; or, if desperate, the lounge of the *Cedar Inn*, MM31 (☎872-4031).

Key West

Much closer to Cuba than mainland Florida, **Key West** can often seem very far removed from the rest of the US. Famed for their tolerant attitudes and laid-back lifestyles, its 30,000 islanders seem adrift in a great expanse of sea and sky and – despite the million tourists who arrive each year – the place resonates with an anarchic and individual spirit that hits you the instant you arrive. Locals (known as *conchs* – after the giant sea snails eaten by early settlers – if they're long-term residents of Key West, or *freshwater conchs* if they're more recent arrivals) ride bicycles, shoot the breeze on street corners and smile at complete strangers. The narrow thoroughfares and alleyways are a blaze of tropical T-shirts, garish hats and extravagant shorts. Even in tourist shops, king-sized cigarette papers and hash pipes are sold next to beachware and sunscreen – and no one turns a hair.

Yet as wild as it may at first appear, Key West today is far from being the drop-outs' and misfits' mecca that it was just a decade or so ago. Much of the sleaziness has been gradually brushed away through a steady process of restoration and revitalization – it takes a lot of money to buy a house here now – paving the way for a sizeable vacation industry that at times seems to revolve around party boats and heavy drinking. Not that Key West is yet near to losing its special identity: it's still non-conformist, and don't dare to suggest otherwise. The liberal attitudes have attracted a large influx of gay people, estimated at one in five of the population, who are not only out of the closet but taking a big role in running the place, sinking thousands of dollars into its future.

If you're in the mood, there's plenty to enjoy over a few days, even if many of the well-hyped "attractions" are less than they're cracked up to be, and the endless tales of drug-runners, Ernest Hemingway (one of a number of writers who have lived here) and the landing of gigantic fish might be taken with a pinch of salt. The sense of isolation from the mainland – much stronger here than on the other keys – and the camaraderie of the locals are best appreciated by adjusting to the mellow pace and joining in; amble the side streets, make meals last for hours, and pause regularly for refreshment in the numerous bars. For all this, Key West is a place one either loves or hates. People are either totally seduced by its uniqueness or can't get away fast enough from what's sometimes seen as just a smug tourist trap.

Some history

Piracy was the main activity around Key West – first settled in 1822 – before Florida joined the US and the navy established a base here. This cleared the way for a substantial **wrecking industry**; millions of dollars were earned through lifting people and cargo off shipwrecks along the Florida Reef, making Key West the wealthiest city in the US by the mid-nineteenth century.

The subsequent building of reef lighthouses sounded the death knell for the wrecking business, but Key West continued to prosper. Many **Cubans** arrived with cigar-making skills, and migrant Greeks established a lucrative sponge enterprise (the highly absorbent sea sponges, formed from the skeletons of tiny marine creatures, were the forerunners of today's synthetic sponges). Industrial unrest and a sponge blight drove these businesses northwards (to Tampa and Tarpon Springs respectively) and left Key West ill-prepared to face the

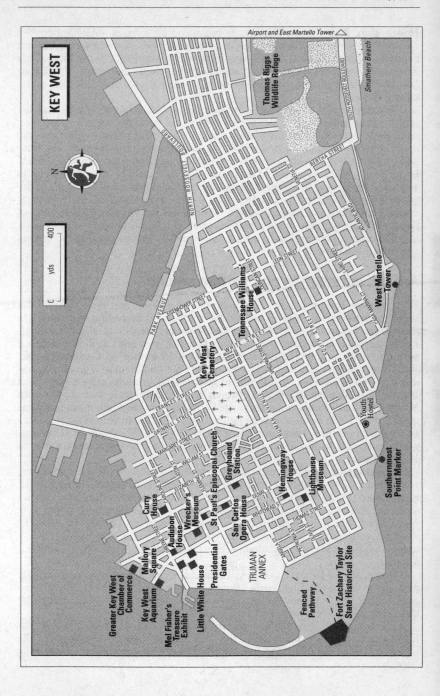

KEY WEST

Airport and East Martello Tower △

N

yds 400

NORTH ROOSEVELT BOULEVARD

SOUTH ROOSEVELT BOULEVARD

Smathers Beach

Thomas Riggs
Wildlife Refuge

PARK AVENUE

EISENHOWER STREET

BERTHA STREET

WHITE STREET

LEON STREET

SOUTH STREET

Tennessee Williams'
House

West Martello
Tower

Key West
Cemetery

FRANCES STREET

GRINNELL STREET

MARGARET STREET

ELIZABETH

WILLIAM ST

FLEMING ST

DARLING STREET

SIMONTON STREET

VIRGINIA STREET

TRUMAN AVENUE

ANGELA ST

PETRONIA ST

DUVAL ST

WHITEHEAD ST

THOMAS STREET

DUVAL ST

Youth
Hostel

Southernmost
Point Marker

Lighthouse
Museum

Hemingway
House

Greyhound
Station

St Paul's Episcopal Church

San Carlos
Opera House

Wrecker's
Museum

Curry
House

Audubon
House

Mallory
Square

Presidential
Gates

Little White House

TRUMAN
ANNEX

Fenced
Pathway

Fort Zachary Taylor
State Historical Site

Mel Fisher's
Treasure
Exhibit

Key West
Aquarium

Greater Key West
Chamber of
Commerce

Depression. By the early Thirties, its remaining inhabitants – die-hard conchs resisting any suggestion that they move to the mainland – were living on fish and coconuts, finally declaring themselves bankrupt in July 1934. Under Roosevelt's New Deal, Key West was tidied up and readied for tourism, but the 1935 Labor Day hurricane blew away the Flagler railway – Key West's only land link to the outside world.

Eventually, it was an injection of naval dollars during World War II, and the island's geographical good fortune to be the US military's eyes and ears on communist Cuba, that saved Key West and provided the backbone of its economy until the **tourists** finally started arriving in force through the Eighties. Far from being swamped by outsiders, however, the community was quick to assert itself. In April 1982, when its pursuit of drugs and illegal aliens led US border patrols to stop all traffic leaving the keys, locals proclaimed the town to be the capital of the "**Conch Republic**". Partly intended as an excuse for a booze-up, this unilateral declaration of independence (followed immediately by surrender and a request for foreign aid) typically made a political point in a humorous way, and symbolized the community's zealously maintained social, as well as geographic, separation from the mainland.

Arrival, information and getting around

The Overseas Highway is the only road into Key West, and runs through the bland eastern section of the island into the much more interesting Old Town. On the way you'll pass the information-packed **Welcome Center** on North Roosevelt Boulevard (daily 9am–5pm; ☎296-4444), though if you don't feel like stopping here, press on and use the **Greater Key West Chamber of Commerce**, 402 Wall Street (daily 8.30am–5pm; ☎294-2587), for free tourist pamphlets and discount vouchers. Four miles east of town is the grandly named Key West International **Airport** (☎296-5439), which actually only deals with flights from Miami and other Florida cities; there are no buses from here into town, but a taxi costs around $8. A novel means of getting from Miami into Key West is *Chalk's International Airlines* **seaplane** service (☎1-800-424-2557; about $190 return), which runs daily to Key West Harbor and includes a free water taxi transfer to Mallory Square.

For **getting around** the narrow, pedestrian-busy streets of the Old Town, you're better off walking than driving. If you're planning to venture further afield, **rent a bike** ($7–10 per day) or moped ($25–30 per day) from *Adventure Scooter & Bicycle Rentals*, at 708 and 925 Duval Street, or from the youth hostel (see "Accommodation"). Remarkably, there is a **bus service** (☎292-8164) on Key West: two routes, one clockwise and the other anticlockwise, loop around the tiny island roughly every fifteen minutes between 7am and 9am and 2.30pm and 5.30pm.

If you're pushed for time, take a ninety-minute **guided tour** of the main sights with either the *Conch Tour Train* (from Mallory Square; every 20–30min 9am–4pm; $12) or the *Old Town Trolley* (board at any of the marked stops around the Old Town; every 30min 9am–4.30pm; $14).

A number of easily found **free publications** list current events: *Solares Hill* (monthly) is the most informative, but look out for *Island Life* (weekly), *The Conch Republic* (monthly), and the gay-oriented gossip sheet *What's Happening* (weekly).

Accommodation

Accommodation costs in Key West are always high – particularly from November to April when the simplest motel room will be in excess of $90 per night. Prices drop considerably at other times but, other than at the hostel, you should expect little change from $50 wherever you stay. Genuine **budget options** are limited to pitching a tent or renting a basic cottage at *Jabour's Trailer Court*, 223 Elizabeth Street (☎294-5723), or the small dorms of the *Key West Hostel*, 718 South Street (☎296-5719; members $14.25, non-members $17.50; weekly $90).

With more money to spend, take advantage of Key West's numerous guest houses, which offer **bed and breakfast** accommodation in century-old buildings at a price no higher than the much less atmospheric **hotels and motels**, some of which are unattractively located on the approach roads into town. Wherever you stay, a reservation is essential during the summer and a sensible precaution for weekends stays at any other time.

Gay and lesbian visitors are unlikely to encounter hostile attitudes wherever they choose to stay. However, the *Curry House*, 806 Fleming Street (☎1-800/633-7439; ④–⑤) and the *Rainbow House*, 525 United Street (☎1 800/749-6696; ④–⑤), are guest houses that are exclusively male and exclusively female respectively. Elsewhere, *Big Ruby's*, 409 Applerouth Lane (☎296-2323; ④–⑤), and *Cypress House*, 601 Caroline Street (☎1-800/525-2488; ③–④), have earned a reputation as classy and relaxing gay-oriented establishments.

Guest houses

Angelina Guest House, 302 Angela St (☎294-4480). Simple, well-priced rooms; paying a little more will get you kitchenettes and suites, good value for four people sharing. ④.

Blue Parrot Inn, 916 Elizabeth St (☎1-800/231-BIRD). Dating from 1884, this offers a heated pool and continental breakfasts, as well as comfortable, nicely furnished rooms. ⑥.

Curry Mansion Inn, 511 Caroline St (☎294-6777). The high price buys a night in a landmark Victorian home furnished with quality antiques; see "Seeing Key West" for an account of its distinguished past. ⑥–⑦.

Duval House, 815 Duval St (☎294-1666). The lower-priced rooms are very good value; extra spending brings a four-poster bed and a balcony overlooking the grounds. ⑤–⑦.

Eden House, 1015 Fleming St (☎1-800/533-KEYS). Wicker furnishings and a fish-filled pool add to the appeal of this thoughtfully renovated and fully modernized 1924 building – one of Key West's most relaxing hideaways. The cheaper rooms share a bathroom; the priciest have jacuzzis. ⑤–⑦.

Island City House, 411 William St (☎1-800/634-8230). This grand mansion, built in the 1880s for a Charleston merchant family, offers studios and one- or two-bedroom apartments overlooking the pool and tropical gardens. ⑦–⑧.

Simonton Court, 320 Simonton St (☎1-800/944-2687). A choice of regular rooms in the main house or well-equipped cottages dotted around the grounds. ⑤–⑦.

Tropical Inn, 812 Duval St (☎294-9977). Large, airy rooms in a charming restored "conch" house. Most of the rooms sleep three, and the more expensive ones have balconies. ④–⑤.

Wicker House, 913 Duval St (☎296-2475). This least costly of Key West's guest houses comprises four restored "conch" houses; the cheaper rooms lack air-conditioning (ceiling fans are installed) and TVs, though there is a communal jacuzzi and a pool. ④–⑤.

Hotels and motels

La Concha Holiday Inn, 430 Duval St (☎1-800/745-2191). Now a link in the *Holiday Inn* chain, this colourful hotel first opened in 1925 and has been refurbished to retain some of its Twenties style; a bigger plus for most guests is the large swimming pool. ⑥–⑦.

Hampton Inn, 2801 N Roosevelt Blvd (☎1-800/426-7866). A branch of a reliable (and usually low-cost) hotel chain, with spacious rooms, a bar and a jacuzzi; rates, however, are far higher than most *Hampton Inns*. ⑦.

Sea Shell Motel, 718 South St (☎296-5719). If the adjoining youth hostel is full or doesn't appeal, this offers standard motel rooms at the lowest rates in the neighbourhood. ④.

Southern Cross, 326 Duval St (☎1-800/533-4891). Key West's oldest hotel offers no-frills rooms; get one at the rear if you want to avoid the night-time hubbub along Duval Street. ⑤.

Southernmost Motel, 1319 Duval St (☎1-800/354-4455). The rooms at the US's most southerly motel are decked out in tropical shades; its poolside tiki bar is the ideal place to meet other guests before taking the ten-minute walk to the heart of Key West. ⑤.

La Terraza de Marti, 1125 Duval St (☎296-6706). Better known locally as "La-Te-Da", The rooms face a beckoning pool, and the tree-studded hotel complex includes several bars, discos and a classy restaurant (see "Nightlife"). Well placed for the town and very popular with gay visitors. ⑥–⑦.

Tilton Hilton, 511 Angela St (☎294-8694). Key West's cheapest hotel but otherwise one with little to recommend it. The rooms are very basic; be sure to see yours before paying for it. ③.

Seeing Key West: along Duval Street

The square mile of the **Old Town** contains virtually everything that you could want to see and is certainly the best place for imbibing Key West's finest feature: its atmosphere. Tourists are plentiful around the main streets, but the relaxed, casually hedonistic mood that draws many to Key West affects everybody, whether they've been here twenty years or twenty minutes. All of the Old Town can be seen on foot in little more than a day, though you should allow at least two or three – dashing about isn't the way to enjoy the place.

Anyone who saw Key West two decades ago would now barely recognize the main promenade, **Duval Street**, which cuts a mile-long swathe right through the Old Town, making it easy to regain bearings after exploring the side streets. Teetering just on the safe side of seedy for many years, much of the street has been transformed into a well-manicured strip of boutiques and beachwear shops catering to the vacationing middle-aged of Middle America. Yet its colourful "local characters" and round-the-clock action mean that Duval Street is still an interesting place to hang out.

Other than shops and bars, few places on Duval Street provide a break from tramping the pavement. One is the **Wrecker's Museum** (daily 10am–4pm; $2), at no. 322, in one of the oldest houses in Key West. This gives some background to the industry on which Key West's earliest good times were based: salvaging cargo from foundering vessels. In the days before radio and radar, wrecking crews simply put out in bad weather and sailed as close as they dared to the menacing reefs, hoping to spot a grounded craft. Judging by the choice furniture that fills the house, Captain Watlington, the wrecker who lived here from the 1830s, did pretty well. On the top floor, modern cartoons recount several Key West folk tales, including the dunking in the sea of a preacher who dwelled too long on the evils of drinking.

A few blocks on, **St Paul's Episcopal Church**, at no. 401, is worth entering briefly for its rich stained-glass windows. If overwhelmed by piety, you might scoot around the corner for a look at the **Old Stone Methodist Church**, 600 Eaton Street, the oldest church in Key West, built in 1877 and shaded by the giant Spanish laurel tree in its front yard.

The San Carlos Opera House and the southernmost point

At 516 Duval Street, the **San Carlos Opera House** (daily 9am–5pm; $3) has played a leading role in Cuban exile life since it opened (on a different site) as the San Carlos Institute in 1871. Financed by a $100,000 grant from the Cuban government, the present building dates from 1924; across its grounds are spread soil from Cuba's six provinces, and a cornerstone was taken from the tomb of legendary Cuban independence campaigner José Martí. Following the break in diplomatic ties between the US and Cuba in 1961, the building fell on hard times – and was briefly used as a cinema, much to the annoyance of local Cubans – until it was revived by a million-dollar restoration project. Now, besides staging opera in its acoustically excellent auditorium and maintaining a well-stocked research library (including, most notably, the records of the Cuban Consulate from 1886–1961), it has a first-rate permanent exhitibion on the history of Cubans in the US and, in particular, Key West.

You'll know when you get near the southern end of Duval Street because, whether it's a house, motel, filling station or restaurant, everything advertises itself as "the Southernmost . . .". Accurately, the **southernmost point** in Key West, and consequently in the continental US, is to be found at the intersection of Whitehead and South streets. Many visitors derive great pleasure from having their photo taken by the daft-looking buoy that marks the spot; if you're not one of them, forget it.

Mallory Square and around

In the early 1800s, thousands of dollars' worth of salvage was landed at the piers, stored in the warehouses and flogged at the auction houses on **Mallory Square**, just west of the northern end of Duval Street. The square's present-day commerce is based on tourism, and little remains from the old times. By day, the square is a plain souvenir market selling overpriced ice cream, trinkets and T-shirts. But return at night for the **sunset celebration**, when buskers, jugglers, fire-eaters and assorted screw-loose types create a merry backdrop to the sinking of the sun. The celebration, which began in the Sixties as a hippie excuse for a smoke-in, is lively and fun, though it, too, has become very tourist-oriented.

Key West Aquarium and Mel Fisher's Treasure Exhibit

More entertaining than the square during the day is the small gathering of sea life inside the adjacent **Key West Aquarium** (daily 10am–7pm; adults $6, under 15s $3), 1 Whitehead Street, where ugly creatures such as porcupine fish and longspine squirrel fish leer from behind glass, and sharks (the smaller kinds such as lemon, blacktip and bonnethead) are known to jump out of their open tanks during the half-hour **guided tours** (11am, 1pm, 3pm and 4.30pm). If you intend to eat conch, a rubbery crustacean sold as fritter or chowder all over Key West, do so before examining the live ones here; they're not the world's most appetizing creatures.

In the wild, the aquarium's fish might make their homes around the remains of sunken galleons that plied the trade route between Spain and its New World colonies during the sixteenth and seventeenth centuries. In **Mel Fisher's Treasure Exhibit**, 200 Greene Street (daily 9.30am–5pm; adults $5, under 13s $2), you'll get a good look at skilfully crafted decorative pieces, a highly impressive emerald cross, a liftable gold bar, plus countless vases and daggers alongside the obligatory cannon, all salvaged from two seventeenth-century wrecks. As engrossing as the collection is, it's really a celebration of an all-American rags-to-riches story. Now the high priest of Florida's many treasure seekers, Fisher was running a surf shop in California before he arrived in the Sunshine State armed with ancient Spanish sea charts. In 1985, after years of searching, he discovered the *Nuestra Señora de Atocha* and *Santa Margarita*, both sunk during a hurricane in 1622, forty miles southeast of Key West – they yielded a haul said to be worth millions of dollars. Among matters you won't find mentioned at the exhibit are the raging dispute between Fisher and the state and federal governments over who owns what, and the ecological upsets that uncontrolled treasure-seeking has caused the keys.

At Greene and Front Streets, the imposing, Romanesque **Custom's House** (☎296-3913) was built in 1891 and used as a post office, customs office and federal court house. Long derelict, the building is being gradually renovated for use as a local history museum – call ahead for details on exhibits and opening hours.

The Truman Annex and Fort Zachary Taylor

The old naval storehouse that contains the Fisher trove was once part of the **Truman Annex** (daily 9am–8pm; free), a decommissioned section of a naval base established in 1822 to keep a lid on piracy around what had just become US territory. Some of the buildings subsequently erected on the base, which spans a hundred acres between Whitehead Street and the sea, were – and still are – among Key West's most distinctive – for example, the dreamy Romanesque-revival-style Customs House (across Front Street from the Mel Fisher Treasure Exhibit).

The most famous among them, however, was the comparatively plain **Little White House** (daily 9am–5pm; adults $6, under 13s $3), by the junction of Caroline and Front streets. This house earned its name by being the favourite holiday spot of President Harry S Truman (after whom the Annex was named), who first visited in 1946 and allegedly spent his vacations playing poker, cruising Key West for doughnuts, and swimming; primitive plumbing meant that no one in the house was allowed to flush the toilet during his visits. The house is now a **museum*** recording, with an immense array of memorabilia, the Truman years .

In 1986, the new owner of the Annex made a lot of friends early on by throwing open the weighty **Presidential Gates** on Caroline Street, which previously only parted for heads of state, and encouraging the public to walk or cycle around the complex. Get the free **walking guide** from the well-signposted sales office and embark on a building-by-building tour – only the exteriors, as yet, are viewable.

The Annex also provides access, along a fenced pathway through the operating naval base, to the less interesting **Fort Zachary Taylor State Historical Site** (daily 8am–sunset; cars $3.25 plus 50c per person, pedestrians and cyclists $1.50), built in 1845 and later used in the blockade of Confederate shipping during the Civil War. Over ensuing decades, the fort simply disappeared under sand and weeds. Excavation work has gradually revealed much of historical worth, though it's hard to comprehend the full importance without joining the 45-minute **guided tour** (daily at noon & 2pm). Most locals pass by the fort on the way to the best **beach** in Key West – a place yet to be discovered by tourists, just a few yards beyond.

Along Whitehead Street

A block west of crowded Duval Street, much quieter **Whitehead Street** has a trio of tourable sights and, with its mix of rich and poor homes, reveals a more down-to-earth side of Key West.

On the corner with Greene Street, the **Audubon House and Tropical Gardens** (daily 9.30am–5pm; $5) was the first of Key West's once-elegant Victorian properties to get a thorough renovation – its success encouraged a host of others to follow suit and sent house prices soaring. The name is taken from a man who actually had nothing at all to do with the place; famed ornithologist John James Audubon spent a few weeks in Key West in 1832, scrambling around the mangrove swamps (now protected as the Thomas Riggs Wildlife Refuge, see p.146), looking for the bird life he later portrayed in his highly regarded *Birds of America* portfolio. Yet Audubon's links with this house go no further than the well-observed lithographs that decorate the walls and staircase; the property belonged to a wrecker called John Geiger. Geiger and his wife took in many children from shipwrecks and broken marriages alongside their own twelve-strong brood, and their enormous stock of family photos provides the only flicker of authentic history in the house, which is otherwise loaded with drab nineteenth-century furniture.

---

* The new museum is part of a dramatic metamorphosis affecting the entire annex following its purchase for $17.25 million in 1986 by a young, postmodern property developer called **Pritam Singh**. Remembered by some Key West residents as a scruffy hippie, Singh, who visited Key West in his long-haired youth and later adopted the Sikh religion, has won plaudits for his public- and environment-friendly building schemes all over the US. His plans for the Truman annex are an ambitious blend of preservation, rehabilitation and development; the intention is for mixed-income housing, shops and restaurants to appear amid what should be a carefully thought out historical site. How it will finally shape up is anyone's guess, but the project is a refreshingly far cry from Florida's traditional hit-and-run property scams.

The Hemingway House

It may be the biggest tourist draw in Key West, but to the chagrin of Ernest Hemingway fans, guided tours of the **Hemingway House**, 907 Whitehead Street (daily 9am–5pm; adults $6. under 13s $1.50), deal more in fantasy than fact. Although Hemingway owned this large, vaguely Moorish-style house for thirty years, he lived in it for barely ten, and the authenticity of the furnishings – a motley bunch of tables, chairs and beds much gloated over by the guide – is hotly disputed by Hemingway's former secretary.

Already established as the nation's foremost hard-drinking, hunting- and fishing-obsessed writer, Hemingway bought the house in 1931, not with his own money but with an $8000 gift from the rich uncle of his then wife, Pauline. Originally one of the grander Key West homes, built for a wealthy nineteenth-century merchant, the dwelling was seriously run down by the time the Hemingways arrived. It soon acquired such luxuries as an inside bathroom and a swimming pool, and was filled with an entourage of servants and housekeepers. Some of the writer's most acclaimed work was produced in the deer-head-dominated study (in an outhouse which Hemingway entered by way of a home-made rope bridge): the short stories *The Short Happy Life of Francis Macomber* and *The Snows of Kilimanjaro*, and the novels *For Whom the Bell Tolls* and *To Have and Have Not*; the latter an interesting though hardly inspired description of Key West life during the Depression. Divorced from Pauline in 1940, Hemingway boxed up his manuscripts and moved them to a back room at the original *Sloppy Joe's* (see "Nightlife") before heading off to a house in Cuba with his new wife, journalist Martha Gellhorn.

To see inside the house (and the study) you have to join the half-hour **guided tour** (ten daily), but afterwards you're free to roam at leisure and play with some of the fifty-odd cats. The story that these are descendants from a feline family that lived here in Hemingway's day is yet another dubious claim: the large colony of inbred cats once described by Hemingway were in Cuba.

The Lighthouse Museum and the Bahama Village

From the Hemingway House, you'll easily catch sight of the **Lighthouse Museum**, 938 Whitehead Street (daily 9.30am–5pm; adults $5, under 12s $1), simply because it *is* an 86-foot lighthouse; one of Florida's first, raised in 1847, and still functioning. There's a tiny collection of lighthouse junk and drawings at ground level and it's possible (though tedious) to climb to the top of the tower, but the view is actually better from the top-floor bar of the *La Concha* hotel (see "Accommodation").

The narrow streets around the lighthouse constitute the so-called **Bahama Village**, immediately striking for its lack of tourists and glossy restoration jobs. Most of the squat, slightly shambolic homes – some of them once small cigar factories – are lived in by hard-up people of Bahamian and Afro-Cuban descent.

Caroline and Greene streets, the dockside area and Key West Cemetery

At the northern end of Duval Street turn right into **Caroline** or **Greene Street**, and you'll come across numerous examples of late-1800s **"conch houses"**, built in a mix-and-match style that fused elements of Victorian, Colonial and Tropical architecture, raised on coral slabs, and rounded off with playful "gingerbread" wood trimming. Erected quickly and cheaply, conch houses were seldom painted, but many here are bright and colourful, evincing their recent transformation from ordinary dwellings to hundred-thousand-dollar winter homes.

In strong contrast to the tiny conch houses, the grand three-storey **Curry Mansion**, 511 Caroline Street (daily 10am–5pm; adults $5, under 12s $1), was the abode of William Curry, Florida's first millionaire. Inside, amid a riot of Tiffany glass and mahogany panelling, are a heady stash of strange and stylish fittings – from an antique Chinese toilet bowl to a lamp designed by Frank Lloyd Wright – added to boost the appeal of the $150 bed and breakfast accommodation on offer and making for an amusing ferret through the premises.

The dockside area

Between Williams and Margaret streets, the **dockside area** has been spruced up into a shopping and eating strip called **Land's End Village**, with a couple of enjoyable bars (see "Nightlife"). One with more than drinking to offer is *Turtle Kraals*, in business as a turtle cannery until the Seventies when harvesting turtles became illegal. There are tanks of touchable sea life inside the restaurant and, just along the short pier, a grim gathering of the gory machines used to slice and mince green turtles – captured off the Nicaraguan coast – into a delicacy known as *Granday's Fine Green Turtle Soup*. Apart from pleasure cruisers and shrimping boats along the docks, you might catch a fleeting glimpse of a naval hydrofoil – vessels of unbelievable speed employed on anti-drug-running missions from their base a mile or so along the coast.

Inland: Key West Cemetery

Leaving the waterfront and heading inland along Margaret Street for five blocks will take you to the **Key West Cemetery** (daily sunrise–6pm; free; guided tours Sun at 10am & 4pm; $5; make a reservation on ☎296-3913), whose residents are buried in vaults above ground (a high water table and solid coral rock prevents the traditional six-feet-under interment). Despite the lack of celebrity stiffs, the numerous mildly witty inscriptions, including "I told you I was sick", encourage a casual stroll around – and suggest that the island's relaxed attitude to life also extends to death.

Unlike his more flamboyant counterparts, Key West's longest residing literary notable, playwright **Tennessee Williams** – famous for steamy evocations of Deep South life in novels such as *A Street Car Named Desire* and *Cat on a Hot Tin Roof* – kept a low profile during his 34 years here (he arrived in 1949 and died in 1934); his modest white clapboard **house** (not open to the public) is a fifteen-minute walk from the cemetery, at 1431 Duncan Street.

The rest of Key West

There's not much more to Key West beyond its compact Old Town. Most of the **eastern section** of the island – encircled by the North and South sections of Roosevelt Boulevard – is residential, but Key West's longest beach is located here, and there are several minor points of botanical, natural and historical interest.

At the southern end of White Street, **West Martello Tower** is one of two Civil War lookout points complementing Fort Zachary Taylor (see p.143). In complete variance to the original military purpose, it's now filled by the intoxicating colours and smells of a **tropical garden** (Wed–Sun 9.30am–3.30pm; free). Though it makes a nice outdoor break, a more worthwhile target is the Tower's sister fort, East Martello (see below).

From the tower, Atlantic Avenue quickly intersects with South Roosevelt Boulevard, which skirts on one side the lengthy but slender **Smathers Beach** – the weekend parade ground of Key West's most toned physiques and a haunt of windsurfers and parasailors – and on the other side, the forlorn salt ponds of the **Thomas Riggs Wildlife Refuge**. From a platform raised above the refuge's mangrove entanglements, you should spot a variety of wading birds prowling the grass beds for crab and shrimp. Save for the roar of planes in and out of the nearby airport, the refuge is a quiet and tranquil place; to gain admission you have to phone the Audubon House (☎294-2116) to learn the combination of the locked gate.

Half a mile further, just beyond the airport, the **East Martello Museum and Gallery** (daily 9.30am–5.30pm; adults $3, under 13s $1) is the second of the two Civil War lookout posts. The solid, vaulted casements now store a fascinating assemblage on local history, plus the wild junk-sculptures of legendary Key Largo scrap dealer Stanley Papio, and the Key West scenes created in wood by a Cuban-primitive artist called Mario Sanchez. There are also displays on local writers, and memorabilia from films shot in Key West; the island's old houses and dependable climate have made it a popular location – in recent years, the final scenes of Sydney Pollack's *Havana* were shot here, and *Crisscross* found Goldie Hawn running amok in the Old Town.

A short distance from the tower, South Roosevelt Boulevard meets the end of the Overseas Highway, which crosses over onto the unexciting Stock Island before continuing (as Hwy-1) on its thousand-mile journey to the Canadian border. Staying on Key West, South Roosevelt Boulevard becomes North Roosevelt Boulevard and loops back towards the Old Town, passing a character-less neighbourhood dominated by chain hotels, run-of-the-mill restaurants and the Chernobyl-like chimneys of the local power station.

Eating

Despite the abundant **restaurants** and **snack stands** along the main streets, it's difficult to eat cheaply and well in Key West, though for special occasions you can spash out on several upmarket outlets serving delectable French, Italian and Asian cuisine. For a lower tab, and to avoid the worst of the crowds, seek out some of the places away from Duval Street. Most menus, not surprisingly, feature fresh **seafood**, and you should make an effort at least once to sample **conch fritter** – a Key West specialty. Don't say no, either, to the local conch chowder.

Restaurants and take-away food

A&B Lobster House, 700 Front St (☎294-2536). Overlooking the town's harbour, there could hardly be a more scenic setting for indulging in fresh seafood or sampling the offerings of the raw bar.

Antonia's, 615 Duval St (☎294-6565). Excellent northern Italian cuisine served in a formal though friendly environment; dinner only – expensive but worth it.

Around the World, 627 Duval St (☎296-2115). Dishes drawn from every corner of the globe; if nothing appeals, tuck into the sizeable salads and sample the extensive selection of wines and beers.

Bo's, 429 Duval St (☎294-9272). Over-the-counter fish'n'chips and conch fritters claimed to be the cheapest in town.

Cafe des Artistes, 1007 Simonton St (☎294-7100). Pricey but tremendous tropical-French cuisine, using the freshest local seafood, lobster and steak.

Cafe Marquesa, 600 Fleming St (☎292-1244). Attractive small café offering an imaginative new American-style vegetarian-based menu at moderate prices.

Camille's, 703 Duval St (☎296-4811). Laid-back lunches and dinners, but best patronized for its locally acclaimed breakfasts – a great, low-cost way to start the day.

Croissants des France, 816 Duval St (☎294-2624). Crepes, soups and freshly baked goods for breakfast or lunch, plus mouthwatering cream cakes and pastries for that decadent snack.

Dim-Sum, 613 Duval St (☎294-6230). Thai, Indonesian and Burmese specialties are the core of an exotic Asian menu; don't expect dinner to be less than $20.

Duffy's Steak & Lobster House, 1007 Simonton St (☎296-4900). As the name suggests, there's an immense selection of steak and lobster dishes, all at very appealing prices.

El Siboney, 900 Catherine St (☎296-4184). Inexpensive traditional Cuban dishes and a casual atmosphere.

Key West Cookie Company, 621 Duval St (☎294-3969). Not only freshly baked cookies to take away, but also inexpensive daily lunch specials and the best *café con leche* – Cuban coffee with milk – between Miami and Havana.

Mangoes, 700 Duval St (☎292-4606). Eat indoors or outdoors under huge umbrellas; seafood and a variety of vegetarian dishes created with a Caribbean slant.

Siam House, 829 Simonton St (☎292-0302). Authentic Thai cuisine served with care in a near-authentic Thai setting. Great food, friendly staff and very reasonable prices.

South Beach Seafood & Raw Bar, 1405 Duval St (☎294-2727). Seafood selections in a casual, ocean-front setting; large portions of chicken, beef and ribs are also on offer.

Yo Sake, 722 Duval St (☎294-2288). Choose from an extensive range of traditional Japanese dishes, sample the sushi bar, or choose one of the daily specials – usually excellent value.

Nightlife

The carefully cultivated "anything-goes" nature of Key West is exemplified by the **bars** that make up the bulk of the island's **nightlife**. Gregarious, rough and ready affairs, often open until 4am and offering a cocktail of yarn-spinning locals, revved-up tourists and (often) live country, folk or rock music, the best bars are grouped around the northern end of Duval Street, no more than a few minutes' stagger apart.

Bars and live music venues

Bull & Whistle Bar, 224 Duval St (no phone). Features the best of local musicians each night. Check the list on the door to see whose playing – or just turn up to drink.

Captain Tony's Saloon, 428 Greene St (☎294-1838). This rustic saloon was the original *Sloppy Joe's* (see below), a noted hang-out of Ernest Hemingway. Live music of various kinds every night.

Full Moon Saloon, 1200 Simonton St (☎294-9090). Another laid-back bar which offers live music – be it blues, jazz, reggae or rap – Thurs–Sat until 4am.

Green Parrot Bar, 601 Whitehead St (☎294-6133). A Key West landmark since 1890, this bar draws local characters to its pool tables, dartboard and pinball machine and offers live music at weekends.

Havana Docks, at the *Pier House Hotel*, 1 Duval St (☎296-4600). An upmarket bar offering unparalleled patio views of the sunset accompanied by the lilting strains of a tropical island band. Inside, there's more live music – usually jazz or Latin – Wed–Sat.

Margaritaville, 500 Duval St (☎292-1435). Owner Jimmy Buffett – a Florida legend for his rock ballads extolling a laid-back life in the sun – occasionally pops up to join the live bands that play here nightly.

Sloppy Joe's, 201 Duval St (☎294-5717). Despite the memorabilia on the walls and the hordes of tourists, this bar – with live music nightly – is not the one made famous by Ernest Hemingway's patronage; for which, see *Captain Tony's Saloon*, above.

Turtle Kraals, Lands End Village, end of Margaret St (☎294-2640). A locals' hangout, offering mellow music from a guitar and vocal duo on Fri and Sat nights.

Two Friends, 512 Front St (☎296-3124). A small, friendly bar with live jazz nightly except Mon.

Viva Zapata, 903 Duval St (☎296-3138). You might start your evening at the happy hour in this lively Mexican restaurant, popular with locals as a drinking spot and for its complimentary nachos.

Predominantly gay bars and venues

Tolerant attitudes ensure that the above bars get plenty of **gay** customers (even if not all tourists leave their redneck attitudes on the mainland), but Key West also has a few specifically gay male hangouts.

The Copa, 623 Duval St (☎296-8521). A busy, progressive gay club with an enjoyable garden bar and, Wed–Sun, a pulsating disco with an excellent floor light show and often live entertainment; cover charge varies.

Eight-O-One Bar, 801 Duval St (☎294-4737). Step in off the street to the downstairs bar or continue up to the rooftop level for a great view over Duval Street and beyond; live entertainment at weekends.

La-Te-Da, 1125 Duval St (☎294-8435). The various bars and discos of this hotel complex have long been a favourite haunt of local and visiting gays; the tea dance craze reached its zenith here in the late 1980s.

Listings

Airport Four miles east of the Old Town, on South Roosevelt Blvd (☎296-5439). No public transport link to the Old Town; a taxi will cost $8–9. *American Airlines, Delta* and *USAir* fly into Key West, with flights mainly serving as feeders to their Miami services.

Bike rental From *Adventure Scooter & Bicycle Rentals*, at 708 and 925 Duval St and the *Youth Hostel*, 718 South St (☎296-5719).

Books The *Key West Island Bookstore*, 513 Fleming St, is packed with the works of Key West authors and keys-related literature, and has an excellent selection of second-hand books. At 538 Truman Ave, *Blue Heron Books* specializes in gay studies and the works of local authors, but also has a good general stock.

Buses Local info: ☎292-8164.

Car rental Only worth it if you're heading off to see the other keys. All companies are based at the airport: *Alamo* (☎294-6675); *Dollar* (☎296-9921); *Hertz* (☎294-1039); *Thrifty* (☎296-6514).

Cigars Key West used to be a major producer of cigars. Now they can only be purchased at *La Tabaqueria* in the lobby of the *Southern Cross Hotel* at 326 Duval St; on Fri, Sat & Sun you can see them being rolled.

Dive shops Diving and snorkelling trips and equipment rental can be arranged all over Key West. Try *Captain Corner's*, Zero Duval St (☎296-8865), or *Reef Raiders*, 109 Duval St (☎294-3635). (See also "Reef trips" and "Ecology tours"; below.)

Ecology tours Dan McConnell, based at *Mosquito Coast Island Outfitters*, 1107 Duval St (☎294-7178), runs six-hour kayak tours of back country mangroves ($48.15 per person) filled with facts on the ecology and history of the keys; there's also an opportunity to snorkel in this unique environment. To explore the reef by boat, join the informative half- or full-day tours aboard the 65-foot schooner *Reef Chief* (phone ☎292-1345 for details).

Greyhound 615$\frac{1}{2}$ Duval St (☎296-9072); to find it, turn right by the fire station off Simonton Street.

Hospitals 24-hour casualty department at *Lower Florida Keys Health System*, 5900 Junior College Rd, Stock Island (☎294-5531).

Late food shops *Owls*, 712 Caroline St, daily until 11pm; *Sunbeam Market*, 500 White Street, never closes.

Library 700 Fleming Ave; book sale on the first Saturday of each winter month.

Newsagents *L. Valladares & Son*, 1200 Duval St, stocks British and Irish newspapers and a vast selection of magazines from the US and elsewhere.

Post office 400 Whitehead St (Mon 8.30am–5pm, Tues–Fri 9.30am–5pm, Sat 9.30am–noon; ☎294-2257; zip code 33040).

Reef trips The glass-bottomed *Fireball* makes 6–7 trips a day from the northern tip of Duval St to the Florida Reef; $17.12 for 2 hours (☎296-6293). For snorkelling and diving, see "Dive shops", above.

Supermarket *Fausto's Food Palace*, 522 Fleming St (Mon–Sat 8am–8pm, Sun 8am–6pm).

Taxi Unlikely to be necessary except to get to the airport (see above); try *Five* (☎296-6666) or *Friendly Cab* (☎292-0000).

Watersports Jet-skiing, waterskiing and parasailing are all possible, in the right conditions, using outlets set up alongside Smathers Beach. For more details phone *Sunset Watersports* (☎296-5545) or *Watersports on the Atlantic* (☎294-2696).

Beyond Key West: the Dry Tortugas

Seventy miles west of Key West in the Gulf of Mexico is a small group of islands that the sixteenth-century Spaniard Ponce de León named the **Dry Tortugas** for the large numbers of turtles he found there (the "dry" was added later to warn mariners of the islands' lack of fresh water). Comprising Garden Key and its neighbouring reef islands, the entire area has been designated a wildlife sanctuary to protect the nesting grounds of the snooty tern – a black-bodied, white hooded bird that's unusual among terns for choosing to lay its eggs in scrubby vegetation and bushes. From early January, these and a number of other winged rarities show up on Bush Key, and they are easily spied with binoculars from Fort Jefferson on Green Key (see below).

Fort Jefferson

Green Key is the last place you'd expect to find the US's largest nineteenth-century coastal fortification, but **Fort Jefferson** (daily during daylight hours), which rises mirage-like in the distance as you approach, is exactly that. Started in 1846 and intended to protect US interests on the Gulf, the fort was never completed, despite thirty years of building work. Instead it served as a prison, until intense heat, lack of fresh water, outbreaks of disease and savage weather made the fort as unpopular with its guards as its inmates; in 1874, after a hurricane and the latest yellow fever outbreak, it was abandoned.

Following the signposted **walk** around the fort and viewing the odds and ends in the small **museum** won't take more than an hour – and spare time should be allocated to **swimming and snorkelling**: get a free map of the best locations from the park ranger's office, by the entrance.

You can **get to the fort** by air in half an hour with *Key West Seaplane* from Sunset Marina, 5603 Junior College Road, Stock Island (☎294-6978; $139 half-day, $239 full day) – a beautiful trip that takes you low over the turquoise water. Less expensive and more relaxed is the *Tortugas Ferry* from Key West Sea Port (☎294-7009; $75; Mon, Wed, Sat), which leaves at 7.30am, allows 4 or 5 hours at the fort, and arrives back in Key West at about 7.30pm. Avid bird-watchers can **camp** at Fort Jefferson for up to twenty days, though given its lack of amenities you have to come well prepared with your own supplies of water and food; only in an emergency can you count on help from park rangers.

travel details

Three **Greyhound** buses a day run between Miami and Key West. Scheduled stops are listed below though the bus can be waved down anywhere on the route – stand by the side of the Overseas Highway and jump about like a maniac when you see the bus coming.

Scheduled stops are in North Key Largo (Central Plaza, 103200 Overseas Highway; ☎451-6280); Islamorada (*Burger King*, MM82; ☎852-4266); Marathon (6363 Overseas Highway; ☎743-3488); Big Pine Key (MM30.2; ☎872-4022); and Key West (615 ½ Duval St; ☎296-9072).

From Miami to Big Pine Key (3hr 50min); Islamorada (2hr 20min); Key West (4hr 30min); Marathon (3hr 20min); North Key Largo (1hr 55min).

CHAPTER THREE

THE SOUTHEAST COAST

S tretching from Miami's northern fringe along almost half the state's Atlantic shoreline, the 130-mile **Southeast Coast** is the sun-soaked Florida of popular imagination, with bodies bronzing on palm-dotted beaches as warm ocean waves lap idly against silky-soft sands. Darkening this vision of paradise, however, is the fact that roughly half the region is the fastest-growing residential area in the state, leaving many of the once pristine and spectacular ocean strips walled by unappealing high-rises. While you can drop your beach towel without a worry just about anywhere, don't spend all your time on the Southeast Coast cultivating a tan. Take the trouble to explore some of the towns and seek out the undeveloped, protected sections, where you'll experience the Florida coastline as nature intended it.

The first fifty-odd miles of the Southeast Coast – **the Gold Coast** – are deep within the sway of Miami, comprising back-to-back conurbations often with little to tell them apart. That said, the first and largest, **Fort Lauderdale**, is certainly distinctive: the reputation for rowdy beach parties – stemming from its years as a student Spring Break destination – is well out of date; the town has cultivated a cleaner cut, sophisticated image of late, aided by an excellent art museum and an ambitious downtown improvement project. Further north, diminutive **Boca Raton** also has a style of its own: Mediterranean Revival architecture has been its hallmark since the Twenties, and it possesses some of the Gold Coast's finest beaches. Unconventional architect Addison Mizner shaped Boca Raton, but is best remembered for his work in **Palm Beach**: inhabited almost exclusively by multi-millionaires, yet accessible even to the most impecunious daytripper.

North of Palm Beach, the population thins and natural Florida asserts itself forcefully throughout the **Treasure Coast**. Here, rarely crowded beaches flank long, pine-coated barrier islands such as **Jupiter Island** and **Hutchinson Island**, whose miles of untainted shoreline are quiet enough for sea turtles to come ashore and lay their eggs.

By car, the scenic route along the Southeast Coast is **Hwy-A1A**, which sticks wherever possible to the ocean side of the **intracoastal waterway**. Beloved of Florida's boat owners, this stretch was formed when the rivers dividing the mainland from the barrier islands were joined and deepened during World War II to

---

ACCOMMODATION PRICE CODES

All **accommodation prices** in this book have been coded using the symbols below. Note that prices are for the least expensive double rooms in each establishment. For a full explanation see p.27 in *Basics*.

① up to $30	③ $45–60	⑤ $80–100	⑦ $130–180
② $30–45	④ $60–80	⑥ $100–130	⑧ $180+

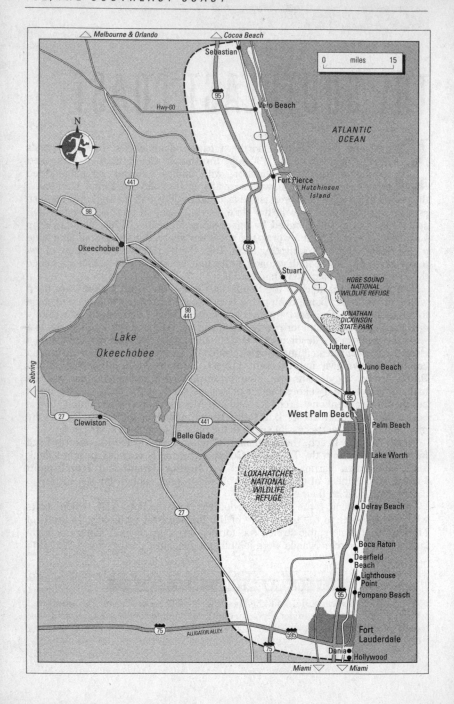

reduce the threat of submarine attack. When necessary, Hwy-A1A turns inland and links with the much less picturesque **Hwy-1**. The speediest road in the region, **I-95**, runs about ten miles west of the coastline, splitting the residential sprawl from the wide-open Everglades, and is only worthwhile if you're in a hurry.

Although most **buses** keep to Hwy-1, the Southeast Coast is good news for non-drivers. Frequent *Greyhound* connections link the bigger towns, and a few daily services run to the smaller communities. Local buses, plentiful from the edge of Miami to West Palm Beach, are nonexistent in the more rural Treasure Coast. Along the Gold Coast, there's the additional option of the dirt-cheap *Tri-Rail* rush hour service, while *Amtrak* has two daily **trains** running as far north as West Palm Beach.

THE GOLD COAST

The widely admired beaches and towns occupying the fifty-mile commuter corridor north from Miami make the **Gold Coast** – named for the booty washed ashore from sunken Spanish galleons – one of the most heavily populated and tourist-besieged parts of the state. The sands sparkle, the nightlife can be fun, and many communities have an assertively individualistic flavour – but if you're seeking peace and seclusion, look elsewhere.

Hollywood and Dania

From Miami Beach, Hwy-A1A runs through undistinguished Hallandale before reaching **HOLLYWOOD** – founded and named by a Californian – with a generous beach and a more cheerful persona than the better-known and much larger Fort Lauderdale, ten miles north. Allocate an hour to the pedestrian-only **Broadwalk**, parallel to Hwy-A1A (known here as Ocean Drive), whose snack bars and skateboarders enliven a casual amble, and the **Art and Culture Center of Hollywood**, 1650 Harrison Street (Tues–Sat 10am–4pm, Sun 1–4pm; $3), which exhibits works by emergent Florida artists.

Modestly priced **motels** line Hollywood's oceanside streets. For good value try the *Stardust*, 915 N Ocean Drive (☎923-5531; ②), or the *Dolphin*, 342 Pierce Street (☎922-4498; ③). As usual, you'll save a few dollars by staying inland, where the *Shell Motel*, 1201 S Federal Highway (☎923-8085; ②), has the best rates.

It was in Hollywood, incidentally, that rap group **2 Live Crew** was arrested for obscenity in June 1990; the group was acquitted, but not before the case became an anti-censorship cause celebre across the country. On the whole, though, Hollywood's nightlife has little at music's cutting edge but plenty to enjoy: solid jazz and R&B are the staple fare of *Club M*, 2037 Hollywood Boulevard (☎925-8396); raunchy rock and roll prevails at the *J & S Restaurant and Lounge*, 5701 Johnson Street (☎966-6196); and country sounds fill the *Southern Fox Tavern*, 6019 Johnson Street (☎961-8964). Blues and food are on offer at the small and rather pricey *Sushi and Blues Café*, 1836 S Young Circle (☎929-9560); and if you fancy a drink right on the beach, accompanied by music and Jamaican food, make for *Sugar Reef*, 600 N Surf Road (☎922-1119). Another cheap, and intimate, place to eat (but without music) is *Try Me Thai*, 2003 Harrison Street (☎926-5585).

> The area code for Hollywood, Dania and Fort Lauderdale is ☎954.

Ocean Drive continues north into **DANIA**, whose prime asset isn't the grouping of pseudo-English antique shops along Hwy-1 but the pine trees and sands of the **John U Lloyd Beach State Recreational Area**, 6503 N Ocean Drive (daily 8am–sunset; cars $3.25, pedestrians and cyclists $1). Situated on a peninsula jutting across the entrance to the shipping terminal of Port Everglades, the park provides an enjoyable, 45-minute nature trail around its mangrove, seagrape and guava trees. If you're around during June and July (Wed & Fri 9pm), you can find out about loggerhead turtle watching; trips include a 20-minute slide presentation and a visit to a nest if one is available, but try to book a month or so in advance as they are immensely popular – and take plenty of insect repellent. Check with a park ranger (☎923-2833) for details on this and other scheduled interpretive activities.

With more time to spare, visit the **Graves Museum of Archeology and Natural History**, 481 S Federal Highway (Tues–Sat 10am–4pm, Sun 1–5pm; $5), which will pursuade any doubters that Florida was inhabited long before *Miami Vice*. In a large and diverse collection, including much from Africa and Egypt, an excellent pre-Columbian section is marked by copious Tequesta Indian artefacts unearthed locally.

Towards Fort Lauderdale: by boat, car or bus

To continue north without a car you can use *BCT*'s **local bus** #1 (which you can catch at any BCT stop on Hwy–1), or the pricier *Greyhound*, 1707 Tyler Street in Hollywood (☎922-8228). Alternatively, if you're not weighed down by luggage, call the *Water Taxi* (☎467-6677) to ferry you from the recreational area to any dockable part of Fort Lauderdale – see "Fort Lauderdale" for more details.

Fort Lauderdale

A thinly populated riverside trading camp at the turn of the century, **FORT LAUDERDALE** came to be known as "the Venice of America" when its mangrove swamps were fashioned into slender canals during the Twenties. From the Thirties, inter-collegiate swimming contests drew the nation's youth here; a fact seized upon by the 1960 teen-exploitation film, *Where The Boys Are*, which instantly made Fort Lauderdale the US's number one Spring Break venue. Hundreds of thousands of students congregated around the seven miles of sand for a six-week pre-exam frenzy of underage drinking and lascivious excess, earning the place a global reputation for rumbustious beach life. By the late Seventies, the students were also bringing six weeks of traffic chaos, and proving a deterrent to regular tourists. Fighting back, the local authorities began a negative advertising campaign across the country's campuses, and enacted strict laws to restrict boozing and wild behavior around the beach.

Subsequently, the students turned their attentions to Daytona Beach (see *The Northeast Coast*), allowing Fort Lauderdale to emerge as an affluent business, historical and cultural centre dominated by a mix of wealthy retirees and affluent yuppies keen to play down the beach-party tag and play up the town's settler-period history. It's not an unpleasant place at all (with a flourishing gay scene, see

"Gay Fort Lauderdale", p.161), despite being a long way from the social inferno you might have been led to expect. **Sports** enthusiasts will find the Greater Fort Lauderdale area a hub of professional activity: you can catch the spring training (in March) of baseball's *New York Yankees* and, during the regular season, watch the *Florida Marlins*. August sees the pre-season training of NFL's *Miami Dolphins* in nearby Davie, and it's not far to Miami to see the *Miami Heat* play professional basketball.

Arrival, transport and information

Known as Federal Highway, Hwy-1 ploughs through the centre of **downtown Fort Lauderdale**, three miles inland from the coast. Just south of downtown, **Hwy-A1A** veers oceanwards off Hwy-1 along SW Seventeenth Street and runs through **beachside Fort Lauderdale**. All the long-distance public transport terminals are in or near downtown: the *Greyhound* **bus station** is at 515 NE Third Street (☎764-6551), while the **train** and *Tri-Rail* station is two miles west at 200 SW 21st Terrace (*Amtrak* ☎1-800/872-7245; *Tri-Rail* ☎1-800-TRI-RAIL), linked to the centre by regular buses #9, #10 and #81.

The handiest service of a thorough **local bus** network (*BCT* ☎357-8400) is #11, which runs twice hourly along Las Olas Boulevard between downtown Fort Lauderdale and the beach; **timetables** are available from Governmental Center, at the corner of Andrews Avenue and Broward Boulevard, or from the bus terminal directly opposite. There is also a free **Downtown Trolley** service, comprising two routes that both run every ten minutes: the Courthouse (on SE Sixth Street) and *BCT* terminal loop (Mon–Fri 7.30am–5.30pm); and the lunchtime express, which travels the length of Las Olas Boulevard (Mon–Fri 11.30am–2.30pm). For a flat fare of $1, you can catch the **Wave Line Trolley** (half hourly 10.15am –10pm; ☎429-3100), which runs along the beach strip – Hwy-A1A between NE 41st Street and 17th Street Causeway.

More expensive than buses – but more fun – are **water taxis** (daily 10am–early hours; ☎467-6677), a series of small boats that will pick up and deliver you almost anywhere along Fort Lauderdale's many miles of waterfront. An all-day pass, allowing unlimited usage, costs $14 (single tickets are $6) and is without doubt the best way to see Fort Lauderdale.

While downtown, gather the latest tourist information from the **Convention and Visitors Bureau**, Suite 1500 in the New River Center at 200 E Las Olas Boulevard (Mon–Fri 8.30am–5pm; ☎765-4466). Also available is a free **entertainments and attractions hotline** (☎527-5600), staffed by operators fluent in five languages.

Accommodation

A handy free booklet, *Superior Small Lodgings Guide,* is available from the Convention and Visitors Bureau (see above), and lists reasonably priced **accommodation** that is inspected annually. Options for staying in downtown Fort Lauderdale are relatively limited, but the scores of **motels** clustered between the intracoastal waterway and the ocean can be exceptionally good value. If money is tight, the well-equipped *Sol Y Mar*, an **AYH hostel** at 2839 Vistamar Street (☎566-1023), has beds for $12 ($15 non-members), as does *International House* (also an AYH hostel), 3811 N Ocean Boulevard (☎568-1615). The closest **camp-**

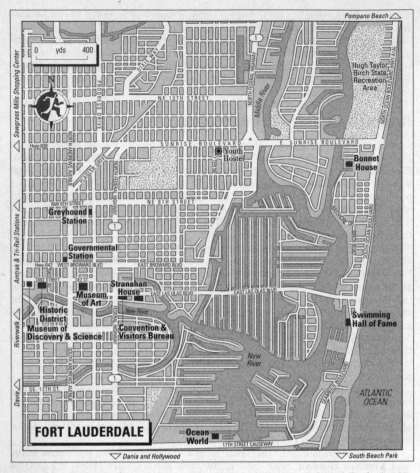

FORT LAUDERDALE

ground is *Easterlin County Park*, 1000 NW 38th Street, Oakland Park (☎938-0610), three miles north of downtown and reached with bus #14.

Bahia Cabana Beach Resort, 3001 Harbor Drive (☎1-800/922-3008). If you came to Fort Lauderdale looking to party, look no further than this tropically themed hotel, restaurant and bar complex, where the fun seldom stops before 2am. ④.

Banyan Marina Apartments, 111 Isle of Venice (☎524-4431). The attractive setting of these apartments, on a waterway a short drive from the beach and close to Las Olas Boulevard, explains the higher price. ④.

Beach Breeze Resort Motel, 550 Breakers Ave (☎1-800/228-4721). A small, inexpensive and friendly motel. ②.

Bermudian Waterfront, 315 N Birch Rd (☎467-0467). North of the centre but handy for the sea. As well as the regular economically priced rooms there are some 1- and 2-bedded suites with fully equipped kitchens. ①–⑦.

Pillars Waterfront Inn, 111 N Birch Rd (☎467-9639). Quiet, relaxing motel with a pool, not far from the ocean. ③.

Riverside Hotel, 620 E Las Olas Blvd (☎1-800/325-3280). Elegant, comfortable, well-placed but over-priced downtown option. ④.

Shell Motel and Apartments, 3030 Bayshore Drive (☎463-1723). This cheerful motel is well-equipped and a stone's throw from the beach. ④.

Downtown Fort Lauderdale

Tall, anonymous, glass-fronted buildings make an uninspiring first impression, but **downtown Fort Lauderdale** has an outstanding modern art museum and a number of restored older buildings to usefully occupy several hours. Lately, too, there's been a multi-million-dollar effort to prettify the district; parks and promenades are linked by the pedestrian-only, one-and-a-half-mile **Riverwalk** along the north bank of the New River, which terminates at the state-of-the-art Museum of Discovery and Science.

The Museum of Art

In a postmodern structure shaped like a slice of pie, the **Museum of Art**, 1 E Las Olas Boulevard (Tues 11am–9pm, Wed–Sat 10am–5pm, Sun noon–5pm, $5; guided tours Tues, Thurs & Fri 1.30pm, free) provides ample space and light for the best art collection in the state, with an emphasis on modern painting and sculpture. The strongest exhibits are drawn from the museum's vast hoard of works under the banner of **CoBrA**, a movement beginning in 1948 with a group of artists from Copenhagen, Brussels and Amsterdam (hence the acronym), and typified by bright expressionistic canvases combining playful innocence with deep emotional power. Important names to look for include Asger Jorn, Carl Henning-Pedersen and Karel Appel, though many later adherents of the genre also produced formidable works – there are plenty of them here to admire.

The Historic District and the Stranahan House

The modern buildings of downtown Fort Lauderdale do little to suggest the community's past. For a quick look at some that do, walk a few blocks west from the Art Museum to the **historic district**, at the centre of which is the **Historical Society**, on Riverwalk at 219 SW Second Avenue (Tues–Fri 10am–4pm, though times may vary $2; ☎463-4431 for the latest info). Here you can pick up details on self-guided walking tours past, and sometimes inside, three of the oldest buildings in Fort Lauderdale, located nearby and in the process of being spruced up for the public: the 1907 **King-Cromartie House**, whose many then-futuristic fixtures include the first indoor bathroom in Fort Lauderdale; the three-storey **New River Inn** (1905), which was the first hotel here; and the **Philomen Bryan House** (1905), once the home of the Bryan family, who constructed many other buildings in this area. To give perspective on the old buildings and the town's past in general, the Historical Society mounts informative temporary displays and stocks plenty of historical books and takeaway pamphlets.

A few minutes' walk east stands a more complete reminder of early Fort Lauderdale life: the carefully restored **Stranahan House (guided tours** Wed, Fri & Sat 10am–3.30pm continuously, closed July & Aug; $3), behind *Wooley's* supermarket on Las Olas Boulevard. Erected in 1901, with high ceilings, narrow windows and wide verandahs, the building is a fine example of the Florida frontier style, and served as the home and trading post of a turn-of-the-century settler, Frank Stranahan. Guided tours of the interior outline the story of Stranahan, a dealer in otter pelts, egret plumes and alligator hides, which he purchased from Seminole Indians trading along the river. Ironically, Stranahan, financially devastated by the late-Twenties Florida property crash, later drowned himself in the same waterway.

The Museum of Discovery and Science

Directly west from the historic district, and marking the end of the Riverwalk, the gleaming **Museum of Discovery and Science** (Mon–Fri 10am–5pm, Sat 10am–8.30pm, Sun noon–5pm; $6) is among the newest and best of Florida's growing number of child-oriented science museums. However, childless adults shouldn't think twice about coming (though they should aim to avoid weekends and school holidays, when the place is packed) because the exhibits present the basics of science in numerous ingenious and entertaining ways. You can even pretend to be an astronaut, rising in an air-powered chair to re-align an orbiting satellite, or making a simulated trip to the moon. The museum also contains an IMAX film theatre (Thurs–Sat, and Sun evenings; $5 or else buy an $8 combination ticket for both museum and IMAX; ☎463-4629).

The Broward Center for the Performing Arts

Continuing west from the Museum of Discovery and Science is the **Broward Center for the Performing Arts**, 201 SW Fifth Avenue (ticket info ☎462-0222), a pleasant, modern, waterfront building that houses Broadway shows and more offbeat productions in its intimate Amaturo Theater.

Around Las Olas Boulevard and the beach

Downtown Fort Lauderdale is linked to the beach by **Las Olas Boulevard** – at the cutting edge of fashion, art, food (from restaurants to sidewalk cafés) – and then by **the Isles**, well-tended canal-side land where residents park their cars on one side of their mega-buck properties and moor their luxury yachts on the other. Once across the arching intracoastal waterway bridge, about two miles on, you're within sight of the ocean and the mood changes appreciably: where Las Olas Boulevard ends, **beachside Fort Lauderdale** begins – T-shirt, sunscreen and swimwear shops are suddenly everywhere.

Along the seafront, **Ocean Boulevard** bore the brunt of Spring Break partying until the clean-up of the Eighties (see above). The whole area has benefited from a multi-million-dollar facelift, and now only a few beachfront bars bear any trace of the carousing of the past, though the sands, flanked by graciously ageing coconut palms and an attractive new promenade, are by no means deserted or dull; joggers, rollerbladers and cyclists create a stereotypical beach scene, and a fair number of whooping students still turn up here each spring.

Since the bulk of Fort Lauderdale's accommodation is here, you'll have no difficulty exploring the beach, the bars, and a few other items of interest in either direction along the main strip.

South along Ocean Boulevard

A short way south of the Las Olas Boulevard junction, the **Swimming Hall of Fame**, 501 Seabreeze Boulevard (Mon–Sat 10am–5pm, Sun 11am–4pm; $4), salutes aquatic sports with a collection even dedicated non-swimmers will enjoy.

The two floors are stuffed with medals, trophies and yellowing press cuttings pertaining to the musclebound heroes and heroines of swimming, diving and many more obscure watery activities.

For a few hours of solitude, thread through the residential streets a mile further south to the placid **South Beach Park**, a restful spot at the tip of Fort Lauderdale's coastline.

North along Ocean Boulevard

In the midst of the high-rise hotels and apartment blocks that now dominate the beachside area, Fort Lauderdale's pre-condo landscape can be viewed in the jungle-like 35-acre grounds of **Bonnet House**, 900 N Birch Road (May–Nov, Wed, Thurs & Fri 10am & 1pm, Sat & Sun 1pm & 2pm; $7), a few minutes' walk off Ocean Boulevard; admission is through guided tours only, for which you'd be advised to turn up fifteen minutes early. The house and its surrounds – including a swan-filled pond and resident monkeys – were designed by Chicago muralist Frank Clay Bartlett and completed in 1921. The tours of the vaguely plantation-style abode highlight Bartlett's eccentric passion for art and architecture – and for collecting ornamental animals, dozens of which fill virtually all of the thirty rooms.

Another green pocket is nearby: beside Sunrise Boulevard, the tall Australian pines of the **Hugh Taylor Birch State Recreation Area** (daily 8am–sunset; cars $3.25, pedestrians and cyclists $1) form a shady backdrop for canoeing on the park's mangrove-fringed freshwater lagoon – a good way to perk yourself up after a morning spent prostrate on the beach.

Eating

Fort Lauderdale has many affordable, enjoyable places to **eat**, featuring everything from exotic Asian creations to homely conch chowder. Restaurants are grouped in different sections of the town, however, and travelling between them can be difficult without a car.

Casablanca Café, intersection of Alhambra and Ocean Blvd, opposite the beach (☎764-3500). An American piano bar in a Moroccan setting with a good, eclectic menu. Expect large portions.

La Crêpe Bretonne, 3025 N Ocean Blvd (☎561-3270). An authentic crêperie overlooking the beach and serving traditional French snacks, high-quality hors d'oeuvres and specialties such as *Canard à l'Orange* (orange duckling) and *Cuisses de Grenouille* (frogs' legs).

Ernie's BBQ Lounge, 1843 S Federal Hwy (☎523-8636). The scruffy but likeable *Ernie's*, south of downtown, is a local legend for its glorious conch chowder (add sherry to taste).

The Floridian, 1410 E Las Olas Blvd (☎463-4041). Downtown coffee shop with a certain flair, serving breakfast, lunch and dinner to a varied and interesting crowd.

Franco & Vinny's Mexican Cantina, 2870 E Sunrise Blvd (☎565-3839). Mexican favourites at giveaway prices near the beach.

Japanese Village, 716 E Las Olas Blvd (☎763-8163). Good Japanese food in a central location.

Lester's Diner, 250 State Rd 84 (☎525-5641). Cheap food first thing in the morning, with the added bonus of coffee served in a 32-ounce cup: a hefty kickstart.

Mangoes, 904 Las Olas Blvd (☎523-5001). Great for burgers; live music and an even livelier atmosphere.

Mistral, 201 S Atlantic Blvd (☎463-4900). Huge plates of sun-drenched, Mediterranean cuisine at the beachfront.

Park Café, 701-B E Broward Blvd (entrance on NE Seventh Avenue; ☎462-1655). Off the beaten track, this friendly and intimate Italian bistro is three blocks from Las Olas and renowned for its homemade tomato pasta sauces. Open from breakfast to dinner; exceptional food and great value for money.

Shirttail Charlie's, 400 SW Third Ave (☎463-3474). Quality seafood and steaks beside the river in the heart of town. In season, alligator and stone crabs feature on the extensive menu.

Shooters Waterfront Café, 3033 NE 37th Ave (☎566-2855). Popular beach-area restaurant drawing large crowds for its generous portions of seafood, burgers and salads.

Southport Raw Bar, 1536 Cordova Rd (☎525-CLAM). Boisterous local bar offering succulent crustaceans and well-prepared fish dishes.

Sukhothai, at *Gateway Plaza*, 1930 E Sunrise Blvd (☎764-0148). Tasty, moderately spiced Thai dishes.

Drinking, live music and nightlife

Some of the restaurants above, particularly *Shooters* and the *Southport Raw Bar*, are also notable **drinking** spots. Other promising libation locations near the beach are the *Parrot Lounge*, 911 Sunrise Lane (☎563-1493), an easy-going bar specializing in over-sized pitchers of beer; and *Elbo Room*, 241 S Atlantic Boulevard (☎463-4615), once a Spring Break favourite but now an ideal place for an evening drink as the ocean breeze ruffles your hair. Inland, try *Shakespeare's Pub & Grille*, 1015 NE 26th Street (☎563-7833), a pseudo-English pub with dart board, decent beer and steak and kidney pies; or the downtown *Nocturnal Café*, 110 SW Third Avenue (☎525-9656), where you'll find goatee beards and Gauloises.

Live music is never far away. To find out who's playing where, call the free *Entertainment Hotline* (☎527-5600), pick up the free *XS* magazine from streetside newsstands, or consult the "*Showtime*" segment of the local *Sun-Sentinel* newspaper's Friday edition. Reliable venues include *Bier Brunnen*, 425 S Ocean Boulevard (☎462-1008), for a variety of musical styles, German beer and bratwurst; *O'Hara's Pub*, 722 E Las Olas Boulevard (☎524-2801), a stylish jazz venue; *Musicians Exchange*, 729 W Sunrise Boulevard (☎764-1912), a less formal space for jazz and rock; and *The Edge*, 109 SW Second Avenue (☎525-9333), which periodically showcases cult indie bands.

Fort Lauderdale's two progressive **nightclubs** are *The Edge* (see above) and *Squeeze*, 2 S New River Drive (☎522-2068). If you're seeking the drunken hedonism of Spring Break, however, you might prefer the regular drink specials and bikini contests at the *Baja Beach Club*, 3200 N Federal Highway (☎561-2432).

Gay Fort Lauderdale

Fort Lauderdale has been one of **gay** America's favourite holiday haunts for years. Predictably, the local conservatism of recent years has caused the scene to quieten, though there's still plenty to delight. For more information, call the *Broward County Gay Hotline* (☎537-0823) or drop into *Out Books*, 1239 E Las Olas Boulevard (☎764-4333).

Accommodation

Fort Lauderdale has a couple of comfortable **guest houses** aimed at gay men: *Midnight Sea*, 3016 Alhambra Street (☎463-4827; ④), and *The Palms on Las Olas*, 1760 E Las Olas Boulevard (☎1-800/858-5182; ⑤). *Big Ruby's*, 908 NE 15th Avenue (☎523-RUBY; ④), has a predominantly gay male clientele but women are also welcome. Of the **mixed** motels, try *La Casa del Mar*, 3003 Granada Street (☎467-2037; ③), or the *Oasis*, 1200 S Miami Road (☎523-3043; ③), whose inland location keeps its prices down.

Bars and clubs

Gay bars and clubs in Fort Lauderdale fall in and out of fashion; read the statewide free weekly newspaper, *TWN*, or the free *XS* magazine for the latest inspots. Usually among the pacesetters are: *Cathode Ray*, 1105 E Las Olas Boulevard (☎462-8611), a video bar that steadily warms up as the evening wears on; *The Copa Cabaret & Disco*, 624 SE 28th Street (☎463-1507), a long-running dance club that draws all ages; *Club Caribbean*, 2851 N Federal Highway (☎565-0402), which has a lively Sunday afternoon tea dance; and *The Hideaway*, 2022 NE 18th Street (☎566-8622), a cruisey bar. For **eating** as well as drinking, you can choose between *Legends Café*, 1560 NE Fourth Avenue (☎467-2233), a BYO restaurant/bar that fills up quickly (it's best to make a reservation); and the popular *Stud Restaurant*, 1000 State Road 84 (☎525-7883).

Inland from Fort Lauderdale

Away from its beach and downtown area, Fort Lauderdale is dismal suburbia all the way to the Everglades. Most people only pass through to reach "Alligator Alley" – the familiar name for I-75, which speeds arrow-straight towards Florida's West Coast a hundred miles distant (see *The West Coast*).

An exception to the prevailing factories, housing estates and freeway interchanges is **DAVIE**, twenty miles from the coast on Griffin Road (take bus #9 from downtown), surrounded by citrus groves, sugar cane and dairy pastures. Davie's 40,000 inhabitants are besotted with the Old West: jeans, plaid shirts and stetsons are the order of the day, and there's even a hitching post (for tethering horses) outside the *McDonald's*. Davie's cowboy origins go back to the 1910s settlers who came here to herd cattle and work the fertile black soil. If you're charmed by the attire, stock up in *Grifs Western*, 6211 SW 45th Street (☎587-9000), a leading purveyor of boots, hats and saddles; otherwise simply turn up for the **rodeo**, held most Saturdays at 8pm at the indoor Rodeo Complex, 6549 SW 45th Street (☎797-1145). A smaller rodeo takes place most Wednesday evenings.

Like its counterparts elsewhere in the state, the **Native Village** at the Seminole Reservation (Mon–Sun 9am–4pm; $5 for a self-guided tour or $6–8 for a guided tour), a mile south of Davie on Hwy-441, is depressing – showing a Native American culture reduced to flogging plastic tomahawks and staging alligator-wrestling shows for tourists. There is some sensitivity to be found, however, in the paintings by Guy LaBree, a local white man who spent time on Seminole reservations during his childhood and whose work is intended to pass legends and history on to younger Seminole generations. More predictably, it's the bingo hall across the road from the village that attracts most white people: laws against high-stakes bingo don't apply to Indian reservations, and you can win $100,000 or more. You can buy your fill of tax-free cigarettes, too.

Twelve miles north of Davie at Coconut Creek, **Butterfly World**, 3600 W Sample Road (Mon–Sat 9am–5pm, Sun 1–5pm; $9.95), stocks, as its name suggests, a massive collection of butterflies. Many are hatched here from larvae – which you'll see in the laboratory – and flap out their short lives around nectar-producing plants inside several aviaries. Spotting Ecuadorian metalmarks, Malay sulpurs and their equally exotic peers, will keep amateur lepidopterists amused for hours.

North from Fort Lauderdale

With a car, stay on Hwy-A1A **north from Fort Lauderdale**: it's a far superior route to Hwy-1 and passes through several sedate beachside communities. One of these, **LAUDERDALE-BY-THE-SEA**, lies around four miles up the coast, and is one of the best places to don scuba-diving gear and explore the reefs.

There are two pleasant **B&Bs** here: *Cristie and Marc's Blue Seas Courtyard*, 4525 El Mar Drive (☎772-3336; ②); and, if you're feeling flush, *A Little Inn by the Sea*, 4546 El Mar Drive (☎1-800/492-0311; ⑤). You'll soon search out the best **eateries**, among them the *Aruba Beach Café*, 1 E Commercial Drive (☎776-0001), where you can tickle your tastebuds with Caribbean and New-World cuisine.

Bus #11 runs this way as far as Atlantic Avenue in **POMPANO BEACH**, two miles on from Lauderdale-by-the-sea. This is one of the larger towns, with a moderately good ocean strip, but if you're independently mobile you should press on.

Three miles further, Hwy-A1A crosses the Hillsboro Inlet, whose 1907 lighthouse gives its name to the posh canal-side community of **LIGHTHOUSE POINT**. There's nothing to detain you here except *Cap's Place*, 2765 NE 28th Court (☎941-0418), which can only be reached from the inland side of the intracoastal waterway; follow directions from NE 24th Street. The food – fresh seafood at affordable prices – is one attraction, but the fact that the restaurant doubled as an illegal gambling den during the Prohibition era is another: Franklin D Roosevelt, Winston Churchill and the Duke of Windsor, remembered by fading photos, are just three of those who have relaxed in the company of owner Cap Knight, a one-time rum-runner whose family presides over the restaurant.

More offbeat history is attached to **DEERFIELD BEACH**, four miles on. As Hwy-A1A twists to the right, you'll catch a glimpse of the triangular **Deerfield Island Park** in the intracoastal waterway. During the Thirties, the island was almost purchased by Al Capone, who, along with his gangster colleagues, frequented the *Riverview Restaurant*'s casino, underneath the Hillsboro Boulevard Causeway at 1741 Riverview Road. Capone's property bid was thwarted by his arrest for tax evasion, and the island, untarnished by development, is occupied today by racoons and armadillos. Its two **walking trails** are reachable only with the free ferry from the *Riverview* on Wednesday and Saturday mornings; call ☎360-1320 for times.

Into Boca Raton

Directly north of Deerfield Beach, Hwy-A1A and Hwy-1 both enter Palm Beach County, the latter becoming the stars-and-stripes-decorated **Blue Memorial Highway**: "a tribute to the armed forces that have served the United States of America", confirming the conservatism of the region. There's plenty of money around, too, much of it in the county's southernmost town, **BOCA RATON** (literally "the mouth of the rat"), populated by golf-mad retirees and the top executives of the numerous hi-tech industries – most famously computer giant IBM – whose headquarters are situated locally. More noticeably, Boca Raton has an abundance of Mediterranean Revival architecture, a style prevalent here since the Twenties and kept alive by strict building codes. The town's new structures have to incorporate arched entrance ways, fake bell towers and red-tiled roofs whenever possible – it may be too contrived for comfort but certainly stands out. Other than the architecture, best seen in downtown Boca Raton around Hwy-1, the town has some under-recognized beaches and parks.

Downtown Boca Raton

The origins of Boca Raton's Spanish-flavoured architecture, which you see all over the **downtown** area, go back to **Addison Mizner**, the "Aladdin of architects", who furnished the fantasies of Palm Beach's fabulously wealthy (see p.170) through the Twenties. Unable to give reign to his megalomaniacal desires elsewhere, Mizner swept into Boca Raton on the tide of the Florida property boom, bought 1600 acres of land and began selling plots of a future community "beyond realness in its ideality". Envisaging gondola-filled canals, a luxury hotel and a great cathedral dedicated to his mother, Mizner's plan was nipped in the bud by the economic crash, and he went back to Palm Beach with his tail between his legs.

The few buildings that Mizner did manage to complete left an indelible mark on Boca Raton. His million-dollar *Cloister Inn* grew into the present **Boca Raton Resort and Club**, a pink palace of marble columns, sculptured fountains and carefully aged wood (the centuries-old effect accomplished by the hobnail boots of Mizner's workmen) that still claims the 160-foot-wide Camino Real – carrying traffic between Hwy-A1A and downtown Boca Raton – as its private driveway. With $200-a-night rooms, the resort is an upper-crust gathering place best viewed on the **guided tours** (Dec–Apr Tues 1.30pm; $5; ☎395-6766) run by the Boca Raton historical society; call to check times and book ahead.

For its part, the historical society resides in a more accessible Mizner work: the dome-topped **Old Town Hall**, 71 N Federal Highway (Mon–Fri 9am–5pm), built in 1927. The society's library, detailing the Mizner times and the rest of Boca Raton's past, is worthy of scrutiny; turn left along the corridor as you enter the building. Nearby, the **old railroad depot**, at the junction of Dixie Highway and SE Eighth Street, is another seminal Mizner-era building but without much allure: the depot (the *Count de Hoernle Pavilion*) is only opened for wedding receptions and meetings, and a couple of post-Mizner streamlined locos stand outside.

The well-heeled of Boca Raton can pay homage to Mizner at **Mizner Park**, off Hwy-1 between Palmetto Park Road and Glades Road, not a park at all, but one of several stylish, open-air shopping malls that have improved downtown Boca Raton in recent years. Decorated by palm trees and waterfalls, and packed with haute couture stores and several affordable places to eat (see "Practicalities", p.165),

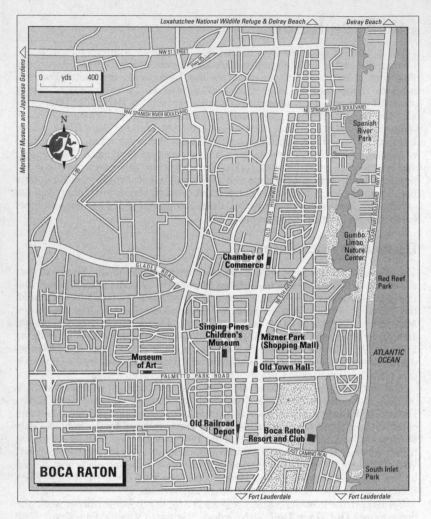

Mizner Park is also home to the new and grandly titled **International Museum of Cartoon Art** (Tues–Sat 11am–5pm Sun noon–5pm; adults $6 children $3).

To escape the Mizner influence altogether, go to the beaches (see below) or turn west into Palmetto Park Road for the **Singing Pines Children Museum**, 498 Crawford Boulevard (Tues–Sat noon–4pm; $1). Housed in a driftwood cracker cottage – the simple abode of early Florida farmers (see *Contexts*) – this stocks entertaining remnants from the pioneer days alongside exhibitions aimed at kids. A mile further, the **Museum of Art**, 801 W Palmetto Park (Mon–Fri 10am–4pm, Sat & Sun noon–4pm; donations), has benefited from donations and inspired curatorship to become one of Florida's finest small art museums.

The area code for Boca Raton and Delray Beach is ☎407.

Besides its temporary exhibitions on leading Florida artists, the museum has a permanent collection that includes the Mayers Collection of drawings by modern masters – Degas, Matisse, Picasso and Seurat are among those represented – and a formidable trove of African art.

Beachside Boca Raton

An air of secrecy hangs over Boca Raton's four **beaches**: all are open to the public but, walled-in by tall rows of Australian pine, it is unlikely that you'll stumble across them by accident. They tend, therefore, to be the preserve of select Floridians rather than long-distance travellers.

The southernmost patch, **South Inlet Park**, is the smallest and quietest of the quartet, often deserted in midweek save for a few people fishing along its short jetty. To reach it, watch for a track turning sharply right off Hwy-A1A, just beyond the Boca Raton Inlet. **South Beach Park**, a mile north, is a surfers' favourite, though the actual beach is a fairly tiny area of coarse sand. **Red Reef Park**, a mile further, is far better for sunbathing and swimming; activities that should be combined with a walk around the **Gumbo Limbo Nature Center** (Mon–Sat 9am–4pm, Sun noon–4pm; donations; ☎338-1473), directly across Hwy-A1A, whose wide boardwalks take you through a tropical hardwood hammock and the mangrove forest beside the intracoastal waterway. Keep your eyes peeled for ospreys, brown pelicans and the occasional manatee lurking in the warm waters. Between May and July you can join the centre's night-time tours to watch sea turtles. These can be extremely popular, however, so you'd be well advised to book as far in advance as possible.

Boca Raton's most explorable beachside area, however, is **Spanish River Park** (daily 8am–sunset; cars $8 weekdays, $10 weekends & holidays, pedestrians and cyclists free), a mile north of Red Reef Park on Hwy-A1A: fifty acres of lush vegetation, most of which is only penetrable on secluded trails through shady thickets. Aim for the 65-foot observation tower for a view across the park and much of Boca Raton. The adjacent beach is a slender but serviceable strip, linked to the park by several tunnels beneath Hwy-A1A.

Boca Raton is also a good place from which to visit Loxahatchee National Wildlife Refuge (see p.174). It's located about ten miles north of here, just off Hwy-441 and two miles south of Boynton Beach Boulevard/Route 804.

Practicalities

There are no *Greyhound* bus terminals in Boca Raton; the nearest are in Pompano Beach (☎305/946-7067) and Delray Beach (☎272-6447). The *Tri-Rail* station is near the Embassy Suites, off Yamato Road and I-95 (☎1-800/TRI-RAIL), and their shuttle buses connect with the town centre. **Local bus** #8 (☎233-4BUS or 930-4BUS) operates from Monday to Saturday and runs from Mizner Park through downtown to the Sandalfoot Shopping Center; $1 one way.

The **Chamber of Commerce**, 1800 N Dixie Highway (Mon–Thurs 8.30am–5pm, Fri 8.30am–4pm; ☎395-4433), supplies the usual info, but don't expect a long list of budget diners and motels – nothing comes cheap in these parts. The cheapest **motels** near the beaches are *Shore Edge*, 425 N Ocean Boulevard (☎395-4491; ④), and *Ocean Lodge*, 531 N Ocean Boulevard (☎395-7772; ④), which also has kitchen units. During the low season you'll save money by sleeping inland at the *Paramount Hotel*, 2901 N Federal Highway (☎395-6850; ② in low season, but ⑥ in high season).

A favourite haunt among locals **eating** out, *Augys*, 1501 NW Second Avenue (☎368-1330), is a family-run concern dishing up southern Italian fare in a lively atmosphere; try their excellent fried calamari or seafood soup. For a good-value breakfast, head for *Tom Sawyer's*, 1759 NW Second Avenue (☎368-4634), where you'll get monstrous helpings. At Mizner Park, the *Bavarian Colony Deli*, 435 Plaza Real (☎393-3989), *Mozarella's Café*, 351 Plaza Real (☎750-3580), and *Ruby Tuesday's*, 409 Plaza Real (☎392-5705), are all worth trying. There's more choice a mile or two further north on the N Federal Highway: standard American fare at the *Boca Diner*, no 2801 (☎750-6744); barbecued ribs and steaks at *Tom's Place*, no. 7251 (☎997-0920); tasty sea fare at *The Seafood Connection*, no. 6998 (☎997-5440); and traditional English food at the English-run eatery *The Ugly Duckling*, no. 5903 (☎997-5929).

Inland from Boca Raton: The Morikami Museum and Japanese Gardens

South Florida is probably the last place you'd expect to find a formal Japanese garden complete with Shinto shrine, teahouse and a museum recording the history of the Yamoto, but ten miles northwest of Boca Raton at the **Morikami Museum and Japanese Gardens**, 4000 Morikami Park Road (Tues–Sun 10am–5pm; $5), you'll find all three. These are reminders of a group of Japanese settlers who came here intending to grow tea and rice and farm silkworms, but finished up selling pineapples until a blight killed off the crop in 1908.

The colony is remembered by artefacts and photographs within the Morikami's older set of buildings. Across the beautifully landscaped grounds, the newer portion of the museum stages themed exhibitions drawn from an enormous archive of Japanese objects and art, and has user-friendly computers ready to impart information about various aspects of Japan and Japanese life. A traditional **teahouse**, assembled here by a Florida-based Japanese craftsman, is periodically used for tea ceremonies.

North towards Palm Beach

Most of the shoulder-to-shoulder towns **north of Boca Raton** have a nice patch of beach, and a couple are putting their modest histories on display, but none should be considered lengthy stops. If you're reliant on public transport, you can take the local *CoTran* **bus** #1S, which runs every hour through towns between Boca Raton and West Palm Beach.

Delray Beach
Five miles north of Boca Raton, **DELRAY BEACH** justifies a half-day visit: its powdery-sanded municipal **beach**, at the foot of Atlantic Avenue, is rightly popular, and is one of the few in Florida to afford a view of the Gulf Stream – a cobalt blue streak about five miles offshore.

Nipping a short way **inland** along Atlantic Avenue, you'll find more to pass the time: on the corner with Swinton Avenue, an imposing school house dating from 1913 forms part of **Old School Square** (Tues–Sat 11am–4pm, Sun 1–4pm; free), a group of buildings restored and converted into a cultural centre. The spacious ground floor of the former school hosts temporary art exhibitions, though a peek upstairs reveals several one-time classrooms still furnished with desks and black-painted walls used to avoid the exorbitant cost of slate blackboards. Within sight, just across NE First Street, the **Cason Cottage** (Tues–Fri 10am–3pm; free), erected in 1920 for Dr John Cason, member of an illustrious local family, warrants a look for its simple woodframe design based on pioneer-era Florida architecture.

Delray Beach makes a sensible **lunch** stop. Near Hwy-1, *The Sundy House*, 106 S Swinton Avenue (☎278-2163), provides midday meals and pots of tea in an antique-filled 1902 home; at the municipal beach, *Boston's on the Beach*, 40 S Ocean Boulevard (☎278-3364), serves fresh seafood. The *Bermuda Inn*, 64 S Ocean Boulevard (☎276-5288; ⑤), is the cheapest beachside **accommodation**.

Lake Worth

If you're pressing on by car, a more inspiring option than Hwy-1 is Hwy-A1A, which charts a picturesque course along twenty-odd miles of slender barrier island, ocean views on one side and the intracoastal waterway – plied by luxury yachts and lined with opulent homes – on the other. Whichever route you take, make a quick stop at **LAKE WORTH** (not to be confused with the actual lake of the same name that divides Palm Beach from West Palm Beach), ten miles north of Delray Beach, for the entertaining clutter of the **Historical Museum**, in the Utilities Department Buildings at 414 Lake Avenue (Tues–Fri 10am–2pm; free). Plant-filled bathtubs, artistically arranged rusting tools and pics aplenty from bygone decades are all infectiously doted over by the museum's curator.

Otherwise, there's nothing to hinder progress to Palm Beach (with Hwy-A1A) or West Palm Beach (with Hwy-1) just a few miles north.

Palm Beach

A small island town of palatial homes, pampered gardens and streets so clean you could eat your dinner off them, **PALM BEACH** has been synonymous for nearly a century with the kind of lifestyle only limitless loot can buy. A bastion of conspicuous wealth whose pomposity – banning washing lines, for example – knows no bounds, Palm Beach is, for all its faults, irrefutably unique.

The nation's nobs began wintering here in the 1890s, after Standard Oil magnate Henry Flagler brought his East Coast railway south from St Augustine and built two luxury hotels on this then secluded, palm-filled island. Throughout the Twenties, Addison Mizner began a vogue for Mediterranean architecture, covering the place with arcades, courtyards and plazas – and the first million-dollar homes. Since then, corporate tycoons, sports aces, jet-setting aristocrats, rock stars and CIA directors have flocked here, eager to become part of the Palm Beach elite and enjoy its aloofness from mainland – and mainstream – life.

Summer is very quiet and easily the least costly time to stay here. The pace hots up between November and May, with the winter months a whirl of elegant balls, fund-raising dinners and charity galas – local residents give more to tax-deductible causes in a year than most people earn in a lifetime. Winter also brings the polo season – watching a chukka or two is the one time Palm Beach

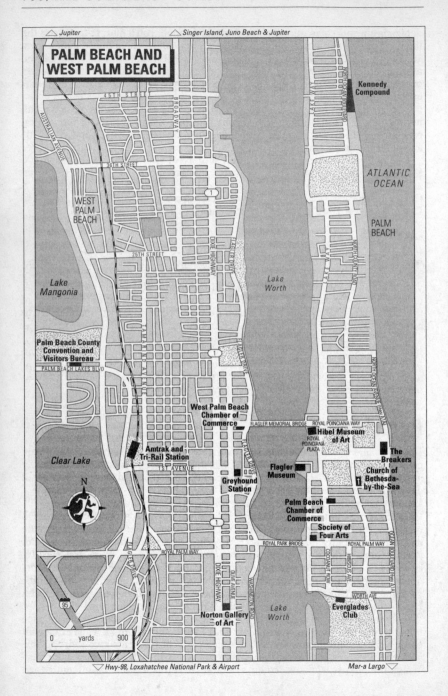

△ Jupiter   △ Singer Island, Juno Beach & Jupiter

PALM BEACH AND WEST PALM BEACH

45TH STREET

BROADWAY

AUSTRALIAN AVENUE

50TH STREET

WEST PALM BEACH

DIXIE HIGHWAY

FLAGLER DRIVE

25TH STREET

1

Lake Mangonia

Lake Worth

ATLANTIC OCEAN

PALM BEACH

NORTH OCEAN BOULEVARD

N LAKE WAY

Kennedy Compound

Palm Beach County Convention and Visitors Bureau

PALM BEACH LAKES BLVD

1

TAMARIND AVENUE

West Palm Beach Chamber of Commerce

FLAGLER MEMORIAL BRIDGE   ROYAL POINCIANA WAY

Hibel Museum of Art

ROYAL POINCIANA PLAZA

Amtrak and Tri-Rail Station

1ST AVENUE

Clear Lake

N

Greyhound Station

Flagler Museum

The Breakers

Church of Bethesda-by-the-Sea

Palm Beach Chamber of Commerce

Society of Four Arts

ROYAL PARK BRIDGE   ROYAL PALM WAY

1

COCOANUT ROW

HIBISCUS AVE

OCEAN BOULEVARD Hwy A1A

NORTH OCEAN AVENUE Hwy A1A

ROYAL PALM WAY

ROYAL PALM WAY

FLAGLER DRIVE

DIXIE HIGHWAY

DIXIE AVENUE

WASHINGTON ROAD

95

WORTH AVE

Everglades Club

Norton Gallery of Art

Lake Worth

0   yards   900

▽ Hwy-98, Loxahatchee National Park & Airport   Mar-a-Largo ▽

denizens show themselves in the less particular environs of West Palm Beach (on the mainland), where the games are held.

Even by walking – much the best way to view the moneyed isle – you'll get the measure of Palm Beach in a day. Either drive in along Hwy-A1A from the south, or use one of the two bridges over Lake Worth from West Palm Beach, the nearest bus and train stop.

The waters off the beach also merit investigation; artificial reefs were created here in the 1960s to protect the coastline by preventing erosion of the natural reef. These are now a spectacular draw for divers; contact the CVB (see p.173) for futher information.

Approaching Palm Beach: the south of the island

Near-neighbours like to think otherwise, but Palm Beach as a byword for wealth, extravagance and exclusivity begins about five miles north of the town of Lake Worth on Hwy-A1A, by the junction with Southern Boulevard (Hwy-98). Here, the **Palm Beach Bath and Tennis Club** is the first of the community's strictly members-only watering holes; its arched windows give sweeping ocean views – passers-by see just the club's guarded entrance. Likewise, for the next couple of miles along this busy two-lane highway (a bad place to cycle or walk, or even stop your car) the high-class homes are shielded from prying eyes by walls of hedges.

You should have no trouble, however, spotting the red-roofed Italianate tower topping **Mar-a-Largo**. Finished in 1926, this was the $8-million winter abode of breakfast cereal heiress Marjorie Merriweather-Post, queen of Palm Beach high society for nearly forty years. On Merriweather-Post's death in 1973, Mar-a-Largo's 118 rooms and eighteen-acre grounds were bequeathed to the US government – who couldn't afford the upkeep; instead, "Florida's most sybaritic private residence" was sold to property tycoon Donald Trump.

Further on, close to the Via La Selva turning, a sprawling property once owned by John Lennon and Yoko Ono can just be glimpsed. Hardly a place to enhance the ex-Beatle's anti-establishment credentials, it earlier belonged to turn-of-the-century multi-millionaire Cornelius Vanderbilt. Half a mile north, Hwy-A1A becomes Ocean Boulevard as it enters the town of Palm Beach.

Palm Beach: the town

The main residential section of Palm Beach – **the town** – is where you should spend most of your time, and **Worth Avenue**, cruised by classic cars and filled with designer stores and high-class art galleries, is a good place to start your stroll.

Other than expense-account acquisition, the most appealing aspect of the street is its architecture: stucco walls, crafted Romanesque facades, and narrow passageways leading to small courtyards where miniature bridges cross non-existent canals and spiral staircases climb to higher levels. On the top floor of one of the courtyard buildings, Via Mizner, situated on the corner with Hibiscus Avenue, sits the former pied-a-terre of the man responsible for the Mediterranean look replicated all over Palm Beach – the flamboyant architect **Addison Mizner**.

After heading up to Worth Avenue's western end to gawp at the vessels moored on Lake Worth – rows of ocean-going yachts with more living space than most people's homes – you should explore the rest of the town along Cocoanut Row or County Road.

PALM BEACH'S ARCHITECT: ADDISON MIZNER

A former miner and prize-fighter, **Addison Mizner** was an unemployed architect when he arrived in Palm Beach in 1918 to recuperate following the recurrence of a childhood leg injury. Inspired by the medieval buildings he'd seen around the Mediterranean, Mizner, financed by the heir to the Singer sewing machine fortune, built the **Everglades Club**, at 356 Worth Avenue. Described by Mizner as "a little bit of Seville and the Alhambra, a dash of Madeira and Algiers", the Everglades Club was the first public building in Florida in the Mediterranean Revival style, and fast became the island's most prestigious social club.

The success of the club, and the house he subsequently built for society bigwig Eva Stotesbury, won Mizner commissions all over Palm Beach as the wintering wealthy decided to swap suites at one of Henry Flagler's hotels for a "million-dollar cottage" of their own.

Brilliant and unorthodox, Mizner's loggias and U-shaped interiors made the most of Florida's pleasant winter temperatures, while his twisting staircases to nowhere became legendary. Pursuing a medieval look, Mizner used untrained workmen to lay roof tiles crookedly, sprayed condensed milk onto walls to create an impression of centuries-old grime, and fired shotgun pellets into wood to imitate worm holes. By the mid-Twenties, Mizner had created the Palm Beach Style – which Florida architecture buff Hap Hattan called "the old world for the new rich". Mizner later fashioned much of Boca Raton, for which see p.163.

Along Cocoanut Row

Four blocks north from its junction with Worth Avenue, **Cocoanut Row** crosses Royal Palm Way, close to the stuccoed buildings of the **Society of the Four Arts** (Mon–Sat 10am–5pm, Sun 2–5pm; suggested donation $3). Between early December and mid-April this holds art shows and lectures of an impressive standard, and its **library** (May–Oct Mon–Fri 10am–5pm; Nov–April Mon–Fri 10am–5pm, Sat 9am–1pm) is worth a browse.

Half a mile further along Cocoanut Row you'll notice the white Doric columns fronting **Whitehall**, also known as the Henry Flagler Museum (Tues–Sat 10am–5pm, Sun noon–5pm; $7; last tour leaves between 3.15pm and 3.30pm). The most overtly ostentatious home on the island, Whitehall was a $4-million wedding present from Henry Flagler to his third wife, Mary Lily Kenan, whom he married (after controversially persuading the Florida legislature to amend its divorce laws) in 1901. Like many of Florida's first luxury homes, Whitehall's interior design was created by pillaging the great buildings of Europe: among the 73 rooms are an Italian library, a French salon, a Swiss billiard room, a hallway modelled on the Vatican's St Peter's and a Louis XV ballroom. All are richly stuffed with ornamentation but – other than mutual decadence – lack any esthetic cohesion. Flagler was in his seventies when Whitehall was built, 37 years older than his bride and not enamoured of the banquets and balls she continually hosted. He often sloped off to bed using a concealed stairway, perhaps to ponder plans to extend his railway to Key West – a display on the project fills his former office. From the 110-foot hallway, informative but not compulsory 45-minute **free guided tours** depart continuously and will leave you giddy with the tales – and the sights – of the earliest Palm Beach excesses.

Whitehall was built beside Flagler's first Palm Beach resort, the *Royal Poinciana Hotel*: a six-storey, Colonial-style structure of 2000 rooms which became the world's largest wooden building on completion in 1894. Other than a small plaque marking the spot, not a trace remains of the hotel, whose hundred-acre grounds spread to what's now Royal Poinciana Way. Here, on the corner with Cocoanut Row, you'll find Royal Poinciana Plaza, a soulless grouping of estate agents' and art dealers' offices, and also the **Hibel Museum of Art**, 150 Royal Poinciana Plaza (Tues–Sat 10am–5pm, Sun 1–5pm; free). Forget Warhol and Rothko, the most commercially successful artist in the US is **Edna Hibel**, a septuagenarian resident of Singer Island (just north of Palm Beach – see p.174), whose works fill this deep-carpeted gallery. Inspired by "love", Hibel has been churning out coy, sentimental portraits, usually of serene Asian and Mexican women, since the late Thirties, often working seven days a week to meet demand. Pay a visit, though, if only to admire the unflappable devotion of the guides, and to figure out why Hibel originals change hands for $50,000.

Along County Road

In terms of things to see, **County Road** is the poor relation of Cocoanut Row – to which it runs parallel – but is still worth a stroll. Along it, two blocks north of Worth Avenue, Mizner's Mediterranean Revival themes are displayed in Palm Beach's very tidy local administration offices and bank buildings. By contrast, the 1926 **Church of Bethesda-by-the-Sea**, a fifteen-minute walk further, is a handsome imitation-Gothic pile replacing the island's first church (see "The North of the Island"): the large stained-glass windows depict Christianity around the world, but ignore them and walk instead through the echoing cloisters to the **Cluett Memorial Gardens** (daily 9am–5pm; free), a peaceful spot in which to take a stone pew and tuck into a picnic lunch.

A little further north, County Road is straddled by the golf course of **The Breakers** hotel, erected in 1926 and the last of Palm Beach's swanky resorts. Inside, the lobby is filled with tapestries, chandeliers, huge fireplaces and painted ceilings; at 3pm on a Wednesday there's a **free guided tour** of the premises.

The North of the island

The limited points of interest beyond Royal Poinciana Way are best viewed from the three-mile **Lake Trail**, a cycle and pedestrian path skirting the edge of Lake Worth, almost to the northern limit of the island. A bicycle is the ideal mode of transport here: rent one from *Palm Beach Bicycle Trail Shop*, 223 Sunrise Avenue (☎659-4583), for $15 a half day.

Most locals use the trail as a jogging strip, and certainly there's little other than exercise and fine views across the lake to make it worthwhile. Keep an eye out, though, for "Duck's Nest", the oldest remaining home in Palm Beach, built in 1891, and the original **Church of Bethesda-by-the-Sea**, dating from 1889. Serving a congregation of early homesteaders across a 125-mile stretch of coast, all of whom had to get here by boat, the shingled church is now a private house, but easily spotted by the clockface hanging from its short tower.

The lake trail expires a few minutes' pedal south of the Lake Worth Inlet, a narrow cut separating Palm Beach from the high-rise-dominated Singer Island; to get to the inlet – for a sight of the neighbouring island and a modest feeling of achievement – weave on through the short residential streets.

For variation, cycle back to central Palm Beach along Ocean Drive (take care as there's no marked cycle path), which passes the two-acre former **Kennedy**

The area code for Palm Beach is ☎407.

Compound, at 1095 N Ocean Boulevard, bought by Joe Kennedy – father of John, Robert and Edward – in 1933. The Kennedys never fully integrated into ultra-conservative Palm Beach life; feeling unwelcome at the Everglades Club, Joe upset the establishment by joining the rival Palm Beach Country Club – and it's said that few Palm Beach tears were shed in 1963 when John (then President) was assassinated. It was on this estate that the most recent scandal to rock Palm Beach occured: the arrest in April 1991 of William Kennedy Smith, nephew of Senator Edward Kennedy, on charges of sexual battery (Florida's legal term for rape), of which he was acquitted.

Practicalities

In a town that often fights shy of tourists, the **Chamber of Commerce**, 45 Cocoanut Row (Mon–Fri 9am–4.30pm in winter, 10am–4.30pm in summer; ☎655-3282) is a welcome provider of free maps and reliable **information**.

You'll need plenty of money to **stay** in Palm Beach: comfort and elegance are the key words, and prices can vary so greatly depending on the time of year that we've noted both high and low season prices below. *Palm Beach Historic Inn*, 365 S County Road (☎832-4009; ④–⑥), is a bed and breakfast spot with the best rates in town, but you'll need to book early. Otherwise, to save money come between May and December, when the lowest prices on the island are found at *The Chesterfield*, 363 Cocoanut Row (☎1-800/CHESTR-1; ④–⑧); the *Colony*, 155 Hammon Avenue (☎1-800/521-5525; ⑤–⑧); the *Heart of Palm Beach*, 160 Royal Palm Way (☎1-800/523-5377; ⑥–⑧); and *The Plaza Inn*, 215 Brazilian Avenue (☎1-800/233-2632; ④–⑥). Obviously, it's far cheaper to stay outside Palm Beach and visit by day – easily done from West Palm Beach even without a car; see below.

Encouragingly, you can **eat** relatively cheaply. *TooJay's*, 313 Royal Poinciana Plaza (☎659-7232), is a top-notch bakery and deli open from breakfast onwards, where you can choose from a wide selection of food, including scrumptious omelettes for less than $6; *Green's Pharmacy*, 151 N County Road (☎832-0304), has a steady supply of diner fare for breakfast and lunch; and *Hamburger Heaven*, 314 S County Road (☎655-5277), dispenses delicious ground-beef burgers. A more expensive option, at between $10 and $15 a throw, is *Testa's*, 221 Royal Poinciana Way (☎832-0992), which serves exquisite seafood and pasta. If money is no object (you'll spend at least $50 a head) and you're dressed to kill, make for the super-elegant French restaurant *Café L'Europe*, 331 S County Road (☎655-4020). Alternatively, the *Publix* supermarket at 265 Sunset Avenue is a useful port of call if the above are closed or you just want picnic fare.

Thrift stores

Amazingly high-class clobber, some of it discarded after only a single use, turns up in Palm Beach's **thrift stores**, though the prices are above normal thrift-store levels. Worth perusing are *The Church Mouse*, 374 S County Road (☎659-2154), *Goodwill Embassy Boutique*, 210 Sunset Avenue (☎832-8199), *Thrift Store Inc*, 231 S County Road (☎655-0520), *Hab Center Boutique & Consignment*, 212B Sunset Avenue (☎832-6913), or *Déja Vu*, 215 Royal Poinciana Way (☎833-6624).

West Palm Beach and further inland

Founded to house the workforce of Flagler's Palm Beach resorts, **WEST PALM BEACH** has long been in the shadow of its glamorous neighbour across the lake. Only during the last two decades has the town gained some life of its own, with smart new office buildings, a scenic lakeside footpath – and less seemly industrial growth sprouting up on its western edge. Above all, West Palm Beach holds the promise of accommodation and food at a lower price than in Palm Beach, and is the closest you'll get to the island using public transport – *CoTran* buses from Boca Raton and *Greyhound* services stop here (details below), leaving a few minutes' walk to Palm Beach over one of the Lake Worth bridges.

Other than basic needs, just the classy collections of the **Norton Gallery of Art**, 1451 S Olive Avenue (Tues–Sat 10am–5pm, Sun 1–5pm; $5 donation suggested), a mile south of the downtown area, provide reason to linger. Together with some distinctive European paintings and drawings by Gauguin, Klee, Picasso and others, the gallery boasts a solid grouping of twentieth-century American works: Mark Tobey's study of stifling urban motion, *The Street*, and Stuart Davis' *New York Mural* impress most. Among a sparkling roomful of Far Eastern pieces are seventh-century sculpted buddhas, absorbingly complex amber carvings and a collection of 1500–500 BC tomb jades.

Information and public transport

The **Chamber of Commerce**, 401 N Flagler Drive, at the corner of Fourth Street (Mon–Fri 8.30am–5pm; ☎833-3711), and the **Palm Beach County Convention and Visitors Bureau**, Second Floor, NationsBank Building at 1555 Palm Beach Lakes Boulevard (Mon–Fri 8.30am–5pm; ☎471-3995), have stacks of free leaflets, and can answer questions on the whole Palm Beach county area. The West Palm Beach **train** (☎1-800/872-7245) and *Tri-Rail* (☎1-800/TRI RAIL) station is at 201 S Tamarind Avenue, and linked by regular shuttle buses to the downtown area. Most *CoTran* **bus** (☎233-1111) routes converge at Quadrille Road; the *Greyhound* station is at 100 Banyan Boulevard (☎833-8534).

Sleeping, eating and nightlife

Most budget chain **motel** prices in West Palm Beach are inflated. The best deals are to be found at *Queens Lodge*, 3712 Broadway (☎842-1108; ②), *Parkview Motor Lodge*, 4710 S Dixie Highway (☎1-800/523-8978; ④), *Mt Vernon Motor Lodge*, 310 Belvedere Road (☎1-800/545-1520; ②), or *Knights Inn*, 2200 45th Street (☎478-1554; ④).

For cheap **eats**, go to *Robinson's Pastry Shop*, 215 Clematis Street (☎833-4259), which sells wonderful freshly baked snacks and sandwiches during the day, or to the *Respectable Café*, 518 Clematis Street (☎832-9999) – also good for an evening **drink** and live music. More tasty, inexpensive food can be found at *Margarita's*, 2030 Palm Beach Lakes Boulevard (☎684-7788), where you can sample Mexican food, and at *New England Lobster & Seafood*, 3420 45th Street (☎686-0040), which serves a variety of reasonably priced seafood sandwiches and burgers. For food and a few laughs, visit *The Comedy Corner*, 2000 S Dixie Highway (☎833-1812), from 8.30pm Wed–Sun, which has a bar and stand-up comics ($1 admission).

Inland from West Palm Beach

If you have a car, West Palm Beach makes a good access point for the **Loxahatchee National Wildlife Refuge** (daily 6am–7.30pm; cars $3.25, pedestrians and cyclists $1; visitor center open Wed–Sun); travel west along Hwy-80 for about five miles, then turn south along Hwy-441, and the well-signposted main entrance is twelve miles ahead. The 200 square miles of sawgrass marshes – the northerly extension of the Everglades (see p.317) – are only marginally penetrable on two easy **walking trails** from the **visitor center** (☎734-8303), one through a Cypress hammock, the other a boardwalk over the marshes to an observation tower. On either, you'll probably see a few snakes and alligators and get a firm impression of what undeveloped inland Florida is all about – and how incredibly flat it is. It's possible to go on guided canoe trails, airboat rides, bird walks and "night prowls": call ☎732-3684 for more information.

African and Asian wildlife is the star attraction of **Lion Country Safari** (daily 9.30am–5.30pm; last vehicles admitted 4.30pm; $12.95), on Southern Boulevard W (15 miles west of I-95 and before the junction of Hwy-98 and 441). Lions, elephants, giraffes, chimpanzees, zebras and ostriches are among the creatures roaming a 500-acre plot where human visitors are confined to their cars. It's awkward to reach and expensive to visit, but if you can't leave Florida without photographing a flamingo, *Lion Country Safari* could well be for you.

Venturing **further inland** to the Lake Okeechobee area (described in *Central Florida*), Hwy-80 from West Palm Beach runs the forty miles to the lakeside town of Belle Glade, a route traversed by *CoTran* bus #10 – but not a good place to be without independent transport.

THE TREASURE COAST

West Palm Beach marks the northern limit of Miami's hinterland and the end of the Southeast Coast's heavily touristed sections. Aside from some small and uninspiring towns, the next eighty miles – dubbed the **Treasure Coast** simply to distinguish it from the Gold Coast – missed out entirely on the expansion seen to the south and to the north, leaving wide open spaces and some magnificent swathes of quiet beach that attract Florida's nature lovers and a small band of well-informed tan-seekers.

Singer Island and Juno Beach

North out of West Palm Beach, Hwy-A1A swings back to the coast at **Singer Island**, a familiar name to anyone who's read Charles Willeford's novel *Sideswipe*: the author's Miami homicide cop, Hoke Moseley, holes up here for a few weeks before boredom drives him back south. The beaches are perfectly adequate but the place lacks life and is predominantly residential, with little budget-range accommodation, apart from *The Sands Hotel Resort*, 2401 Beach Court (☎842-2602; ③). Nearby, on Hwy-A1A, is the **John D. MacArthur Beach State Park** (daily 8am–sunset; visitor center open Wed–Sun 9am–5pm; cars $3.25, pedestrians and cyclists $1), one of the few beach state parks, with worthwhile nature trails and swimming areas.

The next few miles are mostly golf courses and planned retirement communities, but one good stop is **JUNO BEACH**, where Hwy-A1A follows a high coastal bluff and, with luck, you'll find one of the unmarked paths down to the uncrowded sands.

Alternatively, keep going until you reach the beachside **Loggerhead Park**, also the site of the **Marine Life Center** (Tues–Sat 10am–3pm; free), intended for kids but allowing adults to brush up on their knowledge of marine life in general and sea turtles in particular – there's a turtle hatchery here and displays on their life cycles. The only time turtles give up the security of the ocean is between June and July, when they steal ashore to lay eggs under cover of darkness. This is one of several places along the Treasure Coast where expeditions are led to watch them; get the details at the museum or on ☎627-8280. Reservations are essential and taken from May.

Jupiter and Jupiter Island

Splitting into several anodyne districts around the wide mouth of the Tequesta River, **JUPITER**, about six miles north of Juno Beach, was a rum-runners' haven during the time of Prohibition; these days it's better known as the home town of Florida's favourite son, actor Burt Reynolds, markers to whom are everywhere. The first is the *Jupiter Theater*, where Hwy A1A meets Indiantown Road. Founded by the man himself in 1979, the theatre is the base of one of Florida's better professional companies; phone ☎746-5566 for details of their repertoire. Nearby, the Reynolds-owned *Backstage* restaurant, 1061 Indiantown Road (☎747-9533), serves expensive gourmet lunches and dinners beneath walls covered by pics of Burt, Burt's ex-wife and Burt's celebrity friends. Anyone on a Burt pilgrimage will also enjoy a walk through Burt Reynolds Park, near the town centre, beside Hwy-1, where the **Florida History Center and Museum** (Tues–Fri 10am–4pm, Sat & Sun 1–4pm; $4), daringly perhaps, describes pioneer life on and around the Tequesta River long before Burt's time. To gain more insight into how the pioneers lived, walk through an original home located in the grounds and once the property of the DuBois family (Wed & Sun 1pm–4pm; $2) and, if you happen to be here on 8th Oct, join in the rib-eatin', chilli-cookin', beer-swillin', foot-stompin' country dance and hoedown at the **Burt Reynolds Ranch**, two miles south of town at 16133 Jupiter Farms Road (☎746-0393).

The only other thing in Jupiter to merit consideration is the red-brick **lighthouse**, a nineteenth-century beacon on the north bank of the Jupiter inlet, with a small **museum** in the Jupiter Lighthouse Park (Sun–Wed 10am–4pm, $5; Sun afternoons only, free). The lighthouse can be seen from Beach Road, the route Hwy-A1A takes back to the coast after looping through the town. This route skirts the **Jupiter Inlet Colony** – a rich person's billet whose roads are guarded by photo-electric beams, enabling police to check any suspicious traffic cruising the dead-end streets – before heading north along Jupiter Island. If you're feeling peckish, a great place for **seafood** is *Charley's Crab*, 1000 N Hwy-1 (☎744-4710), back at the Jupiter inlet.

Jupiter Island

Two miles into **Jupiter Island** on Hwy-A1A, pull up at the **Blowing Rocks Preserve** (daily 6am–5pm; suggested donation $3), where a limestone outcrop covers much of the beach and powerful incoming tides are known to drive through the rocks' hollows, emerging as gusts of spray further on. At low tide, it's sometimes possible to walk around the outcrop and peer into the rock's sea-drilled cavities. A new education centre (for all ages) includes an exhibit centre, butterfly garden and boardwalk, and in June and July you can take part in night-time walks to watch sea turtles; book ahead on ☎575-2297.

Seven miles further north, the shell-strewn Hobe Sound Beach marks the edge of **Hobe Sound National Wildlife Refuge**, which occupies the remainder of the island. Having achieved spectacular success as a nesting ground for sea turtles during the summer (turtle walks available in June and July; call ☎546-2067), the refuge is also rich in birdsong, with tweeting scrub jays among its tuneful inhabitants. To find out more about the flora and fauna, call in at the small **interpretive center** (Mon–Fri 9–11am & 1–3pm; ☎546-2067), on the mainland where Hwy-A1A meets Hwy-1.

The northern end of Jupiter Island comprises **St Lucie Inlet State Park** (daily 8am–sunset; cars $3.25, pedestrians and cyclists $1), whose 928 acres include mangrove-lined creeks and over two miles of beach. It's occasionally possible to see manatees feeding in the grass beds north of the dock, and the boardwalk is interesting primarily for the skunklike aroma emitted by the aptly named Shite-Stopper, a tropical tree.

Inland: the Jonathan Dickinson State Park

Two miles south of the Hobe Sound interpretive center on Hwy-1, the **Jonathan Dickinson State Park** (daily 8am–sunset; cars $3.25, pedestrians and cyclists $1) preserves a natural landscape quite different from what you'll see at the coast. Step up to the observation platform atop **Hobe Mountain**, an 86-foot-high sand dune, and survey the pines, palmetto (a stumpy, tropical palm fan) flatlands and the mangrove-flanked course of the winding Loxahatchee River. The intrepid can obtain hiking maps from the entrance office and set off along the nine-mile **Kitchen Creek trail**, which starts from the park's entrance and finishes up in a cypress hammock at some basic campgrounds; beware that campground space must be booked in advance (☎546-2771). Cabins, at $50 a night, are also available; phone ahead on ☎1-800/746-1466.

Anyone less adventurous should rent a canoe from the people who rent out the cabins (see above) and paddle along the Loxahatchee River – don't be put off by the preponderance of alligators – to the **Trapper Nelson interpretive center**, named after a Quaker washed ashore near here in 1697. Another way to get there is by taking the two-hour **Loxahatchee River Cruise** (four daily Wed–Sun, 9am–3pm; $10; reservations ☎1-800/746-1466).

Stuart and Hutchinson Island

Another long barrier island lies immediately north of Jupiter Island. To reach it (with either Hwy-1 or Hwy-A1A), you'll first pass through **STUART**, a neat and tidy town on the south bank of the St Lucie River. Stuart has a number of century-old wooden buildings proudly preserved on and around Flagler Avenue – pick up a **free walking guide** from the **Chamber of Commerce**, 1650 S Kanner Highway (Mon–Fri 9am–5pm; ☎287-1088) – and a *Greyhound* station at 757 SE Monterey Road (☎287-7777), but not much else to keep you engaged. There is a

bike rental outlet, however, *Pedal Power*, 1211 SE Port St Lucie Boulevard
(☎335-1310), which you'll need (if you don't have a car) to make the four-mile trip
along Hwy-A1A, over the intracoastal waterway and to Hutchinson Island (though
the cycle path only begins at Jensen Beach – see below). For a bite to **eat** in
downtown Stuart, try the *Riverwalk Café*, 21 SW St Lucie Avenue (☎221-1511) or
The Flagler Grill, 47 SW Flagler Avenue (☎221-9517).

Hutchinson Island

Largely hidden behind thickly grouped Australian pines, several beautiful
beaches line the twenty-mile-long **Hutchinson Island**: keep your eyes peeled for
the public access points. It would be hard, however, to miss **Stuart Beach**, facing
Hwy-A1A as it arrives from the mainland: a low-key stretch of brown sand where
tourists are heavily outnumbered by locals – a fine venue for a few hours of ray
absorption.

Close by, at 825 NE Ocean Boulevard, the **Elliott Museum** (daily 11am–4pm;
$4) exhibits a sizeable hotch-potch of mechanical objects and ornaments, few of
which seem to have much to do with inventor Sterling Elliott, whom the place is
intended to commemorate. A talented inventor active from the 1870s, Elliott's
creations displayed here include an automatic knot-tier and the first addressing
machine, while his quadricycle – a four-wheeled bicycle – solved many of the
technical problems that hindered the development of the car. It's hard, therefore,
to fathom why much of the museum is given over to reconstructed turn-of-the-
century shops, Victorian fashion accessories and a hangar full of vintage cars. A
new addition to this mish-mash is autographed memorabilia of members of the
Baseball Hall of Fame.

A mile south, **Gilbert's House of Refuge** (Tues–Sat 11am–4pm; $2) is a
better stop: a convincingly restored refuge for wrecked sailors that was one of
five erected along Florida's east coast during the 1870s. Furnished in spartan
Victorian style, the rooms of the refuge are best understood with the **free guided
tour** (starting when you're ready, every day except Saturday). There's more
evidence of the refuge's importance in the entrance area – lifeboat equipment,
ship's logs and a modern weather station – along with reminders of the building's
more recent function as a sea turtle hatchery.

Pushing on, roughly halfway along the island, **JENSEN BEACH** has the only
road to the mainland between Stuart and Fort Pierce, as well as a small but pleasant beach. If you feel like sticking around to eat, *Café Coconuts*, 4304 NE Ocean
Boulevard (☎225-6006), provides cheap fare and a bar. For accommodation try
the *Dolphin Motor Lodge*, 2211 NE Old Dixie Highway (☎334-1313; ③). Jensen
Beach also marks the start of a **cycle path**, which continues – passing one of
Florida's two nuclear power stations (which has a visitor center with interactive
exhibits; for opening times call ☎468-4111; free admission) – to the Fort Pierce
Inlet, which divides Hutchinson Island in two. To reach the northern half (known
as North Hutchinson Island), you'll need to pass through the area's biggest town,
Fort Pierce.

The area code for the parts of the Treasure Coast mentioned in this chapter is ☎407.

Fort Pierce

A number of rustic motels, bars and restaurants grouped along Hwy-A1A beside a more than adequate beach make the first taste of **FORT PIERCE** a favourable one. The bulk of the town (looped through by Hwy-A1A) lies two miles away across the intracoastal waterway, where tourism plays second fiddle to processing and transporting the produce of Florida's citrus farms. The convivial coastal section makes an amenable base for island exploration, but the mainland town has only a few features likely to dent your day. Scuba diving off the coast is, however, an entirely different prospect, giving you a chance to explore reefs and wrecks dating back to Spanish galleons; see "Practicalities", p.180 for details.

The Historical Museum

Beside Hwy-A1A, close to the intracoastal waterway bridge at 414 Seaway Drive, the **St Lucie County Historical Museum** (Tues–Sat 10am–4pm, Sun noon–4pm; $2) keeps a cogent assembly of relics. Among them are a full-sized Seminole Indian *chickee* (an open-sided, palm-thatched hut), a hand-carved canoe and a solid account of the Seminole Wars, including the 1835 fort from which Fort Pierce took its name, and a re-creation of *P.P. Cobb's* general store, the hub of the turn-of-the-century town. Outside the museum, a 1907 "cracker" cottage (Gardner House) can be given a once-over; note the tall ceilings and many windows allowing the muggy Florida air to circulate in the days before air conditioning. The museum also contains an exhibitions gallery and a fully restored 1919 fire engine.

Downtown Fort Pierce and around

Entering **downtown Fort Pierce**, your gaze is held by a sewage treatment works and the towers of a cement factory, which provide a stark contrast to Hutchinson Island's raging vegetation. If you've time, however, Hwy-A1A quickly escapes oceanwards to North Hutchinson Island. If you have time in hand, don't bother with the downtown area but make an excursion a few miles north along Hwy-1. From mid-Nov to early April, you may catch sight of manatees in the Indian River Lagoon. A viewing area is located at Moore's Creek at the marina, where Avenue C and North Indian River Drive meet.

The Capron Trail Monument and Indian River Drive

A couple of miles north of downtown Fort Pierce, Hwy-1 crosses St Lucie Boulevard, and a left turn along here leads to a memorial (by the junction with 25th Street) recalling the nineteenth-century soldiers who inched their way from here towards Fort Brooke – the site of present-day Tampa. Their machetes hacked out the **Capron Trail**; one of the first east–west cross-Florida routes. Driving back, stay on St Lucie Boulevard as it crosses Hwy-1 and turn left along **Indian River Drive**, where gracious, rambling wooden homes dating from the early 1900s line the intracoastal waterway.

The Heathcote Botanical Gardens

At 210 Savannah Road, off Hwy-1 and north of Jefferson Plaza, the **Heathcote Botanical Gardens** (Tues–Sat, 9am–5pm. Also open Sun 1–5pm, Nov–April

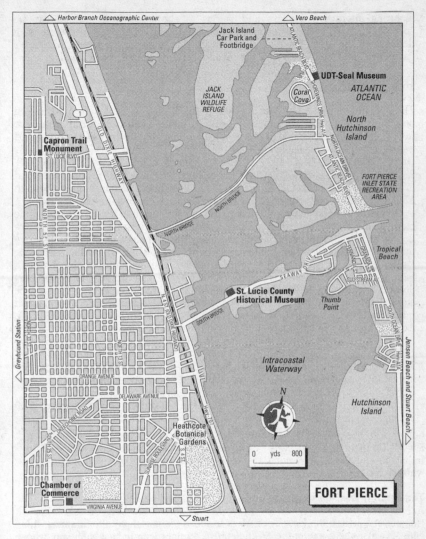

only; $2.50), are an oasis in an otherwise grey setting, and provide a relaxing and surprisingly cool place to while away a couple of hours.

The Harbor Branch Oceanographic Institution

Five miles north of St Lucie Boulevard, on Hwy-1, the **Harbor Branch Oceanographic Institution** (90-min guided tours Mon–Sat 10am, noon & 2pm; $5) is a phenomenally well-equipped deep-sea research and education centre. The highly informative tours depart from the visitor center and cover such highlights as full-scale models of research submersibles and an "Aquaculture" exhibit featuring interactive displays and videos to show you how seafood can be specially cultured for human consumption and thus help to satisfy our increasing demand on the seas. You'll also get the chance to eat in the research centre's canteen: a good feed for $5 – try the meatloaf and, of course, the seafood.

Practicalities

The Fort Pierce *Greyhound* **bus station** (☎461-3299) is six miles from downtown near the junction of Hwy-70 and the Florida Turnpike; a **cab** (☎461-7200) from here to the beach will cost around $12. A group of ordinary but inexpensive **lodging and eating** options are available close to the station. For rooms, try *Days Inn*, 6651 Darter Court off I-95 (☎466-4066; ④), the *Hampton Inn*, 2831 Reynolds Drive (☎460-9855; ③), or *Econo Lodge*, 7050 Okeechobee Road (☎465-8600; ③). Family-style food is available at the *Piccadilly Cafeteria*, 4194 Okeechobee Road, Orange Blossom Mall (☎466-8234), and seafood at *The Gallery Grille*, 927 N Hwy-1 (☎468-2081).

Otherwise, sleeping (with the exception of camping) and dining are best done close to the beach, two miles east of downtown Fort Pierce. Most **motels** are geared up for stays of several nights and many rooms include cooking facilities: try the well-equipped *Days Inn*, 1920 Seaway Drive (☎461-8737; ⑤), or the more basic *Dockside Inn*, 1152 Seaway Drive (☎461-4824; ③). There are further choices along Seaway Drive and the northern part of Ocean Drive; ask on the spot for the best deals. For **camping**, head inland and seven miles south of downtown Fort Pierce along Route 707 to the *Savannas* (☎464-7855), a sizeable square of reclaimed marshland beside the intracoastal waterway where you can pitch a tent for $10. To explore this unspoilt landscape, take one of the nature trails or hire a canoe.

Food options in Fort Pierce include the unpretentious and inexpensive *Captain's Galley*, 825 N Indian River Drive (☎466-8495), whose traditional breakfasts and solid lunches and dinners have earned it a four-star recommendation from the *Miami Herald*; and the more refined *Mangrove Matties*, 1640 Seaway Drive (☎466-1044), which specializes in tasty steaks and seafood.

You can get general **information** from the **Chamber of Commerce**, 2200 Virginia Avenue (Mon–Fri 8.30am–5pm; ☎461-2700). There are various diving packages on offer, among them *Dixie Divers* (☎461-4488) and *Under Sea World* (☎465-4114), who both charge $20 for a 24-hour package.

Port St Lucie

Adjacent to and merging with Southern Fort Pierce lies **PORT ST LUCIE**. The chief attraction here is the *St Lucie County Sports Complex*, at NW Peacock Boulevard, where the New York Mets baseball team complete their spring training. It's also the home of the *St Lucie Mets*, a minor league baseball team, whose season opens in April. At the close of the ninth inning you can rest your head in the nearby *Best Western*, 7900 S Hwy-1, Port St Lucie (☎878-7600; ⑤).

North Hutchinson Island

Convering 340 acres at the southern tip of **North Hutchinson Island** is the **Fort Pierce Inlet State Recreation Area** (daily 8am–sunset; cars $3.25, pedestrians and cyclists $1), on Shorewinds Drive, off Hwy-A1A. Its location, overlooking the

Fort Pierce Inlet and the community's beach, makes this a scenic setting for a picnic, as well as a launch site for local surfers. A mile north, on Hwy-A1A, a footbridge from the car park of the **Jack Island Wildlife Refuge** (same times and fees as above) leads onto the mile-long Marsh Rabbit Run, a boardwalk trail cutting through a thick mangrove swamp to an observation tower on the edge of the Indian River. Among bird life to watch out for are great blue herons and ospreys.

Concern for the environment is not something shared by the **UDT-SEAL Museum** (Tues–Sat 10am–4pm, Sun noon–4pm; $2), on Hwy-A1A between the recreation area and the wildlife refuge, dedicated to the US Navy's frogman demolition teams who've been exploding sea-mines and beach defences since the Normandy landings. During World War II, the UDTs (Underwater Demolition Teams) trained on Hutchinson Island – like most of Florida's barrier islands, it was off-limits to civilians at the time. The more elite SEALs (Sea Air Land), the US equivalent of Britain's SAS, came into being during the Sixties. Some practical stuff covers the technicalities of establishing beachheads, though jingoism is predictably apparent – anyone who can't keep doubts over US foreign policy to themselves should steer clear.

Vero Beach and around

For the next fourteen miles, Australian pines mar Hwy-A1A's ocean view until North Hutchinson Island imperceptibly becomes **Orchid Island** and you reach **VERO BEACH**, the area's sole community of substance and one with a pronounced upmarket image. It makes an enjoyable hideaway, however, with a fine group of beaches around Ocean Drive, parallel to Hwy-A1A. There's little to tempt you from the sands, but it's worth taking the trouble to view the *Driftwood Resort*, 3150 Ocean Drive, a Thirties hotel, now time-share apartments, erected from a jumble of driftwood, flea- market finds and pieces of Palm Beach mansions demolished to avoid taxes.

Vero Beach practicalities

Three miles from the coast, **inland Vero Beach** has a *Greyhound* terminal at the Texaco filling station, 905 Hwy-1 (☎562-6588), and a **Chamber of Commerce** at 1216 21st Street (Mon–Fri 9am–5pm; ☎567-3491). At the beach, exceptions to pricy **accommodation** are the *Riviera Inn*, 1605 S Ocean Drive (☎234-4112; ④), and *Sea Spray Gardens*, 965 E Causeway Boulevard (☎231-5210; ②, self catering only), both with great deals off-season. Cost-effective **eateries** are the *Beachside Restaurant*, opposite the *Driftwood Resort*, at 3125 Ocean Drive (☎234-4477), and *Nino's Café*, 1006 Easter Lily Lane (☎231–9311).

North of Vero Beach: Sebastian Inlet

Tiny beachside communities dot the rest of the island, but you'll find most activity – and campsites ($17 Dec–Apr, $15 May–Nov) – around the **Sebastian Inlet State Recreation Area** (daily 8am–10pm; cars $3.25, pedestrians and cyclists $1), sixteen miles north of Vero Beach. Roaring ocean breakers lure surfers here, particularly over Easter when contests are held, and anglers cram the jetties for the east coast's finest fishing. Without a board or a rod, you can amuse yourself by keeping an eye out for the endangered bird life making sorties from nearby Pelican Island, the oldest wildlife refuge in the country and off-limits to humans. Alternatively, head a couple of miles south of the inlet to the **McLarty Treasure Museum**, at 13180 Hwy-A1A (daily 10am–4.30pm; $2), where you can view treasure salvaged from an eighteenth-century Spanish fleet that was stricken by a hurricane.

Beyond Sebastian you reach the outskirts of the Space Coast, which is covered in *The Northeast Coast*.

travel details

Trains
From Hollywood (2 daily) to Delray Beach (42min); Fort Lauderdale (12min); West Palm Beach (1hr 6min).

Tri-Rail
From Hollywood (5–15 daily) to Boca Raton (39min); Delray Beach (48min); Fort Lauderdale (12min); West Palm Beach (1hr 11min).

Buses
From Fort Lauderdale to Boca Raton (4 daily; 50min); Delray Beach (4 daily; 1hr 10min); Fort Pierce (12 daily; 2hr 50min); Stuart (4 daily; 3hr 15min); Vero Beach (5 daily; 3hr 55min); West Palm Beach (12 daily; 2hr).

From Hollywood to Fort Lauderdale (16 daily; 10–30min); Walt Disney World (1 daily; 5hr 1min).

From West Palm Beach to Belle Glade (1 daily; 1hr 5min); Fort Pierce (7 daily; 1hr 30min); Stuart (6 daily; 1hr); Tampa (1 daily; 6hr); Vero Beach (5 daily; 1hr 50min).

CHAPTER FOUR

THE NORTHEAST COAST

S ubstantially free of commercial exploitation, with washed-up sharks' teeth sometimes more plentiful than people on its beaches, the 190 miles of Florida's **Northeast Coast** are tailor-made for leisurely exploration. You'll often feel like doing nothing more strenuous than settling down beside the ocean, but throughout the region evidence of the forces that have shaped Florida – from ancient Native American settlements to the launch-site of the Space Shuttle – is easy to find and worth exploring. When planning your trip, remember that the Northeast Coast's tourist **seasons** are the reverse of those of the Southeast Coast: the crowded time here is the summer, when accommodation is more expensive and harder to come by than during the winter months.

Besides sharing a shoreline, the towns of the Northeast Coast have surprisingly little in common. Those making up the **Space Coast**, the southernmost area, primarily service the hordes passing through to visit the **Kennedy Space Center**, birthplace and still the launching pad of the nation's space exploits. Its public image is unrelentingly positive, but the Space Center is worth a visit, as is the wildlife refuge that surrounds it. Every March and April, a different kind of blasting-off has traditionally occurred seventy miles north of the Space Coast at **Daytona Beach**, a small town with a big strand which, until a recent bout of soul searching, happily hosted drunken legions of college kids indulging in the legendary excesses of the Spring Break holiday. Although the local authorities are discouraging the event, teenage carousing can still be found around this time; the rest of the year, Daytona is a mellower place to hang out.

Along the northerly section of the coast, the plentiful evidence of Florida's early European landings is nowhere better displayed than in comprehensively restored **St Augustine**, where sixteenth-century Spaniards established North America's earliest foreign settlement. In addition to the attractions of the town itself, there's the surrounding coast, part of a divine strand stretching to the **Jacksonville Beaches**, twenty miles north, where lying in the sun and tuning into the sprightly local nightlife will decadently waste a few days. Just inland, the city of **Jacksonville**, struggling to shrug off its grey and industrial image, merits only a cursory investigation as you strike out towards the state's northeastern extremity. Here, overlooking the coast of Georgia, slender **Amelia Island** is

---

ACCOMMODATION PRICE CODES

All **accommodation prices** in this book have been coded using the symbols below. Note that prices are for the least expensive double rooms in each establishment. For a full explanation see p.27 in *Basics*.

① up to $30	③ $45–60	⑤ $80–100	⑦ $130–180
② $30–45	④ $60–80	⑥ $100–130	⑧ $180+

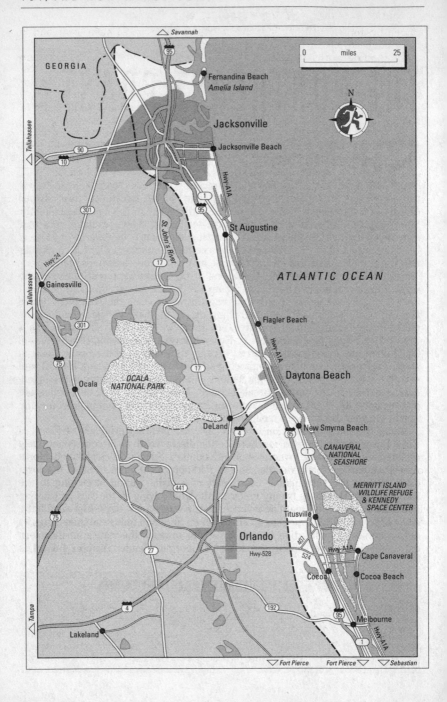

fringed by gorgeous silver sands, has a quirky Victorian-era main town, and is under the beady eye of dollar-crazed developers – arrive before they do.

The **road network** is very much a continuation of the Southeast Coast's system: **Hwy-A1A** hugs the coastline, while **Hwy-1** charts a less appealing course on the mainland and is a lot slower than **I-95**, which divides the coastal area from the eastern edge of Central Florida. *Greyhound* **buses** are frequent along Hwy-1 between the main towns, though the only **local bus services** are in Daytona Beach and Jacksonville. Forget the **train** – only Jacksonville has a station.

The Space Coast

The barrier islands that dominate the Treasure Coast (see *The Southeast Coast*) continue north into the so-called **Space Coast**, the base of the country's space industry and site of the Kennedy Space Center, which occupies a flat, marshy island bulging into the Atlantic just fifty miles east of Orlando. Many of the visitors who flock here are surprised to find that the land from which the Space Shuttle leaves earth is also a sizeable wildlife refuge framed by several miles of rough coastline. Except for the beach-oriented communities on the ocean, the towns of the Space Coast are of little interest other than for low-cost overnight stops or meal breaks.

The Kennedy Space Center and Spaceport USA

Justifiably the biggest attraction in the area, the **Kennedy Space Center** is the nucleus of the US space programme: it's here that space vehicles are developed, tested and blasted into orbit. The first launches actually took place across the water at the US Air Force base on Cape Canaveral (renamed Cape Kennedy between 1963 and 1973), from which unmanned satellites still lift off. After the space programme was expanded in 1964 and the Saturn V rockets proved too large to launch from there, the focus of activity was moved here to Merritt Island, positioned between Cape Canaveral and the mainland and directly north of Cocoa Beach.

The Space Center is well worth a visit for its solid documentation of US achievements, revealing how closely success in space is tied to the nation's sense of well-being.

THE KENNEDY SPACE CENTER: PRACTICAL INFO AND TIPS

The only **public entry roads** into the Kennedy Space Center are Hwy-405 from Titusville, and Route 3 off Hwy-A1A between Cocoa Beach and Cocoa: on either approach, follow signs for **Spaceport USA** (daily 9am–6pm or later; free), which contains the museum, Rocket Garden and IMAX film theatre.

Arrive early to avoid the crowds, which are thinnest on weekends and during May and September. To take one of the two-hour narrated bus tours ("Red" for the Space Center; "Blue" for Cape Canaveral; $7) or see one of the four IMAX films ($4), you should **buy tickets** from the ticket pavilion as soon as you arrive.

To **see a launch** from the Space Center, phone ☎407/867-4636 for recorded schedule information or 407/452-2121 ext. 260 to arrange a $7 pass. **For launch dates and times:** ☎1-800-KSC-INFO. Note, however, that you'll get almost as good a view of a launch from anywhere within a forty-mile radius of the Space Center.

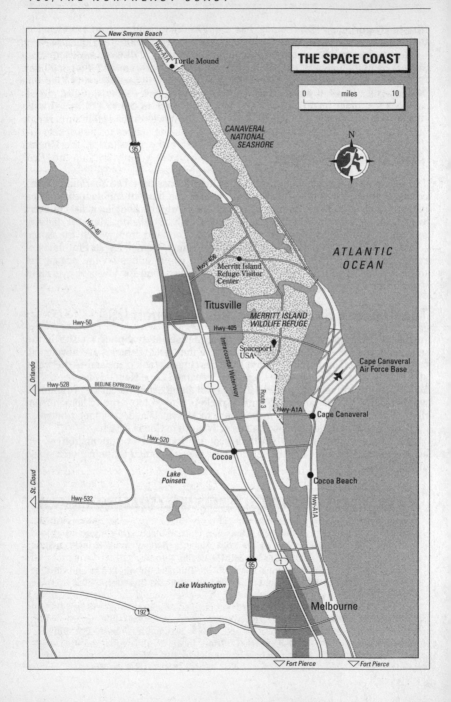

THE SPACE COAST

0   miles   10

New Smyrna Beach

Turtle Mound

CANAVERAL NATIONAL SEASHORE

N

ATLANTIC OCEAN

Hwy-46

Hwy-406

Merritt Island Refuge Visitor Center

Titusville

MERRITT ISLAND WILDLIFE REFUGE

Hwy-50

Hwy-405

Intracoastal Waterway

Spaceport USA

Cape Canaveral Air Force Base

Orlando

Hwy-528

BEELINE EXPRESSWAY

Route 3

Hwy-A1A

Cape Canaveral

St. Cloud

Hwy-520

Cocoa

Lake Poinsett

Cocoa Beach

Hwy-532

Hwy-A1A

Lake Washington

Melbourne

192

Fort Pierce   Fort Pierce

Seeing Spaceport USA

Everything at **Spaceport USA** is within easy walking distance of the carpark, as is the departure point for the bus tours (see below). The **museum** will keep anyone with the faintest interest in space exploration entertained for a good hour. Except for any mention of the Challenger or other disasters, everything you might expect to see is here: actual mission capsules, space suits, detailed models of satellites, lunar modules and the Viking craft used on Mars, a full-sized walk-through mock-up of the Space Shuttle, and a lot more – much of it surprisingly small and deceptively simple in appearance. The same applies to the rockets that launched the early space shots, standing outside the museum in the **Rocket Garden** – they're far daintier than the gigantic Saturn V (only seen on the "Red" bus tour, see below) that launched the Apollo missions.

Next door to the museum, the **Galaxy Theater** shows four IMAX films, using 70mm film projected onto a five-storey screen: using dramatic shots from an orbiting space shuttle, *The Dream is Alive* (37 min) captures the sensations of space

AMERICANS IN SPACE: THE BACKGROUND

The growth of the Space Coast started with the **"Space Race"**, which followed President John Kennedy's declaration in May 1961 to "achieve the goal, before the decade is out, of landing a man on the moon and returning him safely to Earth". This statement came in the chill of the Cold War, when the USSR – which had just put the first man into space following their launch of the first artificial satellite in 1957 – appeared scientifically ahead of the US, a fact which dented American pride and provided great propaganda for the Soviets.

Money and manpower were pumped into **NASA** (National Aeronautics and Space Administration), and the communities around Cape Canaveral expanded with a heady influx of scientists and would-be astronauts. The much-hyped Mercury programme helped restore prestige, and the later Apollo moonshots captured the imagination of the world. The moon landing by Apollo 11 in July 1969 not only turned the dreams of science fiction writers into reality faster than anybody could have predicted, but also meant for the first time – and in the most spectacular way possible – the US had overtaken the USSR.

During the Seventies, as the incredible expense of the space programme became apparent and seemed out of all proportion to its benefits, pressure grew for NASA to become more cost-effective. The country entered a period of economic recession and NASA's funding was drastically slashed; unemployment – unthinkable in the buoyant Sixties – threatened many on the Space Coast.

After the internationally funded Skylab space station programme, NASA's solution to the problem of wasteful one-use rockets was the reusable **Space Shuttle**, first launched in April 1981, able to deploy commercial payloads and carry out repairs to orbiting satellites. The Shuttle's success silenced many critics, but the Challenger disaster of January 1986 – when the entire crew perished during take-off – not only sent a deep sense of loss around the country but highlighted the complacency and corner-cutting that had crept into the space programme after many accident-free years.

More recently, despite numerous satisfactory missions, technical problems and the exercising of stringent safety procedures have caused serious delays to the Space Shuttle programme, illustrating what a colossal accomplishment the manned moon landings actually were. Of equal significance may well be the manned space station in orbit around the earth, planned for completion in the year 2000.

flight as well as the daily business of living in space; *The Blue Planet* (42 min) shows natural disasters viewed from space and signs of man's interference with the Earth's ecosystem; *Hail Columbia* (25 min) is the shortest and least spectacular film, following the first flight of the shuttlecraft, its re-entry and landing; and *Destiny in Space* (40 min), narrated by Leonard Nimoy (*Star Trek*'s Mr Spock), features exterior shots of a space shuttle in flight plus scenes of Mars and Venus.

As far as **eating** goes, both canteens at Spaceport USA provide poor-quality food at a high price; you're better off eating elsewhere.

The bus tours

To see the rest of the Merritt Island space complex, you should take the **"Red" bus tour**. This first crosses the "crawlerway" – the huge tracks along which space shuttles are wheeled to the launch pad – before reaching the 52-storey **Vehicle Assembly Building**, where the shuttles (like Apollo and Skylab before them) are put together and fitted with payloads. Unfortunately, access is prohibited, but if a door is open you'll catch a glimpse inside one of the world's largest structures.

With luck, a space shuttle will be in place for take-off when the bus takes a loop around the **launch pad** – no different in reality from what you've seen on TV, and no more interesting than any other large pile of scaffolding if a shuttle isn't present (obviously, when a countdown is underway there are no bus tours; see the box on p.185 for launch-watching tips). Besides a nose-to-nozzle inspection of a Saturn V rocket, the most impressive part of the bus tour is a simulated Apollo countdown and take-off watched from behind the blinking screens of a realistically mocked-up control room.

Only serious space buffs should take the **"Blue" bus tour**, a much less spectacular trip around the Cape Canaveral Air Force base. The site was developed by the US War Department in the Forties for guided missile testing, pioneering Mercury and Gemini missions blasted off from here, and it's still used for sending weather and communications satellites into orbit.

Air Force Space Museum

If you've not had your fill of space travel at Spaceport, a further attraction in the area is the **Air Force Space Museum** (Mon–Fri 10am–2pm, Sat & Sun 10am–4pm; free), situated a mile inside the gate of Cape Canaveral (on launch pad 26A), and a testament to NASA's skill at making money out of its old hardware The museum consists of a large expanse of land rather akin to the Rocket Garden at

---

SPACEPORT USA: AN UPDATE

Having remained virtually unchanged for thirty years, **Spaceport USA** is currently undergoing a $39 million expansion programme, which at the time of writing was due for completion in November 1997. This marks a radical change from the currently interesting but predictable and rather downbeat operation. A newly built Apollo/Saturn V Center will contain not only the Saturn V rocket, suspended from the ceiling, but also those from the Rocket Garden, old launch towers from Cape Canaveral, simulators used to train astronauts, and other interactive exhibits. The aim is to create a more theme-park-like atmosphere and make Spaceport USA a more competitive tourist attraction.

Spaceport USA (see above), and two buildings containing exhibits and information on rocket development, some of which proves fascinating: one example is the fact that all the extraordinary developments of the space programme stem from V2 rockets, which were originally fired by Nazi Germany against Britain in the closing years of the Second World War, and were subsequently launched into orbit by America in 1950.

For yet another angle on space travel, visit the **Astronaut Hall of Fame** (see Titusville, p.192), just down the road from Spaceport USA.

Merritt Island National Wildlife Refuge

NASA shares its land with the **Merritt Island National Wildlife Refuge** (daily sunrise–sunset; free), entered via Route 402 from Titusville. Here you'll find alligators, armadillos, racoons, bobcats and one of Florida's greatest concentrations of bird life living alongside some of the world's most advanced technology.

Even if you're only coming for a day at the Space Center, it would be a shame to pass up such a spectacular place – though it has to be said that Merritt Island, on first glance, looks anything but spectacular, comprising acres of estuaries and brackish marshes interspersed by occasional hammocks of oak and palm, and pine flatwoods where a few bald eagles construct nests ten feet in circumference. Winter is the **best time to visit**, when the island's skies are alive with thousands of migratory birds from the frozen north, and when mosquitoes are absent. At any other period, and especially in summer, the island's Mosquito Lagoon is worthy of its name; bring ample insect repellent.

Seeing the refuge

Seven miles east of Titusville on Route 406, the six-mile **Black Point Wildlife Drive** gives a solid introduction to the basics of the island's ecosystem. At the entrance you can pick up the highly informative free leaflet, which describes specific stops along the route; from one you'll spot a couple of bald eagle nests, while another by the mudflats provides a good vantage point for watching a wide variety of wading and shore birds swooping on their dinner.

Be sure to do some walking within the refuge, too. Off the wildlife drive, the five-mile **Cruickshank trail** weaves around the edge of the Indian River; if the whole length is too strenuous for you, there's an observation tower just a few minutes' walk from the carpark. For a more varied landscape, drive a few miles further east along Route 402 – branching from Route 406 just south of the wildlife drive – passing the **visitor center** (Mon–Fri 8am–4.30pm, Sat & Sun 9am–5pm; closed Sun April–Oct; ☎861-0667), and tackle the half-mile **Oak Hammock trail** or the two-mile **Palm Hammock trail**, both accessible from the same carpark.

The Canaveral National Seashore

A slender, 25-mile-long beach dividing Merritt Island's Mosquito Lagoon from the Atlantic Ocean, the **Canaveral National Seashore** (winter 6am–6pm, summer 6am–8pm; free) begins at **Playalinda Beach** on Route 402, seven miles east of the refuge's visitor center. The National Seashore's entire length is top-notch beachcombing and surfing territory, and also suitable for swimming. Except when rough seas and high tides submerge it completely, you should take a wind-bitten ramble along the palmetto-lined path to wild **Klondike Beach**,

> The area code for Cocoa Beach and the Space Coast is ☎407.

north of Playalinda Beach, often coated with intriguing shells and marked in summer by the tracks left by sea turtles crawling ashore at night to lay eggs.

At the northern tip of the National Seashore, on **Apollo Beach** (only accessible by road from New Smyrna Beach, eight miles north of Apollo, see "Heading North: New Smyrna Beach", below), is the easily sighted **Turtle Mound**. This thirty-five-foot heap of oyster shells provided a home for Timucua Indians over several generations and was marked on maps by Florida's first Spanish explorers, being visible several miles out to sea. Take a few minutes to walk to the top of the mound, which offers a view over Merritt Island.

Cocoa Beach

A few miles south of the Kennedy Space Center, **COCOA BEACH** comprises just a ten-mile strip of shore and a few residential streets off Atlantic Avenue (Hwy-A1A). As well as being unquestionably the best base from which to see the Space Coast, it's also a favoured haunt of surfers, who are attracted here by some of the biggest waves in Florida. Major (and minor) surfing contests are held here during April and May, and throughout the year the place has a perky, youthful feel. At weekends there's often free music around the pier and beachside parks, and to get an idea of the community's prime concerns you need only take a walk around the original *Ron Jon Surf Shop*, 4151 Atlantic Avenue (☎799-8888), and its two branches a stone's throw away (the *Water Sports Store* and the *Outpost Discount Store*). All are open 24 hours a day and packed with surfboards (rental per day is $10 for a foam board; $20 for fibreglass), bicycles ($3 per hour or $40 per week), kites and extrovert beach attire.

Information and transport

The Cocoa Beach **Chamber of Commerce** is located on Merritt Island at 400 Fortenberry Road (Mon–Fri 9am–5pm; ☎459-2200), though there is also an information desk at the *Ron Jon Surf Shop*. A local **bus** service (*SCAT*; ☎633-1878) runs regularly to and from Cape Canaveral through Cocoa Beach (#9), and #31 runs from downtown Cocoa to Cocoa Beach; both routes cost $1 one way. The *Cocoa Beach Shuttle* (☎784-3831) runs to and from Orlando airport for $18 one way; call to be collected from any hotel on Hwy-A1A. To get around the beach area, hire a **bike** from the *Ron Jon Surf Shop* (details above). The nearest *Greyhound* station is on the mainland in Cocoa at 302 Main Street (☎636-6531).

Accommodation

Accommodation bargains are rare in Cocoa Beach. You can expect prices to be highest during February, July and August – and during space shuttle launches. The lowest rates for motels are with *Fawlty Towers*, 100 E Cocoa Beach Causeway (☎784-3870; ②); *Motel 6*, 3701 N Atlantic Avenue (☎783-3103; ③); *Best Western Ocean Inn*, 5500 N Atlantic Avenue (☎784-2550; ④); and, for bed and breakfast, *Luna Sea*, 3185 N Atlantic Avenue (☎1-800/586-2732; ②). For a longer stay, try the *Cape Colony* resort, 1275 N Atlantic Avenue (☎1-800/795-2252; ⑤), especially good value for several people sharing. To relax in style, stay at *Sea Esta Villas*, 686 S Atlantic Avenue (☎1-800/872-9444; ⑥), whose price includes home-cooked breakfasts and supper. The most tent-friendly **campground** is *Jetty Park*, 400 E Jetty Road (☎783-7111; $14.85), five miles north at Cape Canaveral.

Eating and nightlife

Many inland restaurants strive to undercut each other, resulting in some good **eating** deals if you have your own transport; see "Inland" below for suggestions, and scan free magazines (found in motels and at the Chamber of Commerce) such as *Restaurant Dining Out* for money-saving coupons. Close to the beach, the options are fewer. Open around the clock, the Fifties-style *Herbie K's Diner*, 2080 N Atlantic Avenue (☎783-6740), is as interesting for its after-hours social life as its juicy burgers; for simple basics go to *Roberto's Little Havana*, 26 N Orlando Avenue (☎783-3301); and for great oysters and a $5 lunch buffet, head for *Rusty's Raw Bar*, 2 S Atlantic Avenue (☎783-2401). Good dinner options are *The Pier House*, on the pier (☎783-7549), which has a quality (and somewhat expensive) menu especially strong on seafood; and the cheaper *Old Fish House*, 249 W Cocoa Beach Causeway (☎799-9190).

Nightlife is most enjoyable if you start early at one of the beachside **happy hours**: try *Marlins' Good Time Grill*, also part of the pier complex (☎783-7549), or *Desperados*, 301 N Atlantic Avenue (☎784-3363). As the evening draws on, the *Pig and Whistle*, 801 N Atlantic Avenue (☎799-0724), offering TV soccer and over-priced bitter, is a refuge for homesick Brits; *Coconuts*, 2 Minuteman Causeway (☎784-1422), has drinking and **live music** on the beach; and *New York South*, 900 N Atlantic Avenue (☎784-4811), is a good place to bop the night away.

Inland: Palm Bay, Melbourne, Cocoa and Titusville

The chief attractions of the Space Coast's sleepy **inland towns**, strung along Hwy-1, are cheaper accommodation and food than at the beaches, plus areas of historical interest that provide relief from the usual tourist drag.

Palm Bay

The southernmost town is **PALM BAY**, 30 miles north of Vero Beach (see p.181). Despite boasting a higher population than any of its neighbours, it's the least geared to tourism, being largely a commuter-belt town for Space Coast employees. There's little to detain you here apart from the small **Turkey Creek Sanctuary**, 1502 Port Malabar Boulevard (daily 7am–sunset; free), whose short boardwalk trail winds through three distinct (and simulated) native habitats – hardwood hammock, sand and pine scrub, and wet hardwood forest – that support endangered species of flora and fauna.

Melbourne

Just a few miles north of Palm Bay lies the pretty but dull town of **MELBOURNE**. The collections at its **Brevard Museum of Art and Science**, 1463 Highland Avenue (Tues–Sat 10am–5pm, Sun 1–5pm; $3; free guided tours Tues–Sat 2–4pm), won't hold you here very long, but Melbourne's **restaurants** might: go to *Shooter's*, 707 S Harbour City Boulevard (☎725-4600), for good sand-wiches and a great view of the Indian River; *Mac's Diner*, 1075 N Wickham Road (☎254-8818), for a buffet feed on weekdays or a breakfast buffet at weekends; *Chatterbox*, 850 N Wickham Road (☎254-1111), for all-u-can-eat lunch buffets at $4.95; or *Conchy Joe's*, 1477 Pineapple Avenue (☎253-3131), for seafood and live reggae in the evenings. After eating, you could do worse than take a stroll along **Crane Creek**, a stretch of water between the Hwy-1 road bridge and the railway bridge, which is a **manatee** viewing area. A shoreline boardwalk, lined with oak trees and sabal palms, provides an attractive spot from which to glimpse these shy, endangered creatures.

If you're **staying** overnight, try the *Holiday Inn*, 420 S Harbor City Boulevard (☎723-5320; ②–③), or *Melbourne Harbor Suites*, 1207 E Newhaven Avenue (☎1-800/226-4251; ④), on the harbour – a short walk from Crane Creek. For moving on, catch a *Greyhound* **bus** from 460 S Harbor City Boulevard (☎723-4323).

Cocoa

In **COCOA**, thirty miles north of Melbourne and eight miles inland from Cocoa Beach, the cobblestoned pavements and turn-of-the-century buildings of **Old Cocoa Village** fill several small blocks south of King Street (Hwy-520) and make for a relaxing stroll. Among the twee antique shops and boutiques, seek out the *Porcher House*, 434 Delannoy Avenue (Tues–Fri 10am–1pm; $1), a grand Neoclassical abode of 1916 vintage.

For a greater insight into the town's origins, head a few miles west to the **Brevard Museum of History and Natural Science**, 2201 Michigan Avenue (Tues–Sat 10am–4pm, Sun 1–4pm; $3), whose displays recount Cocoa's birth as a trading post when the first settlers arrived in the 1840s by steamboat and mule. There's also a respectable display on Florida wildlife and some informative leaflets that are particularly useful if you're planning to visit the Merritt Island National Wildlife Refuge (see p.189).

It's worth making a quick stop at the **Astronaut Memorial Hall and Planetarium**, 1519 Clearlake Road (Mon–Fri 10am–4pm, Sat 10.30am–4pm; $3), not for its run-of-the-mill science exhibits but for the **Space Shuttle Park** beside the carpark: an unintentional antidote to the pizzazz of the Kennedy Space Center. Among the various bits of space hardware is – incredibly – an Apollo command module, its cobweb-covered interior strewn with bare wires and plugs: a bizarre fate for something that until recently was at the forefront of space science.

If you're **staying** in Cocoa, there are some small and uninviting motels lining Cocoa Boulevard; a better option is the *Econo Lodge* at no. 3220 N (☎632-4561; ③). For **eating**, try *Norman's Food and Spirits*, 3 Forrest Avenue (☎632-8782), which offers great lunch specials and entertaining karaoke in the evenings; alternatively, *Café Margaux*, 222 Brevard Avenue (☎639-8343), is a stylish spot for a pasta lunch.

To get **to Cocoa Beach** without your own car, a taxi ride (☎636-7017) will cost $15. The *Greyhound* **bus** station is at 302 Main Street (☎636-6531).

Titusville

If you don't visit the Kennedy Space Center, you'll at least get a great view of the towering Vehicle Assembly Building from **TITUSVILLE**, twenty miles north of Cocoa. If you find you have time on your hands here, visit the **Valiant Air Command Museum**, 6600 Tico Road (daily 10am–6pm in summer, 10am–5pm in winter; $6), a celebration of slightly more pedestrian flying machines than those at Spaceport USA. Originally formed to commemorate the US airforce's involvement in preventing Japan's invasion of mainland China in 1941, the museum today exhibits lovingly restored planes, with examples from all wars since that date. The best way to see them is in March, when the VAC holds an air show and most of these war veterans take to the skies.

The area code for Daytona Beach and New Smyrna Beach is ☎904.

Apart from this, all that's commendable about Titusville is ease of access to the Space Center (on Hwy-405) and the Merritt Island National Wildlife Refuge (with Hwy-402). On the way to either place, visit the **Astronaut Hall of Fame** (daily 9am–5pm; $9.95), which offers the chance to experience G-force, shuttle-landing, space flight and weightlessness with the aid of simulators and virtual reality.

For **food**, head for the under-$5 lunch dishes at *Ping On*, 407 Cheney Highway (☎269-2503); the seafood and steaks at *Janet's Café Orleans*, 605 Hopkins Avenue (☎269-6020); or the seafood of *Dixie Crossroads*, 1475 Garden Street (☎268-5000). Inexpensive **motels** are plentiful along Washington Avenue (Hwy-1): *South Wind*, no. 1540 S (☎267-3681; ③), and *Siesta*, no. 2006 (☎267-1455; ③), are just two. Otherwise, try the *Best Western Space Shuttle Inn*, 3455 Cheney Highway (☎269-9100; ④), which also offers eco-tourism packages for exploring the unique flora and fauna of the area. For moving on, the *Greyhound* **bus** station is at 20 N Washington Avenue (☎267-8760).

Heading north: New Smyrna Beach

After the virgin vistas of the Canaveral National Seashore, the tall beachside hotels of **NEW SMYRNA BEACH**, thirty miles north of Titusville on Hwy-1, create the impression of a likeable low-key beach community, where the sea – protected from dangerous currents by offshore rock ledges – is perfect for **swimming**. To reach the beach (or the northern section of the Canaveral National Seashore, see p.189), you have to pass through the inland section of the town, before swinging east on Hwy-A1A.

The town itself has an unusual **history**. A wealthy Scottish physician, Andrew Turnbull, bought land here in the mid-1700s and set about creating a Mediterranean colony, recruiting Greeks, Italians and Minorcans to work for seven years on his plantation in return for fifty acres of land each. The colony didn't last: bad treatment, language barriers, disease and financial disasters hastened its demise, and many of the settlers moved north to St Augustine (see p.201).

The immigrants worked hard, however (by most accounts, they had little choice), laying irrigation canals, building a sugar mill and commencing work on what was to be a palatial abode for Turnbull. Close to Hwy-1, the **ruins** of the mill (at the junction of Canal Street and Mission Road) and his unfinished house (at Riverside Drive and Julia Street) are substantial enough to merit a look, and the nearby **Visitor Center and Chamber of Commerce**, 115 Canal Street (Mon–Sat 9am–5pm during Jan & Feb; otherwise Mon–Fri 9am–5pm, Sat 9am–3pm, Sun 11am–3pm; ☎1-800/541-9621), has a handy historical leaflet, as well as the usual local information.

Greyhound **buses** will drop you here at Steils Gas Station, 600 W Central (☎428-8211); if you want to stay over, the cheapest **motels** are both on Hwy-1 (locally called Dixie Freeway): *Smyrna Motel*, no. 1050 N (☎428-2495; ②), which has an eagle's nest on its property, and *Shangri-La*, no. 805 (☎428-8361; ①).

Continuing north from New Smyrna Beach, Hwy-A1A joins with Hwy-1 for ten miles before splitting off oceanwards near Ponce Inlet, five miles south of mainland Daytona Beach.

Daytona Beach

The consummate Florida beach town, with rows of airbrushed-T-shirt shops, amusement arcades and wall-to-wall motels, **DAYTONA BEACH** owes its existence to twenty miles of light brown sand where the only pressure is to strip off and enjoy yourself.

For decades, Daytona Beach was invaded by half-a-million college kids going through the **Spring Break** ritual of underage drinking and libido liberation until the town controversially decided to end its love affair with the nation's students and emulate Fort Lauderdale (see *The Southeast Coast*) in cultivating a more refined image – an attempt that has been only partially successful. Today this small, medium-paced, down-to-earth resort, with just a day's worth of sights beyond its famous sands, is the centre of three major annual events: the world-famous **Daytona 500** stock-car meeting, held at the Daytona International Speedway; **Bike Week**, when thousands of leather-clad motorcyclists converge for races at the Speedway; and the relatively new **Biketoberfest,** which is much the same idea (see box on p.198 for more info on all three events).

Even before the students and bikers, the beach was a favourite with pioneering auto enthusiasts such as Louis Chevrolet, Ransom Olds and Henry Ford, who came here during the early 1900s to race their prototype vehicles beside the ocean. The land speed record was regularly smashed, five times by millionaire British speedster Malcolm Campbell who, in 1935, roared along at 276mph. As a legacy of these times, Daytona Beach is one of the few Florida towns where **driving on the beach** is permitted: pay $3 at any beach entrance, stick to the marked track, observe the 10mph speed limit, park at right-angles to the ocean – and beware of high tide.

Arrival and getting around

As Ridgewood Avenue, **Hwy-1** steams through **mainland Daytona Beach**, passing the *Greyhound* station, at no. 138 S (☎253-6576). By car, you should keep to **Hwy-A1A** (known as Atlantic Avenue), which enters the beachside area – filling a narrow sliver of land between the ocean and the Halifax River (part of the intracoastal waterway) a mile from the mainland.

Local buses (*Votran* ☎761-7700) connect the beaches with the mainland and the Greater Daytona Beach area, though there are no night or Sunday services. The bus terminal is at the junction of Palmetto Avenue and International Speedway Boulevard in mainland Daytona Beach. At the beach, there are "trolleys" running along the central part of Atlantic Avenue from January to August only. A **taxi** between the mainland and the beach will cost around $7: cab companies include *AA Cab* (☎253-2522) and *Yellow Cab* (☎252-5536).

BUSES BETWEEN DAYTONA BEACH AND ORLANDO AIRPORT

If you're enjoying yourself at the beach but have to fly home from Orlando, you can take advantage of the **Daytona-Orlando Transit Service** (DOTS ☎1-800/231-1965), whose shuttle buses run every 90 minutes between 4.30am and 9pm from the corner of Nova Road and 11th Street to Orlando airport. On request, the buses also make stops in Deland and Sanford. The one-way fare is $20 ($36 return). Call ahead for details and reservations.

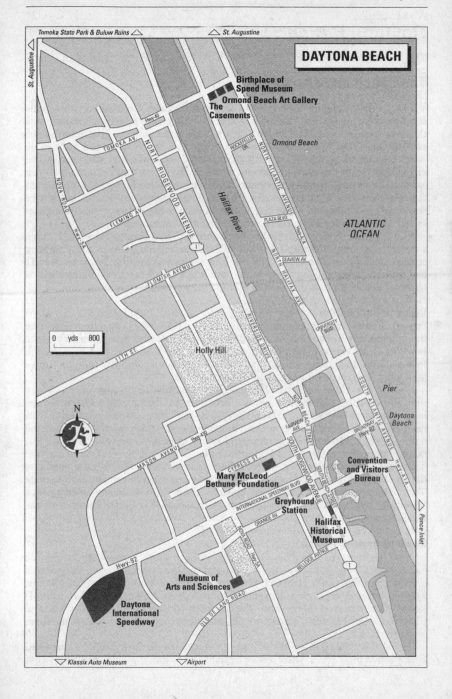

Tomoka State Park & Buluw Ruins △   △ St. Augustine

St. Augustine

DAYTONA BEACH

Birthplace of Speed Museum
Ormond Beach Art Gallery
The Casements

Ormond Beach

ATLANTIC OCEAN

Halifax River

HWY 40

NORTH RIDGEWOOD AVENUE

TOMOKA AV.

NOVA ROAD

HWY 5A

FLEMING AV.

FLOMISH AVENUE

ROCKEFELLER DR.

NORTH ATLANTIC AVENUE

PLAZA BLVD.

HWY A1A

NORTH HALIFAX AVE.

SEAVIEW AV.

RIVERSIDE DRIVE

UNIVERSITY BLVD.

0 yds 800

Holly Hill

11TH ST.

N

MASON AVENUE

HWY 430

NORTH BEACH STREET

FAIRVIEW AV.

SOUTH RIDGEWOOD AVENUE

SOUTH ATLANTIC AVENUE

SOUTH BEACH STREET

BROADWAY HWY 92

Pier

Daytona Beach

Convention and Visitors Bureau

CYPRESS ST.

Mary McLeod Bethune Foundation

INTERNATIONAL SPEEDWAY BLVD.

Greyhound Station

ORANGE AV.

Halifax Historical Museum

1

HWY A1A

△ Ponce Inlet

HWY-92

NOVA ROAD HWY 5A

OLD DE LAND ROAD

BELLEVUE AVENUE

Museum of Arts and Sciences

Daytona International Speedway

▽ Klassix Auto Museum   ▽ Airport

Don't leave mainland Daytona Beach without calling at the **Convention and Visitors Bureau** in the Chamber of Commerce building at 126 E Orange Avenue (Mon–Fri 9am–5pm; ☎1-800/845-1234), for a wealth of free information.

The beach and around

Without a doubt, the best thing about Daytona Beach *is* the **beach**: a seemingly limitless affair – 500 feet wide at low tide and, lengthways, fading dreamily into the heat haze. Although it lives up to its racy reputation during the student mate-seeking season of Spring Break, at other times of the year there's little to do other than develop your tan, take the occasional ocean dip and strut narcissistically about. Even the **pier**, at the end of Main Street, isn't up to much; you can loiter in one of two characterless bars, enjoy panoramic views of the town from the *Space Needle* ($2); take the *Sky Ride*, a cable-car-like conveyance that ferries you slowly from one end of the pier to the other over the heads of patient anglers; or try the *Sky Coaster Ride*, a 60mph amusement arcade affair.

Nearby, Main Street and Seabreeze Boulevard have better **bars and cafés** (see "Eating" and "Nightlife"), but for more diverse pursuits – such as rambling around sand dunes, climbing an old lighthouse or discovering Daytona Beach's history – you need to head twelve miles south to Ponce Inlet, three miles north to Ormond Beach or cross the Halifax River to the mainland.

South to Ponce Inlet

Travelling south along Atlantic Avenue (buses #17A or #17B; only the former goes all the way to Ponce Inlet), small motels and fast-food dives give way to the towering beachside condos of affluent Daytona Beach shores. As you approach **Ponce Inlet**, four miles ahead, the outlook changes again, this time to single-storey beach homes and large sand dunes.

Here, at the end of Peninsula Drive – parallel to Atlantic Avenue – the 175-foot-high **Ponce Inlet Lighthouse** (daily 10am–5pm; $4) illuminated the treacherous inlet giving seaborne access to New Smyrna Beach (see p.193) from the late 1800s until 1970. Stupendous views make climbing the structure worthwhile, and the outbuildings hold surprisingly engaging artefacts from its early days as well as mildly interesting displays on US lighthouses in general. Several **nature trails** scratch a path through the surrounding scrub-covered dunes to a (usually) deserted **beach**; pick up a map from the **ranger station** at the end of Riverside Drive. Once you've trekked up an appetite, drop into *Lighthouse Landing* (see "Eating"), beside the lighthouse, whose cheap seafood is brought ashore at the adjoining marina.

North to Ormond Beach

In 1890, planning to bring his East Coast railway south from St Augustine, oil baron Henry Flagler bought the local hotel, built a beachside golf course and helped give **ORMOND BEACH**, three miles north of Main Street (buses #1A or #1B), a refined tone that it retains to this day. Millionaires like John D Rockefeller wintered here, and the car-potty fraternity of Ford, Olds and Chevrolet used Flagler's garage to fine-tune their autos before powering them along the beach.

Facing the Halifax River at the end of Granada Boulevard, Flagler's **Ormond Hotel** lasted until 1993, when it was demolished to much public mourning. Less depressingly, **the Casements** (Mon–Fri 9am–5pm, Sat 9am–noon; free), a three-storey villa on the other side of Granada Boulevard, which was bought by Rockefeller in 1918, is in fine fettle. **Guided tours** of the house (which, oddly enough, now holds displays of Hungarian folklore and Italian ceramics) run every thirty minutes from 10am, and tell you more than you'll ever need to know about Rockefeller and his time here – mostly spent playing golf and pressing dimes into the hands of passers-by.

Also on Granada Boulevard, the **Birthplace of Speed Museum**, no. 160 (Tues–Sun 1–5pm; $1), makes a convenient stop, though it contains only pictorial records of the early Daytona Beach speed merchants and a few replicas of their machines. Nearby, at no. 78, the Polynesian-style **Ormond Beach Art Gallery** (Tues–Sat 1–5pm; free) puts on reasonable temporary art shows – if they don't appeal, the gallery's jungle-like **gardens**, with shady pathways winding past fish-ponds to a gazebo, just might.

The mainland

When you're tired of the sands or nursing your sunburn, cross the river to **mainland Daytona Beach**, where several waterside parks and walkways contribute to a relaxing change of scene and four museums will keep you out of the sun for a few hours.

Near the best of the parks, on Beach Street, a few turn-of-the-century dwellings have been tidied up and turned into office space. At no. 252 S is the **Halifax Historical Museum** (Tues–Sat 10am–4pm; $2 or free on Sat), which captures – with an absorbing stock of objects, models and photos – the frenzied growth of Daytona Beach and Halifax County. Amid the fine stash of historical fall-out, don't ignore the immense wall paintings of long-gone local landscapes.

One former Daytona Beach resident referred to in the museum is better remembered by the **Mary McLeod Bethune Foundation**, a couple of miles north at 640 Second Avenue. Born in 1875 to freed slave parents, Mary McLeod Bethune was a lifelong campaigner for racial and sexual equality, founding the National Council of Negro Women and serving as a presidential advisor. In 1904, against the odds, she founded the state's first black girls' school here – with savings of $1.50 and five pupils. The white-framed **house** (Mon–Fri 9am–4pm; free), where Bethune lived from 1914 until her death in 1955, contains scores of awards and citations along-side furnishings and personal effects, and sits within the campus of the large community college that has grown up around the original school.

If you're keen on prehistory, stop off at the **Museum of the Arts & Sciences**, 1040 Museum Boulevard (Tues–Fri 9am–4pm, Sat & Sun noon–5pm; $4), a mile south of International Speedway Boulevard (buses #6 and #7 pass close by), to scrutinize the bones and fossils dug up from the numerous archeological sites in the area. These include the ferocious-looking reassembled remains of a million-year-old giant ground sloth (13 foot long). The other sections of the constantly expanding museum are intriguingly diverse: a stash of American paintings, furnishings and decorative arts from the seventeenth century onwards illuminates early Anglo-American tastes; a major African collection displays domestic and ceremonial objects from thirty of the continent's cultures; and Cuban paintings spanning two centuries (donated by Cuba's former dictator, Batista, who spent many years of exile in a comfortable Daytona Beach house) provide a glimpse of the island nation's important artistic movements.

Daytona International Speedway

About three miles west along International Speedway Boulevard (bus #9A & #9B) stands an ungainly configuration of concrete and steel that has done much to promote Daytona Beach's name around the world: the **Daytona International Speedway**, home of the Daytona 500 stock-car meeting and a few other less famous races. When high speeds made racing on Daytona's sands unsafe, the solution was this 150,000-capacity temple to high-performance thrills and spills, which opened in 1959.

Though it can't capture the excitement of a race (for details of which, see the box below), the guided "trolley" **tour** (daily 9.30am–4pm every 30min except on race days; $5) is the only way to get in without buying a race ticket. You'll have a chance to see the sheer size of the place and the remarkable gradient of the curves, which help make this the fastest racetrack in the world – 200mph is not uncommon.

A new attraction at the Speedway, and due to open in July 1996 at an estimated cost of $18 million, is **Daytona USA**, which will provide more information on the Daytona 500. Among the activities planned are virtual reality and interactive displays that will enable you to take part in pit stops, speak to your favourite driver and be a commentator.

Klassix Auto Museum

A mile west of the Speedway, the **Klassix Auto Museum**, at 2909 International Speedway Boulevard (daily 9am–6pm; $7.50), displays pristine examples of every Corvette design from 1953 to the present day, in historically accurate settings. The museum also houses various other collector and "muscle" cars, as well as vintage motorcycles, all engagingly offset by a 1938 Woody Wagon that boasts a top speed of 50mph. You can catch a bus #9A or #9B to get there.

North to Tomoka State Park and the Bulow Ruins

At the meeting point of the Halifax and Tomoka rivers, just off Hwy-1 six miles north of International Speedway Boulevard (bus #3, then a mile's walk), the attractive **Tomoka State Park** (daily 8am–sunset; cars $3.25, cyclists and pedestrians $1) comprises several hundred acres of marshes and tidal creeks, bordered by magnolias and moss-draped oaks. It's ripe for exploration by canoe (rental in the park at $3 per hour or $15 per day) or on foot along trails.

DAYTONA SPEED WEEKS

The Daytona Speedway hosts several major race meetings each year, starting in early February with the **Rolex 24**: a 24-hour race for GT prototype sports cars. A week or so later begin the qualifying races leading up to the biggest event of the year, the **Daytona 500** stock-car race in mid-February. Tickets (see below) for this are as common as Florida snow, but many of the same drivers compete in the **Pepsi 400**, held on the first Saturday in July, for which tickets are much easier to get. As well as cars, the track is also used for motorcycle races: **Bike Week**, in early March, sees a variety of high-powered clashes; **Biketoberfest**, from 19–22 October, is highlighted by AMA championship racing; and the **Daytona Pro-Am** races at the end of October include numerous sprints and a three-hour endurance test.

Tickets (the cheapest are $20–25 for cars, $10–15 for bikes) for the bigger events sell out well in advance, and it's also advisable to book accommodation for those times at least six months ahead. For **information** and ticket details: ☎904/253-6711.

A 1972 addition to the park, the tiny **Fred Dana Marsh Museum** (9.30am–4.30pm; admission included in park entrance fee) details the life and work of the man who, in the 1910s, was the first artist in the US to create large-scale murals depicting "the drama and significance of men at work". In the 1920s, Marsh also designed a then (and in some ways still) futuristic home for himself and his wife in Ormond Beach. Just north of Granada Boulevard on Hwy-A1A, the house can still be seen (no public admission) as, in the park, can Marsh's immense sculpture, *The Legend of Tomokie*.

Take full advantage of the park by camping overnight (see "Accommodation"), which leaves time to visit the **Bulow Plantation Ruins** (daily 9am–5pm; $2 per car), five miles north: the scant and heavily vegetated remains of an eighteenth-century plantation, destroyed by Seminole Indians. A rough, mile-long loop road leads to it off Route 201.

Accommodation

From mid-May to November, scores of small **motels** on Atlantic Avenue slash their rates to $20–30 a double, cheaper for two people sharing than staying at the youth hostel (see below). These rates go up by $10–15 from December to February, and soar to $60 during March and April (though the demise of Spring Break may serve to stabilize prices between December and mid-May). Pick up the free *Superior Small Lodgings Guide* from the Convention and Visitors Bureau for helpful hints on where to stay.

The choice is almost limitless, but any of the following make good beach bases: the welcoming *Tropical Manor Motel*, no. 2237 S (☎252-4920; ②); *Travelers Inn*, no. 735 S (☎253-3501; ②); *Ocean Hut*, no. 1110 N (☎258-0482; ②); *Robin Hood*, no. 1150 N (☎252-8228; ④); *Cove*, no. 1306 N (☎1-800/828-3251; ②); *Cypress Cove Motel*, no. 3245 S (☎761-1660; ②); and *Seascape Motel*, no. 3321 S (☎767-1372; ②).

Prices rise steadily as you move north along Atlantic Avenue towards Ormond Beach, but the *Econo Lodge-on-the-Beach*, 295 S Atlantic Avenue (☎1-800/847-8811; ③), the *Driftwood Beach Motel*, 657 S Atlantic Avenue (☎677-1331; ②), and the *Atlantic Waver Motel*, 1925 S Atlantic Avenue (☎253-7186; ②), have appealing rates.

Bed and breakfast in Daytona Beach means turning your back on the ocean and heading inland. The choices are the homely *Coquina Inn*, 544 S Palmetto Avenue (☎254-4969; ④), the jacuzzi-equipped *Live Oak Inn*, 444–448 S Beach Street (☎252-4667; ⑤), and *The Villa*, 801 N Peninsula Drive (☎248-2020; ④–⑤).

The youth hostel and camping

Large, lively and superbly positioned for the beach, the **youth hostel**, 140 S Atlantic Avenue (☎258-6937), charges $15. The nearest **campgrounds** are less ideally placed: *Nova Family Campground*, 1190 Herbert Street (☎767-0095), ten miles south of mainland Daytona Beach (bus #17A & #17B); and *Tomoka State Park* (☎676-4050), seven miles north of mainland Daytona Beach (bus #3 stops a mile down the road); $17 to pitch a tent.

Eating

Major appetites can be satisfied for modest outlay at several buffet **restaurants**: *Shoney's*, 2558 N Atlantic Avenue (☎255-9054), is open for breakfast, lunch and dinner; *Checkers*, 219 S Atlantic Avenue (☎239-0010), has buffet breakfasts and an all-you-can-eat dinner session; or you can help yourself to the evening spread at the *Manor Buffet*, 747 Ridgewood Avenue (☎253-3359).

If you're watching the calories, forego the buffet blow-outs in favour of the regular diner food offered by the *Main Street Café*, 819 Main Street (☎257-2323), the *Seabreeze Café*, 316 Seabreeze Boulevard (☎258-0510), the Fifties-style *Doo Wop A Doo Diner*, 362 W Granada Boulevard (☎677-5000), and *Café Bravo*, 176 N Beach Street (☎252-7747), which also serves beer.

Slightly pricier but with greater choices for lunch or dinner is *Julian's*, 88 S Atlantic Avenue (☎677-6767), a dimly lit mock-Tahitian lounge with a large and good menu. Also worth trying are the *Lighthouse Landing*, beside the Ponce Inlet lighthouse (☎761-9271), which is strong on fresh seafood, as is *Down the Hatch*, 4894 Front Street, Ponce Inlet (☎761-4831), with a waterfront location and outdoor raw bar. *Brewsters*, 4511 S Atlantic Avenue (☎760-0810), is good for seafood or burgers beside the ocean, and *Aunt Catfish's*, 4009 Halifax Drive, a few miles south of Daytona Beach in Port Orange (☎767-4768), has mighty portions of ribs and seafood prepared to traditional Southern recipes. If you have a sudden desire for Japanese food, head for one of the two branches of *Sapporo*, 501 Seabreeze Boulevard (☎257-4477) and 3340 S Atlantic Avenue (☎756-0480).

Nightlife

Even without the Spring Break invasion of party-crazed students, it seems likely that Daytona Beach will retain its reputation as one of the best spots on Florida's east coast for making merry when the sun goes down. The nucleus of the beach-side **nightlife** is *HoJo's Party Complex*, 600 N Atlantic Avenue (☎255-4471; $3–10), with bars, discos, live rock and reggae and ceaseless wet T-shirt competitions. There's more rabble-rousing at *Razzles*, 611 Seabreeze Boulevard (☎257-6236), *Ocean Deck*, 127 S Ocean Boulevard (☎253-5224), *Kokomos on the Beach* and *Waves*, both at 100 N Atlantic Avenue inside the Adams Mark Daytona Beach Resort (☎254-8200). Danceable **nightclubs** with a less collegiate crowd are the *Checker Café*, 219 S Atlantic Avenue (☎255-0251), and *Coliseum*, 176 N Beach Street (☎257-9982).

Simply for a **drink**, the *Boothill Saloon*, across from the cemetery at 301 Main Street (☎258-9506), can be enjoyable, but if you find its biker clientele threatening, alternatives are *The Oyster Pub*, 555 Seabreeze Boulevard (☎255-6348), where the beer is helped down by dirt-cheap oysters and a loud jukebox, and *The Spot*, a sports bar and part of the *Coliseum* complex (see above). For **live music**, look to *The Other Place*, 642 S Atlantic Avenue (☎672-2461); *Rockin' Ranch* in the Ellinor Village shopping centre, 801 S Nova Road (☎673-0904); the cavernous *Finky's*, 640 N Grandview Avenue (☎255-5059), which features country combos and square dancing; or the *Clocktower Lounge* in the Adams Mark Daytona Beach Resort (see above), an elegant piano bar with an ocean view.

North from Daytona Beach

Assuming you don't want to cut twenty miles inland along I-4 or Hwy-92 to DeLand and the Orlando area (see *Central Florida*), keep on Hwy-A1A **northwards** along the coast towards St Augustine – as usual, *Greyhound* buses take the less interesting Hwy-1.

The first community you'll encounter is **FLAGLER BEACH**, fourteen miles from Daytona Beach, comprising a few houses and shops, a pier and a very tempting beach. Nearby, at the **Flagler Beach State Recreation Area** (daily 8am–sunset; cars $3.25, cyclists and pedestrians $1), a good cross-section of coastal bird life can be spotted, particularly at low tide when freshly exposed sands provide a feast for swift beaks.

Further on, soon after passing the blazing blooms of **Washington Oaks State Gardens** (daily 8am–sunset; cars $3.25, pedestrians and cyclists $1), you can't miss the crumbling Streamline Moderne architecture of **Marineland** (daily 9am–5.30pm; $14.95), Florida's original sea-creature theme park. The state's biggest tourist draw when it opened in 1938, its status has been severely undermined by subsequent imitations such as the far superior Sea World (see *Central Florida*). Established as marine studios for underwater research and photography, the park's highlights include sharks, performing porpoises and a 3-D film depicting an undersea adventure, but none of these justifies the high admission fee.

Hwy-A1A crosses a narrow inlet three miles beyond Marineland onto **Anastasia Island**, close to the Spanish-built seventeenth-century **Fort Matanzas** on Rattlesnake Island. Never conquered, partly due to the sixteen-foot-thick walls and the surrounding moat, even today the fort is accessible only by **ferry** (departures daily except Tuesday every 15min, 9am–4.30pm; free), but it's of minor appeal in comparison to history-packed St Augustine.

A better stop might be the **St Augustine Alligator Farm** (daily 9am–5.30pm; $9.95), a few miles further north along Hwy-A1A. Visitors are greeted by shrieks from a vividly coloured toucan (a tropical bird) and can take a walk through a wildlife-infested swamp. Time your visit to coincide with the "alligator show" (usually twice a day; phone ☎904/824-3337 for exact times), when a keeper drags an alligator around by its tail to demonstrate how the creature expresses anger: it bellows loudly, arches its back and displays a gaping jaw. It's heart-stopping stuff – not least when the handler, sitting on the creature's back, puts his fingers between the gator's teeth.

Once past the Alligator Farm, you're well within reach of St Augustine, whose old centre is just across Matanzas Bay, three miles ahead.

St Augustine

With the size and even some of the looks of a small Mediterranean town, there are few places in Florida as immediately engaging as **ST AUGUSTINE**, the oldest permanent settlement in the US and one with much from its early days still intact. St Augustine's eminently strollable narrow streets are lined by carefully renovated buildings whose architecture carries evidence of Florida's European heritage and the power struggles that led up to statehood. There's plenty here to fill a day or two, and for variation you can visit two alluring lengths of beach located just across the small bay on which the town stands.

Ponce de León, the Spaniard who gave Florida its name, touched ground here in 1513, but it wasn't until Pedro Menéndez de Avilés put ashore on St Augustine's Day in 1565 that settlement began, with the intention of subduing the Huguenots based to the north (at Fort Caroline, see "The Jacksonville beaches", p.209). Repeated battles with the British began when Sir Francis Drake's ships razed St Augustine in 1586, but Spanish control was only relinquished when Florida was

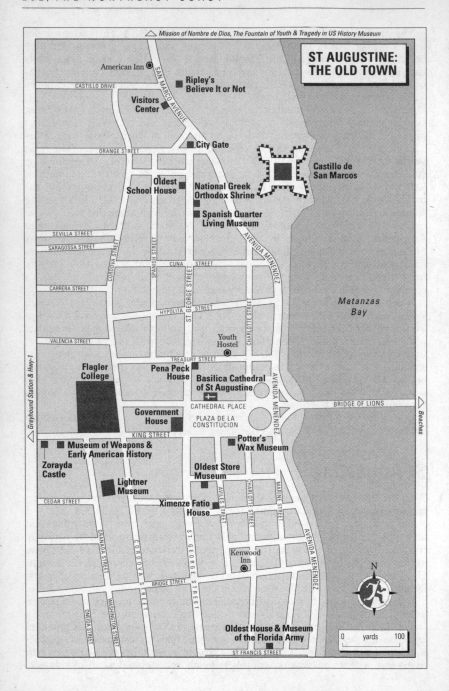

△ Mission of Nombre de Dios, The Fountain of Youth & Tragedy in US History Museum

**ST AUGUSTINE:
THE OLD TOWN**

American Inn ◉

CASTILLO DRIVE

**Ripley's
Believe It or Not**

**Visitors
Center**

SAN MARCO AVENUE

ORANGE STREET

■ **City Gate**

**Castillo de
San Marcos**

**Oldest
School House**

**National Greek
Orthodox Shrine**

**Spanish Quarter
Living Museum**

SEVILLA STREET

SARAGOSSA STREET

CORDOVA STREET

SPANISH STREET

CUNA STREET

CARRERA STREET

AVENIDA MENENDEZ

HYPOLITA STREET

ST GEORGE STREET

*Matanzas
Bay*

CHARLOTTE STREET

VALENCIA STREET

**Youth
Hostel** ◉

TREASURY STREET

Greyhound Station & Hwy-1 △

**Flagler
College**

**Pena Peck
House**

**Basilica Cathedral
of St Augustine** ✝

AVENIDA MENENDEZ

BRIDGE OF LIONS

CATHEDRAL PLACE

Beaches △

**Government
House**

PLAZA DE LA
CONSTITUCION

KING STREET

**Museum of Weapons &
Early American History**

**Potter's
Wax Museum**

**Zorayda
Castle**

**Lightner
Museum**

**Oldest Store
Museum**

CHARLOTTE STREET

MARINE STREET

CEDAR STREET

**Ximenze Fatio
House**

AVILES STREET

GRANADA STREET

CORDOVA STREET

ST GEORGE STREET

AVENIDA MENENDEZ

**Kenwood
Inn** ◉

N

BRIDGE STREET

ONEIDA STREET

WASHINGTON STREET

**Oldest House & Museum
of the Florida Army**

ST FRANCIS STREET

0 yards 100

The area code for St Augustine and Jacksonville is ☎904.

ceded to Britain in 1763, by which time the town was established as an important social and administrative centre – soon to become the capital of East Florida.

Spain regained possession twenty years later, and kept it until 1821, when Florida joined the US. Subsequently, Tallahassee became the capital of a unified Florida, and St Augustine's fortunes waned. A railway and a posh hotel stimulated a turn-of-the-century tourist boom, but otherwise expansion bypassed St Augustine – which inadvertently made possible the restoration programme that started in the Thirties. This has turned the otherwise quiet, residential community into a magnificent historical showcase.

Arrival and information

From Anastasia Island, **Hwy-A1A** crosses over Mantanzas Bay into the heart of St Augustine; **Hwy-1** passes a mile west along Ponce de Leon Boulevard. The *Greyhound* **bus** will drop you at 100 Malaga Street (☎829-6401), a fifteen-minute walk from the centre.

St Augustine has no public transport system, but this poses no problem in the town, which is best seen **on foot**. If you're in a hurry, the **sightseeing train** (tickets from 170 San Marco Ave; daily 8am–5pm; $12) makes an hour-long narrated circuit of the main landmarks. Getting to the beaches means either a two-mile hike, renting a **bike** from *Island Bicycles*, quarter of a mile across the bridge from the mainland at 211 Anastasia Boulevard (☎824-4010), or calling a **taxi** (☎824-8161).

After a few hours of hard exploration, **harbour cruises**, leaving five or six times a day from the City Yacht Pier, near the foot of King Street, make a relaxing break; the 75-minute guided trip around the bay costs $7.

The **visitor center**, 10 Castillo Drive (daily 8.30am–5.30pm; ☎825-1000), offers the usual tourist brochures and discount coupons. It also shows a free film on the history of the town, can recommend a variety of historical guided tours (including those of *Tour St Augustine*, who offer well-organized and informative walking tours, as well as tailored itineraries ☎471-9010), and will fill you in on the numerous local festivals which range from torch-lit processions (third Sat in June) to chowder tastings (last weekend in Oct) and a Menorcan Fiesta (second weekend in September).

Accommodation

St Augustine attracts plenty of visitors, most of whom make short stays between May and October, when costs are $10–20 above the winter rates. The Old Town (see below) has many restored inns offering **bed and breakfast**: *Carriage Way*, 70 Cuna Street (☎829-2467; ③), *Cordova House*, 16 Cordova Street (☎825-0770; ④), and *Kenwood Inn*, 38 Marine Street (☎824-2116; ④), are the best priced. To cut costs considerably, use the *St Augustine Hostel*, 32 Treasury Street (check-in times 8am–10am and 5pm–10pm; ☎808-1999; $12 for everyone).

Alternatively, try the cheap **motels** that ring the Old Town. Least expensive is the *American Inn*, 42 San Marco Avenue (☎829-2292; ③); further along the same road is, *Equinox*, no. 306 (☎829-8569; ③). Across the bay from the Old Town but well within striking distance, you'll find the waterside *Anchorage Motor Inn*, 1

Dolphin Drive (☎829-9041; ③), *Royal Inn*, 420 Anastasia Boulevard (☎824-2831; ②), and the *Friendship Inn*, 107 Anastasia Boulevard (☎826-1700; ④).

Costs are usually higher **at the beaches**, but the laid-back *Vilano Beach Motel*, 50 Vilano Road (☎829-2651; ③), is a great base for enjoying the North Beach; to the south, the busier *St Augustine Beach* has more family-oriented weekly rented apartments than motels, though the small *Sea Shore*, 480 Hwy-A1A (☎471-3101; ③), and *Seaway*, 481 Hwy-A1A (☎471-3466; ③), are reliable.

The best place to **camp** is the *Anastasia State Recreation Area* (☎461-2033), four miles south, off Hwy-A1A (see "The Beaches", p.208), where you can pitch a tent for $17.

The Old Town

St Augustine's historic area – or **Old Town** – along St George Street and south of the central plaza, contains well-tended evidence of the town's Spanish period. Equally worth a look are the lavish structures along King Street, just west of the plaza, remaining from the turn-of-the-century resort times. Although St Augustine is small, there's a lot to see: an early start, around 9am, will give you a lead on the tourist crowds and enable you to get a good look at almost everything inside a day.

The castle
Given the fine state of the **Castillo de San Marcos** (daily 8.45am–4.45pm; $2), on the northern edge of the Old Town beside the bay, it's difficult to believe that the fortress was started in the late 1600s. Its longevity is due to the design: a diamond-shaped rampart at each corner maximized firepower, and fourteen-foot-thick coquina (a type of soft limestone found on Anastasia Island) walls reduced vulnerability to attack – as British troops found when they waged a fruitless fifty-day siege in 1702. Times of free 20-min **talks** on the fort and local history are indicated in the courtyard.

Inside, there's not a lot to admire beyond a small museum and echoing rooms – some of them with military and social exhibits – but venturing along the 35-foot-high ramparts gives an unobstructed view over the low-lying city and its waterborne approaches, which the castle protected so successfully.

Along St George Street
Leaving the castle, the little eighteenth-century **City Gate** marks the entrance to **St George Street**, once the main thoroughfare and now a tourist-trampled pedestrianized strip – but home to plenty of genuine history. At no. 14, the **Oldest Wooden School House** (daily 9am–5pm; $2) still has its original eighteenth-century red cedar and cypress walls and tabby floor (a mix of crushed oyster shells and lime, common at the time). These minor architectural points are the main interest: the building was put into use as a school some years later, thereby inadvertently becoming, as the staff are quick to point out, the oldest wooden schoolhouse in the US. Pupils and teacher are now unconvincingly portrayed by speaking wax models.

Further along, at no. 41, an unassuming doorway leads into the petite **National Greek Orthodox Shrine** (daily 9am–5pm; free), where tapes of Byzantine choirs are played, and icons and candles stand alongside hard-hitting accounts relating the experiences of Greek immigrants to the US – some of whom settled in St Augustine from New Smyrna Beach (see p.193) in 1777.

More directly relevant to the town, and taking up a fair-sized plot at the corner of St George and Cuna streets, the **Spanish Quarter Living Museum** (daily 9am–5pm; $5) includes eight reconstructed homes and workshops. Volunteers disguised as Spanish settlers go about their daily tasks at spinning wheels, anvils and foot-driven wood lathes. The museum should be visited either early in the day or during an off-peak period; crocodile lines of camera-wielding tourists substantially lessen the effect. The main entrance is through the Triay House, on N St George Street.

For a more intimate look at local life during a slightly later period, head for the **Pena Peck House**, at no. 143 (Mon–Sat 10am–4.30pm, Sun 12.30–4.30pm; $2). Thought originally to have been the Spanish treasury, by the time the British took over in 1763 this was the home of a physician and his gregarious spouse, who turned the place into a high society rendezvous. The Pecks' furnishings and paintings, plus the enthusiastic spiel of the guide, make for an enjoyable tour.

The Plaza

In the sixteenth century, the Spanish king decreed that all colonial towns had to be built around a central plaza, and St Augustine was no exception: St George Street runs into **Plaza de la Constitucion**, a marketplace dating from 1598, nowadays attracting shade-seekers and the occasional wino. On the north side of the plaza, the **Basilica Cathedral of St Augustine** (daily 7am–5pm; donation requested) adds a touch of grandeur, though it's largely a Sixties remodelling of the late eighteenth-century original, with murals by Hugo Ohlms depicting life in St Augustine. Periodic **guided tours** (times are sometimes pinned to the door) revel in the painstaking details of the rebuilding and the undistinguished stained-glass windows. Slightly more worthwhile, the ground floor of **Government House** (daily 10am–4pm; $2), on the west side of the plaza, contains small displays of objects from the city's various renovation projects and archeological digs. In contrast, on the south side of the square, seeking shelter from a thunderstorm might be the sole justification for entering **Potter's Wax Museum** (summer daily 9am–9pm; winter 9am–5pm; $5), populated by effigies of people you may have heard of but probably won't recognize.

South of the Plaza

Tourist numbers lessen as you cross south of the plaza into a web of quiet, narrow streets with as much antiquity as St George Street. At 4 Artillery Lane, the **Oldest Store Museum** (summer Mon–Sat 9am–5pm, Sun 10am–5pm; rest of the year Mon–Sat 9am–5pm, Sun noon–5pm; $4) does an excellent job of recreating an 1880s general store, filled to the rafters with the produce of the time: curious foods and drinks, fiery medicinal potions and oversized consumer essentials such as apple peelers, cigar moulders and wooden washing machines.

Close by, at 20 Aviles Street, the **Ximenez Fatio House** (opening hours vary greatly according to season; phone for details on ☎829-3575; free) was built in 1797 for a Spanish merchant and proved popular with the travellers who predated the town's first tourist boom, drawn by the airy balconies added to the original structure. Although the upper floor is a bit rickety, a walk around is safe and quick in the company of a guide who points out illuminating details. At 3 Aviles Street you can spend an interesting fifteen minutes in the small **Spanish Military Hospital** (daily 9am–5pm; $1), built in 1791 and demonstrating the spartan care wounded soldiers could expect.

More substantial history is unfurled a ten-minute walk away at the **Oldest House**, 14 St Francis Street (daily 9am–5pm; $5), occupied from the early 1700s (and, indeed, the oldest house in the town) by the family of an artillery hand at the castle. The second floor was grafted on during the British period, a fact evinced by the bone china crockery belonging to the incumbent, one Mary Peavitt, whose disastrous marriage to a hopeless gambler provided the basis for a popular historical novel, *Maria*, by Eugenia Price (the gift shop has copies). A smaller room shows the pine-stripped "sidecar" style made popular by the arrival of Flagler's railway: it copies the decor of a train carriage.

Entered through the back garden of the house, the less than riveting **Museum of the Florida Army** (entry included with admission to the Oldest House; same hours) gives an inkling, mainly with old uniforms, of the numerous conflicts that have divided Florida over the years. Anybody you might see striding by in modern military garb probably belongs to the Florida National Guard, whose headquarters are across the street.

West of the Plaza: along King Street

A walk west from the plaza along **King Street** bridges the gap between early St Augustine and its turn-of-the-century tourist boom. You'll soon notice, at the junction with Cordova Street, the flowing spires, arches and red-tiled roof of **Flagler College**. Now utilized by liberal arts students, a hundred years ago it was – as the *Ponce de Leon Hotel* – an exclusive winter retreat of the nation's rich and mighty. The hotel was an early attempt by entrepreneur Henry Flagler to exploit Florida's climate and coast, but as he developed properties further south and extended his railway, the *Ponce de Leon* fell from favour – not helped by a couple of freezing winters. There are free guided tours in the summer. You can **walk around** the campus and the ground floor of the main building (daily 10am–3pm) to admire the Tiffany stained glass and the painstakingly restored painted ceiling in the dining room.

In competition with Flagler, the eccentric Bostonian architect Franklin W Smith – seemingly obsessed with poured concrete and Moorish design (see the Zorayda Castle, below) – built a rival hotel of matching extravagance directly opposite the *Ponce de Leon*. He eventually sold it to Flagler, who named it the *Alcazar*. Fronted by a courtyard of palm trees and fountains, the building now holds the **Lightner Museum** (daily 9am–5pm; $4), where you could easily pass an hour poring over the Victorian cut glass, Tiffany lamps, antique music boxes and more. Much of it was acquired by publishing ace Otto C Lightner from once-wealthy estates hard hit by the Depression.

A rather incongruous sight in St Augustine is Franklin W Smith's (see above) recreation of the Alhambra. The architect was so impressed by the Moorish architecture he'd seen in Spain that he built a copy of a wing of the thirteenth-century palace here, at a tenth of the original size. In 1913, forty years after the **Zorayda Castle**, 83 King Street (daily 9am–5pm; $5), was finished, a well-heeled Egyptian consul purchased it to store his ankle-deep carpets and treasures from all points east: a 2300-year-old Sacred Cat Rug, said to put a curse on anyone who stands on it (which is perhaps why it hangs on the wall), and a divinely detailed gaming table inlaid with sandalwood and mother-of-pearl, are just two. As a giant folly stuffed with gems, the Zorayda Castle has much charm; only the 25¢-test-your-sex-appeal machine by the exit shatters the mood.

In stark relief, just across the Zorayda's carpark, a shack contains the **Museum of Weapons and Early American History** (daily 9.30am–5pm; $3.50). Reading the small collection of Civil War diaries gives an interesting personal view of the struggle, but this one-room cache will mainly appeal to survivalist types, with plenty of tools to shoot, stab and batter foes to death.

North of the Old Town: San Marco Avenue and around

Leading away from the tightly grouped streets of the Old Town, the traffic-bearing **San Marco Avenue**, beginning on the other side of the city gate from St George Street, passes the sites of the first Spanish landings and settlements and some remains of the Timucua Indians who greeted them. A couple of other potential stops are of much less relevance to the town but can be good for a laugh.

People either love or loathe them, but if you've never been inside one of the country's several **Ripley's Believe It or Not** collections, you shouldn't pass up the chance. This one, at 19 San Marco Avenue (Memorial Day to Labor day daily 9am–10pm; rest of the year 9am–6pm; $7.50), isn't the best but contains a riveting collection of oddities gathered by Ripley as he travelled around the world in the Twenties and Thirties. Whether it's a grandfather clock made from clothes pegs, the Lord's Prayer printed on the head of a pin or a toothpick model of the Eiffel Tower, each object seems stranger than the last, and it can be hard to tear yourself away.

Half a mile further along San Marco Avenue, don't be discouraged by the dull, modern church that now stands in the grounds of **Mission of Nombre de Dios** (summer daily 7am–8pm; rest of the year 8am–6pm; donation requested). This sixteenth-century mission was one of many established by Spanish settlers in order to convert Native Americans to Christianity, simultaneously exploiting their labour and seeking to earn their support in possible confrontations with rival colonial powers.

A pathway leads to a 208-foot-tall stainless steel cross, glinting in the sun beside the river on the spot where Menéndez landed in 1565. Soon after, Father Francisco Lopez de Mendoza Grajales celebrated the first Mass in North America, recording that "a large number of Indians watched the proceedings and imitated all they saw", which was a bit unfortunate since the arrival of the Spanish signalled the beginning of the end for the Indians. A side-path takes a mildly interesting course around the rest of the squirrel-patrolled lawns, passing a few relics of the mission, on the way to a small, ivy-covered re-creation of the original chapel.

In addition to the prospect of finding gold and silver, it's said that Ponce de León was drawn to Florida by a belief that the fabled life-preserving "fountain of youth" was located here. Rather tenuously, this fact is celebrated at a mineral spring touted as **The Fountain of Youth** (daily 9am–5pm; $4.50) in a park at the end of Williams Street (off San Marco Avenue), very near the point where he landed in 1513, and about half a mile north of the old mission site; it's unlikely, however, you'll live forever after drinking the fresh water handed to you as you enter the springhouse. The expansive acres of the park have far more significance as an archeological site. Besides remains of the Spanish settlement, many Timucua Indian relics have been unearthed, and you'll also come across some of the wiry plants that were the base of the "Black Drink", a thick, highly potent concoction used by the Timucuans to help them achieve mystical states.

Williams Street also holds the morbid and depressing **Tragedy in US History Museum**, at no. 7 (daily 9am–sunset; $4); even self-confessed ghouls won't get much pleasure from looking at President Kennedy's assassination car and the ambulance that took him to hospital, or the bed of his (alleged) assassin, Lee Harvey Oswald. Here, too, are the tangled remains of Jayne Mansfield's death car, the bullet-spattered vehicle of Bonnie and Clyde, a collection of sickeningly racist correspondence and sundry testaments to human cruelty, including an imported Spanish jail cell still containing the bones of an unfortunate inmate.

The beaches

If you've reached St Augustine with Hwy-A1A you'll need no introduction to the fine **beaches** that lie just a couple of miles from the Old Town. Few other people do either, especially on weekends when the bronzers, beachcombers and water-sports fanatics descend in droves. A fine view of St Augustine and up and down the beaches is afforded by the **Lighthouse Museum**, 81 Lighthouse Avenue (daily 9am–5pm; $3.50), which tells the story of keepers and the lights they tended.

Across the bay on Anastasia Island, **St Augustine Beach** is family terrain, but here you'll also find the **Anastasia State Recreation Area** (daily 8am–sunset; cars $3.25, cyclists and pedestrians $1), offering a thousand protected acres of dunes, marshes, scrub and a wind-beaten group of live oaks, linked by nature walks – though most people come here to catch a fish dinner from the lagoon. In the other direction (take May Street, off San Marco Avenue), **Vilano Beach** pulls a younger crowd and marks the beginning of a dazzling strand continuing for twenty undeveloped miles all the way to Jacksonville Beach (see below).

Eating and nightlife

The tourist throng on and around St George Street makes eating in the old town an often pricey affair, particularly for dinner. However, early in the day you could try *Cuzzin's Sandwich Shoppe*, 124 St George Street (☎829-8967), for coffee or **breakfast**; or *The Bunnery*, 35 Hypolita Street (☎829-6166), for economical break-fasts and lunches and specialities that include cinnamon rolls, pecan sticky buns and brownies. South of the plaza, *Café Camacho*, 11 Aviles Street(☎824-7030), is worth a visit for cut-rate breakfasts and good-sized **lunches**. Also good for lunch are the stylish snacks at *Café Alcazar*, 25 Granada Street (☎824-7813), in the antique mall behind the Lightner Museum; the tasty soups and salads at *Scarlett O'Hara's*, 70 Hypolita Street (☎824-6535); and the excellent burgers at *The Oasis*, 4000 Ocean Trace Road (also Hwy-A1A), with access from the beach (☎471-3424) – try the "Gonzo Burger", served with three kinds of cheese and piles of extras.

Most of the above are closed for **dinner** (though *Scarlett O'Hara's* does excel-lent fried crayfish suppers), and an evening meal for under $15 in the Old Town takes some finding. *Matanzas Bay Café*, 12 Avenida Menendez (☎829-8141), and *O.C. Whites*, 118 Avenida Menendez (☎824-0808), may oblige; otherwise head across the bay. On Anastasia Boulevard, *El Toro Con Sombrero*, no. 10 (☎842-8852), is a rowdy bar with Mexican food, jumping until 1am; *O'Steen's*, no. 205 (☎829-6974), serves fish and shrimp until 8.30pm; and the *Gypsy Cab Company*, no. 828 (☎824-8244), provides Greek, Italian and Cajun food in an Art Deco setting.

Nightlife

Try to exhaust yourself during the day because St Augustine has limited **night-life**. In the Old Town, have a **drink** at the tavern-like *White Lion*, 20 Cuna Street (☎829-2388); to a background of floor-singers and (taped) Gregorian chant at *Monk's Vineyard*, 56 St George Street (☎824-5888); during the 5–7pm happy hours at *Scarlett O'Hara's* (see "Eating"); or in the compact *Milltop*, 19 St George Street (☎829-2329). You could also sip a cocktail overlooking the ocean from the deck bar of *Panama Hatties*, 2125 S Hwy-A1A (☎471-2255). If drinking is not on your agenda, then open yourself up to "A Ghostly Experience", a guided **walking tour** of haunted and spook-filled sites (by arrangement on ☎471-9010; $5).

The Jacksonville beaches

However good the beaches around St Augustine may be, they're just the start of an unblemished coastal strip running northwards for twenty miles alongside Hwy-A1A, with nothing but the ocean on one side, and the swamps and marshes of the Talamato River (the local section of the Intracoastal waterway) on the other. The scene begins to change when you near the sculptured golf courses and half-million-dollar homes of **PONTE VEDRA BEACH** – one of the most exclusive communities in northeast Florida. Despite laws to the contrary, there is only one public access point to the beach in Ponte Vedra (off Ponte Vedra Boulevard, which splits from Hwy-A1A near Mickler Landing) but it's worth finding: the crowd-free sands are prime beachcombing terrain, retreating tides often leaving sharks' teeth among the more common ocean debris.

Four miles on, the much less snooty **JACKSONVILLE BEACH** is an affable beachside community whose residents relax here and commute to work in the city of Jacksonville, twelve miles inland. The damage inflicted by a hurricane in 1976 perhaps accounts for the uncluttered feel. As it is, the place is inexplicably neglected by tourists outside of the summer months. The **pier** is the centre of activity, and a fried-fish sandwich from its snack bar is the right accompaniment for observing novice surfers grappling with modest-sized breakers. If you start itching for some action of your own, you could do worse than visit **Adventure Landing**, 1944 Beach Boulevard (daily 10am till late; free), where adults and kids alike can let rip in a glorified adventure playground. You pay as you go to enter the attractions, which include a water park ($13.95), a go-kart race track ($4), a game of laser-tag with pirates in the dark ($6), or the baseball batting cages ($1) where you can indulge fantasies of being Babe Ruth.

Once you cross Seagate Avenue, just under two miles north of the pier, Jacksonville Beach merges with the more commercialized **NEPTUNE BEACH**, which in turn blurs (at Atlantic Boulevard) with the identical-looking **ATLANTIC BEACH**. These last two places are the best to visit for eating and socializing in this area. Just north of Atlantic Beach, downbeat **MAYPORT** is dominated by its naval station, berth to some of the biggest aircraft carriers in the US Navy. It's best seen through a car window on the way to the Mayport ferry, crossing the St John's River, and the barrier islands beyond (see "Towards Amelia Island", p.215).

In contrast to the naval station is the **Kathryn Hanna Park**, 500 Wonderwood Drive (☎249-2316; 50c), just south of Mayport. Besides its mile and a half of unblemished beachfront, the park boasts 450 acres of woodland surrounding a large lake, around which wind ten miles of enjoyable biking and hiking trails. There's also a campsite here (see "Sleeping, eating and nightlife", p.210).

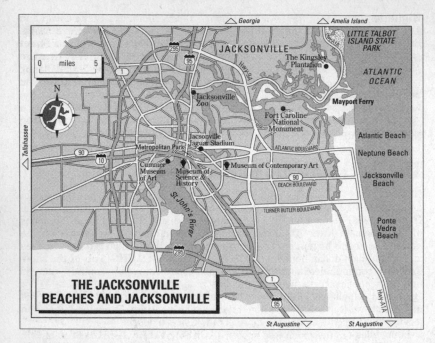

THE JACKSONVILLE
BEACHES AND JACKSONVILLE

Around the beaches

Only two things are likely to drag you away from the beaches. The **American Lighthouse Museum**, 1011 N Third Street (Tues–Sat 11am–4pm; free), has a moderately interesting collection of paintings, drawings, photos, plans and models of lighthouses and ships. Further away, a few miles inland on Girvin Road (off Atlantic Boulevard), the **Fort Caroline National Monument** (daily 9am–5pm; free) offers a more historical interlude: a small museum details the significance of the restored Huguenot fort here, which stimulated the first Spanish settlement in Florida (see "St Augustine" p.201). Another reason to come is the great view from the fort across the mile-wide St John's River and its ocean-going freighters.

Sleeping, eating and nightlife

Along the coast there'll be plenty of bargains in winter, but during the summer be ready to spend $40–55 for a basic **motel** room, and book ahead. *Sea Horse Oceanfront Inn*, 120 Atlantic Boulevard (☎246-2175; ③), *Surfside*, 1236 N First Street, Neptune Beach (☎246-1583; ②), and *Golden Sands*, 127 S First Avenue, Jacksonville Beach (☎249-4374; ①–②), have the lowest rates. If you don't mind staying six miles inland, save a few dollars by using the *Scottish Inn*, 2300 Philips Highway (☎1-800/251-1962; ①), near the junction of I-95 and Hwy-90. Of the more expensive options, try the *Sea Turtle Inn*, 1 Ocean Boulevard, Atlantic Beach (☎1-800/874-6000; ⑤). With a tent, you can **camp** at the Kathryn Hanna Park (see p.209) for $10.

For **eating**, S Third Street at Jacksonville Beach offers two basic, cheap and reliable options: *Beach Hut Café* (no. 1281; ☎249-3516) and *Ellen's Kitchen* (no. 1824; ☎246-1572). Good breakfasts, lunches and dinners are served at *Famous Amos*, at the junction of Atlantic and Third – Hwy-A1A (☎249-7025). Slightly more costly are the fancy variations on deli staples at the *Sun Dog Diner*, 207 S Atlantic Boulevard, Neptune Beach (☎241-8221), or the health-conscious cuisine of *Heaven on Earth*, 363-14 Atlantic Boulevard (☎249-6252).

Nightlife is strong: *Pier 7*, 401 N First Street, Neptune Beach (☎246-6373), is a vibrant disco with big crowds and drink specials; *Einstein A Go Go*, 327 N First Street, Neptune Beach (☎249-4646), is a studenty showcase for alternative sounds and poetry readings; and *Baja Beach Club*, 222 Ocean Front, Atlantic Beach (☎246-7701), hosts anything from Acid House raves to wet T-shirt contests. For a different atmosphere, head for *The Fly's Tie Irish Pub*, 177 E Saltfish Drive, Atlantic Beach (☎246-4293), and enjoy the live Irish music and beer. To escape the beach scene, head for *Tsunarni's*, 2500 Beach Boulevard (☎249-6992), which is on the intracoastal waterway (going inland from Jacksonville Beach) and ideal for dining and dancing.

Jacksonville

With long-established lumber and coffee industries, and the deep St John's River making it a major transit point for seaborne cargo, **JACKSONVILLE** has long been suspicious of anything liable to upset its hard-working traditions; pleasure-seeking visitors are expected to stick to the beaches, twelve miles east, and even the US film industry was scared off in the 1910s when it came here seeking a base, settling instead in California. Lately, with a growing white-collar sector easing the blight of years of heavy industry, there have been efforts to heighten Jacksonville's appeal by creating parks and riverside boardwalks, but the sheer size of the city – at 841 square miles, the largest in the US – dilutes its character and makes it an impossible nut to crack without a vehicle. For all that, Jacksonville is not an unwelcoming place, and will sufficiently consume a day – even if you spend most of it strolling the riverside downtown.

Downtown Jacksonville

Leaning on local businesses to divert some of their profits into area improvement schemes, an enlightened city administration has helped make **downtown Jacksonville** much less the forbidding forest of corporate high-rises that it initially looks. For an overview of downtown Jacksonville, take the **Skyway monorail** (Mon–Thurs 6.30am–9pm, Fri 6.30am–10pm, Sat 9am–10pm; 25¢) from the corner of Bay and Pearl streets to the Conference Center, a five-minute journey at eye-level to the high-rise offices; plans are underway to extend the service to cover more of the city. Another way to get to grips with this sprawling city is to gain a bird's-eye view of it by hitching a ride on a hot-air balloon; *Outdoor Adventures*, 6110-7 Powers Avenue (☎739-1960; see p.213), can take you up for $135 round trip. Otherwise, take a wander along the banks of St John's River, which snakes through the city centre, dividing downtown Jacksonville in two.

The north bank

Within four blocks of Bay Street on the **north bank** of the river, you'll find the few structures that survived the 1901 fire – which claimed much of early Jacksonville – and some of the more distinctive buildings from subsequent decades. These are best examined with the aid of the free *Downtown Walking* leaflet from the Convention and Visitors Bureau (see "Practicalities" below). One noteworthy building is the heavily restored **Florida Theater**, 128 E Forsyth Street, which opened in 1927 and became a centre of controversy thirty years later when Elvis Presley's pelvic thrusts shocked the city's burghers. Another is the **Morocco Temple**, 219 N Newnam Street, built by Henry John Kluthco. This classically minded architect arrived to rebuild Jacksonville after the 1901 fire but later converted to Frank Lloyd Wright-inspired Modernism and erected this sphinx-decorated masterpiece in 1912.

The south bank

To cross to the **south bank** of the river, take the *River Taxi* ($2 one way; $3 return) from the dock beside the gleaming Jacksonville Landing shopping mall, between Water Street and the river. You'll be dropped next to a mile-long pathway called the Riverwalk, west along which is the **Jacksonville Historical Center** (Mon–Sat 10am–5pm, Sun noon–5pm; free), a brief but interesting "walkthrough" account of the city's origins and growth. Further on you'll come to the oversized **Friendship Fountain**, best seen at night when coloured lights illuminate its gushing jets. Finally, the **Museum of Science and History** (Mon–Fri 10am–5pm, Sat 10am–6pm, Sun 1–5pm; $6) has educational hands-on exhibits primarily aimed at kids, plus a planetarium offering hi-tech trips around the cosmos.

Nearby in San Marco on Atlantic Boulevard, dwarfed by neighbouring office towers, the tiny **St Pauls Episcopal Church** is a hundred-year-old example of the "Carpenter Gothic" building style. Don't bother going inside – the church is now used for secular purposes – but read the plaque outside recalling naturalist William Bartram, who passed this way in the 1750s and briefly described "Cowford", as Jacksonville was then known, in his journal; see "Books" in *Contexts*.

Around downtown Jacksonville

With a car, it's easy to zip between the likely points of call scattered about this nebulous city, but it's much harder – and frankly not worth the effort – to do the same thing by bus. A good scrutiny of the art collections will take up an afternoon, but if you feel like being outside, make for Metropolitan Park, the extensive acreage of the zoo, or the thrills at Adventure Landing (see p.209).

Jacksonville Museum of Contemporary Art and the Cummer Museum of Art and Gardens

In this city of commerce and industry, you might not expect much from the **Jacksonville Museum of Contemporary Art** (Tues, Wed & Fri 10am–4pm, Thurs 10am–10pm, Sat & Sun 1–5pm; $3), which you'll find at 4160 Boulevard Center Drive, three miles from downtown Jacksonville and half a mile from the #BH 2 bus stop (from the downtown area, use the weekdays-only "Riverside Shuttle" bus). However, the sizeable stock of ancient Chinese and Korean porcelain turns many knowledgeable heads, and the smaller selection of pre-Columbian objects shouldn't be missed. The museum's main purpose, though, is to provide support and studios for local artists; the workspaces are often open to the public – details from the reception desk.

There's more art across the city, just south of the Fuller Warren river bridge (I-95), in the **Cummer Museum of Art and Gardens**, 829 Riverside Drive (Tues–Fri 10am–4pm, Sat noon–5pm, Sun 2–5pm; free), on the former estate of the wealthy Cummer family. The spacious rooms and sculpture-lined corridors contain works by prominent European masters from the thirteenth to nineteenth centuries, but American art is the strongest feature: Edmund Greacen's smokey cityscape *Brooklyn Bridge East River* and Martin Heade's *St John's River* are particularly evocative. Afterwards, take a stroll through the flower-packed formal English and Italianate **gardens**, which reach down to the river.

Jacksonville Jaguar Stadium and Metropolitan Park

In 1994 Jacksonville was awarded one of the new National Football League franchises, much to the delight of the town, and what was once the Gator Bowl (home of college football) is now the stamping ground of the Jaguars. From all over Jacksonville you can see the floodlights of the 73,000-seat **Jacksonville Jaguar Stadium**, still the scene of the Florida–Georgia college football clash each November (an excuse for 48 hours of city-wide drinking and partying; tickets for the actual match are notoriously hard to get) in addition to the equally exciting Jaguars' home games. Outside of match days, the main reason to visit is the neighbouring **Metropolitan Park**, a plot of riverside greenery that provides a venue for enjoyable free events most weekends plus some big free rock concerts during spring and autumn. In midweek it's often deserted and makes a fine spot for a quiet riverside picnic. The "Northside Connector" **bus** stops close by.

Jacksonville Zoo

Previously a depressing place with restrictive cages and poorly utilized space, **Jacksonville Zoo**, on Hecksher Drive, just off I-95 north of downtown Jacksonville (daily 9am–5pm; $4), is fast developing into one of the best around, giving its inmates plenty of space to prowl, pose and strut. A justifiable source of pride are the white rhinos, seldom bred in captivity, who live in the eleven-acre "African veldt". Bus #NS 10 stops outside – but only on weekends.

Practicalities

In downtown Jacksonville, the **Convention and Visitors Bureau**, 3 Independent Drive (Mon–Fri 8am–5pm; ☎798-9148), has plenty of tourist leaflets and discount vouchers, and is an easy walk from the *Greyhound* **bus** station at 10

OUTDOOR ADVENTURES

If you're interested in exploring out-of-the-way areas in this region, **Outdoor Adventures**, 6110–7 Powers Avenue, Jacksonville (☎739-1960), run a series of reasonably priced canoeing, kayaking, cycling and walking trips throughout an extensive area, ranging from as far afield as the Okefenokee Swamp and Suwanee River down to the Talbot Islands and the rivers and parks around Jacksonville

Pearl Street (☎356-5521). Some *Greyhound* services also stop in the grey surbur-bia of South and West Jacksonville – don't get off at either. The **train** station is an awkward six miles northwest of downtown at 3570 Clifford Lane (☎1-800/872-7245), from which a **taxi** (☎345-5511) downtown will cost around $8. The **local bus** service (☎630-3100) is geared to ferrying locals to and from work, bypassing many useful places and closing down early.

By **bus**, the journey between the **beaches** and downtown Jacksonville takes around fifty minutes with bus #BS 1 (along Atlantic Boulevard), #BS 2 (along Beach Boulevard) or #BS 3 (from Mayport). There's also the "Beaches Flyer", a quicker rush-hour service along Beach Boulevard.

Accommodation

The city's far-flung layout means that the cheapest **accommodation** is repre-sented by the motels around the perimeter, bothersome to get to without a car. The best prices are at the **chain hotels** near the airport, nine miles north of downtown Jacksonville: *Days Inn*, 1181 Airport Road (☎741-4000; ②), *Holiday Inn*, I-95 at Airport Road (☎741-4404); ③), *Red Roof Inn*, 14701 Airport Entrance Road (☎741-4488; ②–③), *Super 8 Motel*, 10901 Hart Road (☎751-3888; ②), and *Scottish Inn*, 1351 Airport Road (☎741-0094; ①). Downtown, beds are suitable primarily for expense-account holders: the *Hospitality Inn*, 901 N Main Street (☎355-3744; ③), is the cheapest. Scenically sited on the south bank of the river, the *Marina*, 1515 Prudential Drive (☎396-5100; ⑤), might be worth a flutter. Another cosy option is **bed and breakfast** at *The House on Cherry Street*, 1844 Cherry Street (☎384-1999; ④), about three miles south of downtown.

Eating

On downtown Jacksonville's north bank, *Chow Down II*, 4 E Bay Street (☎353-2469), and *Akel's Deli*, 130 N Hogan Street (☎356-5628), offer **snacks** and quick **lunches**. Eating in the Jacksonville Landing mall is slightly pricier, though tempt-ing: *The Mill Bakery* is a health-conscious Brew pub, with huge muffins; *Fat Tuesday* offers spicy Cajun lunches (☎353-1229); and *Harry's Oyster Bar* (☎353-4927) has a generous seafood menu. On the south bank, *Worman's Deli*, 1712 San Marco Boulevard (☎396-6592), and *The Loop*, 2014 San Marco Boulevard (☎384-7301), have good-priced general menus, though the healthy lunches concocted by the *Filling Station*, 1004 Hendricks Avenue (☎398-3663), are more adventur-ous. For high-quality liquid refreshment, plus seafood and steaks, call at the *River City Brewing Co.*, 835 Museum Circle (☎398-2299), where you can sample home-brewed beer while listening to **live music**; phone for information on the **free brewery tour**.

The pick of the city's many stylish **dinner** restaurants is the *Wine Cellar*, 1314 Prudential Drive (☎398-8989), where a well-prepared fish or meat meal costs upwards of $15.

Nightlife

Nightlife in Jacksonville is a pale shadow of the rave-ups at the beach (see "The Jacksonville beaches" p.209), but check out the *Milk Bar*, 128 W Adams Street (☎356-MILK), likely to have anything from house and reggae sounds to live bands and 25¢-beer nights; and *Carib*, 43 W Monroe Street (☎359-0134), which has reggae and calypso sounds at weekends.

Towards Amelia Island

Around thirty miles from Jacksonville are the barrier islands that mark Florida's northeast corner, of which **Amelia Island** is particularly appealing. To reach the islands, Hwy-105 will take you from Jacksonville along the north side of the St John's River, but a better route is Hwy-A1A from the Jacksonville beaches, which crosses the river with the tiny **Mayport ferry** (roughly every 30min 6.20am–10pm; cars $2.50, cyclists and pedestrians 50¢). During this short voyage, pelicans swoop overhead to feed off the nearby shrimping boats.

The Kingsley Plantation

Near the ferry's landing point, Hwy-A1A combines with Hwy-105. Continuing north on Hwy-A1A, you'll soon cross onto Fort George Island and, before long, encounter the entrance to the **Huguenot Memorial Park** (daily 6am–sunset; 50¢ per person) on the east side of the road. Here there's a **campground** (☎251-3335), where you can pitch a tent for $5, and the **Natural State Bird Sanctuary**. Hwy-A1A continues past the tree-lined driveway of the **Kingsley Plantation** (daily 9am–5pm; free; ranger talks Mon–Fri 1pm, Sat & Sun 1pm & 3pm), centrepiece of which is the elegant riverside house bought in 1817 by a Scotsman called Zephaniah Kingsley. The house and its 3000 acres were acquired with the proceeds of slavery, of which Kingsley was an advocate and dealer, amassing a fortune through the import and export of Africans. A pragmatic man, he was interested in the rights of freed slaves and wrote a treatise on the virtues of a patriarchal slave system more in keeping with the Spanish approach than the extremely brutal methods of the United States; he simply believed that well-fed, happier and freer (though not free) slaves made better workers. Nonetheless, the restored plantation reveals much about the plight of the forced arrivals and about Kingsley's remarkable wife: a Senegalese woman who ran the plantation and lived in extravagant style – perhaps compensating for her years as Kingsley's servant.

The Talbot Islands

One mile further on from the Kingsley Plantation, Hwy-A1A runs through **Little Talbot Island State Park** (daily 8am–sunset; cars $3.25, cyclists and pedestrians $1), which consumes almost the whole of a thickly forested 3000-acre barrier island inhabited by 194 species of birdlife. The park has two tree-shaded, ocean-facing picnic areas and a superb four-mile **hiking trail**, which winds through a pristine landscape of oak and magnolia trees, wind-beaten sand dunes and a chunk of the park's five-mile-long beach. **Canoes** can be hired for $3 an hour ($12 a day) and **bikes** for $2 an hour ($10 a day). If you're smitten by the natural charms and want to save the bother of finding accommodation on Amelia Island (see below), use the **campground** (☎251-3231) on the western side of the park beside Myrtle Creek.

Alternatively carry on across the creek, onto tiny Long Island and over onto **Big Talbot Island**, which has two points of interest. Firstly, **Bluffs Scenic Shoreline** (signposted off the road), where the bluffs have eroded, depositing entire trees on the beach, some of them still standing upright with all their roots intact. Secondly, the **Black Rock Trail**, a one-and-a-half-mile hike through woods onto the Atlantic coast, to rocks once made from peat. Back on Hwy-A1A, the road continues to Amelia Island.

AMELIA ISLAND HISTORY: THE EIGHT FLAGS

Amelia Island is the only place in the US to have been under the rule of **eight flags**. Following settlement by Huguenots in 1562, the Spanish arrived and founded a mission here. This was destroyed in 1702 by the British, who returned forty years later to govern the island (naming it in honour of King George II's daughter). The ensuing Spanish administration was interrupted by the US-backed "Patriots of Amelia Island", who ruled for a day during 1812; the Green Cross of the Florida Republic flew briefly in 1817; and, oddest of all, the Mexican rebel flag appeared over Amelia Island the same year. US rule has been disturbed only by Confederate occupancy during 1861.

These shifts reflect the ebb and flow of allegiances between the great sea-trading powers, as well as the island's geographically desirable location: for many years offering harbourage for ocean-going vessels outside US control but within spitting distance of the American border.

Amelia Island

Most first-time visitors to Florida would be hard pushed to locate **Amelia Island**, at the state's northeastern extremity, which perhaps explains why this finger of land, thirteen miles long and never more than two across, is so peaceful and only modestly commercialized despite the unbroken silver swathe of Atlantic beach gracing its eastern edge. Matching the sands for appeal, Fernandina Beach, the island's sole town, was a haunt of pirates before transforming itself into an outpost of Victorian high society – a fact proven by its immaculately restored old centre.

Some parts of the island are being swallowed by upmarket resorts (much of the southern half is taken up by the Amelia Island Plantation, a golf and tennis resort with private walking and biking trails, expensive restaurants and $200-a-night rooms), but it's still worth coming here – provided you have a car. In Fernandina, at least, they still concern themselves more with the size of the shrimp catch than with pandering to tourists.

Fernandina Beach

Hwy-A1A runs right into the effortlessly walkable town of **FERNANDINA BEACH**, whose Victorian heyday is apparent in the restored buildings lining the short main drag, Centre Street. The English spelling reflects bygone political to-ing and fro-ing: the Spanish named the town but the British named the streets. Beside the marina, at the western end of Centre Street and adjacent to a vintage train carriage, you'll spot the useful **visitor center** (Mon–Fri 9am–5pm; ☎261-3248), where you can pick up a booklet produced by the Museum of History, highlighting driving and walking tours, as well as points of historical interest.

Remarkably, given the present-day calm, President James Monroe described Fernandina as a "festering fleshpot" after the 1807 US embargo on foreign shipping caused the Spanish-owned town to become a hotbed of smuggling and other illicit activities as ways were sought to circumvent the ban. The acquisition of Florida by the US in 1821 did not diminish Fernandina's importance – this time as a key rail terminal for freight moving between the Atlantic and the Gulf of Mexico.

The Museum of History – and walking around Centre Street

The obvious place to gain insights into the town is the **Museum of History**, 233 S Third Street (Mon–Fri 11am–3pm; donation) – once the county jail – whose scattering of memorabilia is backed up by photographs and maps. The 45-minute **guided tour** of the museum is excellent (Mon–Sat at 11am & 2pm; recommended donation of $2.50), as are the longer **historical walks** (Thurs & Fri at 3pm from the visitor center; suspended June–Aug, except by appointment; $5) which feature many of the old buildings on and around Centre Street.

Even if you miss the tours, **walking around** on your own is far from dull. Centre Street and the immediate area are alive with Victorian-era turrets, twirls and towers, plus many notable later buildings. Among them, the **St Peter's Episcopal Church**, on the corner with Eighth Street, was completed in 1884 by New York architect Robert S Schuyer, whose name is linked to many local structures and who never used the same style twice. The Gothic used for the church is a long way from the heavy-handed Italianate of the **Fairbanks House** (closed to the public), also by Shuyer, situated at the corner of Seventh and Cedar streets. This was commissioned by a newspaper editor as a surprise for his wife, who hated it and refused to step over the threshold.

The beach

Well suited to swimming and busy with beach sports, the most active of the island's **beaches** is at the eastern end of Fernandina's Atlantic Avenue, a mile from the town centre. If you don't mind a long hike with sand between your toes, you can walk along the beach to Fort Clinch State Park, three miles north (see below). In the autumn, you might be lucky enough to spot **whales** in the waters off Amelia Island. The right whale, an endangered species, moves into inland waterways to calve.

North to Fort Clinch State Park

After Florida came under US control, a fort was built on Amelia's northern tip, three miles from Fernandina, to protect seaborne access to Georgia. The fort now forms part of **Fort Clinch State Park** (daily 8am–sunset; cars $3.25, pedestrians and cyclists $1), and provides a home for a gang of Civil War enthusiasts pretending that they're Union soldiers of 1864, the only time the fort saw action. Entrance to the fort itself costs $1, and the most atmospheric way to see it is with the soldier-guided **candle-lit tour** (most Fridays and Saturdays during summer; $2; reservations essential: ☎277-7274). With the pseudo Civil War garrison moaning about their work and meager rations, the tour may sound like a ham job, but in fact it is a convincing, informative – and quite spooky – hour's worth.

The rest of the park can hardly be overlooked: by road, you have to go through three miles of it before reaching the fort, passing an animal reserve (from which overgrown alligators often emerge, so if you do fancy a spot of hiking, stick to the marked 30- and 45-minute **nature trails**) and a turning for the **beach**, where legions of crab-catchers cast their baskets off a long fishing jetty. From both jetty and fort there's an immaculate view of Cumberland Island (only accessible by ferry from St Mary's, on the Georgia mainland, or by canoe or kayak on organized trips run by *Outdoor Adventures* ☎739-1960, see p.213), a Georgian nature reserve famed for its wild horses – if you're lucky, a few will be galloping over the island's sands. You might also catch a glimpse of a nuclear-powered submarine gliding towards Cumberland Sound and the massive Kings Bay naval base.

Accommodation

Cheapest for **accommodation** are the four motels along Fletcher Avenue, a few miles south of Fernandina: *D. J.'s* , no. 3199 (☎261-5711; ④), the *Seaside Inn*, no. 1998 (☎261-0954; ④), *Ocean View*, no. 2801 (☎261-0193; ④), and *Beachside*, no. 3172 (☎261-4236; ④). Should these be full, the next-best budget bet is *Shoney's Inn*, 2707 Sadler Road (☎277-2300; ④).

With a bit more cash, savour Fernandina's historic atmosphere by staying in one of the town's antique-filled **bed and breakfast inns**: the *Bailey House*, 28 S Seventh Street (☎261-5390; ④), *1735 House*, 584 S Fletcher Avenue (☎261-5878; ④), and the *Florida House Inn*, 22 S Third Street (☎261-3300; ④). Booking far in advance might secure you a room in the $175-a-night *Lighthouse*, 748 Fletcher Avenue (☎261-5878), which really *is* a small lighthouse, with space for four people.

Eating and nightlife

For its size, the island has an exceptionally good number of places to **eat**, the bulk of them on and around Fernandina's Centre Street. *Marina*, 101 Centre Street (☎261-5310), is one of the island's oldest restaurants, with a seafood-based menu and a convivial atmosphere. It's renowned for "Fernandina Fantail Fried Shrimp" and as a **breakfast** hot spot, serving fried fish, eggs and cheese grits. Chinese food can be inexpensively sampled from the **lunchtime** buffet at the *Bamboo House*, 614 Centre Street (☎261-0508); and an all-you-can eat lunch is also offered at *Cousin's Pizza & Pasta*, 927 S 14th Street (☎277-4611). An atmospheric, traditional 1950s-style diner, *Maggie's*, 18 N Second Street, (☎261-9976), dishes up lunch buffets on weekdays and Sundays.

A touch more expensive, *Brett's Waterway Café*, at the Fernandina Harbor Marina at the end of Centre Street (☎261-2660), has generous American meals and great views; and *D.J.'s*, 3199 S Fletcher Avenue (☎261-5711), delivers tasty seafood beside the ocean. For a slap-up gourmet **dinner**, try the classy *Beech Street Grill*, corner of Eighth and Beech streets (☎277-3662).

You'll also find a limited menu of plain and simple dishes at the *Palace Saloon*, 117 Centre Street (☎261-6230), though you might prefer to save your visit to what's claimed to be the oldest **bar** in Florida – built in 1878, with a forty-foot hand-carved mahogany bar – for a night-time drink, not least because few other places warrant an after-dark investigation. This was the last tavern in the country to close after Prohibition began, taking two years to deplete its supply of spirits. If you're feeling brave, try a "Pirate's Punch": lemon, lime, orange and pineapple with a gin-and-rum kick.

travel details

Trains

From Jacksonville to Miami (2 daily; 8hr 45min); Orlando (2 daily; 3hr 5min); Pensacola (1 daily; 8hr 50min); Tallahassee (1 daily; 4hr 15min); Tampa (2 daily; 4hr 49min).

Buses

From Cocoa to Daytona Beach (6 daily; 3hr 40min); Jacksonville (6 daily; 5hr 35min); Melbourne (5 daily; 30min); New Smyrna Beach (4 daily; 1hr 45min); Titusville (5 daily; 30min).

From Daytona Beach to Jacksonville (9 daily; 1hr 45min); Orlando (11 daily; 1hr 5min); St Augustine (3 daily; 1hr 5min).

From Jacksonville to Miami (11 daily; 9hr 15min); Orlando (5 daily; 3hr 15min); St Petersburg (8 daily; 8hr 45min); Tallahassee (5 daily; 2hr 54min); Tampa (8 daily; 6hr 35min).

From St Augustine to Jacksonville (3 daily; 45min).

CHAPTER FIVE

CENTRAL FLORIDA

Most of the broad and fertile expanse of **Central Florida**, stretching between the east and west coasts, was self-absorbed farming country when vacation-mania first struck the beachside strips; only as an after-thought to growing citrus and raising cattle were adventurous visitors ferried by steamboat along the region's rivers and across its gushing springs. Over the last two decades, this picture of tranquillity has been shattered: no section of the state has been affected by modern tourism more dramatically.

In the middle of the region, as contradictory as it may seem, the most visited part of Florida is also one of the ugliest: an ungodly clutter of freeway inter-changes, motels, billboards and jumped-up tourist sights arching around the otherwise affable small city of **Orlando**. The blame for the vulgarity lies with Orlando's near-neighbour, **Walt Disney World**, which since the Seventies has sucked millions of people into the biggest and cleverest theme park complex ever created – sparking off a tourist-dollar chase of Gold Rush magnitude on its outskirts. The Disney parks are every bit as polished as their reputation suggests, but their surrounds are no advertisement for Florida, and it's a tragedy that many visitors see no more of the state than this aggressive commercialism.

The rest of Central Florida is markedly less brash. The slow-paced towns of **South Central Florida** make excellent low-cost bases for cruising the Orlando circuit – provided you're driving – and offer plenty of relaxed diversions in their lake-filled vicinity. Much the same can be said of **North Central Florida**, where tiny villages, far more prevalent than towns, hold the century-old homes of Florida's pioneer settlers. The biggest surprise here, however, is **Gainesville**, an outpost of learning and liberalism containing one of the state's two major universi-ties – a welcome sight so deep in rural surrounds.

Since Walt Disney World redefined the geography of the region, **getting around** Central Florida by **car** has become generally easy and quick – but take time to leave the charmless freeways and journey down some of the multitude of minor routes linking the lesser towns and villages. Non-drivers will find that many of the smaller centres have good *Greyhound* **bus** connections, and some even see twice-daily **trains**. Car-less visitors wanting to get to the Disney parks are dependent on the local **shuttle buses** (see "Getting Around", p.223).

ACCOMMODATION PRICE CODES

All **accommodation prices** in this book have been coded using the symbols below. Note that prices are for the least expensive double rooms in each establish-ment. For a full explanation see p.27 in *Basics*.

| ① up to $30 | ③ $45–60 | ⑤ $80–100 | ⑦ $130–180 |
| ② $30–45 | ④ $60–80 | ⑥ $100–130 | ⑧ $180+ |

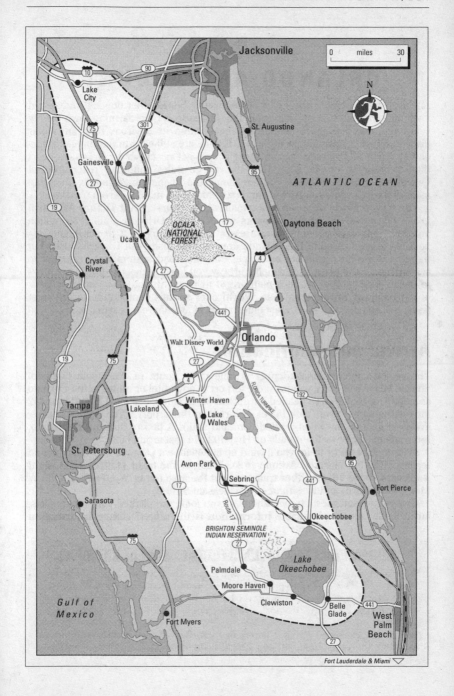

The area code for the Orlando area is ☎407.

ORLANDO AND AROUND

An insubstantial city in the heart of peninsular Florida that doesn't unduly put itself out to attract tourists, it's ironic that **Orlando**, a quiet farming town twenty years ago, now has more people passing through its environs than any other place in the state. Reminders of the old Florida are still easy to find in and immediately north of Orlando, though most people get no closer to Orlando's heart than a string of motels along Hwy-192, fifteen miles south, or **International Drive**, five miles southwest – a long boulevard of mid-range hotels, shopping malls and restaurants so short of character it could be moulded from plastic.

The reason for these apparent anomalies is, of course, **Walt Disney World**, a group of state-of-the-art theme parks southwest of Orlando pulling 35 million people a year to a previously featureless 43-square-mile plot of scrubland. It's possible to pass through the Orlando area and not visit Walt Disney World, but there's no way to escape its influence: even the road system was reshaped to accommodate the place and, whichever way you look, billboards tout more ways to spend your money. Amid a plethora of fly-by-night would-be tourist targets, only **Universal Studios** and **Sea World** offer serious competition to the most finely realized concept in escapist entertainment anywhere on earth.

Arrival and information

The region's international **airport** is nine miles south of downtown Orlando. Shuttle buses will carry you from the airport to any hotel or motel in the Orlando area for $10–15. If you're headed for downtown Orlando, use local bus #11, or #42 for International Drive (both buses depart from the airport's "A Side" concourse, every 60 minutes between around 6am and 9pm). A taxi to downtown Orlando, International Drive or the motels on Hwy-192 will cost around $25.

Arriving by **bus** or train, you'll wind up in downtown Orlando at the *Greyhound* terminal, 555 N Magruder Avenue (☎843-7720), or the **train station**, 1400 Slight Boulevard (☎843-7611). Other train stops in the area are in Winter Park (150 W Morse Boulevard) and Kissimmee (416 Pleasant Street).

Giveaway magazines, strewn wherever you look, are packed with handy facts, but a better source of reliable **information** is the official **visitor information**

ORLANDO AREA ORIENTATION: THE MAJOR ROADS

The major cross-Florida **roads** form a web-like mass of intersections in or around Orlando and Walt Disney World: **I-4** passes southeast–northwest through Walt Disney World and continues in elevated form through downtown Orlando; **Hwy-192** (the **Irlo Bronson Memorial Highway**) crosses I-4 in Walt Disney World and charts an east–west course fifteen miles south of Orlando; **Hwy-528** (the **Beeline Expressway**) stems from I-4, between Walt Disney World and Orlando, bound for the east coast; and the **Florida Turnpike** cuts northwest–southeast between Walt Disney World and Orlando.

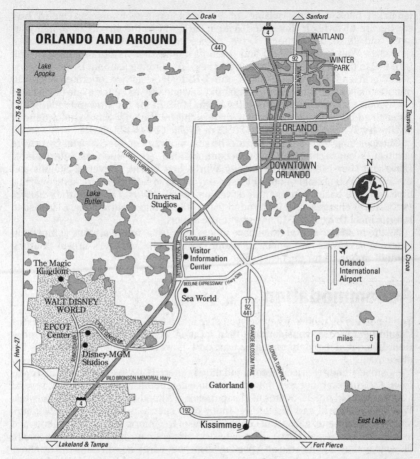

center, 8445 International Drive (daily 8am–8pm; ☎363-5871), where you should pick up the free *Official Visitors Guide to Orlando*, plus any of hundreds of leaflets and discount coupons. Nearer, if you're using the motels along Hwy-192, and equally well stocked, is the **Kissimmee-St Cloud CVB**, no. 1925 (daily 8am–5pm; ☎1-800/327-9159). The best entertainment guide to the area is the Friday "Calendar" section of the *Orlando Sentinel* newspaper.

Getting around

With most routes operating from 6.30am to 6.30pm on weekdays, 7.30am–6pm on Saturdays, and 8am–4pm on Sundays, **local buses** (☎841-8240) converge on the downtown Orlando terminal between Central and Pine streets. You'll need **exact change** (75¢ and 10¢ for a transfer from one route to another) for the buses if you pay on board, or you can buy a ticket from the terminal's information booth. A ten-ticket book is also available for $7, including free transfers. **Useful bus routes** are #1 to Loch Haven and Winter Park; #11 to the airport (a 45-min journey); and #8 to International Drive, where you can catch a shuttle bus (see below) to Walt Disney World and the area's other major tourist parks, or link with #42 to the airport (an hour-long journey). Along International Drive, between Sea World and Universal Studios, the **I-Ride** bus service operates every 10 minutes daily from 7am–midnight, costing 75¢ one way or $2 for a one-day pass.

Orlando **taxis** are expensive: rates begin at $2.75 for the first mile plus $1.50 for each additional mile, but for non-drivers they're the only way to get around at night – try *Town & Country* (☎828-3035) or *Yellow Cab* (☎422-4561).

Cheaper than taxis are the **shuttle buses**, minivans or coaches run by private companies connecting the main accommodation areas such as International Drive and Hwy-192 with Walt Disney World, Sea World, Universal Studios and the airport. You should phone at least a day ahead to be picked up, and confirm a time to come back. You pay the driver on board. *Mears Transportation Service* (☎839-1570) charges $7–9 for a round trip to all the major attractions, $11 or so to International Drive, and $13 one way to the airport.

All the main **car rental** firms have offices at or close to the airport; competition is strong and rates are good, so phone around (the numbers are in "Getting around" in *Basics*) for the best deals.

Accommodation

You'll need to be mobile wherever you stay in the far-flung Orlando area, so price should be a greater consideration than location when looking for **accommodation**. If you're dependent on public transport, however, downtown Orlando is the place to be.

Genuinely budget-priced accommodation is offered only by one hostel in **downtown Orlando**: a quiet area that also has, like neighbouring **Winter Park**, several atmospheric old hotels. Scores of cheap motels are lined **along Hwy-192** between Walt Disney World and Kissimmee; many offer special rates which can be yours simply by picking up a discount coupon at one of the information offices mentioned above. **International Drive**, dominated by pricey chain hotels, is where you're likely to end up if you come on a package trip – but bargains can be found by showing up on spec during the slow winter periods. Campgrounds are plentiful on and around Hwy-192 close to **Kissimmee**. More expensive accommodation is available in **Walt Disney World**; see p.243, for details.

If you *do* have a car, an excellent option is to **rent a villa** from *Sunsplash Rentals Inc.*, 125 Hilltop Street, Davenport, Florida 33837 (☎424-3591 or 6193; from £300 a week if booked from Europe and paid for in sterling). The three- to four-bedroom houses come with their own pools, garages, kitchens, washing machines and so on, and are located in an upmarket residential area 40 minutes from Orlando airport, 15 minutes from Walt Disney World and 15 minutes from the nearest town, Haines City. Staff can provide discount tickets to Disney World and other attractions in the Orlando area, and will even supply a prospective itinerary for your stay. Book as far ahead as possible.

Downtown Orlando

Harley Hotel, 151 E Washington St (☎841-3220). An historic, now completely modernized hotel overlooking Lake Eola. ④.

Orlando International Youth Hostel, 227 N Eola Drive (☎843-8888). In an atmospheric residential area, with beds in small dorms for $12, or single and double private rooms $26. ①.

Winter Park

The Fortnightly Inn, 377 E Fairbanks Ave (☎645-4440). A night or two at this personable 5-room bed and breakfast inn makes a relaxing break from the rampant commercialism of the Orlando area. ⑤.

Langford Resort, 300 E New England Ave (☎644-3400). For this hotel's facilities and service, the price is reasonable, and the location – a leafy Winter Park side street – is great. ②.

Park Plaza, 307 Park Ave (☎647-1072). A Twenties hotel stuffed with wonderful wicker furniture and brass fittings; be sure to book early. Continental breakfast is included. ⑤.

International Drive and around

Days Inn Lakeside, 7335 Sand Lake Rd (☎351-1900). An enormous branch of the nation-wide chain in a winning lakeside location, with a small beach and three pools. ①.

The Floridian, 7299 Republic Drive (☎1-800/445-7299). A mid-sized hotel with an easy-going mood and nicely furnished rooms. ④.

Gateway Inn, 7050 Kirkman Rd (☎351-2000). Good-sized rooms, two pools and free shuttle buses to the major theme parks make this a good base for non-drivers concentrating on the big attractions. ③.

Heritage Inn, 9861 International Drive (☎1-800/447-1890). Plain rooms at modest rates, a pool and a breakfast buffet are reasons for staying in this somewhat kitsch shrine to Southern Victoriana; also has live jazz some evenings. ④.

The Peabody Orlando, 9801 International Drive (☎1-800/PEABODY). Twenty-seven storeys of luxury rooms primarily aimed at delegates using the massive Orange County Convention Center, across the street. If money's no object and you like your in-room luxuries, and access to a fitness centre and floodlit tennis courts, this one's for you. ⑦.

Radisson Barcelo Hotel, 8444 International Drive (☎345-0505). Speed-swimming records have been set at the Olympic-sized pool here, though with relaxation more in mind you'll find the spacious rooms and the location, directly opposite the restaurants of the Mercado Mediterranean Shopping Village (see "Eating", p.230), to be a winning combination. ⑤.

Red Roof Inn, 9922 Hawaiian Court (☎352-1507). Unelaborate but perfectly serviceable budget-range base, with a pool and a coin-op launderette. ③.

Sonesta Villa Resort Orlando, 10000 Turkey Lake Rd (☎352-8051). All rooms are suites with full cooking facilities, and are spread across a ninety-acre lakeside site. ⑥.

Along Hwy-192

A1 Motel, 4030 W Hwy-192/W Vine St (☎662-1920). A medium-sized motel which, being closer to downtown Kissimmee than Walt Disney World, is able to shave a few dollars off the rates of its counterparts a few miles west. ②.

Best Western Kissimmee, 2261 E Hwy-192/E Irlo Bronson Memorial Hwy (☎1-800/944-0062). A good place to be with kids; there's a games room and play area, plus two pools. ④.

Casa Rosa, 4600 W Hwy-192, Kissimmee (☎1-800/432-0665). A generally quiet and relaxing motel with mood-enhancing Mediterranean-style architecture. ②.

Flamingo Inn, 801 E Hwy-192/E Vine St (☎1-800/780-7617). You can rely on this reasonably priced place being clean, tidy and well run; for in-room feasts, microwave ovens are available for $2 a day. ②.

Gemini, 4624 W Hwy-192 (☎1-800/648-4148). Offers free coffee and a free shuttle bus to the main theme parks, also has kitchenettes and microwave ovens. ②.

Golden Link, 4914 W Hwy-192 (☎1-800/654-3957). A comparatively large motel, with heated pool, a self-service launderette and rentable refrigerators. ③.

Holiday Inn Kissimmee, Main Gate East, 5678 Hwy-192 (☎1-800/FON-KIDS). The best hotel for kids, with a full childcare service. Drop them off at "Camp Holiday" and they'll never want to come back. ⑥.

Larson's Lodge Kissimmee, 6075 W Hwy-192 (☎1-800/327-9074). Another good place for kids; the rates might be a touch higher than others in the vicinity but under-18s stay for free in their parents' room and facilities include a games room, tennis court and jacuzzi. ⑤.

Maple Leaf Motel, 4647 W Hwy-192 (☎396-0300). Several people sharing a room will find the special offers here very attractive; cable TV, a pool and coin-op launderette are among the features. ②.

Olympia Inn, 4669 W Hwy-192 (☎396-1890). One of the bigger motels in the area, offering a pool, a coin-op launderette and cable TV, as well as great-value special rates even in high season. ①.

Camping: Kissimmee

Numerous serviceable **campgrounds** stand beside Hwy-192, close to **Kissimmee**. Suited to tents ($15) is the *KOA*, 4771 Hwy-192 (☎1-800/331-1453), which also has **cabins** for $25 and free shuttle buses to Walt Disney World. For a more peaceful setting, choose a site beside Lake Tohopekaliga, where the pace is leisurely and more fuss is made about fishing than visiting Mickey Mouse: try *Merry "D" RV Sanctuary*, 4261 Pleasant Hill Road (☎933-5837), or Richardson's Fish Camp, 1550 Scotty's Road (☎846-6540), where pitching a tent costs $12 for two or $15 respectively.

Orlando

Despite enormous expansion over the last decade, **ORLANDO** remains impressively free of the gross commercialism that surrounds it. Away from the small group of high-rise banks and offices in the downtown area, the bulk of the city comprises smart residential areas enhanced by parks and lakes. Historical leftovers and art collections spread through several sections will fill a day – and, for anyone whose knowledge of the state begins and ends with theme parks, will give at least a brief taste of genuine Florida living. Usefully for non-drivers, bus #1 from downtown Orlando links the key areas.

Downtown Orlando

Except to sample the artificial charms of Church Street Station (see "Nightlife", p.232) or to stay at the hostel (see "Accommodation", p.224), few visitors come to **Downtown Orlando** at all, which, despite the half-dozen corporate towers in its midst, is still redolent, in size and mood, of the tobacco-chewing cow-town that it used to be. Everything of consequence in the tiny district can be visited on foot within an hour.

Begin with a dawdle along **Orange Avenue**, mostly patrolled by lunch-seeking office workers, which passes beneath the Egyptian touches of the late-Twenties *First National Bank*, on the corner with Church Street, and, a few blocks north, the early Art Deco of *McCrory's Five and Dime* building and the *Kress Building*. Pre-dating the Twenties structure, some of the wooden homes built by Orlando's first white settlers stand around **Lake Eola**, a ten-minute walk east of Orange Avenue. Many are undergoing expensive restoration as their owners strive to become bed-and-breakfast moguls. There's a good view of the houses from the oak-filled park that rings the placid lake, overlooked by elevated freeways. Linger here to contemplate the city's first hundred years – and the fact that Orlando's

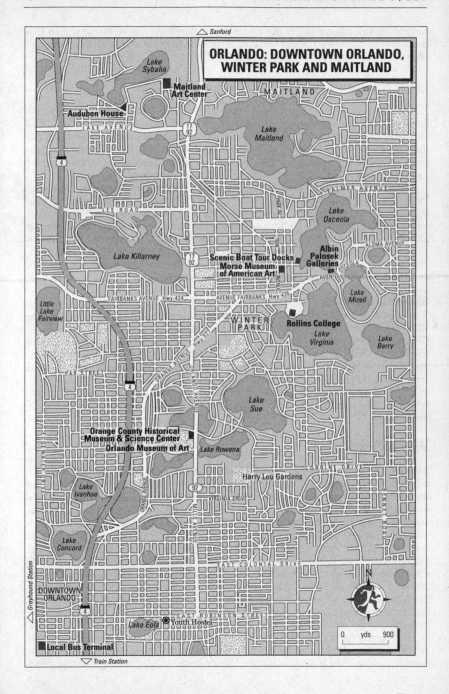

△ *Sanford*

ORLANDO: DOWNTOWN ORLANDO, WINTER PARK AND MAITLAND

Lake Sybalia

■ **Maitland Art Center**

M A I T L A N D

■ **Audubon House**

LAKE AVENUE

Lake Maitland

PALMER AVENUE

LEE ROAD

Lake Osceola

Lake Killarney

ALOMA AVENUE

■ **Albin Palosek Galleries**

Scenic Boat Tour Docks
Morse Museum of American Art ■

Lake Mizell

FAIRBANKS AVENUE Hwy 424

FAIRBANKS Hwy 426

Little Lake Fairview

W I N T E R
P A R K

■ **Rollins College**

Lake Virginia

Lake Berry

PAR STREET

Lake Sue

■ **Orange County Historical Museum & Science Center**
Orlando Museum of Art

Lake Rowena

CORRINE DRIVE

Harry Leu Gardens

Lake Ivanhoe

VIRGINIA DRIVE

Lake Concord

EAST COLONIAL DRIVE

△ *Greyhound Station*

DOWNTOWN ORLANDO

EAST ROBINSON STREET

Lake Eola ● Youth Hostel

■ **Local Bus Terminal**

0   yds   900

▽ *Train Station*

early black inhabitants didn't live in these leafy environs but were consigned to a much less picturesque district west of the railway line, parallel to Orange Avenue; still today, very much the wrong side of the tracks.

Loch Haven Park and Harry P Leu Gardens

A large lawn squeezed between two small lakes, **Loch Haven Park**, three miles north of downtown Orlando, contains three buildings of varied content. The **Orlando Museum of Art** (Tues–Sat 9am–5pm, Sun noon–5pm; suggested donation $4) is likely to take up at least an hour: a permanent collection of pre-Columbian pieces backs up the usually excellent temporary exhibitions of modern American paintings culled from the finest collections in the world.

Across the park, the small **Orange County Historical Museum** (Mon–Sat 9am–5pm, Sun noon–5pm; $3) is more liable to jog the memories of elderly locals than excite out-of-towners, though the artefacts, photos and recreated hotel lobbies and grocers' shops form a picture of the time when, far from being a global tourist mecca, Orlando epitomized the American frontier town. Children will enjoy roaming around the adjacent **Science Center** (Mon–Thurs 9am–5pm, Fri 9am–9pm, Sat noon–9pm, Sun noon–5pm; $4), where hands-on exhibits explain the fundamentals of physics to formative minds.

Harry P Leu Gardens

A mile east of Loch Haven Park, **Harry P Leu Gardens**, 1920 N Forest Avenue (daily 9am–5pm; $3, including a tour of Leu House) was purchased by a green-fingered Orlando businessman in 1936 to show off plants collected from around the world. After seeing and sniffing the orchids, roses, azaleas and the largest camellia collection in the eastern US, take a trip around **Leu House** (guided tours only; on the hour Tues–Sat 10am–3pm, Sun & Mpon 1pm–3pm), a nineteenth-century farmhouse bought and lived in by Leu and his wife, now maintained in the simple but elegant style of their time and laced with family mementoes.

Winter Park

A couple of miles northeast of Loch Haven Park, **Winter Park** has been socially a cut above the rest of the city since it was launched in the 1880s as "a beautiful winter retreat for well-to-do people". For all its obvious money – a mix of new yuppie dollars and old wealth – Winter Park is a very likeable place, with a pervasive sense of community and a scent of California-style New Age affluence.

On Fairbanks Avenue, which brings traffic from Loch Haven into Winter Park, stand the hundred-year-old Mediterranean Revival buildings of **Rollins College**, the oldest college in the state and a tiny but highly regarded seat of liberal arts education. Other than neat landscaping, the campus has just one thing in its favour: the **Cornell Fine Arts Center** (Tues–Fri 10am–5pm, Sat & Sun 1–5pm; free), which offers a staid bundle of modest nineteenth-century European and American paintings, rather more interesting temporary shows, and an eccentric collection of old watch keys.

You'll find a more complete art collection a mile east of the college on Osceola Avenue, at the **Albin Palosek Galleries**, no. 633 (Oct–June Wed–Sat 10am–noon & 1–4pm, Sun 1–4pm; free): the former home of Czech-born sculptor Albin

Palosek, who arrived penniless in the US in 1901 and spent most of his time over the next fifty years winning big-money commissions. The profits were eventually channelled into creating this house and studio, which contain more than two hundred of his technically accomplished, realist pieces.

Along Park Avenue: the Morse Museum and boat tours

Winter Park's upmarket status is compounded by its showcase street, **Park Avenue** (which meets Fairbanks Avenue close to Rollins): a row of top-of-the-range outfitters, jewellers and spick-and-span restaurants. Should window-shopping and fine dining lack appeal, drop into the **Morse Museum of American Art**, just off Park Avenue at 133 E Wolborne Avenue (Tues–Sat 9.30am–4pm, Sun 1–4pm; $2.50), which houses the collections of Charles Hosmer Morse, one of Winter Park's founding fathers. The major exhibits are drawn from the output of Louis Comfort Tiffany – a legend for his innovative Art Nouveau lamps and windows that furnished high-society homes around the turn of the century. Great creativity and craftsmanship went into Tiffany's work: he molded glass while still soft, imbuing it with coloured images of water lilies, leaves and even strutting peacocks. After this brilliant, priceless stuff, the Norman Rockwell paintings and the museum's other possessions seem rather pale.

To discover why people who can afford to live anywhere choose Winter Park as a home, take the **scenic boat tour** from the dock at 312 E Morse Boulevard (departures every 30min daily 10am–4pm; $5.50) – an hour-long voyage over wood-shrouded lakes and their moss-draped connecting canals: a picture-postcard view only otherwise available from the rolling back lawns of big-buck waterside homes.

Maitland

Luscious sunsets over another body of water, Lake Sybelia, in **Maitland**, directly north of Winter Park, inspired a young artist called André Smith to buy six acres on its banks during the Thirties. With the financial assistance of Mary Bok (wealthy widow of Edward Bok; see "South Central Florida"), Smith established what is now the **Maitland Art Center**, 231 W Packwood Avenue (Mon–Fri 10am–4.30pm, Sat & Sun noon–4.30pm; free), a collection of stuccoed studios, offices and apartments grouped around garden courtyards, decorated by Aztec-Mayan murals and bas-reliefs. Smith invited other American artists to spend working winters here, but his abrasive personality scared many potential guests away. The colony continued in various forms until Smith's death in 1959, never becoming the aesthetes' commune he hoped for. There are temporary exhibitions and a permanent collection, but it's the unique design of the place that demands a visit. While here, spare a thought for Smith's ghost, which, according to a number of local painters and sculptors who claim to have felt its presence, dispenses artistic guidance.

A few steps from the art centre are the **Maitland Historical Museum and Telephone Museum**, 221 W Packwood Avenue (Thurs–Sun noon–4pm; free). The front rooms of the combined museums house an ordinary collection of ageing photos and household objects, but the back room is filled with wonderful vintage telephones, commemorating the day in 1910 when a Maitland grocer launched the area's first exchange by installing telephones in the homes of his customers, enabling them to place orders from their armchairs.

The only other thing to make you dally in Maitland is **Audubon House**, 1101 Audubon Way (Tues–Sat 10am–4pm; suggested donation $2): headquarters of the Florida Audubon Society, the state's oldest and largest conservation organization. The house is primarily an educational centre and gift shop, but the small adjacent aviary contains injured or orphaned birds of prey that are being nursed back to health – a chance to see vultures, eagles, falcons and more, close up.

Eating

Given the level of competition among restaurants to attract hungry tourists, **eating** in Orlando is never difficult and need not be expensive. In **downtown Orlando**, choices are comparatively limited, though the need to satisfy a regular clientele of lunch-breaking office workers keeps prices low. With a car, you might also investigate the local favourites dotted around downtown. Affluent **Winter Park** promises more variety, generally with higher standards and prices, though it does have a few serviceable low-cost diners.

Tourist-dominated **International Drive** offers a greater range, if much less atmosphere. The culinary hot-spots are the gourmet ethnic restaurants, but strict-budget travellers will relish the opportunity to eat massive amounts at one of several buffet restaurants – all for less than they might spend on a tip elsewhere. Buffet eating reaches its ultimate expression along **Hwy-192**, where virtually every buffet restaurant chain has at least one outlet, leaving the discerning glutton spoilt for choice.

Discount coupons in tourist magazines bring sizeable reductions at many restaurants, including "Show Restaurants", where $30 per head not only buys a multi-course feed and (usually) limitless beer, wine and soft drinks but also entertainment ranging from cavorting Ninja warriors to medieval knights jousting on horseback.

Downtown Orlando

Jungle Jim's, inside Church Street Market, 55 W Church St (☎872-3111). Local branch of a fast-expanding chain where servers emerge from behind pseudo-jungle decor bearing enormous burgers, gigantic salads and Mexican-style dishes.

Numero Uno, 2499 S Orange Ave (☎841-3840). A small, good-value Cuban restaurant open for lunch and dinner.

Petit Four, 702 N Orange Ave (☎647-0897). An emporium of fresh-baked delights: the featherweight pastries and cakes make decadent snacks.

Le Provence, 50 E Pine St (☎843-1320). Well-presented French cuisine, open for dinner only. Try the after-dinner cheese course.

Taiwan, 5424 S Orange Ave (☎856-8177). Open for lunch and dinner. Don't be put off by the fact that many of the dishes look alike because all have quite distinct flavours. Great prices.

Around Downtown

El Bohio Café, 5756 Dahlia Drive (☎282-1723). One of two local outlets (with *Vega's*, see below) for generous portions of well-priced Cuban food.

Lilia's Philipine Delights, 3150 S Orange Avenue Drive (☎851-9087). A fine selection of Filipino dishes, though quality can vary. If you're seriously hungry, go for the whole pig.

Vega's Café, 1835 E Colonial Drive (☎898-5196). Cuban diner with great-value lunches.

Vihn's, 1231 E Colonial Drive (☎894-5007). Hole-in-the-wall Vietnamese restaurant offering good food at giveaway prices for lunch and dinner.

Winter Park

Brazilian Pavilion, 140 W Fairbanks Ave (☎740-7440). Try the *peixe a Brasileria* or the *frango a Francesca* for the hell of it.

The Briar Patch, 252 Park Ave (☎628-8651). Well-prepared lunches – the salads are huge – and dinners. Eat inside or on the terrace.

The Hutch Coffee Shop, 109 Lyman Ave (☎644-5948). A dependable, budget-priced coffee shop just off fashionable Park Ave.

Maison de Crêpe, Hidden Garden Shops, 348 N Park Ave (☎647-4469). Some people come here solely for the feather-light crêpes, but the lunches and dinners are inventive and tasty.

Park Avenue Grill, 358 Park Ave (☎647-4556). A fairly standard American menu but the window seats are excellent vantage points for people-watching.

Power House, 111 Lyman Ave (☎645-3616). Raise your energy levels with a vitamin-packed fruit juice; or sample one of the tasty soups.

Winter Park Diner, 1700 W Fairbanks Ave (☎644-2343). In business longer than most people can remember, and still serving generous portions of classic diner food at prices to please.

International Drive and around

Bergamo's, Mercado Mediterranean Shopping Village, 8445 International Drive (☎302-3805). Good-quality but slightly expensive freshly prepared pasta and seafood dishes; dinner only.

Butcher Shop Steakhouse, Mercado Mediterranean Shopping Village, 8445 International Drive (☎363-9727). Bigger steaks and chops than you've ever seen in your life; heaven for carnivores.

Cricketers Arms, Mercado Mediterranean Shopping Village, 8445 International Drive (☎254-0686). Fish and chips, pies and pasties complement a range of imported ales and lagers at this inexpensive nook.

Florida Bay Grille, 8560 International Drive (☎352-3315). Don't come here for big portions; the focus is on carefully prepared seafood and meat dishes for the discerning diner.

José O'Day's, Mercado Mediterranean Shopping Village, 8445 International Drive (☎363-0613). Not the best Mexican food you'll ever taste, but portions are large and the atmosphere is enjoyable.

Ming Court, 9188 International Drive (☎351-9988). Chinese cuisine of an exceptionally high standard makes this the best dining spot on International Drive; less costly than you might expect.

Morrison's Cafeteria, 7440 International Drive (☎351-0051). Low-cost self-service eating; load your tray from an immense array of hot dishes, desserts and drinks.

Passage to India, 5532 International Drive (☎351-3456) and 845 Sand Lake Rd (☎856-8362). Indian cuisine served in less spicy forms than is the norm in Europe; *thali* is a house speciality but the lunchtime buffet offers best value.

Ponderosa Steakhouse, 6362, 8510 & 14407 International Drive (☎352-9343; ☎354-1477; ☎238-2526). The biggest appetites will be fully satisfied here, where sizeable buffets – with plenty for non-meat eaters to enjoy – are laid out for breakfast, lunch and dinner.

Sizzler, 9142 International Drive (☎351-5369). Substantial breakfast buffet from 7am to 11am; lunch or dinner brings ample steaks or seafood, plus an all-you-can-eat salad bar.

Western Steer, 6315 International Drive (☎363-0677). Breakfast, lunch and dinner buffets; the latter features five hot courses, as well as soups, salads, vegetables, fruit and ice cream, in limitless supply.

Along Hwy-192

Black-eyed Pea, 5305 W Hwy-192 (☎397-1500). Large portions of Southern-style cooking – catfish, fried chicken and much more – served for lunch and dinner.

Kettle, 7777 W Hwy-192 (☎396-4280). Consistently one of the lowest-priced dinner buffets in the area.

Key W Kool's, 7225 W Hwy-192 (☎396-1166). As a break from buffets, sample the seafood or steaks served for lunch or dinner in this tropically themed restaurant; or show up for the two-dollar breakfast.

New Punjab, 3404 W Vine St/Hwy-192 (☎931-2449). The vegetarian dinner is excellent value.

Ponderosa Steakhouse, 5771 & 7598 Hwy-192 (☎397-2477; ☎396-7721). A gigantic buffet offered all day. Three other branches on International Drive, see above.

Sizzler, 7602 W Hwy-192 (☎397-0997). Most substantial breakfast buffet in the vicinity; also on International Drive, see above.

Show restaurants

Asian Adventure, 5225 International Drive (☎351-5655). Acrobats, magicians and Ninja warriors provide the entertainment as you munch a five-course Chinese dinner.

Capone's Dinner & Show, 4740 Hwy-192 (☎397-2378). Give the secret password and enter this Prohibition-era speakeasy for a Twenties-style song-and-dance revue and an Italian-food buffet.

King Henry's Feast, 8984 International Drive (☎351-5151). Knights duel and jesters amuse as a five-course meal is served and drinks are quaffed from tankards.

Medieval Times, 4510 Hwy-192 (☎1-800/229-8300). Knights swordfight and joust on horseback as you tuck into a feast inside a replica eleventh-century castle.

Sleuth's Dinner Show, 7508 Republic Drive (☎363-1985). If you know red herring isn't a seafood dish, you're well on the way to solving the murder mystery played out in this Agatha-Christie-style set as you eat.

Nightlife

Nightlife in Orlando isn't much to write home about. Although there are exceptions, the choice tends to be between big, brassy discos or restaurant-cum-bars with live music.

Downtown Orlando

Bonkers, 120 N Orange Ave (☎629-2665). An improvised comedy showcase open five nights a week.

Church Street Station, 129 W Church St (☎422-2434). Don't let the crowds who flock here nightly fool you into thinking this complex of bars, restaurants and 1890s-style music hall, *Rosie O'Grady's*, merits the $15.95 admission fee. Once inside, you'll also have to pay well over the odds for drinks.

Howl at the Moon Saloon, 55 W Church St (☎841-9118). It's hard to concentrate on your drink as duelling pianists whizz through a singalong selection of rock and roll classics and songs from the shows.

Sapphire Supper Club, 54 N Orange Ave (☎246-1419). High-quality traditional and contemporary jazz. See the "Calendar" pullout from the *Orlando Sentinel* for the line-up.

Zuma Beach, 46 N Orange Ave (☎648-8363). Covering the widest variety of music, from acid jazz to Latin American, you're sure to find something here to your taste.

Winter Park

Comedy Zone, 626 Lee Road (☎645-5233). A varying line-up of comics doing two-hourly shows from 8.30pm and 10.30pm.

Shooters, 4315 N Orange Blossom Trail (☎298-2955). Lively favourite with locals for its food, drinks and live music (four nights a week) in a pleasant waterside setting.

International Drive, Hwy-192 and around

Bennigan's, 6324 International Drive (☎351-4435). Sprawling sports bar with extended happy hours.

Crazy Horse Saloon, 7050 Kirkham Rd (☎363-0071). Rowdy country and bluegrass music; lots of drinking and high spirits.

Cricketers Arms, Mercado Mediterranean Shopping Village, 8445 International Drive (☎254-0686). English ales, European lagers and the latest soccer scores – and sometimes the matches themselves on giant TV screens.

Fat Tuesday, Mercado Mediterranean Shopping Village, 8445 International Drive (☎647-8719). Just the place to initiate yourself into the joys of the frozen daiquiri, available in many different flavours. Most evenings there's also live music.

JJ Whispers, 5100 Adanson St (☎629-4474). High-tech disco complex which also includes a comedy club, *Bonkerz!*.

Sullivan's, 1108 S Orange Blossom Trail (☎843-2934). Live country music and square-dancing; draws a friendly and enthusiastic crowd.

North from Orlando

Back-to-back residential areas dissolve into fields of fruit and vegetables **north of Orlando**'s city limits. Around here, in slow-motion towns harking back to Florida's frontier days, farming still has the upper hand over tourism. Although it's easy to skim through on I-4, the older local roads connecting the major settlements have far more atmosphere.

Sanford and Mount Dora

A position on the south shore of Lake Monroe, fifteen miles north of Maitland on Hwy-92 (also known as Hwy-17), allows **SANFORD** to grab its share of tourist dollars with riverboat cruises (from $12; ☎1-800/423-7401) from the marina on N Palmetto Avenue. For more of an insight into the modestly sized town – and the turn-of-the-century lawyer and diplomat who created it – dip inside the **Shelton Sanford Memorial Museum**, 520 E First Street (Tues–Fri 11am–4pm; free). Once called "Celery City" on account of its major agricultural crop, Sanford hasn't had a lot going for it since the boom years of the early 1900s, a period lovingly chronicled in the museum. For even more relics of the halcyon days, collect a self-guided tour map from the **Chamber of Commerce**, 400 E First Street (Mon–Fri 9am–5pm; ☎322-2212), and venture around 22 buildings of divergent classical architecture in the adjacent old downtown district, most of them now doing business as drugstores and insurance offices.

On the way back to Hwy-92 at Sanford's southwest corner, the **Seminole County Historical Museum**, 300 Bush Boulevard (Mon–Fri 9am–1pm, Sat & Sun 1–4pm; free), carries a multitude of objects from all over the county including an intriguing selection of medicine bottles. Alternatively, rake around **Flea World** (Fri, Sat & Sun 8am–5pm; free), at the end of Bush Boulevard by the Hwy-92 junction – a large-scale attempt to sell items that nobody in their right mind would ever buy.

To see a Victorian-era Florida village at its most self-consciously quaint, take Route 46 west of Sanford for seventeen miles and feast your eyes on the picket fences, wrought-iron balconies and fancy wood-trimmed buildings that make up

MOUNT DORA. The **Chamber of Commerce**, 341 Alexander Street (Mon–Fri 9am–5pm; ☎904/383-2165), has a free guide to the old houses and the inevitable antique shops that now occupy many of them.

Cassadaga

A village populated by spiritualists conjures up images of weirdos in forbidding mansions, but the few hundred residents of **CASSADAGA**, just east of I-4, ten miles north of Sanford, are disappointingly normal citizens in normal homes, offering contact with the spirit world for a very down-to-earth fee (usually $35 for a half-hour session). A group of northern spiritualists bought this 35-acre site in 1875 and quickly caught the imagination of Florida's early settlers for whom contacting the Other Side was a lot easier than communicating with the rest of the US.

Throughout the year, seminars and lectures cover topics ranging from UFO cover-ups to out-of-body travelling: for more details, visit the **Andrew Jackson Davis Building**, on the corner of Route 4139 and Stevens Street (Mon–Fri 9.30am–5.30pm, Sat 9.30am–6pm, Sun noon–6pm; ☎904/228-2880), which doubles as an information centre and psychic bookshop.

DeLand and around

Intended to be the "Athens of Florida" when founded in 1876, **DELAND**, four miles north of Cassadaga, west off I-4, has turned out a commonplace central Florida town. It does, however, boast one of the state's oldest educational centres: the **Stetson University**, on Woodland Boulevard, whose red-brick facades have stood since the 1880s, partly funded by the profits of the cowboy hat of the university's title. Pick up a free tour map from the easily found DeLand Hall for a walk around the vintage buildings. Also on the campus, on the corner of Michigan and Amelia avenues, the **Gillespie Museum of Minerals** (summer Mon–Sat noon–4pm; free) displays Florida quartz, calcite and limestone, plus gemstones gathered from all over the world.

Assuming you're not rushing towards the east coast (Daytona Beach is twenty miles away on Hwy-92 or I-4; see *The Northeast Coast*) or making haste for the Ocala National Forest, less than ten miles east on Route 44 (see "North Central Florida", p.259), **canoeing** provides a reason to hang around the DeLand area. Organized trips (around $15 a day for a nine-mile trip down the Little Wekiva River Run) are arranged at *Katie's Wekiva River Landing* (☎407/628-1482), five miles west of I-4 on Route 46. For general information, use DeLand's **Chamber of Commerce**, 336 N Woodland Boulevard (Mon–Fri 8.30am–5pm; ☎1-800/749-4350).

North from DeLand: DeLeon Springs and Barberville

Ten miles north of DeLand on Hwy-17, watching thousands of gallons of water emerging for the first time into daylight makes **DeLeon Springs State Recreation Area** (daily 8am–sunset; cars $3.25, pedestrians and cyclists $1) an infinitely pleasurable place – much to the amusement of central and northern Florida residents, for whom springs are a common sight. As well as swimming, canoeing and picnicking in and beside the actual spring, you can make your own pancakes in the *Old Spanish Sugar Mill Restaurant* (☎904/985-5644), a timbered diner beside the park, which opens at 9am on weekdays and at 8am at weekends, and stops serving at 4pm.

Seven miles further on Hwy-17, the tiny crossroads community of **BARBERVILLE** celebrates the rural Florida it personifies with the **Pioneer Settlement for the Creative Arts** (Mon–Fri 9am–4pm, Sat 9am–2pm; $2.50), a turn-of-the-century train station and general store. Here, an assembly of pottery wheels, looms, milling equipment and other tools are put to use in demonstrations of traditional handicrafts on a worthy but informative 45-minute guided tour.

South from DeLand: Blue Spring and Hontoon Island

The naturally warm waters at **Blue Spring State Park** (daily 8am–sunset; cars $3.25, pedestrians and cyclists $1), seven miles from DeLand on Hwy-17, in Orange City, attract **manatees** between mid-November and mid-March. These best-loved of Florida's endangered creatures swim here from the cooler waters of the St Johns River – the colder it is there the more manatees you'll see here. Aside from staking out the manatees from several observation platforms (and watching a 20-minute slide show describing their habits), there's also the chance to see **Thursby House**, a large frame dwelling built by pioneer settlers in 1872. **Accommodation** in the park includes a $16-a-night campground and $55-a-night cabins which sleep up to four people (☎904/775-3663).

Not far from Blue Spring is **Hontoon Island**, a striking dollop of wooded land set within very flat and swampy terrain. Without a private boat, Hontoon Island is reachable only with the sporadic **ferry** running daily from 9am to an hour before sunset from a landing stage on Route 44 (the continuation of DeLand's New York Avenue). Unbelievably, the island once held a boatyard and cattle ranch, but today it's inhabited only by the hardy souls who decide to stay over in one of its six rustic **cabins** (reservations ☎904/736-5309; ②), or at one of its very basic **campsites**.

South from Orlando

Not much fills the rough acres directly **south of Orlando**, though one of the area's oldest and, in its way, most amusing destinations sits on what's called the "Orange Blossom Trail" (known variously as Hwy-92, Hwy-17 and Hwy-441), which runs the sixteen miles between Orlando and Kissimmee.

Gatorland

An oversized alligator mouth serves as the entrance for **Gatorland**, 14501 S Orange Blossom Trail (daily 8am–sunset; $10.95), which has been giving visitors since the Fifties a close look at the state's most feared and least understood animal. Surprisingly lazy beasts, the residents of the park (actually a working farm, licensed to breed alligators for their hides and meat) only show signs of life at the organized feeding – the Gator Jumparoo show – when hunks of chicken are suspended from a wire and the largest alligators, using their powerful tail muscles, propel themselves out of the water to grab their dinner: a bizarre spectacle of heaving animal and ferociously snapping jaws. When you arrive, pick up a schedule of the three main shows: Gator Jumparoo, Gator Wrestling and Snakes of Florida. The latter features some of Florida's most deadly reptiles – coral snakes, pygmy rattlesnakes, cottonmouth moccasins and diamond-back rattlesnakes – none of whom you'd enjoy meeting in the wild, but a handy recognition exercise in case you do.

Kissimmee

A country-bumpkin counterpart to the modern vacation developments that ring it, **KISSIMMEE**, at the end of Orange Blossom Trail, has most of its fun during the Wednesday lunchtime cattle auctions at the **Livestock Market**, 805 E Donegan Avenue. The **motels** close to the town on Hwy-192 (see "Accommodation", p.225) make Kissimmee a cheap place to be, however, and even without a car getting about is relatively simple: **trains** stop at 416 Pleasant Street, *Greyhound* **buses** at 16 N Orlando Avenue (☎847-3911), and **shuttle bus** links to the major Orlando area attractions are frequent (see "Getting around", p.223).

To kill time in Kissimmee, take a walk around the fifty-foot obelisk called **Kissimmee Monument of States**, on Monument Avenue. Comprising garishly painted concrete blocks adorned with pieces of stone, rock and fossil from particular American states or one of 21 other countries, this monument was erected in 1943 to honour the former president of the local All-States Tourist Club.

Walt Disney World

As significant as air conditioning in making the state what it is today, **WALT DISNEY WORLD** turned a wedge of Florida grazing land into one of the world's most lucrative vacation venues within ten years. Bringing growth and money to central Florida for the first time since the citrus boom a century ago, the immense and astutely planned empire (and Walt Disney World really *is* an empire) also pushed the state's media profile through the roof: from being a down-at-heel and slightly seedy mixture of cheap motels, retirement homes and clapped-out alligator zoos, Florida suddenly became a showcase of modern international tourism and in doing so, some would claim, sold its soul for a fast buck.

Whatever your attitude to theme parks, there's no denying that Walt Disney World is the pacesetter: it goes way beyond Walt Disney's original "theme park" – Disneyland, which opened in Los Angeles in 1955 – delivering escapism at its most technologically advanced and psychologically brilliant in a multitude of ingenious guises across an area twice the size of Manhattan. In a crime-free environment where wholesome all-American values hold sway and the concept of good clean fun finds its ultimate expression, Walt Disney World often makes the real world – and all its problems – seem like a distant memory.

Here, litter is picked up within seconds of being dropped, subtle mind-games soften the pain of queueing, the special effects are the best money can buy, and employees grin merrily as snotty-nosed kids puke down their legs. It's not cheap, forward planning is essential, and there are times when you'll feel like a cog in a vast machine – but Walt Disney World unfailingly, and with ruthless efficiency, always delivers what it promises.

Costs* may come as a shock, especially to families (children under three are admitted free of charge, but note that little is designed specifically for their entertainment), but the admission fee allows unlimited access to all the shows and rides in a particular park – and you'll need *at least* a day per park to go on everything in each of the three main ones. There's a strict embargo on bringing **food and drink**

---

*Walt Disney World's **ticket prices** are generally raised by between 50¢ and $1 a year: the theory is that regular small increases won't put people off as much as less frequent big rises. Remember to add Florida's 6 percent sales tax to all prices quoted here.

SOME DISNEY HISTORY

When brilliant illustrator and animator Walt Disney devised the world's first theme park, California's **Disneyland** – which brought to life his cartoon characters, Mickey Mouse, Donald Duck, Goofy and the rest – he left himself with no control over the hotels and restaurants that quickly engulfed it, preventing growth and raking off profits Disney felt were rightly his. Determined that this wouldn't happen again, the Disney corporation secretly began to buy up 27,500 acres of central Florida farmland, and by the late Sixties had acquired – for a comparatively paltry $6 million – a site a hundred times bigger than Disneyland. With the promise of a jobs bonanza for Florida, the state legislature gave the corporation – thinly disguised as the Reedy Creek Improvement District – the rights of any major municipality: empowering it to lay roads, enact building codes, and enforce the law with its own security force.

Walt Disney World's first park, the **Magic Kingdom**, opened in 1971; predictably based on Disneyland, it was an equally predictable success. The far more ambitious **EPCOT Center**, unveiled in 1982, represented the first major break from cartoon-based escapism: millions visited, but the rose-tinted look at the future received a mixed response. Partly due to this, and some cockeyed management decisions, the Disney empire (Disney himself died in 1966) faced bankruptcy by the mid-Eighties.

Since then, clever marketing has brought the corporation back from the abyss – though the wisdom of opening EuroDisney in France in 1992 has yet to be determined – and it now steers a tight and competitive business ship, always looking to increase Walt Disney World's 100,000 daily visitors and stay ahead of its rivals. The recently opened Disney-MGM Studios, for example, aims to put a dent in Universal Studios' trade (see p.245), while Pleasure Island's nightclubs and the recently added *Planet Hollywood* are clearly intended to compete with downtown Orlando's Church Street Station (see p.232). It may trade in fantasy, but where money matters, the Disney corporation's nose is firmly in the real world.

into the parks, where restaurants and snack bars – each as clinically themed as the parks – are plentiful but pricey. Only in Pleasure Island is alcohol served.

Walt Disney World: the main parks

Walt Disney World's three main theme parks are quite separate entities. The **Magic Kingdom** is the Disney park everyone imagines, where Mickey Mouse mingles with the crowds and the emphasis is on fantasy and fun – very much the park for kids. Recognizable for its giant, golfball-like geosphere, **EPCOT Center** is Disney's attempted celebration of science and technology, coupled with a very Disneyfied trip around various countries and cultures: dull for young kids, it's a sprawling area that involves a lot of walking. The newest and most easily assimilated of the three, **Disney-MGM Studios**, suits almost everyone; its special effects are enjoyable even if you've never seen the movies they're based on, and the Backstage Tour, despite moments of tedium, at least visits *real* studios – reality being a rare commodity in Walt Disney World.

Doing justice to all three parks will take at least four days – one should be set aside for rest – and you shouldn't tackle more than one on any single day. If you only have a day to spare, pick the park that appeals most and stick to it: day tickets are only valid for one location anyway.

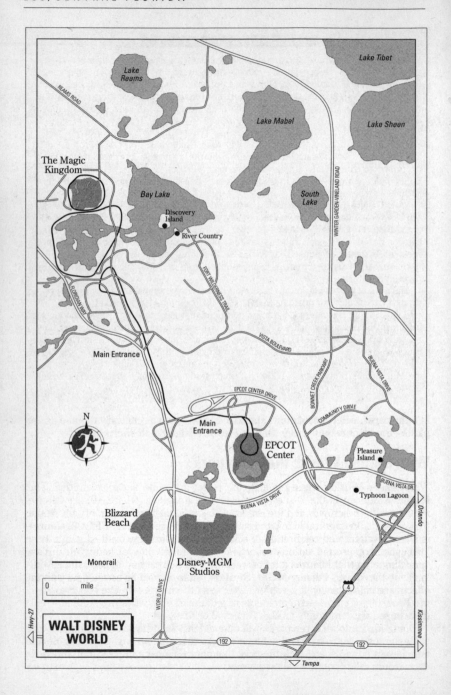

The Magic Kingdom

Lake Reams

Lake Tibet

Lake Mabel

Lake Sheen

REAMS ROAD

Bay Lake

Discovery Island

River Country

South Lake

WINTER GARDEN-VINELAND ROAD

FLORIDIAN WAY

FORT WILDERNESS TRAIL

Main Entrance

VISTA BOULEVARD

BONNET CREEK PARKWAY

BUENA VISTA DRIVE

EPCOT CENTER DRIVE

COMMUNITY DRIVE

N

Main Entrance

EPCOT Center

Pleasure Island

BUENA VISTA DR.

Typhoon Lagoon

Orlando

BUENA VISTA DRIVE

Blizzard Beach

Disney-MGM Studios

4

——— Monorail

WORLD DRIVE

0   mile   1

Hwy-27

WALT DISNEY WORLD

192

192

Kissimmee

▽ Tampa

Disney Information: ☎407/824-4321

When to visit

While EPCOT Center in particular absorbs crowds easily, it's best to avoid the **busiest periods**: during school vacations in the summer, and over Thanksgiving, Christmas and Easter. The busiest days vary from park to park, so plan your itinerary once you've arrived or contact Disney Information for help.

Provided you **arrive early** at the park (just before opening time is best) you'll easily get through the most popular rides before the mid-afternoon crush, when queues can become very long. If you're staying at a Disney World resort, you may be offered early entrance to the parks (before opening time) to help beat the crowds. If you can't arrive early, don't show up until 5 or 6pm, which still leaves time to do plenty before the place shuts up. Each park has regularly updated noticeboards showing the latest **waiting times** for each show and ride – at peak times often about an hour for the most popular rides and up to 15 minutes for others.

Opening times and tickets

The parks are **open** daily from 9am to midnight during the busy periods, and from 9am to 10pm or later for the rest of the year, with extended hours on holidays. A **one-day one-park ticket** costs $39 (children aged 3–9 $32; under 3s go free) from any park entrance, and allows entry to one park only, with unlimited passouts.

For seeing more than two of the parks, spread your visits over four or five days using one of the **passes** that permit entry to all three parks and free use of the shuttle buses around the complex. **Four-day passes** cost $145 (children aged 3–9 $115); **five-day passes** cost $197 (children aged 3–9 $155). There's also a $229 **year-long pass**, strictly for fanatics. If you're staying at a Disney World resort, you are eligible for reductions on all these prices.

As obvious as it may sound, if you arrive by car be sure to follow the signs to the park you want to visit and use its **carpark** (fee $5 a day, which covers you for all the Disney World carparks). These are enormous, so be sure to make a note of exactly where you're parked. Carparks and hotels are linked to the main attractions by a complex and frequent **transport system** of buses and a monorail (free to guests of the Disney World resorts).

The Magic Kingdom

Anyone who's been to Disneyland in LA will recognize much of the **Magic Kingdom**. Like the original Disney theme park, it divides into four sections – **Adventureland, Tomorrowland, Fantasyland** and **Frontierland** – though these divisions become fairly meaningless once you're inside the park. Some rides are identical to their Californian forebears, some are greatly expanded and improved – and a few are much worse. And, like its older relative, the only way to deal with the place is enthusiastically: jump in with both feet and go on every ride you can.

The park

From the main gates, the unprepossessing **Main Street USA**, lined by souvenir shops and food-stands, leads towards **Cinderella's Castle**, a pseudo-Rhineland palace which might look like the most elaborate ride in the park but which, in fact, serves to conceal the electronics and machinery that drive the whole extravaganza. The castle does provide an easily spotted landmark for visitors, however, who are certain to lose their bearings at some point.

If you arrive early, beat the queues by immediately heading for the popular thrills-and-spills rides. The most nerve-jangling of these is **Space Mountain**, in essence an ordinary switchback but one where total darkness makes every jump and jolt unexpected. The ride may last less than three minutes but many people breathe a sigh of relief once it's over. **Splash Mountain** (memorably satirized in an episode of *The Simpsons*) is another glorified switchback, employing water to great effect and culminating in a fifty-foot drop. In a similar but less frenetic vein, **Big Thunder Mountain Railroad** puts you aboard a runaway train hurtling through gold-rush California in about three minutes.

Many of the other rides in the park rely on "AudioAnimatronic" characters – impressive vocal robots of Disney invention – for their appeal. The most up to date are seen in **ExtraTERRORestrial Alien Encounter**, which will appeal to all thrill-seekers, especially those who are fans of the *Alien(s)* films. A wonderful visual treat is **Transportarium**, where you're taken on a trip through time by the archetypal mad professor (whose voice is provided by Robin Williams, with his usual off-the-wall humour). Larger numbers of robots appear in **Pirates of the Caribbean**, a boat-ride through a pirate attack on a Caribbean island complete with drunken debauchery and general mayhem.

Elsewhere, the **Haunted Mansion** is worth a wait, as much for the duration of the ride – one of the longest in the park – as for the clever special effects, from the sliding ceiling in the entrance room to the macabre goings-on as your "doom buggy" passes through a spook-filled cemetery. Almost as entertaining is **20,000 Leagues Under the Sea** (actually about six inches down in an artificial lagoon); keep your nose pressed to the porthole of the submarine and you'll see all manner of curious creatures pass by as Captain Nemo commentates.

The Magic Kingdom does show its age with **Mr Toad's Wild Ride** and **Snow White's Adventures**; though these creaky low-tech amusements are still very popular with young kids, they wouldn't be out of place in a fairground. Another long-term survivor is **The Enchanted Tiki Birds**, with hundreds of AudioAnimatronic tropical birds and Tiki-god statues singing and whistling their way through a programme of South Seas musical favourites.

EPCOT Center

Even before the new Magic Kingdom opened, Walt Disney was developing plans for the **EPCOT Center**, or Experimental Prototype Community of Tomorrow. This was conceived in 1966 as a real community experimenting and working with the new ideas and materials of a technologically advancing US. The idea failed to shape up as Disney had envisaged: EPCOT didn't open its gates until 1982, when global recession and ecological concerns had put paid to utopian notions based on the infallibility of science. One drawback of this park is simply its immense size: twice as big as the Magic Kingdom and, ironically, given its futuristic themes, very sapping on mankind's oldest mode of transport – the feet.

The park

EPCOT's 180-foot-high **geosphere** (unlike a semi-circular geodesic *dome*, the geo*sphere* is completely round) provides information desks and souvenir shops and sits at the heart of the **Future World** section of the park, which keeps close to EPCOT's original concept of exploring the history and researching the future of agriculture, transport, energy and communications.

Future World divides into seven pavilions – each corporately sponsored, so don't expect to learn anything about alternative energy sources or global warming – and each has its own rides, films and interactive computer exhibits. The **Wonders of Life** pavilion has the best of the rides with **Body Wars**, a brief but exciting flight-simulator trip through a human body. While here, be sure to catch the entertaining **Cranium Command**, in which an AudioAnimatronic character is detailed to control the brain of a 12-year-old all-American boy.

Close by, **World of Motion** is completely forgettable. Concentrate instead on beating the queues that often stretch outside **Universe of Energy**: a somewhat dated celebration of the harnessing of the earth's energy, highlight of which is a ride through the the the dinosaur-roamed primeval forests where today's fossil fuels originated.

In the **Journey Into Imagination** pavilion, a 3D cinematic thrill called **Honey I Shrunk the Audience** demands audience participation and keeps you on the edge of your seat – excellent special effects. By contrast, promising an insight into the latest technological advances for the home and at work, with plenty of hands-on activities, the two **Innoventions** pavilions are more like glorified amusement arcades full of corporate advertising. **The Living Seas**, the world's largest artificial saltwater environment, occupied by a multitude of dolphins, sharks and sea lions, has far more to offer – not least for the chance to climb inside a massive diving suit.

Arranged around a forty-acre lagoon, the **World Showcase** section of EPCOT attempts to mirror the history, architecture and culture of eleven different nations. Each is presumably chosen for the ease of replicating an instantly recognisable landmark – Mexico has a Mayan Pyramid, France an Eiffel Tower – or stereotypical scene, such as the UK's pub, Germany's Bavarian village, and Morocco's inevitable bazaar. The elaborate reconstructions show careful attention to detail; highlights include the Viking longboat ride through **Norway**, **Japan**'s cultural museum, and the *Wonders of China* film. The most crowded place, though, is usually **The American Adventure** inside a replica of Philadelphia's Liberty Hall, where AudioAnimatronic versions of Mark Twain and Benjamin Franklin give a somewhat sanitized account of two centuries of US history in under half an hour. It's worth staying on till late evening to witness the lagoon's transformation into the spectacular sound and light show, **IllumiNations**, which starts half an hour before closing.

Disney-MGM Studios

When the Disney corporation began making films and TV shows for adults – most notably *Who Killed Roger Rabbit* – they also, with an eye on the popularity of the Universal Studios tour in California, set about devising a theme park to entertain adults as much as kids. Buying the rights to the gem-filled Metro-Goldwyn-Mayer (MGM) œuvre of films and TV shows, Disney acquired a vast repertoire of instantly familiar images to mould into shows and rides. Opening in 1990, **Disney-MGM Studios** served to mute the opening of Florida's Universal Studios (see p.245), and at the same time found an extra use for the real film studios based here – the people you'll see labouring over storyboards on the Backstage Tour aren't there for show: they are genuinely making films.

The park

The first of several highly sanitized imitations of Hollywood's famous streets and buildings – causing much amusement to anyone familiar with the seedy state of the originals – **Hollywood Boulevard** leads into the park, its length brightened with re-enactments of famous movie scenes, strolling film star lookalikes and the odd Muppet.

Avoid a long wait in the sun later in the day by arriving early and going straight on the half-hour **Backstage Studio Tour**. A narrated tram ride takes you through back lots, whisking you past the windows of film production offices (where you might see costumes and props being created) and animation studios to the climax: the exploding Catastrophe Canyon, an ingenious set that demonstrates special effects disturbingly close to hand. The tour's interest level goes up and down, depending on the movies in production at the time, but you won't feel you've had your money's worth if you miss it. The same applies to two other attractions that were previously part of the Backstage Tour: **The Magic of Disney Animation**, a thirty-minute self-guided tour with a hilarious ten-minute instructional film, again featuring Robin Williams; and **Inside the Magic**, an entertaining one-hour special effects and production tour that reveals the secrets behind making movies. Along the same lines and not to be missed, **The Indiana Jones Epic Stunt Spectacular** recreates and explains many of the action-packed set pieces from the Spielberg films.

Wrong turnings and collisions with asteroids make **Star Tours**, a flight-simulator trip to the Moon of Endor piloted by *Star Wars* characters R2D2 and C-3PO, the most physical ride in the park by a long way – passengers' seatbelts are carefully checked before lift-off. Scariest of the rides is **The Twilight Zone Tower of Terror**, a thirteen-storey drop that's enough to put you off elevators for life. For laughs, go to **Superstar Television**, which plucks volunteers from the crowd to read the news, appear in *The Lucy Show* or team up with *The Golden Girls* – one place in Walt Disney World where the fun is spontaneous. Also good fun is **Jim Henson's MuppetVision 4D**, a three-dimensional film whose special effects put you right inside the Muppet Show.

MGM's only deeply disappointing attraction is **The Great Movie Ride**, repaying a (usually) long queue with a short ride through a few scenes from movie classics.

The rest of Walt Disney World

Several **other Disney-devised amusements** exist to keep people on Disney property as long as possible and to offer therapeutic relaxation to those suffering theme-park burn-out. In addition to those listed below, an Indie-car racetrack is planned for the summer of 1996, on which the **Disney 200** will be held annually.

Blizzard Beach

Near Disney-MGM Studios and All-Star Resorts (see "Walt Disney World Accommodation", below). At peak times daily 9am–8pm, at other times hours vary; adults $23.85, children aged 3–9 $18.02; after 3pm adults $16.96, children $13.25.

A bizarre but immensely popular water park, **Blizzard Beach** is a combination of sand and fake snow surrounding Melt Away Bay, which lies at the foot of a snow-covered "mountain", complete with ski lift and water slides. The quickest way down is via Summit Plummet, designed to look like a ski jump, but in fact a steep water slide 120-feet high. If you don't want to get involved, you can lounge around and soak up some rays, then cool off in one of the pools rippled by wave machines.

Discovery Island
In Bay Lake, near the Magic Kingdom. Daily 10am–5pm in low season, 10am–6pm or later in high season; adults $10, children aged 3–9 $6.

In **Discovery Island**, Disney plays God and attempts to recreate the world by creating a "natural" habitat for a gorgeous variety of bird life. Here you'll find strutting peacocks, gliding swans and a flamingo-filled lagoon reached by prettily landscaped trails. Despite the steep admission price (it makes economic sense to combine it with River Country, see below), if you're not seeing any real Florida wildlife in the real Florida wilds, you'll enjoy this a lot.

River Country
At the Fort Wilderness Campground (see "Walt Disney World accommodation", below). Daily 10am–5pm in low season, 10am–7pm in high season; adults $14.75, children aged 3–9 $12.

River Country, built around the **Ol' Swimming Hole**, is a rustic version of Typhoon Lagoon (see below), offering fewer and less exciting slides – and no wave machines. Yet it scores well with the high-speed, corkscrewing descents from **Whoop-'N-Holler Hollow**, and the enjoyable cruise on inner tubes down the **White Water Rapids**. With a small beach and a nature trail leading to a shady cypress hammock, River Country is more relaxing than Typhoon Lagoon and is a good place to unwind between touring the main parks.

Typhoon Lagoon
Just south of Pleasure Island (see "Disney nightlife", p.245). Daily 10am–5pm in low season, 9am–6pm or later in high season; adults $22.50, children aged 3–9 $18.

Typhoon Lagoon, busiest in the summer and at weekends (often reaching capacity), consists of an imaginatively constructed "tropical island" around a two-and-a-half-acre lagoon, rippled every ninety seconds by artificial waves: bodysurf the breakers, skim over them with a raft (rent one as soon as you arrive; $1 an hour, two-hour minimum), or plunge into them from **Humunga Kowabunga**, a pair of speed-slides fifty feet up the "mountain" beside the lagoon. There are several smaller slides, too, and a saltwater **Shark Reef** where snorkellers fearful of the open seas can explore a "sunken ship" and be sniffed by real (but not dangerous) nurse and bonnethead sharks. When you're exhausted, take an inner tube (provided at the start point) and float around **Castaway Creek**, a half-hour meander through grottoes and caves, only interrupted by a sudden drenching from a tropical storm.

Unlike the major parks, you can bring **food** to Typhoon Lagoon, but no alcohol or glass containers.

Walt Disney World accommodation

If you want to escape the all-pervasive influence and high prices of Walt Disney World for the night, refer to the accommodation listings under "Orlando and around" (p.224); if not, you'll be relieved to find a growing number of Disney-owned **hotels** (most of which are, in fact, fully equipped resorts) within the Walt Disney World complex. Predictably, each follows a particular theme to the nth degree, and, also predictably, prices are much higher – sometimes more than $300 per night – than you'll pay elsewhere. The two All-Star Resorts, however, are specifically intended for the less affluent visitor, costing $69 or $79 a night.

Each resort occupies its own landscaped plot, usually encompassing several swimming pools and a beach beside an artificial lake, and has several restaurants and bars. The Disney resorts are located in several areas, and transport, be it by boat, bus or monorail, is complimentary between them and the main theme parks. Disney guests can also use theme park carparks for free. Theme-park admission tickets are also available at each resort, saving you valuable time otherwise spent queueing up at park ticket booths. The standard of service should be excellent; if it isn't, make a stiff complaint and you'll probably be treated like royalty through the remainder of your stay.

At quiet times, rooms may be available at short notice, but with Disney resorts pitching themselves at convention-goers as much as vacationers, you may turn up on spec to find that there is no space at all, even in 1000-room properties such as the Contemporary Resort. To be assured of a room, book as far ahead as possible – nine months is not unreasonable. **Reservations** can be made through the phone number: ☎**407/W DISNEY** (☎934-7639 from overseas).

Disney Village resort area
Dixie Landings Resort. A moderately priced, Southern-themed hotel, with rooms in the "manor house" or in the "bayou cottages" set in the grounds. ⑤.
Port Orleans Resort. Gaze from your wrought-iron balcony across the mini New Orleans re-created in this resort's courtyard. ⑤.

EPCOT resort area
All-Star Resorts. The newest, largest, most affordable and garish of Disney's resorts, divided into the All-Star Music Resort, which is decorated with giant-sized, brightly coloured cowboy boots, guitar-shaped swimming pools and the like; and the All-Star Sports Resort, complete with huge Coca-Cola cups, American football helmets and so on. Each complex has its own pool and about 1,500 rooms. ④.
Caribbean Beach Resort. Disney's first attempt to create a "budget-priced" hotel still works rather well; rooms at this plushly landscaped property are located in one of five lodges, each with its own pool. ⑤.
The Dolphin. Topped by the giant sculpture of a dolphin and decorated in dizzying pastel shades and reproduction artworks from the likes of Matisse and Warhol. ⑧.
The Swan. Intended as a partner to the *Dolphin*, from which it's separated by an artificial lake and beach, and likewise whimsically decorated and equipped with every conceivable luxury. ⑧.
Yacht and Beach Club Resorts. Turn-of-the-century New England is the cue for these twin hotels, complete with clapboard facades and miniature lighthouse. Amusements include all manner of waterborne activities and a croquet lawn. ⑧.
Boardwalk Resort. A brand-new complex on the scale of the Contemporary and Grand Floridian Beach Resorts (see "Magic Kingdom Area", below), with rooms in the "inn" or – better value for groups of 4 or 5 – in studios. ⑧.

Magic Kingdom area
Contemporary Resort. The Disney monorail runs right through the centre of this hotel, which takes its exterior design from the futuristic fantasies of the Magic Kingdom's Tomorrowland but is disappointingly characterless inside. ⑧.
Fort Wilderness Campground. Here you can pitch your tent ($35), hook up your RV ($54) or rent a six-berth trailer (around $185) – a good deal for larger groups.
The Grand Floridian Beach Resort. Gabled roofs, verandahs and crystal chandeliers are among the frivolous variations on early Florida resort architecture at this elegant and relaxing base. ⑧.

Polynesian Village Resort. An effective, if tacky, imitation of a Polynesian beach hotel; the concept is most effective if you spend your time on the lakeside beach under the shade of coconut palms. ⑧.

Wilderness Lodge. This magnificent, oversized replica of a frontier log cabin is furnished with massive totem poles, a wood-burning fire in the lobby, and Southern-style wooden rocking chairs. ⑧.

Disney nightlife: Pleasure Island

From around 9pm, each Walt Disney World park holds some kind of closing time bash, usually involving fireworks and fountains. For more solid night-time entertainment, the corporation devised the six-acre **Pleasure Island**, exit 26B off I-4 and next to the revamped Disney Village Marketplace. On this remake of an abandoned island, pseudo-warehouses are the setting for a mixture of themed shops, bars and nightclubs. Admission to the island is free from 10am to 7pm; after 7pm a charge of $17 is levied, which allows you limitless entry into the bars and clubs. Anyone under 18 must be accompanied by a parent, and alcohol will only be served to those who are 21 or over. Take your ID and be prepared to pay high prices for food and drink.

The only shows taking place to a timetable are at the *Comedy Warehouse* – whose comedians are genuinely funny and not afraid to send up Mickey Mouse – starting roughly half-hourly. If you're waiting for the curtain to go up, have a drink and lend an ear to the country and bluegrass music inside the *Neon Armadillo*, a Southwestern-style saloon, or check out the competent but unoriginal rock bands at *Rock and Roll Beach Club*. A new addition, *Pleasure Island Jazz Company*, offers live bands, with taped music between shows, plus a limited menu and a wine list. Of the rest, *Mannequins Dance Palace* is a swish disco that doesn't get cracking until midnight; the less ostentatious *8Trax* spins exclusively Seventies music.

The most original – and most enjoyable – place on Pleasure Island is the **Adventurers Club**, loosely based on a 1930s gentlemen's club and furnished with a motley collection of face masks (some of which unexpectedly start speaking), deer heads and assorted fleamarket furniture. Between scheduled shows, actors and actresses move surreptitiously (despite their period attire) among the throng and strike up loud and unusual conversations with unsuspecting audience members. Somthing is always going on.

Back on the mainland, next to Pleasure Island and glowing with neon lights, sits *Planet Hollywood*. Housed in a sphere, it seats 400 people and is the biggest restaurant in the chain so far.

Universal Studios

Half a mile north of Exits 29 or 30B off I-4. Daily from 9am, with closing times varying by season. One-day studio pass $39 for adults, $32 for children aged 3–9; two-day studio pass $58 for adults, $47 for children.

Year-round fine weather, a varied cast of natural landscapes and none of the union rules restricting film-making in California, have helped Florida gain the favour of the US film industry. All the predictions suggest that Florida will be the US moving-image capital of the next century, and the opening of **Universal Studios** in June 1990 did nothing to dampen the speculation.

Obviously a sequel to the long-established and immensely popular Universal Studios tour in Los Angeles, Florida's Universal, like its competitor Disney-MGM, is a working studio, filling over 400 acres with the latest in TV and film production technology and already turning out major features such as *Parenthood*, *Psycho IV* and a bunch of tedious sitcoms – with the prospect of many more to come.

Universal has proved to be extremely popular, becoming the third most visited theme park in the US. Overall, the rides are more spectacular than those at Disney-MGM, with less emphasis on film nostalgia – but the park has a less homely feel and only the very energetic will be able to take in the whole place inside a day. Plans are afoot to ensure you stay much longer: a multi-billion dollar investment is gradually going to expand the park to *twice* its current size, creating a second theme park, a number of hotels, a golf course, and so on. Universal Studios will, in fact, become Universal City.

The park

Street sets replicating New York, Los Angeles and San Francisco – look for the dirt and chewing gum painted onto the walls and pavements – create a striking backdrop to the park, which is arranged around a large lagoon: the scene of the **Dynamite Nights Stuntacular**, a daredevil extravaganza featuring pyrotechnic displays each night.

For sheer excitement, nothing in the park compares to **Back to the Future**, a bone-shaking flight-simulator time trip from 2015 to the Ice Age. Next best is **Ghostbusters**, for its finely judged mix of audience participation (don't let it be you who has to hold the slime) and inventive special effects as the deliberately over-acting cast encourage you to buy a *Ghostbusters* franchise. **Jaws** owes its success to anticipation of horror and classy special effects, but the ride is over all too quickly. The updated **Earthquake – The Big One** gives you a glimpse of what it's like to be caught on a subway train when an 8.3 Richter-scale quake hits.

Moving on, the six-ton version of King Kong in **Kongfrontation**, which attacks your cable car amid cracks of thunder and lightning high above New York's East River, is neither particularly memorable nor worth a lengthy wait. Similarly, **ET's Adventure** is a rather dull ride on pretend bicycles to ET's home planet, although ET speaking your name (which was earlier programmed into a computer) as you leave is a pleasing touch.

Obviously less fun for kids but often more enjoyable than the rides, are the attempts to demystify TV and film production techniques. **Alfred Hitchcock: The Art of Making Movies**, explores some of the outrageous camera angles and visual tricks employed by Hitchcock to send shivers down the spines of millions. Apart from some rather tame efforts to frighten, the tour includes intriguing glimpses of some of his better films, a few startling scenes from the 3D version of *Dial M for Murder*, and a group of actors playing out crucial scenes – including the shower one from *Psycho* – using an unfortunate audience member.

Stress rather than horror is the theme of the often hilarious and intriguing **Murder, She Wrote**, where a yet-to-be-completed episode of the whodunnit blockbuster illustrates different production and post-production processes with the help of audience members.

A more relaxing time might be expected at **The Funtastic World of Hanna-Barbera**, though the excellent simulated cartoon chase from the creators of *The Flintstones* and *Yogi Bear* will have you shaking in your seat; afterwards, using the interactive computers, you can create your own cartoon audio effects – bangs, whoops and crashes – to your heart's content.

Sea World

Sea Harbor Drive, near the intersection of I-4 and 27A, or I-4 and the Bee Line Expwy. Daily 9am–7pm in low season, longer hours in high season; adults $37.95, children aged 3–9 $32.95.

It may have as many souvenir shops as fish, but **Sea World** is the cream of Florida's sizeable crop of marine parks and as such shouldn't be missed. To see it all and get value for money, you'll need to allocate a whole day, and be certain to pick up the free map and show schedule at the entrance.

The big event is the **Shamu** show – twenty minutes of tricks performed by a playful killer whale. The **Wild Arctic** complex (complete with artificial snow and ice) brings you close to beluga whales, walruses and polar bears, while a simulated ride takes you on a stomach-churning helicopter flight through an arctic blizzard. Be sure to check out the launch pad viewing area (on your right as you exit through the gift shop) to gain an insight into the mechanics of simulated rides.

With substantially less razzmatazz, plenty of smaller tanks and displays around the park offer a wealth of information about the undersea world. Among the highlights, the **Penguin Encounter** attempts to re-create Antarctica with scores of the waddling birds scampering over a make-believe iceberg; the occupants of the **Dolphin Pool** assert their advanced intellect by flapping their fins and drenching passers-by; and **Terrors of the Deep** includes a walk through a glass-sided tunnel, offering the closest eye-contact you're ever likely to have with a shark and live to tell the tale. As you might expect in a park devoted to ocean life, there is now a **Bay Watch** water adventure show, which involves water-skiing, speed boats, jet-skis and so on, with a thinly disguised message about ocean safety. It is, however, genuinely spectacular and well worth waiting to see one of the three shows a day.

Finally, if you've never been lucky enough to see a manatee in the wild, don't leave Sea World without taking in **Manatees: the Last Generation?**, where you can see a few of the endangered creatures and learn about the threat faced by their species.

Other attractions around Orlando

The Orlando area's small-time entrepreneurs are nothing if not inventive. No end of tacky, short-lived would-be attractions spring up each year and a large number of them swiftly sink without trace. The list below represents the best – or just the longest-surviving – of the thousand-and-one little places to visit **around Orlando**. Three further highly worthwhile attractions in the Orlando area (Gatorland, Cypress Gardens and Bok Tower Gardens), are detailed on pages 235 and 251.

Splendid China

3000 Splendid China Blvd. Daily from 9.30, with closing times varying by season; adults $23.55, children aged 5–12 $13.90.

The newest and best of these attractions, this park features over sixty authentic replicas celebrating 5000 years of Chinese architecture and history. Painstakingly reconstructed miniatures (including the Great Wall, the Leshan Buddha, and the Terracotta Warriors among others), plus museum exhibits and fascinating displays make this an intriguing place to spend the day. The best time to visit is towards evening when the park is beautifully illuminated.

Flying Tigers Warbird Air Museum

231 N Hoagland Blvd, next to Kissimmee airport. Mon–Sat 9am–5.30pm, Sun 9am–5pm; adults $6; children aged 6–12 $5.

The main hangar contains battle-weary Tiger Moths, Mustangs and assorted bombers and biplanes in various states of repair – all being commercially restored.

Mystery Fun House/Starbase Omega

5767 Major Blvd. Daily 10am–11pm (lobby closes at 9pm); Mystery Fun House $7.95; Starbase Omega $6.95.

The real mystery of Mystery Fun House – with its unprepossessing collection of distorting mirrors, moving floors and talking furniture – is why more people don't ask for their money back. Most fun can be had in the high-tech laser game Starbase Omega where, equipped with a laser gun, you can pretend to be a star trooper to your heart's content.

Reptile World Serpentarium

E Irlo Bronson Memorial Hwy/Hwy 192, just east of St Cloud. Daily 9am–5.30pm; adults $4.25, children aged 6–17 $3.25.

A research centre for the production of snake venoms, which are sold to hospitals and similiar institutions who in turn produce anti-venoms. Visitors are introduced to a caged collection of poisonous and non-poisonous snakes from around the world, and shown demonstrations of venom extraction at 11am, 2pm and 5pm.

Ripley's Believe It or Not!

8201 International Drive. Daily 10am–11pm; $8.95.

A model of the world's tallest man, a chunk of the Berlin Wall and a Rolls-Royce built from a million matchsticks are among the innumerable oddities and curiosities packed into this seemingly lopsided building.

Terror on Church Street

135 S Orange Ave. Daily 7pm–midnight; $12.

The price may be high, but this combination of live actors, hi-tech special effects and imaginative audiotracks, all intended to scare people out of their wits, sometimes works surprisingly well.

Wet'n'Wild

6200 International Drive. Daily 10am–5pm, longer hours in summer; adults $20.95, children aged 3–9 $17.95.

Water slides, chutes, rapids and wave machines – just the job for a day's splashing about when the thermometer soars.

A World of Orchids

2501 Old Lake Wilson Rd, Kissimmee. Daily 10am–6pm. Adults $8.95, children under 15 free if accompanied by a paying adult.

An enthralling air-conditioned tropical rainforest garden that showcases thousands of rare, exotic and beautiful flowering orchids from around the world. Blooms all year round.

SOUTH CENTRAL FLORIDA

Trapped between the holiday haunts of Orlando and the beaches of the Tampa Bay area, the main towns of **South Central Florida** haven't been done any favours, either, by decades of phosphate mining, which have left their surrounds pockmarked with craters. However, matters are gradually being improved. Many of the unsightly holes have been turned into lakes (joining a large number of natural ones), and the prospect of boating, waterskiing and fishing on them is attracting visitors from the grip of Orlando. More interestingly, several of the region's small towns were formerly big towns, around the turn of the century, and are keen to flaunt their past histories – and near them can be found several refreshingly under-hyped attractions, which were bringing tourists into the state when Walt Disney was still in short trousers.

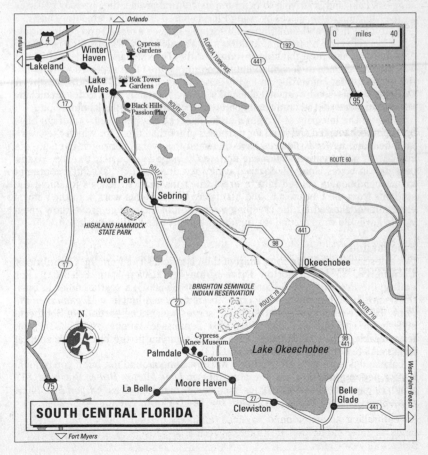

Lakeland and around

A logical place to begin touring the region, **LAKELAND**, fifty miles southwest of Orlando along I-4, plays the suburban big brother to its even more rural neighbours, providing sleeping quarters for Orlando and Tampa commuters, who emerge at weekends to stroll the edges of the town's numerous lakes or ride on them in hideous swan-shaped paddle-boats.

Aided by its busy railway terminal, Lakeland's fortunes rose in the Twenties, and a number of its more important buildings have been maintained as the **Munn Park Historic District** on and close to Main Street – pay heed to the 1927 *Polk Theater*, 124 S Florida Avenue, and the restored balustrades, lampposts and gazebo-style bandstand on the promenade around Lake Mirror, at the east end of Main Street. A few minutes' walk from the town centre, the generous size of the **Polk County Museum of Art**, 800 E Palmetto Street (Tues–Sat 10am–4pm, Sun noon–4pm; free), suggests Lakeland is striving to heighten its cultural profile: the spacious galleries air the latest innovative pieces by rising Florida-based artists on a temporary basis.

A stronger draw, and something of a surprise in such a tucked-away community, is the largest single grouping of buildings by **Frank Lloyd Wright**, who redefined America's architectural thinking throughout the Twenties and Thirties. Maybe it was the rare chance to design an entire communal area that appealed to Wright – the fee he got for converting an eighty-acre orange grove into **Florida Southern College**, a mile southwest of Lakeland's centre, certainly didn't; the financially strapped college paid on credit and got its students to provide the labour.

Much of the integrity of Wright's initial concept has been lost: buildings have been crudely adapted and used for purposes other than those for which they were intended, and newer structures have distorted the overall harmony. Even so, the campus is an inventive statement and easily negotiated using the free **maps** provided in boxes along its covered walkways. Interestingly, Wright's contempt for air conditioning caused him to erect thick masonry structures to shield the students from the Florida sun, and his desire to merge his work with the natural environment allowed for the creeping vegetation of the orange grove (now given way to lawns) to wrap around the buildings and provide further insulation.

Practicalities

Get a descriptive **walking tour map** of the historic district from the **Chamber of Commerce**, 35 Lake Morton Drive (Mon–Fri 8.30am–5pm; 688-8551). For **eating**, the *Reececliff*, 940 S Florida Avenue (☎686-6661), a spartan diner in business since 1934, has ridiculously cheap breakfasts and lunches; *Magnolias in the Park*, 255 N Kentucky Ave (☎686-7275), serves well-priced portions of Southern-style home cooking; and *Silver Ring*, 801 Tennessee Avenue (☎687-3283), proffers sizeable Cuban sandwiches. Also worth sampling is the black bean soup at *Julio's*, 213 N Kentucky Avenue (☎686-1713).

Lakeland doesn't have any nightlife worth waiting around for, but if you're looking for **accommodation**, use the atmospheric *Lake Morton Bed & Breakfast*, 817 South Boulevard (☎688-6788; ③), or inexpensive motels such as *Passport Inn*, 740 E Main Street (☎688-5506; ③), or *Scottish Inn*, 244 N Florida Avenue (☎687-2530; ③).

The area code for the parts of South Central Florida mentioned in this chapter is 941.

Lake Alfred, Winter Haven and Cypress Gardens

The sole reason to visit **LAKE ALFRED**, fifteen miles east of Lakeland on Hwy-17 (also known as Hwy-92), is to rummage about inside the **junk and antique shops** lining Haines Boulevard. While bargains may be few, students of Americana are in for a treat as they sift through the vintage Coke signs, old kitchen tools, yellowing family albums and moth-eaten moose heads.

Like Lake Alfred, **WINTER HAVEN**, seven miles south, struggles to hold onto its passing traffic; the motels (see below) lining Cypress Gardens Boulevard exist for visitors to the long-popular **Cypress Gardens**, at the southeast corner of the town (daily, winter 9.30am–5.30pm, later in summer; $27.95). Gouged from a sixteen-acre swamp by dollar-a-day labourers during the Depression, Cypress Gardens makes a good place to unwind after the tumult of Walt Disney World, especially with kids. The relaxing ambience established by the neatly landscaped setting – a profusion of towering cypress trees and colourful plants arching around a lake – is enhanced by the Southern Belles: young ladies in hooped skirts who sit and fan themselves while being relentlessly photographed. Besides syncopated waterskiing on the lake, the gardens also boast the **Wings of Wonder** butterfly conservatory, a Victorian-style 5,500-foot glass construction filled with rain-forest plants and fifty species of free-flying butterflies (over a thousand in all), together with iguanas, turtles, doves and button quails.

There are snack bars and restaurants inside Cypress Gardens, but it's cheaper to **eat** in the *International House of Pancakes* coffee shop, 1911 Cypress Gardens Boulevard (☎294-4104), purveyors of breakfasts, bounteous lunches and reasonable evening fare. The *Ranch House* is also a good spot for an **overnight stay** (reservations on ☎1-800/366-5996; ②), as is *Ye Olde English Motel*, 1901 Cypress Gardens Boulevard (☎324-5998; ②).

Lake Wales and around

Fourteen miles southeast of Winter Haven on Hwy-27, **LAKE WALES** is a lackadaisical town with more of note on its fringes than in its centre, though the **Lake Wales Depot Museum**, 325 S Scenic Highway (Mon–Fri 9am–5pm, Sat 10am–4pm; free), contains an entertaining collection of train parts, remnants from the turpentine industry on which the town was founded in the late 1800s, and a Warhol-like collection of crate labels from the citrus companies with which it prospered during the early 1900s.

At the museum, confirm directions to **Spook Hill**, an optical illusion that's been turned into a transparently bogus "legend", but one which would be a shame to miss (conveniently, it's on the way to Bok Tower Gardens, see below). By car, cross Central Avenue from the museum and turn right into North Avenue, following the one-way system. Just before meeting Hwy-17A, a sign indicates the spot to brake and put your vehicle into neutral: as you do so, the car appears to slide uphill. Looking back from the junction makes clear the difference in road gradients which creates the effect.

Bok Tower Gardens

"A more striking example of the power of beauty could hardly be found, better proof that beauty exists could not be asked for", rejoiced landscape gardener

William Lyman Phillips upon visiting **Bok Tower Gardens**, two miles north of Lake Wales on Hwy-17A (daily 8am–5pm; last admission 4pm; $4), in 1956. As sentimental as it may sound, Phillips' comment was spot-on. Whether it's the effusive entanglements of ferns, oaks and palms, the bright patches of magnolias, azaleas and gardenias, or just the sheer novelty of a slope (this being the highest point in peninsular Florida), Bok Tower Gardens is one of the state's most lush and lovely places.

Not content with winning the Pulitzer Prize for his autobiography in 1920, Dutch-born office-boy turned author and publisher **Edward Bok** resolved to transform the pine-covered Iron Mountain (as this hump is named) into a "sanctuary for humans and birds", in gratitude to his adopted country for making his glittering career possible. President Coolidge, one of Bok's many famous friends, showed up to declare it open in 1929.

Marvellous though they are, these 128 acres would be just a glorified botanical garden were it not for the **Singing Tower** and the newly opened **mansion**. The tower, two hundred feet of marble and coquina, rises sheerly above the branches, poetically mirrored in a swan- and duck-filled lake. Originally intended to conceal the garden's water tanks, the tower carries finely sculptured impressions of Florida wildlife on its exterior and fills its interior with a 53-bell carillon: richly timbred chimes resound through the garden every half-hour. Only the 3pm recital is "live" (all the others are recordings), but you can discover more about its workings in the **visitor center**, which fills an old "cracker" cottage near the garden's entrance. ("Cracker" was the nickname given to the state's early cattle farmers.) The twenty-room Mediterranean-style mansion was renovated and opened in December 1995, its rooms decorated with 1920s furnishings. Guided tours last for one hour and cost $5.

A portion of the grounds is left in its raw state, allowing wildlife to roam – and be surreptitiously viewed through the glass front of a wooden hut – and visitors to hack their way for twenty minutes along the **Pine Ridge trail**, through the pine trees, saw-edged grasses and wild flowers that once covered the entire hill.

Chalet Suzanne

In 1931, gourmet cook and world traveller Bertha Hinshaw, recently widowed and made penniless by the Depression, moved to an isolated site two miles north of Lake Wales, beside Hwy-17, to open a restaurant called **Chalet Suzanne**. Armed with self-devised recipes and tremendous powers of culinary invention – adding chicken livers to grilled grapefruit, for instance – Bertha created what's now among the most highly rated meal stops in the country, one that's still run by her family.

Aside from the food (a multi-course lunch or dinner costs upwards of $40; reservations on ☎676-6011), the quirky architecture grabs the eye: drunkenly angled buildings painted in clashing pinks, greens and yellows, topped by twisting towers and turrets. You're free to wander through the public rooms – whose furnishings are as loopy as the architecture – even if you're not stumping up for a meal or staying in one of the luxurious guest rooms (⑨).

The one sensible structure is the soup cannery, where "Romaine" soup – another of Bertha's creations – begins its journey to the nation's gourmet food shops. While here, don't be frightened by low-flying aircraft: a small runway beside the cannery is where corporate execs and freeloading food critics breeze in by private plane for a slap-up meal.

Lake Kissimmee State Park

Nineteenth-century Floridian farming techniques may not seem the most inspiring subject in the world, but the 1876 Cow Camp section of **Lake Kissimmee State Park** (daily 8am–sunset; cars $3.25, pedestrians & cyclists $1), fifteen miles east of Lake Wales off Route 60, is an enjoyable and instructive re-creation of a pioneer-era cattle farm, complete with park rangers playing the parts of "crackers" and tending genuine cows and horses.

Elsewhere in the park, an observation point above Lake Kissimmee can be utilized for bird- and alligator-spotting; to get closer to the water, rent a canoe ($15 per half-day) from the marina.

South from Lake Wales: along Hwy-27

The section of Hwy-27 that runs **south from Lake Wales** is among Florida's least eventful roads: a four-lane snake through a landscape of gentle hills, lakes, citrus groves and sleepy communities dominated by retirees. Busy with farm trucks, the highway itself is far from peaceful, but provides an interesting backwoods course if you're making for either coast: smaller roads branch off towards Fort Myers, on the west coast, and, after Hwy 27 twists around the massive Lake Okeechobee, to the big centres of the southeast coast.

Avon Park, Sebring and around

Two miles along Hwy-27 from Lake Wales stands the purpose-built amphitheatre that stages the **Black Hills Passion Play**, a dramatic re-creation of the last week in the life of Christ. Seats for the five performances weekly between mid-February and mid-April cost $6 to $12 and are quickly snapped up. For more details, call ☎676-1495.

Twenty miles further, **AVON PARK** acquired its name from an early English settler born in Stratford-upon-Avon; information on her and the community's general history is available at the **Avon Park Museum**, 3 N Museum Avenue (usually 10am–2pm; free). Once you've worn out the museum, leave Avon Park on Route 17, tracing a ten-mile path around a series of lakes to **SEBRING**, whose unusual semicircular street-plan was devised by its founder, George Sebring: he planted an oak tree here in 1912 to symbolize the sun, and declared that all the town's streets would radiate out from it. They still do, and Route 17 passes the small park now enclosing the great tree just prior to reconnecting with Hwy-27.

As quiet as can be for eleven months of the year, Sebring's tranquillity is shattered each March when tens of thousands of motor-racing fans pack its motels and restaurants, arriving for a twelve-hour endurance contest, the **12 Hours of Sebring**, held at a race track about ten miles east – if you're passing through around this time, plan accordingly.

Well away from the sound of revving engines, the orange grove and cypress swamp trails inside **Highlands Hammock State Park**, six miles west of Sebring on Route 634 (daily 8am–sunset; cars $3.25, pedestrians and cyclists $1), add up to a well-spent afternoon. Keep an eye out for the white-tailed deer, and time your visit to coincide with the informative ranger-guided **tram tour** (for times, call ☎385-0011).

Further homage is paid to cypress trees just beyond Palmdale, forty miles south of Sebring, at the **Cypress Knee Museum** (daily 9am–4pm; $3), which stocks some of the most lifelike specimens of Cypress Knees – a lumpy growth on the tree which enables its submerged roots to breath. Close by, on Hwy-27, **Gatorama** (daily 8am–6pm; $6) is a working alligator farm, licensed to keep thousands of the toothy creatures for public viewing and for turning into handbags, boots and food – if you've already visited Orlando's Gatorland (see "South from Orlando", p.235), this is more of the same.

Moving on from here, Route 29, off Hwy-27 at Palmdale, runs west to La Belle, from which Hwy-80 continues thirty miles to Fort Myers (see *The West Coast*); Hwy-27 ploughs on around the southern edge of Lake Okeechobee.

Lake Okeechobee and around

Until recently, one of the best-kept secrets in Florida has been the outstanding natural beauty of **Lake Okeechobee**, the second-largest freshwater lake in the US. For many years the preserve of sugarcane, beef and dairy farmers, as well as fishermen in search of catfish or large-mouthed bass, the lake (whose name translates from Seminole Indian to mean "Big Water") has started to draw tourists. This is the result of both a state-wide push and the area's abundance of plant- and **wildlife**. Birds feature strongly: over 120 varieties have been spotted, and this is one of the few places in the world where you can still sight a snail kite. Other inhabitants include bobcats, alligators, turtles, otters, snakes and, occasionally, manatees.

Home to Native Americans for centuries, the first farm settlers began arriving in the area in 1910, encouraged by the work carried out by wealthy Philadelphian Hamilton Disston, who, in the nineteenth century, started dredging canals and draining the land for agriculture. Next came the railroads, extending three-quarters of the way round the lake by the late 1920s and providing easy access to the rest of the state. Today the area is also served by three major **highways**, which join to encircle the lake and allow access to the towns dotted around its shores (see below). Staying a few days in one of these will allow you to explore Lake Okeechobee and its environs at your leisure.

Lake Okeechobee

Covering 730 square miles and averaging 14 feet in depth, **Lake Okeechobee** is fed by several rivers, creeks and canals, and has always played an important role in the lives of communities close to its shores and through most of southern Florida, as well as in the life-cycle of the Everglades. Since the completion of the dike, it has served as both a flood-control safety valve during the hurricane season and as a freshwater storage reservoir. Traditionally, the lake's waters have drained slowly south to nourish the Everglades after the summer rains, but the disruption caused by extensive "reclaiming" of land for farming is one of the hottest environmental issues in Florida.

Visiting the lake
The lake itself is best enjoyed **by boat** or from the **walking/cycling trails** (there are several, each 20–36 miles long) that run along the top of the Hoover Dike, which surrounds the lake (rendering it invisible from the road). For more infor-

mation on the trails, call ☎983-3335, and to hire a bike, try *Euler's Cycling Center*, 50 Hwy-441 SE (☎357-0458). An exciting plan for the future is to connect the Okeechobee Scenic Trail with the Appalachian National Scenic Trail to create the longest in the US, joining Maine with Miami by the end of 1997.

A sensitive and instructional way to learn about this habitat and its wildlife is a boat ride with **Swampland Tours**, based near the town of Okeechobee (see below) at the Kissimmee Bridge on 10375 Hwy-78 ($17.50 for two hours; tours depart daily 10am and 1pm, weather permitting; check times and book ahead on ☎467-4411). The 22-mile tours into the 28,000-acre wildlife sanctuary are run by Barry "Chop" Légé in association with the Florida Audubon Society (see p.143), which owns the park. Barry's enthusiasm is infectious, and he will astonish you with his ability to spot all manner of creatures that you might otherwise miss; in any one trip, you're also likely to see at least 35 species of bird.

Okeechobee (the town)

The largest lakeside community, **OKEECHOBEE**, offers a base from which to explore and provides the most alternatives for accommodation, food and entertainment. The town was designed by the pervasive Henry M Flagler (see Palm Beach, p.167), whose grandiose plan demanded wide streets and wooden-framed buildings, some of which remain.

The town has a few places worthy of an hour or two between them, should the weather prevent you from more active pursuits: the **Historical Museum** (in the Historical Park; Thurs only 9am–1pm; free), the 1926 **County Court House**, a pretty example of Mediterranean Revival architecture, a style much favoured by Flagler, and the **Freedman Raulerson House**, on Second Avenue, near the corner with Fourth Street. Details of these and other places of interest, as well as local events, can be found at the **Chamber of Commerce** on 55 S Parrott Avenue (Mon–Fri 9am–5pm; ☎763-6464).

If you're interested in **fishing**, still a primary activity in the area, go to *Garrard Tackle Shop*, 4259 Hwy-441 S (☎763-3416). They will supply all the gear and a guide to help ensure you catch something.

Practicalities

Although the town is easy to get to (*Greyhound*, 106 SW Third Street, ☎763-5328 and *Amtrak* ☎1-800/872-7245 both have depots), there is no local public transport system, and taxis stop running at 9pm. This means that if you don't have a car you'll be pretty much tied to the town in the evenings and may therefore want to limit your time to one or two nights. Of the places to **stay**, the quiet and unassuming *Wanta Linga Motel*, 3225 SE Hwy-441 (☎763-1020; ③) offers reasonably priced rooms. The *Days Inn*, 2200 SE Hwy-441 (☎1-800/874-3744; ③) offers standard clean and comfortable accommodation, plus access to a fishing pier. For **camping**, you'll find the largest *KOA* campsite in the state just outside the town as you're heading towards the lake on Hwy-441 S (☎1-800/845-6846). A tent or RV site costs $24.95, a one-room cabin (sleeping up to four) is $34.95.

For **eating**, *Lightsey's Fish Co.*, Okee-Tantie Hwy-78 W (☎9763-4276), serves a selection of fresh fish and home-made American fare at reasonable prices. Keep an eye out for their specials. *Old Habits*, 4865 SE Hwy-441 (☎763-9924), offers home-made Southern-style food and hospitality. Alternatively, gorge yourself on the all-you-can-eat breakfast, lunch or dinner at *Pogey's*, SE Hwy-441 (☎763-7222), or on the cheap buffet dinner at *Michael's Restaurant*, 1001 S Parrott Avenue (☎763-2069). The *Angus Restaurant*, 2054 Hwy-70 at junction 98 (☎763-2040), specializes in beef, for which the area is famous.

The west side of the lake

Leaving Hwy-27 just west of Moore Haven, Route 78 charts a 34-mile course along the **west side of the lake**, passing through Fisheating Creek and continuing into the treeless expanse of Indian Prairie, part of the 35,000-acre **Brighton Seminole Indian Reservation**.

The Seminole Indians migrated here in the eighteenth century from Georgia and Alabama, replacing the already decimated original Native American population. After they, too, became the target of aggression, a small number managed to establish themselves here on the western side of the lake, where about 450 remain, as successful cattle farmers. Although they live in houses rather than traditional Seminole chickees, the residents here have remained faithful to long-held beliefs – handicrafts may be offered from the roadside, but you won't find any of the tacky souvenir shops common to reservations in more populous areas.

On this side of the lake, **accommodation** is limited to several well-equipped **campgrounds**, the best of which is *Twin Palms Resort* (☎946-0977), located thirteen miles from Moore Haven and 21 miles from the town of Okeechobee. This RV park offers self-contained cottages for $45 and tent sites for $12.50 per night.

Clewiston, Belle Glade and around

From Moore Haven, Hwy-27 is walled by many miles of sugar cane – half of all the sugar grown in the US, in fact – harvested between March and November by Jamaican labourers who are flown in, housed in hostels and notoriously underpaid for their physically demanding and even dangerous work. Many in Florida, particularly the 43,000 locally employed in the sugar industry, seem content to turn a blind eye to the scandalous treatment of the migrants. Their plight is not a subject wisely brought up in **CLEWISTON**, fourteen miles from Moore Haven, dominated by the US Sugar Corporation and, through the company's multi-million-dollar profits, enjoying the highest income per capita in the country – or in **BELLE GLADE**, a small town twenty miles east, which has the biggest sugar mill in the country and numerous trailer parks aimed largely at attracting fishermen. In its otherwise quiet history, one event stands out: the loss of 2000 lives when the lake was whipped up by a hurricane in 1928. The Belle Glade **Chamber of Commerce** is at 540 S Main Street (Mon–Fri 9am–5pm; ☎305/996-2745).

Acommodation is relatively plentiful, though squarely aimed at fishing folk – if that's not your scene you may as well stay away: on Torrey Island, two miles west of Belle Glade on Route 717, *The City of Belle Glade's Marina Campground* (☎407/996-6322) has lots of campervan space and a tent area ($15.40 a night).

Moving on from here, Hwy-27 swings south from just ouside Belle Glade towards Miami, eighty miles distant, while Hwy-441 cuts east forty miles to West Palm Beach.

NORTH CENTRAL FLORIDA

Millions of people each year hammer through **North Central Florida** towards Orlando, almost all of them oblivious to the fact that a few miles east of the unrelentingly ordinary I-75 are the villages and small towns that typified Florida before the arrival of interstate highways and made-to-measure vacations. The region has just two appreciably sized towns, one of which holds a major university, and a terrain that varies from rough scrub to resplendent grassy acres lubricated by dozens of natural springs. Giving it a few days won't waste your time or break your budget: costs here are extremely low.

The area code for North Central Florida is ☎904.

Ocala and around

Known throughout the US for the champion runners bred and trained at the thoroughbred horse farms occupying its green and softly undulating surrounds, **OCALA** itself is a town without much to shout about – though it makes an agreeable base for seeing more of the immediate area. The **Chamber of Commerce**, 110 E Silver Springs Boulevard (Mon–Fri 8.30am–5pm; ☎629-8051), can supply local facts, issue walking maps of the town's mildly interesting historic districts and tell you which of the **horse farms** are open for free self-guided tours. The two contrasting museums on either side of the town are also worth a visit.

The Garlits and Appleton museums

Ten miles from Ocala, Exit 67 off I-75, the **Don Garlits Museum of Drag Racing** (daily 9am–5.30pm; $7.50) parades dozens of low-slung drag-racing vehicles, including the "Swamp Rat" machines that propelled local legend Don Garlits to 270mph over the drag tracks during the mid-Fifties. Yellowing press cuttings and grainy films chart the rise of the sport, and a subsidiary display of Chevys, Buicks and Fords – and the classic hits pumped out by a Wurlitzer jukebox – evoke an *American Graffiti* atmosphere.

An outstanding assembly of art and artefacts sits on the other side of Ocala, inside the **Appleton Museum of Art**, 4333 NE Silver Springs Boulevard (Tues–Sat 10am–4.30pm, Sun 1–5pm; $3). Spanning the globe and five thousand years, the exhibits, collected by a wealthy Chicago industrialist, go together with remarkable cohesion, and there's barely a dull moment over two well-filled floors. Early Rembrandt etchings, a Rodin *Thinker* cast from the original mould and paintings by Jules Breton amid an exquisite stock of nineteenth-century French canvases, are admirable enough, but the handicrafts are really special: look for the Turkish prayer rugs, the brightly coloured Naxco ceramics, the wooden Tibetan saddle and the massed ranks of "Toggles" – Japanese *netsuke* figures carved from ivory.

Silver Springs

Approximately one mile east of Ocala on SR-40/Silver Springs Boulevard, **Silver Springs** (daily 9am–5.30pm, longer hours in summer; $26.95 adults, children

HORSEBACK RIDING

A visit to this area isn't really complete without seeing one of its numerous **horse ranches**, but you'll need a car to reach them. If you want to go horseback riding rather than just looking around, try **Young's Paso Fino Ranch**, four miles along SR-326, off I-75, at no. 8075 NW (☎867-5305 or 5273; book ahead). One of the country's top ranches for breeding and training Paso Fino horses (the name means "fine gait" in Spanish), they offer instruction before taking you out on a trail ($25 for 1hr 30min, including instruction). The horses' easy disposition and exceptionally smooth gait make them an ideal choice for beginners as well as more advanced riders. If you're lucky, you'll meet Barbara Young, the owner, whose charm and enthusiasm know no bounds.

A very different experience can be had at **The Happy Wrangler Dude Ranch**, about 25 miles south of Ocala, near Bushnell, off I-75 (☎793-DUDE for directions and to book ahead), where you can fully indulge in the cowboy fantasy. For $50 you can stay overnight (breakfast included) and go on a two-hour trail ride. Phone for information on various other options. All rooms are devoid of TVs and phones, leaving you free to amuse yourself by spinning yarns with your fellow cowhands around the fire.

An ideal place to rest your saddle-sore butt after a hard day's horseback riding is the **Heritage Country Inn**, set in ranch country at 14343 W Hwy-40, off I-75 (☎489-0023). The $74 for bed and breakfast is money well spent for the loving care and attention you'll receive in this turn-of-the-century converted farmhouse, with its six unique bedrooms, ranging from the *Plantation Room* to the *English Thoroughbred Room*. A favourite among guests is the home-baked cinnamon bread.

$18.95) has been winning admirers since the late 1800s when Florida's first tourists came by steamboat to stare into the spring's deep, clear waters.

During the 1930s and 1940s, six of the original *Tarzan* films were shot here, starring Johnnie Weissmuller. Today, the park operates as a highly commercial enterprise: piped Muzak along its walkways, a menagerie of imported animals such as monkeys, giraffes and llamas, plus the inevitable petting zoo mar an otherwise attractive spot where you can happily while away half a day. In addition, the admission fee is high, especially considering the proliferation of springs all across central and northern Florida, some of them just a few miles east in the Ocala National Forest (see opposite). From a conservationist point of view, Wakulla Springs (near Tallahassee, see p.338) is a far better bet. However, if you do decide to visit Silver Springs, you'll get the most from the **Glass-Bottomed Boat Tour** (the best of three boat rides available) and the **Jeep Safari**, both of which run regularly through the day. If you feel like cooling off or have kids in tow, buy a combo ticket, allowing entry to the adjacent **Wild Waters** (daily 10am–5pm), a typical water park with slides, wave pools, amusement arcades and so on.

Rainbow Springs State Park

A more natural setting for a walk and a swim is **Rainbow Springs State Park**, located about 20 miles west of Ocala and 3 miles north of Dunnellon, off Hwy-41 (☎489-5201; daily 8am–sunset; $1). From 1890 until the 1960s, this park rivalled Silver Springs as a commercial venture, but has thankfully been allowed to return to its natural state. A popular haunt for locals, it's busy at weekends, with families picnicking on the grass and splashing around in the springs. At other times you can enjoy exploring woodland **trails** in peace and quiet, keeping an eye out for bobcats, racoons, wild pigs, otters and a great variety of birdlife, then have a swim in the cool, crystal-clear waters. Phone ahead to take advantage of the **ranger-led walks**, **snorkelling** or **scuba diving**, which allow views of otherwise restricted areas. Inner-tube rentals are also available for a leisurely drift down the Blue Run River.

Practicalities

Motels line Silver Springs Boulevard between Ocala and Silver Springs: *Silver Springs Motel*, no. 4121 E (☎236-4243; ①); *Sun Plaza*, no. 5461 NE (☎236-2343; ②); *Cloister Court Motel*, no. 5460 NE (☎236-0799; ②); *Southland Motel*, no. 1260 E (☎351-0113; ①); and the *Holiday Inn–Ocala*, no. 3621 W (☎629-0381; ④), are all worth trying. For comparative luxury, try the *Ramada Inn*, 3810 NW Blitchton Road (☎732-3131; ④). The only local **campground** to allow tents is the *KOA* (☎237-2138), five miles southwest of Ocala on Route 200. You can pitch a tent for $22 or rent a cabin for $40.

You'll seldom spend more than $5 for a filling **meal** in the town, with a wide selection along E Silver Springs Boulevard. For hearty all-American food, go to the *Stage Stop Restaurant*, no. 5131 (☎236-1060), for breakfast or lunch only, *Morrison's Cafeteria*, no. 1600 (☎622-7447); or *Sonny's*, no. 4102 (☎236-1012). Slightly more expensively, *Richard's Place* (no. 316; ☎351-2233) does tasty things with vegetables; for something meaty and out of the ordinary, sample the large helpings of bratwurst and schnitzel at the *German Kitchen* (no. 5340; ☎236-3055).

Ocala National Forest

Translucent lakes, bubbling springs and a splendid 65-mile hiking trail bring weekend adventurers to the **Ocala National Forest**, five miles east of Silver Springs on Route 40. Steer clear of the busy bits, and you'll find plenty to savour in seclusion – alternatively, if you only have time for a quick look, take a spin along Route 19 (meeting Route 40, 22 miles into the forest), running north–south in the shade of overhanging hardwoods near the forest's eastern edge.

Juniper, Alexander and Salt springs

For undemanding nature, with swimming, canoeing (rent on the spot, for $15 per half-day), very gentle hiking – and lots of other people, especially on weekends and holidays – thrown in, the forest has three warm-water springs that fit the bill; and each of them has a campground. The easiest to reach from Silver Springs is **Juniper Springs** (info: ☎625-2520), twenty miles ahead on Route 40, particularly suited to hassle-free canoeing with a seven-mile marked course. **Alexander Springs** (info: ☎669-7495), on Route 445 off SR-19 about ten miles southeast of Juniper Springs, has good canoeing, too, and its see-through waters are perfect for snorkelling and scuba-diving.

To the north of the forest, reachable with Route 314 or Route 19, the most developed site – it even has a filling station and launderette – is **Salt Springs**

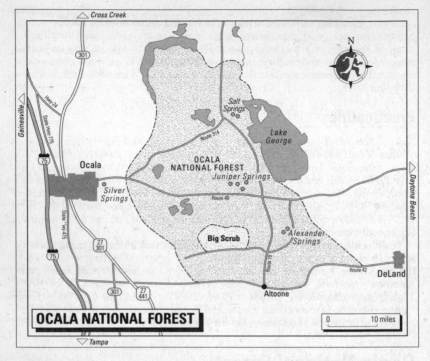

(info: ☎685-2048 or 3070). Despite the name, the springs here pump up 52 million gallons of fresh water a day, and the steady 72°F temperature stimulates a semi-tropical surround of vividly coloured plants and palm trees. Swimming and canoeing are as good here as at the other two springs, but people come mainly for the **fishing**, casting off in anticipation of catfish, large-mouthed bass and speckled perch.

The Ocala hiking trail

The 67-mile **Ocala hiking trail** runs right through the forest, traversing many remote, swampy areas, and passes beside the three springs mentioned above. Very **basic campgrounds** appear at regular intervals (be warned that these are closed during the mid-Nov to early Jan hunting season). At the district rangers' offices (see the box opposite), pick up the excellent leaflet describing the trail, which is part of the Florida State Scenic Trail.

However keen you might be, you're unlikely to have the time or stamina to tackle the entire trail, though one exceptional area that merits the slog required to get to it is **Big Scrub**, an imposingly severe landscape with sand dunes – and sometimes wild deer – moving across its semi-arid acres. The biggest problem at Big Scrub is lack of shade from the scorching sun, and the fact that the nearest facilities of any kind are miles away – don't come unprepared. Big Scrub is in the southern part of the forest, seven miles along Forest Road 573, off Route 19, twelve miles north of Altoona.

OCALA NATIONAL FOREST INFORMATION

The Ocala **Chamber of Commerce**, 110 E Silver Springs Boulevard (daily 9am–5pm; ☎629-8051), has maps and general information. The latest **camping updates** are available by phoning the camping areas at Juniper, Alexander and Salt springs (see p.259). For specialist hiking tips, call at one of the **district ranger offices** – the northern and southern halves of the forest are administered respectively by the Lake George Ranger District, 17147 E Hwy-405, Silver Springs (☎625-2520), and the Seminole Ranger District, 40929 Route 19, Umatilla (☎669-3153).

North from Ocala

From the monotonous I-75, you'd never guess that the thirty or so miles of hilly, lakeside terrain just to the east contain some of the most distinctive and insular villages in the state. Beyond the bounds of public transport, they can be reached only by driving; head **north from Ocala** on Hwy-301.

Cross Creek and the Marjorie Kinnan Rawlings Home

Native Floridians often wax lyrical about Marjorie Kinnan Rawlings, author of *The Yearling*, the Pulitzer prize-winning tale of the coming of age of a Florida farmer's son, and *Cross Creek*, describing the daily activities of country folk in **CROSS CREEK**, about twenty miles from Ocala on Route 325 (off Hwy-301). Leaving her husband in New York, Rawlings spent her most productive years – the Thirties – writing and tending a citrus grove here; a time inaccurately re-created in Martin Ritt's 1983 film, *Cross Creek*.

The restored **Marjorie Kinnan Rawlings Home** (Thurs–Mon 10–11.30am & 1–4.30pm; guided tours of up to ten people on the half-hour, with afternoon tours often fully booked; $2) gives an eye-opening insight into the toughness of the "cracker" lifestyle, but more surprising is the refusal of the self-reliant community to cash in on their literary associations.

Micanopy, McIntosh and Paynes Prairie

Four miles north of Cross Creek, Route 346 branches off to meet Hwy-441 just outside **MICANOPY**: a voguish vacation destination during the late 1800s, of late making efforts to win back visitors by turning itself, and many of its century-old brick buildings, into antique and craft shops. They're okay for a quick browse, but if it's a weekend, you'd be much better travelling a few miles south along Hwy-441 to another village, **McINTOSH**, whose 400-strong population dresses up in Victorian costumes for the **1890 festival**, held every October, to escort visitors around the restored homes.

In contrast to such conviviality, the marshy landscapes of the **Paynes Prairie State Preserve** (daily 8am–sunset; cars $3.25, cyclists and pedestrians $1), filling a broad sweep of land (18,000 acres) between Micanopy and Gainesville, can't help but strike a note of foreboding. It's an eerie place in many ways, though one well stocked with wildlife: cranes, hawks, waterfowl, otters, turtles and various wading birds all make homes here, as do many alligators. During weekends from October to March, **ranger-led hikes** (reservations: ☎466-4100; free) uncover the fascinat-

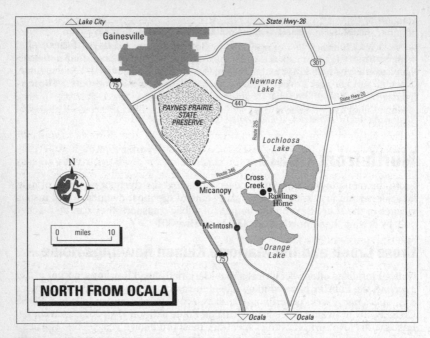

ing natural history of the area – and some of the social history: habitations have been traced back to 10,000 BC. Without a guide, you can bone up on the background at the **visitor center** (daily 9am–5pm), four miles from Micanopy off Hwy-441, and peer into the moody wilderness from the nearby **observation tower**.

Gainesville and around

Without the University of Florida, **GAINESVILLE**, 35 miles north of Ocala, would be just another slow-paced rural community nodding off in the Florida heartland. As it is, the daintily sized place, once called Hogtown, is given a boost by its 40,000 students, who bring a lively, liberal spirit and account for the only decent **nightlife** in Central Florida outside Orlando. This, combined with a few low-key targets in and around the town, and plentiful cheap accommodation, make Gainesville a deserving base for a day or two.

On a sadder note, Gainesville hit the national headlines for all the wrong reasons in August 1990 when the bodies of five murdered and mutilated students were discovered in off-campus apartment blocks. Incredibly, despite the incarceration of a suspect, two similar killings took place in June 1991, and these horrific crimes are likely to haunt Gainesville for some time to come.

The town and university

Impressive sights are few in Gainesville's quiet centre, where most of the people you'll see are office workers going to or from work or nipping out to lunch. At the junction of University Avenue and NE First Street you'll spot the **Clock Tower**, an undramatic relic culled from Gainesville's nineteenth-century courthouse; inside are the clock workings and some photos from the old days. If these whet your historical appetite, explore northwards along Third Street, which reveals many of the showcase homes of turn-of-the-century Gainesville – Queen Anne, Colonial and various Revival styles dominate – and the palm-fronted **Thomas Center**, 306 NE Sixth Avenue (Mon–Fri 9am–5pm, Sat & Sun 1–4pm; free), once a plush hotel and restaurant, which now hosts small-scale art and historical exhibitions.

The old buildings are easily tracked down with the *Historic Gainesville* brochure issued by the **Visitors and Convention Bureau**, at 30 E University Avenue (Mon–Fri 8.30am–5pm; ☎374-5231). From the town centre, it's an easy fifteen-minute walk along University Avenue to the university; though if you're feeling very lazy, take a **bus** (any number from #1 to #10) from beside the Clock Tower. The *Greyhound* station is centrally placed, at 516 SW Fourth Avenue (☎376-5252).

The University of Florida

Most of Gainesville's through-traffic passes half a mile west of the town centre along 13th Street (part of Hwy-441), from which the **University of Florida (UF)** campus stretches three miles west from its main entrance by the junction with University Avenue. Call at the **information booth**, facing SW Second Street, for a free map, without which it's easy to get lost in the expansive grounds.

After it opened in 1906, the university's early science alumni gave Florida's economy a leg-up by pioneering the state's fantastically successful citrus farms. These days, the curriculum is broader based and modern buildings dominate the campus, though the first you'll see are the red-brick "Collegiate Gothic" structures favoured by US turn-of-the-century academic institutions. In the centre of the campus, styled in imitation of the Collegiate style, the 1953 **Century Tower** serves as a navigational aid and a time-keeping device – its electric bells issue a nerve-shattering carillon every hour.

Beyond the tower, the 83,000-seat **Florida Field/Ben Hill Griffin Stadium** – home of the Gators football team and a monument to the popularity of college sports in Florida – can hardly be missed, and neither can the adjacent **O'Connel Center**, an indoor sports venue, entering which is akin to walking into a giant balloon. Aside from staging evening volleyball and basketball games, and entertaining design buffs, the building offers only a cool, refreshing breather.

A couple of other places also offer quick respites from the sun. The temporary shows in the **University Gallery** (Mon–Sat 9am–5pm, Sun 1–5pm; free), inside the Fine Arts Building, capture the best student art, while nearby, on Museum Road, the **Florida Museum of Natural History** (Mon–Sat 10am–5pm, Sun 1–5pm; free) is much larger but disappointing, with shallow displays and texts on Florida's prehistory and wildlife. The best feature is the Object Gallery's pull-out drawers, containing some weird and wonderful (dead) insects.

Back outdoors, walk about a mile west along Museum Road to the tidy University Garden, where a concealed footpath leads to **Lake Alice**, overlooked by a wooden observation platform gradually losing its battle against the surrounding vegetation. You could come here for a picnic, but the roar of insects, the constant scampering of lizards and the knowledge that alligators are plentiful, means keeping your guard up as you gaze over the sizeable lake.

Accommodation

Although Gainesville has rows of low-cost **motels** a couple of miles out of the centre along SW 13th Street, be warned that these fill quickly when the Gators are playing at home. The closest tent-friendly **campground** is ten miles south at the Paynes Prairie State Preserve (see p.261; ☎466-3397).

Bambi, 2119 SW 13th St (☎1-800/34BAMBI). Slightly nearer to downtown than most of the inexpensive motels. ③.

Comfort Inn, 2435 SW 13th St (☎373-6500). One of the newer budget options. ③.

Econo Lodge, 2469 SW 13th St (☎1-800/424-4474). Reliable chain motel. ③.

Gainesville Lodge, 413 W University Ave (☎376-1224). Much the most convenient place to stay, near downtown Gainesville and the campus. ③.

Eating

Gainesville is not a difficult place in which to find a good meal, with plenty of restaurants around the town centre and the university.

Emiliano's Café, 7 SE First St (☎375-7381). Fresh-baked delights and substantial Costa Rican-style lunches.

Ernesto's Tex-Mex Café, 6 S Main St (☎376-0750). Reasonably priced standard American Mexican food.

Harry's Seafood Bar and Grill, 110 SE First St (☎372-1555). A sidewalk café serving New Orleans-style seafood, pasta, chicken, burgers and salads.

Snuffy's, 1017 W University Ave (☎376-8899). Gourmet burgers, steaks and fresh seafood.

Wolfgang's Bistro, 11 SE First St (☎378-7850). A student favourite, offering food from all over the world.

Nightlife

The town's students keep a bright **nightlife** in motion, live rock music being especially easy to find. For **what's on** details, check the "Scene" section of Friday's *Gainesville Sun*, or the free *Moon* magazine, found in most bars and restaurants.

Hardback Café, 232 SE First St (☎372-6248). The best of the live music venues, attracting "alternative" acts at weekends and assorted painters and poets on other nights.

Lilian's, 112 SE First St (☎372-1010). Live bands or comedy and a 2–8pm happy hour.

Loungin, 6 E University Ave (☎377-8080). The hippest of Gainesville's clubs. Comics and acoustic acts early in the week, and house, acid, techno and classic disco grooves Thurs–Sun.

Market Street Pub, 120 SW First St (☎377-2927). Brews its own beer and provides acoustic country and bluegrass music to help it down.

Richenbacher's, 104 S Main St (☎375-5363). Live blues, rock or reggae bands nightly and a 4–8pm happy hour.

Around Gainesville

Three places close to Gainesville will help flesh out a day. Two of them are neighbours and served by local buses; the third can only be reached by car – unless you're feeling energetic and **rent a bike** from *Chain Reaction Bicycles*, 1630 W University Avenue ($5 per hour or $12 per day; ☎373-4052).

Kanapaha Botanical Gardens and the Fred Bear Museum

Flower fanciers shouldn't miss the 62-acre **Kanapaha Botanical Gardens** (Mon, Tues & Fri 9am–5pm, Wed, Sat & Sun 9am–sunset; $1.50), five miles southwest of central Gainesville on Route 24, reachable with bus #1. The summer months more than most are a riot of colour and fragrances, although the design of the gardens means there's always something in bloom. Besides vines and bamboos, and special sections planted to attract butterflies and hummingbirds, the highlight is the herb garden, whose aromatic bed is raised to nose-level to encourage sniffing.

Across the road from the gardens, a signpost points to the **Fred Bear Museum** (Wed–Sun 10am–6pm; $2.50): a mass of mounted, skinned and stuffed animals, and some (such as the elephant's ear table with hippo legs) turned into furniture. Many of the unfortunate creatures were caught and killed by Fred Bear himself, who runs the adjoining archery factory: not a place for animal lovers.

The Devil's Millhopper

Of thousands of sinkholes in Florida, few are bigger or more spectacular than the **Devil's Millhopper**, set in a state geological site (daily 9am–sunset; cars $3.25, pedestrians and cyclists $1; free guided tour Sat 10am), seven miles northwest of Gainesville, off 53rd Avenue. Formed by the gradual erosion of limestone deposits and the collapse of the resultant cavern's ceiling, the lower reaches of this 120-foot-deep bowl-shaped dent have a temperature significantly cooler than the surface, allowing species of alpine plant and animal life to thrive. A winding boardwalk delivers you into the thickly vegetated depths.

North of Gainesville

Travelling **north of Gainesville** puts you in easy striking distance of the Panhandle to the west, and Jacksonville, the major city of the Northeast Coast. If you're uncertain of which way to turn, relax for a few hours at **Ichetucknee Springs** (daily 8am–sunset; cars $3.25, pedestrians and cyclists $1), the birthplace of the Ichetucknee River, whose chilled waters lend themselves to canoeing or inner-tube rafting along a six-mile course. Canoe rental costs $20 a day, plus $4.25 per person to go on the river. Weekdays, when beavers, otters and turtles sometimes share the river, are the best time to come; weekend crowds scare much of the wildlife away. The springs are 35 miles northwest of Gainesville, on Route 238, off I-75, and five-and-a-half miles north of Fort White.

There's no point in stopping in the unremarkable Lake City, thirteen miles north of the springs, nor in the Osceola National Forest, to the east of Lake City. This smallest of the state's three federally protected forests is mostly visited by hardened fishermen bound for its Ocean Pond, and you should aim instead for a couple of more fulfilling attractions in the near vicinity.

The Stephen Foster State Culture Center

Twelve miles north of Lake City, off Hwy-41, the **Stephen Foster State Culture Center** (daily 9am–sunset; cars $3.25, pedestrians and cyclists $1) offers a tribute to the man who composed Florida's state song, *Old Folks At Home*, immortalizing the waterway ("Way down upon the S'wanee river. . .") that flows by here on its

250-mile meander from Georgia's Okefenokee Swamp to the Gulf of Mexico. As it happens, Foster never actually saw the river but simply used "S'wanee" as a convenient Deep South-sounding rhyme. Besides exploring Florida's musical roots, the Center has a sentimental display about Foster, who penned a hatful of classic American folk songs including *Camptown Races, My Old Kentucky Home* and *Oh! Susanna* – instantly familiar melodies which ring out through the oak-filled park from a belltower – before dying in New York in 1863, aged 37.

The Olustee Battlefield Site

The **Olustee Battlefield Site**, thirteen miles west of Lake City beside Hwy-90 (Thurs–Mon 9am–5pm; free), is a sure sign you're approaching the Panhandle, a Confederate power base during the Civil War. The only major battle of the conflict in Florida took place here in February 1864, when 5000 Union troops pressing west from Jacksonville squared up to a similar-sized Confederate force. The five-hour battle, which left three hundred dead, nearly two thousand wounded and both sides claiming victory, is marked by a monument and a small interpretive centre at the entrance (closed Tues & Wed), and by a trail around the respective troop positions – hard to imagine the carnage that took place in what's now, as then, an otherwise peaceful pine forest.

travel details

Trains

From Orlando to DeLand (2 daily; 58min); Jacksonville (2 daily; 3hr 12min); Kissimmee (7 daily; 18min); Lakeland (7 daily; 1hr 28min); Sanford (2 daily; 38min); Tampa (7 daily; 2hr 17min); Winter Park (2 daily; 15min).

From Winter Haven to Fort Lauderdale (2 daily; 3hr); Miami (2 daily; 4hr 2min); Sebring (2 daily; 38min); West Palm Beach (2 daily; 2hr 9min).

Buses

From Clewiston to Belle Glade (1 daily; 30min); West Palm Beach (1 daily; 1hr 35min).

From Lakeland to Avon Park (1 daily; 3hr 5min); Cypress Gardens (1 daily; 45min); Lake Wales (1 daily; 1hr 5min); Sebring (1 daily; 3hr 30min); West Palm Beach (1 daily; 5hr); Winter Haven (1 daily; 30min).

From Orlando to Daytona Beach (4–6 daily; 2hr 35min); DeLand (4–6 daily; 1hr); Fort Lauderdale (7 daily; 5hr 20min); Fort Pierce (7 daily; 2hr 25min); Gainesville (4 daily; 2hr 50min); Jacksonville (4–6 daily; 3hr 30min); Lakeland (5 daily; 1hr 35min); Kissimmee (2 daily; 40min); Miami (7 daily; 5hr 55min); Ocala (4 daily; 1hr 30min); Sanford (4–6 daily; 35min); Tallahassee (4 daily; 5hr 30min); Tampa (5 daily; 3hr 15min); West Palm Beach (7 daily; 4hr); Winter Haven (5 daily; 1hr 5min).

CHAPTER SIX

THE WEST COAST

In the three hundred miles from the state's southern tip to the border of the Panhandle, Florida's **West Coast** embraces all the extremes. Buzzing, youthful towns neighbour placid fishing hamlets; mobbed holiday strips are just minutes from desolate swamplands. Surprises are plentiful: search for a snack bar and you'll stumble across a world-class art collection; doze off on an empty beach and you'll wake to find it packed with shell-collectors. The West Coast's one constant is proximity to the Gulf of Mexico – and sunset views rivalled only by those of the Florida Keys.

The heavily populated **Tampa Bay area**, midway along the coast, is the obvious first stop if you're arriving from Central Florida. The West Coast's largest city, **Tampa** probably won't detain you long, though it has more to offer than its power-dressers and corporate towers initially suggest, not least a long-established Cuban community.

Directly across the bay, **St Petersburg** once took pride in being the archetypal Florida retirement community: lately it has recast itself in a younger mould and is riding high on its acquisition of a major collection of works by surrealist artist Salvador Dalí. For the mass of visitors, though, the Tampa Bay area begins and ends with the **St Petersburg beaches**, whose miles of sea, sun and sand are undiluted vacation territory – but also a useful base for exploring the Greek-dominated community of **Tarpon Springs**, just beyond.

Far from the beach crowds, and indeed far from beaches, the **Big Bend** consumes the coast **north of Tampa**. No settlement numbers more than a few thousand amid the area's dead-flat marshes, large chunks of which are wildlife refuges with little public access. Within the scattered communities, it's easy to discover evidence of busier times: from a prehistoric site of sun-worship at **Crystal River**, to the long-defunct railway that made **Cedar Key** a thriving cargo port over a century ago.

A string of barrier-island beaches runs the length of the Gulf **south from Tampa**. The mainland towns that provide access to them have a lot in their favour, too: **Sarasota**, the first of any size, is the custodian of a fine-arts legacy passed down by a turn-of-the-century circus boss; further south, Thomas Edison was one of a number of scientific pioneers who took a fancy to palm-studded **Fort**

ACCOMMODATION PRICE CODES

All **accommodation prices** in this book have been coded using the symbols below. Note that prices are for the least expensive double rooms in each establishment. For a full explanation see p.27 in *Basics*.

① up to $30	③ $45–60	⑤ $80–100	⑦ $130–180
② $30–45	④ $60–80	⑥ $100–130	⑧ $180+

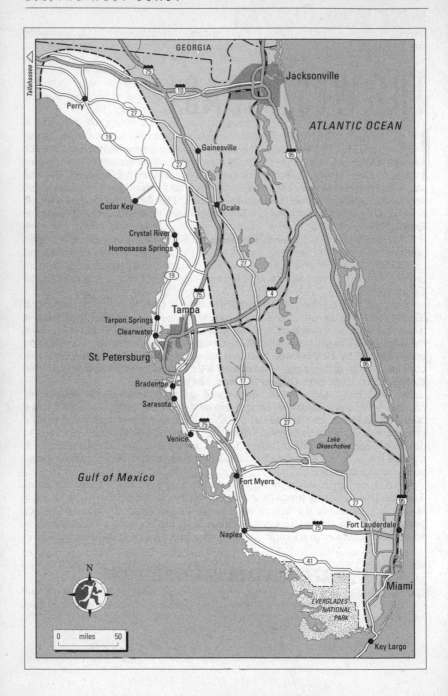

Myers, which neighbours **Sanibel** and **Captiva** – two atmospheric islands justifying a few days' relaxed discovery. As you pass through, take the opportunity to strike inland: the southwest coast backs onto the **Everglades,** a vast expanse whose swamps and prairies are brimming with natural life. The window on it all is the **Everglades National Park,** spreading east almost to the edge of Miami; explorable on simple walking trails, by canoeing, or by spending the night at backcountry campgrounds with only the alligators for company.

The West Coast is easy to **get around.** The region's **major roads,** and **I-4** from Central Florida, converge close to Tampa. From Tampa through the Big Bend, **Hwy-19** is the only route, served by two *Greyhound* buses daily in each direction. **Hwy-41** connects the main southwest coast settlements, and is often known as the **Tamiami Trail,** a nickname from its time as the only road link crossing the Everglades between Tampa and Miami; these days it's superseded for speed by the bland **I-75.** *Greyhound* services number five daily each way through the southwest coast, and a few towns are also connected by *Amtrak* buses from Tampa. The bigger centres have adequate **local bus services,** though the barrier islands and the Big Bend towns rarely have any public transport.

THE TAMPA BAY AREA

The geographic and economic nerve centre of the region, with a population almost on a par with that of Miami, the **Tampa Bay area** is easily the busiest and most congested part of the West Coast. People do live here for reasons other than work, however. The wide waters of the bay provide a scenic backdrop for Tampa itself, a stimulating city, while the barrier-island beaches along the coast let the locals swap metropolitan bustle for luscious sunsets and miles of glistening sands, which are also lapped up by large numbers of holidaymakers.

Tampa

TAMPA is a small city with an infectious upbeat mood; you'll only need a day or two to explore it thoroughly but you'll depart with a lasting impression of a city on the rise. The West Coast's undisputed business hub, it has been one of the major benefactors of the recent flood of people and money into Florida – and lavishes an impressive amount on a highbrow cultural diet envied by many larger communities. Yet in spite of this and the international airport that brings them to its doorstep, many people give Tampa only a brief glance before heading out to Busch Gardens, a theme park on the city's outskirts, and the Gulf coast beaches half an hour's drive west – missing out totally on one of Florida's most youthful and energetic urban communities.

Tampa began as a small settlement beside Fort Brooke, a US Army base built to keep an eye on local Seminole Indians during the 1820s, and remained tiny, isolated and insignificant until the 1880s, when the railway arrived and the

The area code for the Tampa Bay and St Petersburg areas is ☎813.

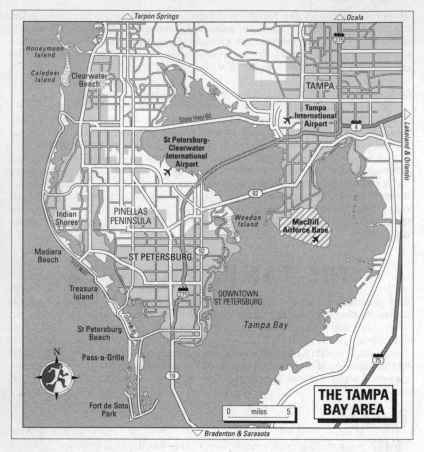

Hillsborough River – on which the city stands – was dredged to allow sea-going vessels to dock. Tampa became a booming port and simultaneously acquired a major tobacco industry as thousands of Cubans moved north from Key West to the new cigar factories of neighbouring Ybor City. Although the Depression saw off the economic surge, the port remained one of the busiest in the country, tempering the decline Tampa endured during the postwar decades. While the social problems that blight any US city are evident, there seems little to stand in the way of Tampa's continued emergence as a forward-thinking and financially secure community.

Regardless of the deals being struck in its towering office blocks, **downtown Tampa** is surprisingly quiet and compact, with an art museum and the *Tampa Bay Hotel* – one of the few reminders of times gone by – forming the basis of a three-hour ramble. Downtown Tampa may lack atmosphere and history, but there's plenty of both three miles northeast in the **Ybor City** quarter, whose Latin American character originated with migrant cigar workers; it now boasts myriad markers to the heady days of Cuban independence struggles. With more time to spare, you can venture into **Hyde Park**, containing the homes of Tampa's wealthiest early settlers, out to **Busch Gardens** or the **Museum of Science and Industry**, or into the wild, open country that appears remarkably quickly just north of the busy city.

Arrival, information and getting around

The city's international **airport** (☎870-8700) is five miles northwest of downtown Tampa. Local bus #30 (see "City transport", below) is the least costly connection ($1.15), or use the around-the-clock *Limo Inc* vans (☎572-1111 or 1-800/282-6817), whose representatives have desks in the baggage reclaim area; book the day before you fly. They also cover St Petersburg, Clearwater and the beaches. The flat fare to any Busch Boulevard or coastal accommodation is $13 per person, or $22 for a return ticket. **Taxis** – the main firms are *United* (☎253-2424) and *Yellow* (☎253-0121) – are abundant but expensive: to downtown Tampa or a Busch Boulevard motel costs $13–24; to St Petersburg or the St Petersburg Beaches, $30–45. All the major **car rental** companies have desks at the airport.

Long-distance public transport terminates in downtown Tampa: *Greyhound* **buses** at 610 Polk Street (☎229-2174 or 1-800/231-2222), and **trains** at 601 N Nebraska Avenue (☎221-7600 or 1-800/872-7245). The main routes **by car** into Tampa are I-275 and I-4 (intersecting with I-75, ten miles east of the city), which converge a few miles north of downtown Tampa. Be warned that downtown Tampa has a fiendish one-way system.

Information

In downtown Tampa, collect vouchers, leaflets and general information from the **visitors information center**, Suite 1010, 111 Madison Street (Mon–Sat 9am–5pm; ☎1-800/44-TAMPA). In Ybor City, visit the **Ybor City Chamber of Commerce**, 1800 Ninth Avenue (Mon–Fri 9am–5pm; ☎248-3712). Opposite Busch Gardens, the **Tampa Bay Visitor Information Center**, 3601 E Busch Boulevard (daily 10am–6pm; ☎985-3601) has local and state-wide information. For **nightlife** listings, read the free *Weekly Planet*, buy the Friday edition of the *Tampa Tribune*, or call the free *Nightlife* phone service on ☎854-8000.

Getting around

Although downtown Tampa and Ybor City are easily covered on foot, to travel between them – or to reach Busch Gardens or the Museum of Science and Industry – without a car, you'll need to use **local buses** (HARTline ☎254-4278), whose routes fan out from Marion Street in downtown Tampa. **Useful numbers** are #8 to Ybor City; #5, #14 or #18 to Busch Gardens; #6 to the Museum of Science and Industry; and #30 to the airport. Only rush-hour commuter (express) buses run **between Tampa and the coast**: #100X to St Petersburg (for schedule info for this bus only, call ☎530-9911) and #200X to Clearwater. Alternatives are the numerous daily *Greyhound* buses or the twice-daily *Amtrak* bus. Another way to travel between downtown Tampa and Ybor City is on the **Tampa-Ybor Trolley** (☎254-4278), which runs Mon–Fri 9am–4pm, every twenty minutes; weekends and holidays 7.30am–5.30pm, every thirty minutes. The route takes you via Harbour Island and the Florida Aquarium (see p.274), costing 50¢ one way.

Accommodation

Except for the area around Busch Gardens, Tampa is not generously supplied with low-cost **accommodation**, and you're likely to save money by sleeping in St Petersburg or at the beaches, and treating the city as a daytrip.

The cheaper **motels** are all on E Busch Boulevard close to Busch Gardens: *Best Western Resort* no. 820 (☎933-4011; ③); *Econo Lodge* no. 1701 (☎933-7681; ③); or *Howard Johnson's* no. 4139 (☎1-800/874-1768; ③) are the best of a substantial bunch. Right by the Museum of Science and Industry, the *Days Inn Busch Gardens*, 2520 N 50th Street (☎247-3300; ③) is another economical option.

Any of the above makes a reasonable base for seeing the city by car; if you're dependent on buses, however, and downtown Tampa and Ybor City are your main interests, choice is much more limited. You'll need to use one of the downtown business-traveller-orientated hotels, such as the convenient *Riverside*, 200 N Ashley Drive (☎223-2222; ④–⑥) or, ten minutes' walk from downtown, the *Days Inn*, 2522 N Dale Mabry (☎1-800/448-4373; ④).

Other than the site at the Hillsborough River State Park (see "Around Tampa", p.277), the only local **campground** where tents are welcome is the *Camp Nebraska RV Park*, 10314 N Nebraska Avenue/Hwy-41 (☎971-3460), lying a mile and a half north of Busch Gardens.

Downtown Tampa

Downtown Tampa's current prosperity is demonstrated by its upright office towers; aside from riverside warehouses in various states of dilapidation and renovation around the northern end of the pedestrianized **Franklin Street** (once the compact district's pulsating main drag and still the best place to get your bearings), recalling the city's past is largely left to text-bearing plaques detailing everything from the passage of sixteenth-century explorer Hernando DeSoto to the site of Florida's first radio station. The single substantial relic of bygone days is the **Tampa Theatre**, 711 Franklin Street (☎223-8981), one of the few surviving "atmospheric theaters" erected by Mediterranean-mad designer John Eberson during the Twenties. When silent movies enthralled the masses, Eberson's cinemas heightened the escapist mood: ceilings became star-filled skies, balconies were chiselled into Moorish arches, gargoyles leered from stuccoed walls, and replica Greek and Roman statuary filled every nook and cranny. Having fallen on hard times with the arrival of TV, the Tampa Theatre is enjoying a new lease of life as the home of the Tampa Film Club, sporting a full programme of very viewable movies – a $4 ticket for one (see "Nightlife", p.279) is the only way to gain access to the splendidly restored interior.

None of the contemporary buildings in downtown Tampa better reflects the city's striving for cultural recognition than the **Tampa Museum of Art**, on the banks of the Hillsborough River, at 600 N Ashley Drive (Mon–Tues and Thurs–Sat 10am–5pm, Wed 10am–9pm, Sun 1–5pm; $5 or free Sun 1–5pm and Wed 5–9pm; free guided tours on Wed and Sat at 1pm, Sun at 2pm). The highly regarded museum specializes in an incongruous mix of classical antiquities and twentieth-century American art: selections from the permanent modern stock are cleverly blended with loaned pieces from the cream of recent US painting, photography and sculpture. A third gallery is devoted to major travelling exhibitions, often of an excellent standard. The museum also runs free **guided walking tours** of art

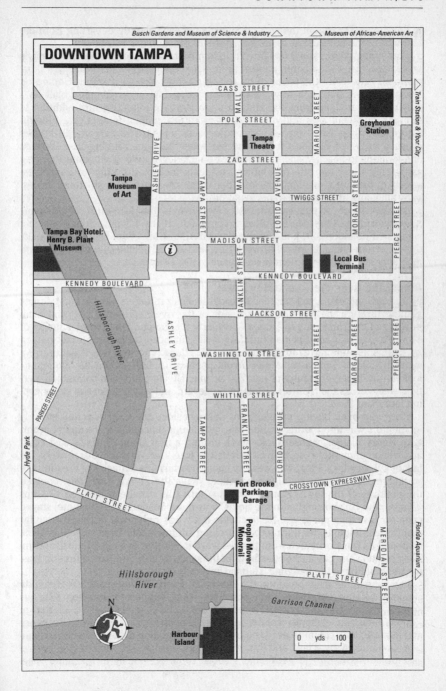

DOWNTOWN TAMPA

Busch Gardens and Museum of Science & Industry △   △ Museum of African-American Art

Train Station & Ybor City

CASS STREET

MALL

POLK STREET

MARION STREET

Greyhound
Station

ASHLEY DRIVE

Tampa
Theatre

ZACK STREET

Tampa
Museum
of Art

TAMPA STREET

MALL

FLORIDA AVENUE

TWIGGS STREET

MORGAN STREET

PIERCE STREET

Tampa Bay Hotel:
Henry B. Plant
Museum

MADISON STREET

FRANKLIN STREET

Local Bus
Terminal

KENNEDY BOULEVARD

KENNEDY BOULEVARD

Hillsborough River

JACKSON STREET

ASHLEY DRIVE

WASHINGTON STREET

MARION STREET

MORGAN STREET

PIERCE STREET

PARKER STREET

WHITING STREET

FRANKLIN STREET

TAMPA STREET

FLORIDA AVENUE

Hyde Park

PLATT STREET

Fort Brooke
Parking
Garage

CROSSTOWN EXPRESSWAY

People Mover
Monorail

MERIDIAN STREET

Florida Aquarium

PLATT STREET

Hillsborough
River

Garrison Channel

N

Harbour
Island

0   yds   100

in downtown Tampa, on the second Saturday of each month, departing from the entrance of the museum at 10am. For more information call ☎274-8130.

Continuing south, you'll feel like an insignificant speck at the feet of the city's tallest structures: for a better view of them – and their surrounds – take the short monorail ride (from the terminal on top of the Fort Brooke Parking Garage on Whiting Street; 50¢ each way) to **Harbour Island**, a large shopping mall on a small island dredged from the Hillsborough Bay. An attractive new addition to Tampa's dockland area and the product of an $84 million budget, the **Florida Aquarium** (daily 9am–6pm; $13.95; audio wands an extra $2; carpark $3) houses lavish displays of Florida's fresh- and salt-water habitats, ranging from springs and swamps to beaches and coral reefs. You can learn quite a bit about Florida's animal life here, too: the permanent residents include not only an impressive variety of fish but also all manner of other native creatures such as otters, turtles, baby alligators and countless species of bird.

Another place of cultural interest downtown is the **Museum of African-American Art**, 1308 Marion Street (Tues–Sat 10am–4.30pm, Sun 1–4.30pm; suggested donation $2), housing the Barnett-Aden Collection. Dating from 1800, the collection contains over 142 works by, and about, people of African descent, including art from the Harlem Renaissance of the Twenties.

Across the river: the Tampa Bay Hotel

From Harbour Island you can't fail to spot the silver minarets, cupolas and domes glinting through the trees on the far side of the river, sprouting from the main building of the University of Tampa – formerly the **Tampa Bay Hotel**, a fusion of Moorish, Turkish and Spanish building styles financed to the tune of $2 million by steamship and railway magnate, **Henry B. Plant**. The structure is as bizarre a sight in today's Tampa as it was on its opening in 1891, when its 500 rooms looked out on a community of just 700 people. Be sure to make a closer inspection: walk across the river on Kennedy Boulevard and climb down the steps leading into Plant Park.

Plant had been buying up bankrupt railways since the Civil War and steadily inching his way into Florida to meet his steamships unloading at Tampa's harbor. Like Henry Flagler, whose tracks were forging a trail along Florida's east coast and whose upmarket resorts in St Augustine (see *The Northeast Coast*) were the talk of US socialites, Plant was wealthy enough to turn his fantasies of creating the world's most luxurious hotel into practice. While the *Tampa Bay Hotel* boosted the prestige of the town, Plant's boast to "turn this sandheap into the Champs Elysées, the Hillsborough into the Seine" was never realized, and the hotel stayed open for less than ten years. Neglect (the hotel was only used during the winter months and left to fester during the scorching summer) and Plant's death in 1899, hastened its transformation from the last word in comfort to a pile of musty, crumbling plaster. The city authorities bought the place in 1905 and halted the rot, leasing the building to the fledgling Tampa University 23 years later.

In a wing of the main building, the **Henry B. Plant Museum**, 401 W Kennedy Boulevard (Tues–Sat 10am–4pm, Sun noon–4pm; suggested donation $3), has several rooms containing what's left of the hotel's furnishings: a clutter of Venetian mirrors, elaborate candelabras, ankle-deep rugs, Wedgewood crockery and intricate teak cabinets were the fruits of a half-million-dollar shopping expedition undertaken by Plant and his wife across Europe and Asia. Note the reassembled *Rathskellar*, a gentleman's social room previously in the hotel basement (now a student snack bar, see below), complete with German wine cooler, card and billiard tables; and the final room which reveals Mrs Plant's affection for over-sized ornamental swans.

A few strides from the museum, the former lobby is a popular rendezvous point for the university's two thousand students, who display their tans from the hotel's old wicker chairs surrounded by its antique French statuary. You can roam around much of the building at will, but the details only fall into place on the free **guided tour**, departing from the lobby (Sept–May Tues & Thurs at 1.30pm; call ☎253-3333 for more info). After the tour, call into the *Rathskellar*, which looks nothing like its forebear re-created in the Plant Museum, but has cheap food and serves beer from 4pm.

Hyde Park

If they don't ensconce themselves in a bay-view condo, Tampa's yuppies snap up the old wooden homes of **Hyde Park**, a mile southwest of downtown Tampa just off Bayshore Boulevard. Attracted by the glamour of the newly opened *Tampa Bay Hotel*, well-heeled 1890s arrivals raised several blocks in the architectural modes that defined the wealthier sections of turn-of-the-century American towns: a mishmash of Mediterranean, Gothic, Tudor and Colonial revival jobs, inter-spersed with Queen Anne cottages and prairie-style bungalows – rocking-chair-equipped porches being the sole unifying feature. Such complete blasts from the past are rare in Tampa and, provided you're driving (they don't justify a slog around on foot), the old homes are easy to appreciate on a twenty-minute drive on and around Swann and Magnolia avenues and Hyde Park and South boulevards. Even Tampans who prefer modern living quarters descend on Hyde Park to lay waste to their wages in the fashionable stores of Olde Hyde Park Village, beside Snow Avenue, where several classy restaurants offer affordable refreshment; see "Eating", p.279.

Continuing south from Hyde Park, incidentally, brings you to the gates of **Mac Dill Air Force Base**. This, the nerve centre of US operations during the 1991 Gulf War, was where the Queen knighted General "Stormin' Norman" Schwarzkopf later the same year.

Ybor City

In 1886, as soon as Henry Plant's ships (see above) ensured a regular supply of Havana tobacco into Tampa, cigar magnate Don Vincente Martinez Ybor cleared a patch of scrubland three miles northeast of present-day downtown Tampa and laid the foundations of **Ybor City**. Around 20,000 migrants, mostly Cubans drawn from the strife-ridden Key West cigar industry, joined by a smattering of Spaniards and Italians, settled here, creating an enclave of Latin American life and producing the top-class hand-rolled cigars that made Tampa the "Cigar Capital of the World" for forty years. Mass-production, the popularity of cigarettes and the Depression proved a fatal combination for skilled cigar makers: as unemployment struck, Ybor City lost its *joie de vivre*, and while the rest of Tampa expanded, its twenty tight-knit blocks of cobbled streets and red-brick buildings became surrounded by drab and dangerous low-rent neighbourhoods.

Over the last few years, efforts to mould Ybor City into a tourist attraction have brought improvements and saved many older buildings from dereliction. As yet, visitors are too few to over-commercialize the place: shops still sell hand-rolled cigars, the smells of newly baked Cuban bread and freshly brewed coffee are never far off, and many relics from the eventful past remain. Taking their cue from the craftsmen who created the Spanish ceramics decorating many neighbourhood structures, new faces are beginning to appear, too, opening arts and crafts galleries and helping make Ybor City one of Tampa's trendiest – and most enjoyable – quarters.

Walking around Ybor City

The Latin roots are instantly apparent and explanatory background texts adorn many buildings, but Ybor City's sights are never dramatic and its mood is surprisingly subdued. Take it in by leisurely strolling the ten blocks of **Seventh and Eighth avenues** east of 13th Street: the heart of this individual yet very small community. The **Ybor City State Museum**, 1818 Ninth Avenue (Tues–Sat 9am–5pm; $2), offers just enough to help you grasp the main points of Ybor City's creation and its multi-ethnic make-up. Enormous wall photographs show the cigar rollers at work: thousands sat in long rows at bench-tables on a 25¢-per-cigar piece-work rate, cheering or heckling the *lector* (or reader) who recited the news from Spanish-language newspapers. Standing in the grounds, a cigar-worker's cottage, which you can enter, is more worthy than riveting, demonstrating the unelaborate turn-of-the-century domestic arrangements. The museum also organizes free **walking tours** around Ybor City from Ybor Square (see below) at 10.30am on Thursday and Saturday (call ☎247-6323 for more info).

There's more activity in the factory where the cigar-rolling actually took place, now called **Ybor Square**, 1901 13th Street (Mon–Sat 10am–6pm, Sun noon–5.30pm). This cavernous structure – three storeys supported by sturdy oak pillars – has been converted into a collection of tourist-aimed shops and restaurants, and a peek inside will complement the museum's photo. You should also pause at one of the snack bars for an invigorating Cuban coffee and perhaps even purchase a hand-rolled cigar from *Tampa Rico* on the first floor.

Standing on the factory's iron steps in 1893, the famed Cuban poet and independence fighter José Martí spoke to thousands of Ybor City's Cubans, calling for pledges of money, machetes and manpower for the country's anti-Spanish pro-independence struggles*. It's estimated that expatriate Cuban cigar workers contributed ten percent of their earnings, most of which was spent on the illicit purchase and shipment of arms to rebels in Cuba. A stone marker at the foot of the steps records the event and, across the street, the **José Martí Park** remembers Martí with a statue.

From the earliest days, each of Ybor City's ethnic communities ran its own social clubs, published newspapers and even organized a medical insurance scheme which led to the building of two hospitals. The hospitals still function today, as do several of the social centres. Stepping inside one of the centres (opening hours vary wildly) reveals patriotic paraphernalia and sometimes, in the basement, men-only dens of dominoes and drinking: if you can, call into *Centro*

---

*A few years after Martí's speech, Tampa became the embarkation point for the US's Cuban Expeditionary Forces, with thousands of US soldiers housed in tents waiting to join the Spanish-American War. On January 1, 1899, the Spanish pulled out of Cuba, along with the US – not without retaining a lot of power and influence – and Cuba acquired its independence.

Español, at 1526 E Seventh Ave, *The Cuban Club*, 2010 Avenida Republica de Cuba N, or *Centro Asturiano*, 1913 N Nebraska Avenue, for a look at Ybor City life that most visitors miss. One Ybor City institution out-of-towners invariably do find is the *Columbia* restaurant, 2117 Seventh Avenue (see "Eating", p.279). Now filling a whole block, the *Columbia* opened in 1905 as a humble coffee stop for tobacco workers; inside, wall-lining newspaper cuttings recount its rise and rise.

Around Tampa

The collar of suburbia around downtown Tampa contains few reasons to stop. Hereabouts, though, the city's least expensive motels cluster around a theme park – **Busch Gardens** – ranking among the state's top tourist attractions. While as enjoyable as any of its ilk, you might be inclined to skip the park and divide your attentions between the **Museum of Science and Industry** and (provided you're driving; it's unreachable by public transport) the 3000 pristine acres of the **Hillsborough River State Park**. On the way, don't be tempted by the Seminole Indian Village (5221 N Orient Road), part of a Seminole reservation where a token collection of native American arts and crafts is on sale to tourists and high-stakes bingo is played.

Busch Gardens

Incredible as it may seem, most people are drawn to Tampa by a theme park re-creation of colonial-era Africa in the grounds of a brewery, at 3000 E Busch Boulevard. In glossing over the questionable tarting up of a period of imperial exploitation in the name of entertainment – and the garden's subtitle, "The Dark Continent", which caused justifiable outrage within the local black community – **Busch Gardens** (daily 9am–6.30pm; longer hours in high season; adults $32.50, children $28) brazenly reshapes world history just as much as its arch rival, Walt Disney World. It costs a packet and is as tacky as hell, but if you do come you'll need to stick around all day to get your money's worth, go on everything in the park (all the rides are included in the admission fee) – and learn to love the kitsch without dwelling on its implications.

Traversable on foot or by pseudo-steam train, the 300-acre gardens divide into several areas. You'll first enter *Morocco*, where Moroccan crafts are sold at un-Moroccan prices, snake-charmers and belly dancers weave through the crowds, and the Mystick Sheiks Marching Band blast their trumpets into the ears of passers-by. Then comes the *Myombe Reserve*, where a collection of chimps and gorillas are kept in a tropical environment. Follow the signs to *Nairobi* and you'll find small gatherings of elephants, giant tortoises, alligators, crocodiles and monkeys in varying states of liveliness, and the animal hospital and children's zoo inhabited by cute, cuddly creatures that are happy to be stroked by kids. Directly ahead in *Timbuktu*, animals are less in evidence than amusements; a small roller-coaster and a children's fairground ride called "Sandstorm", neither of which is a patch on "Kumba" (see below). If the Ubanga-Banga bumper cars in the *Congo* don't hold lasting appeal, gird your loins for the swirling raft trip around the Congo River Rapids – which may encourage you to cross Stanleyville Falls on a roller-coaster, the best feature of neighbouring *Stanleyville*. Whatever you do, don't miss the devastating "Kumba", the largest and fastest roller-coaster in the southeastern US. The biggest single section of the gardens, the *Serengeti Plain*, roamed by giraffes, buffalos, zebras, antelopes, black rhino and elephants, is the closest the place gets to showing anything genuinely African; see the beasts from the all-too-brief monorail ride. After all this, retire to the *Hospitality House* of the **Anheuser-Busch Brewery,** purveyors of *Budweiser* to the masses and owners of the park, where the beer is free but limited to two drinks (in a paper cup) per person.

The Museum of Science and Industry

Two miles northeast of Busch Gardens, at 4801 E Fowler Avenue, the **Museum of Science and Industry** (daily 9am until late afternoon – closing hours are seasonal; ☎987-6100; $8) will entertain adults as much as kids. Intended to reveal the mysteries of the scientific world, the hands-on displays and machines are hard to resist and will easily fill half a day.

To get the most from your visit, study the programme schedule carefully on arrival: the main (and most interesting) features run at fixed times throughout the day. Plan your time around the *Challenger Learning Center* (an engrossing simulated space craft and mission control); the *Gulf Coast Hurricane* (a convincing demonstration, allowing begoggled participants to feel the force of the strongest winds known); *Energy Pinball* (a massive walk-through pinball machine that lets you follow the ball along 700 feet of track); the *Saunders Planetarium*, and, for an extra $6 (or do better by buying a combo ticket for $11 on arrival at the museum) the unmissable MOSIMAX, Florida's first IMAX (or "maximum image") film theatre in a dome, which shows films of outstanding visual clarity and sound quality.

Hillsborough River State Park

Twelve miles north of Tampa on Hwy-301, shaded by live oaks, magnolias and sable palms, the **Hillsborough River State Park** (daily 8am–sunset; cars $3.25, pedestrians and cyclists $1) holds one of the state's rare instances of rapids – outside of a theme park – as the Hillsborough River tumbles over limestone outcrops before pursuing a more typical meandering course. Rambling the sizeable park's walking trails and canoeing the gentler sections of the river could nicely fill a day (and the park makes an enjoyable **camping** place; ☎986-1020; $13 to pitch a tent), but on a Saturday or Sunday you should devote part of the afternoon to the **Fort Foster Historic Site**, a reconstructed 1836 Seminole War fort only viewable with the **guided tour** (departures from the park entrance on Sat, Sun & major holidays only, 9–11am & 1–4pm; $1.75). Stemming from the US attempts to drive Florida's Seminole Indians out to reservations in the Midwest and make the state fit for the white man, the Seminole Wars raged throughout the nineteenth century and didn't end officially until 1937. Period-attired enthusiasts occupy the fort and recount historical details, not least the fact that more

---

CANOEING ON THE HILLSBOROUGH RIVER

To spend a half or whole day gliding past the alligators, turtles, wading birds and other creatures who call the Hillsborough River home, contact *Canoe Escape*, 9335 E Fowler Avenue (☎1-800/448-2672), who have devised a series of novice-friendly routes along the tea-coloured river. Cost is $24 for two people for two hours, including instruction (extra person; $8), and you should make a reservation at least 72 hours in advance.

soldiers died from tropical diseases than in battle; over the river, the occupants of the Seminole camp unfurl a somewhat different account of the conflict: both sides make interesting listening.

Eating

Choice and quality are features of Tampa **eating** with the exception of **downtown Tampa**, where street stands dispensing snacks to lunching office workers are the culinary norm. Nonetheless, *Ole Style Deli*, 110 E Madison Street (☎223-4282) is a likely venue for a breakfast of a good sandwich or salad; *Gladstone's Grilled Chicken*, 502 Tampa Street (☎221-2988), serves poultry like you've never tasted it before; and at *Café Pepé*, 2006 W Kennedy Boulevard (☎253-6501), a Tampa landmark for years, you can enjoy favourites such as *filete salteado* and *paella*. On a tour around the *Tampa Bay Hotel* (see p.274), drop into the student-patronized *Rathskellar* for a cheap, light meal.

There's more choice elsewhere. In and around **Hyde Park**, budget breakfasts are found at *Café DeSoto*, 504 E Kennedy Boulevard (☎229-2566), located between downtown and Hyde Park. Look out also for their Cuban lunch specials, such as roast chicken, black beans, rice and Cuban bread for only $3.95. For lunch or dinner, *J. B. Winberie's*, 1610 W Swann Avenue (☎253-6500), serves healthy fish and salad dishes; take a table on the sidewalk and watch Hyde Parkers shop. *Ho Ho Chinois*, 720 Howard Avenue (☎254-9557), lays out a sizeable Chinese lunch buffet; and the *Cactus Club*, 2413 Bayshore Boulevard, located at 1604 Snow Avenue (☎254-1111), offers succulent hickory-smoked ribs, huge salads and excellent burgers.

In **Ybor City**, the *Café Creole & Oyster Bar*, 1330 E Ninth Avenue (☎876-7836), excels in spicy Cajun dishes, best value of which is the filling gumbo seafood soup; there's also live Bourbon Street jazz on Friday and Saturdays nights. *Carmine's*, 1802 Seventh Avenue (☎298-3126), provides Spanish and Italian food in an atmospheric setting, with live music on weekends. The *Silver Ring*, 1831 E Seventh Avenue (☎248-2549), has been serving simple but authentic Cuban sandwiches for nearly fifty years; the *Columbia*, 2117 E Seventh Avenue (☎248-4961), has been going even longer, with refined Spanish and Cuban food that's become a fixture on the tourist circuit (see "Ybor City", p.275) – its eleven rooms hold nearly 2000 people, entertained six nights a week by spirited flamenco dancers. *Frankie's Patio*, 1920 E Seventh Avenue (☎248-3337) is Ybor City's only rooftop open-air bar, serving inexpensive and imaginative American variations. For something out of the ordinary, head for *El Sol de Cuba*, 3101 N Armenia Avenue (☎872-9880), whose combination Chinese/Cuban ("Chino-Latino") cuisine is served up in huge portions at bargain-basement prices.

Nightlife

Tampa **at night** has always been strong on drinking and live rock music; of late, the cultural profile has been raised with regular high-quality shows in a state-of-the-art performance venue. For details of forthcoming arts and cultural events, phone the *Artsline* on ☎229-ARTS; general nightlife listings are available for free on the *Nightlife* line ☎854-8000 (use your touch-tone phone to access details on comedy clubs, sports bars, local bands and more). For **tickets** to any major event, call *Ticketmaster*, ☎287-8844.

Drinking

Many live music venues and nightclubs (see below) have tempting **drink** reductions, though the most cost-effective way to booze, as ever, is at the **happy hours** taking place all over the city – just watch for the signs. For later drinking, head to Ybor City for the *Irish Pub*, 1721 E Seventh Avenue (☎248-2099), or the Gothic-inspired *Castle*, at the corner of Ninth Avenue and 15th Street (☎247-7547). If you like to yell at TV sport shows after downing a few, sample the city's biggest **sports bars**: *Sidelines Sports Emporium*, 11425 N Dale Mabry Highway (☎960-2398), *Grand Slam* at the *Sheraton Grand Hotel* (☎286-4400), and *Baker's Billiards*, 1811 N Tampa Street (☎226-6541), which has 14 full-sized pool tables.

Live music, nightclubs and the performing arts

The *Weekly Planet* and the Friday edition of the *Tampa Tribune* (see "Information", p.271 and the *Nightlife* line, see above) have **live music** listings. Tampa's most dependable club is the blues- and reggae-dominated *Skipper's Smokehouse*, 910 Skipper Road (☎971-0666). Overall, though, it's no-nonsense hard rock that keeps Tampa jumping into the small hours: *Killans Lounge*, 4235 W Waters Avenue (☎884-8965), and *Kasey's Cove*, 2025 E Fowler Avenue (☎977-2683), are the places to hear it. Another place to hear live music – often featuring cult indie bands – is the *Ritz*, see below.

Of a bunch of average **nightclubs** (for a full list, call *Nightlife*, see above), with varying drink specials, karaoke singalongs and theme nights, the *Green Iguana*, 4029 S Westshore Boulevard (☎837-1234), and *Hammerjax*, 901 N Franklin Street (☎221-JAXX), are the ones to try; cover varies from nothing to $8.

The big names in rock, jazz, funk and soul are becoming frequent visitors to Tampa's **major venues**: the *USF Sun Dome*, 4202 S Fowler Avenue (☎974-3002), and the *Tampa Stadium*, 4201 Dale Mabry Highway (☎872-7977). Another large and ultra-modern auditorium is the *Tampa Bay Performing Arts Center*, 1010 N MacInnes Place (☎221-1045), where **opera**, **classical music** and **ballet** programmes feature the top US and international names. Ticket prices for big shows range from $10 to $45.

Oddly, given the weight placed on promoting the arts, the city has just one purpose-built **theatre**: the *Ritz*, 1503 E Seventh Avenue, in Ybor City (☎247-PLAY), whose two stages see a mix of fringe and bigger-budget mainstream productions, as well as live music (see above).

Film, comedy clubs and poetry readings

For a full list of **films** playing around the city, read the Friday edition of the *Tampa Tribune*. Foreign-language, classic or cult films crop up only at the *Tampa Theatre*, 711 Franklin Street (see "Downtown Tampa", p.272); pick up a schedule from the building itself or phone the 24-hour information line: ☎223-8981; tickets are $5. Tampa has one notable **comedy club**: *Comedy Works*, 3447 W Kennedy Boulevard (☎875-9129), where the cover charge is $4–12. If it's Thursday, forsake the gags and get stuck into the **poetry readings** at the "Thirsty Ear Poetry Series" at the *Trolley Stop*, 1327 E Seventh Avenue (☎237-6302), a hangout for Tampa's coffee-drinking literary crowd.

Gay and lesbian Tampa

Gay and lesbian life in Tampa is improving all the time, with constant additions to a number of established bars, clubs and resource centres. Get general information by calling *The Line* (☎247-2006), the *Gay Information Service* (☎586-4297), or the *Gay and Lesbian Community Center* (☎273-8919). You can also pick up useful information from *Encounter Magazine*, published in Tampa twice a month and available free in all gay and lesbian bars.

Bars, clubs and restaurants

Easily the most popular, and most enjoyable, **nightspot** is *Tracks/El Goya*, at 1430 E Seventh Avenue in Ybor City (☎247-2711), a predominantly gay-male disco with state-of-the-art lighting and cutting-edge sounds. Of the exclusively or mainly **gay male bars**, *City Side*, 3810 Neptune Street (☎254-6466), and *Twenty Six-O-Six*, 2606 N Armenia Avenue (☎875-6993), are cruisey watering holes. Primarily geared towards lesbians is *The Cherokee Club*, 1320 E Ninth Avenue (☎247-9966). Enjoyable **mixed bars and clubs** include; *The Parthenon*, 802 E Whiting Street, and *Paradise*, 14802 N Nebraska Avenue (☎971-2132).

Listings

Airport Five miles northwest of downtown Tampa (☎870-8700); reach it with local bus #30, see "Arrival, information and transport".

Dentists For referral: ☎886-9040.

Doctor For referral: ☎870-4444.

Left luggage At the *Greyhound* station, 610 Polk Street; the train station, 601 Nebraska Avenue; and at the airport.

Local bus information ☎254-4278.

Pharmacy *Eckerd Drugs*, 11613 N Nebraska Avenue (☎978-0775), is open around the clock.

Police Emergencies ☎911. To report something lost or stolen: ☎223-1515.

Sport The city's professional football team, *Tampa Bay Buccaneers*, play at Tampa Stadium, 4201 Dale Mabry Highway (box office and match details: ☎879-BUCS); cheapest tickets are $15–35. Tampa's soccer team, the *Rowdies* (☎877-7800), play outdoor matches at Tampa Stadium and indoors at the Bayfront Center in St Petersburg, 400 First Street; tickets are $8–50.

Taxis Main operators are *United* (☎253-2424) and *Yellow* (☎253-8871).

Thomas Cook Nearest branch is in St Petersburg: Paragon Crossing, 11300 Fourth Street North (☎577-6556).

Ticketmaster Branches around the city: ☎287-8844.

Weather ☎622-1212.

St Petersburg

Declared the healthiest place in the US in 1885, **ST PETERSBURG**, twenty miles from Tampa on the eastern edge of the Pinellas peninsula, wasted no time in attracting the recuperating and the retired to its paradisiacal climate – at one point putting five thousand green benches on its streets to take the weight of elderly backsides. By the early 1980s, few people under fifty lived in the town (which, incidentally, was named by a homesick Russian), and no one was surprised when it became the setting for the 1985 film *Cocoon*, in which a group of local geriatrics magically regain the vigour of their youth. Right now, St Petersburg seems to be emulating them. The average age of its residents has been almost halved, the revamped pier is a great place for open-air socializing, and – most remarkably of all – the town has acquired the major collection of works by the controversial surrealist artist **Salvador Dalí**: reason enough to be in St Petersburg, if only as a day's break from the beaches nine miles west on the Gulf coast (see "The St Petersburg beaches", p.285).

Arrival, information and accommodation

The main route **by car** into St Petersburg is I-275; don't leave it before the "Downtown St Petersburg" exit or you'll face interminable traffic lights. The *Greyhound* **bus** station is centrally located at 180 Ninth Street (☎1-800/231-2222). There are no trains between Tampa and St Petersburg, just a twice-daily *Amtrak* bus link (☎221-7600 or 1-800/872-7245). You can reach the St Petersburg beaches with **local buses** (PSTA; ☎530-9911), though these are not always direct – see the "Buses between St Petersburg and the beaches" box on p.286. Most services arrive and depart from the Williams Park terminal, at the junction of First Avenue N and Third Street N, where an information booth gives route details.

Gather the usual tourist **information** and discount coupons from the **Chamber of Commerce**, 100 Second Avenue N (Mon–Fri 8.30am–5pm; ☎821-4715), and look out for the "Weekend" section of the *St Petersburg Times* for entertainment and nightlife listings. The ground floor of the pier – see below – also has a well-stocked tourist counter.

Accommodation
Sleeping in St Petersburg can be less costly than doing so at the beaches. The *St Petersburg International Youth Hostel*, in the historic *McCarthy Hotel*, at 326 First Avenue N (☎822-4141), charges $10 for members, $15 for others; single and double rooms are also available from $32. **Motels** are plentiful and can be inexpensive – up to $39 all year round. Of dozens along Fourth Street, the closest to the centre are *The Banyan Tree* no. 610 N; (☎822-7072; ①–②), *Landmark* no. 1930 (☎895-1629; ①–②), and *Kentucky* no. 4246 (☎526-7373; ①–②).

The town

To get your bearings of downtown St Petersburg, you might wish to undertake a a self-guided **walking tour** around the area's historic buildings; pick up the *St Petersburg Preservation Program* brochure at the Chamber of Commerce (see above) and use the *Central Business District* map enclosed in it. Alternatively, you might be lucky enough to find a copy of the (discontinued) *Historic Downtown Walking Tour* brochure, which gives in-depth information about the various sites. Not all of the old buildings listed are much to look at, but at least walk along **Fourth Avenue**, passing the grandstands of the **Shuffleboard Club**, no. 536 N, spiritual home of this amazingly popular sport, and, directly across Fourth Avenue N, the Mediterranean Revival facade of the **Coliseum Ballroom**, built in 1924 and still throbbing to big band sounds – see "Nightlife", p.285. If the wide streets of downtown St Petersburg (around the junction of Central Avenue and Fourth Street) seem deserted, this is because everyone gravitates to the quarter-mile-long **pier** jutting from the end of Second Avenue N, a few minutes' walk east. Browsable arts and crafts exhibitions often line the pier, and you'll find stacks of tourist information at the Chamber of Commerce desk (Mon–Sat 10am–8pm, Sun 11am–6pm; ☎821-6164), by the entrance to the inverted-pyramid-like building, whose five storeys are packed with restaurants, shops, fast-food counters and an aquarium.

Around the pier: the Museum of History

Opposite the entrance to the pier is the **Museum of History**, 335 Second Avenue NE (Mon–Sat 10am–5pm, Sun 1–5pm; $4.50). Modest displays recount St Petersburg's early twentieth-century heyday as a winter resort (which lasted until the wider and sandier Gulf coast beaches became accessible), and the inaugural flight of the world's first commercial airline, which took off from St Petersburg in 1914. There's documentation, too, on Weedon Island, five miles north of the town and once the base of a small film industry. Significant pottery finds were unearthed from Native American burial mounds here, until they were ransacked by looters in the 1960s. Now a state-protected wildlife refuge, the island is mostly used for fishing and doesn't merit a visit for any other purpose.

The Museum of Fine Arts

One block west of the pier, a group of Mediterranean Revival buildings houses the **Museum of Fine Arts** at 255 Beach Drive NE (Tues–Sat 10am–5pm, Sun 1–5pm; donation $5; regular free guided tours). For years this has been one of the state's better art collections; now, however, given the giant strides made by other, newer museums and the new rival Dalí Museum (see below), it looks increasingly outmoded.

Inside, the works of seventeenth-century art are competent rather than imposing, though Monet's *Houses of Parliament* and Daumier's amusing *Connoisseur of Prints* are two that shine. Also on display are pre-Columbian pieces, plus ceramics, glasswork and antiquities from Europe and Asia. More inspiring is the section on modern European art, featuring drawings by Kandinsky; and the American contemporary room displays some of Georgia O'Keeffe's flowers, as well as George Luks' simple and emotive *The Musician*.

Florida International Museum

A short walk south of the Museum of Fine Arts is the imposing **Florida International Museum**, 100 Second Street N (daily during exhibition periods only, 9am–6pm; $14.50; tickets and info on ☎1-800/777-9882), which encompasses an entire block. Taking its inspiration from abroad, the museum opened in 1995, with the first of its exhibitions, "Treasures of the Czars", containing works from the Moscow Kremlin museums. It's certainly worth investigating what's on here, as the exhibitions, which last for about a year at a time, are grand in scale and often sumptuous. To gain entry (and to ensure an easy flow of people around the museum), you must book ahead on the number given above.

The Dalí Museum and Great Explorations

Few places make a less likely depository for the biggest collection of works by maverick artist Salvador Dalí than St Petersburg, but this is exactly what's on show at the **Salvador Dalí Museum**, 1000 S Third Street (Mon–Sat 9.30am–5.30pm, Sun noon–5.30pm; $6), a mile and a half south of the pier. It stores more than a thousand Dalí works from the collection of a Cleveland industrialist who struck up a friendship with the artist in the Forties, bought stacks of his works and ran out of space to show them – until this purpose-built gallery opened in 1982.

Hook up with the **free tours**, which begin whenever sufficient people are mustered. These trace a fact-filled path around the chronologically arranged paintings (some shown on rotation), from early experiments with Impressionism and Cubism to the soft watches of the seminal surrealist canvas, *Persistence of Memory*, and on to works from Dalí's "Classic" period, from 1943, which grapple with the fundamentals of religion, science and history. Some – such as the overwhelming *Discovery of America by Christopher Columbus*, and the multiple double-images of the *Hallucinogenic Toreador* – are so big they have been hung in a specially deepened section of the gallery.

Dalí never visited the museum, though if he had it's easy to imagine him nipping across the street to explore the hands-on exhibits of **Great Explorations**, 1120 Fourth Street S (Mon–Sat 10am–5pm, Sun noon–5pm; $5), which, like Tampa's much larger Museum of Science and Industry, strives to make the rudiments of science accessible with inventive games. The technology of fun includes bubbles that can be climbed inside, an elaborate test-your-fitness display, and a chance to feel your way through a pitch-black tunnel.

The Sunken Gardens

If you've had your fill of culture, head for the **Sunken Gardens**, 1825 Fourth Street (daily 10am–5pm; $14), a mile north of the pier. Nearly seventy years ago, a water-filled sinkhole here was drained and planted with thousands of tropical plants and trees, which now form the shady and sweet-scented gardens. For a crash-course in exotic botany, scrutinize the texts along the pathway that descends gently through bougainvillea, hibiscus and staghead ferns. Only the parrot shows and the depressingly small cages housing some of the resident animals dim an hour's unhurried pleasure.

Eating

The Eating Place, 320 First Avenue NE (☎894-3496), is the top spot for filling **breakfasts** and **lunches**, closely rivalled by the very basic *Gold Coffee Shop*, 336 First Avenue (☎822-4922), and *A.J.'s Deli Café* at the Plaza on 111 Second Avenue NE, Suite 106 (☎821-4151), where you can sample some of the most innovative omelettes in town. For an excellent and inexpensive seafood lunch or **dinner**, head for *The Shrimp Store*, 1006 Fourth Street N (☎822-0325), or *Ted Peters' Famous Smoked Fish*, 1350 Pasadena Avenue (☎381-7931), where you can indulge in hot smoked-fish dinners with all the trimmings. Best of all is *The Chattaway*, 358 22nd Avenue (☎823-1594), a one-time grocery store, filling station and trolley

---

THE PINELLAS TRAIL

If you're looking for an intriguing alternative to the usual beach-hopping progress of tourists up or down the coast, take the **Pinellas Trail,** a 34-mile hiking/cycling track that runs between St Petersburg and Tarpon Springs. You can pick up a free, informative and highly portable guide to the trail at any of the Chambers of Commerce or visitor centers between these two destinations. The guide describes the route and picks out points of interest, providing easy-to-manage maps of sections of its inland course. Numerous exit and entry points encourage a leisurely approach, so allow yourself time to meander off the well-marked confines of the trail, and if you don't feel inclined to tackle its entirety, you can take a bus or drive to various pre-selected areas for day excursions. Despite some uglier sections through urban centres (tricky on a bike) the trail offers enjoyable scenery along its rural portions and a chance for contemplation away from tanning and watersports.

stop that's now a great American diner; try the "Chattaburger" with all the trimmings, and the coldest draft beer in St Petersburg. At the pier you'll find a number of acceptable fast-food stands: the more salubrious *Cha Cha Coconuts* (☎822-6655), whose Caribbean dishes are accompanied by tall, frosty island drinks and live entertainment; and the *Columbia* (☎822-8000), providing high-quality Cuban and Spanish food for $10–15.

Nightlife

If you're at the pier, start the evening in *Alessi's* (☎894-1133), whose weekday **happy hour** lasts from noon to 7pm, then go up to roof level to hear the free band playing at *Cha Cha Coconut's* (☎822-6655) – the cool ocean breeze and St Petersburg skyline making the lightweight rock sounds palatable. Elsewhere, a steady procession of **rock** bands appear at *Club Detroit*, 16 Second Street N (☎896-1244), and *The Big Catch*, 9 NE First Street (☎821-6444). For an evening with a difference, turn up with your own booze (there's no bar) at the *Coliseum Ballroom*, 535 Fourth Avenue (☎892-5202), a **big band** venue for decades, which boasts one of the biggest dance floors in the US; weekend cover is $9, less during the week, and $4 for the tea dance. If you're a **jazz** fan, try *The Silver King Tavern*, 1114 Central Avenue (☎821-6470); **country**-music enthusiasts should head for *The Bull Pen Lounge*, 3510 34th Street N (☎526-3366).

The St Petersburg beaches

The drab suburbs stretching west from St Petersburg cover virtually all of the Pinellas peninsula, a bulky thumb of land poking between Tampa Bay and the Gulf of Mexico. Framing the Gulf side of the peninsula, a 25-mile chain of barrier islands form the **St Petersburg beaches***, one of Florida's busiest coastal strips. When the famed resorts of Miami Beach lost their allure during the Seventies, the St Petersburg beaches grew in popularity with Americans. More recently they've become a major destination for package-holidaying Europeans – English accents and the *Daily Mirror* are commonplace. The sands are broad and beautiful, the sea is warm and the sunsets are fabulous – but in no way is this Florida at its best. Despite that, staying here can be very cost-effective (especially during the summer); a few of the islands have been kept in their pre-tourism state and deserve exploration; and it's quite feasible to combine lazing on the beach with daytrips to the more interesting inland areas.

Information

Several beach areas have **Chambers of Commerce** readily dispensing handy information: St Petersburg Beach, 6990 Gulf Boulevard (Mon-Fri 9am–5pm; ☎360-6957); Treasure Island, 152 108th Avenue (Mon–Fri 8am–4.30pm; ☎367-4529); Madeira Beach, 501 150th Avenue (Mon–Fri 9am–5pm; ☎391-7373). In

A convenient name in the absence of an official collective title; each beach area has a name of its own, though you're likely to hear them branded "the Holiday Isles", or the "Pinellas County Suncoast".

BUSES BETWEEN ST PETERSBURG AND THE BEACHES

From the Williams Park terminal in St Petersburg, take PSTA bus #12, #29 or #35 to the Palms of Pasadena Hospital stop, just off Gulf Boulevard, where *Bats* buses (☎367-3086) cross the Corey Causeway **to St Petersburg Beach and Pass-a-Grille** (Mon–Sat 7.15am–5.50pm, Sun & holidays 7.45am–5.50pm). PSTA bus #3 from the Williams Park terminal runs to the junction of Central Avenue and Park Street, where the *Treasure Island Transit* (☎360-0811) continues **to Treasure Island**, plying Gulf Boulevard between 79th and 125th avenues (hourly Mon–Sat 8.15am–4.15pm except 12.15pm; $1 one way). There's a direct connection from Williams Park **to Madeira Beach and Indian Shores** with #71, and **to Clearwater** with #18 and #52, from where #80 continues **to Clearwater Beach**. PSTA bus fares cost $1.50 one way; transfers are free. For further transport details, see "Buses and boats around Clearwater Beach", p.289.

Clearwater Beach, call at the **Welcome Center**, 40 Memorial Causeway (Mon–Fri 9am–5pm; ☎446-2424). At any of the above, and in shops, restaurants and motels, look for **free magazines** such as the *St Petersburg Official Visitors Guide* and *See St Pete and Beaches*; if you want the latest nightlife listings, buy the Friday edition of the *St Petersburg Times*.

Accommodation

With the exception of camping, you're spoilt for choice when seeking **somewhere to sleep** around the beaches. **Hotels** are plentiful but tend to be filled with package tourists and pricier than motels; two unusual but expensive options are the luxurious *Don Cesar*, 3400 Gulf Boulevard (☎360-1881; ⑦), described on p.287, or the fetchingly restored *Clearwater Beach Hotel*, 500 Mandalay Avenue (☎441-2425; ⑦).

Better value is represented by the **motels** that line mile after mile of Gulf Boulevard and the neighbouring streets – typically $40–55 in winter, $10–15 less during the summer, though if you're staying long enough, many offer discounted weekly rates. Some have only a few standard rooms and will offer **self catering** accommodation for $5–10 above the basic room rate. Remember, too, that a room on the beach side of Gulf Boulevard costs $5–10 more than an identical room on the inland side.

Lack of competition causes prices in **Pass-a-Grille** to be around $10 higher than you might pay a few miles north, but the district makes an excellent base. Try the *Pass-a-Grille Beach Motel*, 709 Gulf Way (☎1-800/544-4184; ④), or, for a lengthy stay, opt for the cottages at *Gamble's Island's End Resort*, 1 Pass-a-Grille (☎360-5023; ⑤). For the best deals in **St Petersburg Beach**, check out *Blue Horizon*, 3145 Second Street W (☎360-3946; ④); *Carlton House*, 633 71st Avenue (☎367-4128; ④); *Florida Dolphin*, 6801 Sunset Way (☎360-7233; ④); *Gulf Tides Motel*, 600 68th Avenue (☎367-2979; ④); or the *Ritz*, 4237 Gulf Boulevard (☎360-7642; ④).

Further north on **Treasure Island**, try *Beach House*, 12100 Gulf Boulevard (☎360-1153; ④); *Green Gables*, 11160 Gulf Boulevard (☎360-0206; ③); *Jolly Roger*, 11525 Gulf Boulevard (☎360-5571; ④); or *Sunrise*, 9360 Gulf Boulevard (☎360-9210; ④). In **Madeira Beach**, choose from *Beach Plaza*, 14560 Gulf Boulevard (☎391-8996; ④); *Gulf Stream*, 13007 Gulf Boulevard (☎391-2002; ④); or *Skyline*, 13999 Gulf Boulevard (☎391-5817; ④).

In **Clearwater Beach**, the lowest rates are with *Bay Lawn*, 406 Hamden Drive
(☎443-4529; ④); *Cyprus Motel Apts*, 609 Cyprus Avenue (☎442-3304; ④); *Gulf
Beach*, 419 Coronado Drive (☎447-3236; ④), and *Olympia Motel*, 423 E Shore
Drive (☎446-3384; ④). Although savings over a motel room may be slim,
Clearwater Beach also offers a **youth hostel**, at the *Sands Motel*, 606 Bay
Esplanade (☎443-1211), with beds for $12.

Camping
There are no **campgrounds** along the main beach strip, though the nearest and
nicest spot, at Fort DeSoto Park (see p.288; ☎866-2662), is adjacent to sand and
sea. The alternatives are inland: *St Petersburg KOA*, 5400 95th Street W (☎1-800/
848-1094), five miles east of Madeira Beach; *Clearwater/Tarpon Springs KOA*,
37061 Hwy-19 N (☎937-8412), six miles north of Clearwater, is handier for
Clearwater Beach and surrounds – though neither site is much use without
private transport (both charge $16.50 to pitch a tent).

The southern beaches

In twenty or so miles of heavily touristed coast, just one section has the looks and
feel of a genuine community: the slender finger of **PASS-A-GRILLE**, at the very
southern tip of the barrier island chain. One of the first beach communities on
the West Coast, settled by fishermen in 1911, modern Pass-a-Grille comprises
two miles of tidy houses, well-kempt lawns, small shops and a cluster of bars and
restaurants. On weekends, informed locals come to Pass-a-Grille's beach to enjoy
one of the area's liveliest set of sands and unobstructed views of the tiny islands
that dot the entrance to Tampa Bay. There is no bus service to Pass-a-Grille; your
best bet is to take a bus to St Petersburg Beach (see p.286) and then a cab, or
hire a bike.

A mile and a half north of Pass-a-Grille, at St Petersburg Beach, you won't need
a signpost to locate the **Don Cesar Hotel**, 3400 Gulf Boulevard (free guided tours
Fri 11.30am; details on ☎360-1881), a grandiose pink castle with white-trimmed
arched windows and vaguely Moorish turrets, rising above Gulf Boulevard and filling seven beachside acres. Conceived by a Twenties property speculator, Thomas
J Rowe, the *Don Cesar* opened in 1928, but its glamour was short-lived. The
Depression forced Rowe to use part of the hotel as a warehouse, and later drove
him to allow the uncouth New York Yankees baseball team to make it their spring
training base. After decades as a military hospital and then as federal offices, the
building received a $1- million face-lift during the Seventies, and regained its hotel
function – a vacation base for anyone with upwards of $150 a night to spare. The
present interior bears little resemblance to its original appearance, but you should
stride past the marble columns and crystal chandeliers of the lobby into the
lounge, where you can soak up the understated elegance from the depths of a sofa
or, just outside, from the poolside – often in demand as a film set and used as a
location for much of Robert Altman's satirical film *Health*.

Just beyond the *Don Cesar*, Pinellas County Bayway cuts inland and makes a
good route to take to Fort DeSoto Park (see below). Keeping to Gulf Boulevard
brings you into the main section of **ST PETERSBURG BEACH**, uninspiring
rows of hotels, motels and eating places grouped along Gulf Boulevard and
continuing for several miles. A very short break in the monotony is provided by a
batch of pseudo-English shops around Corey Avenue. Further north,

TREASURE ISLAND is even less varied, culminating in an arching drawbridge that crosses over to **MADEIRA BEACH** and the wood-walled, tin-roofed shops, restaurants and bars of **John's Pass Village**, 12901 Gulf Boulevard. Linked by a creaking boardwalk, the shops and the local fishing and pleasure-cruising fleet moored close by are mildly entertaining if you're at a (very) loose end. Madeira Beach itself is another sleepy place – though if you can't make it to Pass-a-Grille (see above), the local beach justifies a weekend fling.

Four miles north of Madeira Beach, at **INDIAN SHORES**, the **Suncoast Seabird Sanctuary**, 18328 Gulf Boulevard (daily 9am–sunset; donations requested; free guided tours Tues 2pm), offers a break from bronzing. The sanctuary is a respected treatment centre for sick birds: convalescing pelicans, herons, turkey vultures and many other winged creatures bearing the brunt of human incursions into their natural habitat.

Fort DeSoto Park

If you have a car, you can soak up some of the history surrounding the St Petersburg beaches by heading across the Pinellas County Bayway, immediately north of the *Don César*, then turning south along Route 679 to spend a day on the five islands comprising **Fort DeSoto Park** (sunrise–sunset; free). The Spaniard credited with discovering Florida, Ponce de León, is thought to have anchored here in 1513, and again in 1521 when the islands' indigenous inhabitants inflicted on him what proved to be a fatal wound. Centuries later, the islands became a strategically important Union base during the Civil War, and in 1898 a fort was constructed to forestall attacks on Tampa during the Spanish-American War. The remains of the fort – which was never completed – can be explored on one of several **walking trails**, which wind through an impressively untamed, thickly vegetated landscape featuring Australian pines and oaks.

Three miles of swimmer-friendly **beaches** line the park, which in midweek possess an intoxicating air of isolation – a far cry from the busy beach strips. The best way to savour the area is by **camping**, see "Accommodation", p.286.

The northern beaches

Much of the **northern section** of Sand Key, the longest barrier island in the St Petersburg chain, is lined by stylish condos and time-share apartments – this is one of the wealthier portions of the coast. It ends with the pretty **Sand Key Park**, where tall palm trees frame a scintillating strip of sand. The classic beach vista is marred only by the nearby high-rises, which include the *Sheraton Sand Key Resort*; custom at this hotel was given a temporary boost by the calamitous liaison that took place here in 1987 between TV evangelist Jim Bakker and the model Jessica Hahn.

Sand Key Park occupies one bank of Clearwater Pass, across which a belt of sparkling white sands characterize **CLEARWATER BEACH**, yet another community devoted to the holiday industry. Motels fill its side streets and European package tourists are everywhere, but an endearing small-town ambience makes this a pleasant place to spend a couple of days. A crucial plus for non-drivers are the regular bus links between Clearwater Beach and the mainland town of **CLEARWATER** – reached by a two-mile causeway – where you'll find connections to St Petersburg and Tarpon Springs, and a *Greyhound* station (see box opposite).

BUSES AND BOATS AROUND CLEARWATER BEACH

Clearwater Beach is good news for travellers without cars. **Around the beach strip**, the free *Clearwater Beach Trolley* runs half-hourly during the day between Sand Key (from the *Sheraton Sand Key Resort*) and Clearwater Beach (along Gulfview Boulevard, Mandalay Avenue and Acacia Street). **To the mainland**, the cheapest option is the *Jolly Trolley*, which stops at various points along the beach and will take you to downtown Cleawater for 50¢. Alternatively, catch bus #80, which operates between Clearwater Beach and Clearwater's Park Street terminal (info: ☎530-9911). **Useful routes** from the terminal are: #80 to Honeymoon Island; #18 and #52 to St Petersburg; #66 to Tarpon Springs; and #200X (rush hours only) to Tampa. A much less frequent, mainland link is provided by two daily *Amtrak* buses, running from Tampa in lieu of trains; they stop in Clearwater at 657 Court Street, and at Clearwater Beach's Civic Center. The *Greyhound* station in Clearwater is at 2811 Gulf to Bay Boulevard (☎796-7315).

To combine a trip between the Clearwater Beach Marina and Caladesi Island (see below) with a dolphin encounter, take a ride on the *Caladesi Connection* ferry, operating twice daily (at 1am and 1pm, except Monday; $15 return). The same company also runs outings to Tarpon Springs (see "Tarpon Springs") every Tuesday and Thursday; $21.75 one way including lunch, $5 more for the return leg by boat or bus.

Beyond its sands and two long piers, there's not much to do in Clearwater Beach: if the brine beckons, take the two-hour *Captain Memo* "pirate cruise" (leaving at 10am, 2pm, 4.30pm and, April–Sept only, 7pm; $28; ☎446-2587) from the marina just south of the causeway; or, more adventurously, make a daytrip to the Caladesi or Honeymoon islands, a few miles north.

Listed on the national register of historic places and a short trip inland from the intracoastal waterway is the 1897 **Belleview Mido Resort Hotel**, 25 Belleview Boulevard, Clearwater (☎442-6171), a beautiful wooden construction in the grand tradition, sitting high on a bluff and consisting of 145 rooms. Originally owned by the railroad magnate Henry B. Plant, who entertained important shippers and celebrities here, the *Belleview* has been immaculately preserved and is well worth a look inside and out. To best appreciate the place, join one of the **historic tours** (daily 11am; $5, or $13.50 including lunch).

Honeymoon and Caladesi islands

In 1921, a hurricane ripped apart a five-mile-long island directly north of Clearwater Beach to create the aptly named Hurricane Pass and two islands which, now protected state parks (both charging admission of $3.25 per car; $1 pedestrians and cyclists), offer a chance to see the jungle-like terrain that covered the whole coast before the bulldozers arrived. Of the two, only **Honeymoon Island** can be reached by road; take Route 586 off Hwy-19 just north of Dunedin (or bus #80 from Clearwater). The condos that sprout from Honeymoon Island dent its natural impact – maintained in a wild pocket to the end of the road, viewable by a looping foot trail.

For a more authentic experience of untouched Florida make for **Caladesi Island**, just to the south. From a signposted landing stage beside Route 586 on Honeymoon Island, a **ferry** ($4 return) crosses between the islands daily between 10am and 6pm (hours may vary, check on ☎734-1501); Caladesi Island can also be acessed from Clearwater Beach with the *Caladesi Connection* ferry (see box on p.289). Once ashore at Caladesi's mangrove-fringed marina, boardwalks lead to a beach of unsurpassed tranquility: perfect for swimming, sunbathing and shell collecting. While here, though, summon up the strength to tackle the three-mile **nature trail**, which cuts inland through saw palmetto and slash pines to an observation tower. Be certain to bring food and drink to the island; without them, the poorly stocked snack bar at the marina is the sole source of sustenance.

Eating

It's easy to find a decent place to **eat** around the beaches. At 807 Gulf Way, the *Hurricane Restaurant* (☎360-9558; $16.50 to pitch a tent) sports a well-priced menu of the freshest seafood; further north, the *Sea Horse*, 800 Pass-a-Grille (closed Tues; ☎360-1734), is strong on sandwiches; *Pep's Sea Grille*, 5895 Gulf Boulevard (☎367-3550), creates inspired combinations of pasta and seafood; *Debby's*, 7370 Gulf Boulevard (☎367-8700), serves substantial breakfasts and lunches at insubstantial prices; *46th South Beach*, 46 46th Avenue, St Pete's Beach (☎360-9414), offers nightly specials such as the "one-pound you-peel-em shrimp dinner" and Bloody Marys for just $1; and *O'Malley's Bar*, 7745 Blind Pass Way (☎360-2050), grills the thickest, juiciest burgers around. If you're feeling wealthy, and inordinately hungry, on a Sunday, show up in smart attire for the lunchtime **buffet** at the *Don Cesar*, 3400 Gulf Boulevard (☎360-1881), which starts at 10.30am and costs $27 per head.

In Clearwater Beach, *Alex*, 305 Coronado Drive (☎447-4560), and *Coca Cabana Motel*, 669 Mandalay Avenue (☎446-7775), are good for cheap breakfasts; *Frenchy's Shrimp and Oyster Café*, 41 Baymont Street (☎446-3607), cooks up grouper burgers and shrimp sandwiches; *Seafood & Sunsets*, 351 S Gulfview Boulevard (☎441-2548), provides inexpensive seafood, ideally consumed while watching the sun sink. Larger appetites should be sated by the **dinner buffets** for under $10 spread out at the *Hilton Resort*, 715 S Gulfview Boulevard (☎447-9566).

Nightlife

As you'd expect, most **nightlife** is aimed at tourists, though there are exceptions. Many hotel and restaurant bars have lengthy **happy hours** and lounges designed for watching the sunset while sipping a cocktail – look for the signs and ads in the free tourist magazines. For more cut-rate boozing, investigate *Jammins*, 470 Mandalay Avenue (☎441-2005), or the *Beach Bar*, 454 Mandalay Avenue (☎446-8866).

Bland pop bands are two-a-penny in the hotels. For better **live music**, aim for one of the following: the *Hurricane Restaurant*, 807 Gulf Way (☎360-9558), featuring some of the area's top **jazz** musicians; the *Harp and Thistle*, 650 Corey Avenue (☎360-4104), hosting Irish folksters most nights; *Bennigan's*, 4625 Gulf Boulevard (☎367-4521), for the **reggae** bands on Saturday nights. In Clearwater Beach, there's reggae of fluctuating standards at *Cha Cha Coconuts*, 1241 Gulf Boulevard (☎569-6040), and **jazz and blues** at *Zapps*, 138 Island Way (☎449-8282), five nights a week. **Country** music can be heard every night at *Joyland*, 11225 Hwy-19 S (☎573-1919).

North of Clearwater: Tarpon Springs

Greek sponge-divers driven out of Key West by protectionist locals during the early 1900s resettled in **TARPON SPRINGS**, ten miles north of Clearwater off Hwy-19 (buses #19 and #66), the first of what became a sizeable Greek community in a town previously the preserve of wealthy wintering northerners. Demand for sponges was unprecedented during World War II (among other attributes, sponges are excellent for mopping up blood), but later the industry was devastated by a marine blight and the development of synthetic sponges. The Greek presence in Tarpon Springs remains strong, however, and is most evident in January when 40,000 participate in the country's largest Greek Orthodox Epiphany celebration. Each year an even greater number of tourists traipse around the souvenir shops lining the old sponge docks, largely neglecting the rest of the small town which – from restored buildings to weeping icons – has much more to intrigue.

Practicalities

Collect general **information** and a map guide to historical sites and points of interest in downtown from the **Chamber of Commerce** at Suite 120, 11 E Orange Street, opposite the cathedral (Mon–Fri 8.30am–5pm; ☎937-6109). Cheap breakfasts can be found at *Bread and Butter Deli*, 1880 Pinellas Avenue (☎934-9003). In the Arcade at 210 Pinellas Avenue, the *Times Square Deli & Café* (☎934-4026) has sandwiches and snacks to eat in or take away. For a fuller sit-down meal, sample the inexpensive Greek dishes at *Costa's*, 510 Athens Street (☎938-6890), or *Plaka*, 769 Dodecanese Boulevard (☎934-4752), where you can watch them make their own gyro; or try the pricier *Pappas* at 10 W Dodecanese Boulevard (☎937-5101) for fresh seafood and their famous Greek Salad ($5 for two people).

Tarpon Springs makes a sensible **overnight stop** if you're continuing north. A number of motels dot the junctions with Hwy-19; more central are *Scottish Inn*, 110 Tarpon Avenue (☎937-6121; ②); *Sunbay Motel*, 57 W Tarpon Avenue (☎934-1001; ②); and *Gulf Manor Motel*, 548 Whitcomb Boulevard (☎937-4207; ③), in a beautiful setting overlooking the Bayou.

The town

Symbols of the Greek community fill Tarpon Springs, by far the strongest being the resplendent Byzantine Revival **St Nicholas Orthodox Cathedral**, on the corner of Pinellas Avenue and Orange Street (daily 8am–4pm; free), partly funded by a half-percent levy on local sponge sales and finished in 1943. The full significance of the cathedral's ornate interior is inevitably lost on those not of the faith, though the icons and slow-burning incense create an intensely spiritual atmosphere.

After leaving the cathedral, drop into the nearby **Tarpon Springs Cultural Center**, 101 S Pinellas Avenue (Mon–Fri 8am–5pm, Sat 10am–5pm; free except for special events), which regularly stages imaginative exhibitions about Tarpon Springs' past and present as well as art exhibitions. This Neoclassical building served as the city hall from 1915, a period when Tarpon Avenue, a street away, was a bustling commercial strip: butchers, bakers and grocers plied their trade from stumpy masonry structures, many of which still stand, several converted into curio-filled antique shops – good enough for a half-hour amble.

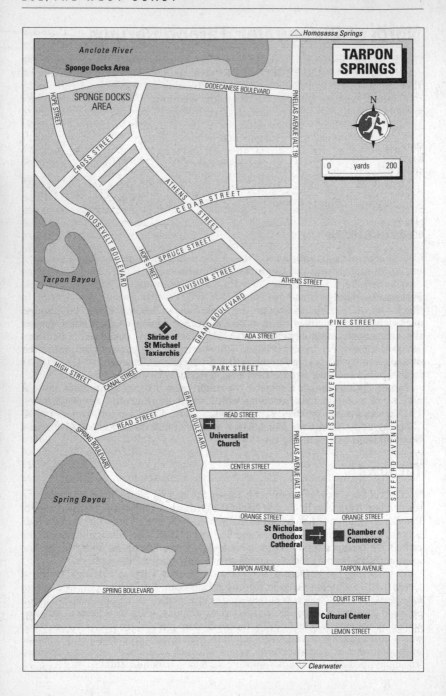

Homosassa Springs

TARPON SPRINGS

Anclote River

Sponge Docks Area

DODECANESE BOULEVARD

SPONGE DOCKS AREA

N

0   yards   200

HOPE STREET

CROSS STREET

ATHENS STREET

CEDAR STREET

ROOSEVELT BOULEVARD

HOPE STREET

SPRUCE STREET

Tarpon Bayou

DIVISION STREET

ATHENS STREET

GRAND BOULEVARD

PINELLAS AVENUE (ALT 19)

ADA STREET

PINE STREET

Shrine of St Michael Taxiarchis

HIGH STREET

CANAL STREET

PARK STREET

HIBISCUS AVENUE

READ STREET

GRAND BOULEVARD

READ STREET

SPRING BOULEVARD

SAFFORD AVENUE

✚ **Universalist Church**

CENTER STREET

PINELLAS AVENUE (ALT 19)

Spring Bayou

ORANGE STREET

ORANGE STREET

St Nicholas Orthodox Cathedral

Chamber of Commerce

TARPON AVENUE

TARPON AVENUE

SPRING BOULEVARD

COURT STREET

Cultural Center

LEMON STREET

Clearwater

Walking west along Tarpon Avenue will take you downhill to **Spring Bayou**, a crescent-shaped lake around which many homes of Tarpon Springs' pre-sponge-era residents – a mix of tycoons and artists – remain, their gabled roofs, shady porches and latticework decor an imposing sight from the lakeside path. Among the early residents was George Innes, a famed landscape painter, who rented a property eventually purchased by his son, George Jnr, also a noted landscape artist. George Jnr's primary legacy to the town can be viewed inside the nearby **Universalist Church**, 57 Read Street (Oct–May Tues–Sun, rest of the year daily, 2–5pm; free); the church, espousing utopian notions of peace, love and understanding, had its windows blown out by a hurricane in 1918, and George made six large-scale works to replace them. Take a look if the church is open, but don't fret about missing them if not; size is their most impressive aspect.

Keeping to a religious theme, a few minutes' walk from the Universalist Church, the simple wooden **Shrine of St Michael Taxiarchis**, at 113 Hope Street (always open), was erected by a local woman in gratitude for the unexplained recovery of her "terminally ill" son in 1939. Numerous instances of the blind regaining their sight and the crippled throwing away their walking sticks after visiting the shrine have been reported, all detailed in a free pamphlet. While here, study the icons closely for tear-tracks; several allegedly began crying – regarded as a bad omen – during 1989.

The sponge docks

Along Dodecanese Boulevard, on the banks of the Anclote River, the **sponge docks** are a disappointing conglomeration of one-time ships' supply stores turned into gift shops touting cassettes of Greek "belly-dancing music" and, of course, sponges ($2–3 for a small specimen). A boat departs regularly throughout the day on a half-hour **sponge-diving trip** (*St Nicholas Boat Line*; ☎942-6425; $4) purely for the benefit of camera-toters. The trip includes a cruise through the sponge docks, a talk on the history of sponge diving, and a demonstration of harvesting performed in a traditional brass-helmeted divingsuit; these days only a few sponge boats still operate commercially.

You'll pay less, and learn more about the local community and sponge diving at the docks, among a group of shops at 510 Dodecanese Boulevard, whose **Spongerama Exhibition** (daily 10am–5pm; free) traces the roots and growth of Tarpon Springs' Greek settlers, and shows the primitive techniques still used in the industry. Don't bother with the less satisfying **museum** (daily 10am–5pm; free) down the street at the **Sponge Exchange**, where piles of freshly found sponges were once auctioned off (and a few still are early on Thursday mornings to wholesalers) in an area that's become little more than a dull, Greek-themed shopping mall.

THE NORTHWEST COAST: THE BIG BEND

Popularly known as the **Big Bend** for the way it curves towards the Panhandle, Florida's **northwest coast** is an oddity in as much as it has no beaches. Instead, thousands of mangrove islands form a fractured and almost unmappable shoreline, infrequently interrupted by snoozing villages, natural springs and – in one instance – an outstanding Native American ceremonial site. Sand-crazy visitors miss it all by barrelling towards the Tampa Bay beaches on Hwy-19, the region's only major road, leaving the Big Bend one of the few sections of coastal Florida undisturbed by mass tourism – and one of the most rewarding for inquisitive visitors who want more from the state than a tan.

Homosassa Springs and around

As you leave the Tampa Bay area on Hwy-19, the roadside clutter of filling stations and used-car lots recedes north of New Port Richey, an uninteresting place of condos and time-share properties, and gives way to a more soothing, if often monotonous, landscape of hardwood and pine forests along with uncharitable expanses of swamp. After sixty or so miles, watch out for the amusing dinosaur-shaped roof of *Harold's Auto Center* and, just ahead by the junction with Route 50, two parks. Entertainment at **Weeki Wachee** (daily 9.30am–5.30pm in winter, longer hours in summer; $16.95), includes a thoroughly kitsch underwater choreography routine performed by "mermaids" in one of the Big Bend's many natural springs, and a trip through a wildlife preserve (park grounds open 8am–sunset; free). Buying a combination ticket will allow you access to the adjacent Buccaneer Bay water park, where you can swim and play on the water slides to your heart's content.

Any thirst for animals and (real) sea life is better sated twenty miles north at **HOMOSASSA SPRINGS**, the first community of any size on Hwy-19. Here, at the **Homosassa Springs State Wildlife Park** (daily 9am–5.30pm; $6.95), squirrel-infested walking trails lead to another gushing spring, and an underwater observatory offers eye-to-gill sightings of the numerous fish and manatees swimming through it. To get a feel for the town, go a couple of miles west along the oak-lined Route 490, passing the crumbling walls and rusting machinery of the **Yulee Sugar Mill**, originally owned by David Yulee. Florida's first Congressman and the financier of the 1860s Cedar Key to Fernandina Beach rail line (see "Cedar Key", p.296), Yulee extended a section south to Homosassa Springs; the closest the place has ever been to civilization. With the railway long gone, the tranquil town's old wooden houses are finding favour with young artists: drop into the *Riverworks Gallery*, 10844 W Yulee Drive, to see some of the better works.

Crystal River and around

Seven miles further along Hwy-19, **CRYSTAL RIVER** is among the region's bigger communities despite a population of just four thousand; many residents are retirees fearful of the crime in Florida's urban areas and unable to afford the more southerly sections of the coast. You'd never guess it from the drab Hwy-19, but quite a few arrivals are also drawn here by the sedate beauty of the clear river from which the town takes its name. **Manatees** take a shine to it as well: they can be seen all year round here, but during the winter greater numbers are found in the numerous inlets of **Kings Bay**, a section of the river just west of Hwy-19. By snorkelling or scuba diving, you stand a fair chance of meeting one of these friendly, walrus-like creatures; **guided dives** are set up for around $25 an hour by dive shops in the vicinity. Check with the Chamber of Commerce (see below) for the best deals.

Crystal River's present dwellers are by no means the first to live by the waterway; it provided a source of food for Native Americans from at least 200 BC. To

The area code for Crystal River, Yankeetown and Cedar Key is ☎904.

gain some insight into their culture, take State Park Road off Hwy-19 just north of the town to the **Crystal River State Archeological Site** (daily 8am–sunset; cars $3.25, pedestrians and cyclists $1), where the temple, burial and shell midden mounds are still visible. Inside the **visitor center** (daily 9am–5pm), there's an enlightening assessment of finds from the 450 graves discovered here, indicating trade links with tribes far to the north. More fascinating, however, are the connections with the south: the site contains two *stele*, or ceremonial stones, much more commonly found in Mexico. The engravings – thought to be faces of Sun deities – suggest that large-scale solar ceremonies were conducted here. The sense of the past and the serenity of the setting make the site a highly evocative, as well a historically instructive, place – don't pass it by.

Practicalities

Other than diving and visiting the archeological site, Crystal River doesn't have much to justify a long stop, though if you're travelling by *Greyhound* (the station is at 200 N Hwy-19; ☎795-4445), it's useful as an overnight stop. The cheapest **accommodation** is provided by *Days Inn*, just north of the town on Hwy-19 (☎795-2111; ②); more expensive but more relaxing is the *Plantation Inn*, on Route 44 (☎1-800/632-6262; ④). If you're planning some diving and an overnight stay, check out the dive-and-accommodation packages offered by the *Best Western*, 614 NW Hwy-19 (☎795-3774; ③). The closest **campground** is *Sun Coast*, half a mile south on Hwy-19 (☎795-9049), where it costs $15 to pitch a tent. For **food**, use the basic but dependable *Crystal Paradise Restaurant*, 508 Citrus Avenue (☎563-2620). The **Chamber of Commerce**, 28 N Hwy-19 (Mon–Thurs 8.30am–5pm, Fri 8.30am–4pm; ☎795-3149), can supply general facts on Crystal River and around.

Yankeetown and around

Ten miles north of Crystal River, Hwy-19 spans the **Florida barge canal**. Conceived in the 1820s to provide a cargo link between the Gulf and Atlantic coasts, work on the canal only started in the 1930s and – thanks largely to the efforts of conservationists – was abandoned in the 1970s with just six miles completed. The bridge offers a view of the Crystal River nuclear power station; the area's major employer and the reason why local telephone books carry instructions on how to survive a nuclear catastrophe.

Further on, taking any left turn off Hwy-19 will invariably lead to some tiny, eerily quiet community, where fishing on the local river is the only sign of life. One such place is **YANKEETOWN**, five miles west of Inglis on Route 40, reputedly named after some Yankee soldiers who moved here following the Civil War. To get the complete middle-of-nowhere effect, spend a night at the *Izaak Walton Lodge*, at the corner of Riverside Drive and 63rd Street (☎447-2311; ③), an angler's billet and restaurant since 1923 and still the fomenting place of local gossip.

This area contains many parks and preserves, most with something to recommend them. Two of the largest are **Withlacoochee State Forest** (south of Route 44) and **Chassahowitzka National Wildlife Refuge** (west of Hwy-19), either of which are huge enough to give you a humbling experience.

Further north, the protected wildlife habitats of the **Wacassassa State Preserve** cover the salt marshes and tidal creeks on the coastal side of Hwy-19 as you travel on from Yankeetown. A breeding ground for deer and turkey, and sometimes visited by black bear and Florida panthers, these swampy lands are intended to allow the state's indigenous creatures to replenish their numbers: human accessibility is not a pressing concern, although there are periodic ranger-guided **canoe trips** through the area: details on ☎543-5567.

Cedar Key

One left turn you you must certainly make is onto Route 24 at the hamlet of Otter Creek, along which you should continue west for twenty miles until the road runs out in the centre of **CEDAR KEY**. In the 1860s, the railroad from Fernandina Beach (see *The Northeast Coast*) ended its journey here, turning this isolated community – which occupies one of several small islands – into a thriving port. When ships got bigger and required deeper harbours, Cedar Key stayed solvent by cutting down its cypress, pine and cedar trees to fuel a pencil-producing indus-try. Inevitably, the trees were soon all gone, and by the turn of the century – not aided by a devastating hurricane – Cedar Key was all but a ghost town. The few who stayed eked out a living from fishing and harvesting oysters, as many of the thousand-strong population still do.

Only during the last ten years have there been signs of a revival: many decay-ing timber-framed warehouses have been turned into restaurants and shops, and more holiday homes are appearing. Given the town's remoteness, however (there's no public transport from other communities in the area), it's unlikely that Cedar Key will ever be deluged with visitors – the only remotely busy periods are during the seafood festival in October and the arts and crafts show during April – and the place remains a fascinating example of old Florida.

Practicalities

The **Chamber of Commerce**, inside the former city hall on Second Street (daily 9am–3pm; ☎543-5600), can supply the usual neighbourhood information and keep you up to date on the increasing number of places offering **accommodation** in the town. Bed and breakfast at the 130-year-old *Island Hotel*, corner of Second and B streets (☎543-5111; ④), is a great way to soak up the local atmosphere. For a standard room, try the *Beach Front Motel*, corner of First and G streets (☎543-5113; ②); *Faraway Inn*, corner of Third and G streets (☎543-5330; ②–③), whose cottages or rooms with kitchens are better value than the standard rooms; or *Bayside Cottages*, half a mile from the centre on Route 24 (☎543-5141; ②). **Tents** can be pitched at *Sunset Isle RV Park*, three miles away on Route 24 (☎543-5375; $12), or at the secluded and basic *Shell Mound Park*, five miles away on Route 326, off Route 347 (☎543-6153; $3.50–5).

Eating freshly caught seafood is a pleasurable way to while away a few hours in Cedar Key: oysters, smoked mullet and fried trout are among the local, rather expensive specialities. Three likely spots to sample the goods are close to each other along Dock Street (and too conspicuous to have street numbers): *The Captain's Table* (☎543-5441), *Seabreeze* (☎543-5738) and the *Brown Pelican* (☎543-5428). A cheaper alternative, away from the dock, is *Annie's Café*, on the corner of Hwy-24 and Sixth Street (☎543-6141), serving good, home-style break-fasts and lunches.

Around Cedar Key

Pass the time by strolling the ramshackle waterfront structures of Dock Street and the old wooden houses on and around Second Street, and be sure to drop into the **Historical Society Museum**, on the corner of D and Second streets (Mon–Sat 11am–4pm, Sun 1–4pm; $1). Here you can scan newspaper clippings attesting to the halcyon days of yore, and view the scraps of historical fallout, such as the long poles used in oyster harvesting. The museum also supplies various leaflets, including a 50¢ map of Cedar Key, and a **historic walking tour** leaflet for $2. More remains are stored a mile away at the **State Historical Museum**, at the end of Museum Drive (Mon & Thurs–Sat, times vary; 50¢), in an unprepossess-ing residential section of the town: you needn't feel uncomfortable about neglect-ing it. And, if possible, stick around long enough to admire the blazing sunset.

If you're staying a couple of days or more, you can make a boat trip out to the many islands nearby that make up a **wildlife refuge**. *Island Hopper*, at the City Marina on Dock Street (☎543-5904), hire out a variety of boats (minimum three people; prices from $30 for a half day, $50 all day). At Norwood's Marina (☎543-6148), just outside town on Route 24, prices are much the same. Bear in mind that deposits of $30 upwards are also required at both places. Alternatively, take a ninety-minute *Island Hopper Scenic Cruise* from City Marina to the **bird sanctu-ary** on Seahorse Key for $10 return, which allows you a stay of about fifteen minutes on the beach. Better still, opt for their "Island Drop-Off" to Seahorse Key ($15 return) and simply arrange a collection time, leaving you free to enjoy the island at your leisure.

North towards the Panhandle

Back on Hwy-19, there's a featureless ninety-mile slog to the next noticeable town, **PERRY**. The lumber industry for which the place is famous is celebrated in the **Forest Capitol State Museum**, one mile south of the town, at 204 Forest Park Drive (Thurs–Mon 9am–5pm; $1); exhibits include an 1860 furnished "cracker" home. Otherwise, nothing breaks the journey **north towards the Panhandle**, fifty miles distant. To reach Tallahassee, stick to Hwy-19 (from here also known as Hwy-27), or, for the Panhandle coast, branch west with Hwy-98. The Panhandle is fully detailed in Chapter Seven.

THE SOUTHWEST COAST

Flavouring the 150 miles of coast south of Tampa Bay are several individualistic towns with origins dating back to the early days of Florida's incorporation into the US. Residents here lead enviable lives away from the big city hurly-burly and until recently had an easy job preserving their seclusion. Nowadays, newer communi-ties in the vicinity are beginning to expand at a colossal rate, and large-scale tour-ism is creeping steadily southwards, yet the southwest coast is still one of Florida's most quietly absorbing sections: a fine balance of mainland sights and beaches begging for exploration, with the prize of the Everglades National Park at its end.

South from Tampa Bay

Taking I-275 south from St Petersburg (a preferable route to the lacklustre I-75 or Hwy-41 from Tampa), you'll soar over Tampa Bay on the new **Sunshine Skyway Bridge**, high enough to allow ocean-going ships to pass beneath and for the outlines of land and sea to become blurred in the heat haze. It was built to replace the original Sunshine Skyway, which was rammed by a phosphate tanker during a storm in May 1980, causing the central span of the southbound section to collapse. With visibility down to a few feet, drivers on the bridge failed to spot the gap, and 35 people, including the occupants of a *Greyhound* bus, plunged 250 feet to their deaths; this tragedy was the worst of several fatal accidents on the Sunshine Skyway. The southern and northern sections have now been turned into fishing piers (access costs $3 per vehicle), while the central section, submerged in the waters at the mouth of Tampa Bay, creates an artificial reef. The new Sunshine Skyway Bridge is rife with tales of phantom hitch-hikers: they thumb rides across, only to vanish into thin air before reaching the other side. For the dollar toll, it beats anything at Walt Disney World.

The Gamble Plantation

The bridge comes to earth about five miles north of Palmetto, an uninteresting dormitory community of Bradenton (see below). If you have time to spare, veer east from Palmetto along Tenth Street (Hwy-301) to Ellenton, a riverside settlement where the 1840s **Gamble Plantation**, 3708 Patten Avenue (grounds Mon–Thurs 9.30am–5pm; $3), is one of the oldest homes on Florida's west coast and the only slave-era plantation this far south. Composed of thick, tabby walls (a mixture of crushed shell and molasses) and girded on three sides by sturdy columns, the house belonged to a Confederate major, Robert Gamble, a failed Tallahassee cotton planter who ran a sugar plantation here before financial uncertainty in the run-up to the Civil War forced him to leave. An excellent showcase of wealthy (and white) Old South living, the house – stuffed to the rafters with period fittings – can only be seen on the free **guided tour** (at 10.30am, then on the hour 1–4pm) which, besides describing the building, its contents and owners, offers a thought-provoking Confederate view of the Civil War.

Bradenton and around

A major producer of tomato and orange juice, **BRADENTON**, across the broad Manatee River from Palmetto, is a hard-working town whose centre comprises several unlovely miles of business buildings along the river's south bank. To see Bradenton at its best you need to travel eight miles west to the **beaches** that line Anna Maria Island, the northernmost of a chain of barrier islands running from here to Fort Myers – by car, this is a better (if slightly longer) route to Sarasota than the inland options. It's inevitable, however, that you'll pass through Bradenton and, particularly if you've missed the Gamble Plantation (see above), you might find the town's historical collections briefly entertaining.

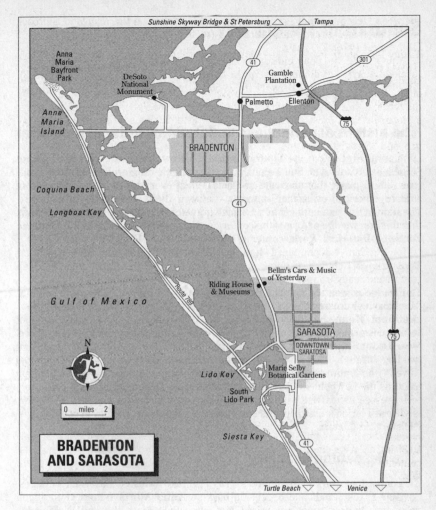

Sunshine Skyway Bridge & St Petersburg △   △ *Tampa*

Anna
Maria
Bayfront
Park

DeSoto
National
Monument

*Anne
Maria
Island*

Gamble
Plantation

Palmetto   Ellenton

BRADENTON

Coquina Beach

Longboat Key

Gulf of Mexico

Bellm's Cars & Music
of Yesterday

Riding House
& Museums

SARASOTA

DOWNTOWN
SARATOSA

N

Lido Key

Marie Selby
Botanical Gardens

South
Lido Park

0   miles   2

Siesta Key

**BRADENTON
AND SARASOTA**

Turtle Beach ▽   ▽ *Venice* ▽

Practicalities

In central Bradenton, the **Chamber of Commerce**, 222 Tenth Street (Mon–Fri
8.30am–4.30pm; ☎748-3411), has the usual tourist information; better for beach
facts is the **Anna Maria Island Chamber of Commerce**, 503 Manatee Avenue
(Mon–Fri 9am–5pm; ☎778-1541).

   Accommodation on a budget is a problem within walking distance of the
beach: *Silver Surf Motel*, 1301 Gulf Drive (☎1-800/441-7873; ③) and *Queensgate*,
1101 Gulf Drive (☎/78-7153; ③), are possibilities. Costlier but cosier – and you'll
need to book ahead – is bed and breakfast at the *Duncan House*, 1703 Gulf Drive
(☎778-6858; ④). If beach prices are too high or there's no space (as often occurs

between December and April), use one of the motels on the mainland approach roads, such as *Baxter's*, 3225 14th Street (☎746-6448; ③), or *Hoosier Manor*, 1405 14th Street (☎768-7935; ③).

You should do your **eating** on Anna Maria Island. Top choices for fresh seafood lunches or dinners are *Rotten Ralph's*, 902 S Bay Boulevard (☎778-3953), *Harbor House*, 200 Gulf Drive N (☎778-5608), and *Fast Eddie's*, 101 S South Bay Boulevard (☎778-2251).

The historical collections and DeSoto National Memorial

In central Bradenton, the **South Florida History Museum**, 201 Tenth Street (Tues–Sat 10am–5pm, Sun 1–6pm; $5), takes a wide-ranging look at the region's past; its displays, dioramas and artefacts reflect every phase of habitation from Native American civilization onwards – among them a credibility-straining re-creation of the sixteenth-century Spanish home of Hernando DeSoto (see below). Further knowledge of turn-of-the-century settlers can be acquired at the **Manatee Village Historical Park**, corner of Manatee Avenue E and Fifteenth Street E (Mon–Fri 9am–4.30pm, Sun 1–4pm, July–Aug closed Sat & Sun; free), which has a courthouse, church, general store and cracker cottage dating from Florida's rough-and-ready frontier days.

Five miles **west of central Bradenton**, Manatee Avenue (the main route to the beaches) crosses 75th Street W, at the northern end of which is the **DeSoto National Memorial** (daily 9am–5pm; free). This is believed to mark the spot where Spanish conquistador Hernando DeSoto came ashore in 1539. The three-year DeSoto expedition, hacking through Florida's dense subtropical terrain and wading through its swamps, led to the European discovery of the Mississippi River – and numerous pitched battles with Native Americans. An exhibition records the key points of DeSoto's trek, and, from December to April, park rangers dressed as sixteenth-century Spaniards add informative pointers to the lifestyles of Florida's first adventurers. For more about the DeSoto expedition, see "History" in *Contexts*.

The Bradenton beaches

In contrast to central Bradenton's greyness, the ramshackle beach cottages, seaside snack stands and beachside bars on **Anna Maria Island**, onto which Manatee Avenue runs, are bright and convivial. From the end of Manatee Avenue, turn left along Gulf Drive for **Coquina Beach**, where the swimming is excellent and the weekend social life youthful and merry; with a quieter time in mind, take a right turn along Marina Drive for the calm **Anna Maria Bayfront Park**.

South of Anna Maria Island, **Longboat Key** is all about privacy: its pricey homes are shielded by rows of tall Australian pines, and, while all the sands along this nineteen-mile-long island are public property, access to them is almost impossible for non-residents. Not until you reach Lido Key, further south, are there more useable beaches – described on p.304 under "The Sarasota Beaches".

Sarasota and around

Rising on a gentle hillside beside the blue waters of Sarasota Bay, **SARASOTA** is one of Florida's better-off and better-looking towns, and also one of the state's leading cultural centres: home to numerous writers and artists, and the base of several respected performing arts companies. Despite periodic conservative flappings (such as recent attempts to outlaw skimpy swimwear at the local beaches), the community is far less stuffy than its wealth, and the abundance of Neoclassical statues, fountains and manicured lawns decorating it, suggest. Save for an excellent grouping of bookshops, downtown Sarasota has less impact than the Ringling estate on the town's northern edge – home of the art-loving millionaire from whom modern Sarasota takes its cue – and the barrier island beaches, a couple of miles away across the bay.

> The area code for the Sarasota area is ☎941

Arrival, transport and information

From the north, **Hwy-41** skirts the Ringling estate before running through downtown Sarasota, passing the main causeway to the islands. In downtown Sarasota, *Greyhound* **buses** stop at 575 N Washington Boulevard (☎955-5735), and the *Amtrak* bus from Tampa ends its trip at the local bus terminal – see below.

   Local bus (*SCAT*; information ☎316-1234, 4.30am–8.30pm, except Sun) routes radiate out from the downtown Sarasota terminal on Lemon Avenue, between First and Second streets. **Useful routes** are #2 or #10 to the Ringling estate; #4 to Lido Key; #18 to Longboat Key; and #11 to Siesta Key. If you're around for a week or more, a good way to explore the town and the islands is by **renting a bike** for around $20 per day from *Sarasota Bicycle Center*, 4048 Bee Ridge Road (☎377-4505); the *Village Bike Shop*, on Siesta Key at 5101 Ocean Boulevard (☎346-2111); or the *Backyard Bike Shop*, on Longboat Key at 5610 Gulf of Mexico Drive (☎383-5184). To see the islands cheaply and with the minimum of exertion, take the trolley for $2 (you can hop on and off as many times as you like), which runs three times a day (9.30am, 12.30pm & 3.30pm), starting at the Best Western Siesta Beach Resort. It takes you to all the islands, making plenty of stops along the way. (For schedule info call ☎346-3115.)

   For **information** in Sarasota, call at the **Visitors and Convention Bureau**, 655 N Tamiami Trail (Mon–Sat 9am–5pm; ☎1-800/522-9799), or the **Chamber of Commerce**, 1819 Main Street (Mon–Fri 9am–5pm; ☎955-8187). On **Siesta Key**, you'll find a Chamber of Commerce at 5100 Ocean Boulevard (Mon–Fri 9am–5pm; ☎349-3800). Besides the customary discount coupons and leaflets, look for the free magazines, *Sarasota Visitors Guide* and *See*, and the Friday edition of the *Sarasota Herald Tribune*, whose pull-out section, "Ticket", has entertainment listings.

Accommodation

On the **mainland**, motels run the length of Hwy-41 between the Ringling estate and downtown Sarasota, typically charging $35–50. You can take your pick:

Sarasota Motor Inn, no. 7251 (☎1-800/282-6827; ③), *Cabana Motor Inn*, no. 525 (☎955-0195; ②); and *Knights Inn*, no. 5340 (☎355-8867; ③).

At the **beaches**, prices are higher. Lowest rates on Lido Key are with the *Gulf Side Motel*, 138 Garfield Drive (☎388-2590; ④), and the *Lido Apartment Vacation Rentals*, 528 S Polk Drive (☎388-1004; ④). Otherwise, be prepared to fork out substantially for a night at the *Harley Sandcastle*, 1540 Benjamin Franklin Drive (☎388-2181; ⑤), or the *Half Moon Beach Club*, 2050 Benjamin Franklin Drive (☎388-3694; ⑥). In general, Siesta Key is even more expensive, with many places renting out fully equipped apartments for a week in preference to motel rooms by the night. Two on Midnight Pass Road that may be worth a try are *Surfrider Beach Apartments*, no. 6400 (☎349-2121; ⑤), and *Gulf Sun Apartments & Motel* no. 6722 (☎349-2442; ⑤). The only budget alternative is the *Gulf Beach Travel Trailer Park*, 8862 Midnight Pass Road (☎349-3839), though it consists almost exclusively of RV sites; if you can get a **tent** site, be prepared to pay upwards of $20.

Northern Sarasota: the Ringling Museum Complex

As you reach Sarasota from the north, don't fail to tour the house and art collections of **John Ringling**, a multi-millionaire who not only poured money into the fledgling community from the 1910s but also gave it a taste for fine arts that it's never lost. One of the owners of the fantastically successful *Ringling Brothers Circus*, which toured the US from the 1890s, Ringling – an imposing figure over six feet tall and weighing nearly twenty stone – ploughed the circus's profits into railways, oil and land, by the Twenties acquiring a fortune estimated at $200 million. Charmed by Sarasota and recognizing its investment potential, Ringling built the first causeway to the barrier islands and made the town his circus's winter base, saving a fortune in northern heating bills and generating tremendous publicity for the town in doing so. His greatest gift to Sarasota, however, was a Venetian Gothic mansion – a combination of European elegance and American-millionaire extravagance – and an incredible collection of European Baroque paintings, displayed in a purpose-built museum beside the house. Grief-stricken following the death of his wife, Mable, in 1927, and losing much of his wealth through the Wall Street crash two years later, Ringling died in 1936, reputedly with just $300 to his name. The **Ringling Museum Complex** is two miles north of downtown Sarasota beside Hwy-41 at 5401 Bay Shore Road (daily 10am–5.30pm; $8.50, free admission to the art museum on Sat). The buildings are linked by pathways over a 66-acre site, though all are easy to walk between and clearly signposted. To get here from downtown Sarasota, use **buses** #2 or #10.

The Ringling House: Ca' d'Zan

Begin your exploration of the Ringling estate by walking through the gardens to the former Ringling residence, **Ca' d'Zan** ("House of John", in Venetian dialect), a gorgeous piece of work serenely situated beside the bay. Completed in 1925, reputedly at a cost of $1.5 million, the house was planned around an airy, two-storey living room marked on one side by a fireplace of carved Italian marble and on the other by a $50,000 organ belonging to the musical Mable. The other rooms are similarly filled with expensive items, but unlike their mansion-erecting contemporaries elsewhere in Florida, John and Mable Ringling knew the value of restraint: their spending power never exceeded their sense of style, and the house remains a triumph of taste and proportion – and an exceptionally pleasant place to walk around. Take the free **guided tour** departing regularly from the entrance, then roam on your own.

The Art Museum

The mix of inspiration and caution that underpinned Ringling's business deals also influenced his art purchases. On trips to Europe to scout for new circus talent, Ringling became obsessed with **Baroque art** – then wildly unfashionable – and over five years, largely led by his own sensibilities, he acquired more than five hundred Old Masters; a collection now regarded as one of the finest of its kind in the US. To display the paintings, many of them as epic in size as they were in content, Ringling selected a patch of Ca' d'Zan's grounds and erected a spacious **museum** around a mock fifteenth-century Italian palazzo, decorated by his stockpile of high-quality replica Greek and Roman statuary. As with Ca' d'Zan, the very concept initially seems absurdly pretentious but, like the house, the idea works: the architecture matching the art with great aplomb. Here also, you should take the free **guided tour** departing regularly from the entrance, before wandering around at your leisure.

Five enormous paintings by **Rubens**, commissioned in 1625 by a Hapsburg archduchess, and the painter's subsequent *Portrait of Archduke Ferdinand*, are the undisputed highlights of the collection, though they shouldn't detract from the excellent canvases in succeeding rooms: a wealth of talent from Europe's leading schools of the mid-sixteenth to mid-eighteenth centuries. Watch out, in particular, for the finely composed and detailed *The Rest on the Flight to Egypt*, by Paolo Veronese, and the entertaining *Building of a Palace* from Piero de Cosimo. In contrast, recently acquired contemporary works include sculpture from Joel Shapiro and John Chamberlain, and paintings by Frank Stella and Philip Pearlstein.

The Circus Gallery and the Asolo Theater

The Ringling fortune may have its origins in the Big Top, but the **Circus Gallery** is an unworthy afterthought to the house and art museum: a dull bunch of leftovers – parade wagons, old costumes, a human-firing cannon – with only the antique illustrations of balancing tricks and, from a time when physical abnormalities were a feature of circus entertainment, some clothes and memorabilia from Tom Thumb, the celebrated nineteenth-century dwarf.

Elsewhere in the grounds, try the door of the **Asolo Theater** (sometimes locked) for a peek at the interior of a genuine eighteenth-century Italian court playhouse. As well as plays it hosts lectures and art films – for a full programme of events phone ☎355-7115. Don't confuse this with the larger Asolo Center for the Performing Arts, 5555 N Tamiami Trail, the present home of the *Asolo Theater Company* (see "Nightlife", p.306), which was previously based here.

Bellm's Cars & Music of Yesterday

Only vintage car enthusiasts and devotees of old music boxes will derive any pleasure from **Bellm's Cars and Music of Yesterday**, across Hwy-41 from the entrance to the Ringling Estate (daily 9.30am–5.30pm; $8). Nearly 200 aged vehicles – a few Rolls-Royces among them – are gathered together with hurdy-gurdies, cylinder discs and an enormous Belgian pipe organ, combining to make an awful racket.

Downtown Sarasota

The allure of the Ringling estate and the nearby beaches keeps many visitors (except those travelling by public transport, who have no choice) away from **downtown Sarasota**, missing out on the restaurants, bars, boutiques and antique shops lining the strollable **Main Street**. Admittedly, other than eating and drinking, window shopping is the sole pursuit, though anyone bemoaning the lack of decent **bookshops** in Florida should take heart: here you'll find the biggest and most varied selection in the state. The best-filled shelves are at *Book Bazaar/A. Parkers*, no. 1488, *Charlie's News*, no. 341, and *Main Bookshop*, no. 1962.

Away from Main Street, most of downtown Sarasota is an unrewarding mix of public buildings and offices, and you should head south, following the curve of the bay for half a mile, to the **Marie Selby Botanical Gardens**, 811 S Palm Avenue (daily 10am–5pm; $6). The walled perimeter gives little inkling of the small but startling gathering of growths inside, and time spent meandering along the fragrant pathways can't fail to improve your mood. There's always something in bloom.

The Sarasota beaches

Increasingly the stamping ground of European package tourists spilling south from the St Petersburg beaches, the powdery white sands of the **Sarasota beaches** – fringing two barrier islands, which continue the chain beginning off Bradenton – haven't been spared the attentions of property developers either, losing much of their scenic appeal to towering condos. For all that, the Sarasota beaches are worth a day of anybody's time – either to lie back and soak up the rays, or to seek out the few remaining isolated stretches. Both islands, Lido Key and Siesta Key, are accessible by car or bus from the mainland, though there's no link directly between them.

Lido Key

Financed by and named after Sarasota's circus-owning sugar daddy, the Ringling Causeway – take buses #4 or #18 – crosses the yacht-filled Sarasota Bay from the foot of Main Street to **Lido Key** and flows into **St Armands Circle**, a glorified roundabout ringed by upmarket shops and restaurants, and dotted with some of John Ringling's replica classical statuary – muscle-bound torsos surrealistically emerging from behind palm fronds. Other than staging entertaining arts and crafts events on weekends and offering a safe place to stroll after dark, St Armands Circle has little to occupy anyone without a limitless budget and – after a look around – you should continue south along Benjamin Franklin Drive. This route passes the island's most easily accessible beaches, fine in themselves though bearing a pronounced holiday-maker bias. After two miles, it ends at the more attractive **South Lido Park** (daily 8am–sunset; free): a belt of dazzlingly bright sand beyond a large grassy park, with walking trails shaded by Australian pines. Busy with barbecues and tanned bodies on Saturday and Sunday, the park is a delightfully subdued spot for weekday rambles.

Away from the beaches, the only place of consequence on Lido Key is a mile north of St Armands Circle at City Island Park, just off John Ringling Parkway: the **Mote Marine Aquarium**, 1600 Ken Thompson Parkway (daily 10am–5pm;

$6), the public offshoot of a marine laboratory studying the ecological problems
threatening Florida's sea life. Some of the work – such as research into the
mysterious "red tide", an unexplained algae that appears every few years,
devastating sea life and causing sickness among people along the coast – is
outlined, and there's a great assortment of live creatures, from seahorses to
loggerhead turtles. The centrepiece of the 22 aquariums is a massive outdoor
shark tank, where you can view several species up close through underwater
windows.

Adjacent to the Mote Aquarium, you'll find **Pelican Man's Bird Sanctuary**,
1708 Ken Thompson Parkway (daily 10am–5pm; free, though donations are
welcomed). Injured and sick migratory birds from all over the world, together
with native Floridian species, are cared for here by over 200 volunteers. You'll
come away furnished with facts about the various ways our feathered friends
come to grief (usually at the hands of man) and how they are nursed back to
health before being re-released into the wild.

Siesta Key

The bulbous northerly section of **Siesta Key**, reached by Siesta Drive off Hwy-41
about five miles south of downtown Sarasota (bus #11), contains the bulk of the
tadpole-shaped island's resident population on streets twisting around a complicated network of canals. Beach-lovers should hit **Siesta Key Beach**, beside
Ocean Beach Boulevard, a wide white strand that can – and often does – accommodate thousands of partying sun-worshippers. To escape the crowds, continue
south past Crescent Beach, which meets a second road (Stickney Point Road)
from the mainland, and follow Midnight Pass Road for six miles to **Turtle Beach**,
a small body of sand that has the islands' only campground; see p.302.

Eating

In **downtown Sarasota**, **eating** should be done along Main Street. *Willie's
Backstage Café*, no. 1371 (☎954-2226), delivers high quality international fare; *El
Greco Café*, no. 1592 (☎365-2234), serves extremely cheap Greek dishes besides
the usual array of American breakfasts and lunches; *First Watch*, no. 1395 (☎954-
1395), serves reasonably priced hearty breakfasts, salads and sandwiches; and
Gordo's Burritos, no. 1430 (☎366-9439), provides a wide choice of low-fat Tex-Mex
food. For home-made food cooked to old-fashioned recipes, venture slightly
further afield to one of the local Amish restaurants: *Yoder's*, 3434 Bahia Vista
Street (☎955-7771), winner of several awards and a local favourite; *Sugar & Spice*,
1850 Tamiami Trail (☎953-3340); or *Der Dutchman*, 3713 Bahia Vista Street
(☎955-8007).

Food is dearer at the **beaches**, especially on Lido Key. Around St Armands
Circle, only *The Buttery*, 470 John L. Ringling Boulevard (☎388-1523), offers
round-the-clock respite from ritzy eating spots. Siesta Key is better news: *The
Broken Egg*, 210 Avenida Madera (☎346-2750), is favourite with locals for
breakfast and lunch; *The Old Salty Dog*, 5023 Ocean Boulevard (☎349-0158),
offers "English-style" fish and chips, alongside regular seafood and hot dogs;
while *Turtles*, 8875 Midnight Pass Road (☎346-2207), and *Surfrider*, 6400
Midnight Pass Road (☎346-1199), both provide outstanding seafood dinners for
under $15.

Nightlife

Some of the state's top small theatrical groups are based in Sarasota: **drama** devotees should scan local newspapers for play listings or phone the theatres directly. The major repertory, the *Asolo Theater Company*, based at the Asolo Center for the Performing Arts, 5555 N Tamiami Trail (☎351-8000), has a strong programme throughout the year (tickets $15–30). The other companies (tickets $10–30) stick to a winter season: *Florida Studio Theater*, 1241 N Palm Avenue (☎366-9796; $15–25); *Golden Apple Dinner Theater*, 25 N Pineapple Avenue (☎366-5454; $29); and *Players of Sarasota*, 838 N Tamiami Trail (☎365-2494; $15.50).

Otherwise, Sarasota's **nightlife** is a bit limp. **Beer drinkers** will find solace at the *Sarasota Brewing Company Bar & Grill*, 6607 Gateway Avenue (☎925-2337), which home-brews beers to traditional German specifications, and at *The Old Salty Dog* (address under "Eating", above), where a variety of British ales are sold by the pint. If you feel like mixing with an intellectually high-octane crowd, try the Greenwich-Village atmosphere of *Kanega*, 1528 Main Street (☎957-0813), a coffee-house bar owned by a New York photographer. Elsewhere, there's **live music**: jazz and blues most nights at *The Brass Parrot*, 555 Palm Avenue (☎316-0338); *The Lost Kangaroo Pub*, 427 12th Street W (☎747-8114), where "The Yellow Dog Jazz Band" appears regularly; and *The Gator Club*, 1490 Main Street (☎366-5969), which is popular among locals. Outdoor live rock and roll at weekends is played on the corner of Main Street and Lemon Avenue (usually packed). For reggae, look in at *Cha Cha Coconuts*, 417 St Armands Circle (☎388-3300).

Inland from Sarasota: Myakka River State Park

Should your knowledge of Florida be limited to beaches and theme parks, broaden your horizons fourteen miles inland from Sarasota on Route 72. Here you'll find a great tract of rural Florida barely touched by humans, whose marshes, pinewoods and prairies form **Myakka River State Park** (daily 8am–sunset; cars $3.25, pedestrians and cyclists $1). On arrival, drop into the **interpretive center** for an insight into this fragile (and threatened) ecosystem, before you begin exploring it by walking along numerous paths or canoeing on the calm expanse of the Upper Myakka Lake. If you're equipped for **hiking**, following the forty miles of trails through the park's **wilderness preserve** is a better way to get to close to the cotton-tailed rabbits, deer, turkey, bobcats and alligators who live in the park; before commencing, register at the entrance office and get maps and weather conditions – be ready for wet conditions during the summer storms.

Other than five basic campgrounds on the hiking trails, park **accommodation** (details and reservations: ☎361-6511) comprises two well-equipped **campgrounds** and a few four-berth **log cabins** for $50 a night.

South from Sarasota: Venice and around

In the Fifties, the Ringling Circus moved its winter base twenty miles south from Sarasota to **VENICE**, a small town modelled on its European namesake: a place of broad avenues and Italianate architecture surrounded by water. However, it's the **beaches** that make the town. Used by a mix of sunbathers, water-sports enthusiasts and stooping beachcombers hunting for the fossilized sharks teeth commonly washed ashore, the best strands are along the Venice Inlet, a mile west of Hwy-41.

If you have your own transport, you can also explore around the underexploited coastline around **Englewood beaches**, south of Venice on Route 775, pockmarked by small islands and creeks. Sooner or later, though, you'll have to rejoin Hwy-41, which, out of Venice, turns inland to chart an unremarkable fifty-mile course through retirement communities such as Punta Gorda and Port Charlotte, before reaching the far more appetitizing Fort Myers (see below).

Practicalities

If you're arriving in Venice by *Greyhound* bus, you'll be dropped at 225 S Tamiami Trail (☎485-1001), from which your first port of call might be the **Chamber of Commerce**, 257 N Tamiami Trail (Mon–Fri 8.30am–5pm; Nov–March also Sat 9am–12pm; ☎488-2236), for local information. **Local buses** (*SCAT*; ☎316-1234) #13 and #16 (25¢ fare) link Venice with the beaches and surrounding areas.

Spending a night in this quiet community might seem an attractive proposition, though prices aren't low outside of summer: of the motels, try the *Kon-Tiki*, 1487 Tamiami Trail (☎485-9696; ④), or the *Gulf Tide*, 708 Granada Avenue (☎484-9709; ⑤). More luxurious is the *Inn at the Beach Resort*, 101 The Esplanade (☎1-800/255-8471; ③). The *Venice Campground* is at 4085 E Venice Avenue (☎488-0850; $20), in an oak hammock by the river.

For **eating**, *James Place*, 117 W Venice Avenue (☎485-6742), provides great, cheap breakfasts and daily hot lunch specials in an Anglo-Irish setting; *The Crow's Nest*, 1968 Tarpon Center Drive (☎484-9551), is a marina pub with a waterfront view, serving fresh seafood, sandwiches and snacks.

Fort Myers

Lacking the elan of Sarasota, **FORT MYERS**, fifty miles south, is nonetheless one of the up-and-coming communities of the southwest coast, recently undergoing considerable expansion and looking set for a prosperous future. Fortunately, most of the growth has occurred on the north side of the wide Caloosahatchee River, which the town straddles, allowing the traditional centre, along the waterway's south shore, to remain relatively unspoiled. The home and workplace of inventor Thomas Edison, who lived in Fort Myers for many years, provide the strongest interest in a town that otherwise relies on its scenery – making the most of its riverside setting and regimental lines of palm trees lining the main thoroughfares – to delay your progress towards the local beaches, fifteen miles south, or the islands of Sanibel and Captiva, a similar distance west.

Arrival and information

Even without a car, Fort Myers is easy to get around. The mile between the downtown area and the Edison home is covered by **local buses** (☎277-5012) and a trolley (old-fashioned, single-carriage buses) service. To get from downtown Fort Myers to the beaches, take any bus to the Edison Square Mall, then use #50 to Summerlin Square, from where a trolley continues to Estero Island and Carl Johnson Park. Note that there's no local public transport on Sundays. The *Greyhound* station is at 2275 Cleveland Avenue (☎334-1011), just south of downtown Fort Myers. Stacks of **information** await you at the **Visitor and Convention Bureau**, 2180 W First Street (Mon–Fri 8am–5pm; ☎1-800/237-

6444), and the **Chamber of Commerce**, 661 Estero Boulevard (Mon–Fri 8am–5pm; ☎1-800/782-WAVE), at the beaches.

Accommodation

Accommodation costs in and around Fort Myers are low between May and mid-December, when $10–20 is lopped off the standard rates given here. For a motel **in downtown Fort Myers**, look along First Street: *Sea Chest*, no. 2571(☎332-1545; ②), *Ta Ki-Ki*, no. 2631 (☎334-2135; ③), and *Tides,* no. 2621 (☎334-1231; ③). There are many more along Cleveland Avenue, though if you're driving, aim for the rustic cottages a mile east of Hwy-41 at *Rock Lake Motel*, 2930 Palm Beach Boulevard (☎334-3242; ②).

At the beaches, seek a room along the motel-lined Estero Boulevard and be prepared to spend $70. Midweek you may find cheaper deals at *Beacon*, no. 1240 (☎463-5264; ④), *Gulf*, no. 2700 (☎463-9247; ④), *Laughing Gull*, no. 2890 (☎463-1346; ④), *The Outrigger Beach Resort*, no. 6200 (☎463-3131; ⑤), or a few miles inland at *Island*, 201 San Carlos Boulevard (☎463-2381; ③). Of the **campgrounds**, only *Red Coconut*, 3001 Estero Boulevard (☎463-7200), is an easy walk from the beach. Two others further inland are *Gulf Air Travel Park*, 17279 San Carlos Road (☎466-8100), and *San Carlos*, 18701 San Carlos Boulevard (☎466-3133).

Downtown Fort Myers

Once across the Caloosahatchee River, Hwy-41 (here called Cleveland Avenue) strikes **downtown Fort Myers**, picturesquely nestled on the river's edge. Aside from a few restored homes and storefronts around Main Street and Broadway, modern office buildings predominate and you'll need to look to the creditable exhibitions of the **Fort Myers Historical Museum**, 2300 Peck Street (Tues–Sat 10am–4pm; $2.50), for thorough insights into the past. These include the exploits of Doctor Franklin Miles, a Fort Myers inhabitant who developed *Alka Seltzer*. The invention of the world's great hangover cure was overshadowed, however, by the deeds of Thomas Edison, comprehensively recalled a mile west of downtown Fort Myers on McGregor Boulevard (see below) – also the route to the Fort Myers beaches and the Sanibel Island causeway.

Along McGregor Boulevard

In 1885, six years after inventing the light bulb, workaholic **Thomas Edison** collapsed from exhaustion and was instructed by his doctor to find a warm working environment or face an early death. While on holiday in Florida, the 37-year-old Edison noted a patch of bamboo sprouting from the banks of the Caloosahatchee River and bought fourteen acres of it. Having cleared a section, he established what became the **Edison Winter Home**, 2350 McGregor Boulevard (guided tours every 30min; Mon–Sat 9am–5pm, Sun noon–5pm; $8; an extra $2 allows you entry into the Ford Winter Home, see below), where he spent each winter until his death at the age of 84.

A liking for bamboo was no idle fancy: Edison was a keen horticulturalist and often utilized the chemicals produced by plants and trees in his experiments. The **gardens** of the house, where the tours begin (get a ticket from the signposted office across McGregor Boulevard), provided Edison with much raw material: a variety of tropical foliage, from the extraordinary African sausage tree to a profusion of wild orchids nurtured by the inventor, intoxicatingly scented by frangipani. By contrast, Edison's **house** is an anticlimax: a palm-cloaked wooden structure with an ordinary collection of period furnishings glimpsed only through the windows. A reason for the plainness of the abode may be that Edison spent most of his waking hours inside the **laboratory**, attempting to turn the latex-rich sap of *solidago Edisoni* (a giant strain of goldenrod weed which he developed) into rubber – anticipating the shortage caused by the outbreak of World War II. A mass of test tubes, phials and tripods are scattered over the benches, unchanged since Edison's last experiment, performed just before his death in 1931.

Not until the tour reaches the **museum** does the full impact of Edison's achievements become apparent. A design for an improved ticker-tape machine provided him with the funds for the experiments which led to the creation of the phonograph in 1877, and financed research into passing electricity through a vacuum that resulted in the incandescent light bulb two years later. Scores of cylinder and disc phonographs with gaily painted horn-speakers, bulky vintage light bulbs, and innumerable spin-off gadgets, make up an engrossing collection; here, too, you'll see some of the ungainly cinema projectors derived from Edison's *Kinetoscope* – bringing the inventor a million dollars a year in patent royalties from 1907.

A close friend of Edison's since 1896, when the inventor had been one of the few people to speak admiringly of his ambitious car ideas, **Henry Ford** bought the house next door to Edison's in 1915, by which time he was established as the country's top automobile manufacturer. Unlike the Edison home, you can go inside the **Ford Winter Home** (tour hours as for Edison home; to view *this* house you must buy a combination ticket to the Edison House also, $10), though the interior, restored to the style of Ford's time but lacking the original fittings, hardly justifies the admission price: despite becoming the world's first billionaire, Ford lived with his wife in modest surroundings.

Before leaving the old homes, pause to admire the sprawling **banyan tree** outside the ticket office: grown from a seedling given to Edison by tyre-king Harvey Firestone in 1925, it's now the largest tree in the state.

The Fort Myers beaches

Still being discovered by the holidaying multitudes, the **Fort Myers beaches**, fifteen miles south of downtown Fort Myers, are appreciably different in character from the West Coast's more commercialized beach strips, with a cheerful seaside mood that's worth getting acquainted with. Accommodation (see above) is plentiful on and around Estero Boulevard – reached by San Carlos Boulevard, off McGregor Boulevard – which runs the seven-mile length of **Estero Island**; the hubs of activity being the short fishing pier and the **Lynne Hall Memorial Park**, at the island's northern end.

Estero Island becomes quieter and increasingly residential as you press south, Estero Boulevard eventually swinging over a slender causeway onto the barely developed **San Carlos Island**. A few miles ahead, at the **Carl Johnson Park** (daily 8am–5pm; $1.50), a footpath picks a trail over a couple of mangrove-fringed islands and several mullet-filled creeks – a domain of weekend fishing enthusiasts – to **Lovers Key**, a spectacularly secluded beach where occasional washed-up drink cans are the only signs of human existence: a perfect base for stress-free beachcombing and sunbathing. If you don't fancy the half-mile walk, a free trolley-bus will transport you between the park entrance and the beach.

Inland from Fort Myers

Just as the beaches are kept in good condition, so much of the eastern perimeter of the town, verging on the open lands of central Florida, is protected by a series of parks: scenic spots for picnicking, with canoeing and walking trails often thrown in. For a more informative look at the local landscape, spend a couple of hours at the **Nature Center of Lee County**, 3450 Ortiz Avenue (Mon–Sat 9am–5pm, Sun 11am–5pm; $3), on boardwalk trails through cypress and pine woods. Cast an eye, too, around the aviary – where injured birds regain their strength before returning to the wild – and the indoor **museum**: alongside general geological and wildlife exhibits, you'll find a caged specimen of each of the state's four varieties of poisonous snake; the facial expressions of the mice, fed to each snake once a day, are not a sight for the faint-hearted.

Further inland, forty miles northeast of Fort Myers on Route 31, and fifteen minutes from Exit 26 on I-75, natural Florida rears up in even more decisive fashion with **Babcock Wilderness Adventures** (90-min tours run 9am–3pm Nov–April, mornings only May–Oct reservations essential on ☎1-800/500-5583; for info call ☎338-6367), which penetrate a section of a 90,000-acre ranch belonging to the phenomenally wealthy Babcock family (their fortune built on household supply stores). Turkey vultures circle overhead and buffalo roam in the distance as you bump around the rough terrain aboard a "swamp buggy", pausing to look for the rare Florida panther from a glass-fronted observation hut and to walk into a primordial cypress swamp. It's not an inexpensive tour, but it's probably as close as you'll get to the wildlands without a carefully planned expedition.

Eating

Inexpensive breakfasts, snacks and lunches are easily found in **downtown Fort Myers**: try *Melanie's Restaurant*, 2158 McGregor Boulevard (☎334-3139), *Dolly's Bites and Delights*, 2235 First Street (☎332-1600), or pick up a fresh-baked goodie from *Mason's*, 1615 Hendry Street (☎334-4525). For a fuller lunch or dinner, head for the *Oasis Restaurant*, 2222 McGregor Boulevard (☎334-1566) or, for good country cooking using fresh ingredients from the State Farmers' Market, *Farmers' Market Restaurant*, 2736 Edison Avenue (☎334-1687). **At the beaches**, the laid-back *Café du Monde*, 1740 Estero Boulevard (☎463-8088), produces tempting morsels from homemade recipes; *Top O' The Mast*, 1028 Estero Boulevard (☎463-9424), is a solid bet for seafood; with a massive appetite, go to *The Reef*, 2601 Estero Boulevard (☎463-4181), for all-you-can-eat nightly specials, ranging from catfish to frogs' legs.

Sanibel and Captiva islands

When the Lee County authorities (who control the whole Fort Myers area) decided to link **Sanibel Island**, the most southerly of an island grouping around the mouth of the Caloosahatchee River, by road to the mainland in 1963, Sanibel's thousand or so occupants fought tooth and nail against the scheme, but eventually lost. A decade later, they got their own back by seceding from the county, becoming a self-governing "city" and passing strict land-use laws to prevent their island sinking beneath holiday homes and hotels.

Those who remember the old days insist that the island has gone to the dogs: motels and restaurants are more numerous than ever before, and visitors always outnumber the present 7000 residents. But Sanibel is a credit to those who run it: high-rises have been kept out, the beaches are superb, and sizeable areas are set aside as nature preserves. Other than the complete lack of public transport from the mainland, there's no excuse not to visit the twelve-mile-long, two-mile-wide island: arrive for a few hours and you could find yourself staying several days (though if you do, you'll need a fat wallet – living expenses are high here).

North of Sanibel, a road continues to **Captiva Island**, even less populated, its only concession to modern-day economics being an upmarket holiday resort at its northern tip, from which boat trips render some of the neighbouring islands accessible.

Practicalities

Your first stop on Sanibel should be the **Chamber of Commerce**, 1159 Causeway Boulevard (Mon–Sat 9am–7pm, Sun 10am–5pm; ☎472-1080), packed with essential **information** and numerous free publications. The only **public transport** is a "trolley" (info: ☎472-6374) operating from December to April between the Chamber of Commerce and the *South Seas Plantation*; one-day tickets are $2 for Sanibel and $4 to cover Sanibel and Captiva (see p.314). If your stay on Sanibel is a brief one, you'll get a good sense of what makes the place tick from the **guided trolley tour** (Nov–April Mon, Wed & Fri at 10am & 12.30pm; $8). A better way to get about is by **bike**: *Finnimore's Cycle Shop*, 2353 Periwinkle Way (☎472-5577), and *The Bike Rental Inc*, 2330 Palm Ridge Road (☎472-2241), are the cheapest places to rent one.

Accommodation on the islands is always more expensive than on the mainland, though rates are less between May and November. *Kona Kai*, 1539 Periwinkle Way (☎472-1001; ⑤), is among the least costly; if you'd rather be on the beach, use *West Wind Inn*, 3345 W Gulf Drive (☎1-800/282-2831; ⑦), or *Best Western*, 3287 W Gulf Drive (☎472-1700; ⑧). A good alternative to standard rooms are the wooden cottages, sleeping two to four, at *Seahorse*, 963 Kings Crown Road (☎472-4262; ④). Sanibel also has a **campground**, *Periwinkle Trailer Park*, 1119 Periwinkle Way (☎472-1433; $22 to pitch a tent).

For **eating**, you can get a filling breakfast at *Calamity Jane's Café*, 630 Tarpon Bay Road (☎472-6622)); the *Lighthouse Café*, 362 Periwinkle Way (☎472-0303), serves good-value meals throughout the day; and *Cheeburger Cheeburger*, 2413 Periwinkle Way (☎472-6111), has a variety of burgers. For a more substantial lunch or dinner, you'll find a wide selection of seafood at *The Mucky Duck*, Andy Rosee Lane (closed Sun; ☎472-3434), and at *Fast Eddie's*, 1975 Periwinkle Way (☎472-8445); alternatively, mouthwatering pasta and Cajun dishes are a speciality of the slightly more expensive *Jacaranda*, 1223 Periwinkle Way (☎472-1771).

Sanibel Island

From the mainland, Causeway Boulevard ($3 outbound toll) – a continuation of Route 876, fifteen miles west from downtown Fort Myers and just north of the town's beaches – meets Periwinkle Way, the main route through the southern half of Sanibel Island. Erected in 1884, the undramatic **Sanibel lighthouse**, a mile to the left, is a relic most arrivals feel obliged to inspect (from the outside

only) before spending a few hours on the presentable beach at its foot. More productively, retrace a course along Periwinkle Way and turn right into Dunlop Street, acknowledging the island's tiny city hall on the way to the **Island Historical Museum** (mid-Oct to mid-Aug Wed–Sat 10am–4pm; free): a century-old pioneer settler's home with furnishings and photos of early Sanibel arrivals – those who weren't seafarers tried agriculture until the soils were ruined by salt-water blown up by hurricanes – and displays on the pre-European dwellers, the Calusa Indians, including a thousand-year-old skeleton.

Continuing along Periwinkle Way, Tarpon Bay Road cuts west to the coast, passing the rampant vegetation of the **Bailey Tract**, a jungle-like rectangle of untamed land in the midst of a residential area: poorly marked trails will take you deeper in, among the alligators and the wildfowl – for the careful and courageous only. In either direction from the end of Tarpon Springs Road, resorts and tour-ists mark the beaches; turning left along Casa Ybel Road and Algiers Lane leads to the more promising **Gulfside City Park**, a slender sandy strip shaded by Australian pines and bordered by a narrow canal, with a nicely secluded picnic area. Before you leave, follow the bike path off Algiers Road for a few yards to a tiny **cemetery**, where a few wooden markers remember those who perished, some a hundred years ago, in their attempts to forge an existence on the then inhospitable island.

The J N "Ding" Darling Wildlife Refuge

In contrast to the smooth beaches along the Gulf side of the island, the opposite edge comprises shallow bays and creeks, a vibrant wildlife habitat under the protection of the **J N "Ding" Darling Wildlife Refuge** (daily except Fri sunrise–sunset; cars $4, cyclists and pedestrians $1); the main entrance and **information center** are just off the Sanibel–Captiva Road – chief artery of Sanibel's northern section. Alligators, brown pelicans and ospreys are usually easy to spy, but much of what you'll see at the refuge is determined by when you come: during the autumn, migrating songbirds are plentiful, thousands of winter-ing ducks show up in subsequent months, and in spring, graceful roseate spoon-bills sweep by just before sunset.

The five-mile **Wildlife Drive** requires slow speeds and plenty of stops if you're to see the well-camouflaged residents by car. If you're cycling, take heed of the wind direction before entering: you'll usually keep the wind at your back and not in your face by pedalling north to south. You'd do better, though, to plod the four miles of the **Indigo trail**, beginning just beyond the information center. There's a second, much shorter, foot route close to the north end of Wildlife Drive: the **Indian Shell trail**, which twists between mangrove and buttonwood, and passes a few lime trees (remaining from the efforts to cultivate the island) to a Native American **shell mound** – a hump in the ground, much less spectacular than you might hope.

Bailey-Matthews Shell Museum and C.R.O.W.

Taking the local love of shells to its logical conclusion, the newly opened, non-profit-making **Bailey-Matthews Shell Museum**, at 3075 Sanibel-Captiva Road (Tues–Sun 10am–4.30pm; $4), is devoted entirely to molluscs from all over the world. A cornucopia of colours, shapes and sizes is spread before you in such a way as to inform as well as entertain, revealing the formation of shells, their diversity and uses, past and present. The museum's several rooms merit an hour or two of quiet contemplation.

Still on Sanibel-Captiva Road, near the entrance to the J N "Ding" Darling Wildlife Refuge (see above), you'll find a "hospital" for injured, orphaned and sick native wildlife from all over southwest Florida. Since most of the several thousand patients treated here each year are the result of human interference, **C.R.O.W.** (Care and Rehabilitation of Wildlife Inc.) puts some of its energy into educating the public about the threats we often, unwittingly, pose. This ten-acre sanctuary, established thirty years ago and largely staffed by volunteers, recently opened its doors to the public and offers **guided tours** for small groups (Mon–Fri at 11am, Sun at 1pm; donation requested; book ahead on ☎472-3644). A short but enlightening talk on the dangers posed by carelessly discarded fishing lines and other detritus, is followed by a walk around the sanctuary's outdoor enclosures, which contain a multitude of mammals, birds, amphibians and reptiles until they are (hopefully) ready for release back into the wild. It all serves as a poignant reminder of man's impact on the environment, as well as the healing powers of nature.

Bowman's Beach

One of Sanibel's loveliest swathes of sand, **Bowman's Beach**, lies to the north of the island; to reach it, watch for Bowman's Beach Road off the Sanibel–Captiva

---

SHELLING ON SANIBEL AND CAPTIVA ISLANDS

Something Sanibel and Captiva share are **shells**. Literally tons of them are washed ashore with each tide, and the popularity of shell collecting has led to the bent-over condition known as "Sanibel Stoop". The potential ecological upset of too many shells being taken away has led to laws forbidding the removal of any live shells (ie one with a creature living inside), on pain of a $500 fine or a prison sentence. Novices and seasoned conchologists alike will find plenty to occupy them on the beaches; to identify your find, use one of the shell charts drawn in most of the giveaway tourist magazines – or watch the experts at work during the **Sanibel Shell Festival** in early March.

Road just prior to Blind Pass. Popular with the shell-hunting crowds, this is also an excellent spot for sunset-watching, and, in the more secluded sections, **naturists** perfect their all-over tans.

Captiva Island

Immediately north of Bowman's Beach, the Sanibel–Captiva Road crosses Blind Pass by bridge and reaches **Captiva Island**, markedly less developed than Sanibel and inhabited only by a few hundred people. If you're not going to call on one of them, the sole site of note is the tiny **Chapel-by-the-Sea**, at 11580 Chapin. Mostly used for weddings, the chapel is unlikely to be open and you should walk instead around the **cemetery**, just opposite, where many of the island's orginal settlers are buried. With crashing waves a shell's throw away and the graves protected from the sun by a roof of seagrape, it's a fitting final resting place for an islander.

A few miles further, Captiva's northern tip is covered by the tennis courts, golf courses and Polynesian-style villas of the ultra-posh *South Seas Plantation*, where the cheapest beds are $150 a night. There's no point in hanging around here, except for the **boat trips** to the neighbouring islands.

Beyond Captiva Island: Cabbage Key

Of a number of small islands just north of Captiva, **Cabbage Key** is the one to visit. Even if you arrive on the lunch cruise from Captiva (see the box below), skip the unexciting food in favour of prowling the footpaths and the small marina: there's a special beauty to the isolated setting and the views across Pine Island Sound. Do take a peep into the **restaurant**, though, to see the most expensive wallpaper in Florida: an estimated $25,000 worth of dollar bills, each one signed by the person who left it pinned up in observance of a Cabbage Key tradition. If you get the urge **to stay** longer, the inn has six simple rooms on offer at $65 and, more expensively, a few rustic cottages in the grounds; reserve on ☎282-2278 at least a month in advance.

BOAT TRIPS FROM CAPTIVA ISLAND

Several organized **boat trips** begin from the docks at the *South Sea Plantation*. The best of them is the lunch cruise, departing at 10.30am and returning at 3pm, allowing two hours ashore at either Cabbage Key (see above) or at a gourmet restaurant on Useppa Island; cost is $27.50. A dinner cruise to the same destinations, departing at 6pm and returning at 10.30pm, costs $38. Neither price includes food while ashore – there's no obligation to eat once you land, but taking your own food on the boat isn't allowed. Other cruises include an hour-long breakfast voyage around Captiva, departing at 9am and costing $22 with a light meal provided; and an hour-long sightseeing cruise at 3.30pm for $16.50.

Whenever you sail, you're likely to see **dolphins**: many of them live in the warm waters around the islands, sometimes leaping above the water to turn somersaults for your benefit.

To obtain further **details** and to make **reservations** for all sailings, call ☎472-7549.

South of Fort Myers

While Sanibel and Captiva islands easily warrant a few days of exploration, there's less to keep you occupied on the mainland on the seventy-mile journey **south from Fort Myers** towards the Everglades National Park. The towns you'll pass will carry less appeal than the nearby beaches, or the vistas of Florida's interior at the end of inland detours. Set aside a few hours, however, to examine one of the stranger footnotes to Florida's history: the oddball religious community of the Koreshans.

The Koreshan State Historic Site

Around the turn of the century, some of the nation's radicals and idealists began viewing Florida as the last earthly wilderness; a subtropical Garden of Eden where the wrongs of modern society could be righted. Much to the amusement of hard-living Florida farmers, some of them came south to experiment with utopian ways, though few braved the humidity and mosquitoes for long. One of the more significant arrivals was also the most bizarre: the **Koreshan Unity** community, which came from Chicago in 1894 to build the "New Jerusalem" on a site now preserved as the **Koreshan State Historic Site**, 22 miles from Fort Myers, just south of Estero beside Hwy-41 (daily 8am–sunset; cars $3.25, pedestrians and cyclists $1).

The flamboyant leader of the Koreshans*, **Cyrus Teed**, was an army surgeon when he underwent the "great illumination": an angel appearing and informing him that the Earth was concave, lining the inner edge of a hollow sphere, at the centre of which was the rest of the universe. Subsequently, Teed changed his name to "Koresh" and gained a following among Chicago intellectuals who, like him, were disillusioned with established religions and were seeking a communal, anti-materialistic way of life. Among the tenets of the Koreshan creed were celibacy outside marriage, shared ownership of goods, and gender equality. The aesthetes who came to this desolate outpost, accessible only by boat along the alligator-infested Estero River, quickly learned new skills in farming and house building, and marked out thirty-foot-wide boulevards, which they believed would one day be the arteries of a city inhabited by ten million enlightened souls. In fact, at its peak in the three years from 1904, the community numbered just two hundred. After Teed's death in 1908, the Koreshans fizzled out, the last member – who arrived in 1940, fleeing Nazi Germany – dying in 1982.

The Koreshan library and museum

The Koreshan site will be a disappointment unless you first call at the **Koreshan library and museum**, 8661 Corkscrew Road (tours Mon–Fri at 1pm, 2pm, 3pm & 4pm; $1; four person minimum; details on ☎992-0311), for background on the Koreshans' beliefs, plus the chance to see numerous photos and portraits of Teed, some of his esoteric books, and copies of the still-published Koreshan newspaper, *The American Eagle*. Along the broad thoroughfares at the neigh-

---

*There is no link between the Koreshans and David Koresh, leader of the religious cult who barricaded themselves into their Waco, Texas, headquarters and battled with federal troops before they and their compound were incinerated in April 1993.

bouring **site**, several of the Koreshans' buildings have been restored. Among them are Teed's home; the Planetary Court, meeting place of the seven women – each named after one of the seven known planets – who governed the community; and the Art Hall, where the community's cultural evenings were staged, where Koreshan celebrations (such as the solar festival in October and the lunar festival in April) still occur, and where the *rectilinator*, a device which "proved" the Koreshan theory of the concave Earth, can be seen.

Bonita Springs and the Corkscrew Swamp Sanctuary

A fast-growing residential community, **BONITA SPRINGS**, seven miles south of the Koreshan site, has negligible appeal besides providing access to **Bonita Beach**, along Bonita Beach Road, and the less impressive **Everglades Wonder Gardens**, on the corner of Terry Street and Hwy-41 (daily 9am–5pm; $8), keeping a multitude of the state's indigenous creatures in cramped confinement.

Make more of an effort and you'll get a better impression of natural Florida twenty miles **inland** on Route 846 (branching from Hwy-41 a few miles south of Bonita Springs) at the National Audubon Society's **Corkscrew Swamp Sanctuary** (May–Nov daily 8am–5pm; Dec–April 7am–5pm; $6.50), an enormous gathering of Spanish-moss-draped cypress trees rising through a dark and moody swamp landscape. Tempering the strange joy of the scene, though, is the knowledge that all of the much larger area presently safeguarded by the Big Cypress Swamp National Preserve (see "The Everglades", below) used to look like this; uncontrolled logging felled the five-hundred-year-old trees and severely reduced Florida's wood stork population, who nest a hundred feet up in the tree tops. The remaining wood stork colony is still the largest in the country, but is now faced with the threat of falling water levels.

The two-hour **guided tour** is excellent, especially with the help of the leaflet from the visitor center. A unique facet of this park, though, is found at the outset, on the way to the restrooms. Here an ingenious, though remarkably simple "living machine" aids water management in the park by recycling waste matter from the restrooms through a purely natural environment to produce purified water. Within a visually pleasing plant-filled glasshouse construction, the cycle relies on sunlight, bacteria, algae and snails to break down the waste, a process that is later continued by vegetation, such as alligator flag, arrowhead, and small insects and animals. The result is purified water that fulfils statutory hygiene standards. At the time of writing, plans were afoot to introduce butterflies into the "garden", eventually creating a colony, and it's mildly amusing to think that if you avail yourself of the facilities in Corkscrew Swamp, a part of you will remain here for some time to come, helping to preserve it.

Continuing south: Naples and Marco Island

A place of million-dollar homes and $500-a-ticket costume balls, **NAPLES** has little to thrill the cost-conscious traveller except many miles of public **beaches**, which make the pervading social snobbishness bearable. You'll get the hang of the place on Fifth Avenue, where the boat yards from the town's fishing community origins have been turned into upmarket clothes shops, art galleries and restaurants – press on swiftly to **Lowdermilk Park**, about two miles north of the pier, which, on weekends, is the most gregarious of the local sands. If you do want **information**, then try the Golden Gate Visitor Center at 8801 Davis Boulevard (daily 9am–5pm; ☎352-0508).

Greyhound buses do stop in Naples (at 2669 Davis Boulevard; ☎774-5660), but it's no great loss that they don't go anywhere near **MARCO ISLAND**, directly south, where artificial bald eagle nests are among the techniques dreamed up by property developers to bring back the wildlife their high-rise condos have driven away. At the northern end of the island, the old village of Marco has some charm, and **Tigertail Beach Park**, at the end of a boardwalk from Hernando Drive, is a fine place to relax – though neither really makes the journey (seven miles along Route 951 off Hwy-41) worthwhile. The Everglades, within easy striking distance, are a far superior target.

The Everglades

Nothing anywhere else is like them: their vast glittering openness, wider than the enormous visible round of the horizon, the racing free saltness and sweetness of their massive winds, under the dazzling blue heights of space. They are unique also in the simplicity, the diversity, the related harmony of the forms of life they enclose. The miracle of the light pours over the green and brown expanse of sawgrass and of water, shining and slow-moving below, the grass and water that is the meaning and the central fact of the Everglades of Florida. It is a river of grass.

Marjory Stoneman Douglas, *The Everglades: River of Grass*

Whatever scenic excitement you might anticipate from one of the country's more celebrated natural areas, no mountains, canyons nor even signposts herald your arrival in the **Everglades**. From the straight and monotonous ninety-mile course of Hwy-41, the most dramatic sights are small pockets of trees poking above a completely flat sawgrass plain that stretches to the horizon. It looks dead and empty; you wonder what all the fuss is about. Yet these wide open spaces resonate with life, forming part of an immensely subtle and ever-changing ecosystem that has evolved through a unique combination of climate, vegetation and wildlife.

Originally encompassing everything south of Lake Okeechobee, throughout this century the Everglades' boundaries have steadily been pushed back by human demands for farmland, fresh water and urban development; only a comparatively small section around Florida's southeastern corner is under the federal protection of the **Everglades National Park**. It's here, where public access is designed to inflict minimum damage, that the vital links holding the Everglades together become apparent: the all-important cycle of wet and dry seasons; the ability of alligators to discover water and dig for it with their tails; and the tree islands providing sanctuaries for animals during the flood period. None of this can be comprehended from a car window, or with a half-hour ride through the sawgrass on an airboat: noisy, destructive contraptions touted all along Hwy-41 but banned inside the park.

Don't expect to fathom it all: the Everglades are a constant source of surprise, even for the few hundred people who live in them. Use the visitor centers, read the free material, take the guided tours and, above all, explore slowly. It's then that the Everglades begin to reveal themselves, and you'll realise you're in the middle of one of the natural world's most remarkable ecosystems.

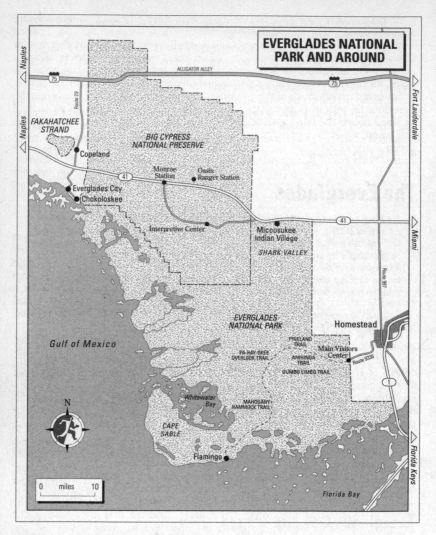

Some geology and natural history

Appearing as flat as a table-top, the oolitic limestone (once part of the seabed) on which the Everglades stand actually tilts very slightly – by a few inches over seventy miles – towards the southwest. For thousands of years, water from summer storms and the overflow of Lake Okeechobee has moved slowly through the Everglades towards the coast. The water replenishes the sawgrass, which grows on a thin layer of soil – or "marl" – formed by decaying vegetation on the limestone base, and gives birth to the algae at the foot of a complex food chain that sustains much larger creatures, most importantly alligators.

Alligators earn their "keepers of the Everglades" nickname during the dry winter season. After the summer floodwaters have reached the sea, drained through the bedrock or simply evaporated, the Everglades are barren except for the water accumulated in ponds or "gator holes" – created when an alligator senses water and clears the soil covering it with its tail. Besides nourishing the alligator, the pond provides a home for other wildlife until the summer rains return.

Sawgrass covers much of the Everglades, but where natural indentations in the limestone fill with marl, tree islands – or "hammocks" – appear, just high enough to stand above the flood waters and fertile enough to support a variety of trees and plants. Close to hammocks, often surrounding gator holes, you'll find wispy green-leafed willows. Smaller patches of vegetation, like small green humps, are called "bayheads". Pinewoods grow in the few places where the elevation exceeds seven feet; and in the deep depressions that hold water the longest, dwarf cypress trees flourish, their treetops forming a distinctive "cypress dome" when large numbers cover a extensive area.

Human habitation and exploitation

Before dying out through contact with Europeans, several Native American tribes lived hunter-gatherer existences in the Everglades; the shell mounds they built can still be seen in sections of the park. In the nineteenth century, Seminole Indians, who'd fled white settlers in the north, also lived peaceably in the area (for more on them, see "Miccosukee Indian Village", p.322). By the late 1800s, a few white settlements – such as those at Everglades City and Flamingo – had sprung up, peopled by fugitives, outcasts and loners, who, unlike the Indians, looked to exploit the land rather than live in harmony with it.

As Florida's population grew, the damage caused by uncontrolled hunting, road building and draining the Everglades for farmland gave rise to a significant conservation lobby. In 1947, a section of the Everglades was declared a national park, but unrestrained commercial use of nearby areas continued to upset the Everglades' natural cycle; a problem acknowledged – if hardly alleviated – by the preservation in the Seventies of the Big Cypress Swamp, just north of the park.

As human understanding increases, so the severity of the problems faced by the Everglades becomes ever more apparent. The 1500 miles of canals built to divert the flow of water away from the Everglades and towards the state's expanding cities, the poisoning caused by agricultural chemicals from the farmlands around Lake Okeechobee, and the broader changes wrought by global warming, could yet turn Florida's greatest natural asset into a wasteland – with wider ecological implications that can only be guessed at.

Everglades City and around

Purchased and named in the Twenties by an advertising executive dreaming of a subtropical metropolis, **EVERGLADES CITY**, thirty miles from Naples and three miles south off Hwy-41 along Route 29, has a population of under five hundred living around a disproportionately large city hall. Most who visit are solely intent on diminishing the stocks of fish living around the mangrove islands – the aptly titled **Ten Thousand Islands** – arranged like jigsaw-puzzle pieces around the coastline.

For a closer look at the mangroves that safeguard the Everglades from surge tides, ignore the ecologically dubious tours advertised along the roadside and

Orientation

A busy two-lane road, not the scenic drive you might expect, **Hwy-41** (the **Tamiami Trail**) runs east from Naples around the northern edge of the park, providing the only land access to the Everglades City, Shark Valley and Chekika (at the end of Richmond Drive, nine miles south of Hwy-41, on Route 997) park entrances, and to Fakahatchee Strand, the Big Cypress National Preserve and the Miccosukee Indian Village. To reach the Flamingo entrance, touch the edge of Miami and head south. **No public transport** of any kind runs along Hwy-41 or to any of the park entrances, though daytrips are available from Miami (see p.118). Between Naples and Fort Lauderdale, *Greyhound* buses use "Alligator Alley", the popular title for Route 84, twenty miles north of Hwy-41 and recently converted into a section of I-75.

When to visit

Though open all year, the park changes completely between its **wet** (summer) and **dry** (winter) seasons. The best time to visit is **winter** (Nov to April), when receding floodwaters cause wildlife, including migratory birds, to congregate around gator holes and sloughs (fresh water channels); ranger-led activities – such as guided walks, canoe trips and talks – are frequent; and the mosquitoes are bearable.

The picture is entirely different in **summer** (May to Oct), when afternoon storms flood the sawgrass prairies and pour through the sloughs, leaving only the hammocks visible above water. Around this time, mosquitoes become a severe annoyance, rendering the backcountry campgrounds almost uninhabitable; organized activities are substantially reduced; migratory birds have gone; and the park's wildlife spreads throughout the park due to a plentiful supply of food.

A clever compromise is a visit **between the seasons** (late April to early May or late Oct to early Nov), which avoids the worst of the mosquitoes and the winter

take one of the park-sanctioned **boat trips** (departures every 30min 8.30am–5pm; the last trip departing at 4.30pm or 5pm depending on sunset time; tours last 90–105min; $11) from the dock on Chokoloskee, a blob of land – actually an Indian shell mound – marking the end of Route 29. The dockside **visitor center** (daily 8.30am–4.30pm in summer, 7.30am–5pm in winter; ☎941/695-3311) provides information on the cruises and the excellent ranger-led **canoe trips** (Sat 10am in winter). Anybody adequately skilled with the paddle, equipped with rough camping gear, and with a week to spare, should have a crack at the hundred-mile **wilderness waterway**, a marked trail through Whitewater Bay to Flamingo (see below), with numerous backcountry campgrounds en route.

Other than boat-accessed camping, there's no **accommodation** inside this section of the park. In Chokoloskee, though, you can rent an RV by the night for $45–60 at *Outdoor Resorts* (☎695-2881), or get a simple cottage in the grounds of the *Everglades Rod & Gun Lodge*, 200 Riverside Drive (☎941/695-4211; ③).

Big Cypress National Preserve

The completion of Hwy-41 in 1928 led to the destruction of thousands of towering bald cypress trees – whose durable wood is highly marketable – lining the roadside sloughs. By the Seventies, attempts to drain these acres and turn them into saleable residential plots had caused enough damage to the national park for the tourist crowds, but at the same time reveals plenty of wildlife and the park's changing landscapes.

Entering the park and accommodation
Entering the park is free at Everglades City (though you can only see it by boat or canoe). At Shark Valley ($4), Flamingo ($5) and Chekika ($5) you **pay** per car; tickets are valid for seven days and can be used at all sites. Only Shark Valley closes for the night. With the exception of the wilderness waterway canoe trail between Everglades City and Flamingo, you can't travel from one section of the park into another.

Apart from the two organized campgrounds and hotel at Flamingo, park **accommodation** is limited to backcountry campgrounds. In most cases these are raised wooden platforms with a roof and chemical toilet, accessible by boat or canoe; to stay, you need a permit, issued free from the relevant visitor center. One backcountry site at Flamingo, Pearl Bay, is accessible to **disabled visitors**.

Practical tips
In the park, wear a hat, sunglasses and loose-fitting clothes with long sleeves and long trousers, and carry plenty of **insect repellent**. Besides the hazards of sunburn (there's very little shade) and mosquitoes, you need take no special measures for the walking trails, most of which are short trots along raised boardwalks.

Travelling and camping in the **backcountry** requires more caution. Most exploration is done by boat or canoe along marked trails, with basic campgrounds situated on the longer routes. Take a **compass**, **maps** (available from visitor centers) and ample provisions, including at least a **gallon of water** per person per day. Supplies should be carried in **hard containers**, as racoons can chew through soft ones. Be sure to leave a **detailed plan** of your journey and its expected duration with a park ranger. Finally, pay heed to the latest **weather forecast**, and note the tidal patterns if you're canoeing in a coastal area.

government to create the **Big Cypress National Preserve** – a massive chunk of protected land mostly on the northern side of Hwy-41. Sadly, neither the bald cypress trees nor the wood storks that once flourished here are present in anything like their previous numbers (a better place to observe both is the Corkscrew Swamp Sanctuary; see p.316). The only way to traverse the Big Cypress Swamp is on a very rugged 29-mile hiking trail, beginning twenty miles east on Hwy-41 at the **Oasis Ranger Station** (Thurs–Mon 9am–4pm; ☎941/695-4111).

While it's not actually part of the national preserve, be sure to visit the nearby **Fakahatchee Strand**, directly north of Everglades City on Route 29: a water-holding slough sustaining dwarf cypress trees (much smaller than the bald cypress; grey and spindly during the winter, draped with green needles in summer), a stately batch of royal palms, and masses of orchids and spiky-leafed air plants. If possible, see it on a **ranger-guided walk** (details on ☎941/695-4593).

If your car's suspension is dependable, turn right at Monroe Station, four miles west of the Oasis Ranger Station, onto Loop Road, a gravel road that's potholed in parts and prone to sudden flooding. This winds its way through cypress and pine-woods to Pinecrest, where an **interpretive center** makes sense of the varied terrains all around. The road rejoins Hwy-41 at Forty Mile Bend, just west of the Miccosukee Indian Village.

The Miccosukee Indian Village

Driven out of central Florida by white settlers, several hundred Seminole Indians retreated to the Everglades during the nineteenth century to avoid forced reset-tlement in the Midwest. They lived on hammocks in open-sided "chickees" built from cypress and cabbage palm, and traded, hunted and fished across the wetlands by canoe. Descendants of the Seminoles, and of a related tribe, the **Miccosukee** still live in the Everglades, though the coming of Hwy-41 – making the land accessible to the white man – brought another fundamental change in their lifestyle as they set about grabbing their share of the tourist dollars.

Four miles east of Forty Mile Bend, the **Miccosukee Indian Village** (daily 9am–5pm; $5) symbolizes their uneasy compromise. In the souvenir shop, good quality traditional crafts and clothes stand side-by-side with blatant tat, and in the "village", men turn logs into canoes and women cook over open fires: despite the authentic roots, it's such a contrived affair that anyone with an ounce of sensitiv-ity can't help but feel uneasy – the arrow-shooting gallery and the awful alligator wrestling don't help. Since it's the only chance you're likely to get to discover anything of Native American life in the Everglades, it's hard to resist taking a look; though a plateful of traditional pumpkin bread from the *Miccosukee Restaurant* (☎305/223-8388), across the road, and a read of the *Seminole Tribune* newspaper, describing present-day concerns, might serve you better. From the marina beside the restaurant, the tribe run **airboat rides** ($7 for 30min) to another "village", situated on a hammock about fifteen minutes away through the sawgrass – another chance to buy dismal souvenirs and not a lot else.

Shark Valley

In no other section of the park does the Everglades' "River of Grass" tag seem as appropriate as it does at **Shark Valley** (daily 8.30am–6pm; cars $4, pedestrians and cyclists $2), a mile east of the Miccosukee Indian Village. From here, dotted by hardwood hammocks and the smaller bayheads, the sawgrass plain stretches as far as the eye can see. It's here, too, that the damage wrought by humans on the natural cycle can sometimes be disturbingly clear. The thirst of Miami coupled with a period of drought can make Shark Valley resemble a stricken desert.

Seeing Shark Valley

Aside from a few simple walking trails close to the **visitor center** (winter daily 8.30am–5.15pm; reduced hours during the summer; ☎305/221-8776), you can see Shark Valley only from a fourteen-mile loop road. Too lengthy and lacking in shade to be covered comfortably on foot, and off-limits to cars, the loop is ideally covered by **bike** (rental; costs $3.25 an hour; return by 4pm). Alternatively, a highly informative two-hour **tram tour** (departures hourly from 9am in winter; at 9am, 11am, 1pm & 3pm in summer; $6; reservations necessary March–July ☎305/221-8455) will get you around and stop frequently to view wildlife, but won't allow you to linger in any particular place.

Set out as early as possible (the wildlife is most active in the cool of the morn-ing), ride slowly and stay alert: otters, turtles and snakes are plentiful but not always easy to spot, and the abundant alligators often keep uncannily still. During September and October you'll come across female alligators tending their young;

the brightly striped babies often sun themselves on the backs of their extremely protective mothers; watch them from a safe distance. More of the same creatures – and a good selection of bird life – can be seen from the **observation tower** overlooking a deep canal and marking the far point of the loop.

It may seem hard to believe but Shark Valley is only seventeen miles from the western fringes of Miami. To **see more of the park**, continue east on Hwy-41, turn south along Route 997, and head west for eleven miles along Route 9336 from Homestead to the park's main entrance.

Pine Island

Everglades City has the islands and Shark Valley has the sawgrass, but the **Pine Island** section of the park – the entire southerly portion, containing Cape Sable and Flamingo (see below) – holds virtually everything that makes the Everglades tick: spend a well-planned day or two here and you'll quickly grasp the fundamentals of its complex ecology. From the **park entrance** (always open; cars $5, pedestrians and cyclists $3), the road passes the **main visitor center** (daily 8am–5pm; ☎305/242-7700) and continues for 38 miles to the tiny coastal settlement of Flamingo, a one-time pioneer fishing colony now comprising a marina, hotel and campground. There's no compulsion to drive the whole way, and the short walking trails (none more than half a mile) along the route will keep you engaged for hours; sensibly, though, you should devote one day to walking and another to the canoe trails close to Flamingo.

Accommodation

There are well-equipped **campgrounds** at Long Pine Key, near the main visitor center, and Flamingo ($4 to pitch a tent; $8 to hook up your RV), as well as many backcountry sites (free) on the longer walking and canoe trails. Reservations are not accepted for any of the campgrounds: spare space at Flamingo (which invariably fills first) or Long Pine Key can be checked on the board just inside the park entrance. If there is space and the visitor center is closed, you can use the site but should pay at the visitor center before 10am the following day. For the backcountry sites, you will, of course, need a permit: these are issued free at the visitor centers. The only **rooms** within the park are at *Flamingo Lodge* (☎941/695-3101 or ☎305/253-2241; ③, including a continental breakfast) – you'll need to make a reservation months in advance if arriving between November and April.

Towards Flamingo: walking trails

A good place to gather information on the Everglades' various habitats is the Royal Palm **visitor center** (summer daily 8am–4.15pm, winter 8am–5pm; down the Royal Palm turn-off, a mile from the main park entrance). Apparently unimpressed by the multitudinous forms of nature and animal life throughout the Everglades, large numbers of park visitors simply want to see an alligator, and most are satisfied by walking the **Anhinga Trail**, a mile from the main visitor center. Turtles, marsh rabbits and the odd raccoon are also likely to turn up on the route, but you should watch for the bizarre anhinga, a black-bodied bird resembling an elongated cormorant, which, after diving for fish, spends ages drying itself on rocks and tree branches with its white-tipped wings fully spread. Beat the crowds to the Anhinga Trail and then peruse the adjacent but very different **Gumbo Limbo Trail** (much of the vegetation along the trail was destroyed by Hurricane Andrew in 1992 and is now beginning to grow back), a hardwood hammock packed with exotic subtropical growths: strangler figs, gumbo limbos, royal palms, wild coffee and resurrection ferns. The latter appear dead during the dry season, but "resurrect" themselves in the summer rains to form a lush collar of green.

By comparison, the **Pinelands Trail**, a few miles further by the Long Pine Key campground, offers an undramatic ramble through a forest of slash pine, though the solitude comes as a welcome relief after the busier trails: the hammering of woodpeckers is often the loudest sound you'll hear. More bird life – including egrets, red-shouldered hawks and circling vultures – is viewable six miles ahead from the **Pa-hay-okee Overlook Trail**, which emerges from a stretch of dwarf cypress to face a great tract of sawgrass – a familiar sight if you've arrived from Shark Valley.

Although related to California's giant redwoods, the mahogany trees of the **Mahogany Hammock Trail**, eight miles from the overlook, are disappointingly small despite being the largest of the type in the country; a greater draw are the colourful snails and golden orb spiders lurking amongst their branches. The sight of the red mangrove trees – recognizable by their above-ground roots – rising from the sawgrass is a sure indication that you're approaching the coast.

Flamingo and around

A century ago, the only way to reach **FLAMINGO** was by boat, a fact that failed to deter a small bunch of settlers who came here to fish, hunt, smuggle and get paralytic on moonshine whisky. It didn't even have a name until the opening of a post office made one necessary: "The End of the World" was favoured by those who knew the place, but "Flamingo" was eventually chosen due to an abundance of roseate spoonbills – pink-plumed birds, killed for their feathers – wrongly identified by locals. The completion of the road to Homestead in 1922 was expected to bring boom times to Flamingo, but as it turned out, most people seized on this as a chance to leave. None of the old buildings remain, and present-day Flamingo does a brisk trade servicing the needs of sports fishing fanatics. On land, the **visitor center** (summer daily 9am–5pm; winter 7.30am–5pm; ☎941/695-2945) and the marina of the *Flamingo Lodge* (see p.323), are the activity bases.

There are several walking trails within reach of Flamingo, but more promising are the numerous **canoe trails**. Rent a canoe ($25 a day) from the marina, and get maps and advice from the visitor center. Obviously, you should pick a canoe trail that suits your level of expertise; a likely one for novices (though not alone if you've no experience whatsoever) is the three-mile **Noble Hammock Trail**, passing through sawgrass and around mangroves, using a course pioneered by bootleg booze-makers. For polished paddlers, the hundred-mile **wilderness waterway** to Everglades City (see p.319), lined by plentiful backcountry campgrounds, is the trip you've been waiting for.

If you lack faith in your own abilities, take one of the **guided boat trips** from the marina. The most informative, the **Pelican Backcountry Cruise** (daily 12.30pm & 3.30pm; $12; reservations on ☎305/253-2241), makes a two-hour foray around the mangrove-enshrouded Whitewater Bay, offering good views of **Cape Sable**, a strip of deserted beach and rough prairie hovering uncertainly between land and sea. An alternative, and a must for birdwatchers, is the **Bald Eagle Florida Bay Sunset Cruise** (daily 7pm and sunset; $8.50), a ninety-minute tour of the marine feeding and nursery grounds.

travel details

Trains

From Tampa to Bradenton (2 daily; 1hr 10min); Clearwater (2 daily; 45min); Clearwater Beach (2 daily; 1hr); DeLand (2 daily; 3hr 14min); Jacksonville (2 daily; 5hr 28min); Kissimmee (2 daily; 1hr 36min); Lakeland (2 daily; 32min); Orlando (2 daily; 12hr 16min); Palatka (2 daily; 4hr 1min); Sanford (2 daily; 2hr 54min); Sarasota (2 daily; 1hr 40min); St Petersburg (2 daily; 30min); Treasure Island (2 daily; 1hr); Winter Park (2 daily; 2hr 31min).

From St Petersburg to Tampa (2 daily; 35min); Treasure Island (1 daily; 30min); Winter Haven (2 daily; 2hr 45min).

Buses

From Tampa to Avon Park (1 daily; 3hr 5min); Bradenton (5 daily; 1hr); Clearwater (6 daily; 30min); Crystal River (3 daily; 3hr 13min); Fort Lauderdale (5 daily; 7hr 5min); Fort Myers (5 daily; 2hr 5min); Lake Wales (1 daily; 1hr 55min); Lakeland (1 daily; 1hr); Miami (5 daily; 8hr 55min); Naples (5 daily; 4hr 5min); Orlando (7 daily; 1hr 30min); Sarasota (5 daily; 1hr 35min); Sebring (1 daily; 3hr 30min); St Petersburg (15 daily; 35min); Tallahassee (3 daily; 6hr 35min); Venice (5 daily; 2hr 10min); West Palm Beach (1 daily; 6hr); Winter Haven (1 daily; 1hr 30min).

From St Petersburg to Clearwater (11 daily; 30min); Tampa (11 daily; 35min–1hr).

CHAPTER SEVEN

THE PANHANDLE

Rubbing hard against Alabama in the west and Georgia in the north, the long, narrow **Panhandle** has much more in common with the states of the Deep South than with the rest of Florida. Cosmopolitan sophisticates in Miami and Tampa have countless jokes lampooning the folksy life-styles of the people here – undeniably more rural and down-to-earth than their counterparts around the rest of the state – but the Panhandle has more to offer than many give it credit for; certainly, you won't get a true picture of Florida without seeing at least some of it.

A century ago, the Panhandle actually *was* Florida. At the western edge, **Pensacola** was a busy port when Miami was still a swamp; fertile soils lured wealthy plantation owners south and helped establish **Tallahassee** as a high-society gathering place and administrative centre – a role which, as the state capital, it retains; and the great Panhandle forests fuelled a timber boom that brought new towns and unrivalled prosperity. But the decline of cotton, the felling of too many trees and the coming of the East Coast railway eventually left the Panhandle high and dry.

The region today divides neatly in two. Much of the **inland Panhandle** still seems neglected: small farming towns that see few visitors despite the proximity of springs, sinkholes and the **Apalachicola National Forest**, perhaps the best place in Florida to disappear into the wilderness. The **coastal Panhandle**, on the other hand, is enjoying better times. Rows of hotels and condos mark the most popular, money-spinning sections, though much of its spectacular shoreline is shielded from developers, leaving many untainted miles of blindingly white sands. Each grain is almost pure quartz, washed down over millions of years from the Appalachian mountains, causing the beaches to squeak when you walk on them. Not to be outshone, the Gulf waters here are two-tone: emerald green close to the shore and deep blue further out.

Provided you're driving, **getting around** presents few problems. Across the inland Panhandle, **I-10** carries the through traffic, and **Hwy-90** links the little places and many of the natural sights between Tallahassee and Pensacola. It's easy, too, to turn south off I-10 or Hwy-90 and get to the coast in under an hour. The main route along the coast is **Hwy-98**, with a number of smaller, scenic

---

ACCOMMODATION PRICE CODES

All **accommodation prices** in this book have been coded using the symbols below. Note that prices are for the least expensive double rooms in each establishment. For a full explanation see p.27 in *Basics*.

① up to $30	③ $45–60	⑤ $80–100	⑦ $130–180
② $30–45	④ $60–80	⑥ $100–130	⑧ $180+

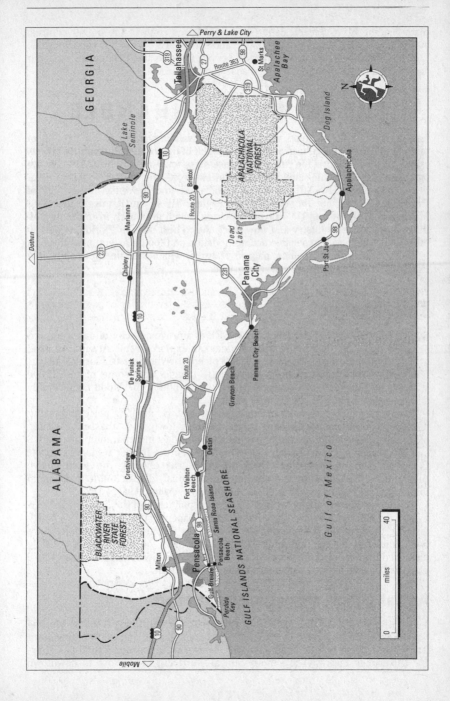

roads leading off it. Several daily *Greyhound* buses connect the bigger centres, but rural and coastal services are fewer, and some parts see no bus services at all. The Los Angeles–Jacksonville *Amtrak* service crosses the Panhandle, stopping once a day in each direction at Tallahassee and Pensacola.

THE INLAND PANHANDLE

Vast tracts of oak and pine trees, dozens of winding rivers and a handful of moderately sized agricultural bases make much of the **inland Panhandle** powerfully evocative of Florida in the days before mass tourism took hold. Despite the presence of the sociable state capital, **Tallahassee**, it's the insular rural communities strung along Hwy-90 – between Tallahassee and the busy coastal city of **Pensacola** – that set the tone of the region. These small towns, including **Marianna**, **Chipley** and **De Funiak Springs**, which grew rich from the turn-of-the-century timber industry and now work the richest soils in Florida, generally offer little – beyond inexpensive accommodation and food – as you pass through to the area's more compelling natural features, which include the state's only explorable caverns, and two massive forests.

Tallahassee

State capital it may be, but **TALLAHASSEE** is a provincial city of oak trees and soft hills that won't take more than two days to explore in full. Around its small grid of central streets – where you'll find plentiful reminders of Florida's formative years – briefcase-clutching bureaucrats mingle with some of the 25,000 students at Tallahassee's two universities, who brighten the mood considerably and keep the city awake late into the night.

Though built on the site of an important prehistoric meeting place and taking its name from Apalachee Indian ("talwa" meaning town; and "ahassee" meaning old), Tallahassee's **history** really begins with Florida's incorporation into the US and the search for an administrative base between the former regional capitals, Pensacola and St Augustine. Once this site was chosen, the local Native Americans – the Tamali tribe – were unceremoniously dispatched to make room for a trio of log cabins in which the first Florida government sat in 1823.

The scene of every major wrangle in Florida politics, and the home of an ever-expanding white-collar workforce handling the paperwork of the country's fourth fastest-growing state, Tallahassee's own fortunes through recent decades have been hindered by the lightning-paced development of south Florida. Oddly distanced from most of the people it now governs, the city remains a conservative place with a slow tempo – and a strong sense of the past.

Arrival, getting around and information

I-10 cuts across Tallahassee's northern perimeter; turning off along Monroe Street takes you past most of the budget accommodation and on into downtown Tallahassee, three miles distant. **Hwy-90** (known as Tennessee Street) and **Hwy-27** (Apalachee Parkway) are more central – arriving in or close to downtown

> The area code for Tallahassee and the rest of the Panhandle area
> covered in this chapter is ☎904

Tallahassee. Coming by **bus** presents few problems: the *Greyhound* terminal is at 112 S Tennessee Street (☎222-4240), within walking distance of downtown Tallahassee and opposite the local bus station. The *Amtrak* station is housed in a historic (1855) building at the intersection of Gaines Street and Railroad Avenue (☎224-2779), one block from Railroad Square in downtown Tallahassee. Tallahassee's **airport** is twelve miles southwest of the city (☎891-7800); frustratingly, no public transport services link it to the town. A **taxi** to the centre will cost around $15 (try *City Taxi*, ☎562-4222, or *Yellow Cab*, ☎222-3070); some motels offer a free pick-up service.

Getting around

Downtown Tallahassee can be seen **on foot**, and **local buses** (*TalTran* ☎891-5200) need only be used to reach outlying destinations. Collect a **route map and timetable** from the **bus station** (officially known as "Transfer Plaza") at the corner of Tennessee and Duval streets. You can get a **free ride** into downtown Tallahassee from the bus station with the **Old Town Trolley**, which runs to the Civic Center (near the New Capitol Building) and back at ten-minute intervals on weekdays between 7am and 6pm; hop on at any of the "Trolley Stop" signs. The *Old Town Trolley Tour Guide* leaflet also gives a brief history of each of the eighteen stops and their surrounds.

Information

The **Chamber of Commerce**, 100 N Duval Street (Mon–Fri 8.30am–5pm; ☎224-8116), has stacks of leaflets relating to the city and the surrounding area. For material covering Tallahassee, the rest of the Panhandle and much of the rest of the state, use the **Tallahassee Area Visitor Information Center** (Mon–Fri 8am–5pm, Sat & Sun 8.30am–4.30pm; ☎1-800/628-2866) on the ground floor of the New Capitol Building – see "Downtown Tallahassee", below. Be sure to pick up the engaging *Walking Guide to Historic Downtown Tallahassee* booklet, a comprehensive guide to the buildings and history of the area, the highlights of which are listed below.

Accommodation

Finding **accommodation** in Tallahassee is only problematic during two periods: the sixty-day sitting of the state legislature from early April – if you're arriving then, try to turn up on a Friday or Saturday when the power-brokers have gone home; and on autumn weekends when the Seminoles (Florida State University's immensely well-supported football team) are playing at home. If you can't avoid these periods, book well ahead.

The cheapest **hotels** and **motels** are on N Monroe Street about three miles from downtown: the *Econo Lodge*, no. 2681 (☎1-800/424-4777; ③), *Super 8*, no. 2702 (☎1-800/800-8000; ③), and the *Days Inn*, no. 2800 (☎1-800/325-2525; ③). Staying downtown is dearer, except during the summer when there are $28-a-night rooms on the FSU campus inside *Osceola Hall*, 500 Chapel Drive (☎222-

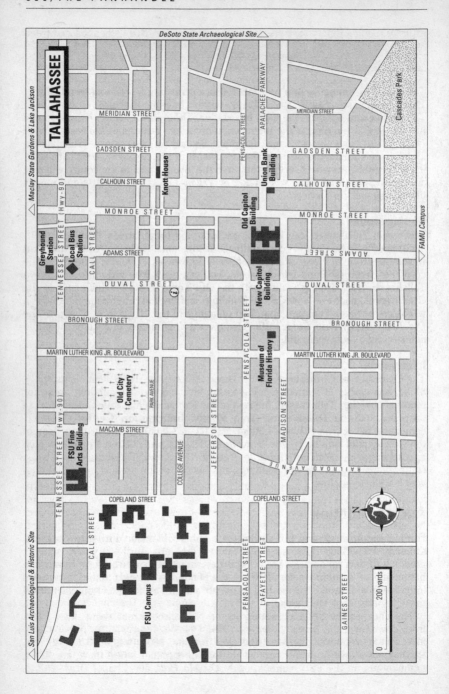

TALLAHASSEE

DeSoto State Archaeological Site

Maclay State Gardens & Lake Jackson

MERIDIAN STREET
GADSDEN STREET
CALHOUN STREET
MONROE STREET
ADAMS STREET
DUVAL STREET
BRONOUGH STREET
MARTIN LUTHER KING JR. BOULEVARD
MACOMB STREET
COPELAND STREET

Knott House

TENNESSEE STREET (Hwy-90)

CALL STREET

Greyhound Station
Local Bus Station

Old City Cemetery

PARK AVENUE

FSU Fine Arts Building

COLLEGE AVENUE

JEFFERSON STREET

FSU Campus

San Luis Archaeological & Historic Site

PENSACOLA STREET
APALACHEE PARKWAY
MERIDIAN STREET
GADSDEN STREET
CALHOUN STREET
MONROE STREET
ADAMS STREET
DUVAL STREET
BRONOUGH STREET
MARTIN LUTHER KING JR. BOULEVARD

Union Bank Building
Old Capitol Building
New Capitol Building
Museum of Florida History

MADISON STREET
RAILROAD AVENUE
COPELAND STREET

PENSACOLA STREET
LAFAYETTE STREET
GAINES STREET

FAMU Campus

Cascades Park

N

200 yards
0

5010; ③). Failing that, you're stuck with the *Holiday Inn*, 316 W Tennessee Street (☎1-800/HOLIDAY; ⑥), the *Governors Inn*, 209 S Adams Street (☎1-800/342-7717; ⑦), or the *Comfort Inn*, 1302 Apalachee Parkway (☎877-3141; ②).

There are no **campgrounds** within the city. The nearest to accept tents are beside Lake Talquin to the west, the closest being the *Tallahassee RV Center & Campground*, 6401 W Tenesee Street (Exit 28 off I-10; ☎575-0145; $16 to pitch a tent). Alternatively, the nearest **RV-only** sites are *Tallahassee RV Park* (☎878-7641; $18–20), five miles east on Hwy-90, and *Bell's Campground* (☎576-7082; $18–20), five miles west on Hwy-90.

Downtown Tallahassee

The soul of Tallahassee is the mile-square **downtown** area, where the main targets – the two Capitol Buildings, the State Museum of History and the two universities – are within walking distance of **Adams Street**, a peaceful and partly pedestrianized main drag, whose restored Twenties storefronts more often than not conceal attorneys' offices. A day will cover everything with ease.

The Capitol buildings and around

Downtown Tallahassee is dominated by a fifty-million-dollar eyesore, the towering **New Capitol Building**, at the junction of Apalachee Parkway and Monroe Street (Mon–Fri 8.30am–5pm; free; Visitor Information Center open in lobby Sat & Sun 8.30am–4.30 pm, see "Information", above), whose vertical vents make the seat of the Florida legal system resemble a gigantic air-conditioning machine. The only way to escape the sight of the structure, unveiled to much outrage in 1977, is to go inside. The twenty-second-floor **observation level** provides an unobstructed view over Tallahassee and its environs – and if you're visiting during April or May, stop off at the fifth floor for a glance at the House of Representatives or the Senate in action. Should you feel the need to learn more about the building's architecture and role, join the free 45-minute **guided tours** (on the hour, Mon–Fri 9–11am & 1–4pm, Sat & Sun 9am–3pm).

Florida's growing army of bureaucrats made the New Capitol Building necessary. Previously, they'd been crammed into the ninety-year-old **Old Capitol Building** (Mon–Fri 9am–4.30pm, Sat 10am–4.30pm, Sun noon–4.30pm; free; main entrance facing Apalachee Parkway) that stands in the shadow of its replacement. Designed on a more human and welcoming scale than its modern counterpart, with playful red and white awnings over its windows, it's hard to credit that the Old Capitol's walls once echoed with the decisions that shaped modern Florida. Proof is provided, however, by the political history contained within the side rooms: absorbing exhibits lifting the lid on the state's juiciest scandals and controversies.

Look along Apalachee Parkway from the Old Capitol's entrance to locate the nineteenth-century **Union Bank Building** (Tues–Fri 10am–1pm, Sat & Sun 1–4pm; free). The bank's past has been unsteady: going bust in the 1850s after giving farmers too much credit; re-opening to administer the financial needs of emancipated slaves after the Civil War; and later serving variously as a shoe factory, a bakery and a cosmetics shop. If the curator's on hand, he'll deliver an enthusiastic account of the background, otherwise you'll need to make do with the pictures and texts, and the small collection of period furniture in the director's office.

The Museum of Florida History

For a more rounded history – easily the fullest account of Florida's past anywhere in the state – visit the **Museum of Florida History**, 500 S Bronough Street (Mon–Fri 9am–4.30pm, Sat 10am–4.30pm, Sun noon–4.30pm; free). Detailed accounts of Paleo-Indian settlements, and the significance of their burial and temple mounds – some of which have been found on the edge of Tallahassee (see "Around Tallahassee", below) – are valuable tools in comprehending Florida's prehistory; and the imperialist crusades of the Spanish, both in Florida and across South and Central America, are outlined with copious finds. Other than portraits of hard-faced Seminole chiefs, whose Native American tribes were driven south into Florida backcountry, there's disappointingly little on the nineteenth-century Seminole Wars – one of the sadder and bloodier skeletons in Florida's closet. There's plenty, though, on the turn-of-the-century railroads that made Florida a winter resort for wealthy northerners, and on the subsequent arrival of the "tin can tourists", whose nickname referred to the rickety Ford camper-vans (forerunners of the modern Recreational Vehicles) they drove to what was by then called "the Sunshine State" – an ironic epithet for a region that had endured centuries of strife, feuding and almost constant warfare.

Tallahassee's universities: FSU and FAMU

West from Adams Street, graffiti-coated fraternity and sorority houses along College Avenue line the approach to **Florida State University (FSU)**. This has long enjoyed a strong reputation for its humanities courses, taught from the late 1800s in the Collegiate Gothic classrooms you'll see as you enter the wrought-iron gates, but has recently switched emphasis to science and business, hence the newer, less characterful buildings on the far side of the campus. Shady oaks and palm trees make the grounds a pleasant place for a stroll, but there's little cause to linger. The student art of the **University Gallery and Museum** (Mon–Fri 9am–4pm; free), in the Fine Arts Building, might consume a few minutes, but you'd be better occupied rummaging around inside *Bill's Bookstore*, just across Call Street at 107 S Copeland Street (☎224-3178), whose large stock includes many student cast-offs at reduced prices.

The more interesting of Tallahassee's two universities, in spite of being financially much the poorer, is the **Florida Agriculture and Mechanical University (FAMU)**, about a mile south of the Capitol buildings: Florida's major black educational centre since its founding in 1887. FAMU's **Black Archives Research Center and Museum** (Mon–Fri 9am–4pm; free) gives an illuminating insight into the situation of black people in Florida and the US, with a display of leg-irons from slavery times and many small but revealing items from the segregation era. Among these are letters and memorabilia of those who helped bring about change, including Martin Luther King and Booker T Washington, and two Florida women who contributed to the rise of black awareness: educator and folklorist Mary McLeod Bethune (see "Daytona Beach", *The Northeast Coast*), and author Zora Neale Hurston (see "Books" in *Contexts*). The archives are in the centre of the otherwise bleak campus, in an easily spotted nineteenth-century wooden building.

The Knott House

Another important landmark in Florida's black history, and one of the city's most evocatively restored Victorian homes, is the **Knott House Museum**, 301 E Park Avenue (Wed–Fri 1–4pm, Sat 10am–4pm; $3). This was built by a free Black in

1843 and later became home to Florida's first black physician; Florida's slaves were officially emancipated in May 1865 by a proclamation read from its very steps. The house takes its name, however, from the Knotts, a white couple who bought it in 1928. State treasurer during a period of economic calamity (Florida had been devastated by two hurricanes as the country entered the Depression), William Knott became one of Florida's most respected and influential politicians until his retirement in 1941. His wife, Luella, meanwhile, devoted her energies to the temperance movement (partly through her efforts, alcohol was banned in Tallahassee for a fifty-year period) and to writing moralistic poems, many of which you'll see attached to the antiques and furnishings that fill this intriguing relic. The absence of intrusive ropes cordoning off the exhibits allows for an unusually intimate experience of the house and its history.

Old City Cemetery

A somewhat different perspective on Tallahassee's past is provided by a walking tour around the **Old City Cemetery**, between Macomb Street and M.L. King Jnr Boulevard (daily sunrise–sunset; free), which was established outside the city's original boundaries in 1829, and restored in 1991. Its layout, consisting of four quadrants, is striking as a testament to segregation, even unto death: graves of Union soldiers lie in the southwest quarter, while those of Confederates are kept at a distance in the southeast portion; slaves and free Blacks were consigned to the western half of the ground, while whites occupied the eastern part. Among the names marked on gravestones, you'll find many of Tallahassee's former leading figures: their stories are told by an informative leaflet, *Walking Tour of Old City Cemetery*, available from the Visitor Information Center.

Around Tallahassee

Scattered around the fringes of Tallahassee, half a dozen diverse spots deserve brief visits: prehistoric mounds, archeological sites and lakeside gardens. All are easily accessible by car, though most are much harder to reach by bus.

The archeological sites

Slowly being unearthed at the **San Luis Archaeological and Historic Site**, 2020 W Mission Road, about three miles west of downtown Tallahassee (bus #21), the village of San Luis de Talimali was a hub of the seventeenth-century Spanish mission system, second only to St Augustine. At its zenith in 1675 its population numbered 1,400. Call at the **visitor center** (Mon–Fri 9am–4.30pm, Sat 10am–4.30pm, Sun noon–4.30pm; free) for a general explanation and to see some of the finds – or join the hour-long free **guided tour** (Mon–Fri at noon, Sat at 11am & 3pm, Sun at 2pm) to appreciate the importance of the place. On some weekends, period-attired individuals re-enact village life – it sounds tacky but can be fun.

The historical associations may be more dramatic, but there's much less tangible evidence of the past – just a few holes in the ground, in fact, on a site which is closed to the public except for special events – at the **DeSoto State Archaeological Site**, two miles east of downtown Tallahassee at the corner of Goodbody Lane and Lafayette Street, thought to have been where Spanish explorer Hernando de Soto set up camp in 1539 and held the first Christmas celebration in North America. The de Soto expedition also saw the first European crossing of the Mississippi River: see "History" in *Contexts* for the full story.

Tallahassee Museum of History and Natural Science

Three miles southwest of the city, the **Tallahassee Museum of History and Natural Science** (Mon–Sat 9am–5pm, Sun 12.30–5pm; $5), off Lake Bradford Road (bus #15) at 3945 Museum Drive, is primarily aimed at kids, though it could fill an hour even if you don't have young minds to stimulate. The centrepiece is a working nineteenth-century-style farm, complete with cows and wandering roosters. Elsewhere, there's a short nature walk, a few cases of snakes and a couple of old buildings of moderate note – a 1937 Baptist Church and a vintage schoolhouse.

Maclay State Gardens

For a lazy half-day, journey four miles northeast of downtown Tallahassee to **Maclay State Gardens**, set in a lakeside park at 3540 Thomasville Road, north of I-10, Exit 30 (park: daily 8am–sunset, cars $3.25; garden: daily 9am–5pm, Jan– April $3, rest of year free) – bus #16 stops close by. New York financier and amateur gardener Alfred B Maclay bought this large piece of land in the Twenties and planted flowers and shrubs in order to create a blooming season from January to April. It worked: for four months of each year the gardens are alive with the fragrances and fantastic colours of azaleas, camellias, pansies and other flowers, framed by dogwood and redbud trees and towered over by huge oaks and pines. Guided tours of the gardens are conducted at weekends around mid-March (call ☎487-4556 for details and times), but they're worth visiting at anytime, if only to retire to the lakeside pavilion for a snooze as lizards and squirrels scurry around your feet.

The admission fee to the gardens also gets you into the **Maclay House** (open Jan–April only), filled with the Maclays' furniture and countless books on horticulture.

While you're here, take your time to explore **the rest of the park** and Lake Hall. A picnic area gives great views of the lake, as does the short **Big Pine Nature Trail**, which meanders through the wooded hillside overlooking it. There's also a swimming area close to the carpark nearest the park's entrance.

Lake Jackson and the Indian Mounds

Most boat-owning locals moor their vessels beside the sizeable **Lake Jackson**, five miles north of downtown Tallahassee. On an inlet known as Meginnis Arm is the **Lake Jackson Mounds State Archaeological Site**, off Hwy-27 at Crowder Road (daily 8am–sunset; free), where rich finds, such as copper breastplates and ritual figures, suggest that this eighty-acre site was once an important Native American ceremonial centre. Other than large humps of soil and a sense of history, all that's here now are a few picnic tables and an undemanding nature trail over a small ravine. By car, follow the signs off Monroe Street; on foot, the site's a three-mile trek from the #1 bus stop.

Eating

One of the few places to get **breakfast** in downtown Tallahassee is *Goodies*, 116 E College Avenue (☎681-3888), which also serves **lunch** (sandwich specials and big salads). Other lunch options are the stylish New York deli *Andrew's Adams Street Café*, 228 S Adams Street (☎222-3444), and *Andrew's Second Act*, at the same address – an elegant restaurant also offering more expensive dinners. The

Uptown Café, 111 E College Avenue (☎222-3253), provides reasonably priced sandwiches and salads at lunchtime and bagels for breakfast; or you could try the $5–6 lunch and **dinner** buffets on offer at a couple of Chinese restaurants: *Ouy Lin*, 220 W Tennessee Street (☎222-0876), and *China Garden*, 435 W Tennessee Street (☎561-8849).

Out of downtown Tallahassee, *Mom and Dad's*, 4175 Apalachee Parkway (closed Mon; ☎877-4518), has delicious and affordable home-made Italian food; and the *Wharf Seafood Restaurant*, 4141 Apalachee Parkway (☎656-2332), carries a great range of what its name suggests. There's more low-cost seafood – with a riotous atmosphere and live Fifties music – at *Barnacle Bill's*, 1830 N Monroe Street (☎385-8734). Another cheap and fun place for seafood, gumbo and Newcastle Brown is *Paradise Grill*, 1406 N Meridian Road (☎224-2742). *The Mill*, 2329 Apalachee Parkway (☎656-2867) and 2136 N Monroe Street (☎877-4848), has burgers, salad buffets, sandwiches and exquisite pizzas to accompany its home-brewed beers.

Nightlife

Bolstered by its students, Tallahassee has a strong **nightlife**, with a leaning to social drinking and live rock music (see below). There's also **comedy** at the *Comedy Zone*, *Ramada Inn North*, 2900 N Monroe Street (☎386-1027), and a fair amount of **drama**, headed by the student productions at the *University Theater*, on the FSU campus (☎644-6500), and the *Tallahassee Little Theatre*, 1861 Thomasville Road (☎224-8474). Find out **what's on** from the "Entertainments" section of the Friday *Tallahassee Democrat* newspaper; the *Florida Flambeau*, the FSU student paper containing listings and recommendations; or, for live music details, listen to radio station *WUFS* on 89.7 FM.

Bars
On nights leading up to Seminole football matches, *Doc's*, 1921 W Tennessee Street (☎224-5946), is packed with clean-cut collegiate sports fans. Other strongly collegiate hang-outs are *Po' Boys Creole Café*, 224 E College Avenue (☎224-5400) and 679 W Tennessee Street (☎681-9191), *Potbelly's*, 459 W College Avenue (☎224-2233), and *Poor Paul's Pourhouse*, 618 W Tennessee Street (☎222-2978).

Less student-dominated, *Calico Jack's*, 2745 Capitol Circle NE (☎385-6653), offers beer, oysters and stomping southern rock'n'roll records; *Halligan's*, 1700 Halstead Boulevard (☎668-7665), is popular for its pool tables and chilled mugs of beer; and *Clyde's & Costello's*, 210 S Adams Street (☎224-2173), pulls a smart and very cliquey crowd, except on Thursdays when the four-for-one drinks offer strips away inhibitions.

Live music and clubs
Big name **live bands** appear at *The Moon*, 1020 E Lafayette Street (☎222-6666 for recorded info), or at the vast *Leon County Civic Center*, at the corner of Pensacola Street and Martin Luther King Jnr Boulevard (☎222-0400). For a taste of the past, try the *Americal Legion Hall*, 229 Lake Ella Drive (☎222-3382), which hosts a big-band dance night every Tuesday and good ole-boy country for the rest of the week; *Andrew's Upstairs*, 228 S Adams Street (☎222-3444), hosts modern jazz combos; and there's rock and blues at the log-cabin-like *Bullwinkle's*, 620 W Tennessee Street (☎224-0651). The *Cow Haus*, 836 Lake Bradford Road (☎574-

COWS), showcases known and unknown indie acts, as do *The Cab Stand*, 1019 N Munroe Street (☎224-0322), which also features blues, and *East Side Mario's*, 2576 N Munroe Street (☎385-1774).

Finally, *Top Flight Club*, 623 Osceola Street (☎575-7365), or *Club Diamond and Pearls*, 2011 S Adams Street (☎224-7004), are the pick of the local **nightclubs**, with different themes on different nights – always good for a drink, dance or laugh. The coolest spot in town is the *Waterworks*, 104½ S Munroe Street (☎224-1887), an intimate venue that you won't want to leave.

Listings

Art galleries Tallahassee has a credible arts scene: around Railroad Square, close to the junction of Springhill Road and Gaines Street, near the FSU campus, are some innovative galleries, and several local artists have open studios there. Other contemporary art showcases are the *Nice Picture Company*, 100 W Seventh Avenue; *Nomads*, 508 W Gaines Street; and the *La Moyne Gallery*, 125 N Gadsden St.

Canopy roads The name applied to thoroughfares where oak-tree branches form an arch across the road and you drive beneath a drooping fringe of Spanish moss. Miccossukee, Centerville, Old St Augustine, Meridian and Old Bainbridge roads are good examples.

Car rental Most companies have branches at the airport (see p.329), and at the following locations: *Alamo*, 1720 Capitol Circle (☎576-6134); *Avis*, 3300 Capitol Circle (☎331-1212); *Budget*, 1415 Capitol Circle (☎1-800/527-0700); *Lucky's*, 2539 W Tennessee St (☎575-0632); *Ugly Duckling*, 3120 W Tennessee St (☎575-0400).

Dentist Dental Information Service: ☎1-800/282-9117.

Hospital Non-emergencies: Capitol Medical Center ☎877-9018.

Pharmacy *Walgreens*, in the Tallahassee Mall, 2415 N Munroe Street (☎385-7145), open Mon–Sat 10am–9pm, Sun 12.30–5.30pm.

Sports Tickets for FSU baseball (March–May) and football (Sept–Nov) matches are on sale at the stadiums two hours before the games begin: ☎644-1073 and ☎644-1830 respectively. For info on FAMU sports teams, all known as the *Rattlers*, call ☎599-3200. There's a full fixture list in the local telephone book.

Western Union 460 W Tennessee St (☎224-4096); 1717 Apalachee Parkway (☎878-7990); 3111 Mahan Drive (☎877-0783).

North from Tallahassee

The Georgia border is only twenty miles **north of Tallahassee**, and reached via several routes, but the journey to it is a dour one. Twelve miles northwest along Hwy-27, tiny **HAVANA** tries to lure drivers with several blocks of Olde Worlde antique shops and art galleries. You'd do better to head twelve miles northeast from Tallahassee on Route 151 (Centerville Road) to **Bradley's Country Store** (Mon–Fri 9am–6pm, Sat 9am–5pm; free; guided tours on request; $1.50), which has been peddling Southern-style food for seventy years; unusual delicacies include country-milled grits, hogshead cheese and liver pudding.

A more time-filling destination is just across the state line on Hwy-319, twenty miles north of Tallahassee and five miles south of Thomasville, where the **Pebble Hill Plantation** (Tues–Sat 10am–5pm, Sun 1–5pm, $2; closed most of Sept; hour-long guided tour of house, with the last tour leaving at 4pm, $5) remains from the times of cotton picking and slavery, and shows how comfortable things were for the wealthy Whites who ran the show. Much of the original Pebble Hill burnt down in the Thirties, and what you see is a fairly faithful rebuilding of the sumptuous main house, complete wih the extensive fine art, antique, crystal and porcelain collection that belonged to the house's final owner, Elisabeth Ireland Poe, and was rescued from the fire. Note that babies and children aged 6 or under are not allowed into the house. Each April the house comes back to life as people throng to a spring plantation ball.

South from Tallahassee

At weekends, many Tallahassee residents head south to the Panhandle's beaches (see "The Coastal Panhandle", p.344). If you're not eager to join them, make a slower trek south along **routes 363** or **61**, tracking down a few isolated pockets of historical or geological significance; or take **Hwy-319** and lose yourself in the biggest and best of Florida's forests.

One of the most enjoyable ways to explore is by **cycling or roller-blading** the 16-mile Tallahassee–St Marks Historic Railroad Trail, a flat and straight course through placid woodlands following the route of a long-abandoned railroad. Bikes and blades can be rented for four hours from *Cyclelogical Bicycle Rentals*, 4780 Woodville Highway (☎656-0001; $16 and $15 respectively).

Leon Sinks Geological Area

Seven miles south of Tallahassee on Route 319 is the **Leon Sinks Geological Area** (8am–8pm; free), a fascinating karst (terrain that has been altered by rain and ground water dissolving underlying limestone bedrock). The area contains several prominent sinkholes, numerous depressions, a natural bridge and disappearing stream, which give a unique glimpse of the area before man's interference. There are three manageable trails of between half a mile and three miles, described in a guide leaflet available from the ranger station at the entrance.

The Natural Bridge Battlefield Site and St Marks

Ten miles southeast of Tallahassee, a turning off Route 363 at Woodville leads to the **Natural Bridge Battlefield Site** (daily 8am–sunset; free) where, on March 4, 1865, a motley band of Confederates saw off a much larger group of Union soldiers, preventing Tallahassee from falling into Yankee hands. Not that it made much difference – the war ended a couple of months later – but the victory is celebrated by a monument and an annual re-enactment on or close to the anniversary: several hours of shouting, loud bangs and smoke.

Twelve miles south of Woodville, Route 363 expires at the hamlet of **ST MARKS**, where the **San Marcos de Apalache Historic Site** (Thurs–Mon 9am–5pm, free; museum $1) offers decent pickings for students of Florida history – this sixteenth-century Spanish-built fort was visited by early explorers such as Pánfilo de Narváez and Hernando de Soto, and two hundred years later became Andrew Jackson's headquarters when he waged war on the Seminole Indians.

Round off a visit at one of the nearby fishcamp eating places, such as *Posey's* (no phone), on Old Fort Drive.

If you prefer wildlife to history, backtrack slightly along Route 363 and turn east along Hwy-98: at Newport you'll locate the main entrance to **St Marks National Wildlife Refuge** (daily sunrise–sunset; cars $3, pedestrians and cyclists $1), which spreads out over the boggy outflow of the St Marks River. Bald eagles and a few black bears are resident in the refuge, though from the various roadside look-out points and observation towers you're more likely to spot otters, white-tailed deer, raccoons and a wealth of bird life. Just inside the entrance, a **visitor center** doles out useful information (Mon–Fri 8am–4.15pm, Sat & Sun 10am–5pm).

Wakulla Springs

Fifteen miles south of Tallahassee, off Route 61 on Route 267, **Wakulla Springs State Park** (daily 8am–sunset; cars $3.25, pedestrians and cyclists $1), contains what is believed to be one of the biggest and deepest natural springs in the world, pumping up half a million gallons of crystal-clear pure water from the bowels of the earth every day – difficult to guess from the calm surface. The principal reason for visiting Wakulla Springs is to enjoy the barely touched scenery and to appreciate a part of Florida that is still intact after hundreds of years.

It's refreshing to **swim** in the cool waters (do so only in the marked area), but to learn more about the spring, you should take the fifteen-minute narrated **glass-bottomed boat tour** ($4.50) and peer down to the swarms of fish hovering around the 180-foot-deep cavern through which the water comes. Join the forty-minute **river cruise** ($4.50) for glimpses of some of the park's other inhabitants: deer, turkeys, turtles, herons and egrets – and the inevitable alligators. If *déjà vu* strikes, it may be because a number of films have been shot here, including several of the early *Tarzan* flics and parts of *The Creature from the Black Lagoon*. To see the alligators and snakes at their most active, take the **moonlight cruise** at twilight ($4.50).

You shouldn't leave without strolling through the **Wakulla Lodge**, a hotel built beside the spring in 1937, which retains many of its original features: Moorish archways, stone fireplaces and fabulous hand-painted Toltec and Aztec designs on the lobby's wooden ceiling. Take the opportunity, also, to pay your respects to the stuffed carcass of "Old Joe", one of the oldest and largest alligators ever known, who died in the Fifties, measuring eleven feet long and supposedly aged 200; he's in a glass case by the reception desk.

Spending a night here is actually comparatively cheap (☎224-5950; ③). The lodge and its surrounds have a relaxing ambience that can prove quite addictive. An added bonus is that once the daytrippers have departed, you'll have the springs and wildlife all to yourself.

Further South: the Apalachicola National Forest

With swamps, savannahs and springs dotted liberally about its half-million acres, the **Apalachicola National Forest** is the inland Panhandle at its natural best. Several roads enable you to drive through a good-sized chunk, and many undemanding spots offer a rest and a snack, but to see more of the forest than its

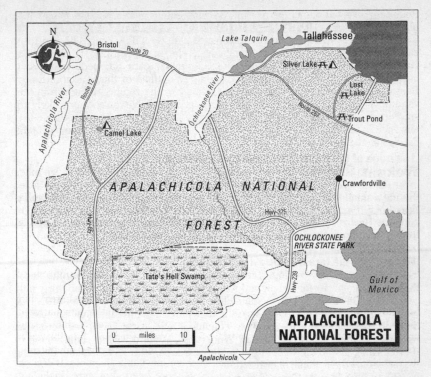

picnic tables and litter bins you'll have to make an effort: leaving the periphery and delving into the pristine interior, exploring at a leisurely pace, following hiking trails, taking a canoe on one of the rivers, or simply spending a night under the stars at one of the basic campgrounds.

Practicalities

The northeast corner of the forest almost touches Tallahassee's airport, fanning out from there to the edge of the Apalachicola River, about 35 miles west. Most of the northern edge is bordered by Hwy-20, the eastern side by Hwy-319 and Hwy-98, and to the south lies the gruesome no-man's-land of Tate's Hell Swamp (see below).

The main **entrances** are off Hwy-20 and Hwy-319, and three minor roads, Routes 267, 375 and 65, form cross-forest links between the two highways. **Accommodation** is limited to camping. With the exception of Silver Lake (see below), all the sites are free with basic facilities – usually just toilets and drinking water. For more information, call ☎643-2282. The only place to **rent a canoe** near the forest is *TNT Hideaway* (☎925-6412), on Route 2 near Crawfordville, on Hwy-319.

One section of the forest, Trout Pond (open April–Oct only; $2 per car), on Route 373, is intended for **disabled visitors** and their guests, with a wheelchair-accessible lakeside nature trail and picnic area.

The edge of the forest: Lost Lake and Silver Lake

For a brief taste of what the forest can offer, make for **LOST LAKE**, seven miles from Tallahassee along Route 373, where there's little except a few picnic tables beside a small lake. The area's well suited to a nibble and a waterside laze, and is less busy than the campervan-infested **SILVER LAKE**, nine miles east of the city, off Hwy-20. Swimming or camping at Silver Lake will cost you $2 and $5 respectively; anticipate the company of too many other people.

Deeper into the forest: hiking and canoeing

Several short, clearly marked **nature walks** lie within the forest, but the major **hiking trail**, strictly for ardent and well-equipped backpackers, is the thirty-mile **Apalachicola trail**, which begins close to Crawfordville, on Hwy-319. This passes through the heart of the forest and includes a memorable (and sometimes difficult, depending on the weather conditions and water level) leg across an isolated swamp, the Bradwell Bay Wilderness. After this, the campground at Porter Lake, just to the west of the wilderness area, with its toilets and drinking water, seems the epitome of civilization.

The trail leads on to **Camel Lake**, whose campground has drinking water and toilets, and the less demanding nine-and-a-half-mile **Camel Lake Loop trail**. By vehicle, you can get directly to Camel Lake by turning off Hwy-20 at Bristol and continuing south for twelve miles, watching for the signposted turn-off on the left.

Although there are numerous put-in points along its four rivers, **canoeists** can paddle right into the forest from the western end of Lake Talquin (close to Hwy-20), and continue for a sixty-mile glide along the Ochlockonee River – the forest's major waterway – to the Ochlockonee River State Park, close to Hwy-319. Obviously, the length of trip means that to do it all you'll have to use the riverside **campgrounds** (info from the Supervisor's Office, National Forests Florida, 325 John Knox Road, Tallahassee). Those with drinking water are at Porter Lake, Whitehead Lake and Mack Landing; be warned that these are often concealed by dense foliage, so study your map carefully.

South of the forest: Tate's Hell Swamp

Driving through the forest on Route 65 or Route 67, or around it on Hwy-319 (which merges with Hwy-98 as it nears the coast), you'll eventually pass the large and forbidding area called **Tate's Hell Swamp**. According to legend, Tate was a farmer who pursued a panther into the swamp and was never seen again. It's a breeding ground for the deadly water moccasin snake, and gung-ho locals sometimes venture into the swamp hoping to catch a few snakes to sell to less reputable zoos; you're well advised to stay clear.

West from Tallahassee

To discover the social character of the inland Panhandle, take Hwy-90 **west from Tallahassee** all the way to Pensacola: 180 miles of frequently tedious rural landscapes and time-locked farming towns that have been down on their luck since the demise of the timber industry fifty years ago. When it gets too much to bear, you can easily switch to the speedier I-10, or cut south to the coast. But the compensations are the endless supply of rustic eating places, low-cost accommodation, several appealing natural areas – and a chance to see a part of Florida that the travel brochures rarely reveal.

Lake Seminole and the Three Rivers State Recreational Area

Fifty miles out of Tallahassee, within spitting distance of the Georgia border, Hwy-90 reaches Sneads, a small town dominated by the large **Lake Seminole**, created by a Fifties hydroelectric project. On the lake's Florida side (other banks are in Georgia and Alabama), spend an enjoyable few hours in the **Three Rivers State Recreational Area** (daily 8am–sunset; cars $3.25, pedestrians and cyclists $1), two miles from Sneads on Route 271. A mile-long **nature walk** from the park's **camping area** (☎482-9006) leads to a wooded, hilly section where squirrels and alligators are two-a-penny, and white-tailed deer and grey foxes lurk in the shrubbery. Primarily, though, the lake is popular for its massive and abundant catfish, bream and bass. To spend a night by the lake without camping, use the ten-room *Seminole Lodge* (☎593-6886; ③), at the end of Legion Road, just outside Sneads.

Marianna and the Florida Caverns State Park

Twenty-five miles further along Hwy-90, **MARIANNA** is one of the larger inland Panhandle settlements, despite having a four-figure population for whom the twice-monthly horse sale is the only source of excitement. There isn't much to commend the place, though the **Chamber of Commerce**, 2928 Jefferson Street (Mon–Fri 8am–5pm; ☎482-8061), will give you a walking-tour map of the town's elegant Old South homes (the Chamber of Commerce itself sits inside one), and there's a more-than-filling lunch buffet of Chinese and Vietnamese specialties at *Kim's*, 4157 Lafayette Street (☎482-2257). Inexpensive **lodgings** can be found at *Motel Sandusky*, 918 W Lafayette Street (☎1-800/238-2552; ②).

The best thing about Marianna is its proximity to **Florida Caverns State Park** (daily 8am–sunset; cars $3.25, pedestrians and cyclists $1), three miles

---

CROSSING THE TIME ZONE

Crossing the Apalachicola River, which flows north–south across the Inland Panhandle, roughly 45 miles west of Tallahassee, takes you into the **Central Time Zone**, an hour behind Eastern Time and the rest of Florida. In the Coastal Panhandle, the time shift occurs about ten miles west of Port St Joe, on the boundary between Gulf and Bay counties.

north on Route 167, where hourly **guided tours** (9am–5pm; $4) venture through 65-foot-deep caverns filled with strangely shaped calcite formations. The caves are not new discoveries, they were mentioned in Spanish accounts of the area and used by Seminole Indians to hide from Andrew Jackson's army in the early 1800s – an unnerving experience in the days before electric lights illuminated the booming rock chambers. Back in the sun, the park has a few other features to fill a day comfortably. From the **visitor center** (☎482-9598) by the caverns' entrance, a **nature trail** leads around the floodplain of the Chipola River, curiously dipping underground for several hundred feet as it flows through the park. At the **Blue Hole Spring**, at the end of the park road, you can swim, snorkel or scuba-dive – and sleep at its **campground** ($14).

Chipley and Falling Waters State Recreation Area

Continuing west, the next community of any size is **CHIPLEY**, 26 miles from Marianna. The town takes its name from William D Chipley, who put a railroad across the Panhandle in the mid-1800s to improve the timber trade, and gave rise to little sawmill towns such as Chipley. The railroad is still here (restricted locally to freight), but the boom times are long gone, and it's a smart idea to leave the town along Route 77 for **Falling Waters State Recreation Area** (daily 8am–sunset; cars $3.25, pedestrians and cyclists $1), three miles south, to inspect Florida's only waterfall. The so-called fall is in fact a 100-foot drop into a tube-like sinkhole topped by a viewing platform. A trail passes several other sinks (without waterfalls), and another leads to a decaying oil well – remaining from an unsuccessful attempt to strike black gold in 1919. The park has a **campground** (☎638-6130; $8), but for accommodation under a roof use *Wilburn's Motel*, 700 Hwy-90 (☎638-1850; ②), back in Chipley.

De Funiak Springs

The railroad that carried timber also brought the Panhandle's first tourists a century ago, many of them drawn to a large, naturally circular lake in **DE FUNIAK SPRINGS** (on Hwy-90, forty miles from Chipley), around which the Chautauqua Alliance – a benevolent religious society espousing free culture and education for all – had set up a winter base. With the death of its founders and the coming of the Depression, the Alliance faded away, but its four-thousand-seat auditorium for great speakers of the day still stands beside the lake, one of several turn-of-the-century wooden structures whose Doric columns and raised balconies seem entirely at odds with the dozy character of the modern town. Amongst all the grandeur, it's the smallest building that's most worth seeking out: at 3 Circle Drive, the **Walton-De Funiak Library** (Mon 9am–7pm, Tues, Wed & Fri 9am–6pm, Sat 9am–3pm; free) has been lending books since 1886, and more recently acquired the Panhandle's most unexpected sight – a small stash of medieval European weaponry, donated by a local collector.

Another unlikely find is the **Chautauqua Vineyards**, on Hwy-331 near the junction with I-10, whose diverse wines may not be the world's finest but have picked a few awards in their seven years of existence and await your considered assessment (free tours and tastings, Mon–Sat 9am–5pm, Sun noon–5pm).

Stopping over in De Funiak Springs is a sound move if you're aiming for the more expensive coastal strip 25 miles south along Hwy-331. The *Econo Lodge*, 1325 S Freeport Road (☎892-6615; ②), has good rates but is closer to I-10 than the town; to stay in step with the historical mood, opt instead for the good-value **bed and breakfast** at the *Sunbright Manor*, 606 Live Oak Avenue (☎892-0656; ③). While in town, **eat lunch** amid the antiques at the *Busy Bee Café*, 2 N Seventh Street (☎892-6700).

The Blackwater River State Forest

Between the sluggish towns of Crestview and Milton, thirty miles west of De Funiak Springs, the creeks and slow-flowing rivers of **Blackwater River State Forest** are jammed each weekend with waterborne families enjoying what's officially dubbed "the canoe capital of Florida". In spite of the crowds, the forest is by no means overcommercialized, being big enough to absorb the influx and still offer peace, isolation and unruffled nature for anyone intrepid enough to hike through it. Alternatively, if you're not game for canoeing or hiking but just want a few hours' break, the **Blackwater River State Park** (daily 8am–sunset; cars $2, pedestrians and cyclists $1), within the forest four miles north of Harold off Hwy-90, has some easy walking trails.

From Milton, Hwy-90 and I-10 both offer a mildly scenic fifteen-mile drive over Escambia Bay to the hotels and freeways on the northern fringes of Pensacola, the city marking Florida's western extremity (see "Pensacola and around", p.354).

Accommodation in the forest

With the exception of the restored 1800s "cracker" **cabins** at Tomahawk Landing (see below; ①–⑤, depending on the comfort level), forest accommodation is limited to **camping** ($8–10). There are fully equipped sites at the Krul Recreation Area (☎957-4201), near the junction of Forest Road 4 and Route 19, and at the Blackwater River State Park (see above; ☎623-2363). Free basic sites intended for hikers lie along the main trails.

Hiking and canoeing

Hardened **hikers** carrying overnight gear can tackle the 21-mile **Jackson Trail** through wiregrass, named after Andrew Jackson who led his invading army this way in 1818, seeking to wrest Florida from Spanish control. On the way, two very basic shelters have handpumps for water. The trail runs between Karick Lake, off Hwy-189, fourteen miles north of Hwy-90, and the Krul Recreation Area. The shorter **Sweetwater Trail** is a good substitute if your feet aren't up to the longer hike: an enjoyable four-and-a-half-mile walk, it leaves the Krul Recreation Area and crosses a swingbridge and the Bear Lake dam before joining the Jackson trail.

Canoeing in the forest is centred around *Adventures Unlimited*, at **Tomahawk Landing** on Coldwater Creek (☎623-6197 or 1-800/239-6864), twelve miles north of Milton on Hwy-87; here you can rent tubes, canoes and kayaks for around $8, $13 and $20 respectively per day. Two- and three-day trips, with overnight gear and food provided, can also be arranged for around $28 per person.

THE COASTAL PANHANDLE

Lacking the glamour and international renown of Florida's other beach strips, the **coastal Panhandle** is nonetheless no secret to residents of the Southern states, who descend upon the region in their thousands throughout the summer. Consequently, a few sections of the region's 180-mile-long coastline are nightmarishly overdeveloped: **Panama City Beach** revels in its "redneck riviera" nickname, and smaller **Destin** and **Fort Walton Beach** are only marginally more refined. By contrast, little **Apalachicola**, and the **South Walton beaches**, both easily reached by car (they're inaccessible by bus) but out of the main tourist corridor, have much to recommend them: beautiful unspoilt sands, and off-shore islands where people are a rarer sight than wildlife.

Apalachicola and around

A few miles south of the Apalachicola National Forest (p.338), and the first substantial part of the coast you'll hit on Hwy-98 from central Florida, the **Apalachicola area** contains much of value. Mainland beaches may be few, but sand-seekers are compensated by the brilliant strands of three barrier islands, and the small fishing communities you'll pass through are untainted by the aggressive tourism that scars the coast fifty miles west.

Apalachicola

Now a tiny port with an income largely derived from harvesting oysters (nine out of every ten eaten in Florida are farmed here), **APALACHICOLA** once rode high on the cotton industry, which kept its dock busy and its populace affluent during the early 1800s. A number of stately columned buildings attest to former wealth; one, at 84 Market Street, is occupied by the **Chamber of Commerce** (Mon–Fri 9.30am–4pm, Sat 10am–3pm; ☎653-9419), where you can pick up a map to find the others along an enjoyable half-hour's stroll.

To reach Apalachicola, Hwy-98 crosses the four-mile Gorrie Memorial Bridge, which commemorates a man held in high regard by present-day Floridians. Arriving in the town in 1833, physician **John Gorrie** was seeking a way to keep malaria patients cool when he devised a machine to make ice (previously transported in large blocks from the north). Gorrie died before the idea took off and become the basis of the modern refrigerator and air-conditioning machine. The **John Gorrie State Museum**, on the corner of Sixth Street and Avenue D (Thurs–Mon 9am–noon & 1–5pm; $1), remembers the man and his work, as well as the general history of Alpachicola. Only a replica of the cumbersome ice-making device stands here – the original is in the Smithsonian Institute in Washington DC.

Accommodation and eating

There isn't a lot to Apalachicola, but the town makes a good base for visiting the barrier islands (see below). The crusty *Rainbow Inn*, 123 Water Street (☎653-8139; ③), has the least expensive rooms, and **bed and breakfast** can be had at *Coombes House Inn*, 80 Sixth Street (☎653-9199; ③), and the *Gibson Inn*, 57 Market Street (☎653-2191; ④). The latter also offers murder-mystery weekends

and a full lunch and dinner menu in their own somewhat pricey restaurant. You'll find lower prices just outside town (one-and-a-half miles west) at the *Rancho Inn*, 240 Hwy-98 (☎653-9435; ②). Good places to eat in town are the *Apalachicola Seafood Grill and Steakhouse*, 100 Market Street (☎653-9510), for a wide range of lunch and dinner specials; and the *Boss Oyster Bar*, 125 Water Street (☎653-8139), where you can tuck into fresh Apalachicola oysters. Adjacent to the *Rancho Inn* (see above), you'll find the *Red Top Café* (☎653-8612), which serves inexpensive, Southern cooking for lunch and dinner.

The barrier islands: St George, Dog and St Vincent

A few miles off the coast, framing the Apalachicola Bay and the broad, marshy outflow of the Apalachicola River, the three Apalachicola **barrier islands** are well endowed with beaches and creatures – including thousands of birds who use them as rest stops during migration – and two of them hold what must qualify as the most isolated communities in Florida. It's worth seeing one of the islands if you have the chance: all three can be visited with *Jeanni's Journeys* (☎927-3259), who provide a variety of instructional guided canoe trips and hikes; but only the largest island, St George, is accessible by road – Route 1A, which leaves Hwy-98 at Eastpoint.

Twenty-seven miles of powdery white sands and wide ocean vistas are not the only reason to come to **St George Island**, where shady live oak hammocks and an abundance of osprey-inhabited pine trees add colour to a day's lazy sunning. A few restaurants, beach shops, the eight-room *St George Inn* (☎927-2903; ④) and the *Buccaneer Inn* (☎927-2585; ④) occupy the island's central section; but in the eastern sector is the raccoon-infested **St George Island State Park** (daily 8am–sunset; cars $3.25, pedestrians and cyclists $1), where a three-mile **hiking trail** leads to a very basic **campground**, costing $4 (there's a better-equipped site at the start of the hike, costing $9; ☎927-2111).

A couple of miles east of St George, **Dog Island**, only accessible by boat (signs advertising crossings are all over the marina in Carrabelle, on Hwy-98), has a small permanent population living in little cottages nestled among Florida's tallest sand dunes. Several footpaths lead around the windswept isle, which won't take more than a few hours to cover. The only **accommodation** is pricey bed and breakfast at the *Pelican Inn* (☎1-800/451-5294); reservations are essential.

The freshwater lakes and saltwater swamps of **St Vincent Island**, almost within a shell's throw of St George's western end, form a protected refuge for loggerhead turtles, wild turkeys and bald eagles, among many other creatures. In November **guided trips** set out to see them (info: ☎653-8808); at any other time, you'll have to negotiate a boat ride from the mainland.

St Joseph Peninsula State Park and Port St Joe

For a final taste of virgin Florida coast before hitting heavily commercial Panama City Beach, take Route 30 – eighteen miles from Apalachicola, off Hwy-98 – to the **St Joseph Peninsula State Park** (daily 8am–sunset; cars $3.25, pedestrians and cyclists $1). A long finger of sand with a short **nature trail** at one end and a spectacular nine-mile **hiking route** at the other, the park has rough **camping** ($7) at its northern tip and better-equipped sites ($15) and **cabins** ($55; ☎227-1327) about halfway along near Eagle Harbor.

The peninsula wraps a protective arm around **PORT ST JOE** on the mainland, another dot-on-the-map fishing port that has seen better days. One such came in 1838 when a constitution calling for statehood (which Florida didn't acquire until seven years later) and liberal reforms was drawn up here*, only to be deemed too radical by the legislators of the time. At the **Constitution Convention State Museum** (Mon–Sat 9am–noon & 1–5pm; $1), signposted from Hwy-98 as you enter the town, daft, battery-powered waxworks re-enact the deed, alongside more credible mementoes of the town's colourful past, which show how it earned the title "wickedest city in the Southeast" during its early years.

Panama City Beach

An orgy of motels, go-kart tracks, mini-golf courses and amusement parks, **PANAMA CITY BEACH** is entirely without pretensions, capitalizing as blatantly as possible on the appeal of its 27-mile beach. The whole place is as entirely commercial, but with the shops, bars and restaurants all trying to undercut one another, there are some great bargains to be found – from air-brushed T-shirts and cut-price sunglasses to cheap buffet food. With everybody out to have a good time, there's some fine cruising to be done, too; not least during the Spring Break months of March and April when thousands of students from the Deep South states arrive to drink and dance themselves into oblivion. As vulgar and crass as it often is, Panama City Beach cries out to be seen. Come here once, if only as a voyeuristic daytrip – you may well be smitten enough by its tacky charm to stay longer.

---

*Strictly speaking, the constitution was drawn up in the town of St Joseph (later devastated by yellow fever, two hurricanes and a fire), whose site Port St Joe now occupies.

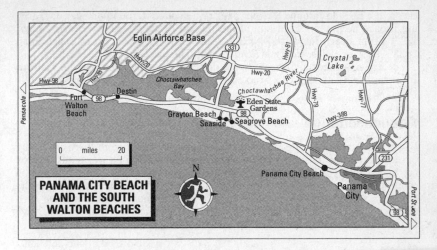

PANAMA CITY BEACH AND THE SOUTH WALTON BEACHES

Seasons greatly affect the mood. Throughout the lively **summer** (the so-called "100 Magic Days"), accommodation costs are high and advance bookings essential. In **winter**, prices drop and visitors are fewer; most are Canadians and – increasingly – northern Europeans, who have no problems sunbathing and swimming in the relatively cool (typically around 65°F) temperatures.

What Panama City Beach doesn't have is any **history** worth mentioning. It began as an offshoot of **Panama City**, a dull place of docks and paper mills eight miles away over the Hathaway Bridge (which Hwy-98 crosses). Today there's little love lost between the two communities; they have nothing in common besides a name.

Arrival, getting around and information

Panama City Beach being essentially a very long beach, **getting your bearings** could hardly be simpler, even if there are only two real, if rather similar landmarks (City Pier to the west, County Pier to the east). **Front Beach Road** (part of Hwy-98A, which starts at the foot of the Hathaway Bridge) is the main track, a two-lane highway, often called "the Strip", that's very much the place to cruise at crawling pace on weekends. The speedier, four-lane **Middle Beach Road** loops off Front Beach Road for a few blocks around County Pier from the junction with **Thomas Drive** (which links the eastern extremity of the beach). If you don't want to see gaudy Panama City Beach at all, **Back Beach Road** (Hwy-98) will take you straight through its anonymous residential quarter.

Greyhound **buses** pick up and drop off at the Shell station, 17325 W Hwy 98, leaving a fifteen-minute walk to the nearest motels. Travelling by other bus lines, however, you may well end up in Panama City (917 Harrison Avenue; ☎785-7861), rather than Panama City Beach, and you'll need to use one of the four daily *Greyhound* services linking them.

Panama City Beach is incredibly bad for **walking**; **public transport** is non-existent and **taxis** are prohibitively expensive, even for a short journey. Without a car, rent a **bicycle** (around $12 per day) or a **scooter** (around $30 per day; driving licence necessary) from any of the myriad beach shops; try *Beach Things*, 13226 Front Beach Road (☎234-0520), *Uncle Harvey's*, 17280 Front Beach Road (☎235-9963), or *California Cycle Rentals*, 8906 Thomas Drive (☎230-8080).

For free news-sheets, magazines and discount coupons, drop into the **Visitors Information Center**, 12015 Front Beach Road (Mon–Sun 8am–5pm; ☎1-800/PCBEACH).

Accommodation

Visitors to Panama City Beach outnumber residents, and though there are plenty of **places to stay**, these fill with amazing speed, especially on weekends. **Prices** are higher than you'll pay elsewhere in the Panhandle – $60–80 for a basic motel room in summer – so if you're counting the bucks, stay inland and drive to the beach. In winter prices drop by 30–40 percent, with monthly rentals being even cheaper. Camping is the only way to cut costs; sites are rarely more expensive than their equivalents elsewhere, though only a couple are good for tents.

Motels

As a very general rule, **motels** at the eastern end of the beach are smarter and slightly pricier than those in the centre, and those at the western end are quiet and family-orientated. That said, you're unlikely to find much to complain about at any place that takes your fancy.

To the **east**, you could try *Bay Villa*, 4501 W Hwy-98 (☎785-8791; ③); *Lagoon*, 5915 N Lagoon Drive (☎235-1800; ③); or *Pana Roc*, 5507 Thomas Drive (☎234-2775; ③). In the **centre** on Front Beach Road there's *Barney Gray* no. 10901 (☎234-2565; ③); *Beachside* no. 10710 (☎234-3997; ③); *Driftwood Lodge* no. 15811 (☎234-6601; ③); or *Siesta* no. 9113 (☎234-2510; ③). To the **west** on Front Beach Road, five worth recommending are *Blue Dolphin* no. 19919 (☎234-5895; ④); *Desert Palms* no. 17729 (☎234-2140; ③); *Impala* no. 17751 (☎234-6462; ③); *Sea Witch* no. 21905 (☎234-5722; ③); or *Sugar Sands Motel* no. 20723 (☎1-800/367-9221; ③).

Campgrounds

Several large and busy **campgrounds** cater mainly to RVs: the most central are *Miracle Strip RV Resort*, 10510 W Hwy 98 (☎234-3833; $20), and *Raccoon River*, 12405 Middle Beach Road (☎234-0181; $18). Quieter, and better for **tents**, are *Magnolia Beach*, 7800 Magnolia Road (☎235-1581; $16), and the *St Andrews State Recreation Area*, 4415 Thomas Drive (☎234-5140; $18).

Around the beach

Getting a tan, running yourself ragged at beach sports, and going hammer-and-tongs at the nightlife are the main concerns in Panama City Beach – you'll be regarded as a very raw prawn indeed if you go around demanding history, art and culture.

If you remain dissatisfied, try go-karting (around $7 for ten minutes), visiting one of the amusement parks (usually $17 for an all-inclusive day ticket), going on a fishing trip (take your pick of the party boats on the Thomas Drive Marina, from around $30 a day), scuba-diving (several explorable shipwrecks litter the area; details from any of the numerous dive shops), a waverunner trip to Shell Island (see below; $69), parasailing ($25 for a ten-minute ride), bungee jumping ($18) or a four-mile helicopter ride (starting at $30 for two people). Otherwise, the following provide the only variation.

Gulf World Marine Park
15412 Front Beach Road. Daily 9am–7pm; $10.95.

A cramped marine park, which has performing sea lions and dolphins, shark feeding sessions, and stingrays ripe for petting. Mildly more unusual is the "parrot show", featuring a roller-skating parrot and a high-wire-walking parakeet.

Museum of Man in the Sea
17314 W Hwy-98. Daily 9am–5pm; $5.

All you ever needed to know about diving is contained in this large collection that includes enormous eighteenth-century underwater helmets, bulky airpumps and matching bodysuits, deep-sea cutting devices, and torpedo-like propulsion vehicles. A separate display documents *Sealab*, the US Navy's underwater research vessel, the first of which was fitted out in Panama City and now stands outside the museum. This entertaining stop makes an ideal prelude to a day's snorkelling.

St Andrews State Recreation Area
4415 Thomas Drive. Daily 8am–sunset; cars $3.25, pedestrians and cyclists $1.

Get here early and you'll spot a variety of hopping, crawling and slithering wildlife by following one of the nature trails around the pine forest and salt marshes within the park. By noon the hordes have arrived to swim, fish and prepare picnics. If you're with kids, they'll enjoy splashing in the shallow lagoon sheltered by an artificial reef known as The Jetties, rated the number one beach for beauty and cleanliness in 1995. Take advantage of the campground (see "Accommodation", above) to enjoy the quietest times in this spot.

Shell Island
Half an hour by ferry from the Capt. Anderson Marina, foot of Thomas Drive. Boat departures at 9am, 1pm & 3.45pm; return ticket $8; or five minutes from St Andrews State Recreation Area, departing every 30mins 9am–5pm in summer, and 10am–3pm in winter; $7.

This seven-mile strip of sand is a haven for shell collectors and sun worshippers alike. With little shade on the undeveloped island, dark glasses are essential; the glare off the sands can be blinding. There are numerous boat trips from Captain Anderson Marina, most of which include a brief stop at Shell Island. The standard and prices vary wildly, so shop around.

Zoo World
9008 Front Beach Road. Daily 9am–dusk; $8.95.

If you're not opposed to animals being incarcerated, you'll enjoy this small collection of lions, tigers, orang-utans and other creatures. Many of the inmates prefer to sleep through the midday heat, so try to time your visit for early morning or late afternoon.

Eating

With an emphasis on basic wholesome cooking, and lots of it, the cheapest places to **eat** are the **buffet** restaurants, charging $4–10 for all you can manage. Try *Bishop's Family Buffet*, 12628 Front Beach Road (☎234-6457), for substantial meals three times daily; the *Golden Anchor*, 11800 Front Beach Road (☎234-1481), for sizeable seafood lunches and dinners; or *Katman'du*, at the intersction of Hwy-79 and Front Beach Road (☎235-9866), offering cheap and tasty break-fasts and catfish to die for.

Wherever you can get a buffet it's also possible to order from the menu, but if that's your real intention you're better off having **lunch or dinner** at one of the places below.

Cajun Inn at the Edgewater Beach Resort Shopping Center (☎235-9987). Mouth-watering selection of Cajun and Creole American cuisine.

Hamilton's, 5711 N Lagoon Drive (☎234-1255). Blackened alligator nuggets among the more regular dishes. Dinner only.

Mikato, 7724 Front Beach Rd (☎234-1388). Japanese food prepared by knife-throwing chefs.

Mike's Diner, 17554 Front Beach Rd (☎234-1942). Honest-to-goodness coffee shop that opens early, closes late and is great value throughout the day.

Ruthie T's, two blocks east of Joan Avenue on Thomas Drive (☎234-2111). Soul food with heart and a house special of blackened prime rib with attitude.

Shuckum's Oyster Pub & Seafood Grill, 15618 W Hwy-98 (☎235-3214). Cheap oysters in many styles, including fried in a sandwich.

Sweet Basil's, 11208 Front Beach Rd (☎234-2855). Classy Italian food combined with the freshest seafood.

The Treasure Ship, 3605 Thomas Drive (☎234-8881). A seafood restaurant built to resemble a wooden sailing ship, with pirates hopping around the tables.

Nightlife

Even if you only stay a few minutes, you should visit one of the two beachside **nightlife** fleshpots: *Club La Vela*, 8813 Thomas Drive (☎234-3866), or *Spinnaker*, 8795 Thomas Drive (☎234-7822) – both open 10am to 4am, with free entry. Each has dozens of bars, several discos, live bands and a predominantly under-25 clientele eagerly awaiting the weekend bikini and wet T-shirt contests, and thrice-weekly "hunk shows". Because competition between the two clubs is so intense, there'll often be free beer in the early evening. During the day, the action is by the clubs' open-air pools, where you're overdressed if covering anything more than your genitalia.

Everywhere else is tranquil by comparison. Although they may also have live music, a number of **bars** are worth a call simply for a drink. Check out *Sharky's*, 15201 Front Beach Road (☎235-2420), a massive tiki bar right on the beach; *Schooner's*, 5121 Gulf Drive (☎234-9074), for its ocean-view beachside tables; or *Pineapple Willy's Beachside Restaurant & Beach Bar*, 9900 S Thomas Drive (☎235-0928), where you can munch barbecue ribs steeped in Jack Daniels to the sound of Sixties and Seventies classic rock bands.

---

*It makes no difference to travellers, but for official purposes the South Walton Beaches don't include Fort Walton Beach, which is in adjoining Okaloosa County.

West from Panama City Beach

West of Panama City Beach, motels eventually give way to a more rugged, less developed terrain: the **beaches of South Walton County***, comprising fifty miles of some of Florida's best-kept coast. With a few exceptions, accommodation here is in resort complexes with sky-high rates, but it's a great area to spend a day gliding through. **Route-30A** links the region's small beach communities – a superior course to Hwy-98 (also known as Route 30), which takes an inland route. For **general information** on the South Walton beaches and surrounding area, phone the South Walton Development Council: ☎1-800/822-6877.

Along Route 30A: Seaside and Grayton

An exception to the casual, unplanned appearance of most South Walton beach towns, **SEASIDE**, forty miles from Panama City Beach, is an experiment in urban architecture, begun in 1981 by a rich, idealistic developer called Robert Davies. The theory is that Seaside's pseudo-Victorian cottages foster village-like neighbourliness and instil a sense of community: in reality, they do nothing of the sort. The picket fences and pastel paintwork of the cottages, and the aseptic red-brick streets – on which it seems antisocial to leave so much as a footprint – make for a place too expensive and exclusive to ever feel a part of.

Fortunately, the antidote to Seaside's sterility is just a few miles further along Route 30A at **GRAYTON**, whose secluded position (hemmed in by protected land) and ramshackle wooden dwellings have taken the fancy of a number of artists, who now reside here. Some of their work is regularly on show at the beachside *Gallery at Grayton* (Tues–Sat 9.30am–5pm). Also worth a visit is the workshop of **Joe Elmore**, on S Hwy-331, two miles past the Chamber of Commerce at the junction of Hwy-331 and Hwy-98 (daily 8.30am–4.30pm; ☎267-3511). Elmore is a wood sculptor who works with a chainsaw; his remarkably detailed creations can be admired here – as can several of his chainsaws.

Many who come to Grayton skip straight through to the **Grayton Beach State Recreation Area** (daily 8am–sunset; cars $3.25, pedestrians and cyclists $1), just east of the village. Walled by sand dunes and touching the banks of a large brackish lake, a night at the park's **campground** ($14) leaves plenty of time for a slow exploration of the village and its natural surrounds. Route 30A rejoins Hwy-98 seven miles west of Grayton.

Inland: Eden State Gardens

Away from the coast road, only **Eden State Gardens** (Thurs–Mon 8am–sunset; free), reached by Route 395 from Seagrove Beach a mile east of Seaside, are worth a visit. Their peace now disturbed only by the buzz of dragonflies, the gardens were once the base of the Wesley Lumber Company, which helped decimate Florida's forests during the turn-of-the-century timber boom. Impressed with the setting, the company boss pinched some of the wood to build himself a grandiose two-storey plantation-style home, the **Wesley house** (guided tours on the hour 9am–4pm Thurs–Mon; $2), rife with period architectural details and stuffed with the eighteenth-century antiques and curios of a later owner.

Destin and around

Once a small fishing village and a cult name among anglers for the fat marlin and tuna lurking in an undersea canyon a few miles offshore, **DESTIN** now features towering condos, which emerge through the heat haze as you approach on Hwy-98, and bear witness to two decades of unrestrained exploitation that have stripped away much of the town's character. Pick up tourist information at the **visitors center**, 1021 Hwy-98 (Mon–Fri 9am–5pm; ☎837-6241), signposted to your right as you arrive on Hwy-98.

Accommodation

You'll seldom find accommodation under $60 a night among the monolithic hotels in central Destin, so head around four miles east to the **motels** along Route 2378, also known as old Hwy-98 or Beach Road. The lowest rates are with *Sun'n'Sand* no. 4080; (☎837-6724; ④), *Crystal Beach Motel* no. 2931 E; (☎837-4770; ④) and *Surf High* no. 3000; (☎837-2366; ⑦, but reasonable prices in low season). For several people planning a **long stay**, *Surfside* no. 4701; (☎837-4700; ⑥) is an option. Reasonably priced alternatives include the *Hampton Inn*, 1625 Hwy-98 E (☎654-2677; ⑤), and *Silver Beach Motel & Cottages*, eight miles east of Fort Walton Beach (see below), 1050 Hwy-98 (☎837-6125; ③ for motel rooms).

Of the **campgrounds**, only two accept tents: *Destin RV Resort*, 3175 Cobia Street (☎837-6215; $18); and, in central Destin, *Destin Campground*, 209 Beach Drive (☎837-6511; $17).

The town and beach

Evidence of Destin's sudden expansion can be found amid the fading photos of bygone days in the **Old Destin Post Office Museum** (Mon & Wed 1.30–4.30pm; free), opposite the library on Stahlman Avenue; while the **Fishing Museum**, at 20009 Emerald Coast Parkway (Mon–Sat 11am–4pm; $2), with its mounted record-breaking catches, and thousands of pictures of landed fish with their grinning captors, is proof of Destin's high esteem among hook-and-line enthusiasts.

An escape from the condo overkill is provided by enticing white sands situated just east of Destin. The **beach** here is family territory, but it offers relaxation, excellent sea swimming and classic Gulf-coast sunsets. To reach it, take **Route 2378**, lined by unobtrusive motels and beach shops, which makes a coast-hugging loop off Hwy-98, starting about four miles from Destin.

While in the vicinity, resist any temptation to visit the **Museum of the Sea and Indian**, at 4801 Beach Drive (winter daily 9am–4pm summer 8am–6pm; $3.75), an entirely uninspiring place where you're loaned a cassette player and pointed to a dull batch of sea creatures, shells and Native American artefacts.

Eating and nightlife

On Hwy-98, the 24-hour *Destin Diner*, 1083 Hwy-98 (☎654-5843), dishes up hearty and economical breakfasts, burgers and frothy milkshakes in surrounds of neon and chrome; later in the day, there's a buffet at the *Seafood Factory*, 21 Hwy-98 (☎837-0999); fresh pasta, seafood and hand-tossed pizzas at *Sweet Basil's*, 104 Hwy-98 (☎654-5124); and seafood and steaks prepared on a California open grill at *Sunset Bay Café*, 9300 Hwy-98 (☎267-7108). Along Route 2378 you can munch a fish sandwich or shrimp salad at *Captain Dave's* no. 3769; (☎837-2627), while gazing over the ocean; and at *The Back Porch* no. 1740; (☎837-2022), a delicious vegetable platter complements the usual seafood dishes.

Destin's **nightlife** has little vigour: a few of the beachside bars and restaurants offer nightly drink specials – look for the signs – or you can drink to the accompaniment of undistinguished rock bands at the *Hog's Breath Saloon*, 1239 Siebert Street (☎244-2199); dance the night away at *Nightown*, 140 Palmetto Avenue, two blocks east of the Destin Bridge (see below, ☎837-6448); or enjoy the floor shows accompanied by Fifties and Sixties music at *Yesterday's*, 1079 E Hwy-98 (☎837-1954), easy to spot with its classic Chevy and Thunderbird out front.

Okaloosa Island and Fort Walton Beach

Hwy-98 leaves Destin by rising over the **Destin Bridge**, giving towering views of the two-tone ocean and intensely white sands, before hitting the crazy golf courses and amusement parks of **Okaloosa Island**. The island's **beaches**, immediately west, are a better sight, kept in their raw state by their owner – the US Air Force – and making a lively weekend playground for local youths and high-spirited beachbums.

A mile west, the neon motel signs that greet arrivals to **FORT WALTON BEACH** offer no indication that this was the site of a major religious and social centre during the Paleo-Indian period; so important were the finds made here that the place gave its name to the "Fort Walton Culture" (see "History", in *Contexts*, for more). These days it's military culture that dominates, as the town is home to Eglin, the country's biggest Air Force base. Aside from a few crewcuts and topless bars, however, you'll see little evidence of the base close to Hwy-98, and much of Fort Walton Beach has a more downbeat and homely feel – and slightly lower prices – than Destin. The local **visitors center**, 1540 Hwy-98 E (Mon–Sat 8am–5pm; ☎1-800/322-3319), has abundant information on eating and accommodation.

Accommodation

The cheapest **motels** are along Miracle Strip Parkway (the local section of Hwy-98): *Super 8*, no. 333 SW; (☎244-4999; ③), *Knights Inn* no. 209; (☎244-5137; ④), *Days Inn* no. 135; (☎1-800/325-2525; ④), or *Greenwood*, 1340 Hwy-98 (☎244-1141; ③). The nearest **campground** is the RV-only *Playground RV Park*, four miles north on Hwy-189 (☎862-3513); campers with **tents** should make for *Gulf Winds Park*, ten miles west on Hwy-98 (☎939-3593), or, slightly further on, *Navarre Beach Family Campground* (☎939-2188), just outside Navarre.

The Indian Temple Mound and Air Force Armament museums

If you were inspired by the sizeable temple mound standing incongruously beside the busy highway into Fort Walton Beach, then you might wish to inspect the small **Indian Temple Mound Museum** (June–Aug Mon–Sat 9am–5pm; Sept–May Mon–Sat 11am–4pm; $2), at the junction of Hwy-98 and Route 85, which is crammed with elucidating relics.

For an insight into more contemporary culture, the **Air Force Armament Museum** (daily 9.30am–4.30pm; free), six miles north of Fort Walton Beach on Route 85, has a large stock of what the local Air Force base is famous for: guns, missiles and bombs – and the planes that carry them. The first guided missiles were put together here in the Forties, and work on developing and testing (non-nuclear) airborne weaponry has continued unabated ever since.

Eating and nightlife

For $4 you can get all the breakfast you can eat at *Peppers*, 1120 Santa Rosa Boulevard (☎243-3395), or opt for their delicious cinnamon rolls. Visit later in the day for remarkably cheap buffet lunches and dinners. More healthily, *Mother Earth's Good Time Café*, 512 Eglin Parkway (☎863-3092), uses nothing but fresh natural ingredients and country recipes; and *Thai Saree*, 163 Eglin Parkway (☎244-4600) serves excellent Thai food for lunch and dinner. The pricier *Royal Orchid*, 238 N Eglin Parkway (☎864-3344), dishes up great Indian dinners. Seafood buffets are on offer at *Sam's Oyster House*, 1214 Siebert Drive, just off Santa Rosa Boulevard (☎244-3474), as well as a full seafood menu. High-quality steak and seafood dinners are provided at the *Coach-N-Four*, 1313 Lewis Turner Boulevard (☎863-3443).

Fort Walton Beach **nightlife** amounts to little more than the usual **beachfront bars**, mostly on Okaloosa Island, with some good happy hours. The best are *Pandora's*, 1120 Santa Rosa Boulevard (☎244-8669), drawing tourists and locals to its nightly specials; *Fudpucker's Beachside Bar & Grill*, 108 Santa Rosa Boulevard (☎243-3833), with live entertainment on "The Deck"; and *Harpoon Hanna's Ship Deck/The Soggy Dollar Saloon*, 1450 Miracle Strip Parkway, offering live beach rock and reggae.

West from Fort Walton

If you're driving, travel **west from Fort Walton** along Hwy-98 and branch off on Route 399 for sixty scenic miles along **Santa Rosa Island** to the Gulf Islands National Seashore, near Pensacola Beach (see "Pensacola and around" below). The parallel route, the continuation of Hwy-98, is much duller, but is the one the daily *Greyhound* **bus** takes from the station at 101 SE Perry Avenue (☎243-1940). A worthy stop if you're peckish, for tasty food at rock-bottom prices in a friendly yet idiosyncratic setting; is *Hazel's Country Kitchen*, one mile west of the Navarre Bridge on Hwy-98 (☎939-3437).

Pensacola and around

Tucked away at the western end of the Panhandle, you might be inclined to overlook **PENSACOLA**, built on the northern bank of the broad Pensacola Bay and five miles inland from the nearest beaches, particularly as its prime features are a naval aviation school and some busy dockyards. Pensacola is, however, an historic centre: occupied by the Spanish from 1559 – only the hurricane that ended their settlement prevented it becoming the oldest city in the US – it repeatedly changed hands between the Spanish, French and British before becoming the place where Florida was officially ceded by Spain to the US in 1821. The city has retained enough evidence of its seesawing past to give substance to a short visit, but it also makes a good and economical base for exploring one of the prettiest and least spoilt parts of the Coastal Panhandle; just cross the Bay Bridge to the coast, you'll find Pensacola Beach neighbouring the wild, protected beaches of the Gulf Islands National Seashore.

Arrival, information and getting around

Unless you're arriving from the inland Panhandle on I-10 or Hwy-90, aim to take the scenic route to Pensacola, along Santa Rosa Island on **Route 399** (also known here as Via De Luna Drive). Doing this, you'll first strike Pensacola Beach, from which Pensacola Beach Road swings north, crossing the Santa Rosa peninsula and joining **Hwy-98** before crossing the three-mile-long Pensacola Bay Bridge into the city. At the foot of the bridge, on the city side, is the **visitor information center** (daily 8am–5pm; ☎1-800/874-1234), packed with the usual worthwhile handouts.

Unusually, the *Greyhound* **bus** station is far from central, being seven miles north of the city centre at 505 W Burgess Road (☎476-4800); bus #10 links it to Pensacola proper. **Local buses** (info: ☎436-9383) serve the city but not the beach; the main terminal is at the junction of Gregory and Palafox streets. To get from the city to the beach without your own transport, take a **taxi** (*ABC* ☎438-8650, or *Yellow* ☎433-3333): the fare will be roughly $10–12.

Accommodation

The main approach roads from I-10, N Davis Boulevard and Pensacola Boulevard, are both lined with unmissable billboards advertising **budget chain hotels** for $30–50 a night. **Central** options are more limited: cheapest is the *Seville Inn*, 223 E Garden Street (☎1-800/277-7275; ②); the *Civic Inn*, 200 N Palafox Street (☎432-3441; ②), and *Days Inn*, 710 N Palafox Street (☎438-4922; ②), are slightly dearer. A few miles west of the centre is the *Mayfair Motel & RV Park*, 4540 Mobile Highway (☎455-8561; ①).

At **Pensacola Beach**, the lowest prices are at *Barbary Coast*, 24 Via De Luna Drive (☎932-2233; ④), *Gulf Aire*, 21 Via De Luna Drive (☎932-2319; ③), and the *Sandpiper Inn*, 23 Via De Luna Drive (☎932-2516; ③). *The Hampton Inn*, 2 Via De Luna Drive (☎932-6800; ⑤) is a comfortable, though pricier alternative, but you do benefit from a continental breakfast included in the cost.

The closest **campground** is the *Fort Pickens Campground* (☎932-5018), on the Gulf Islands National Seashore, a few miles west of Pensacola Beach (see p.359). Two others are further out: *Big Lagoon*, ten miles southwest on Route 292A on Perdido Key (☎492-1595; $8); and *Circle G* (☎944-1096), on the city's forested fringe, near Exit 2 off I-10, about twelve miles from the centre.

On **Perdido Key**, accommodation other than camping is pricey: choose from *The Best Western*, 13585 Perdido Key Drive (☎492-2755; ③), and the *Perdido Bay Golf Resort*, 1 Doug Ford Drive (☎492-1243; ④).

The city

Pensacola's past was much livelier than its present, and virtually everything worth seeing lies within three adjoining **districts** in the centre of the city: the Palafox District, North Hill, and the Seville District. Apart from the restored buildings and museums here, there are just a small number of offices and shops, and

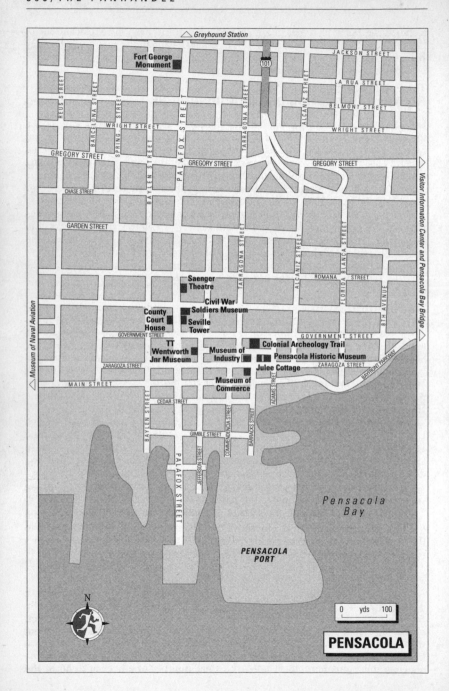

△ Greyhound Station

JACKSON STREET

Fort George
Monument

101

LA RUA STREET

BELMONT STREET

REUS STREET

BARCELONA STREET

SPRING STREET

BAYLEN STREET

PALAFOX STREET

TARRAGONA STREET

ALCANIZ STREET

WRIGHT STREET

WRIGHT STREET

GREGORY STREET

GREGORY STREET

GREGORY STREET

CHASE STREET

GARDEN STREET

TARRAGONA STREET

ALCANIZ STREET

FLORIDA BLANCA STREET

8TH AVENUE

ROMANA STREET

Visitor Information Center and Pensacola Bay Bridge △

Saenger
Theatre

Civil War
Soldiers Museum

County
Court
House

Seville
Tower

GOVERNMENT STREET

GOVERNMENT STREET

TT
Wentworth
Jnr Museum

Museum of
Industry

Colonial Archeology Trail

Pensacola Historic Museum

ZARAGOZA STREET

Julee Cottage

ZARAGOZA STREET

ADAMS STREET

BAYFRONT PARKWAY

MAIN STREET

Museum of Naval Aviation △

Museum of
Commerce

BAYLEN STREET

CEDAR STREET

PALAFOX STREET

JEFFERSON STREET

GIMBLE STREET

COMMENDENCIA STREET

BARRACKS STREET

*Pensacola
Bay*

N

**PENSACOLA
PORT**

0   yds   100

PENSACOLA

surprisingly few people. Elsewhere, only a naval aviation museum – the city's major single tourist attraction – offers any inducement to delay heading out to Pensacola Beach for some serious sunbathing and nature exploration.

The Palafox District

Already a booming port by the turn of the century, the opening of the Panama Canal was expected to boost Pensacola's fortunes still further. Sadly, the surge in wealth never came, but the optimism of the era is apparent in the delicate ornamentation and detail in the turn-of-the-century structures around the southerly section of Palafox Street – the **Palafox District**.

Take a look first at the **County Court House**, at the junction of Palafox and Government streets, which, besides its legal function, has also seen service as a customs house, a post office and tax offices. Opposite, the slender form and vertically aligned windows of the **Seville Tower** exaggerate the height of what, in 1909, was the tallest building in Florida. A block further north, at 118 Palafox Place, the Spanish Baroque **Saenger Theater** is now the base of the Pensacola Symphony Orchestra; if the door is open, take the opportunity to have a peek at the interior – twice as evocative as the outside.

Also meriting a look, the **Civil War Soldiers Museum**, 108 S Palafox Place (Mon–Sat 10am–4.30pm; $4), houses a collection of uniforms, weaponry and many unsettling medical tools – all of which saw action in the Civil War – which graphically illustrate the conditions endured by soldiers during the conflict between the States. Ask at the entrance, which doubles as a well-stocked bookstore specializing in the Civil War, about the thirty-minute videos that put the exhibits into context. Note the newspaper article on the wall behind the counter, which mentions Myrtle, a volunteer who occasionally works here and whose father and grandfather served in the Confederate Army.

North Hill

Between 1870 and 1930, Pensacola's professional classes took a shine to the **North Hill** area, just across Wright Street from the Palafox district, and commissioned elaborate homes in a plethora of fancy styles. Strewn across the tree-studded fifty-block area are pompous Neoclassical porches, cutesy Tudor-Revival cottages, low-slung California bungalows, and rounded towers belonging to the finest Queen Anne homes. Being private residences, none is open to the public, and the best way to see them is by driving around Palafox, Spring, Strong and Brainerd streets.

The clamour to build houses in this fashionable neighbourhood led to the ruin of **Fort George**, which once barracked two thousand British troops and fell to the Spanish at the Battle of Pensacola in 1781. Only an imitation cannon and a plaque at the corner of Palafox and LaRua streets locates the spot.

The Seville District: Historic Pensacola Village

As a commercial centre, Pensacola kicked into gear in the late 1700s, with a cosmopolitan mix of Native Americans, early settlers and seafaring traders gathering here to swap, sell and barter on the waterfront of the **Seville District**, about half a mile east of Palafox Street. Those who did well took up permanent residence, and many of their homes remain in fine states of repair, forming – together with several museums – the **Historic Pensacola Village** (daily 10am–4pm; $5.50). Each ticket is valid for two days and allows access to all of the museums and former homes (and you should see them *all*, the effect of the whole is far greater than the sum of its parts) in an easily navigated four-block area. Although it's easy to take the self-guided tour, the free **guided excursions** (winter daily 11.30am & 1.30pm; summer 10.30am, 11.30am, 1.30pm & 2.30pm) will help you gain a more intimate view of the area.

Start at the **Museum of Commerce**, next door to the visitor center on the corner of Zaragoza and Tarragona streets, an entertaining indoor re-creation of Palafox Street in its turn-of-the-century heyday, using many of the original store-fronts and shop fittings. Much of the prosperity of Pensacola was based on the timber industry, a point celebrated by a noisy, working sawmill in the **Museum of Industry**, just across Zaragoza Street, where there's also an immense pile of fishing tackle and other reminders of how the city stayed on its uppers for many years.

To catch up on earlier local history, cross Church Street to the sedate **Colonial Archeology trail**, where bits of pottery and weapons suggest the lifestyles of the city's first Spanish inhabitants, and a marked path leads around the site of the British-era Government House, an outpost of empire which collapsed in the 1820s. Virtually next door, the 1809 **Julee Cottage** belonged to Julee Panton, a "freewoman of color" – a euphemism for being black and not a slave – who had her own land and business, and even her own slave: the building's exhibits record her life and deeds, and the achievements of later black people with Pensacola associations.

Other **restored homes** in the vicinity signify the mishmash of architectural styles, from Creole to Greek Revival, favoured by wealthier Pensacolians in the late 1800s. Filled with period furnishings, they make for an enjoyable browse – despite the somewhat twee attendants who sit in them, dressed in period costume during the summer season.

If you have neither the energy nor inclination to visit all the museums and old homes of the Historic Village, head instead to the **Pensacola Historic Museum** (Mon–Sat 9am–4.30; $2), inside the Old Christ Church at 405 S Adams Street, easily spotted by its sturdy masonry tower. Built in 1832, the church now keeps an imposing clutter, from fossils and Native American pottery to cut-glass ornaments owned by the well-to-do settlers of the early 1900s, which helps make Pensacola's complicated history comprehensible.

Similar historical detritus can be found inside the **T T Wentworth Jnr Museum**, on Plaza Ferdinand (Mon–Sat 10am–4pm; $5; free admission with Historic Pensacola Village ticket), a yellow-brick Renaissance affair built as the city hall in 1907. Its arched corridors and rooms are filled with photos, maps and markers to the city's past, while the upper floor has a room with hands-on exhibits to amuse restless kids. It was in Plaza Ferdinand, incidentally, that Florida was officially accepted into the US – a statue to Andrew Jackson, the state's first governor, salutes the fact.

The Museum of Naval Aviation and Fort Barrancas

You don't have to be a military fanatic to enjoy the **Museum of Naval Aviation** (daily 9am–5pm; free; ID must be shown; bus #14), inside the US naval base on Navy Boulevard, about eight miles southwest of central Pensacola, though harbouring *Biggles* fantasies will help: visitors can climb into many of the full-sized training cockpits and play with the controls.

The main purpose of the museum, however, is to collect and display US naval aircraft, from the first flimsy seaplane acquired in 1911 to the Phantoms and

Hornets of more recent times. Among them are a couple of oddities: a small Vietnamese plane, which carried a Vietnamese family onto a US carrier during the Fall of Saigon, and the Command Module from the first Skylab mission, whose crew were naval pilots. It's all rather impressive, and serves to underline Pensacola's role as the home base of US naval aviation – the training ground for thousands of new pilots each year.

On the other side of the road lies the visitor center for **Fort Barrancas** (daily 9.30am–5pm; guided tours on Sat & Sun 2pm; cars $4, pedestrians and cyclists $2), part of the National Seashore area (see below). It's worth spending an hour or so at this well-preserved 1698 Spanish fort, whose design includes a fascinating system of connecting interior vaults.

Around Pensacola

On the other side of the bay from the city, the glistening quartz beaches of two **barrier islands** are ideal for sunbathing: Santa Rosa Island, running fifty miles from Fort Walton and containing Pensacola Beach; and Perdido Key, to the west of Santa Rosa. Also demanding investigation is the **Gulf Islands National Seashore**, a generic name for several parks, each with a specific point of interest (natural or historical), stretching 150 miles along the coast from here to Mississippi, and including, in this part, the Naval Live Oaks Reservation, the western section of Santa Rosa Island, Fort Barrancas, and the eastern section of Perdido Key.

Gulf Breeze and the Naval Live Oaks Reservation

En route to Santa Rosa Island, via the three-mile-long Pensacola Bridge, you'll pass through **GULF BREEZE**, on the Santa Rosa peninsula: a well-scrubbed, well-off community that's going all-out to attract homebuyers. The only reason to give it more than a passing thought is the **Naval Live Oaks Reservation** (daily 8am–sunset; free), about two miles east along Hwy-98. In the 1820s, part of this live oak forest was turned into a tree farm, intended to ensure a supply of ship-building material for years to come. Precise calculations were made as to how many trees would be needed for a particular ship, and the requisite number of acorns then planted – followed by a fifty-year wait. Problems were plentiful: the oak was too heavy for road transportation, wood rustlers cut down trees and sold them to foreign navies, and the final blow for the farm was the advent of iron-built ships.

The **visitor center** (daily 8.30am–4.30pm), near the entrance, has exhibits and explanatory texts on the intriguing forest, where fragments from Native American settlements from as far back as 1000 BC have been found. To escape the glare of the sun for an hour or so, take one of the short but shady **forest trails**, which include a two-mile section of what was, in the early 1800s, Florida's major roadway, linking Pensacola and St Augustine.

Pensacola Beach

From Gulf Breeze, another (shorter) bridge ($1 toll) leads across a narrow waterway to Santa Rosa Island and the epitome of a Gulf Coast strand, **Pensacola Beach**. Featuring mile after mile of fine white sands, rental outlets for beach and water-sports equipment, a pier lined with fishermen, and beachside bars and snack stands, it's hard to beat for uncomplicated oceanside recreation. With its sprinkling of motels and hotels (see p.355) Pensacola Beach also makes an alternative if pricier base to Pensacola, back on the mainland.

Fort Pickens

From Pensacola Beach, it's just two and a half miles along Fort Pickens Road (9am–sunset; cars $4, pedestrians and cyclists $2) to the western end of Santa Rosa Island and the entrance to a part of the Gulf Islands National Seashore. Here, vibrant white sands are walled by a nine-mile stretch of high, rugged dunes, and the only reminder of civilization – other than the road – is a foliage-encircled campground. Hoofing over the dunes is strictly forbidden, but several tracks lead from the road to the beach, where you'll find plenty of space and seclusion – and sometimes even dolphins. To learn more about the dunes, and the curious ecology of the island, join one of the frequent **ranger-led walks**; for details call ☎934-2600, or read the bulletin boards situated around the park.

At the western tip of the island are the substantial remains of **Fort Pickens** (daily 9.30am–4pm; free), built by slaves in the early 1800s to protect Pensacola from seaborne attack. Plenty can be gleaned by walking around the fort's creepy passageways and rooms on your own: pick up the free tour leaflet at the visitor center. A small **museum** explains the origins of the structure, details the flora and fauna of the national seashore area, and records the travails of the seventeen Apache Indians who were imprisoned here in 1886. Among their number was a chief, Goyahkla, better known as **Geronimo**, who served his sentence roaming the sands. The Apaches, whose tribal lands covered much of the southwestern US, were one of the last Native American tribes to surrender to the advancing White settlers, signing a peace treaty with the sympathetic General Crook in 1886. Soon after, the higher-ranking General Sheridan reneged on the terms of the surrender and incarcerated Geronimo and his fellows, leading Crook to resign from the army in protest.

Beside the fort, some crumbling concrete walls remain from seacoast batteries erected in the Forties, which, together with the pillboxes and observation posts that litter the area, are a reminder that the fort's defensive function lasted until the end of World War II, only becoming obsolete with the advent of guided missiles.

Perdido Key

Another barrier island, to the west of Santa Rosa, **Perdido Key** offers yet more pristine beaches. Its eastern section, protected as part of the Gulf Islands National Seashore, provides five miles of island untouched by roads. A one-and-a-quarter-mile nature trail allows you to explore the area, and if you're smitten by the seclusion, stick around to swim or pitch your tent at one of the primitive campsites. Note that you need a permit to use the island's carpark ($4 for up to seven days; arrange one by calling ☎492-1595, at the Big Lagoon State Recreation Area). The remainder of Perdido Key is much like Santa Rosa Island: a hotbed of sport, drinking and suntanning rituals.

Eating

Central Pensacola boasts a large number of restaurants; *Elise's*, 11 S Palafox Street (☎432-5100), has inexpensive breakfasts and lunches, as does *EJ's*, 232 E Main Street (☎432-5886), with well-priced daily specials and a big salad bar; *Hall's Catfish & Seafood*, 920 E Gregory Street (☎438-9019), has fish-laden dinner buffets; *McGuire's Irish Pub*, 600 E Gregory Street (☎433-6789), serves immense portions and draft porter in a lively atmosphere; the *Founaris Brothers Greek Restaurant*, 1015 N Ninth Avenue (☎432-0629), dishes up cheap and cheerful fare; and for a touch of class, the *1912 Restaurant* at the *Pensacola Grand Hotel*, 200 E Gregory Street (☎433-3336), offers high-quality, highly priced cuisine.

You'll find more choice at **Pensacola Beach**: *Butler's*, 27 Via De Luna Drive (☎932-6537), and *The Sundeck Sidewalk Café*, 12 Via De Luna Drive (☎932-0835), do well-priced breakfasts and lunches; while *Boy on a Dolphin*, 400 Pensacola Beach Boulevard (☎932-7954), and the pricier *Flounder's Chowder & Ale House*, 800 Quietwater Beach Road (☎932-2003), both offer hearty seafood dinners. For inexpensive, unspectacular but good-quality food, try *Chan's Market Café*, 16a Via De Luna Drive (☎932-8454), for breakfast, lunch and dinner, plus tasty pastries.

Nightlife

In **central Pensacola**, avoid the *Seville Quarter*, 130 E Government Street (☎434-6201), a tourist-orientated bar and disco decked out to reflect Pensacola's history, but too expensive and contrived to be fun. Better is *McGuire's Irish Pub*, 600 E Gregory Street (☎433-6789; see "Eating", above), which serves home-brewed ale.

At **Pensacola Beach** the action centres on *Flounder's Chowder & Ale House* (see "Eating", above), which draws as many drinkers as diners and has live music about once a week; and *The Dock* (☎934-3314), beside the pier, which is packed every Friday and Saturday night. For a rum cocktail, drop into *Sandshaker Lounge*, 731 Pensacola Beach Boulevard (☎932-2211).

travel details

Trains

From Pensacola to Jacksonville (Mon, Wed, Fri; 8hr 50min); Tallahassee (Tues, Thurs, Fri, Sun; 4hr 15min).

From Tallahassee to Jacksonville (Mon, Wed, Fri; 4hr 20min); Pensacola (Tues, Thurs, Fri, Sun; 4hr 15min).

Buses

From Panama City Beach to Destin (2 daily; 50min); Fort Walton Beach (2 daily; 1hr 10min); Panama City (2 daily; 30min); Pensacola (2 daily; 2hr 15min).

From Pensacola to Destin (2 daily; 1hr 25min); Fort Walton Beach (2 daily; 1hr 5min); Mobile (8 daily; 1hr); New Orleans (6 daily; 4hr 15min); Panama City Beach (2 daily; 2hr 15min); Tallahassee (7 daily; 4hr 25min).

From Tallahassee to Chipley (1 daily; 1hr 30min); De Funiak Springs (1 daily; 2hr 25min); Gainesville (5 daily; 2hr 40min); Jacksonville (5 daily; 3hr 40min); Marianna (5 daily; 35min); Miami (5 daily; 11hr 55min); New Orleans (6 daily; 8hr 30min); Orlando (4 daily; 6hr 30min); Panama City Beach (4 daily; 2hr 30min); Pensacola (7 daily; 2hr 35min); Tampa (5 daily; 5hr); Thomasville (1 daily; 1hr 5min).

PART THREE

THE
CONTEXTS

THE HISTORICAL FRAMEWORK

Contrary to popular belief, Florida's history goes back far beyond Walt Disney World and motel-lined beaches. For thousands of years, its aboriginal inhabitants lived in organized social groupings with contacts across a large section of the Americas. During the height of European colonization, it became a Spanish possession and, for a time, was under British control. Only in the nineteenth century did Florida become part of the US: the beginning of a period of unrestrained exploitation and expansion and the start of many of the problems with which the state continues to grapple today.

ORIGINS OF THE LAND

Over billions of years, rivers flowing through what's now **northern Florida** carried debris from the Appalachian mountains to the coast, their deposits of fine-powdered rock forming the beaches and barrier islands of the Panhandle. Further south, the highest section of a seabed plateau – the **Florida peninsula** – altered in shape according to the world's ice covering. The exposed land sometimes measured twice its present size; during other periods, the coastline was far inland of its current position, with wave action carving out still-visible

bluffs in the oolitic limestone base. In the **present era**, beginning about 75 million years ago, rotting vegetation mixed with rainfall to form acid that burned holes in the limestone, and natural freshwater springs emerged; the underground water accumulated from heavy rains which preceded each Ice Age. Inland forests of live oak and pine became inhabited 20,000 years ago by mastodons, mammoths and saber-toothed tigers, thought to have travelled – over many generations – across the ice-covered Bering Strait from Siberia.

FIRST HUMAN INHABITATION

Two theories exist regarding the origins of Florida's **first human inhabitants**. It's commonly believed that the earliest arrivals followed the same route as the animals from Siberia, crossing North America and arriving in northern Florida around 10,000 years ago. A minority of anthropologists take the alternative view that the first Floridians were the result of migration by aboriginal peoples in South and Central America. Either way, the **Paleo** (or "Early") **Indians** in Florida lived hunter-gatherer existences – the spear tips they used are widely found across the central and northern parts of the state.

Around 5000 BC, social patterns changed: settlements became semi-permanent and diet switched from meat to shellfish, snails and molluscs, which were abundant along the rivers. Travelling was done by dugout canoe and, periodically, a community would move to a new site, probably to allow food supplies to replenish themselves. Discarded shells and other rubbish were piled onto the **midden mounds** still commonly seen in the state.

Though pottery began to appear around 2000 BC, not until 1000 BC was there a big change in lifestyle, as indicated by the discovery of **irrigation canals**, patches of land cleared for **cultivation**, and cooking utensils used to prepare grown food. From the time of the Christian era, the erection of **burial mounds** – elaborate tombs of prominent tribespeople, often with sacrificed kin and valuable objects also placed inside – became common. These suggest strong religious and trading links across an area stretching from Central America to the North American interior.

Spreading east from the Georgian coastal plain, the **Fort Walton Culture** became prevalent from around 200 AD. This divided society into a rigid caste system and people lived in villages planned around a central plaza. Throughout Florida at this time, approximately 100,000 inhabitants formed several distinct tribal groupings: most notably the **Timucua** across northern Florida, the **Calusa** around the southwest and Lake Okeechobee, the **Apalachee** in the Panhandle and the **Tequesta** along the southeast coast.

EUROPEAN DISCOVERY AND SETTLEMENT

After Christopher Columbus located the "New World" in 1492, Europe's great sea powers were increasingly active around the Caribbean. One of them, Spain, had discovered and plundered the treasures of ancient civilizations in Central America, and all were eager to locate other riches across these and neighbouring lands. The **first European sighting** of Florida is believed to have been made by John and Sebastian **Cabot** in 1498, when they set eyes on what is now called Cape Florida, on Key Biscayne in Miami.

In 1513, the **first European landing** was made by **Juan Ponce de León**, a Spaniard previously employed as governor of Puerto Rico, a Spanish possession, and who was eager to carve out a niche for himself in the expanding empire. While searching for Bimini, Ponce de León sighted land during *Pascua Florida*, the Spanish Festival of the Flowers, and named what he saw *La Florida* – or "Land of Flowers". After putting ashore somewhere between the mouth of the St John's River and present-day St Augustine, Ponce de León sailed on around the Florida Keys, naming them *Los Martires*, for their supposed resemblance to the bones of martyred men, and *Las Tortugas* (now the Dry Tortugas), named for the turtles he saw around them.

Sent to deal with troublesome natives in the Lower Antilles, it was eight years before Ponce de León returned to Florida, this time with a mandate from the Spanish king to **conquer and colonize** the territory. Landing on the southwest coast, probably somewhere between Tampa Bay and Fort Myers, Ponce de León met a hostile reception from the Calusa Indians and was forced to withdraw, eventually dying from an arrow wound received in the battle.

Rumours of gold hidden in Apalachee, in the north of the region, stimulated several Spanish incursions into Florida, all of which were driven back by the aggression of the indigenes and the ferocity of the terrain and climate. The most successful undertaking – even though it ended in death for its leader – was the **Hernando de Soto expedition**, a thousand-strong band of war-hardened knights and treasure seekers, which landed at Tampa Bay in May 1539. Recent excavations in Tallahassee have located the site of one of de Soto's camps, where the first Christmas celebration in North America is thought to have taken place before the expedition continued north, later making the first European crossing of the Mississippi River – for a long time marking Florida's western boundary.

Written accounts of the expeditions are a major source of information about the aboriginal life of that period, though anthropology was not a major concern of the Spanish, and the news that Florida did not harbour stunning riches caused interest to wane. Treasure-laden Spanish ships sailing off the Florida coast between the Americas and Europe proved attractive to pirate ships, however, many of them British and French vessels hoisting the Jolly Roger. The Spanish failure to colonize Florida made it a prime base for attacks on their vessels, and a small group of **French Huguenots** landed in 1562, building Fort Caroline on the St John's River.

The French presence forced the Spanish into a more determined effort at settlement. Already commissioned to explore the Atlantic coast of North America, **Pedro Menéndez de Avilés** was promised the lion's share of whatever profits could be made from Florida. Landing south of the French fort on August 28, 1562, the day of the Spanish Festival of San Augustín, Menéndez named the site **St Augustine** – founding what was to become the longest continuous site of European habitation on the continent. The French were quickly defeated, their leader **Jean Ribault** and his crew massacred after being driven ashore by a hurricane; the site of the killing is still known as *Matanzas*, or "Place of Slaughter".

THE FIRST SPANISH PERIOD (1585–1763)

Only the enthusiasm of Menéndez held Florida together during the early decades of Spanish rule. A few small and insecure settlements were established, usually around **missions** founded by Jesuits or Franciscans bent on Christianizing the Indians. It was a far from harmonious setup: homesick Spanish soldiers frequently mutinied and fought with the Indians, who responded by burning St Augustine to the ground. Menéndez replaced St Augustine's wooden buildings with "tabby" (a cement-like mixture of seashells and limestone) structures with palm-thatched roofs, a style typical of early European Florida. While easily the largest settlement, even St Augustine was a lifeless outpost unless a ship happened to be in port. Despite sinking all his personal finances into the colony, Menéndez never lived to see Florida thrive, and he left in 1571, ordered by the king to help plan the Spanish Armada's attack on Britain.

Fifteen years later, as war raged between the European powers, St Augustine was razed by a naval bombardment led by **Francis Drake**, a sign that the **British** were beginning to establish their colonies along the Atlantic coast, north of Florida. Aware that the Indians would hold the balance of power in future colonial power struggles, a string of Spanish missions were built along the Panhandle from 1606; besides seeking to earn the loyalty of the natives, these were intended to provide a defensive shield against attacks from the north. By the 1700s the British were making forays into Florida, ostensibly to capture Indians to sell as slaves. One by one, the missions were destroyed, and only the timely arrival of Spanish reinforcements prevented the fall of St Augustine to the British in 1740.

With the French in Louisiana, the British in Georgia and the Spanish clinging to Florida, the scene was set for a bloody confrontation for control of North America. Eventually, the **1763 Treaty of Paris**, concluding the Seven Years' War in Europe, settled the issue: the British had captured the crucial Spanish possession of Havana, and Spain willingly parted with Florida to get it back.

THE BRITISH PERIOD (1763–1783)

Despite their two centuries of occupation, the Spanish failed to make much impression on Florida. It was the British, already developing the colonies further north, who grafted a social infrastructure onto the region. They also divided Florida (then with only the northern section inhabited by whites) into separate colonies: **East Florida** governed from St Augustine, and **West Florida** governed from the growing Panhandle port of **Pensacola**.

By this time, aboriginal Floridians had largely died out through contact with European diseases, to which they had no immunity, and Florida's Indian population was becoming composed of disparate tribes arriving from the west, collectively known as the **Seminoles**. Like the Spanish, the British acknowledged the numerical importance of the Indians and sought good relations with them. In return for goods, the British took Indian land around ports and supply routes, but generally left the Seminoles undisturbed in the inland areas.

Despite attractive grants, few settlers arrived from Britain. Those with money to spare bought Florida land as an investment, never intending to develop or settle on it, and only large holdings – **plantations** growing corn, sugar, rice and other crops – were profitable. Charleston, to the north, dominated sea trade in the area, though St Augustine was still a modestly important settlement and the gathering place of passing British aristocrats and intellectuals. West Florida, on the other hand, was riven by political factionalism and often the scene of skirmishes with the Seminoles, who received worse treatment than their counterparts in the east.

Being a new and sparsely populated region, the discontent that fuelled the **American War of Independence** in the 1770s barely affected Florida, except to bring British Royalists fleeing into St Augustine, many of them moving on to the Bahamas or Jamaica. Pensacola, though, was attacked and briefly occupied in 1781 by the Spanish, who had been promised Florida in return for helping the American rebels defeat the British. As it turned out, diplomacy rather than gunfire signalled the end of British rule in Florida.

THE SECOND SPANISH PERIOD (1783–1821)

The **1783 Treaty of Paris**, with which Britain recognized American independence, not only returned Florida to Spain, but also gave it Louisiana and the prized port of New Orleans. Spanish holdings in North America were now larger than ever, but with Europe in turmoil and the Spanish colonies in Central America agitating for their own independence, the country was ill-equipped to capitalize on them. Moreover, the complexity of Florida's melting pot, comprising the British, smaller numbers of ethnically diverse European settlers, and the increasingly assertive Seminoles (now well established in fertile central Florida, and often joined by Africans escaping slavery further north), made it impossible for a declining colonial power to govern.

As fresh European migration slowed, Spain was forced to **sell land to US citizens**, who bought large· tracts, confident that Florida would soon be under Washington's control. Indeed, in gaining Louisiana from France in 1800 (to whom it had been ceded by Spain), and moving the Georgia border south, it was clear the US had Florida in its sights. Fearful of losing the commercial toehold it still retained in Florida, and aligned with Spain through the Napoleonic wars, Britain landed troops at Pensacola in 1814. In response, a US general, **Andrew Jackson**, used the excuse of an Indian uprising in Alabama to march south, killing hundreds of Indians and pursuing them – unlawfully and without official sanction from Washington – into Pensacola, declaring no quarrel with the Spanish but insisting that the British depart. The British duly left, and Jackson and his men withdrew to Mobile (a Floridian town that became part of Alabama as the Americans inched the border eastwards), soon to participate in the Battle of New Orleans, which further strengthened the US position on the Florida border.

THE FIRST SEMINOLE WAR

Jackson's actions in 1814 had triggered the **First Seminole War**. As international tension heightened, Seminole raids (often as a result of baiting on the US side) were commonly used as excuses for US incursions into Florida. In 1818, Jackson finally received what he took to be presidential approval (the "Rhea Letter", thought to have been authorized by President Monroe) to march again into Florida on the pretext of subduing the Seminoles but with the actual intention of taking outright control.

While US public officials were uneasy with the dubious legality of these events, the American public was firmly on Jackson's side.

The US government issued an ultimatum to Spain, demanding that either it police Florida effectively or relinquish its ownership. With little alternative, Spain formally **ceded Florida to the US** in 1819, in return for the US assuming the $5 million owed by the Spanish government to American settlers in land grants (a sum which was never repaid). Nonetheless, it took the threat of an invasion of Cuba for the Spanish king to ratify the treaty in 1821; at the same time Andrew Jackson was sworn in as Florida's first American governor.

TERRITORIAL FLORIDA AND THE SECOND SEMINOLE WAR

In territorial Florida it was soon evident that the East and West divisions were unworkable, and a site midway between St Augustine and Pensacola was selected as the new administrative centre: **Tallahassee**. The Indians living on the fertile soils of the area were rudely dispatched towards the coast – an act of callousness that was to typify relations between the new settlers and the incumbent Native Americans for decades to come.

Under Spanish and British rule, the Seminoles, notwithstanding some feuding between themselves, lived peaceably on the productive lands of northern central Florida. These, however, were precisely the agriculturally rich areas that US settlers coveted. Under the **Treaty of Moultrie Creek** in 1823, most of the Seminole tribes signed a document agreeing to sell their present land and resettle in southwest Florida. Neither side was to honour this agreement: no time limit was imposed on the Seminole exodus, and those who did go found the new land to be unsuitable for farming; the US side, meanwhile, failed to provide promised resettlement funds.

Andrew Jackson spent only three months as territorial governor, though his influence on Florida continued from the White House when he became US president in 1829. In 1830 he approved the **Act of Indian Removal**, decreeing that all Native Americans in the eastern US should be transferred to reservations in the open areas of the Midwest. Two years later, James Gadsen, the newly appointed Indian commissioner, called a meeting of the Seminole tribes at Payne's Landing on the Oklawaha River, near Silver Springs, urging them to cede their land to the US and move west. Amid much acrimony, a few did sign the **Treaty of Payne's Landing**, which provided for their complete removal within three years.

THE SECOND SEMINOLE WAR (1821–1842)

A small number took what monies were offered and resettled in the west, but most Seminoles were determined to stay and the **Second Seminole War** ensued, with the Indians repeatedly ambushing the US militiamen who had arrived to enforce the law, and ransacking the plantations of white settlers, many of whom fled and never returned. Trained for set-piece battles, the US troops were rarely able to deal effectively with the guerrilla tactics of the Seminoles. It was apparent that the Seminoles were unlikely to be defeated by conventional means and in October 1837, their leader, **Osceola**, was lured to St Augustine with the promise of a truce – only to be arrested and imprisoned, eventually to die in jail. This treachery failed to break the spirit of the Seminoles, though a few continued to give themselves up and leave for the west, while others were captured and sold into slavery.

It became the policy of the US to drive the Seminoles steadily south, away from the fertile lands of central Florida and **into the Everglades**. In the Everglades, the Seminoles linked up with the long-established "Spanish Indians" to raid the Cape Florida lighthouse and destroy the white colony on Indian Key in the Florida Keys. Even after bloodhounds were – controversially – used to track the Indians, it was clear that total US victory would never be achieved. With the Seminoles confined to the Everglades, the US formally **ended the conflict** in 1842, when the Seminoles agreed to stay where they were – an area earlier described by an army surveyor as "fit only for Indian habitation".

The six-year war crippled the Florida economy but stimulated the growth of a number of **new towns** around the army forts. Several of these, such as Fort Brooke (Tampa), Fort Lauderdale, Fort Myers and Fort Pierce, have survived into modern times.

STATEHOOD AND SECESSION (1842–1861)

The Second Seminole War forestalled the possibility of Florida **attaining statehood** –

which would have entitled it to full representation in Washington and to appoint its own administrators. Influence in Florida at this time was split between two camps. On one side were the wealthy slave-owning plantation farmers, concentrated in the "cotton counties" of the central section of the Panhandle, who enjoyed all the traditions of the upper rung of Deep South society. They were anxious to make sure that the balance of power in Washington did not shift towards the non-slave-owning "free" states, which would inevitably bring a call for the abolition of slavery. Opposing statehood were the smallholders scattered about the rest of the territory – many of whom were Northerners, already ideologically against slavery and fearing the imposition of federal taxes.

One compromise mooted was a return to a divided Florida, with the West becoming a state while the East remained a territory. Eventually, based on a narrowly agreed **constitution** drawn up in Port St Joseph on the Panhandle coast (on the site of present-day Port St Joe), Florida **became a state** on March 3, 1845. The arrival of statehood coincided with a period of material prosperity: the first railroads began spidering across the Panhandle and central Florida; an organized school system became established; and Florida's 60,000 population was doubled within twenty years.

Nationally, things were less bright. The issue of slavery was to be the catalyst that led the US into civil war, though it was only a part of a great cultural divide between the rural Southern states – to which Florida was linked more through geography than history – and the modern industrial states of the North. As federal pressure intensified for the abolition of slavery, Florida formally **seceded from the Union** on January 10, 1861, aligning itself with the breakaway Confederate States in the run-up to the Civil War.

FLORIDA IN THE CIVIL WAR (1861–1865)

Inevitably, the **Civil War** had a great effect on Florida, although most Floridians conscripted into the Confederate army fought far away from home, and rarely were there more than minor confrontations within the state. The relatively small number of Union sympathizers generally kept a low profile, concentrating on protecting their families. At the start of the war, most of Florida's **coastal forts** were occupied by Union troops as part of the blockade on Confederate shipping. Lacking the strength to mount effective attacks on the forts, those Confederate soldiers who remained in Florida based themselves in the interior and watched for Union troop movements, swiftly destroying whatever bridge, road or railroad lay in the invaders' path – in effect creating a stalemate, which endured throughout the conflict.

Away from the coast, Florida's primary contribution to the war effort was the **provision of food** – chiefly beef and pork reared on the central Florida farms – and the transportation of it across the Panhandle towards Confederate strongholds further west. Union attempts to cut the supply route gave rise to the only major battle fought in the state, the **Battle of Olustee**, just outside Live Oak, in February 1864: 10,000 participated in an engagement that left 300 dead and both sides claiming victory.

The most celebrated battle from a Floridian viewpoint, however, happened in March 1865 at **Natural Bridge**, when a youthful group of Confederates defeated the technically superior Union troops, preventing the fall of Tallahassee. As events transpired, it was a hollow victory; following the Confederate surrender, the war ended a few months later.

RECONSTRUCTION

Following the cessation of hostilities, Florida was caught in an uneasy hiatus. In the years after the war, the defeated states were subject to **Reconstruction**, a re-arrangement of their internal affairs determined by, at first, the president, later by a much harder-line Congress intent on ensuring the southern states would never return to their old ways.

The Northern ideal of free-labour capitalism was an alien concept in the South, and there were enormous problems. Of paramount concern was the future of the **freed slaves**. With restrictions on their movements lifted, many emancipated slaves wandered the countryside, often unwittingly putting fear into all-white communities that had never before had a black face in their midst. Rubbing salt into the wounds, as far as the Southern whites were concerned, was the occupation of many towns

by black Union troops. As a backlash, the white-supremacist **Ku Klux Klan** became active in Tennessee during 1866, and its race-hate, segregationist doctrine soon spread into Florida.

Against this background of uncertainty and trepidation, Florida's **domestic politics** entered a period of unparalleled chicanery. Suddenly, not only were black men allowed to vote, but there were more black voters than white. The gullibility of the uneducated blacks and the power of their votes proved an irresistible combination to the unscrupulous and power hungry. Double dealing and vote-rigging were practised by diverse factions united only in their desire to restore Florida's statehood and acquire even more power. Following a constitution written and approved in controversial circumstances, Florida was **re-admitted to the Union** on July 21, 1868.

Eventually, in Florida as in the other Southern states, an all-white, **conservative Democrat government** emerged. Despite emancipation and the hopes for integration outlined by the Civil Rights Act passed by Congress in 1875, blacks in Florida were still denied many of the rights reasonably regarded as basic. In fact, all that distanced the new administration from the one that led Florida into secession was awareness of the power of the federal government and the need to at least appear to take outside views into account. It was also true that many of the former slave-owners were now the employers of freed blacks, who remained very much under their white masters' control.

A NEW FLORIDA TAKES SHAPE (1876–1914)

Florida's bonds with its neighbouring states became increasingly tenuous in the years following Reconstruction. A fast-growing population began spreading south – part of a gradual diminishing of the importance of the Panhandle, where ties to the Deep South were strongest. Florida's identity became forged by a new **frontier spirit**. Besides smallholding farmers, loggers came to work the abundant forests, and a new breed of wealthy settler started putting down roots, among them Henry DeLand and Henry S Sanford, who each bought large chunks of central Florida and founded the towns that still bear their names.

As northern speculators invested in Florida, they sought to publicize the region, and a host of articles extolling the virtues of the state's climate as a cure for all ills began to appear in the country's newspapers. These early efforts to promote **Florida as a tourist destination** brought the wintering rich along the new railroads to enjoy the sparkling rivers and springs, and naturalists arrived to explore the unique flora and fauna.

With a fortune made through his partnership in Standard Oil, **Henry Flagler** opened luxury resorts on Florida's northeast coast for his socialite friends, and gradually extended his Florida East Coast Railroad south, giving birth to communities such as **Palm Beach** and making the remote trading post of **Miami** an accessible, expanding town. Flagler's friendly rival, **Henry Plant**, connected *his* railroad to **Tampa**, turning a desolate hamlet into a thriving port city and a major base of cigar manufacture. The **citrus industry** also got into top gear: Florida's climate enabled oranges, grapefruits and other fruits to be grown during the winter and sold to an eager market in the cooler north. The **cattle farms** went from strength to strength, Florida becoming a major supplier of beef to the rest of the US: cows were rounded up with a special wooden whip which made a gunshot-like sound when used – hence the nickname **"cracker"**, which was applied to rural settlers.

One group that didn't benefit from the boom years were the blacks: many were imprisoned for no reason, and found themselves on chaingangs building the new roads and railroads; punishments for refusing to work included severe floggings and hanging by the thumbs. Few whites paid any attention, and those who were in a position to stop the abuses were usually too busy getting rich. There was, however, the founding of **Eatonville**, just north of Orlando, which was the first town in Florida – and possibly the US – to be founded, governed and lived in by black people.

FLORIDA AND THE SPANISH-AMERICAN WAR

By the 1890s, the US was a large and unified nation itching for a bigger role in the world. As the drive in **Cuba** for independence from Spain gathered momentum, an opportunity to participate in international affairs presented itself. Florida already had long links with Cuba – the capital, Havana, was just ninety miles from Key West, and several thousand Cuban migrants were employed in the Tampa cigar factories. During 1898, tens of thousands of US troops – the Cuban Expeditionary Force – arrived in the state, and the **Spanish-American War** was declared on April 25. As it turned out, the fighting was comparatively minor; Spain withdrew, and on January 1, 1899, Cuba attained independence (and the US a big say in its future). But the war was also the first of several major conflicts that were to prove beneficial to Florida. Many of the soldiers would return as settlers or tourists, and improved railroads and strengthened harbours at the commercially significant ports of Key West, Tampa and Pensacola did much to boost the economy.

THE BROWARD ERA

The early years of the 1900s were dominated by the progressive policies of **Napoleon Bonaparte Broward**, state governor from 1905. In a nutshell, Broward championed the small man against corporate interests, particularly the giant land-owning railroad companies. Among Broward's aims were an improved education system, a state-run commission to oversee new railroad construction, a tax on cars to finance road building, better salaries for teachers and the judiciary, a state-run life assurance scheme, and a ban on newspapers – few of which were well-disposed towards Broward – knowingly publishing untruths. Broward also enacted the first **conservation laws**, protecting fish, oysters, game and forests; but at the same time, in an attempt to create new land to rival the holdings of the rail barons, he conceived the drainage programme that would cause untold damage to the Everglades.

By no means all of Broward's policies became law, and he departed Tallahassee for a US Senate seat in 1910. Nonetheless, the forward-thinking plans of what became known as the **Broward Era** were continued through subsequent administrations – a process that went some way to bringing a rough-and-ready frontier land into the twentieth century.

WORLD WAR I AND THE FLORIDA LAND BOOM

World War I continued the tradition of the Spanish-American War by giving Florida an economic shot in the arm as the military arrived to police the coastline and develop sea-warfare projects. Despite the influx of money and the reforms of the Broward years, there was little happening to improve the lot of Florida's blacks. The Ku Klux Klan was revived in Tallahassee in 1915, and the public outcry that followed the beating to death of a young black on a chaingang was answered only by the introduction of the sweatbox as punishment for prisoners considered unruly.

Typically, most visitors to Florida at this time were less concerned with social justice than with getting drunk. The coast so vigilantly protected from advancing Germans during the war was left wide open when **Prohibition** was introduced in 1919; the many secluded inlets became secure landing sites for spirits from the Caribbean. The illicit booze improved the atmosphere in the new resorts of **Miami Beach**, a picture-postcard piece of beach land-scaping replacing what had been a barely habitable mangrove island just a few years before. Drink was not the only illegal pleasure pursued in the nightclubs: gambling and prostitution were also rife, and were soon to attract the attention of big-time **gangsters** such as Al Capone, initiating a climate of corruption that was to scar Florida politics for years.

The lightning-paced creation of Miami Beach was no isolated incident. Throughout Florida, and especially in the southeast, new communities appeared almost overnight. Self-proclaimed architectural genius **Addison Mizner** erected the "million dollar cottages" of Palm Beach and began fashioning **Boca Raton** with the same mock-Mediterranean excesses, on the premise: "get the big snob and the little snob will follow"; visionary **George Merrick** plotted the superlative **Coral Gables** – now absorbed by Miami – which became the nation's first pre-planned city and one of the few schemes of the time to age with dignity.

In the rush of prosperity that followed the war, it seemed everyone in America wanted a piece of Florida, and chartered trains brought in thousands of eager buyers. The spending frenzy soon meant that for every genuine offer there were a hundred bogus ones: many people unknowingly bought acres of empty swamp-land. The period was satirized by the Marx Brothers in their first film, *Cocoanuts*.

Although millions of dollars technically changed hands each week during the peak year of 1925, little hard cash actually moved: most deals were paper transactions with buyers paying a small deposit into a bank. The inflation inherent in the system finally went out of control in 1926: with buyers failing to keep up payments, banks went **bust**, quickly followed by everyone else. A **hurricane** devastated Miami the same year – the city's house-builders never thought to protect the structures against tropical storms – and an even worse hurricane in 1928 caused Lake Okeechobee to burst its banks and flood surrounding communities.

With the Florida land boom well and truly over, the **Wall Street Crash** in 1929 proceeded to make paupers of the millionaires, such as Henry Flagler and Sarasota's **John Ringling**, whose considerable investments had helped to shape the state.

THE DEPRESSION, WORLD WAR II AND AFTER

At the start of the **Thirties**, even the major rail-roads that had stimulated Florida's expansion were in receivership, and the state government only avoided bankruptcy with a constitutional escape clause. Due to the property crash, Florida had had a few extra years to adjust to grinding poverty before the whole country experienced the **Depression**, and a number of recovery measures – making the state more active in citizens' welfare – pre-empted the national **New Deal** legislation of President Roosevelt.

No single place was harder hit than **Key West**, which was not only suffering the Depression but hadn't been favoured by the property boom either. With a population of 12,000, Key West was an incredible $5 million in debt, and had even lost its link to the main-land when the Overseas Railroad – running across the Florida Keys between Key West and Miami – was destroyed by the 1935 Labor Day hurricane.

What saved Key West, and indeed brought financial stability to all of Florida, was **World War II**. Once again, thousands of troops arrived to guard the coastline – off which there was an immense amount of German U-boat activity – while the flat inland areas made a perfect training venue for pilots. Empty tourist hotels provided ready-made barracks, and the soldiers – and their visiting families – got a taste of Florida that would bring many of them back.

In the immediate **postwar period**, the inability of the state to plan and provide for increased growth was resoundingly apparent, with public services – particularly in the field of education – woefully inadequate. Because of the massive profits being made through illegal gambling, corruption became endemic in public life. State governor **Fuller Warren**, implicated with the Al Capone crime syndicate in 1950, was by no means the only state official suspected of being in cahoots with criminals. A wave of attacks against blacks and Jews in 1951 caused Warren to speak out against the Ku Klux Klan, but the discovery that he himself had once been a Klan member only confirmed the poison flowing through the heart of Florida's political system.

A rare upbeat development was a continued commitment to the conservation measures introduced in the Broward era, with $2 million allocated to buying the land that, in 1947, became the **Everglades National Park**.

FLORIDA IN THE FIFTIES AND SIXTIES

Cattle, citrus and tourism continued to be the major components of Florida's economy as, in the ten years from 1950, the state soared from being the twentieth to the tenth most populous in the country, home to five million people. While its increased size raised Florida's profile in federal government, within the state the demographic changes – most dramatically the shift from rural life in the north to urban living in the South – went unacknowledged, and **reapportionment** of representation in state government became a critical issue, one only resolved by the **1968 constitution**, which provided for automatic reapportionment in line with population changes.

The fervent desire for growth and the need to present a wholesome public image prevented the state's conservative-dominated assembly from fighting as hard as their counterparts in the other Southern states against **de-segregation**, following a ruling by the federal Supreme Court on the issue in 1956. Nonetheless, blacks continued to be banned from Miami Beach after dark and from swim-

ming off the Palm Beach coast. In addition, they were subject to segregation in restaurants, buses, hotels, schools – and barely represented at all in public office. As the **Civil Rights** movement gained strength during the early Sixties, bus boycotts and demonstrations took place in Tallahassee and Daytona Beach, and a march in St Augustine in 1964 resulted in the arrest of the movement's leader, Martin Luther King Jnr. The success of the Civil Rights movement in ending legalized discrimination did little to affect the deeply entrenched racist attitudes among much of Florida's longer-established population. Most of the state's blacks still lived and worked in conditions that would have been intolerable to whites: a fact that, in part, accounted for the **Liberty City riot** in August 1968, the first of several violent uprisings in Miami's depressed areas.

The ideological shift in Florida's near-neighbour, **Cuba** – declared a socialist state by its leader Fidel Castro in 1961 – came sharply into focus with the 1962 **missile crisis**, which triggered a tense game of cat and mouse between the US and the USSR over Soviet missile bases on the island. After world war was averted, Florida become the base of the US government's covert anti-Castro operations. Many engaged in these activities were among the 300,000 **Cuban migrants** who had arrived following the Castro-led revolution. The Bay of Pigs fiasco in 1961 proved that there was to be no quick return to the homeland, and while not all of the new arrivals stayed in Florida, many went no further than Miami, where they were to totally change the social character – and eventually the power balance – of the city.

Another factor in Florida's expansion was the basing of the new civilian space administration, **NASA**, at the military long-range missile testing site at Cape Canaveral. The all-out drive to land a man on the moon brought an enormous influx of space industry personnel in the early Sixties – quadrupling the population of the region soon to become known as the **Space Coast**.

Although it didn't open until 1971, **Walt Disney World** got off the drawing board in the mid-Sixties and was to have a terrific impact on the future of Florida. The state government bent over backwards to help the Disney Corporation turn a sizeable slice of central Florida into the biggest theme park complex ever known. Throughout its construction, debate raged over the commercial and ecological effects of such a major undertaking on the rest of the region. Undeterred, smaller businesses rushed to the area, eager to capitalize on the anticipated tourist influx, and the sleepy cow-town of **Orlando** suddenly found itself the hub of one of the state's fastest-growing population centres – soon to become one of the world's best-known holiday destinations.

CONTEMPORARY FLORIDA

The great commercial success of Walt Disney World, and a fortuitous set of circumstances – American fears of terrorism reducing foreign travel and price-wars between tour operators and airlines encouraging overseas visitors – have helped solidify Florida's place in the **international tourist market**: directly or indirectly, one in five of the state's twelve million inhabitants now makes a living from tourism. Simultaneously, the general swing from heavy to **high-tech industries** has resulted in many American corporations forsaking their traditional northern bases in favour of Florida, bringing their white-collar workforces with them.

Behind the optimistic facade, however, lie many problems. Taxes kept low to stimulate growth have reduced funding for public services, leaving the apparently booming state with appalling levels of adult illiteracy, infant mortality and crime. Efforts to **raise taxes** during the late Eighties met incredible resistance and forced a U-turn by the state governor, Bob Martinez. A further cause for concern is the broadening **gap** between the relative liberalism of the big cities and the arch-conservatism of the bible-belt rural areas. While Miami is busy promoting its modernity and multicultural make-up (glossing over some severe inter-ethnic conflicts in doing so), the Ku Klux Klan holds picnics in the Panhandle, a children's storybook is removed from a north Florida school's reading list for containing the words "damn" and "bitch", and in Pensacola a doctor is shot dead by anti-abortion activists.

GUNS AND DRUGS

Contradictions are also apparent in efforts to reduce crime. In 1976, Florida became the first state to **restore the death penalty**, declaring it the ultimate deterrent to murder; yet the state's

gun laws remain notoriously lax. Some districts impose a "cooling off" period of a few days while the background of a potential gun purchaser is checked; but in most, firearms can be bought over the counter on production of the flimsiest ID.

The multi-million-dollar **drugs trade** active in the state shows few signs of abating. Geographically highly convenient for the exporters of Latin America, estimates suggest that at least a quarter of the cocaine entering the US arrives through Florida. In Miami, around ninety separate drug-law enforcement agencies are operative, but fear of corruption causes them to act alone and not pool information. Ironically, a recent switch of emphasis from capturing dealers to clamping down on **money-laundering** (the filtering of illegal profits through legitimate businesses) has begun to threaten many of Miami's financial institutions, built on – and it's an open secret – the drugs trade.

RACIAL ISSUES

Racial issues continue to be vexed. Black–white relations are often strained, and many Anglo-Americans are rueful of the powerful positions attained by Cubans who've steadily worked their way up the system since the Sixties. At the other end of the spectrum, large-scale immigration – legal and otherwise – into south Florida from the poor and unstable countries of Latin America and the Caribbean has put considerable pressure on the state's social services (such as they are), and played into the hands of right-wingers, who favour strict measures to curtail the influx and advocate a hardening of attitudes towards the state's ethnic minorities.

President Clinton sought to gain support for the Democrats in Florida by involving himself in the Cuban situation. In 1994 it was decided that all Cubans trying to reach Florida would be interned at the US Navy's Guantanamo base in Cuba, though little thought was given to the fate of those refused entry. In 1995, the Cubans detained at Guantanamo were allowed into the US, but it was decreed that any future refugees would be returned to Cuba. This was a major policy shift that angered right-wing Cuban exiles. For the first time since Castro gained power, the US was officially saying that Cubans were not being persecuted en masse; it was up to individuals to prove that they were in danger.

In 1996, in an attempt to appease right-wing elements of the Cuban exile community,

Clinton agreed to accept the Helms-Burton law threatening sanctions on foreign businesses with interests in Cuba. Yet in so doing, he infuriated the governments of Canada, Britain, Mexico and other important US allies and trading partners, and it's unlikely that he will have converted many right-wingers in Florida to vote Democrat in the November 1996 elections.

VIOLENCE AGAINST TOURISTS

Repeated incidents of violence against European tourists, including the murders of German and British holiday makers, earned the state much adverse publicity. Governor Lawton Chiles (a liberal successor to Martinez, and elected against the odds in November 1990) responded in February 1993 by creating the Task Force on Tourist Safety. The task force launched pilot schemes in Miami and Orlando which entailed improved road signs (to show more clearly routes to major attractions), new tourist information centres at key arrival points, and an ending of the giveaway "Y" and "Z" licence plates on rental cars.

While the task force is a step forward, nobody seriously thinks that crime against the Florida tourist can ever be completely eradicated — the murder in 1996 of a Dutch tourist asking for directions at a Miami filling station is a reminder of this. State officials are swift to point out, however, that if European visitors heeded the routine safety precautions (outlined in *Basics*) that most Americans take for granted, the risks would be greatly lessened.

CONSERVATION

Increased protection of the state's **natural resources** has been a more positive feature of the last decade. Impressive amounts of land are under state control and, overall, wildlife is less threatened now than at any time since white settlers first arrived. Most spectacular of all has been the revival of the state's alligator population. On the downside, the Everglades — and its dependent animals — could still be destroyed by south Florida's ever-increasing need for drinking water.

HURRICANE ANDREW

In August 1992, **Hurricane Andrew** brought winds of 168mph tearing through the southern regions of Miami (blowing down the radar of the National Hurricane Center in the process). Although the hurricane was no surprise — scores of potential hurricanes develop off Florida's shores each year between June and November and are closely observed; most die out well before striking the coast — roofs were ripped off homes, supermarkets were gutted, 150,000 were left homeless or living in ruins, 230,000 more had no power supply, and the cost of damage was estimated at $30 billion.

Governor Chiles declared the stricken region a disaster area, deployed 1500 National Guardsmen to stem looting, and warned that Florida would be bankrupt if left to foot the bill alone. As criticism of the sluggishly paced and disorganized federal response to the emergency mounted, the then president, George Bush, made two child-hugging tours of the devastated area, eventually deploying 20,000 marines and a naval convoy in what became the biggest relief operation ever mounted.

Even four years after the hurricane struck, signs of its handiwork are still apparent in the form of abandoned homes and destroyed businesses. Nevertheless, some good has emerged from the disaster — many parks have replaced uprooted trees with species endemic to Florida, which are much more likely to survive future hurricanes.

While older Floridians remembered the series of hurricanes that hit the state in the Twenties and Thirties, later arrivals had a tendency to play down the threat of hurricanes, with few people bothering to stock emergency provisions or take heed of evacuation warnings. Post-Andrew, however, this attitude has dramatically changed, and hurricane preparation events — which give tips on preparing for and surviving a hurricane — now attract very big crowds indeed.

NATURAL FLORIDA

The biggest surprise for most people in Florida is the abundance of undeveloped, natural areas throughout the state and the extraordinary variety of wildlife and vegetation within them. From a rare hawk that eats only snails to a vine-like fig that strangles other trees, natural Florida possesses plenty that you've probably never seen before, and which – due to drainage, pressures from the agricultural lobby, and the constant need for new housing – may not be on view for very much longer.

BACKGROUND

Many factors contribute to the unusual diversity of **ecosystems** found in Florida, the most obvious being **latitude**: the north of the state has vegetation common to temperate regions, which is quite distinct from the subtropical flora of the south. Another crucial element is **elevation**: while much of Florida is flat and low-lying, a change of a few inches in elevation drastically affects what grows, due in part to the enormous variety of soils.

THE ROLE OF FIRE

Florida has more thunderstorms than any other part of the US, and the resulting lightning frequently ignites **fires**. Many Florida plants have adapted to fire by developing thick bark or the ability to regenerate from stumps. Others,

such as cabbage palmetto and sawgrass, protect their growth bud with a sheath of green leaves. Fire is necessary to keep a natural balance of plant species – human attempts to control naturally ignited fires have contributed to the changing composition of Florida's remaining wild lands.

FORESTS AND WOODLANDS

Forests and woodlands aren't the first thing people associate with Florida, but the state has an impressive assortment, ranging from the great tracts of upland pine common in the north to the mixed bag of tropical foliage found in the southern hammocks.

PINE FLATWOODS

Covering roughly half of Florida, **pine flatwoods** are most widespread on the southeastern coastal plain. These pine species – longleaf, slash and pond – rise tall and straight like telegraph poles. The Spanish once harvested products such as turpentine and rosin from Florida's flatwood pines, a practice that continued during US settlement: some trees still bear the scars on their trunk. Pine flatwoods are airy and open, with abundant light filtering through the upper canopy of leaves, allowing thickets of shrubs such as saw palmetto, evergreen oaks, gallberry and fetterbrush to grow. **Inhabitants** of the pine flatwoods include white-tailed deer, cotton rats, brown-headed nuthatches, pine warblers, eastern diamondback rattlesnakes and oak toads. Although many of these creatures also inhabit other Florida ecosystems, the **fox squirrel** – a large and noisy character with a rufous tinge to its undercoat – is one of the few mammalian denizens more or less restricted to the pine flatwoods.

UPLAND PINE FORESTS

As the name suggests, **upland pine forests** – or high pinelands – are found on the rolling sand ridges and sandhills of northeastern Florida and the Panhandle; conditions that tend to keep upland pine forests dryer and therefore even more open than the flatwoods. Upland pine forests have a groundcover of wiregrass and an overstorey of (mostly) longleaf pine trees, which creates a park-like appearance. Red-headed woodpeckers, eastern bluebirds,

Florida mice, pocket gophers (locally called "salamanders", a distortion of "sand mounder") and gopher tortoises (amiable creatures often sharing their burrows with gopher frogs) all make the high pine country their home. The latter two, together with scarab beetles, keep the forest healthy by mixing and aerating the soil. The now-endangered red-cockaded woodpecker is symbolic of old-growth upland pine forest; logging and repression of the natural fire process have contributed to its decline.

HAMMOCKS

Wildlife tends to be more abundant in hardwood **hammocks** than in the associated pine forests and prairies (see below). Hammocks consist of narrow bands of (non-pine) hardwoods growing transitionally between pinelands and lower, wetter vegetation. The make-up of hammocks varies across the state: in the south, they chiefly comprise tropical hardwoods (see the "South Florida Rocklands", below); in the north, they contain an overstorey of oaks, magnolia and beech, with a few smaller plants – red-bellied woodpeckers, red-tailed and red-shouldered hawks and barred owls nest in them, and you can also find eastern wood rats, striped skunks and white-tailed deer.

SCRUB AND PRAIRIE

Scrub ecosystems once spread to the southern Rocky Mountains and northern Mexico, but climatic changes reduced their distribution and remnant stands are now found only in northern and central Florida. Like the high pines, scrub occurs in dry, hilly areas. The vegetation, which forms an impenetrable mass, consists of varied combinations of drought-adapted evergreen oaks, saw palmetto, Florida rosemary and/or sand pine. The **Florida bonamia**, a morning-glory with pale blue funnel-shaped blossoms, is one of the most attractive plants of the scrub, which has more than a dozen plant species officially listed as endangered. Scrub also harbours some unique animals, including the Florida mouse, the Florida scrub lizard, the sand skink and the Florida scrub jay. The **scrub jay** has an unusual social system: pairs nest in co-operation with offspring of previous seasons, who help carry food to their younger siblings. Although not unique to scrub habitat, other

inhabitants include black bear, white-tailed deer, bobcats and gopher tortoises.

Some of Florida's inland areas are covered by **prairie**, characterized by love grass, broomsedge and wiregrass – the best examples surround Lake Okeechobee. The **bison** that roamed here some two hundred years ago were destroyed by settlers, but herds are now being reintroduced to some state parks. A more diminutive prairie denizen is the **burrowing owl**: most owls are active at night, but burrowing owls feed during the day and, equally unusually, live in underground dens and bow nervously when approached – earning them the nickname the "howdy owl". Eastern spotted skunks, cotton rats, black vultures, eastern meadowlarks and box turtles are a few other prairie denizens. Nine-banded **armadillos** are also found in prairie habitats and in any non-swampy terrain. A recent invader from Texas, the armadillos usually forage at night, feeding on insects. Due to poor eyesight, they often fail to notice a human's approach until the last minute, when they will leap up and bound away noisily.

THS SOUTH FLORIDA ROCKLANDS

Elevated areas around the state's southern tip – in the Everglades and along the Florida Keys – support either pines or tropical hardwood hammocks on limestone outcrops collectively known as the **south Florida rocklands**. More jungle-like than the temperate hardwood forests found in northern Florida, the **tropical hardwood hammocks** of the south tend to occur as "tree islands" surrounded by sparser vegetation. Royal palm, pigeon plum, gumbo limbo (one of the most beautiful of the tropical hammock trees, with a distinctive smooth red bark) and ferns form dense thickets within the hammocks. The **pine forests** of the south Florida rocklands largely consist of scragglylooking slash pine. Wet prairies or mangroves surround the hammocks and pine forests.

EPIPHYTIC PLANTS

Tropical hammocks contain various forms of **epiphytic plants** – which use other plants for physical support but don't depend on them for nutrients. In southern Florida, epiphytes include orchids, ferns, bromeliads (**Spanish moss** is one of the most widespread bromeliads, hanging from tree branches throughout the state and forming the "Canopy Roads" in Tallahassee, see *The Panhandle*). Seemingly the most aggressive of epiphytes, **strangler figs**, after germinating in the canopy of trees such as palms, parasitize their host tree: they send out aerial roots that eventually reach the soil and then tightly enlace the host, preventing growth of the trunk. Finally, the fig produces so many leaves that it chokes out the host's greenery; the host dies leaving only the fig.

OTHER PLANTS AND VERTEBRATES

The south Florida rocklands support over forty plants and a dozen vertebrates found nowhere else. These include the crenulate lead plant, the Key tree cactus, the Florida mastiff bat, the Key deer and the Miami black-headed snake. More common residents include **butterflies and spiders** – the black and yellow yeliconia butterflies, with their long paddle-shaped wings and a distinctive gliding flight pattern, are particularly elegant. Butterflies need to practise careful navigation as hammocks are laced with the foot-long webs of the banana spider. Other wildlife species include sixty types of land snail, green tree frogs, green anoles, cardinals, opossums, raccoons and white-tailed deer. Most of these are native to the southeastern US, but a few West Indian bird species, such as the mangrove cuckoo, gray kingbird and white-crowned pigeon, have colonized the south Florida rocklands.

FRESHWATER SWAMPS AND MARSHES

Although about half have been destroyed due to logging, peat removal, draining, or sewage outflow, **swamps** are still found all over Florida. Trees growing around swamps include pines, palms, cedars, oaks, black gum, willows and bald cypress. Particularly adapted to aquatic conditions, the **bald cypress** is ringed by knobby "knees", or modified roots, providing oxygen to the tree, which would otherwise suffocate in the wet soil. Epiphytic orchids and bromeliads are common on cypresses, especially in the southern part of the state. Florida's official state tree, the **sabal palm**, is another swamp/hammock plant: "heart of palm" is the gourmet's name for the vegetable cut from its insides and used in salads.

Florida swamps also have many species of **insectivorous plants**; sticky pads or liquid-filled funnels trap small insects, which are then digested by the nitrogen-hungry plant. Around the Apalachicola National Forest is the highest diversity of carnivorous plants in the world, among them pitcher plants, bladderworts and sundews. Other swamp-dwellers include dragonflies, snails, clams, fish, bird-voiced tree frogs, limpkins, ibis, wood ducks, beavers, raccoons and Florida panthers.

Wetlands with relatively few trees, **freshwater marshes** range from shallow wet prairies to deep-water cattail marshes. **The Everglades** form Florida's largest marsh, most of which is sawgrass. On higher ground with good soils, sawgrass (actually a sedge) grows densely; at lower elevations it's sparser, and often an algal mat covers the soil between its plants. Water beetles, tiny crustaceans such as amphipods, mosquitoes, crayfish, killifish, sunfish, gar, catfish, bullfrogs, herons, egrets, ibis, water rats, white-tailed deer and Florida panthers can all be found. With luck, you might see a **snail kite**: a brown or black mottled hawk with a very specialized diet, entirely dependent on large apple snails. Snail and snail kite numbers have drastically fallen following the draining of marshes for agriculture and flood control: so far, 65 percent of the Everglades has been irreversibly drained.

WETLAND DENIZENS: ALLIGATORS AND WADING BIRDS

Alligators are one of the most widely known inhabitants of Florida's wetlands, lakes and rivers. Look for them on sunny mornings when they bask on logs or banks. If you hear thunder rumbling on a clear day, it may in fact be the bellow of territorial males. Alligators can reach ten feet in length and primarily prey on fish, turtles, birds, crayfish and crabs. Once overhunted for their hides and meat, alligators have made a strong comeback since protection was initiated in 1973; by 1987, Florida had up to half a million of them. They are not usually dangerous – in the fifteen years following 1973 there were only four fatal attacks. Most at risk are people who swim at dusk and small children playing unattended near water. To many creatures, alligators are a life-saver: during the summer, when the marshes dry up, they use their snouts, legs and tails to enlarge existing pools, creating a refuge for themselves and for other aquatic species. In these "gator holes", garfish stack up like cordwood, snakes search for frogs, and otters and anhingas forage for fish.

Wading birds are conspicuous in the wetlands. Egrets, herons and ibis, usually clad in white or grey feathers, stalk frogs, mice and small fish. Turn-of-the-century plume-hunters decimated these birds to make fanciful hats, and during the last few decades habitat destruction has caused a ninety percent reduction in their numbers. Nonetheless, many are still visible in swamps, marshes and mangroves. Cattle egrets, invaders from South America, are a common sight on pastures, where they forage on insects disturbed by grazing livestock. Pink waders – roseate spoonbills and, to a much lesser extent, flamingoes – can be also found in southern Florida's wetlands.

LAKES, SPRINGS AND RIVERS

Florida has almost 8000 freshwater **lakes**. Game fish such as bass and bluegill are common, but the waters are too warm to support trout. Some native fish species are threatened by the introduction of the **walking catfish**, which has a specially adapted gill system enabling it to leave the water and take the fish equivalent of cross-country hikes. A native of India and Burma, the walking catfish was released into southern Florida canals in the early Sixties and within twenty years had "walked" across twenty counties, disturbing the indigenous food chain. A freeze eliminated a number of these exotic fish, though enough remain to cause concern.

Most Florida **springs** release cold fresh water, but some springs are warm and others emit sulphur, chloride or salt-laden waters. Homosassa Springs (see *The West Coast*), for example, has a high chloride content, making it attractive to both freshwater and marine species of fish.

Besides fish, Florida's extensive **river** system supports snails, freshwater mussels and crayfish. Southern river-dwellers also include the lovable **manatee**, or sea cow, which inhabits bays and shallow coastal waters. The only totally aquatic herbivorous mammal, manatees sometimes weigh almost a ton but only eat aquatic plants. Unable to tolerate cold conditions, manatees are partial to the warm water discharged by power plants, taking some of them as far north as North Carolina. In Florida during the winter, the large springs at Crystal River (see *The West Coast*) attract manatees, some of which have become tame enough to allow divers to scratch their bellies. Although they have few natural enemies, manatees are on the decline, often due to power-boat propellers injuring their backs or heads when they feed at the surface.

THE COAST

There's a lot more than sunbathing taking place around Florida's **coast**. The sandy beaches provide a habitat for many species, not least sea turtles. Where there isn't sand, you'll find the fascinating mangrove forests, or wildlife-filled salt marshes and estuaries. Offshore, coral reefs provide yet another exotic ecosystem, and one of the more pleasurable to explore by snorkelling or diving.

SANDY BEACHES

Waves bring many interesting creatures onto Florida's **sandy beaches**, such as sponges, horseshoe crabs and the occasional sea horse. Florida's **shells** are justly famous – fig shells, moon snails, conches, whelks, olive shells, red and orange scallops, murex, cockles, pen and turban shells are a few of the many varieties. As you beachcomb, beware of stepping barefoot on purplish fragments of **man-of-war** tentacles: these jellyfish have no means of locomotion, and their floating, sail-like bodies often cause them to be washed ashore – their tentacles, which sometimes reach to sixty feet in length, can deliver a painful sting. More innocuous beach inhabitants include wintering birds such as black-bellied plovers and sanderlings, and nesting black skimmers.

Of the seven species of **sea turtle**, five nest on Florida's sandy beaches: green, loggerhead, leatherback, hawksbill and olive ridley. From February to August, the female turtles haul out at night, excavate a beachside hole and deposit a hundred-plus eggs. Not many of these will survive to adulthood: raccoons eat a lot of the eggs, and hatchlings are liable to be crushed by vehicles on the coastal highways when they become disoriented by their lights. Programmes to hatch the eggs artificially have helped offset some of the losses. The best time to view sea turtles is during June — peak nesting time — with one of the park-ranger-led walks offered along the southern portion of the northeast coast (see *The Northwest Coast*).

MANGROVES

Found in brackish waters around the Florida Keys and the southwest coast, Florida has three species of **mangrove**. Unlike most plants, mangroves bear live young: the "seeds", or propagules, germinate while still on the tree; after dropping from the parent, the young propagule floats for weeks or months until it washes up on a suitable site, where its sprouted condition allows it to put out roots rapidly. Like bald cypress, mangroves have difficulty extracting oxygen from their muddy environs and solve this problem with extensive aerial roots, which either dangle finger-like from branches or twist outwards from the lower trunk. Various fish species, such as the mangrove snapper, depend on mangroves as a nursery; other **mangrove inhabitants** include frogs, crocodiles, brown pelicans, wood storks, roseate spoonbills, river otters, mink and raccoons.

SALT MARSHES AND ESTUARIES

Like the mangrove ecosystem, the **salt marsh and estuary** habitat provides a nursery for many fish species, which in turn fodder larger fish, herons, egrets and the occasional dolphin. **Crocodiles**, with narrower and more pointed snouts than alligators, are seldom sighted, and confined to salt water at the state's southernmost tip. In a few southern Florida salt marshes, you might find a **great white heron**, a rare and handsome form of the more common great blue heron. Around Florida Bay, great white herons have learned to beg for fish from local residents, each of these massive birds "working" a particular neighbourhood — striding from household to household demanding fish by rattling window blinds with their bills or issuing guttural croaks. A less appealing salt marsh denizen is the **mosquito**: unfortunately, the more damaging methods of mosquito control, such as impounding salt water or spraying DDT, have inflicted extensive harm on the fragile salt marshes and estuaries.

THE CORAL REEF

A long band of living **coral reef** frames Florida's southeastern corner. Living coral comes in many colours: star coral is green, elkhorn coral orange, and brain coral red. Each piece of coral is actually a colony of hundreds or thousands of small, soft animals called **polyps**, related to sea anemones and jellyfish. The polyps secrete limestone to form their hard outer skeletons, and at night extend their feathery tentacles to filter seawater for microscopic food. The filtering process, however, provides only a fraction of the coral's nutrition — most is produced via the photosynthesis of algae that live within the polyps' cells. In recent years, influxes of warmer water, possibly associated with global warming, have killed off large numbers of the algal cells. The half-starved polyp then often succumbs to disease, a phenomenon known as "bleaching". Although this has been observed throughout the Pacific, the damage in Florida has so far been moderate: the impact of the tourist industry on the reef has been more pronounced, though reef destruction for souvenirs is now banned.

Coral reefs are home to a kaleidoscopic variety of brightly coloured fish — beau gregories, porkfish, parrot fish, blennies, grunts and wrasses — which swirl in dazzling schools or lurk between coral crevices. The **damselfish** is the farmer of the reef: after destroying a polyp patch, it feeds on the resultant algae growth, fiercely defending it from other fish. Sponges, featherduster worms, sea fans, crabs, spiny lobsters, sea urchins and conches are among the thousands of other creatures resident in the coral reef.

BOOKS

Florida's perennial state of social and political flux has always promised rich material for historians and journalists eager to pin the place down. Rarely have they managed this, though the picture of the region's unpredictable evolution that emerges can make for compulsive reading. Many established fiction writers spend their winters in Florida, but few have convincingly portrayed its characters, climate and scenery. Those that have succeeded, however, have produced some of the most unique and gripping literature to emerge from any part of the US.

HISTORY

Edward N Akin *Flagler: Rockefeller Partner & Florida Baron.* Solid biography of the man whose Standard Oil fortune helped build Florida's first hotels and railroads.

Howard Kleinberg *The Way We Were.* Oversized overview of Miami's history: colourful archival photos and text by a former editor-in-chief of the city's newspaper of 92 years, *The Miami News.*

Helen Muir *Miami, USA.* An insider's account of how Miami's first developers gave the place shape during the land boom of the Twenties.

John Rothchild *Up for Grabs: A Trip Through Time and Space in the Sunshine State.* Irreverent look at Florida's chequered career as a vacation spa, tourist trap and haven for scheming ne'er-do-wells.

Charlton W Tebeau *A History of Florida.* The definitive academic tome, but not for casual reading.

Garcilaso de la Vega *The Florida of the Inca.* Comprehensive account of the sixteenth-century expedition led by Hernando de Soto through Florida's prairies, swamps and aboriginal settlements; extremely turgid in parts, but overall an excellent insight into the period.

Lawrence E Will *Swamp to Sugarbowl: Pioneer Days in Belle Glade.* A "cracker" account of early times in the state, written in first-person redneck vernacular. Variously oafish and offensive – but never dull.

NATURAL HISTORY

Jon L Dunn & Eirik A T Blom *Field Guide to the Birds of North America, Second Ed.* The best country-wide guide, with plenty on Florida, and excellent illustrations throughout.

Harold R Holt *Lane's "A Birder's Guide to Florida".* Detailed accounts of when and where to find Florida's birds, including maps and seasonal charts. Aimed at the expert but excellent value for the novice bird-watcher.

Ronald L Myers & John J Ewel *Ecosystems of Florida.* Technical yet highly readable treatise for the serious ecologist.

Marjory Stoneman Douglas *The Everglades: River of Grass.* Concerned conservationist literature by one of the state's most respected historians, describing the nature and beauty of the Everglades from their beginnings. A superb work that contributed to the founding of the Everglades National Park.

TRAVEL IMPRESSIONS

T D Allman *Miami: City of the Future.* Excellent, incisive look at modern Miami, which becomes bogged down when going further back than *Miami Vice.*

William Bartram *Travels.* The lively diary of an eighteenth-century naturalist rambling through the Deep South and on into Florida during the period of British rule. Outstanding accounts of the indigenous people and all kinds of wildlife.

Edna Buchanan *The Corpse had a Familiar Face.* Sometimes sharp, often sensationalist account of the author's years spent pounding the crime beat for the *Miami Herald* – five thousand corpses and gore galore. The subsequent *Vice* is more of the same.

Joan Didion *Miami* A riveting though ultimately unsatisfying voyage around the impenetrably complex and wildly passionate *el exilio* politics of Cuban Miami.

Lynn Geldof *Cubans*. Passionate and rambling interviews with Cubans in Cuba and Miami, which confirm the tight bond between them.

Henry James *The American Scene*. Interesting waffle from the celebrated novelist, including written portraits of St Augustine and Palm Beach as they thronged with wintering socialites at the turn of the century.

Norman Mailer *Miami and the Siege of Chicago*. A rabid study of the American political conventions of 1968, the first part frothing over the Republican Party's shenanigans at Miami Beach when Nixon beat Reagan for the presidential ticket.

Roxanne Pulitzer *The Prize Pulitzer: The Scandal that Rocked Palm Beach*. A small-town girl who married into the jet-set lifestyle of Palm Beach describes the mud-slinging in Florida's most moneyed community when she seeks a divorce.

David Rieff *Going to Miami: Exiles, Tourists and Refugees in the New America*. An exploration of Miami through the minds of its conservative Cubans, its struggling black and Haitian communities, and its resentful Anglos – but with too many sexist musings to be credible.

Alexander Stuart *Life on Mars*. "Paradise with a lobotomy" is how a friend of the author described Florida. This is an often amusing series of snap shots of both the empty lives led by the beautiful people of South Beach and the red-neck "white trash" of up-state.

John Williams *Into the Badlands: A Journey through the American Dream*. The author's trek across the US to interview the country's best crime writers begins in Miami, "the city that coke built", its compelling strangeness all too briefly revelled in.

ARCHITECTURE AND PHOTOGRAPHY

Barbara Baer Capitman *Deco Delights*. A tour of Miami Beach's Art Deco buildings by the woman who championed their preservation, with definitive photography.

Laura Cerwinske *Miami: Hot & Cool*. Coffee-table tome with text on high-style south Florida living and glowing, colour pics of Miami's beautiful homes and gardens. By the same author, *Tropical Deco: The Architecture & Design of Old Miami Beach* delivers a wealth of architectural detail.

Donald W. Curl *Mizner's Florida: American Resort Architecture*. An assessment of the life, career and designs of Addison Mizner, the self-taught architect responsible for the "Bastard Spanish Moorish Romanesque Renaissance Bull Market Damn the Expense Style" structures of Palm Beach and Boca Raton.

Hap Hatton *Tropical Splendor: An Architectural History of Florida*. A readable, informative and effectively illustrated account of the wild, weird and wonderful buildings that have graced and disgraced the state over the years.

Alva Johnston *The Legendary Mizners*. A racy biography of Addison Mizner and his brother Wilson, telling how they wined, dined and married into the lifestyles of the rich and famous of the Twenties.

Gary Monroe *Life in South Beach*. A slim volume of monochrome photos showing Miami Beach's South Beach before the restoration of the Art Deco district and the arrival of globe-trotting trendies.

FICTION

Pat Booth *Miami*. It had to happen: best-selling author uses the glitz-and-glamour of Miami's South Beach as a backdrop to a pot-boiling tale of seduction and desire.

Edward Falco *Winter in Florida*. Flawed but compulsive story of a cosseted New York boy seeking thrills on a central Florida horse farm.

Ernest Hemingway *To Have and Have Not*. Hemingway lived and drank in Key West for years but set only this moderate tale in the town, describing the woes of fishermen brutalized by the Depression.

Carl Hiaasen *Double Whammy*. Ferociously funny fishing thriller that brings together a classic collection of warped but believable Florida characters; among them a hermit-like ex-state governor, a cynical Cuban cop and a corrupt TV preacher. By the same author, *Skin Tight* explores the perils of unskilled plastic surgery in a Miami crawling with mutant hitmen, bought politicians and police on gangsters' payrolls, and *Native Tongue* delves into the murky goings-on behind the scenes at a Florida theme park.

Zora Neale Hurston *Their Eyes Were Watching God*. Florida-born Hurston became one of the bright lights of the Harlem Renaissance in the Twenties. This novel describes the founding of Eatonville – her home town and the state's first all-black town – and the labourers' lot in Belle Glade at the time of the 1928 hurricane. Equally hard to put down are *Jonah's Gourd Vine* and the autobiography, *Dust Tracks on a Road*.

David A. Karfelt *American Tropic*. Overblown saga of passion and power set during several key eras in Florida's history; just the job for idle hours on the beach.

Peter Matthiessen *Killing Mister Watson*. Thoroughly researched story of the early days of white settlement in the Everglades. Slow-paced but a strong insight into the Florida frontier mentality.

Thomas McGuane *Ninety-Two in the Shade*. A strange, hallucinatory search for identity by a young man of shifting mental states who aspires to become a Key West fishing guide – and whose family and friends are equally warped. *Panama*, by the same author, is also set in Key West.

Theodore Pratt *The Barefoot Mailman*. A Forties account of the long-distance postman who kept the far-flung settlements of pioneer-period Florida in mail by hiking the many miles of beach between them.

John Sayles *Los Gusanos*. Absorbing, if long-winded novel set around the lives of Cuban exiles in Miami – written by a cult film director.

Daniel Vilmure *Life in the Land of the Living*. Only the vigour of the writing lifts this purposeless story of two brothers rampaging through an unnamed Florida port town on a blisteringly hot Friday night.

CRIME FICTION

Edna Buchanan *Nobody Lives Forever*. Tense, psycho-killer thriller played out on the mean streets of Miami. See also "Travel impressions".

Liza Cody *Backhand*. London's finest female private investigator, Anna Lee, follows the clues from Kensington to the West Coast of Florida – highly entertaining.

James Hall *Under Cover of Daylight; Squall Line; Hard Aground*. Taut thrillers with a cast of crazies that make the most of the edge-of-the-world landscapes of the Florida Keys.

Elmore Leonard *Stick; La Brava; Gold Coast*. The pick of this highly recommended author's Florida-set thrillers, respectively detailing the rise of an opportunist black through the money, sex and drugs of Latino Miami; low-life on the seedy South Beach before the preservation of the Art Deco district; and the tribulations of a wealthy gangster-widow alone in a Fort Lauderdale mansion.

Charles Willeford *Miami Blues*. Thanks to an uninspired film, the best-known but not the best of a highly recommended series starring Hoke Mosely, a cool and calculating, but very human, Miami cop. Superior titles in the series are *The Way We Die Now, Kiss Your Ass Goodbye* and *Sideswipe*.

COOKERY

Sue Mullin *Nuevo Cubano Cooking*. Easy-to-follow instructions and mouth-watering photographs, of recipes fusing traditional Cuban cooking with nouvelle cuisine.

Steven Raichleu *Miami Spice*. Latin American and Caribbean cooking meets Florida and the "Deep South", resulting in some of the tastiest dishes in America. Clear recipes and interesting background information.

INDEX

direct orders from

Amsterdam	1-85828-086-9	£7.99	US$13.95	CAN$16.99
Andalucia	1-85828-094-X	8.99	14.95	18.99
Australia	1-85828-141-5	12.99	19.95	25.99
Bali	1-85828-134-2	8.99	14.95	19.99
Barcelona	1-85828-106-7	8.99	13.95	17.99
Berlin	1-85828-129-6	8.99	14.95	19.99
Brazil	1-85828-102-4	9.99	15.95	19.99
Britain	1-85828-208-X	12.99	19.95	25.99
Brittany & Normandy	1-85828-126-1	8.99	14.95	19.99
Bulgaria	1-85828-183-0	9.99	16.95	22.99
California	1-85828-181-4	10.99	16.95	22.99
Canada	1-85828-130-X	10.99	14.95	19.99
Corsica	1-85828-089-3	8.99	14.95	18.99
Costa Rica	1-85828-136-9	9.99	15.95	21.99
Crete	1-85828-132-6	8.99	14.95	18.99
Cyprus	1-85828-182-2	9.99	16.95	22.99
Czech & Slovak Republics	1-85828-121-0	9.99	16.95	22.99
Egypt	1-85828-075-3	10.99	17.95	21.99
Europe	1-85828-159-8	14.99	19.95	25.99
England	1-85828-160-1	10.99	17.95	23.99
First Time Europe	1-85828-210-1	7.99	9.95	12.99
Florida	1-85828-074-5	8.99	14.95	18.99
France	1-85828-124-5	10.99	16.95	21.99
Germany	1-85828-128-8	11.99	17.95	23.99
Goa	1-85828-156-3	8.99	14.95	19.99
Greece	1-85828-131-8	9.99	16.95	20.99
Greek Islands	1-85828-163-6	8.99	14.95	19.99
Guatemala	1-85828-045-1	9.99	14.95	19.99
Hawaii: Big Island	1-85828-158-X	8.99	12.95	16.99
Hawaii	1-85828-206-3	10.99	16.95	22.99
Holland, Belgium & Luxembourg	1-85828-087-7	9.99	15.95	20.99
Hong Kong	1-85828-066-4	8.99	13.95	17.99
Hungary	1-85828-123-7	8.99	14.95	19.99
India	1-85828-104-0	13.99	22.95	28.99
Ireland	1-85828-179-2	10.99	17.95	23.99
Italy	1-85828-167-9	12.99	19.95	25.99
Kenya	1-85828-043-5	9.99	15.95	20.99
London	1-85828-117-2	8.99	12.95	16.99
Mallorca & Menorca	1-85828-165-2	8.99	14.95	19.99
Malaysia, Singapore & Brunei	1-85828-103-2	9.99	16.95	20.99
Mexico	1-85828-044-3	10.99	16.95	22.99
Morocco	1-85828-040-0	9.99	16.95	21.99
Moscow	1-85828-118-0	8.99	14.95	19.99
Nepal	1-85828-190-3	10.99	17.95	23.99

New York	1-85828-171-7	9.99	15.95	21.99
Pacific Northwest	1-85828-092-3	9.99	14.95	19.99
Paris	1-85828-125-3	7.99	13.95	16.99
Poland	1-85828-168-7	10.99	17.95	23.99
Portugal	1-85828-180-6	9.99	16.95	22.99
Prague	1-85828-122-9	8.99	14.95	19.99
Provence	1-85828-127-X	9.99	16.95	22.99
Pyrenees	1-85828-093-1	8.99	15.95	19.99
Rhodes& the Dodecanese	1-85828-120-2	8.99	14.95	19.99
Romania	1-85828-097-4	9.99	15.95	21.99
San Francisco	1-85828-185-7	8.99	14.95	19.99
Scandinavia	1-85828-039-7	10.99	16.99	21.99
Scotland	1-85828-166-0	9.99	16.95	22.99
Sicily	1-85828-178-4	9.99	16.95	22.99
Singapore	1-85828-135-0	8.99	14.95	19.99
Spain	1-85828-081-8	9.99	16.95	20.99
St Petersburg	1-85828-133-4	8.99	14.95	19.99
Thailand	1-85828-140-7	10.99	17.95	24.99
Tunisia	1-85828-139-3	10.99	17.95	24.99
Turkey	1-85828-088-5	9.99	16.95	20.99
Tuscany & Umbria	1-85828-091-5	8.99	15.95	19.99
USA	1-85828-161-X	14.99	19.95	25.99
Venice	1-85828-170-9	8.99	14.95	19.99
Wales	1-85828-096-6	8.99	14.95	18.99
West Africa	1-85828-101-6	15.99	24.95	34.99
More Women Travel	1-85828-098-2	9.99	14.95	19.99
Zimbabwe & Botswana	1-85828-041-9	10.99	16.95	21.99
Phrasebooks				
Czech	1-85828-148-2	3.50	5.00	7.00
French	1-85828-144-X	3.50	5.00	7.00
German	1-85828-146-6	3.50	5.00	7.00
Greek	1-85828-145-8	3.50	5.00	7.00
Italian	1-85828-143-1	3.50	5.00	7.00
Mexican	1-85828-176-8	3.50	5.00	7.00
Portuguese	1-85828-175-X	3.50	5.00	7.00
Polish	1-85828-174-1	3.50	5.00	7.00
Spanish	1-85828-147-4	3.50	5.00	7.00
Thai	1-85828-177-6	3.50	5.00	7.00
Turkish	1-85828-173-3	3.50	5.00	7.00
Vietnamese	1-85828-172-5	3.50	5.00	7.00
Reference				
Classical Music	1-85828-113-X	12.99	19.95	25.99
Internet	1-85828-198-9	5.00	8.00	10.00
World Music	1-85828-017-6	16.99	22.95	29.99
Jazz	1-85828-137-7	16.99	24.95	34.99

THE LOWEST PRICE CAR RENTAL AROUND THE

AND THAT'S A PROMISE†

For convenient, low-price car rental – all around the world – choose Holiday Autos. With a network of over 4,000 locations in 42 countries, when you're off globetrotting you won't have to go out of your way to find us.

What's more, with our lowest price promise, you won't be flying round and round in circles to be sure you're getting the best price.

With Holiday Autos you can be sure of the friendly, efficient service you'd expect from the UK's leading leisure car rental company. After all, we've won the Travel Trade Gazette 'Best Leisure Car Rental Company' award and the Independent Travel Agents' 'Top Leisure Car Rental Company' award time and time again. So, we've quite a reputation to maintain.

With Holiday Autos you simply don't need to search the globe for down-to-earth low prices.

For further information see your local Travel Agent or call us direct on **0990 300 400**

Holiday Autos
WE KNOW YOU HAVE A CHOICE

†Our lowest price promise refers to our pledge to undercut by £5 any other equivalent offer made at the same price or less by an independent UK car rental company for a booking made in the UK prior to departure. Holiday Autos undercut offer is valid unless and until withdrawn by Holiday Autos.